R. Gupta's®

POPULAR MASTER GUIDE

DSSSB–TEACHERS

PGT

MATHS

Recruitment Exam

by

RPH Editorial Board

2026
EDITION

RAMESH PUBLISHING HOUSE, NEW DELHI

Published by
O.P. Gupta *for* Ramesh Publishing House

Admin. Office
12-H, New Daryaganj Road, Opp. Officers' Mess,
New Delhi-110002 ✆ 23275224, 23245124

E-mail: info@rameshpublishinghouse.com
For Online Shooping: www.rameshpublishinghouse.com

Showroom
- Balaji Market, Nai Sarak, Delhi-6 ✆ 23253720, 23282525
- 4457, Nai Sarak, Delhi-6, ✆ 23918938

Book Code: R-1309

ISBN: 978-93-5012-008-8

Price: ₹ 320

Printed at: Deepak Offset, Delhi

CONTENTS

❑❑❑

Previous Paper (Solved)

DSSSB–TEACHERS PGT MATHS

Recruitment Exam, 2021*

1. 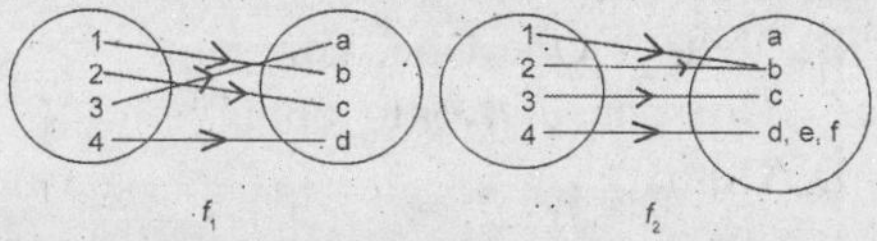

Which of the following is correct if the above image represents the functions f_1 and f_2?
A. f_1 is one-one, f_2 is one-one
B. f_1 is onto, f_2 is one-one
C. f_1 is one-one, f_2 is onto
D. f_1 is onto, f_2 is onto

2. If $f : R \to R$ defined by $f(x) = x^2 - 3x + 2$, then $f(f(x)) =$
A. $x^4 + 6x^3 - 13x^2 + 3x$
B. $x^4 - 6x^3 + 10x^2 - 3x$
C. $x^4 + 6x^3 + 10x^2 + 3x$
D. $x^4 - 6x^3 - 13x^2 + 3x$

3. If $U_n > 0$ for all $n \in N$, then $\lim_{n\to\infty} U_n^{1/n}$ is equal to:
A. $\lim_{n\to\infty} \frac{U_n + 1}{U_n}$
B. $\lim_{n\to\infty} \frac{U_{n-1}}{U_n}$
C. $\lim_{n\to\infty} \frac{U_n}{U_{n-1}}$
D. $\lim_{n\to\infty} \frac{U_n}{U_{n+1}}$

4. If $f : R \to R$ and $g : R \to R$ are given by $f(x) = \cos x$, and $g(x) = 3x^2$, then:
A. gof = fog
B. Can't be determined
C. gof and fog both do not exist
D. gof ≠ fog

5. A conditionally convergent series is a series which is:
A. Absolutely Convergent
B. Convergent but not absolutely
C. Not convergent but absolutely convergent
D. Absolutely divergent

6. A Relation in R is defined as $R = \{(a, b) : a \le b^2\}$ is ____.
A. Transitive
B. Reflexive
C. Symmetric
D. Not an Equivalence Relation

7. Which of the following is incorrect?
A. Every sequence has a monotone subsequence
B. Every sequence has a limit point
C. Every bounded sequence has a convergent subsequence
D. Every sequence has a countable number of terms

8. The greatest integer function $f : R \to R$ given by $f(x) = [x]$, (where $[x]$ denotes the greatest integer), is ____.
A. One-One, onto
B. One-One, but not onto
C. Neither One-One nor onto
D. Onto, but not one-one

9. If a binary operation * on N is defined as $a * b = a^3 + b^3$, then:
A. * is commutative but not associative
B. * is both associated and commutative
C. * is neither commutative nor associative
D. * is associative but not commutative

10. Which one of the following tests does not give absolute convergence of a series?
A. Ratio Test
B. Comparison Test
C. Root Test
D. Leibnitz's Test

11. The domain of convergence for $x - \frac{x}{2} + \frac{x}{3} - \frac{x}{4} + ...$ is:
A. (–1, 1)
B. [–1, 1)
C. [–1, 1]
D. (–1, 1]

* Exam held on 10/07/2021

12. Which one of the following series is divergent?

A. $\sum \sin \frac{1}{n}$ B. $\sum \frac{1}{n^3}$

C. $\sum \sin \frac{1}{n^2}$ D. $\sum \frac{1}{\sqrt{n}} \tan \frac{1}{n^2}$

13. The series $\sum (-1)^{n+1} \frac{1}{n}$ is:

A. Unbounded

B. Conditionally Convergent

C. Divergent

D. Absolutely Convergent

14. If Σa_n^2 and Σb_n^2 are convergent series of positive real number then, $\Sigma \sqrt{a_n \cdot b_n}$

A. must be convergent

B. may or may not be convergent

C. is divergent

D. may be convergent

15. The sequence $\{x_n\}$, where

$x_n = 1 + \frac{1}{3} + \frac{1}{5} + ... + \frac{1}{2n-1}$ is:

A. Not Cauchy sequence

B. Oscillatory

C. Monotonically decreasing

D. Convergent

16. If S = $\{a, b, c, d\}$ and $p = \{(a, a), (b, b), (c, c), (d, d), (a, b), (b, a), (b, c), (c, d)\}$, then p is:

A. Reflexive and symmetric

B. Equivalence

C. Symmetric and transitive

D. Reflexive and transitive

17. If $f: R \to R$ given by $f(x) = 4x + 3$, then inverse of f is:

A. $f^{-1} = \frac{3-y}{4}$ B. $f^{-1} = \frac{y-4}{3}$

C. $f^{-1} = \frac{4-y}{3}$ D. $f^{-1} = \frac{y-3}{4}$

18. Let $f: R \to R$ be defined as $f(x) = 8x$. Choose the correct answer:

A. f is neither one-one nor onto

B. f is one-one onto

C. f is one-one but not onto

D. f is many-one onto

19. If a sequence $\{a_n^2\}$ converges to a^2, then the sequence $\{a_n\}$ converges to:

A. Not convergent B. $\sqrt{a}$

C. a D. a^2

20. If $f: A \to B$ and $g: B \to C$ are one-one, then gof : A → C is :

A. One-one

B. Neither One-One, nor onto

C. One-one and onto both

D. Onto

21. Which one of the following is true?

A. $A \times (B \cup C) = (A \times B) \cap (A \times C)$

B. $A \times (B \cap C) = (A \times B) \cup (A \times C)$

C. $(A - B) \times C = (A \times C) - (B \times C)$

D. $A \times (B - C) = (A \times C) - (A \times B)$

22. Which of the following is not true?

A. If $f(z) = u + i.v$ is an analytic function, then u and v are both harmonic functions

B. If a function does not satisfy Cauchy – Riemann equations, then it is not analytic

C. If u and v are both harmonic functions, then $f(z) = u + i.v$ is analytic

D. If $f(z) = u + i.v$ is an analytic function, then $u(x, y) = c_1$ and $v(x, y) = c_2$ are orthogonal

23. If $(x, y) = x^3 - 3xy^2$ of an anlytic function $f(z) = u + i.v$, then:

A. v is its harmonic conjugate and $v(x, y) = 3x^2y - y^3 + c$, c is any constant

B. v is its harmonic conjugate and $v(x, y) = 3x^2y - y^3 + c$, c is real constant

C. $-v$ is its harmonic conjugate and $v(x, y) = y^2 - 3x^2y + c$, c is real constant

D. $-v$ is its harmonic conjugate and $v(x, y) = y^3 - 3x^2y + c$, c is any constant

24. If a set A = φ, then how many elements are there in P(A)?

A. 1 B. 3

C. 2 D. No element

25. If three non-empty sets A, B and C are having relation $A \cap B = A \cap C$ and $A \cup B = A \cup C$, then:

A. A = C B. B = C

C. A = B D. A = B = C

26. Let X be a complete metric space then no non-empty open sub-set of X is of first category. Which theorem states this?
A. Cauchy's Theorem
B. Bolzano-Weierstrass Theorem
C. The Baire category Theorem
D. Intermediate Value Theorem

27. Let $f(z) = \frac{1}{z}, z \neq 0$, then
A. f satisfies Cauchy – Riemann equation, but not analytic for all $z \neq 0$
B. f is continuous only but nowhere differentiable
C. f does not satisfy Caucy – Riemann equation for all $z \neq 0$
D. f is analytic for all $z \neq 0$

28. If n is real number and $f = r^n (\cos n\theta + i. \sin n\theta)$, then:
A. f is analytic everywhere except possibly at $r = 0$
B. f is analytic nowhere
C. f is analytic everywhere except possibly at $\theta = 0$
D. f is analytic everywhere

29. If X and Y are two non-empty sets such that $n(X) = 17$, $n(Y) = 23$ and $n(X \cup Y) = 38$, then $n(X \cap Y)$ is;
A. 10 B. 16
C. 6 D. 2

30. The radius of convergence of the power series $\sum_{n=0}^{\infty} \frac{(n!)^2}{2n!} z^n$ is:
A. 1/4 B. 1/2
C. 2 D. 4

31. The value of the integral $\int_c \frac{z^2 e^{2z}}{z^2+1} dz$, where c is a circle IzI is:
A. $2\pi \cdot i \cdot \sin^2$ B. $-2\pi \cdot i$
C. $-2\pi \cdot i \cdot \sin^2$ D. 0

32. Which of the following represents De Morgan's Law?
A. $A \cap B = A' \cup B'$
B. $(A' \cup B') = A \cap B'$
C. $(A \cup B') = A' \cap B$
D. $(A \cup B)' = A' \cap B'$

33. In a group of 400 players, 250 play football and 200 play cricket, then how many people play both the games?
A. 200 B. 50
C. 100 D. 250

34. If $f(z) = u(x, y) + i.v(x, y)$ be analytic everywhere and $u - v = (x - y) \cdot (x^2 + 4xy + y^2)$, then:
A. $f(z) = -i.z^3 + c$, c is arbitrary constant
B. $f(z) = i.z^3 + c$, where c is arbitrary constant
C. $f(z) = z^2(1 + i) + c$, c is arbitrary constant
D. $f(z) = z(1 - i.z) + c$, c is arbitrary constant

35. $[A \cup (B \cup C)] \cap [A' \cap (B' \cap C']$ is equal to:
A. Universal set B. $A \cap (B' \cap C')$
C. null set D. $A' \cup (B \cup C)$

36. The value of the integral $\int_c \frac{ze^2}{(z-1)^3} dz$, where c is a circle $|z| = 2$ is:
A. $\frac{2\pi ic}{3}$ B. $2\pi i c$
C. $3\pi. i. c$ D. $\pi i c$

37. If $f(z) = |z^2|$, then:
A. f is differentiable only at zero
B. f is differentiable everywhere except 0
C. f is differentiable everywhere
D. f is differentiable nowhere

38. If $Z_1 = \{3x : x \in \mathbb{Z}\}$
$Z_2 = \{3x + 1 : x \in \mathbb{Z}\}$
$Z_3 = \{3x + 2 : x \in \mathbb{Z}\}$ then:
A. Z_1, Z_2, Z_3 form a partition of $\mathbb{Z}$
B. $Z_1 \cap Z_2 \cap Z_3 = \mathbb{Z}$
C. Z_1, Z_2, Z_3 form a group under multiplication
D. Z_1, Z_2, Z_3 form a partition of $\mathbb{R}$

39. If $U = \{1, 2, 3, 4, 5, 6, 7, 8, 9\}$
$A = \{1, 2, 3, 4\}$
$B = \{2, 4, 6, 8\}$, then $(A \cup B)'$ is:
A. {2, 4, 6, 8} B. {1, 3, 5, 7, 9}
C. {1, 2, 3, 4, 6, 8} D. {5, 7, 9}

40. If $f(z) = \begin{cases} \frac{|z|}{\text{Re}(z)}, & \text{if } \text{Re}(z) \neq 0 \\ 0, & \text{if } \text{Re}(z) = 0 \end{cases}$, then:

A. f is not continuous nowhere
B. f is not continuous at 0
C. f is not continuous only at 0
D. f is not continuous everywhere

41. If $lx + my + n = 0$ be the normal to the circle $x^2 + y^2 + a^2$ then:
A. $n = a$ B. $n = a^2$
C. $n = 1$ D. $n = 0$

42. The image of the point (–3, 8, 4) in the plane $6x - 3y - 2z + 1 = 0$, is:
A. (1, 2, –2) B. (0, 2, 9)
C. (9, 2, 0) D. (–2, 1, 3)

43. The general equation of the cone which passes through the co-ordinate axes is:
A. $x^2y^2 + y^2z^2 + z^2x^2 = 0$
B. $hxy + fyz + gzx = 0$
C. $xy + yz - zx = 0$
D. $ax^2 + b^2 + cz^2 + 2hxy + 2fyz + 2gzx = 0$

44. The surface of revolution of the straight line $z^2 = y, x = 0$ about the y-axis is:
A. $x^2 + z^2 = y$ B. $y^2 + z^2 = x$
C. $z^4 = x^2 + y^2$ D. $y^4 = x^2 + z^2$

45. If the normals at the point $\left(ct_1, \frac{c}{t_1}\right)$ on the hyperbola $xy = c^2$ meets it again at the point $\left(ct_2, \frac{c}{t_2}\right)$ then:
A. $t_2t_1^3 = -1$ B. $t_2^2t_1 = -1$
C. $t_1^2t_2 = -1$ D. $t_2^3t_1 = -1$

46. Equation of the sphere that passes through the points (0, 0, 0), $(a, 0, 0)$, $(0, b, 0)$, $(0, 0, c)$ is:
A. $(x-a)^2 + (y-b)^2 + (z-c)^2 = \frac{1}{2}\sqrt{(a^2+b^2+c^2)}$
B. $\left(x-\frac{a}{2}\right)^2 + \left(y-\frac{b}{2}\right)^2 + \left(z-\frac{c}{2}\right)^2 = \frac{1}{2}(a^2+b^2+c^2)$
C. $x^2 + y^2 + z^2 = a^2 + b^2 + c^2$
D. $\left(x-\frac{a}{2}\right)^2 + \left(y-\frac{b}{2}\right)^2 + \left(z-\frac{c}{2}\right)^2 = \frac{1}{4}(a^2+b^2+c^2)$

47. The equation $ax^2 + by^2 + cz^2 + 2ux + 2vy + 2wz + d = 0$, represents a cone if:
A. $au^2 + bv^2 + cw^2 = d$
B. $bcu + acv + abw = d$
C. $(b + c) \cdot u^2 + (a + c) \cdot v^2 + (a + b) \cdot w^2 = d$
D. $\frac{u^2}{a} + \frac{v^2}{b} + \frac{w^2}{c} = d$

48. In three dimension, the equation $x^2 = 2 \cdot \lambda \cdot y$, $\lambda \neq 0$ represents:
A. an elliptic cylinder
B. a cylinder
C. a hyperbolic cylinder
D. a parabolic cylinder

49. Two conjugate diameters of the hyperbola are such that:
A. Both meet the curve at real point
B. Both meet the curve at imaginary points
C. They meet the curve at infinity
D. One meets the curve at real point and another meets at imaginary point

50. A plane passes through a point (1, –2, 1) and is perpendicular of two planes $2x - 2y + z = 0$ and $x - y + 2z = 4$. The distance of the plane from the point (1, 2, 2) is:
A. $2\sqrt{2}$ B. 1
C. $\sqrt{2}$ D. 2

51. The polar co-ordinate of a centre of the circle $r = 4 \cdot \cos\theta + 3 \cdot \sin\theta$ is:
A. $\left(\frac{3}{4}, \tan^{-1}\frac{2}{3}\right)$
B. $\left(\frac{5}{2}, \tan^{-1}\frac{3}{4}\right)$
C. $\left(5, \tan^{-1}\frac{3}{4}\right)$
D. $\left(\frac{5}{2}, \tan^{-1}\frac{2}{3}\right)$

52. The angle between the lines represented by $x^2 - 2xy - y^2 + 2x + 3y - 1 = 0$ is:
A. $\frac{\pi}{2}$ B. $\tan^{-1}\left(\frac{1}{4}\right)$
C. $\tan^{-1}\left(\frac{1}{2}\right)$ D. $\frac{\pi}{4}$

53. If any tangents to the ellipse $\frac{x^2}{a^2}+\frac{y^2}{b^2}=1$ makes intercepts of lengths h and k on the axis, then:

A. $\frac{h^2}{a^2}+\frac{k^2}{b^2}=1$ B. $\frac{h^2}{a^2}-\frac{k^2}{b^2}=1$

C. $\frac{a^2}{h^2}-\frac{b^2}{k^2}=1$ D. $\frac{a^2}{h^2}+\frac{b^2}{k^2}=1$

54. Let l be the focal chord of a parabola and d be the distance from vertex, then:

A. $l \propto \frac{1}{d^2}$ B. $l \propto \frac{1}{d}$

C. $l \propto d^2$ D. $l \propto d$

55. The eccentricity and semi-latus rectum of the curve $\frac{1}{r}=8+5.\cos\theta$, are respectively:

A. $\frac{5}{8}, 8$ B. $\frac{5}{8}, \frac{1}{8}$

C. $\frac{1}{8}, \frac{5}{8}$ D. $\frac{1}{8}, 8$

56. If $S_1 = 0$ and $S_2 = 0$ are the equations of a sphere, then $S_1 + \lambda \cdot S_2 = 0$ represents:

A. a sphere passing through the circle of intersection of the spheres

B. a sphere passing through the plane of intersection

C. a plane

D. circle

57. The equation $xy - ax - by + ab = 0$ represents:

A. a pair of straight lines

B. a hyperbola

C. a circle

D. an ellipse

58. The equation of the plane through the point (1, 2, –3) and normal to the straight line joining the points (–1, 3, 4) and (5, 2, –1) is:

A. $3x - 2y - 5z - 9 = 0$

B. $6x - y - 5z - 19 = 0$

C. $6x - y + 5z + 19 = 0$

D. $x - 2y - 3z - 17 = 0$

59. From a hyperbola or ellipse how many normals can be drawn?

A. Four B. Two

C. One D. Three

60. The shortest distance between the z-axis and the line $\frac{x-2}{1}=\frac{y-1}{2}=\frac{z+1}{2}$ is:

A. $3\sqrt{5}$ B. $\frac{3}{\sqrt{5}}$

C. $\frac{5}{\sqrt{3}}$ D. $\frac{2}{\sqrt{5}}$

61. If $\operatorname{cosec}\alpha + \cot\alpha = 2+\sqrt{5}$, then value of $\cos\alpha$ is:

A. $\frac{\sqrt{5}}{2}$ B. $\sqrt{3}$

C. $\frac{1}{\sqrt{3}}$ D. $\frac{2}{\sqrt{5}}$

62. What should be a necessary and sufficient condition for the curve v = constant to be a Geodesic on the general surface?

A. $EE_2 - FE_1 + 2EF_1 = 0$

B. $EE_2 + FE_1 - 2EF_1 = 0$

C. $EE_2 + FE_1 + 2EF_1 = 0$

D. $EE_2 - FE_1 - 2EF_1 = 0$

63. The element of surface ds is given by:

A. $ds = H^2\sqrt{du^2+dv^2}$

B. $ds = H\sqrt{du^2+dv^2}$

C. $ds = H.dudv$

D. $ds = H^2dudv$

64. If $X = \cot\theta + \cos\theta$ and $Y = \cot\theta - \cos\theta$, then find the value of $\frac{X^2-Y^2}{\sqrt{XY}}$.

A. 4 B. 0

C. 1 D. 2

65. If $\cos^{-1}\left(\frac{p}{a}\right)+\cos^{-1}\left(\frac{q}{b}\right)=\alpha$, then $\frac{p^2}{a^2}+k\cos\alpha$, $+\frac{q^2}{b^2}+\sin^2\alpha$ where k is equal to:

A. $-\frac{pq}{ab}$ B. $\frac{2pq}{ab}$

C. $\frac{pq}{ab}$ D. $-\frac{2pq}{ab}$

66. The value of $\sqrt{3}\sin 10°$ is equal to:
A. cos 50° – cos 70°
B. cos 50° + cos 70°
C. sin 20° + sin 40°
D. sin 70° + sin 50°

67. Value of $\cot\left(7\frac{1}{2}\right)°$ is:
A. $2+\sqrt{3}+\sqrt{5}+\sqrt{6}$
B. $\sqrt{2}+\sqrt{3}+\sqrt{5}+\sqrt{6}$
C. $3+\sqrt{2}+\sqrt{3}+\sqrt{6}$
D. $2+\sqrt{2}+\sqrt{3}+\sqrt{6}$

68. sin 6° · sin 66° is:
A. $\frac{3-\sqrt{5}}{8}$ B. $\frac{3-\sqrt{5}}{4}$
C. $\frac{\sqrt{5}-1}{4}$ D. $\frac{\sqrt{5}-1}{8}$

69. On the surface $xyz = 4$, what shall be the equation of the tangent plane at the point (1, 2, 2)?
A. $x - 2y - z + 1 = 0$
B. $x + 2y + z = 2$
C. $2x + y + z = 6$
D. $x + 2y + z - 1 = 0$

70. If sin 3A = cos (A – 30), where 3A and (A – 30) are acute angles, find the value of (sin 2A + cos 2A):
A. $\frac{\sqrt{3}+1}{2}$ B. $\frac{\sqrt{3}+1}{3}$
C. $\frac{\sqrt{3}-1}{3}$ D. $\frac{\sqrt{3}-1}{2}$

71. Equation of asymptotic lines is given by:
A. $-\mathrm{L}du^2 - 2\mathrm{M}\, dudv + \mathrm{N}dv^2 = 0$
B. $\mathrm{L}du^2 - \mathrm{N}dv^2 = 0$
C. $\mathrm{M}\, dudv = 0$
D. $\mathrm{L}du^2 + 2\mathrm{M}\, dudv + \mathrm{N}dv^2 = 0$

72. For a curve to be a helix which of the following should be the most necessary sufficient condition?
A. The ratio of the curvature and the torsion is constant
B. The torsion is constant
C. The product of the curvature and the torsion constant
D. The curvature is constant

73. What shall be the appropriate matrix of the coefficient of Frenet-Serret formula?
A. $\begin{bmatrix} 0 & k & 0 \\ -k & 0 & \tau \\ 0 & -\tau & 0 \end{bmatrix}$ B. $\begin{bmatrix} 0 & -k & 0 \\ k & 0 & -\tau \\ 0 & \tau & 0 \end{bmatrix}$
C. $\begin{bmatrix} 0 & \tau & 0 \\ -\tau & 0 & k \\ 0 & -k & 0 \end{bmatrix}$ D. $\begin{bmatrix} 0 & -\tau & 0 \\ \tau & 0 & -k \\ 0 & k & 0 \end{bmatrix}$

74. Let there be a surface, $x = u \cos v$, $y = u \sin v$, $z = cv$. The first fundamental coefficient are respectively:
A. 0, 0, $u^2 + c^2$
B. cos v, sin v, $u^2 + 1$
C. 1, 0, $\sqrt{u^2+c^2}$
D. 1, 0, $u^2 + c^2$

75. Find the value of $\frac{\cot^3 2\mathrm{A} + 3\cot 2\mathrm{A}\,\mathrm{cosec}^2 2\mathrm{A}}{\mathrm{cosec}^3 2\mathrm{A}(\cos^6 \mathrm{A} - \sin^6 \mathrm{A})}$.
A. 2 B. 3
C. 4 D. 1

76. If A lies in the first quadrant and $2\sqrt{3}\sin \mathrm{A}\cos \mathrm{A} = \cos^2 \mathrm{A} - \sin^2 \mathrm{A}$, then the value of cos A cos (A/2) sin (A/2) is:
A. 4 B. $\frac{1}{8}$
C. $\frac{1}{4}$ D. 8

77. If $\mathrm{P}(\vec{r})$ is a point on a surface, then P will be a singularity of the surface if:
A. $r_1 \times r_2 \neq 0$ B. $r_1 = r_2$
C. $r_1 = r_2 = 0$ D. $r_1 \times r_2 = 0$

78. Find the value of: $\frac{\sec 8A(\tan 10\mathrm{A} + \tan 6\mathrm{A})}{4(\tan 10\mathrm{A} - \tan 6\mathrm{A})}$.
A. sin 4A B. cos 4A
C. tan 4A D. sin 2A

79. For a paraboloid of revolution $z = x^2 + y^2$, the asymptotic lines is given by:
A. $u^2du^2 + v^2dv^2 = 0$
B. $du^2 + u^2dv^2 = 0$
C. $du^2 - dv^2 = 0$
D. $du^2 + dv^2 = 0$

80. Express the relation between readius of spherical-curvature R and the radius of curvature ρ of the curve P and σ (the reciprocal of the torsion).

A. $R^2 = \sigma^2 + (\rho'\rho)^2$
B. $R^2 = \rho'^2 + (\rho\sigma)^2$
C. $R^2 = \sigma^2 + \left(\frac{p^1}{\sigma}\right)^2$
D. $R^2 = \rho^2 + (\rho'\sigma)^2$

81. Find the sum of coefficient of the expansion $(1 + x - 3x^2)^{4165}$.

A. 2 B. 1
C. 0 D. –1

82. Find by using binomial theorem $(2^{3n} - 7n - 1)$ is divisible by which of the following numbers?

A. 49 B. 27
C. 7 D. 15

83. The CTFT of a continuous time signal $x(t) = e^{-A|t|}$, A > 0 is ____.

A. $\frac{2A}{(A^2+\omega^2)}$ B. $\frac{A}{(\omega^2)}$
C. $\frac{A}{(A^2+\omega^2)}$ D. $\frac{2A}{(\omega^2)}$

84. If f is a continuous function, then $\lim_{n\to\infty} \sum_{r=0}^{n-1} \frac{1}{n} f\left(\frac{r}{n}\right)$ can be expressed as:

A. $\int_0^1 f(x)\, dx$ B. $\int_0^1 xf(x)\, dx$
C. $\int_0^1 \frac{1}{x} f\left(\frac{1}{x}\right) dx$ D. $\int_0^1 f\left(\frac{1}{x}\right) dx$

85. The running integrator given by $y(t) = \int_{-\infty}^{\infty} x(t)dt$:

A. Produces an abounded output for every causal bounded input
B. Produces a bounded output for every anti-causal bounded input
C. Has no finite zeros in its double-sided Laplace transform Y(s).
D. Has no finite singularities in its double sided Laplace transform Y(s).

86. A signal $x(t)$ is given by $x(t) = \begin{cases} 1, & \frac{-T}{4} < t \le \frac{3T}{4} \\ -1, & \frac{3T}{4} < t \le \frac{7T}{4} \\ -x(t+T) & \end{cases}$

Which among the following gives the fundamental Fourier terms of $x(t)$?

A. $\frac{4}{\pi}\sin\left(\frac{\pi t}{T} - \frac{\pi}{4}\right)$ B. $\frac{4}{\pi}\sin\left(\frac{\pi t}{T} + \frac{\pi}{4}\right)$
C. $\frac{4}{\pi}\cos\left(\frac{\pi t}{T} + \frac{\pi}{4}\right)$ D. $\frac{4}{\pi}\cos\left(\frac{\pi t}{T} - \frac{\pi}{4}\right)$

87. Which of the following is true?

A. Every integrable function is monotone increasing
B. Every integrable function is continuous
C. Every monotone function is integrable
D. Every discontinuous function is integrable

88. Find the remainder when 2^{252} is divided by 210?

A. 208 B. 141
C. 106 D. 1

89. The largest coefficient of $(x + 1)^{20}$ is:

A. $\frac{(20)!}{5!4!}$ B. $\frac{(20)!}{(10!)^2}$
C. $\frac{(20)!}{10!5!}$ D. $\frac{(20)!}{6!4!}$

90. Root of the number $(6+4\sqrt{3})$.

A. $3(\sqrt{2}+1)^2$ B. $\sqrt{3}(\sqrt{3}-1)^2$
C. $3(\sqrt{3}+1)^2$ D. $\sqrt{3}(\sqrt{3}+1)^2$

91. $y(t)$ is a real valued function of a real variable with period T. Its trigonometric Fourier series expansion contains no terms of frequency $w = 2\pi\left(\frac{2k}{T}\right)$, k = 1, 2, ... Also no terms are present. Then $y(t)$ satisfies the equation:

A. $y(t) = y(t - T) = y(t - T/2)$
B. $y(t) = y(T - t) = -y(t - T/2)$
C. $y(t) = y(t + T) = y(t + T/2)$
D. $y(t) = y(t - T) = -y(t - T/2)$

92. If $(a + b) = 2$, then the value of $\sum_{r=0}^{n} {}^nC_r a^r b^{n-r}$

A. 0 B. -2^n
C. 2^n D. 1

93. Coefficient of x^{-2} of this expansion $\left(2x^3 - \frac{7}{x}\right)^8$:

A. 40 B. 90
C. 72 D. 60

94. The middle term in the expansion of $\left(x^2 + \frac{1}{x^2} + 2\right)^n$ is:

A. $\frac{(2n!)}{\left[\left(\frac{n}{2}\right)!\right]^2}$ B. $\frac{(2n)!}{(n!)^2}$

C. $\frac{n}{\left[\left(\frac{n}{2}\right)!\right]^2}$ D. $\frac{1.2.5..(2n+1)}{n!}2^n$

95. Which of the following is true?

1. $(1.01)^{1000000} > 10000$
2. $(98)^55 > 9500000000$

A. Only 1
B. Both 1 and 2
C. Neither 1 nor 2
D. Only 2

96. The remainder when $75^{75^{75}}$ is divided by 37:

A. 7 B. 0
C. 5 D. 1

97. The continuous time system described by the equation $y(t) = x(t)^2$ comes under the category of:

A. Non-causal, linear and time-variant
B. Causal, non-linear and time-varying
C. Causal, linear and time-varying
D. Non-causal, non-linear and time-variant

98. The Fourier series for the function $f(x) = \sin^2(x)$ is:

A. 0.5 + 0.5 sin 2x B. 0.5 + 0.5 cos 2x
C. 0.5 – 0.5 sin 2x D. 0.5 – 0.5 cos 2x

99. If $4.5^x = 500$, then the value of x^x is:

A. 27 B. 8
C. 1 D. 64

100. The system characterized by the differential equation $\frac{d^2y(t)}{dt^2} - \frac{dy}{dt} - 2y(t) = x(t)$ is:

A. Non-linear and stable
B. Linear and unstable
C. Non-linear and unstable
D. Linear and stable

101. Find the value of statement P(n) : 1.6 + 2.9 + 3.12 + ... + $n(3n + 3)$.

A. $n(n + 1)(n + 2)$ B. $(n + 1)(n + 2)(n + 3)$
C. $n(n + 6)$ D. $(n + 3)(n + 6)$

102. By mathematical ascending method the value of 1 + 2 + 3 + ... + n is ____.

A. $\frac{(n+1)(n+2)}{2}$ B. $\frac{n(n+1)}{2}$

C. $\frac{n(n+1)}{3}$ D. $\frac{(n+1)(n+2)}{3}$

103. For what value of n, the statement P(n) : $n! < \left(\frac{n+1}{2}\right)^n$, is true? Where n is a positive whole number?

A. 3 B. 2
C. 4 D. 1

104. Which of the following improper integral is convergent?

A. $\int_2^{\infty} \frac{1}{\log x} dx$ B. $\int_0^1 \frac{1}{\sqrt{x}(x+1)} dx$

C. $\int_1^2 \frac{\sqrt{x}}{\log x} dx$ D. $\int_0^{\pi} \frac{1}{1-\cos x} dx$

105. General form of the statement is $\left(1+\frac{1}{1}\right)\left(1+\frac{1}{2}\right)\left(1+\frac{1}{3}\right)...\left(1+\frac{1}{n}\right)$ is:

A. $(n + 1)^2$ B. $\left(1+\frac{1}{n}\right)$

C. $\left(n+\frac{1}{n}\right)$ D. $(n + 1)$

106. The integral $\int_0^1 \frac{x^3 \cos 3x}{2+x^2}$ lies between?

A. $-\frac{1}{2}$ and $\frac{1}{2}$ B. -1 and 1

C. $-\frac{3}{2}$ and $\frac{3}{2}$ D. $-\frac{1}{3}$ and $\frac{1}{3}$

107. The statement $(x^n - y^n)$ is divisible by:
A. $(x + y)$ B. $(x^2 + y^2)$
C. $(x - y)$ D. $(x + y)(x - y)$

108. Which of the following is true?
Let $f : [0, 1] \to R$ be defined by

$$f(x) = \begin{cases} (-1)^{r-1}, & \text{when } \frac{1}{r+1} < x \le \frac{1}{r}, r = 1, 2, 3, ... \\ 0, & \text{when } x = 0 \end{cases}$$

A. f is not integrable in [0, 1]
B. f is integrable on [0, 1], but f in bounded
C. f is integrable on [0, 1], but f in unbounded
D. f is integrable on [0, 1]

109. Which statement is true?

A. $n! < \left(\frac{n+1}{2}\right)^n$ B. $n! > \left(\frac{n+1}{2}\right)^n$

C. $n! < \left(\frac{n}{2}\right)^n$ D. $n! > (n)^n$

110. If $I_n = \int_0^{\frac{\pi}{2}} x^n \sin x \, dx, n > 1$, then $I_n + n(n-1)I_{n-2}$ is equal to:

A. $n\left(\frac{\pi}{2}\right)^{n-1}$ B. $n\left(\frac{\pi}{2}\right)^n$

C. $\left(\frac{\pi}{2}\right)^{n-1}$ D. $\left(\frac{\pi}{2}\right)$

111. $P(n) : 1.1! + 2.2! + 3.3! + n.n! = (n + 1)! - 1$, then $P(n)$ statement is true:
A. For $n > 1$
B. For $n > 4$
C. For all negative values of n
D. For all values of n

112. Let $I_n = \int \tan^n x \, dx, (n > 1)$. $I_4 + I_6 = a \tan^5 x + bx^5 + c$, where c is a constant of integration, then the order pair (a, b) is equal to:

A. $\left(-\frac{1}{5}, -1\right)$ B. $\left(\frac{1}{5}, \frac{4}{5}\right)$

C. $\left(\frac{1}{5}, 0\right)$ D. $\left(-\frac{1}{5}, 1\right)$

113. Which one of the inequality is true?

A. $-1 < \int_0^1 e^{x^2} dx < 1$ B. $\frac{1}{e} < \int_0^1 e^{x^2} dx < \frac{1}{2}$

C. $e < \int_0^1 e^{x^2} dx < 1$ D. $1 < \int_0^1 e^{x^2} dx < e$

114. Which of the following improper integral is convergent?

A. $\int_1^\infty \frac{1}{x^2} dx$ B. $\int_1^\infty \frac{1}{\sqrt{x}} dx$

C. $\int_1^\infty \frac{1}{x^3} dx$ D. $\int_1^\infty \frac{1}{x^{3/2}} dx$

115. The solution of the differential equation $(2D + 1)^2 y = 0$ is:
A. $y = (A + B)e^{-x/2}$ B. $y = (A + Bx)e^{-x/2}$
C. $y = (A + Bx)e^{-x}$ D. $y = Ae^{-x/2}$

116. The solution of the differential equation

$$X^2 \frac{d^2y}{dx^2} - 3X\frac{dy}{dx} + 4y = 0 \text{ is:}$$

A. $y = (c_1 + c_2 \log x)x$
B. $y = (c_1 + c_2 \log x)e^x$
C. $y = (c_1 + c_2 \log x)x^2$
D. $y = (c_1 + c_2 \log x)e^{2x}$

117. The statement $(5^{2n} - 1)$ is always divisible by:
A. 25 B. 15
C. 42 D. 24

118. The statement $1.2 + 2.2^2 + 3.2^2 + ... n.2^2$ can be written in the form of:
A. $(n - 1)2^n + 2$ B. $(n + 1)2^n + 2$
C. $(n - 1)2^{n+1} + 2$ D. $(n + 1)2^{n+1} + 2$

119. $(3^{2n+1} + 2^{n+2})$ is divisible by:
A. 7 B. 3
C. 5 D. 2

120. If $f(x) = x|x|$, then for any real numbers a and b with $a < b$, the value of $\int_a^b f(x)dx$ equals:

A. $\frac{1}{3}(a^3 - b^3)$ B. $\frac{1}{3}(a^3 + b^3)$

C. $\frac{1}{3}(|b|^3 - |a|^3)$ D. $\frac{1}{3}(|b^3 - a^3|)$

121. The number of onto homomorphism from Z_8 to Z_4 is:

A. 3 B. 2
C. 4 D. 1

122. If $y = x$ is a solution of the differential equation $x^2y'' + xy' - y = 0$, then the second linearly independent solution of the above equation is:

A. x^2 B. x^3
C. $\frac{1}{x}$ D. x^{-2}

123. If $x = A\,(mt - \alpha)$, then the differential equation satisfying the relation is:

A. $\frac{d^2x}{dt^2} = -m^2x$ B. $\frac{dx}{dt} = 1 - x^2$

C. $\frac{d^2x}{dt^2} = m^2x$ D. $\frac{d^2x}{dt^2} = -\alpha^2 x$

124. If ${}^{2n+1}P_{n-1} : {}^{2n-1}P_n = 3 : 5$, then what is the value of n?

A. 2 B. 3
C. 0 D. 4

125. Let H be a subgroup of a group G and K be a normal subgroup of a group G, then:

A. K is a normal subgroup of HK $\cap$ KH
B. K is a normal subgroup of HK
C. K is a normal subgroup of KH
D. K is not a normal subgroup of HK.

126. Let (G, o) and (G′, *) be two groups and f: G $\to$ G′ be a homomorphism, then f(G):

A. Is a cyclic subgroup of G′ is commutative
B. Is a cyclic subgroup of G′ if G may not be cyclic
C. Is a cyclic subgroup of G′
D. Is not a cyclic subgroup of G′ if G is cyclic

127. If G is a group such that $a^2 = c$ for all $a \in$ G, then G is:

A. Field B. Non-abelian group
C. Abelian Group D. Ring

128. $e^x(c_1 \cos\sqrt{3x} + c_2 \sin\sqrt{3x}) + c_3e^{2x}$ is the general solution of:

A. $\frac{d^2x}{dy^2} + 4y = 0$

B. $\frac{d^3y}{dx^3} - 2\frac{d^2y}{dx^2} + \frac{dy}{dx} - 2y = 0$

C. $\frac{d^3x}{dy^3} + x\frac{dx}{dy} - 3x = 0$

D. $\frac{d^2x}{dy^2} + 8y = 0$

129. Let (G, o) and (G′, *) be two groups and ϕ : G $\to$ G′ be an epimorphism then:

A. O(G) is not a divisor of O(G′).
B. O(G) is a divisor of O(G′).
C. O(G′) is a divisor of O(G).
D. O(G′) is not a divisor O(G).

130. Using digit 1, 2, 3, 4, 5 and 6 how many numbers between 3000 and 4000 can be made if no digit should be repeated?

A. 90 B. 70
C. 100 D. 60

131. A commutative group G is simple if and only if:

A. O(G) = n, n is a positive integer
B. O(G) = n, n is an even integer
C. O(G) = n, n is an odd integer
D. O(G) = n, n is a prime integer

132. The particular integral of $(D^2 + a^2)y = \sin ax$ $\left(D \equiv \frac{d}{dx}\right)$ is:

A. $-\frac{x}{2a}\cos ax$ B. $\frac{x}{2a}\cos ax$

C. $-\frac{xa}{2}\cos ax$ D. $\frac{xa}{2}\cos ax$

133. Let (G, o) and (G′, *) be two groups and ϕ : G $\to$ G′ be a epimorphism. Then ϕ is an isomorphism if and only if:

A. Ker $\phi \subset \{eG'\}$
B. Ker $\phi \subset \{eG\}$
C. Ker $\phi = \{eG'\}$
D. Ker $\phi = \{eG\}$

134. Which of the following is not true?

A. Let G be a group in which $(ab)^3 = a^3b^3$ for all $a, b \in G$, then $H = \{x^3, x \in G\}$ is normal subgroup of G.

B. Every commutative subgroup of a group is normal subgroup of the group.

C. If H is normal subgroup of a finite group G, then [G : H] = 2.

D. Let G is non-commutative group of order $2p$, p is prime and there exists at least one element a of order p, then $\langle a \rangle$ is normal in G.

135. The linearly independent solutions of the differential equation $4\dfrac{d^2y}{dx^2}+4\dfrac{dy}{dx}+5y=0$ is:

A. $e^{x/2}\cos x$ and $e^{x/2}\sin x$

B. $e^{x/2}\cos x$ and $e^{-x/2}\sin x$

C. $e^{-x/2}\cos x$ and $e^{x/2}\sin x$

D. $e^{-x/2}\cos x$ and $e^{-x/2}\sin x$

136. A particular solution of differential equation $\dfrac{d^2y}{dx^2}-\dfrac{dy}{dx}-2y=\cos x+3\sin x$ is:

A. $-\cos x$ B. $\cos x$

C. $-\sin x$ D. $\sin x$

137. If f is continuous mapping of compact metric space X into a metric space Y then:

A. f is uniformly continuous

B. f is not continuous

C. f has a jump at $x = \theta$

D. f is a step function

138. If ${}^9P_5 + 5 \cdot {}^9P_4 = {}^{10}P_r$, then r is:

A. 8 B. 5

C. 9 D. 10

139. The general solution of the differential equation $\dfrac{d^2y}{dx^2}+2\dfrac{dy}{dx}+y=e^x\cos x$ is:

A. $(c_1+c_2x)e^{-x}+\dfrac{e^x}{25}(4\sin x+3\cos x)$

B. $(c_1+c_2x)e^{-x}+\dfrac{e^x}{4}(4\sin x+3\cos x)$

C. $(c_1+c_2x)e^{-x}+\dfrac{e^x}{9}(4\sin x-3\cos x)$

D. $(c_1 + c_2x + \sin x)e^{-x}$

140. The solution of the differential equation is $\dfrac{d^2y}{dx^2}-3\dfrac{dy}{dx}+2y=e^{3x}$ is:

A. $y=c_1e^x+c_2e^{-2x}+\dfrac{1}{2}e^{3x}$

B. $y=c_1e^{-x}+c_2e^{2x}+\dfrac{1}{2}e^{-3x}$

C. $y=c_1e^x+c_2e^{-2x}+\dfrac{1}{2}e^{-3x}$

D. $y=c_1e^x+c_2e^x+\dfrac{1}{2}e^{3x}$

141. Find the unit vector which is paralleled to the addition of two vectors $\vec{r_1}=3\vec{i}-2\vec{j}$ and $\vec{r_2}=-4\vec{i}+4\vec{j}$.

A. $1/5(-\vec{i}-2\vec{j})$ B. $1/\sqrt{5}(\vec{i}+2\vec{j})$

C. $1/\sqrt{5}(-\vec{i}+2\vec{j})$ D. $1/5(\vec{i}-2\vec{j})$

142. There is a group of 11 cricketers, 4 can bat and 7 can ball. In how many ways can a group of 5 cricketers be selected if the group has at least one batsman and bowler?

A. 441 B. 669

C. 237 D. 745

143. If $(\vec{x}-\vec{a})(\vec{x}+\vec{a})=8$ and $\vec{a}$ is a unit vector, then $\vec{x}$ will have value of:

A. 4 B. 3

C. 8 D. 9

144. The function $f(x) = x \sin(1/x)$, if $x = 0$ and $f(0) = 1$ has discontinuity at ____.

A. 2 B. 0

C. 1 D. 3

145. If no two '–' signs can be repeated, then in how many ways a line can be made from six '+' signs and four '–' signs?

A. 50 B. 53

C. 15 D. 35

146. (1, 1), (–1, –1) and (–√3, √3) are vectors of:

A. Isosceles triangle

B. Equilateral triangle

C. Collinear points

D. Right angle triangle

147. If ${}^nP_r = 336$ and ${}^nC_r = 56$, then what is the value of n and r?

A. $n = 3, r = 2$ B. $n = 8, r = 3$
C. $n = 14, r = 4$ D. $n = 7, r = 8$

148. The ring of Matrix $S = \left\{ \begin{pmatrix} 2a & 0 \\ 0 & 2b \end{pmatrix} : a, b \in Z \right\}$ contains:

A. divisors of zero without unity
B. divisors of zero with unity
C. no divisors of zero with unity
D. no divisors of zero without unity

149. If $\vec{a}$ is a non-zero vector of magnitude 'a' and λ is a non-zero scalar, then $\lambda\vec{a}$ is unit vector if:

A. $a = \frac{1}{|\lambda|}$ B. $a = |\lambda|$
C. $\lambda = 1$ D. $\lambda = -1$

150. If $|m\vec{a}| = 2$, then what is the value of m?

A. $-\frac{2}{|\vec{a}|}$ B. $\frac{2}{|\vec{a}|}$
C. 2 D. $\pm\frac{2}{|\vec{a}|}$

151. If ${}^{25}C_r = {}^{25}C_{2r+1}$, then what is the value of ${}^rC_5$?

A. 56 B. 64
C. 65 D. 50

152. Find the intervals in which the function f given by strictly increasing $f(x) = 2xx^2 - 3x$:

A. $\frac{3}{4}, \infty$ B. $\infty, \frac{3}{4}$
C. $-\frac{3}{4}, \infty$ D. $-\infty, \frac{3}{4}$

153. The points

$A(-2\vec{i} + 3\vec{j} + 5\vec{k}), B(\vec{i} + 2\vec{j} + 3\vec{k}), C(7\vec{i} - 5\vec{k})$

are:

A. Collinear
B. Formed a equilateral triangle
C. Formed a Right angle triangle
D. Non-Collinear

154. If two vectors $p\vec{i} + 2\vec{j}$ and $3\vec{i} - 3\vec{j}$ are aligned, then what is the value of p?

A. 2 B. −1
C. −2 D. 1

155. In how many of the distinct permutation of letters in JUXTAPOSED do the four vowels come together?

A. 102960 B. 182900
C. 190026 D. 120960

156. The position-vectors of point A, B, C and D are $3\vec{i} - \vec{j}, 2\vec{i} + 2\vec{j}, -2\vec{i} - 3\vec{j}, 4\vec{i} + 3\vec{j}$, respectively such that AB || CD, then what is the ratio of their modulus?

A. 2 : 3 B. 3 : 2
C. 2 : 1 D. 1 : 2

157. Find the number of diagonals of a polygon whose number of sides is "n".

A. $(n - 2)(n - 5)/3$
B. $n(n - 3)/2$
C. $n(n - 1)/2$
D. $(n - 1)(n - 2)/3$

158. Let $R = (Z_2 \times Z_2, +, .)$ forms a ring of module 2 such that $(a, b) + (c, d) = (a + c, d + d)$ and $(a, b)(c, d) = (a \cdot c, b \cdot d)$ for $(a, b), (c, d) \in Z_2 \times Z_2$ then:

A. R is a commutative ring with unity and it contains divisor of zero
B. R is a commutative ring with unity and it contains no divisor of zero
C. R is a commutative ring without unity and it contains no divisor of zero
D. R is a non commutative ring with unity and it contains divisor of zero

159. If two position-vectors of A and B are $8\vec{i} + 3\vec{j}$ and $2\vec{i} - 5\vec{j}$, then determine the direction of AB vector:

A. $\cos^{-1}(-3/5)$
B. $\cos^{-1}(3/5)$
C. $\sin^{-1}(-5/3)$
D. $\sin^{-1}(5/3)$

160. If the Ring R is a commutative with unity, then the polynomial ring $R|x|$ is:

A. a non commutative ring without unity
B. a commutative ring with unity
C. a commutative ring without unity
D. a non-commutative ring with unity

161. $f : R - \{-2\} \rightarrow R$ defined by

$f(x) = \dfrac{x+1}{x+2}, \forall x \in R - \{-2\}$ is an example of:

A. Rational Function
B. Signum Function
C. Modulus Function
D. Polynomial Function

162. Which one of the following is TRUE?

A. The sequence $\{n \cos 1/n\}$ has a convergent sequence
B. Every sequence that has a convergent subsequence is a Cauchy sequence
C. The sequence $\{\sin n\}$ has a convergent subsequence
D. Every sequence that has a convergent sequence is a bounded sequence

163. Which one of the following ring of matrix is not a field?

A. $\left\{\begin{pmatrix} a & b \\ -b & a \end{pmatrix} : a, b \in R\right\}$

B. $\left\{\begin{pmatrix} a & b \\ 3b & a \end{pmatrix} : a, b \in Q\right\}$

C. $\left\{\begin{pmatrix} a & b \\ 2b & a \end{pmatrix} : a, b \in R\right\}$

D. $\left\{\begin{pmatrix} a & b \\ 2b & a \end{pmatrix} : a, b \in Q\right\}$

164. Let ΣU_n be a convergent series of positive terms and let ΣV_n be a divergent series of positive terms. Then

A. The sequence $\{V_n\}$ diverges to ∞
B. Both the sequence $\{U_n\}$ and $\{V_n\}$ are convergent
C. The sequence $\{U_n\}$ is convergent and the sequence $\{V_n\}$ is divergent
D. The sequence $\{U_n\}$ converges to 0

165. Suppose the matrix

$$A = \begin{pmatrix} 40 & -29 & -11 \\ -18 & 30 & -12 \\ 26 & 24 & -50 \end{pmatrix}$$

has a certain eigen value $\lambda \neq 0$. Which of the following must be eigen value of A?

A. $\lambda - 20$ B. $\lambda + 20$
C. $20 - \lambda$ D. $-20 - \lambda$

166. The integral $\int_0^\infty \sin x \, dx$:

A. Exists and is equal to 0
B. Exists and is equal to 1
C. Exists and is equal to –1
D. Does not exist

167. The series $\sum_{n=1}^{\infty}\left[\dfrac{1}{\sqrt{n}} + \dfrac{(-1)^n}{n^{3/2}}\right]$ is:

A. oscillatory B. divergent
C. bounded D. convergent

168. Let $\{U_n\}$ be a sequence of real number such that $\lim_{n\to\infty} U_n$ exist, then:

A. $\lim_{n\to\infty} U_{2n}$ does not exist but $\lim_{n\to\infty} U_{2n+1}$ exists
B. both $\lim_{n\to\infty} U_{2n}$ and $\lim_{n\to\infty} U_{2n+1}$ do not exist
C. $\lim_{n\to\infty} U_{2n}$ exists but $\lim_{n\to\infty} U_{2n+1}$ does not exist
D. both $\lim_{n\to\infty} U_{2n}$ and $\lim_{n\to\infty} U_{2n+1}$ exist

169. Let M_2 (R) be the set of all 2 × 2 matrices, then $(M_2(R), +, .)$ is:

A. a commutative ring without zero divisors
B. a non commutative ring with zero divisors
C. a commutative ring with zero divisors
D. a non commutative ring without zero divisors

170. The integral $\int_0^\infty \dfrac{|\sin x|}{x} dx$:

A. is not convergent
B. is absolutely convergent
C. is divergent
D. is convergent but not absolutely

171. The set of all units in a ring R with unity forms ____.

A. an integral domain
B. a field
C. a ring with unity
D. a group with respect to multiplication

172. If $\lim_{n\to\infty} \frac{U_n}{n} = 1 \neq 0$, then the sequence $\{U_n\}$.
A. may or may not be bounded
B. is not bounded
C. is convergent
D. is bounded

173. The ring of residue classes (mod m) is an integral domain if m is:
A. prime B. a natural number
C. an integer D. a rational number

174. The sequence $\left\{P + \frac{(-1)^n q}{n}\right\}$ is:
A. oscillatory B. divergent
C. Unbounded D. bounded

175. The sequence $\{2 + (-1)^n\}$ has:
A. exactly one constant subsequence
B. exactly two constant subsequence
C. no constant subsequence
D. exactly three constant subsequence

176. The ring $(Z_n, +, .)$ is an integral domain if and only if:
A. n is positive integer
B. n is odd prime
C. n is odd
D. n is prime

177. $\lim_{n\to\infty} \left(\frac{2}{1}\cdot\frac{3}{2}\cdot\frac{4}{3}\cdot\ldots\cdot\frac{n+1}{n}\right)^{\frac{-1}{n}}$ is equal to:
A. 0 B. e
C. 1 D. ∞

178. The value of
$$\lim_{n\to\infty} \frac{1}{n}\left[\left(\frac{1}{2}\right)^n + \left(\frac{1}{2}\right)\left(\frac{1}{2}\right)^{n-1} + \ldots + \left(\frac{1}{n}\right)\left(\frac{1}{2}\right)\right]$$ is
A. 1 B. 0
C. ∞ D. does not exist

179. Which of the following ring is an integral domain?
A. $(Z \times Z, +, .)$ B. $(\rho, +, .)$
C. $(2Z, +, .)$ D. $(Z_8, +, .)$

180. Let M be non-zero $n \times n$ real matrix with $n \geq 2$. Which of the following statements is true?
A. det (M) = 0 $\Rightarrow$ rank (M) = 0
B. rank (M) = n $\Rightarrow$ det (M) $\neq$ 1
C. rank (M) = 1 $\Rightarrow$ det (M) $\neq$ 0
D. det (M) = 1 $\Rightarrow$ rank (M) $\neq$ 0

181. Which of the following subject/s Mathematics is a part of?
A. Geography
B. Geography, Economics and Commerce
C. Economics
D. Commerce

182. Who said, that "Mathematics is the language in which God has written the universe"?
A. Marshal Stone B. Aryabhatta
C. Galileo Galilei D. Bertrand Russell

183. Which one of the following is not a problem-solving strategy in mathematics?
A. rote learning B. drawing
C. trial and error D. solving backwards

184. Which one of the following statements is correct?
A. Sum of two prime numbers is always a prime number
B. There is no even prime numbers
C. 1 is the smallest prime number
D. A composite number cannot be prime

185. Who of the following invented the letter system?
A. Arya-Bhatta-1 B. Kumargupta
C. Bhahmagupta D. Sidhanta

186. The term Mathematics was coined by:
A. Pythayoreans B. Pythamasciour
C. Pythabactus D. Pythanorean

187. Cooperative learning is an alternative to:
A. Competitive models
B. Teaching models
C. Microteaching
D. Lesson plan

188. Educational objectives have been divided into:
A. Four domains B. Two domains
C. Three domains D. Five domains

189. Which is not true about lesson plan?
A. It saves from haphazard teaching
B. It is developed by students
C. It helps in orderly delivery to content
D. It develops confidence in teacher

190. Which of the following is not related to early number concept?
A. measurement B. classification
C. conservation D. class inclusion

191. Which one of the following is not a mathematical process?
A. Memorization B. Estimation
C. Measurement D. Visualization

192. The hypothesis underlying team teaching is:
A. A single teacher cannot control the class
B. The best teachers in schools are shared by more students
C. Teachers are not competent
D. Teachers feel bore while marking alone

193. A learner exhibiting difficulty in sorting, recognising pattern, orienting numbers and shape, telling time and measurement may have dyscalculia with difficulty in:
A. Visual motor coordination
B. Language processing
C. Visual motor skills
D. Visual memory

194. According to Piaget when the child is at formal operational stage, it is appropriate to introduce:
A. Geometry
B. Data handling
C. Numbers
D. Ratio and proportion

195. A good mathematics teacher is one who:
A. encourages convergent thinking
B. remains helpful, insightful and explain things well
C. gives only a lot of problems to practice with
D. follows the same method always

196. In a mathematics classroom emphasis is placed on:
A. mathematical content process and reasoning
B. mathematical content
C. mathematical algorithm and process
D. problem solving strategies

197. The number of students in cooperative learning groups are:
A. Ten to fifteen B. Eight to ten
C. Three to four D. Five to six

198. Which of the following is/ are not the principle of Curriculum-construction of mathematics?
A. Integrity of theory with practice
B. Principle of unit
C. Should not be child-centric
D. The principle of preparation for life

199. Which of the following is/are true regarding the aims of teaching mathematics?
1. To develop a good ability to solve problem.
2. To develop the ability to make decision.
3. To develop a good understanding of numbers and number system.
A. Only 1 and 3 B. 1, 2 and 3
C. Only 1 and 2 D. Only 2 and 3

200. Who said— "instructional objectives are best described in terms of the terminal behaviour expected from the learners"?
A. Sumit Samele B. Robert Miller's
C. Robert Wadra D. Robert Mager

ANSWERS

1	2	3	4	5	6	7	8	9	10
C	B	C	D	B	D	B	C	A	D
11	**12**	**13**	**14**	**15**	**16**	**17**	**18**	**19**	**20**
D	A	B	D	A	A	D	B	A	A
21	**22**	**23**	**24**	**25**	**26**	**27**	**28**	**29**	**30**
C	C	B	A	B	C	D	A	D	D
31	**32**	**33**	**34**	**35**	**36**	**37**	**38**	**39**	**40**
C	D	B	A	C	C	A	A	D	B

41	42	43	44	45	46	47	48	49	50
D	C	B	A	A	D	D	D	B	A
51	**52**	**53**	**54**	**55**	**56**	**57**	**58**	**59**	**60**
B	A	D	A	B	A	A	B	A	B
61	**62**	**63**	**64**	**65**	**66**	**67**	**68**	**69**	**70**
D	B	C	A	D	A	D	A	C	A
71	**72**	**73**	**74**	**75**	**76**	**77**	**78**	**79**	**80**
D	A	A	D	C	B	D	B	B	D
81	**82**	**83**	**84**	**85**	**86**	**87**	**88**	**89**	**90**
D	A	A	A	A	A	C	C	B	D
91	**92**	**93**	**94**	**95**	**96**	**97**	**98**	**99**	**100**
A	C	D	B	A	D	A	D	A	B
101	**102**	**103**	**104**	**105**	**106**	**107**	**108**	**109**	**110**
A	B	B	B	D	A	D	D	A	A
111	**112**	**113**	**114**	**115**	**116**	**117**	**118**	**119**	**120**
D	C	D	B	B	C	D	C	A	C
121	**122**	**123**	**124**	**125**	**126**	**127**	**128**	**129**	**130**
B	C	A	D	B	B	C	B	C	D
131	**132**	**133**	**134**	**135**	**136**	**137**	**138**	**139**	**140**
D	A	A	C	D	C	A	A	A	D
141	**142**	**143**	**144**	**145**	**146**	**147**	**148**	**149**	**150**
C	A	B	B	D	B	B	A	A	D
151	**152**	**153**	**154**	**155**	**156**	**157**	**158**	**159**	**160**
A	A	A	C	D	D	B	A	A	D
161	**162**	**163**	**164**	**165**	**166**	**167**	**168**	**169**	**170**
A	C	C	D	C	D	B	D	B	D
171	**172**	**173**	**174**	**175**	**176**	**177**	**178**	**179**	**180**
D	B	A	D	B	D	C	B	B	D
181	**182**	**183**	**184**	**185**	**186**	**187**	**188**	**189**	**190**
B	C	A	D	A	A	A	C	B	C
191	**192**	**193**	**194**	**195**	**196**	**197**	**198**	**199**	**200**
A	B	A	D	B	A	C	C	B	D

EXPLANATORY ANSWERS

5. In mathematics, a series or integral is said to be conditionally convergent if it converges, but it does not converge absolutely.

More precisely a series of real numbers $\sum_{n=0}^{\infty} a_n$ is said to converge conditionally if $\lim\limits_{m\to\infty} \sum_{n=0}^{m} a_n$ exists (as finite real number, *i.e.*, not ∞ or −∞), but $\sum_{n=0}^{\infty} |a_n| = \infty$.

A classic example is the alternating harmonic series given by

$$1-\frac{1}{2}+\frac{1}{3}-\frac{1}{4}+\frac{1}{5}-\ldots=\sum_{n=1}^{\infty}\frac{(-1)^{n+1}}{n},$$

which converges to ln(B), but is not absolutely convergent.

7. ***Theorem 1:*** Let (s_n) be a monotonic bounded sequence in $\mathbb{R}$. Then (s_n) converges to some $L \in \mathbb{R}$.

Proof: Suppose first that (s_n) is increasing. The set $S = \{s_n : n \in \mathbb{N}\}$ is non-empty (since $s_1 \in S$) and bounded above, so it has a least upper bound, L say. We claim that $s_n \to L$ as $n \to \infty$. So let $\varepsilon > 0$. Then there is some $s \in S$ with $L - \varepsilon < s \le L$. Now, $s \le S$ so $s = s_N$ for some $N \in \mathbb{N}$. Let $n > N$. Then $s_N \le s_n$, since (s_n) is increasing, so we have $L - \varepsilon < s_N \le s_n \le L < L + \varepsilon$, so $L - \varepsilon < s_n < L + \varepsilon$, so $|s_n - L| < \varepsilon$. Thus $s_n \to L$, as claimed.

Theorem 2: Let (s_n) be a sequence in $\mathbb{R}$. Then (s_n) has a subsequence which is monotonic.

The idea is as follows: we give a method for constructing an increasing subsequence in (s_n), which will work unless some particular thing goes wrong. We will then give an alternative method which gives a decreasing subsequence, and which will work if that particular thing went wrong with the first method.

10. The alternating series $\sum_{n=1}^{\infty} \frac{(-1)^n}{n}$ converges, as you note, conditionally, and by the Leibnitz test. It does not converge absolutely. Please note that $\sum_{n=1}^{\infty} \frac{(-1)^n}{n} \neq \sum_{n=1}^{\infty} \frac{1}{n}$.

Alternating series are not equivalent to their non-alternating couterparts. The alternating series test, aka the Leibnitz Test, is precisely for series like this: series that do not converge absolutely, but converge nonetheless. The fact that alternating terms are negative negates the divergence of the sum in the case of the absolute term.

Absolute convergence simply means the series consisting of the absolute values of the terms converges. It does not mean "definitely" converges. A conditionally convergent series still very much converges, for a different reason, but converges just the same.

12. $\sum_{n=1}^{\infty} \sin\left(\frac{1}{n}\right)$

We have $a_n = \sin(1/n)$

Let $b_n = 1/n$

Then using limit comparison test

$$\lim_{n\to\infty} \frac{a_n}{b_n} = \lim_{n\to\infty} \frac{\sin(1/n)}{(1/n)}$$

Let $\frac{1}{n} = \theta$ so $\theta \to 0$ as $n \to \infty$

Then $\lim_{n\to\infty} \frac{a_n}{b_n} = \lim_{\theta\to 0} \frac{\sin\theta}{\theta} = 1$

So $\lim_{n\to\infty} \frac{a_n}{b_n} = 1 > 0$

Since $\sum_{n=1}^{\infty} b_n = \sum_{n=1}^{\infty} \frac{1}{n}$ is a harmonic series which is divergent

So the series $\sum_{n=1}^{\infty} \sin(1/n)$ is also divergent.

13. If Σa_n converges but $\Sigma|a_n|$ does not, we say that Σa_n converges conditionally. Recall that the alternating harmonic series $\sum_{n=1}^{\infty} \frac{(-1)^{n-1}}{n}$ converges, but that the corresponding series of absolute values, namely the harmonic series $\sum_{n=1}^{\infty} \frac{1}{n}$, diverges. Hence, the alternating harmonic series is conditionally convergent.

26. Let $\{N_n\}_{n=1}^{\infty}$ be an arbitrary sequence of nowhere dense sets in X. It suffices to show that if $A = \cup_{n=1}^{\infty} N_n$, then $U \setminus A \neq \varnothing$. Note first that by the foregoing proposition there exists an open ball $D_1 = D_{r1}(x_1)$ with radius $r_1 \le 1$ such $D_1^- \subset U$ and $D_1^- \cap N_1 = \varnothing$. Continuing via mathematical induction, one easily constructs a nested sequence $D_1 \supset D_2 \supset \ldots \supset D_n \supset \ldots$ of open balls $D_n = D_{rn}(x_n)$ such that $r_n \le 1/n$ and such that $D_n^- \cap N_n = \varnothing$ for every n. The sequence of centers $\{x_n\}$ is then obviously a Cauchy sequence, and since X is complete, $\{x_n\}$ must converge to some limit x_0. Since x_0 is also the limit of every tail $\{x_n\}_{n=m}^{\infty}$, and since this tail lies in D_m, it follows that $x_0 \in D_m^-$ for $m = 1, 2, ...$ Thus $x_0 \notin A$, and since $x_0 \in D_1^-$ and $D_1^- \subset U$, we have $x_0 \in U \backslash A$.

30. Let $a^n = \dfrac{(n!)^2 z^n}{(2n)!}$. Then have

$$\lim_{n\to\infty} \frac{a_n+1}{a_n} = \lim_{n\to\infty}\left(\frac{(n+1)!^2 z^{n+1}}{(2n+2)!}\right)\left(\frac{(2n)!}{(n!)^2 z^n}\right)$$

$$= \lim_{n\to\infty} \frac{(n+1)^2}{(2n+1)(2n+2)} z = \frac{z}{4}$$

Thus, the radius of convergence is $r = 4$. This diverges on the boundary points since if $|z| = 4$, then the terms do not go to 0.

32. Let $P = (A \cup B)'$ and $Q = A' \cap B'$

Let x be an arbitrary element of P then $x \in P$

$\Rightarrow \quad x \in (A \cup B)'$

$\Rightarrow \quad x \notin (A \cup B)$

$\Rightarrow \quad x \notin A$ and $x \notin B$

$\Rightarrow \quad x \in A'$ and $x \in B'$

$\Rightarrow \quad x \in A' \cap B'$

$\Rightarrow \quad x \in Q$

Therefore, $P \subset Q$ ...(*i*)

Again, let y be an arbitrary element of Q then $y \in Q$

$\Rightarrow \quad y \in A' \cap B'$

$\Rightarrow \quad y \in A'$ and $y \in B'$

$\Rightarrow \quad y \notin A$ and $y \notin B$

$\Rightarrow \quad y \notin (A \cup B)$

$\Rightarrow \quad y \in (A \cup B)'$

$\Rightarrow \quad y \in P$

Therefore, $Q \subset P$ ...(*ii*)

Now combine (*i*) and (*ii*)

We get; $P = Q$ *i.e.*, $(A \cup B)' = A' \cap B'$.

34. Here, $f(z) = u + iv$ ...(*i*)

$if(z) = iu - v$ ...(*ii*)

Adding (*i*) and (*ii*) we get

$$f(z) + if(z) = u + iv + iu - v$$

$$(1 + i) f(z) = (u - v) + i(u + v)$$

Let $(1 + i) f(z) = F(z)$, $u - v = U$ and $u + v = V$, then

$$F(z) = U + iV$$

If $U = u - v = (x - y)(x^2 + 4xy + y^2)$

So, $\dfrac{\partial U}{\partial x} = x^2 + 4xy + y^2 + x - y(2x + 4y)$

$= 3x^2 + 6xy - 3y^2 = (x_1, y_1)$

And, $\dfrac{\partial U}{\partial x} = -(x^2 + 4xy + y^2) + (x - y)(4x + 2y)$

$= 3x^2 - 6xy + 3y^2 = (x_2, y_2)$

Now $(z_1, 0) = 3z^2$

and $(z_2, 0) = 3z^2$

$$F(z) = \int [3z^2 - i(3z^2)]dz + c$$

$$F(z) = (1 - i)z^3 + c$$

$$(1 + i)f(z) = (1 - i)z^3 + c$$

$$f(z) = -iz^3 + c_1.$$

41. Line, $lx + my + n = 0$ is normal to the circle, $x^2 + y^2 = a^2$

We know that every normal passes through the centre of the circle

Here center of the circle = (0, 0)

Point (0, 0) passing through $lx + my + n = 0$

$l(0) + m(0) + n = 0 \Rightarrow n = 0$.

42. The given plane is $6x - 3y - 2z + 1 = 0$.

Direction ratio's of the normal to the plane are 6, –3, –2

Equation of plane passing through point P = (–3, 8, 4) and $\perp$ar to the plane $6x - 3y - 2z + 1 = 0$ is

$$\frac{x-(-3)}{6} = \frac{y-8}{-3} = \frac{z-4}{-2} = K$$

$\therefore\ x = 6K - 3,\ y = 8 - 3K,\ z = 4 - 2K$

$\therefore$ Co-ordinate of any point lies on this plane is $P'(x, y, z) = (6K - 3, 8 - 3K; 4 - 2K)$

Mid-point of line PP'

$$= \left(\frac{6K-3-3}{2}, \frac{8-3K+8}{2}, \frac{4-2K+4}{2}\right)$$

$$= \left(3K-3, 8-\frac{3K}{2}, 4-K\right)$$

This mid-point lies on the plane

$6x - 3y - 2z + 1 = 0$

$\therefore\ 6(3K-3)-3\left(8-\frac{3K}{2}\right)-2(4-K)+1 = 0$

$$18K+\frac{9K}{2}+2K-18-24-8+1 = 0$$

$$\frac{49K}{2}-49 = 0 \Rightarrow K = 2$$

$\therefore$ Co-ordinate of image point

$$P' = (6\times 2-3,\ 8-3\times 2,\ 4-2\times 2)$$
$$= (9, 2, 0).$$

43. The equation of the cone of the second degree is $ax^2 + by^2 + cz^2 + 2fyz + 2gzx + 2hxy = 0$ ...(*i*)

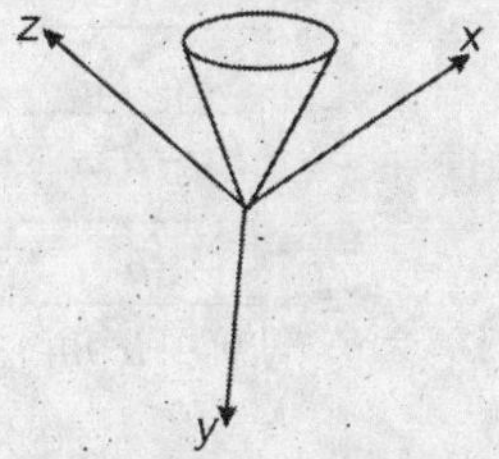

X-axis is a generator of the cone.

$\Rightarrow$ the direction cocines (1, 0, 0) of the X-axis satisfies (1) $\Rightarrow a = 0$.

Similarly, Y-axis is a generator $\Rightarrow b = 0$.

Similarly, Z-axis is a generator $\Rightarrow c = 0$.

Hence the general equation of the cone containing the three axes is $fyz + gzx + hxy = 0$.

44.

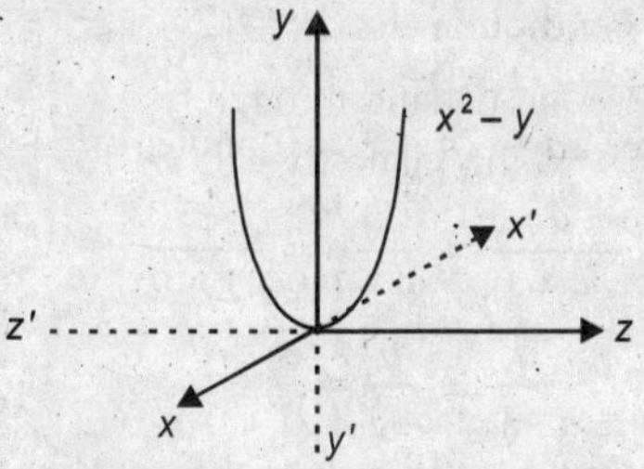

$\therefore$ Surface of revolution of the given lines are $x^2 + z^2 = y$.

45. The equation of hyperbola is $xy = C^2$ and point $\left(ct_1, \frac{c}{t_1}\right)$ lies on it.

Let us find the equation of the normal.

Equation of hyperbola can be written as $y=\frac{c^2}{x}$ and therefore slope of tangent is given by first derivative *i.e.*, $\frac{dy}{dx}=-\frac{c^2}{x^2}$

Hence slope of normal is given by $\frac{x^2}{c^2}$ and at $\left(ct_1, \frac{c}{t_1}\right)$ is t^2 and its equation is

$$y = t_1^2(x-ct_1)+\frac{c}{t_1}$$

or $xt_1^3 - yt_1 - ct_1^4 + c = 0$

As this passes through $\left(ct_2, \frac{c}{t_2}\right)$

$$ct_2t_1^3-\frac{c}{t_2}t_1-ct_1^4+c = 0$$

or $ct_1^3(t_2-t_1)+\frac{c}{t_2}(t_2-t_1) = 0$

as $t_1 = t_2$, $t_1 - t_2 = 0$ and dividing by it we get

$$ct_2^3 = -\frac{c}{t_2}$$

or $\qquad t_2^3t_2 = -1.$

46. Let the coordinates of A, B, C be $(a, 0, 0)$, $(0, b, 0)$ and $(0, 0, c)$ respectively. Let the sphere be

$x^2 + y^2 + z^2 + 2ux + 2vy + 2wz + d = 0$

If it passes through $(a, 0, 0)$, $(0, b, 0)$ and $(0, 0, c)$ and $(0, 0, 0)$ we have

$$a^2 + 2ua + d = 0$$
$$b^2 + 2vb + d = 0$$
$$c^2 + 2wz + d = 0$$

and $\qquad d = 0$

$\therefore u = -\frac{a}{2},\ v = -\frac{b}{2},\ w = -\frac{c}{2}$ and $d = 0$.

$$\text{Radius} = \sqrt{\left[\frac{a^2}{4}+\frac{b^2}{4}+\frac{c^2}{4}\right]}$$

Hence the equation of the sphere is $x^2 + y^2 + z^2 - ax - by - cz = 0$.

47. Let $F(x, y, z, t) \equiv ax^2 + by^2 + cz^2 + 2uxt + 2vyt + 2wzt + dt^2 = 0$ ...(1)

$$\left.\begin{array}{l}\frac{\partial F}{\partial x}=2ax+2ut,\ \frac{\partial F}{\partial y}=2by+2vt \\ \frac{\partial F}{\partial z}=2cz+2wt,\ \frac{\partial F}{\partial t}=2ux+2vy+2wz+2dt\end{array}\right\}\text{...(A)}$$

Putting $t = 1$ in each of the relations in (A) and then equation them to zero, we have

$$\frac{\partial F}{\partial x} = 0 \Rightarrow 2ax + 2u = 0,$$

$$\frac{\partial F}{\partial y} = 0 \Rightarrow 2by + 2v = 0,$$

$$\frac{\partial F}{\partial z} = 0 \Rightarrow 2cz + 2w = 0,$$

and $$\frac{\partial F}{\partial t} = 0 \Rightarrow 2ux + 2vy + 2wz + 2d = 0.$$

From the first three equations, we have

$$x = -\frac{u}{a},\ y = -\frac{v}{b},\ z = -\frac{w}{c}$$

Putting these values of x, y, z in the fourth equation namely

$$2ux + 2vy + 2wz + 2d = 0,$$

we have

$$2u\left(-\frac{u}{a}\right) + 2v\left(-\frac{v}{b}\right) + 2w\left(-\frac{w}{c}\right) + 2d = 0$$

or $$\frac{u^2}{a} + \frac{v^2}{b} + \frac{w^2}{c} = d \qquad ...(3)$$

Hence (3) is the required condition that the given equation (1) represents a cone.

48. Given equation $x^2 = 2 \cdot \lambda y$

In 2-dimension this is a equation of parabola that passes through the origin.

Again, In 3-D, this is a equation of a parabolic cylinder.

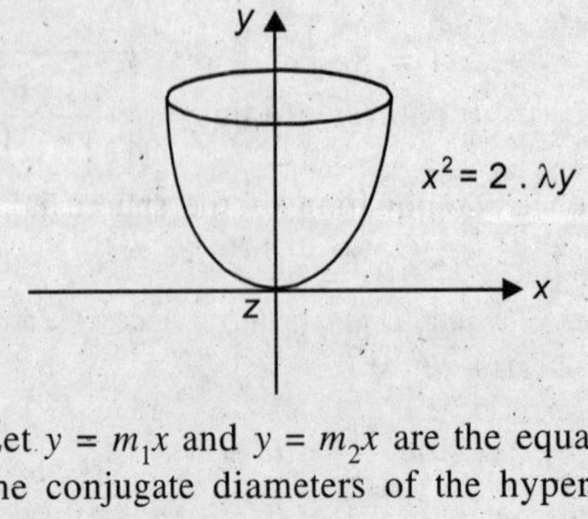

49. Let $y = m_1 x$ and $y = m_2 x$ are the equations of the conjugate diameters of the hyperbola

$$\frac{x^2}{a^2} - \frac{y^2}{b^2} = 1 \qquad ...(1)$$

$$\therefore \qquad m_1 m_2 = \frac{b^2}{a^2}$$

Point of intersection of (1) and $y = m_1 x$ is given by

$$x = \sqrt{\frac{a^2 b^2}{b^2 - a^2 m_1^2}}$$

and $$y = \sqrt{\frac{a^2 b^2 m_1^2}{b^2 - a^2 m_1^2}} \qquad ...(2)$$

Point of intersection of (1) and $y = m_2 x$ is given by

$$x = \sqrt{\frac{-a^4 m_1^2}{b^2 - a^2 m_1^2}}$$

and $$y = \sqrt{\frac{-b^4}{b^2 - a^2 m_1^2}} \qquad ...(3)$$

clearly,

if $b^2 > a^2 m_1^2$, then (2) gives real points and (3) gives imaginary points.

if $b^2 < a^2 m_1^2$, then (2) gives imaginary points and (3) gives real points.

50. The equation of a plane passing through (1, –2, 1) is

$a(x - 1) + b(y + 2) + c(z - 1) = 0 \qquad ...(i)$

It is perpendicular to $2x - 2y + z = 0$ and $x - y + 2z = 4$

Therefore, $2a - 2b + c = 0$ and $a - b + 2c = 0$

$$\Rightarrow \qquad \frac{a}{-4+1} = \frac{b}{4-1} = \frac{c}{-2+2}$$

$$\Rightarrow \qquad \frac{a}{-3} = \frac{b}{-3} = \frac{c}{0}$$

On substituting the values of a, b and c in equation (i), we get

$-3(x - 1) - 3(y + 2) + 0(z - 1) = 0$

$\Rightarrow \qquad x + y + 1 = 0$

Distance of this plane from (1, 2, 2) is given by,

$$d = \frac{1+2+1}{\sqrt{1+1}} = 2\sqrt{2}.$$

51. $r = 3 \cos \theta + 4 \sin \theta$

Converting into cartesian form by using $r^2 = x^2 + y^2$ and $x = r \cos \theta$, $y = r \sin \theta$, we get

$$r^2 = 3x + 4y$$

$$\Rightarrow \quad x^2 + y^2 = 3x + 4y$$

Coordinates of centre of this circle in cartesian form: $\left(\frac{3}{2}, 2\right)$

Converting into polar form, we get

$$r = \frac{5}{2}, \theta = \tan^{-1}\frac{4}{3}.$$

52. General equation of pair of straight lines is
$ax^2 + by^2 + 2hxy + 2gx + 2fy + c = 0$
$x^2 - 2xy - y^2 + 2x + 3y - 1 = 0$
Comparing above with general equation
$ax^2 + by^2 + 2hxy + 2gx + 2fy + c = 0$
$a = 1;\ b = -1;\ h = -1;\ g = 1;\ f = 1.5;\ c = 1$
Angle will be

$$\theta = \tan^{-1}\left|\frac{2\sqrt{h^2 - ab}}{a+b}\right|$$

$$= \tan^{-1}\left|\frac{2\sqrt{(-1)^2 - (1\times -1)}}{1-1}\right|$$

$$\theta = \tan^{-1}\left|\frac{2\sqrt{2}}{0}\right| = \tan^{-1}|\infty|$$

$$\theta = \tan^{-1}\left(\tan\left(\frac{\pi}{2}\right)\right)$$

$$\theta = \frac{\pi}{2}.$$

53. Let point be $P(a \cos \theta, b \sin \theta) = (x_1, y_1)$

Equation of tangent to ellipse $\frac{x^2}{a^2} + \frac{y^2}{b^2} = 1$ at (x_1, y_1) is given by:

$$\frac{xx_1}{a^2} + \frac{yy_1}{b^2} = 1$$

$$\Rightarrow \quad \frac{x \cdot a\cos\theta}{a^2} + \frac{y \cdot b\sin\theta}{b^2} = 1$$

$$\Rightarrow \quad \frac{x\cos\theta}{a} + \frac{y\sin\theta}{b} = 1$$

For x-axis intercept, $y = 0$

$$\Rightarrow \quad \frac{b\cos\theta}{a} = 1$$

$$\Rightarrow \quad \cos\theta = \frac{a}{h} \quad \ldots(i)$$

For y-axis intercept, $x = 0$

$$\Rightarrow \quad \frac{k\sin\theta}{b} = 1$$

$$\Rightarrow \quad \sin\theta = \frac{b}{k} \quad \ldots(ii)$$

$(i)^2 + (ii)^2$

$$\Rightarrow \quad \frac{a^2}{h^2} + \frac{b^2}{k^2} = \cos^2\theta + \sin^2\theta$$

$$\Rightarrow \quad \frac{a^2}{h^2} + \frac{b^2}{k^2} = 1.$$

54.

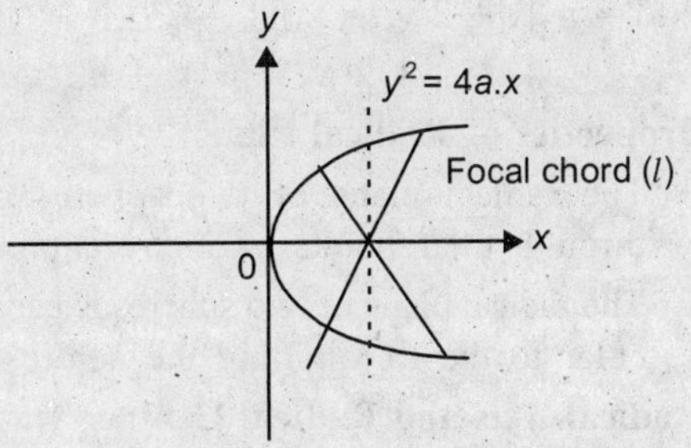

Here, Focal chord $(l) \propto \frac{1}{d^2}$.

55. Let $x = r\cos\theta,\ y = r\sin\theta$

$$\Rightarrow x^2 + y^2 = r^2 \Rightarrow r = \sqrt{x^2 + y^2}$$

$$\frac{1}{r} = 8 + 5\cos\theta$$

$$1 = 8r + 5r\cos\theta$$

$$1 = 8\cdot\sqrt{x^2 + y^2} + 5\cdot x$$

$$(1 - 5x) = 8\cdot\sqrt{x^2 + y^2}$$

Squaring both sides, we get

$$(1 - 5x)^2 = \left\{8\cdot\sqrt{x^2 + y^2}\right\}^2$$

$$1 + 25x^2 - 10x = 64 \times (x^2 + y^2)$$

$$39x^2 + 10x + 64y^2 = 1$$

$$\left(\sqrt{39}x\right)^2 + \frac{2.5}{\sqrt{39}}\cdot\sqrt{39}x + \left(\frac{5}{\sqrt{39}}\right)^2 + (8y)^2 = 1 + \left(\frac{5}{\sqrt{39}}\right)^2$$

$$\left(\sqrt{39}x - \frac{5}{\sqrt{39}}\right)^2 + (8y)^2 = \frac{64}{39}$$

Here, eccentricity $(e) = \frac{5}{8}$

Semi-latus rectum $= \frac{1}{8}$.

56. **Radical Plane:** The radical plane of two spheres is defined as the locus of a point whose powers with respect to the spheres are equal. The radical plane of the spheres.

$S_1 \equiv x^2 + y^2 + 2u_1x + 2v_1y + 2w_1z + d_1 = 0$
$S_2 \equiv x^2 + y^2 + 2u_2x + 2v_2y + 2w_2z + d_2 = 0$
is given by

$$S_1 - S_2 = 0 \text{ i.e.,}$$

$$2(u_1 - u_2)x + 2(v_1 - v_2)y + 2(w_1 - w_2)z + d_1 - d_2 = 0$$

Properties of Radical Plane:

- The radical plane of two spheres passes through their points of intersection.
- The radical plane of two spheres is perpendicular to the line joining the centres.

Radical Axis and Radical Centre: The three radical planes of the three spheres $S_1 = 0$, $S_2 = 0$, $S_3 = 0$, taken in pairs, intersect in a line. This line is called the radical line (axis) of the spheres.

The four radical planes of four spheres $S_1 = 0$, $S_2 = 0$, $S_3 = 0$, $S_4 = 0$, taken in pairs pass through a *common point*. This point is called the *radical centre* of the spheres.

Coaxial System of Spheres: A system of spheres is said to be *coaxial system of spheres* if any *two spheres of the system have the same radical plane*.

If $S_1 = 0$ and $S_2 = 0$ be the equations of two spheres, then the system of spheres determine a coaxial system of spheres.

$S_1 + \lambda S_2 = 0 (\lambda \neq -1)$ or, $S_1 + \lambda(S_2 - S_1) = 0$.

57. The equation $xy - ax - by + ab = 0$ represents a pair of straight lines.

58. Point A = (–1, 3, 4) and B = (5, 2, –1)

$$\overrightarrow{AB} = (5-(-1))\hat{i} + (2-3)\hat{j} + (-1-4)\hat{k}$$
$$= 6\hat{i} - \hat{j} - 5\hat{k}$$

$\overrightarrow{AB}$ is normal to the plane

$\therefore$ Direction of normal (6, –1, –5)

$\therefore$ equation $6x - y - 5z = K$

Point (1, 2, –3) passes through the plane

$\therefore \quad 6(1) - 2 - 5(-3) = K$

$\therefore \quad K = 19$

Hence, equation of the plane

$$6x - y - 5z = 19$$

or, $\quad 6x - y - 5z - 19 = 0$.

59. Let $S \equiv x^2/a^2 + y^2/b^2 - 1 = 0$

Be the ellipse and P(h, k) be a point in the plane of the ellipse.

$ax \sec\theta - by \operatorname{cosec}\theta = a^2 + b^2$

$$\Rightarrow \frac{ax[1+\tan^2(\theta/2)]}{1-[\tan^2(\theta/2)]} - \frac{by[1+\tan^2(\theta/2)]}{2\tan(\theta/2)} = a^2 - b^2$$

$$\Rightarrow \frac{ax(1+t^2)}{1-t^2} - \frac{by(1+t^2)}{2t} = a^2 - b^2 \quad \left(\text{where } t = \tan\frac{\theta}{2}\right)$$

$$\Rightarrow ax(1 + t^2)2t - by(1 - t^4) = 2t(1 - t^2)(a^2 - b^2) = 2t(1 - t^2)a^2e^2$$

$$\Rightarrow byt^4 + 2(ax + a^2e^2)t^3 + 2(ax - a^2e^2)t - by = 0$$

This normal passes through P(h, k). This implies

$$bkt^4 + 2(ah + a^2e^2)t^3 + 2(ah - a^2e^2)t - bk = 0 \quad ...(1)$$

Since Eq. (1) is a fourth-degree equation in t, it has four roots t_1, t_2, t_3 and t_4 (not necessarily distinct) so that there exist four points on the ellipse (t_r, $r = 1, 2, 3, 4$) at which the normals drawn are concurrent at P(h, k). Also, we have the set of equations

$$t_1 + t_2 + t_3 + t_4 = -\frac{2(ah + a^2e^2)}{bk}$$

$$\Sigma t_1t_2 = 0$$

$$\Sigma t_1t_2t_3 = -\frac{2(ah - a^2e^2)}{bk}$$

and $t_1t_2t_3t_4 = \frac{-bk}{bk} = -1$.

60. Equation of line

$$\frac{x-2}{1}=\frac{y-1}{2}=\frac{z+1}{2}=P$$

$$\therefore \quad \vec{v} = (P+2)\hat{i}+(2P+1)\hat{j}+(2P-1)\hat{k}$$

Point $z = (0, 0, 1)$

Now, shortest point

$$= \frac{|(v-z)\cdot(z*v)|}{|z*v|}=\frac{3}{\sqrt{5}}.$$

62. Given, $v = c \Rightarrow \dot{v} = 0$

Also $u = t \Rightarrow \dot{u} = 1$

$\therefore$ $\dot{v} = 0,\ \dot{u} = 1$

Hence

$$2T = E\dot{u}^2+2F\dot{u}\dot{v}+G\dot{v}^2$$
$$= E + 2F \cdot 1 \cdot 0 + G \cdot 0 = E$$

$$\Rightarrow \quad \frac{\partial T}{\partial u} = \frac{1}{2}E_1$$

In the same way, $\dfrac{\partial T}{\partial \dot{u}} = E\dot{u}+F\dot{v},$

$$\frac{\partial T}{\partial \dot{v}} = F\dot{u}+G\dot{v}$$

When $\dot{u} = 1,\ \dot{v} = 0$

$$\Rightarrow \quad \frac{\partial T}{\partial \dot{u}} = E,\ \frac{\partial T}{\partial \dot{v}} = F$$

$$\therefore \quad U = \frac{d}{dt}\left(\frac{\partial T}{\partial \dot{u}}\right)-\frac{\partial T}{\partial u}=\frac{\partial E}{\partial t}-\frac{1}{2}E_1$$
$$= \left(\frac{\partial E}{\partial u}\frac{\partial u}{\partial t}+\frac{\partial E}{\partial v}\frac{\partial v}{\partial t}\right)-\frac{1}{2}E_1$$
$$= E_1\dot{u}+E_2\dot{v}-\frac{1}{2}E_1$$
$$= E_1\cdot 1-\frac{1}{2}E_1+E_2\cdot 0$$
$$= E_1-\frac{1}{2}E_1=\frac{1}{2}E_1$$

$$\text{Also } V = \frac{d}{dt}\left(\frac{\partial T}{\partial \dot{v}}\right)-\frac{\partial T}{\partial v}=\frac{dF}{dt}-\frac{1}{2}E_2$$
$$= F_1-\frac{1}{2}E_2$$

Hence, from $-U\dfrac{\partial T}{\partial \dot{v}}+V\dfrac{\partial T}{\partial \dot{u}} = 0$

or, $V\dfrac{\partial T}{\partial \dot{u}}-U\dfrac{\partial T}{\partial \dot{v}} = 0$

We get,

$EE_2 + FE_1 - 2EF_1 = 0$, when $v = c$ (const.).

63. *Element of area:* Consider the figure with vertices (u, v), $(u + \delta u, v)$, $(u + \delta u, v + \delta v)$, and $(u, v + \delta v)$ joined by parametric curves (Fig.). When δu and δv are small and positive, this figure is approximately a parallelogram with adjacent sides given by the vectors $r_1\,\delta u$, $r_2\,\delta v$, and area $|r_1\delta u \times r_2\delta v| = H\ \delta u\delta v$. This formula, with du, dv in place of δu, δv is taken to bet the element of area dS for the surface, so that $dS = H\ dudv$.

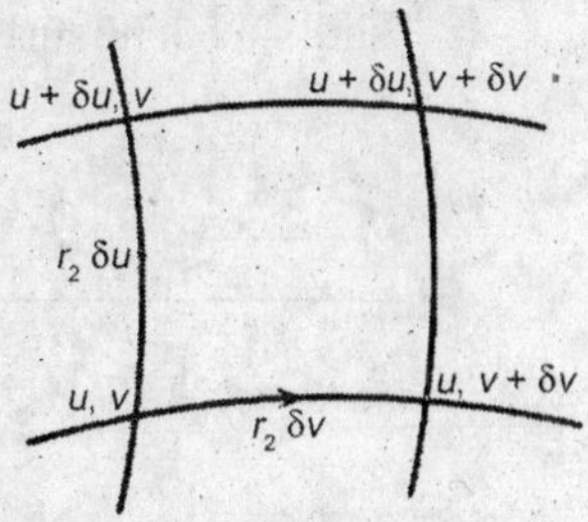

65. $\cos^{-1}\left(\dfrac{p}{a}\right)+\cos^{-1}\left(\dfrac{q}{b}\right)=\alpha$

$$\cos^{-1}\left(\frac{p\cdot q}{a\cdot b}-\frac{\sqrt{a^2-p^2}}{a}\cdot\frac{\sqrt{b^2-q^2}}{b}\right)=\alpha$$

$$\left(\frac{p\cdot q-\sqrt{a^2-p^2}\cdot\sqrt{b^2-q^2}}{ab}\right)=\cos\alpha$$

Squaring on both sides, we get

$$\cos^2\alpha = \left(\frac{p\cdot q-\sqrt{a^2-p^2}\cdot\sqrt{b^2-q^2}}{a^2\cdot b^2}\right)^2$$

$$= \frac{p^2\cdot q^2+(a^2-p^2)\cdot(b^2-q^2) - 2p\cdot q\sqrt{(a^2-p^2)(b^2-q^2)}}{a^2b^2}$$

$$= 1-\frac{2pq\cdot\sqrt{(a^2-p^2)(b^2-q^2)}}{a^2b^2}$$

$$1-\cos^2\alpha = \frac{p^2}{a^2}-\frac{2p\cdot q}{ab}\cdot\left\{\frac{p\cdot q}{ab}-\frac{\sqrt{a^2-p^2}\cdot\sqrt{b^2-q^2}}{ab}\right\}+\frac{q^2}{b^2}$$

$$\sin^2\alpha = \frac{p^2}{a^2}-\frac{2p\cdot q}{ab}\cos\alpha+\frac{q^2}{b^2}$$

$$\therefore \quad K = \frac{-2pq}{ab}.$$

67. L.H.S. = $\cot 7\frac{1}{2}^\circ = \cot \frac{15}{2}^\circ$

$$= \frac{\cos\left(\frac{15}{2}\right)^\circ}{\sin\left(\frac{15}{2}\right)^\circ} = \frac{2\cos\left(\frac{15}{2}\right)^\circ}{2\sin\left(\frac{15}{2}\right)^\circ}$$

$$= \frac{2\cos^2\left(\frac{15}{2}\right)^\circ}{2\sin\left(\frac{15}{2}\right)^\circ \cos\left(\frac{15}{2}\right)^\circ} = \frac{1+\cos 15^\circ}{\sin 15^\circ}$$

$$\left[\because 1+\cos 2\theta = 2\cos^2 \frac{2\theta}{2}\right]$$

$$\left[\& \; 2\sin\frac{\theta}{2}\cdot\cos\frac{\theta}{2} = \sin\frac{2\theta}{2}\right]$$

$$\Rightarrow \quad \cos 15^\circ = \frac{1}{4}\left(\sqrt{6}+\sqrt{2}\right)$$

$$\& \quad \sin 15^\circ = \frac{1}{4}\left(\sqrt{6}-\sqrt{2}\right)$$

$$\therefore \quad \text{LHS} = \frac{1+\frac{1}{4}\left(\sqrt{6}+\sqrt{2}\right)}{\frac{1}{4}\left(\sqrt{6}-\sqrt{2}\right)}$$

$$= \frac{4+\sqrt{6}+\sqrt{2}}{\sqrt{6}-\sqrt{2}}$$

Apply componendo and dividendo, we get

$$\Rightarrow \text{LHS} = \frac{\left(4+\sqrt{6}+\sqrt{2}\right)\left(\sqrt{6}+\sqrt{2}\right)}{\left(\sqrt{6}-\sqrt{2}\right)\left(\sqrt{6}+\sqrt{2}\right)}$$

$$= \frac{4\sqrt{6}+4\sqrt{2}+6+\sqrt{12}+\sqrt{12}+2}{6-2}$$

$$= \frac{4\sqrt{6}+4\sqrt{2}+8+2\sqrt{3}+2\sqrt{3}}{4}$$

$$= \frac{8}{4}+\frac{4\sqrt{2}}{4}+\frac{4\sqrt{3}}{4}+\frac{4\sqrt{6}}{4}$$

$$= 2+\sqrt{2}+\sqrt{3}+\sqrt{6}.$$

68. $\sin 6^\circ \cdot \sin 66^\circ$

$$\frac{2\cdot\sin 6^\circ\cdot\sin 66^\circ}{2}$$

$$= \frac{\cos(66^\circ-6^\circ)-\cos(66^\circ+6^\circ)}{2}$$

$$= \frac{\cos(60^\circ)-\cos(72^\circ)}{2}$$

$$= \frac{\frac{1}{2}-\cos(90^\circ-18^\circ)}{2}$$

$$= \frac{1}{4}-\frac{\sin 18^\circ}{2}$$

$$= \frac{1}{4}-\frac{\left(\frac{\sqrt{5}-1}{4}\right)}{2} = \frac{3-\sqrt{5}}{8}.$$

69. Equation of the surface is

$F(x, y, z) \equiv xyz - 4 = 0$

$\therefore \quad \frac{\partial F}{\partial x} = yz = 4$ at (1, 2, 2);

$\frac{\partial F}{\partial y} = xz = 2$ at (1, 2, 2) and

$\frac{\partial F}{\partial z} = xy = 2$ at (1, 2, 2).

Therefore equation of the tangent plane at (1, 2, 2) is

$(x-1)(4) + (y-2)(2) + (z-2)(2) = 0$ or

$4x + 2y + 2z = 12$ or $2x + y + z = 6$.

70. $\sin(3A) = \cos(A - 30^\circ)$

$\sin(3A) = \sin(90^\circ - (A - 30^\circ))$

$3A = 90^\circ - (A - 30^\circ)$

$4A = 120^\circ \Rightarrow A = 30^\circ$

Now, $\sin 2A + \cos 2A$

$= \sin(2 \times 30^\circ) + \cos(2 \times 30^\circ)$

$= \sin 60^\circ + \cos 60^\circ$

$$= \frac{\sqrt{3}}{2}+\frac{1}{2}=\frac{\sqrt{3}+1}{2}.$$

71. A direction $(du : dv)$ at a given point $P(u, v)$ on the surface $S(\bar{r}\,(u,v)) \subseteq \mathbb{E}^3$ is called *asymptotic* if in this direction the *normal curvature* k_n is equal to zero. From (1) it follows that the asymptotic directions $(du : dv)$ on a surfae are given by the differential relation

$$k_n = \left(\frac{\mathrm{II}(u,v)}{\mathrm{I}(u,v)}\right)\Bigg|_{(du:dv)}$$

$$= \left(\frac{\mathrm{L}du^2 + 2\mathrm{M}dudv + \mathrm{N}dv^2}{\mathrm{E}du^2 + 2\mathrm{F}dudv + \mathrm{G}dv^2}\right)\Bigg|_{(du:dv)} \quad ...(1)$$

$$\mathrm{L}(u, v)du^2 + 2\mathrm{M}(u, v)dudv + \mathrm{N}(u, v)dv^2 = 0 \quad ...(2)$$

Further, (2) yields an important consequence for the ensuing analysis: at any hyperbolic point P of the surface (where $(\mathrm{LN} - \mathrm{M}^2)|_{P \in S} < 0$, there always exists two distinct asymptotic directions.

Recall that a line on a surface is called an *asymptotic line,* if at each of its points its direction is asymptotic. We list two important properties of asymptotic lines:

- If a surface in $\mathbb{E}^3$ contains a *straight line,* then this straight line is an asymptotic line on the surface.
- The tangent plane to the surface at any point of an asymptotic lines is the osculating plane of the surface at that point.

72. A curve is called a cylindrical helix or general helix if its tangent makes a constant angle with a fixed line in space. A curve is a general helix if and only if the ratio of curvature to torsion is constant.

In other words, a cylindrical helix is a space curve which lies on a cylinder and cuts the generators at a constant angle. Its tangent makes a constant angle α with afixed line known as the axis of the helix. The axis of the helix is also called the axis of the cylinder (generator).

To prove this, let a be a unit vector along the direction of axis of the helix and t be the unit tangent vector (See in Fig. 1). Since the helix intersects the generators at a constant angle α, so we have

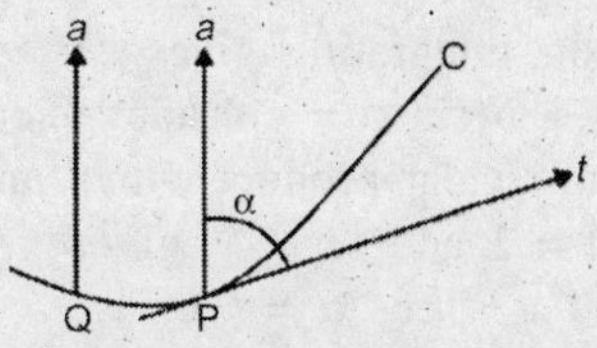

Fig. 1: *A unit vector a makes a constant angle α with its tangent*

$$t.\, a = \cos\alpha = \text{constant},$$

which on differentiation with respect to s gives

$$t'.\, a = 0,$$

which in view of Serret-Frenet formulae gives

$$kn.\, a = 0$$

But $k \neq 0$. Therefore $n.\, a = 0$, which shows that a is perpendicular to n, that is, a lies in the rectifying plane (that is, the plane containing t and b). Since a makes an angle α with t, so it must make angle (90° – α) with b (see in Fig. 2), this a expressed as a linear combination of t and b is given by

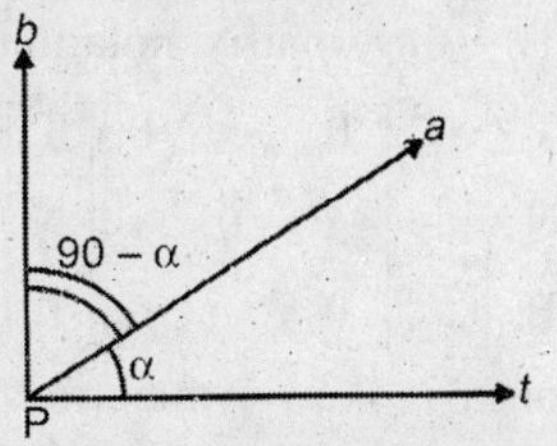

Fig. 2: *The vector a lies in the rectifying plane*

$$a = t\cos\alpha + b\sin\alpha,$$

which on differentiating with respect to s gives

$$a' = t'\cos\alpha + b'\sin\alpha,$$

which in view of $a' = 0$, and Serret-Frenet formulae reduces to

$$kn\cos\alpha - \tau n\sin\alpha = 0$$

or $(k\cos\alpha - \tau\sin\alpha)n = 0$

But $n \neq 0$. Therefore $k\cos\alpha - \tau\sin\alpha = 0$

or $\dfrac{k}{\tau} = \tan\alpha = \text{constant}$, since a = constant.

Conversely, let $\dfrac{k}{\tau} = \tan\alpha$ (say) or $k\cos\alpha - \tau\sin\alpha = 0$ or $(k\cos\alpha - \tau\sin\alpha)n = 0$, since $n \neq 0$, which in view of Serret-Frenet formula reduces to

$$t'\cos\alpha + b'\sin\alpha = 0$$

or $\dfrac{d}{ds}(t\cos\alpha + b\sin\alpha) = 0,$

which on integrating gives
$t \cos \alpha + b \sin \alpha$ = constant vector = a(say)
which on scalar product with t and using the facts $t.t = 1$ and $t.b = 0$, gives

$$\cos \alpha = t.a.$$

Hence, the curve makes a constant angle with direction of fixed vector a and the curve is thus a helix.

73. The Frenet-Serret formulas are:

$$\frac{dT}{ds} = \kappa N$$

$$\frac{dN}{ds} = -\kappa T + \tau B$$

$$\frac{dB}{ds} = -\tau N$$

where κ is the curvature and τ is the torsion. The Frenet-Serret formulas are also known as *Frenet-Serret theorem,* and can be stated more concisely using matrix notation:

$$\begin{bmatrix} T' \\ N' \\ B' \end{bmatrix} = \begin{bmatrix} 0 & \kappa & 0 \\ -\kappa & 0 & \tau \\ 0 & -\tau & 0 \end{bmatrix} \begin{bmatrix} T \\ N \\ B \end{bmatrix}$$

This matrix is skew-symmetric.

74. $r = (u \cos v, u \sin v, cv)$

$r_1 = (\cos v, \sin v, 0)$

$r_2 = (-u \sin v, u \cos v, c)$

$E = r_1^2 = (\cos v, \sin v, 0) \cdot (\cos v, \sin v, 0)$

$= \cos^2 v + \sin^2 v = 1$

$F = r_1 \cdot r_2$

$= (\cos v, \sin v, 0) \cdot (-u \sin v, u \cos v, c)$

$= -u \cos v \sin v + u \sin v \cos v + 0 = 0$

$G = r_2^2$

$= (-u \sin v, u \cos v, c) \cdot (-u \sin v, u \cos v, c)$

$u^2 \sin^2 v + u^2 \cos^2 v + c^2 = u^2 + c^2.$

76. $2\sqrt{3} \cdot \sin A \cdot \cos A = \cos^2 A - \sin^2 A$

$\sqrt{3}(2 \sin A \cdot \cos A) = \cos 2A$

$\sqrt{3} \cdot (\sin 2A) = \cos 2A$

$\cot 2A = \sqrt{3}$

$\cot 2A = \cot 30°$

$\therefore \quad 2A = 30°$

Now, $\cos A \cdot \left\{\sin \frac{A}{2} \cdot \cos \frac{A}{2}\right\}$

$= \frac{1}{2} \cdot \cos A \left\{2 \cdot \sin \frac{A}{2} \cdot \cos \frac{A}{2}\right\}$

$= \frac{1}{4} \cdot 2 \cos A \cdot \{\sin A\}$

$= \frac{1}{4} \sin 2A = \frac{1}{4} \sin 30°$

$= \frac{1}{4} \times \frac{1}{2} = \frac{1}{8}.$

77. An ordinary point is defined as, $r_1 \times r_2 \neq 0$. A point which is not an ordinary point is called a singularity. At a singularity $r_1 \times r_2 = 0$.

78. $\dfrac{\sec 8A \cdot (\tan 10A + \tan 6A)}{4(\tan 10A - \tan 6A)}$

$= \dfrac{\sin 10A \cdot \cos 6A + \sin 6A \cdot \cos 10A}{4 \cdot \cos 8A \cdot (\sin 10A \cdot \cos 6A - \sin 6A \cdot \cos 10A)}$

$= \dfrac{\sin (10+6)A}{4 \cdot \cos 8A \cdot \sin 4A} = \dfrac{\sin 16A}{4 \sin 4A \cdot \cos 8A}$

$= \dfrac{2 \sin 8A \cdot \cos 8A}{4 \sin 4A \cdot \cos 8A} = \dfrac{\sin 8A}{2 \sin 4A}$

$= \dfrac{2 \sin 4A \cdot \cos 4A}{2 \sin 4A} = \cos 4A.$

79. Take the parametric equations to be

$$x = u \cos v,\ y = u \sin v,\ z = u^2$$

Then $\quad r = u \cos v\, i + u \sin v\, j + u^2 k$

$r_u = \cos v\, i + \sin v\, j + 2uk$

$r_v = -u \sin v\, i + v \cos v\, j,$

whence $E = 1 + 4u^2$, $F = 0$, $G = u^2$
and $(EG - F^2)^{1/2} = u(1 + 4u^2)^{1/2}$
Further $r_{uu} = 2k,$

$r_{uv} = -\sin v\, i + \cos v\, j,$

$r_{vv} = -u \cos v\, i - u \sin v\, j$

So $[r_u, r_v, r_{uu}] = 2u, \quad L = 2/(1 + 4u^2)^{1/2},$

$[r_u, r_v, r_{uv}] = 0, \quad M = 0,$

$[r_u, r_v, r_{vv}] = 2u^3, \quad N = 2u^2/(1 + 4u^2)^{1/2}.$

Since, F = M = 0, the lines of curvature are u = constant and v = constant.

The asymptotic lines are given by $du^2 + u^2dv^2 = 0$. These are imaginary since $LN > M^2$. All points on the surface are elliptical.

80. The sphere which has four point contact at a point P of a given curve is called the osculating sphere of the curve at that point P. It is also known as the sphere of curvature at P of the curve. Let us find the equation of the sphere is given by

$$(r - c)^2 = R^2 \quad ...(1)$$

Suppose that equation of the curve be

$$r = r(s) \quad ...(2)$$

Thus, the points of intersection of (1) and (2) are given by

$$F(s) = (r(s) - c)^2 - R^2 = 0 \quad (A)$$

As (1) has four point contact with (2), we have

$$F = 0, F' = 0, F'' = 0, F''' = 0 \text{ at P}$$

Thus, in view of (A), we get

$F = 0$ gives $(r - c)^2 - R^2 = 0$ ...(3)

$$F' = 0 \Rightarrow (r - c) \cdot r' = 0$$

or $(r - c) \cdot t = 0$ ...(4)

$$F'' = 0 \Rightarrow t^2 + (r - c) \cdot t' = 0$$

or $1 + (r - c) \cdot kn = 0$ ...(5)

$$F''' = 0 \Rightarrow r' \cdot kn + (r - c) \cdot kn' + (r - c) \cdot k'n = 0 \quad ...(6)$$

or $k \cdot (r - c) \cdot (\tau t - kt) + (r - c) \cdot k'n = 0$

by Serret-Frenett formulae.

Now in view of equation (4), $r - c$ is $\perp t$. Thus, $r - c$ lies in the normal plane. Hence, $r - c$ can be expressed linearly in terms of n and b.

Hence, let $r - c = \lambda n + \mu b$, λ, μ being scalar (B)

Now, in view of (5) and (6), we have

$$1 + (\lambda n + \mu b) \cdot kn = 0$$

or $$\lambda = -\frac{1}{k} - \rho \quad (C)$$

and $k \cdot (\lambda n + \mu b) \cdot (\tau b - kt) + k'(\lambda n + \mu b) \cdot n = 0$

or $$k\tau\mu + k'\lambda = 0$$

or $$\frac{\mu}{\rho\sigma} - \frac{1}{\rho^2}\rho'\lambda = 0 \quad (D)$$

Hence, in view of (C), we have

$$\frac{\mu}{\rho\sigma} = -\frac{\rho}{\rho'} \text{ or } \mu = -\sigma\rho' \quad (E)$$

Using (C) and (E) in (B), we get

$$r - c = -\rho n - \sigma\rho' b$$

or $$c = r + \rho n + \sigma\rho' b$$

Thus in view of (3)

$$R^2 = (\rho n + \sigma\rho' b)^2 = \rho^2 + \sigma^2\rho'^2.$$

81. Given, expression $= (1 + x + 3x^2)^{4165}$

To obtain sum of co-efficient of the expression we put $x = 1$,

then, sum of the co-efficient

$= (1 + 1 - 3)^{4165} = (-1)^{4165} = -1.$

82. Given expression: $(2^{3n} - 7n - 1)$

$= \{(2)^3\}^n - 7n - 1$

$= 8^n - 7n - 1$

$= (1 + 7)^n - 7n - 1$

$\{{}^nC_0 (1)^n + {}^nC_1 \cdot 7 + {}^nC_2 \cdot (7)^2 + ... + {}^nC_n \cdot (7)^n\} - 7n - 1$

$= 1 + 7n + \{{}^nC_2 \cdot (7)^2 + ... + {}^nC_n \cdot (7)^n\} - 7^{n-1}$

$= (7)^2 \{{}^nC_2 + {}^nC_3 \cdot 7 + {}^nC_4 \cdot (7)^2 ... {}^nC_n (7)^{n-3}\}$

This is divisible by 49.

83. CTFT $\{x(t)\} = X(j\omega) = \int_{-\infty}^{\infty} x(t)e^{-j\omega t} dt$

$$= \int_{-\infty}^{\infty} e^{-A|t|}e^{-j\omega t} dt$$

$$= \int_{-\infty}^{0} e^{-A(-t)}e^{-j\omega t} dt + \int_{0}^{\infty} e^{-At}e^{-j\omega t} dt$$

$$= \int_{-\infty}^{0} e^{-At}e^{-j\omega t} dt + \int_{0}^{\infty} e^{-At}e^{-j\omega t} dt$$

$$= \int_{-\infty}^{0} e^{(A-j\omega)t} dt + \int_{0}^{\infty} e^{-(A+j\omega)t} dt$$

$$= \left[\frac{1}{A - j\omega}e^{(A-j\omega)t}\right]_{-\infty}^{0} + \left[\frac{1}{-(A + j\omega)}e^{-(A+j\omega)t}\right]_{0}^{\infty}$$

$$= \left[\frac{1}{A - j\omega} + \frac{1}{A + j\omega} = \frac{2A}{A^2 + \omega^2}\right]$$

$$\therefore x(j\omega) = \frac{2A}{(A^2 + \omega^2)}.$$

84. As f is continuous function

$$\lim_{n\to\infty}\sum_{r=0}^{(n-1)}\frac{1}{n}\cdot f\left(\frac{r}{n}\right)=\int_0^1 f(x)\,dx.$$

85. The running integrator $\int_{-\infty}^{t} x(t)dt = 0$ for every causal system. As causal systems have no memory and the initial value is zero, the output is followed by input. So, $y(t)$ will always be bounded if this function is causal bounded system.

86. $$x(t) = \begin{cases} 1, & \frac{-T}{4} < t \le \frac{3T}{4} \\ -1, & \frac{3T}{4} < t \le \frac{7T}{4} \\ -x(t+T) & \end{cases}$$

Now, by property of symmetry of Fourier-transform of $x(t)$, we got the Fundamental Fourier term

$$= \frac{4}{\pi}\sin\left(\frac{\pi t}{T}-\frac{\pi}{4}\right).$$

87. Assume that f is increasing on an interval $[a, b]$. Thus, $f(a) \le f(x) \le f(b)$, and f is bounded on $[a, b]$. Given $\varepsilon > 0$, there exists $k > 0$ such that $k[f(b) - f(a)] < \varepsilon$.
Let $P = \{x_0, x_1, ..., x_n\}$ be a partition of $[a, b]$ such that $\Delta x_i \le k$ for all i. Since f is increasing, it follows that $m_i = f(x_{i-1})$ and $M_i = f(x_i)$, $i = 1, 2, ..., n$.
Where m_i is the greatest lower bound of f on $[x_{i-1}, x_i]$, and M_i is the least upper bound of f on $[x_{i-1}, x_i]$.

$$U(f, P) - L(f, P) = \sum_{i=1}^{n}[f(x_i)-f(x_{i-1})]\Delta x_i$$

$$\le k\sum_{i=1}^{n}[f(x_i)-f(x_{i-1})](*)$$

$$= k[f(b) - f(a)] < \varepsilon.$$

By Theorem f is integrable on $[a, b]$. In the case that f is monotone decreasing, we may use the same argument on $-f$.

89. $$(x + 1)^{20} = {}^{20}C_0\,(x)^{20} + {}^{20}C_1\,x^{19} + {}^{20}C_2\,x^{18} + ... + {}^{20}C_{20}$$

Largest Co-efficient = Co-efficient of middle term = ${}^{20}C_{10}$

$$= \frac{20!}{10!(20-10)!} = \frac{20!}{10!10!}.$$

90. Let $$y^2 = \left(6+4\sqrt{3}\right)$$

$$= \left(\sqrt{3}\times 2\sqrt{3}+4\sqrt{3}\right)$$

$$= \sqrt{3}\left(2\sqrt{3}+4\right)$$

$$= \sqrt{3}\left\{2\sqrt{3}+(1)^2+\left(\sqrt{3}\right)^2\right\}$$

$$= \sqrt{3}\left(\sqrt{3}+1\right)^2.$$

91. Since, the fourier expansion of $x(t)$ contains no sine terms, therefore.

$x(t) = x(-t)$

or, $x(t) = x(T - t)$

as $x(t)$ is periodic with T

Now, as signal $x(t)$ contains odd harmonics.

Then $x(t) = -x\left(t-\frac{T}{2}\right)$

Thus $x(t) = x(T - t) = -x\left(t-\frac{T}{2}\right)$.

92. $$\sum_{r=0}^{n} {}^{n}C_r a^r b^{n-r}$$

$$= {}^{n}C_0 a^0 b^n + {}^{n}C_1 ab^{n-1} + {}^{n}C_2 a^2 b^{n-2} + ... + {}^{n}C_n a^n b^0$$

$$= (a + b)^n = (2)^n.$$

94. $$\left(x^2+\frac{1}{x^2}+2\right)^n = \left(x^2+\frac{1}{x^2}+2\cdot x\cdot\frac{1}{x}\right)^n$$

$$= \left\{\left(x+\frac{1}{x}\right)^2\right\}^n = \left(x+\frac{1}{x}\right)^{2n}$$

$$\therefore \text{ Middle term } = {}^{2n}C_n (x)^n\cdot\left(\frac{1}{x}\right)^n$$

$$= {}^{2n}C_n = \frac{2n!}{n!n!}$$

95. 1. $(1.01)^{1000000} = \left(\frac{101}{100}\right)^{(100)^3}$

$= \left(1+\frac{1}{100}\right)^{(100)^3}$

Now, $\left(1+\frac{1}{100}\right)^{(100)^3} > (100)^2$ {True}

2. $(98)^5 \cdot 5 > 95 \times 10^8$ is false.

96. Since 75 ≅ 1 modulo 37
75 × 75 ≅ 1 * 1(= 1) modulo 37
75 × 75 × 75 ≅ 1 * 1 * 1(= 1) modulo 37
So 75 any integer ≅ 1 modulo 37$$
So $75^{75^{75}}$ ≅ 1 modulo 37
The remainder is 1.
*The digits (=1) are the remainder when divided by 37.

97. Time-variance check:

$$y(t) = x(t)^2$$

Shifting the input first,

$$y(t, k) = x(t^2 - k)$$

Shifting the output,

$$y(t - k) = x((t - k)^2)$$

$$y(t, k) \neq y(t - k)$$

Given system is time variant.

Applications:

The continuous-time system described by

$$y(t) = x(t^2)$$

The system depends on the future inputs and hence it is **non-causal**.

A time shift of t_0 in the input does not give the t_0 shift in the output and hence it is **time-variant**.

As there are no non-linear operators present, it is **linear**.

Therefore, the given system is non-causal, linear and time-variant

98. $f(x) = \frac{a_0}{2} + \sum_{n=0}^{\infty}(a_n \cos nx + b_n \sin nx)$

$\sin^2(x)$ is even function so $b_n = 0$

Only we need to compute a_0 and a_n

$$f(x) = \frac{a_0}{2} + \sum_{n=0}^{\infty} a_n \cos nx$$

$$a_0 = \frac{1}{\pi}\int_{-\pi}^{\pi} f(x)dx$$

$$a_0 = \frac{1}{\pi}\int_{-\pi}^{\pi} \sin^2(x)dx$$

$$a_0 = \frac{2}{\pi}\int_{0}^{\pi} \sin^2(x)dx$$

Since, $\sin^2(x) = \left(\frac{1-\cos(2x)}{2}\right)$

$$a_0 = \frac{2}{\pi}\int_{0}^{\pi}\left(\frac{1-\cos(2x)}{2}\right)dx$$

$$a_0 = \frac{1}{\pi}\int_{0}^{\pi} 1-\cos(2x)dx$$

$$a_0 = \frac{1}{\pi}\int_{0}^{\pi} 1dx - \frac{1}{\pi}\int_{0}^{\pi}\cos(2x)dx$$

$$a_0 = \frac{1}{\pi}[x]_0^{\pi} - \frac{1}{\pi}\left[\frac{\sin(2x)}{2}\right]_0^{\pi}$$

$$a_0 = \frac{1}{\pi}[\pi - 0] - \frac{1}{2\pi}[\sin(2\pi) - \sin(0)]$$

$$a_0 = \frac{1}{\pi}[\pi] - \frac{1}{2\pi}[0]$$

[∵ $\sin(2x) = \sin(0) = 0$]

$$a_0 = 1 - 0$$

$$a_0 = 1$$

$$a_n = \frac{1}{\pi}\int_{-\pi}^{\pi} f(x)\cos(nx)dx$$

$$a_n = \frac{1}{\pi}\int_{-\pi}^{\pi} \sin^2(x)\cos(nx)dx$$

$$a_n = \frac{2}{\pi}\int_{0}^{\pi} \sin^2(x)\cos(nx)dx$$

$$a_n = \frac{2}{\pi}\int_{0}^{\pi}\left(\frac{1-\cos(2x)}{2}\right)\cos(nx)dx$$

$$a_n = \frac{1}{\pi}\int_{0}^{\pi}(1-\cos(2x))\cos(nx)dx$$

$$a_n = \frac{1}{\pi}\int_0^\pi \cos(nx)dx$$

$$- \frac{1}{\pi}\int_0^\pi \cos(2x)\cos nx dx$$

$$2\cos(m\theta)\cos(n\theta) = \cos(m+n)\theta + \cos(m-n)\theta$$

$$a_n = \frac{1}{\pi}\int_0^\pi \cos(nx)dx$$

$$-\frac{1}{2\pi}\int_0^\pi 2\cos(2x)\cos nx\, dx$$

$$a_n = \frac{1}{\pi}\int_0^\pi \cos(nx)dx$$

$$-\frac{1}{2\pi}\int_0^\pi \cos(2+n)x + \cos(2-n)x\, dx$$

$$a_n = \frac{1}{\pi}\left[\frac{\sin(nx)}{n}\right]_0^\pi$$

$$-\frac{1}{2\pi}\left[\frac{\sin(2+n)x}{2+n} + \frac{\sin(2-n)x}{2-n}\right]_0^\pi$$

$$a_n = \frac{1}{\pi}\left[\frac{\sin(n\pi) - \sin(0)}{n}\right]$$

$$-\frac{1}{2\pi}\left[\frac{\sin(2+n)\pi}{2+n} + \frac{\sin(2-n)\pi}{2-n} - \frac{\sin(0)}{2+n} - \frac{\sin(0)}{2-n}\right]$$

$a_n = 0$ where $n > 2$

This equation is not true for $n = 1$ and 2, so we will compute a_1 and a_2 separately.

When we will solve for a_1, we will get

$$a_1 = 0$$

And when we will solve for a_2, we will get

$$a_2 = -\frac{1}{2}$$

$$f(x) = \frac{a_0}{2} + \sum_{n=0}^{\infty} a_n \cos nx$$

$$f(x) = \frac{a_0}{2} + a_1\cos(x)$$

$$+ a_2\cos(x) + a_3\cos(3x)$$

$$f(x) = \frac{a_0}{2} + a_2\cos(2x)$$

$$f(x) = \frac{1}{2} - \frac{1}{2}\cos(2x)$$

$$\sin^2(x) = \frac{1}{2} - \frac{1}{2}\cos(2x).$$

99. $4 \times 5^x = 500$

$4 \times 5^x = 4 \times 125 = 4 \times 5^3$

$\therefore \quad x = 3$

Now $(x)^x = (3)^3 = 27$.

100. $\frac{d^2y(t)}{dt^2} - \frac{dy(t)}{dt} - 2y(t) = x(t)$

$\Rightarrow (D^2 - D - 2)y = x(t)$

AE $\Rightarrow (m^2 - m - 2) = 0$

$(m-2)(m+1) = 0$

$\therefore \quad m = -1$ and 2

Thus system characterstics are linear and unstable.

101. $P(n) = 1.6 + 2.9 + 3.18 + ... + n(3n + 3)$

$= 3.1.2 + 2.3.3 + 3.3.4 + ... + 3.n.(n + 1)$

$= 3[1.2 + 2.3 + 3.4 + ... + n.(n + 1)]$

nth term $= 3(n)(n + 1)$

$= 3[n^2 + n]$

Now $P(n) = 3[\Sigma n^2 + \Sigma n]$

$$= \left[\frac{n(n+1)(2n+1)}{6} + \frac{n(n+1)}{2}\right]$$

$$= \frac{n(n+1)}{2}[2n+1+3]$$

$$= \frac{n(n+1)(2n+4)}{2}$$

$$= n(n+1)(n+2).$$

102. $S_1 = 1$

$$S_2 = 1 + 2 = \frac{2(2+1)}{2} = 3$$

$$S_3 = 1 + 2 + 3 = \frac{3(3+1)}{2} = 6$$

....

$$S_n = 1 + 2 + 3 + ... + n = \frac{n(n+1)}{2}.$$

103. $P(n) : n! < \left(\frac{n+1}{2}\right)n$

For, $n = 1,\ 1! = 1$

and $\left(\frac{1+1}{2}\right)\cdot 1 = 1 \Rightarrow$ for $1! \nleq 1$

For, $n = 2;\ 2! = 2$

and $\left(\frac{2+1}{2}\right)\cdot 2 = 3 \Rightarrow 2! < 3$

For, $n = 3;\ 3!$

$= 2 \times 3 = 6$

and $\left(\frac{3+1}{2}\right) = 6$

$3! \nleq 6$

For, $n = 4;\ 4!$

$= 2 \times 3 \times 4 = 24$

and $\frac{4(4+1)}{2} = 10$

$\therefore$ $4! \nleq 10$

Hence, this is true for $n = 2$.

104. $I = \int_0^1 \frac{1}{\sqrt{x}(x+1)}dx$

Let $\sqrt{x} = 2,\ \frac{dx}{2\sqrt{x}} = dz$

$\Rightarrow$ $dx = 2z\ dz$

Now, $\int \frac{1}{\sqrt{x}(1+x)}dx = \int \frac{2z\ dz}{z(1+z)^2}$

$= 2\int \frac{dz}{(1+z^2)} = 2\tan^{-1}(z)$

$= 2\tan^{-1}(\sqrt{x})$

Applying the limit

$$I = \left[2\tan^{-1}\left(\sqrt{x}\right)\right]_0^1$$

$$= 2\left[\tan^{-1}(1) - \tan^{-1}(0)\right]$$

$$= 2\left[\frac{\pi}{4} - 0\right] = \frac{\pi}{2}$$

This, integral is convergent.

105. Here,

$$P(n) = \left(1+\frac{1}{1}\right)\left(1+\frac{1}{2}\right)\left(1+\frac{1}{3}\right)\left(1+\frac{1}{4}\right)...\left(1+\frac{1}{n}\right)$$

$$= \left(\frac{1+1}{1}\right)\left(\frac{2+1}{2}\right)\left(\frac{3+1}{3}\right)\left(\frac{4+1}{4}\right)...\left(\frac{n+1}{n}\right)$$

General term $P(n) = (n + 1)$.

107. For n = even integer

$(x^2 - y^2) = (x - y)(x + y)$

$(x^4 - y^4) = (x^2 - y^2)(x^2 + y^2)$

$= (x - y)(x + y)(x^2 + y^2)$

$(x^6 - y^6) = (x^2 - y^2)(x^4 + x^2y^2 + y^4)$

$= (x - y)(x + y)(x^4 + x^2y^2 + y^4)$

Hence, $(x^n - y^n)$ is divisible by $(x - y)(x + y)$.

108. As $f(x)$ is continuous between $0 \le x \le 1$ and also differentiable between $0 \le x \le 1$.

So, $f(x)$ is integrable on $[0, 1]$.

109. For $n = 2, 3, 4, ..., \infty$

$2! < \left(\frac{2+1}{2}\right)^2 \Rightarrow 2 < \frac{9}{4}$

$3! < \left(\frac{3+1}{2}\right)^3 \Rightarrow 6 < 8$

$4! < \left(\frac{4+1}{2}\right)^4 \Rightarrow 24 < \frac{625}{16}$

Hence, $n! < \left(\frac{n+1}{2}\right)^n$ is true.

110. $I_n = \int_0^{\frac{\pi}{2}} x^n \sin x\ dx$

For $n = 3$,

$$I_3 = \int_0^{\frac{\pi}{2}} x^3 \sin x\ dx$$

$$= x^3(-\cos x) - \int 3x^2(-\cos x)dx$$

Now for $x = 0,\ \frac{\pi}{2}$

$\left[x^3 \cos x\right]_0^{\frac{\pi}{2}} = 0 - 0 = 0$

$$\therefore \quad I_3 = \int_0^{\frac{\pi}{2}} 3x^2 \cos x\, dx$$

$$= 3x^2 \int \cos x\, dx - \int \frac{d}{dx}(3x^2) \int (\cos x\, dx) dx$$

$$= 3x^2 \sin x - \int 6x \sin x\, dx$$

$$= \left[3x^2 \sin x\right]_0^{\frac{\pi}{2}} - 6\int_0^{\frac{\pi}{2}} x \sin x\, dx$$

As, $I_1 = \int_0^{\frac{\pi}{2}} x \sin x\, dx$

and $[3x^2 \sin x]_0^{\pi/2} = 3\left(\frac{\pi}{2}\right)^2 - 0 = 3\left(\frac{\pi}{2}\right)^2$

$$\therefore \quad I_3 = 3\left(\frac{\pi}{2}\right)^2 - 6I_1$$

$$= 3\left(\frac{\pi}{2}\right)^{(3-2)} - 3(3-1)I_1$$

$$\Rightarrow I_3 + 3(3-1)I_1 = 3\left(\frac{\pi}{2}\right)^{(3-2)}$$

Hence, $I_n + n(n-1)\, I_{(n-2)} = n\left(\frac{\pi}{2}\right)^{n-1}$.

113. $I = \int_0^1 e^{x^2} dx$

On expression of $e^{x^2} = 1 + x^2 + \frac{x^4}{2} + \frac{x^6}{6} ...$

Now $\int_0^1 e^{x^2} dx = \int_0^1 \left(1 + x^2 + \frac{x^4}{2} + \frac{x^6}{6} ...\right) dx$

$$= \left[x + \frac{x^3}{3} + \frac{x^5}{10} + \frac{x^7}{42} + ...\right]_0^1$$

$$= 1 + \frac{1}{3} + \frac{1}{10} + \frac{1}{42} + ...$$

$\therefore 1 < I < e$.

114. $I = \int_1^{\infty} \frac{1}{\sqrt{x}} dx = \left[\frac{\sqrt{x}}{\frac{1}{2}}\right]_1^{\infty} = \left[2\sqrt{x}\right]_1^{\infty}$

This is convergent.

115. D.E.: $(2D + 1)^2 y = 0$

$\therefore \; 2D + 1 = 0 \Rightarrow D = -\frac{1}{2}, -\frac{1}{2}$

Solution of this D.E.

$$= (A + Bx)e^{-\frac{x}{2}}.$$

116. D.E.: $x^2 \frac{d^2y}{dx^2} - 3x\frac{dy}{dx} + 4y = 0$

Let $x = e^z$, then $z = \log x$

then, $x\frac{dy}{dx} = Dy$ and $x^2 \frac{d^2y}{dx^2} = D(D-1)y$

So given equation

$$x^2 \frac{d^2y}{dx^2} - 3x\frac{dy}{dx} + 4y = 0$$

$$= D(D-1)y - 3Dy + 4y = 0$$

$(D^2 - 4D + 4)y = 0$

$(D - 2)^2 y = 0$

$\therefore$ A.E. is $(m - 2) = 0$

then, $m = 2, 2$

C.F. $= (c_1 + c_2 z)e^{2z}$

$= (c_1 + c_2 \log x)e^{2 \log x}$

$= (c_1 + c_2 \log x)x^2$.

117. $(5^{2n} - 1) = \{(5^2)^n - (1)^n\}$

$= ((25)^n - (1)^n)$

As, $(x^n - y^n)$ is alway divisible by $(x - y)$

$\therefore \{(25)^n - (1)^n\}$ is alway divisible by $25 - 1 = 24$.

120. $f(x) = x|x|$

$$I = \int_a^b f(x)dx = \int_a^b \left|x^2\right| \cdot dx$$

$$= \left|\int_a^b x^2 dx\right| = \left|\frac{x^3}{3}\right|_a^b$$

$$= \frac{1}{3}\left(\left|b^3\right| - \left|a\right|^3\right).$$

121. Here order of the image must divide the order of Z_8.

G.c.d. of (4, 8) = 4

Hence, number of onto homomorphism Z_8 to Z_4 = 2.

122. Given D.E. = $x^2y'' + xy' - y = 0$

Let $\quad x = e^z$ or, $z = \log x$

$$x^2 \frac{d^2y}{dx^2} = D(D-1) \text{ and } x\frac{dy}{dx} = D$$

$\therefore\ x^2y'' + xy' - y = 0$

$\Rightarrow D(D-1)y + Dy - y = 0$

$(D^2 - 1)y = 0$

Then A.E.: $m^2 - 1 = 0 \Rightarrow m = \pm 1$

$\therefore$ Solution of D.E. $y = e^z$ and $y = e^{-z}$

$y = e^{\log x}$ and $y = e^{-\log x}$

$\Rightarrow \quad y = x$ and $y = 1/x$.

123. $x = A\cos(mt - \alpha)$

$$\frac{dx}{dt} = -mA\sin(mt-\alpha)$$

$$\frac{d^2x}{dt^2} = -mA(m)\cos(mt-\alpha)$$

$$\frac{d^2x}{dt^2} = -m^2 A\cos(mt-\alpha)$$

$$\frac{d^2x}{dt^2} = -m^2 x.$$

124. ${}^{(2n+1)}P_{(n-1)} : {}^{(2n-1)}P_n = 3 : 5$

$$\frac{\dfrac{(2n+1)!}{(2n+1-n+1)!}}{\dfrac{(2n-1)!}{(2n-1-n)!}} = \frac{3}{5}$$

$$\frac{(2n+1)!(n-1)!}{(n+2)!(2n-1)!} = \frac{3}{5}$$

$$\frac{(2n+1)(2n)}{(n+2)(n+1)(n)} = \frac{3}{5}$$

$$10(2n+1) = 3(n+2)(n+1)$$

$$20n + 10 = 3n^2 + 9n + 6$$

$$3n^2 - 11n - 4 = 0$$

$$(n-4)(3n+1) = 0$$

$$\therefore \quad n = 4.$$

125. We show that

1. HK is closed under multiplication
2. For $x \in HK$, we should have $x^{-1} \in HK$
3. $e \in HK$

Let $x, y \in HK \Rightarrow x = h_1k_1, y = h_2k_2$, where $h_1, h_2 \in H$; $k_1, k_2 \in K$

Consider $xy = h_1k_1h_2k_2 = h_1h_2(h_2^{-1}k_1h_2)k_2 \in HK$

Let $h_2 \in H \Rightarrow h_2^{-1} \in H \subseteq G \Rightarrow h_2^{-1} \in G$

Since K is a normal subgroup of G, and $k_1 \in K$,

$\therefore\ h_2^{-1}k_1h_2 \in K$

$\Rightarrow (h_2^{-1}k_1h_2)k_2 \in K$

$\Rightarrow h_1h_2(h_2^{-1}k_1h_2)k_2 \in HK$

Thus HK is closed under multiplication.

Further, For $x \in HK$, we have

$x^{-1} = (h_1k_1)^{-1} = k_1^{-1}h_1^{-1} = h_1^{-1}(h_1k_1^{-1}h_1^{-1})$

Let $h_1 \in H \subseteq G \Rightarrow h_1 \in G$. Also $k_1 \in K$

$\Rightarrow k_1^{-1} \in K$

Since K is a normal subgroup of G

$\therefore\ h_1k_1^{-1}h_1^{-1} \in K$

$\Rightarrow h_1^{-1}(h_1k_1^{-1})h_1^{-1} \in HK$

Thus $x^{-1} \in HK$

Finally, $e \in H, e \in K \Rightarrow e \cdot e \in HK \Rightarrow e \in HK$

Thus HK is a subgroup of G.

126. Let a be a generator of G. Let (S, *) be a subgroup of G. Then $\{a^n/n \in Z_1 \text{ and } Z_1 \subseteq Z\}$. Let m be the smallest positive integer in Z_1. Consider any element a^n in S. By division algorithm, $n = qm + r$ where $0 \le r < m$. $a^r = a^n - q^m = a^n * (a^m)^{-q}$. As $a^n, a^m \in S$, $a^n * (am)^{-q} \in S$. This forces a^r to be in S. As $r < m$, this is a contradiction to the property of m. Hence $a^n = (a^m)^q$. Thus each element of S is generated by a^m and hence (S, *) is cyclic.

127. Let $a, b \in G$

Then $\quad a^2 = e$ and $b^2 = e$

Since G is a group $a, b \in G$ [by associative law]

Then $(ab)^2 = e$

$\Rightarrow \quad (ab)^2 = a^2$ [Since $a^2 = e$]

$= (ab)(ab) = a.a$

$\Rightarrow \quad bab = a$ [let cancellation law]

Multiply right side by b we get

$$bab^2 = ab$$

$\Rightarrow$ $ba.e = ab$ [Since $b^2 = e$]

$\Rightarrow$ $ba = ab$

Therefore, G is an abelian group.

128. D.E. $= \frac{d^3y}{dx^3} - 2\frac{d^2y}{dx^2} + \frac{dy}{dx} - 2y = 0$

$(D^3 - 2D^2 + D - 2)y = 0$

A.E. $\Rightarrow (m^3 - 2m^2 + m - 2) = 0$

$(m^2 + 1)(m - 2) = 0$

$\therefore$ $m = 2$ and $\pm i$

Hence, general solution

$$e^x\left(c_1 \cos\sqrt{3}x + c_2 \sin\sqrt{3}x\right) + c_3 e^{2x}.$$

131. Since G is simple, we must have $(g) = G$. If the order of g is not finite, then (g^2) is a proper normal subgroup of $(g) = G$, which is impossible since G is simple.

Thus the order of g is finite, and hence $G = (g)$ is a finite group.

Let p be the order of g (hence the order of G). Seeking a contradiction, assume that $p = mn$ is a composite number with integers $m > 1$, $n > 1$. Then (g^m) is a proper normal subgroup of G. This is a contradiction since G is simple. Thus p must be a prime number.

Therefore, the order of G is a prime number.

133. Let $K = ker(\phi)$. To show that K is a normal subgroup of G we need, to show that $xkx^{-1} \in K$ for all $x \in G$, and $k \in K$.

So fix $x \in G$ and $k \in K$, and let $g = xkx^{-1}$. We want to show that $g \in K$. We have

$$\begin{aligned}\phi(g) &= \phi(xkx^{-1})\\ &= \phi(x)\phi(k)\phi(x^{-1})\\ &= \phi(x)e_H\phi(x^{-1})\\ &= \phi(xx^{-1}) = \phi(e_G) = e_H,\end{aligned}$$

and so g is in K, the kernel of ϕ.

134. Option (C) is correct as the statement, given in option (C) is not correct.

Theorem: If the index of H in G is equal to 2, then H is a normal subgroup of G and the quotient group G/H is isomorphic to $\mathbb{Z}_2$.

Proof: We show that $xH = Hx$ for every $x \in G$. This is clear when $x \in H$. If $x \in G - H$, the left cosets H, xH form a partition of G. But H and Hx also partition G. Therefore, xH must equal Hx as required. As there are only two distinct cosets, the quotient group G/H has order 2 and isomorphic to $\mathbb{Z}_2$.

137. Let $\{V_\alpha\}$ be an open covering of $f(X)$. Because f is continuous, each of the sets $f^{-1}(V_\alpha)$ is open, by Theorem. Because X is compact, there are finitely many indices, say $\alpha_1, ..., \alpha_n$, such that

$$X \subset f^{-1}(V_{\alpha_1}) \cup f^{-1}(V_{\alpha_2}) \cup ... \cup f^{-1}(V_{\alpha_n})$$

Because $f(f^{-1}(E)) = E$, for every $E \subset Y$, implies that

$$f(X) \subset V_{\alpha_1} \cup V_{\alpha_2} \cup ... \cup V_{\alpha_n}$$

This completes the proof.

144. If a function is continuous at a point a, then

$$\lim_{x\to a} f(x) = f(a)$$

$\sin(\infty) = a$, where $-1 \le a \le 1$

Given:

$$f(0) = 1$$

$$f(x) = x\sin(1/x)$$

Checking continuity at $x = 0$

$$\lim_{x\to 0} f(x) = f(0)$$

L.H.L.

$$= \lim_{x\to 0} f(x) = \lim_{x\to 0} x\sin\left(\frac{1}{x}\right)$$

$$= 0 \times \sin\left(\frac{1}{0}\right)$$

$$= 0 \times \sin(\infty) = 0$$

R.H.L.

$$= f(0) = 1$$

$$\text{L.H.L.} \ne \text{R.H.L.}$$

Hence, function is discontinuous at $x = 0$.

145. + + + + +

$\therefore$ 4 negative sign has seven places to be arranged

$\Rightarrow$ ${}^7C_4 = 35.$

148. A division ring is a ring which every non-zero element has a multiplicative inverse (that is, every non-zero element is a unit). (Equivalently, a division ring is a ring in which the non-zero elements form a multiplicative group). A non-commutative division ring is called a *skew field.*

$+_2$	0	1
0	0	1
1	1	0

$\times_2$	0	1
0	0	0
1	0	1

From above (R, $+_2$) is commutative group (can be easily verified)

$\times_2$ is associative.

as $(0 \times_2 1) \times_2 1 = 0 \times_2 (1 \times_2 1)$

$\times_2$ is distributive over $+_2$.

as $1 \times_2 (0 +_2 1) = 1 \times_2 1 = 1$

$= 1 \times_2 0 + 1 \times_2 1$

$= 0 + 1 = 1$

From table it clear that R is without zero divisors.

149. Vector $|a| = a$

Given, $\lambda\vec{a}$ is a unit vectors

$$\Rightarrow \quad |\lambda\vec{a}| = 1$$

$$\Rightarrow \quad |\lambda||\vec{a}| = 1$$

$$\Rightarrow \quad |\lambda|a = 1$$

$$\Rightarrow \quad a = \frac{1}{|\lambda|}$$

Hence, option (A), is correct.

152. A. $f'(x) > 0$ if $4x - 3 > 0$ *i.e.,* $x > \frac{3}{4}$

$\therefore f^x$ is strictly increasing on $\left[\frac{3}{4}, \infty\right)$

B. $f'(x) < 0 \Rightarrow 4x - 3 < 0$

$\Rightarrow x < \frac{3}{4}$

$\therefore$ function is decreasing in $\left(-\infty, \frac{3}{4}\right]$.

160. Facts about rings

- The set of all units of a ring is a group under the multiplication defined on the ring.
- Every principal ideal domain is a unique factorization domain.
- If R is a commutative ring with unity, then every maximal ideal is a prime ideal.
- If R is commutative ring with unity, the R is a field if and only if the only ideals of R are R and $\{0\}$.
- If R is a commutative ring with unity and $I \neq R$ is an ideal, then R/I is an integral domain if and only if I is a prime ideal.
- If R is a commutative ring with unity, then I is a maximal ideal if and only if R/I is a field.
- If $f(x) \in F|x|$ (where F is a field) and the ideal generated by $f(x)$ is not $\{0\}$, then the ideal is maximal if and only if $f(x)$ is irreducible over F.
- There are exactly four normed division rings, they have dimensions 1, 2, 4 and 8. They are the real numbers, the complex numbers, the quaternions, and the octonions. The quaternions are non-commutative and the octonions are non-associative.

162. ***Step 1:*** One half of $[-M, M]$, either $[-M, 0]$ or $[0, M]$, call it I_1, contains a_n for infinitely many n (if both halves do, then it does not matter which one we pick). One half of I_1, call, it I_2, contains a_n for infinitely many n. Continuing, we obtain a sequence $I_1 \supset I_2 \supset I_3 \supset \ldots$ of closed bounded intervals such that each I_k contains a_n for inifinitely many n.

Step 2: Choose $n_1 \in \mathbb{N}$ with $a_{n1} \in I_1$. Choose $n_2 > n_1$ with $a_{n2} \in I_2$. This is possible because $a_n \in I_2$ for infinitely many n: these n cannot all be less than or equal to n_1. Continue and obtain a subsequence (a_{ni}) of (a_n) with $a_{nk} \in I_k$ for all k. We want to prove that this subsequence converges.

Step 3: There is $b \in \bigcap_{k-1}^{\infty} I_k$ by the nested interval property (Theorem). We claim that $a_{nk} \to b$. Let $e > 0$. By the Archimedean property, there is $N \in \mathbb{N}$ such that the length of I_N, which is $M/2^N$, is smaller than e. Thus for $k \geq N$, $|a_{nk} - b| < e$ since a_{nk} and b both lie in $I_k \subset I_N$.

166. An integral is (C, 0) summable precisely when it exists as an improper integral. However, there are integrals which are (C, α) summable for α > 0 which fail to converge as improper integrals (in the sense of Riemann or Lebesgue). One example is the integral.

$$\int_0^\infty \sin x\, dx$$

which fails to exist as an improper integral but is (C, α) summable for every α > 0. This is an integral version of Grandi's series.

172. If the limit the graph is approaching is infinity, the limit is unbounded. A limit does not exist if the graph is approaching a different value from opposite directions. Here given limit

$$\lim_{n \to \text{infinity}} \frac{\text{U}n}{n} = 1 \text{ is not bounded.}$$

173. Suppose $\mathbb{Z}_p$ is an integral domain. Assume (by way of contradiction) that n is not prime. Then $n = ab$ for some, $a, b \in \mathbb{Z}$ where $1 < a$ and $b < n$, meaning $ab \equiv 0 \pmod{n}$. This is a contradiction since $\mathbb{Z}_p$ is assumed to be an integral domain and therefore does not contain any zero divisors. Therefore p must be prime. ($\Leftarrow$) Assume p is prime. Then a does not divide n for any $1 < a < n$ where $a \in \mathbb{Z}_p$. Thus $\mathbb{Z}_p$ does not contain any zero divisors and is therefore an integral domain.

176. Since $\mathbb{Z}_n$ is a commutative ring with identity for any n, it will be an integral domain if and only if it has no zero divisors.

Suppose first that n is a prime and suppose that $ab = 0$ in $\mathbb{Z}_n$. Then in $\mathbb{Z}$ we have

$$ab \equiv 0 \bmod n \Rightarrow n|ab$$

Since n is prime, by Euclid's lemna $n|a$ or $n|b$. In terms of congruences, then,

$$a \equiv 0 \bmod n \Rightarrow a = 0 \text{ in } \mathbb{Z}_n$$

$$\text{or } b \equiv 0 \bmod n \Rightarrow b = 0 \text{ in } \mathbb{Z}_n$$

Therefore $\mathbb{Z}_n$ is an integral domain if n is prime. Suppose n is not prime. Then $n = m_1 m_2$ with $1 < m_1 < n$, $1 < m_2 < n$. Then $n|m_1$, $n|m_2$, but $n|m_1 m_2$. Translating this into $\mathbb{Z}_n$, we have $m_1 m_2 = 0$ but either $m_1 \neq 0$ or $m_2 \neq 0$. Therefore $\mathbb{Z}_n$ is not an integral domain if n is not prime.

179. In mathematics, specifically abstract algebra, an integral domain is a non-zero commutative ring in which the product of any non-zero elements is non-zero integral domains are generalizations of the ring of integers and provide a natural setting for studying divisibility. In an integral domain, every non-zero element a has the cancellation property, that is if $a \neq 0$, an equality $ab = ac$ implies $b = c$. Here (0, +, ρ) ring is an integral domain.

181. Geography, Economics and Commerce are a part of subject Mathematics.

182. The Italian astronomer and physicist Galileo Galilei said: "*Mathematics is the language in which God has written the universe.*"

The universe cannot be read until one has learned the language and become familiar with the characters which they have been written. This mathematical language is geometry. The letters are triangles, circles, and other geometrical figures. Some traditions call this sacred geometry. Without these figures, it is impossible to comprehend a single word.

Math is a universal language. The symbols and organization to form equations are the same in every country of the world.

183. Mathematics is the study of numbers, shape, quantity, and patterns. Teaching methods of mathematics include problem-solving, lecture, inductive, deductive, analytic, synthetic, and heuristic or Discovery Method. The teacher adopts any method according to the needs and interests of students.

Problem Solving Strategy in Mathematics: In a mathematics class, students at the primary level enjoy learning, solving problems, develop mathematical curiosity and become confident in using mathematics to analyze and solve problems.

- Problem-solving is a learner-centred approach that emphasizes learner's active involvement in the learning process. In this approach, teachers create a problematic situation for students and then assist them in perceiving, defining, and stating the problems in a fear-free classroom environment.

- An effective problem-solving strategy is a plan of action used to find a solution. Different strategies have different action plans associated with them. For example, a well-known problem-solving strategy is the trial and error principle.
- Solving problems in a backward manner and drawing is also part of problem-solving strategy in mathematics.

Note: Learning should never facilitate the rote method. Mathematics always discourages rote learning and makes the whole process better by including hands-on-experiences.

Hence, from the above mentioned points, it becomes clear that Rote learning is not a problem-solving strategy in mathematics.

184. A. Sum of two prime numbers is always a prime number. But 5 + 7 = 12, which is not a prime number.

B. There is no even prime numbers. But 2 is even prime number.

C. 1 is the smallest prime number. But 2 is the smallest prime number.

D. A composite number cannot be prime. This is true.

185. Early man used to hunt animals. He needed to identify them and count their numbers. He used a system of drawing and later on his ten fingers to count from one to ten. Even today this system of counting on fingers is popular. This method of counting was developed in India and later on adopted by Arabs, Romans and other Europeans. The Romans used seven letters to write numbers. These were M, D, C, L, X, V and I. This system is taught in the schools even now. Sumerians used special shapes, but they counted in 60's.

The number system that we use today is the Hindu-Arabic system. This system of numbers is used all over the world. Ancient Indian scholar Aryabhatta invented Zero which made the counting possible and most difficult calculation easy. The Arabs took this system of numbers from 0 to 9 to Europe. We should be proud of contributions made by our country.

186. The study of mathematics as a "demonstrative discipline" began in the 6th century BC with the Pythagoreans, who coined the term "mathematics" from the ancient Greek (*mathema*), meaning "subject of instruction". Greek mathematics greatly refined the methods (espically through the introduction of deductive reasoning and mathematical rigor in proofs) and expanded the subject matter of mathematics.

187. Cooperative learning is an alternative to competitive models. Cooperative learning settings compared to those in individualistic or competititve learning settings, achieve more, reason better, gain higher self-esteem, like classmates and the learning tasks more, and have more perceived social support.

188. Educational and instructional objectives, the specific outcomes of the teaching-learning act are related with all the three aspects or domains of the learner's behaviour cognitive, affective and conative or psychomotor. For the specification of these educational and instructional objectives a number of taxonomies have been suggested.

Taxonomy means a system of classification and in this sense Bloom's Taxonomy presents a system of classification of the objectives in the similar way as Dewey's Decimal system tends to classify a number of books in a library.

The taxonomy, of educational and instructional objectives has been worked out on the assumption that the teaching-learning process may be conceived as an attempt to change the behaviour of the pupils with respect to some subject matter or learning experiences. Since behaviour is divided into three domains—Cognitive (knowing), effective (feeling) and psychomotor (doing): The taxonomy of educational and instructional objectives has also been considered to be belonging to these three domains.

The taxonomy related to cognitive domain has been presented by Bloom (Bloom, et al., 1956), the second related to affective domain by Krathwohl, Bloom and Masia (Krathwohl, et al., 1964) and the third related to psychomotor domain by Harrow (Harrow, 1972) and Simpson (1966).

189. Good lesson planning is essential to the process of teaching and learning. A teacher who is prepared is well on his/her way to a successful instructional experience. The development of interesting lessons takes a great deal of time and effort. As a new teacher you must be committed to spending the necessary time in this endeavour.

It is also important to realize that the best planned lesson is worthless if interesting delivery procedures, along with good classroom management techniques, are not in evidence.

190. Early number knowledge provides an essential foundation for learning basic arithmetic. It includes the following:

Classification: To group according to properties

Conservation: To keep something in mind for future

Class inclusion: Inclusion of the whole class, *for example*: while teaching counting, students are asked to count one by one or sometimes in chorus.

Learning early numbers

Mental calculations

Number acquisition

Place of counting

Oral works

Hence, we can conclude that Measurement is not an early number concept. It is a part of the evaluation.

191. Visualization:

- Any technique to create images, scenes, diagrams, or animations to convey a message is visualization.
- Visualization through visual imagery is an effective way to communicate abstract or concrete ideas. Hence it is considered as a Mathematical process.

Estimation:

- It is the process to find approx. or extimate values or the process of approximation is termed as an estimation. It is one of the most effective processes used in Mathematics.
- *For example*, getting an estimated solution of $72.13 \times 5 + 40 = ?$ While solving the above problem a student will think like $70 \times 5 = 350 + 40$ so the estimated value of the solution will be around 400.

Transposition:

- The process in which transfer or exchange of two or more elements or data takes place is called transposition.
- It is the most effective process used in algebra in Mathematics.

Memorization refers to remembering something by heart which is not a mathematical process memorization has no relation to the mathematical process.

It is a passive process and can be done only where you know prior events and then memorize the answers accordingly. But this method cannot be opted in a situation where you don't know exactly what the question will ask.

192. Team teaching involves a group of instructors working purposefully, regularly, and cooperatively to help a group of students of any age learn. Teachers together set goals for a course, design a syllabus, prepare individual lesson plans, teach students, and evaluate the results. They share insights, argue with one another, and perhaps even challenge students to decide which approach is better.

193. A learner exhibiting difficulty in sorting, recognizing patterns, orienting numbers and shapes, telling time and measurement may have dyscalculia with difficulty in visual-spatial skills.

Some students have disturbances in the **visual-spatial-motor organization**, which may result in weak or lacking understanding of concepts, very poor "number sense", specific difficulty with pictorial representations and/or poorly controlled handwriting and confused arrangements of numerals and symbols. Students with profoundly impaired conceptual understanding often have substantial perceptual-motor deficits and are presumed to have right hemisphere dysfunction.

194. Jean Piaget argued that when the child is at formal operational stage, it is appropriate to introduce 'Ratio and Proportion' as in this stage:

- children's mental capabilities are developed to the maximum level.
- children become capable of hypothetical and deductive reasoning.
- children are capable of creating logical combinations and verifying hypotheses.
- children develop abstract thinking and understand the structure of mathematical problems.
- children gain the ability to reason proportionally and to work in probabilities and possibilities.
- children can segregate the variable, eliminates contradictions, and combines variables in a logical way.

195. A good mathematics teacher is expected to possess to good habits like hard work, self-confidence, patience, strong will power, systematic working, outlook, sweet speaking etc. He is also expected to have rational and scientific attitude. The Mathematics teacher should clearly know the use of the knowledge of his subject in various fields of real life. If he has a good knowledge of the application of mathematics in real life, in various vocations, in other subjects etc., he can communicate and transfer it to his students.

196. In a Mathematics classroom, the emphasis is placed on mathematical content, process, and reasoning. Mathematical reasoning is an ability to provide a justification for a mathematical procedure. It also involves the ability to think logically and systematically.

197. **Cooperative learning** is an educational approach which aims to organize classroom activities into academic and social learning experiences.. Students must work in groups to complete tasks collectively toward academic goals.

There are a great number of cooperative learning techniques available. Some cooperative learning techniques utilize student pairing, while others utilize small groups of four or five students.

198. **Principles of curriculum construction in Mathematics are:**

- should be child-centred-makes it easy to understand and interested in learning.
- should be activity-based-make students learning by doing and playing.
- should have teachers' acceptance.
- Logically & psychologically arranged curriculum improves the child's critical thinking over it.

199. The aims of teaching and learning mathematics are to encourage and enable students to:

- recognize that mathematics permeates the world around us;
- appreciate the usefulness, power and beauty of mathematics;
- enjoy mathematics and develop patience and persistence when solving problems;
- understand and be able to use the language, symbols and notation of mathematics;
- develop mathematical curiosity and use inductive and deductive reasoning when solving problems;
- become confident in using mathematics to analyse and solve problems both in school and in real-life situations;
- develop the knowledge, skills and attitudes necessary to pursue further studies in mathematics;

- develop abstract, logical and critical thinking and the ability to reflect critically upon their work and the work of others
- develop a critical appreciation of the use of information and communication technology in mathematics;
- appreciate the international dimension of mathematics and its multicultural and historical perspectives.

200. Robert Mager's Approach: According to Robert Mager (1962), instructional objectives are best described in terms of the terminal behaviour expected from the learners. He recommends the following things for the writing of the objectives:

- Identification of the terminal behaviour or performance and its naming.
- Description of the important conditions under which the behaviour is expected to occur.
- Specification of the criteria of acceptable performance (desired terminal behaviour) by describing how good a learner's performance must be for being acceptable.

Previous Paper (Solved)

DSSSB—TEACHERS PGT MATHS
Recruitment Exam, 2018*

1. Let R be a relation from a set A = {1, 2, 3, 4} to a set B = {u, v, w, x} defined by R = {(1, u), (1, v), (3, v), (3, x), (4, v)}. The domain of R and range of R, are, respectively:
A. {1, 2, 3, 4}; {u, v, w, x}
B. {1, 3, 4}; {u, v, x}
C. {1, 2, 4}; {u, v, x}
D. {1, 3, 4}; {u, w, x}

2. Consider n(U) = 20, n(A) = 12, n(B) = 9 and (A ∩ B) = 4. Then the value of $n\left(\dfrac{A}{B}\right)$ is:
A. 11 B. 17
C. 3 D. 8

3. Let A = {1, 2, 3}. A function f from A to A is defined by f(1) = 2, f(2) = 1 and f(3) = 3. The inverse of the function f is:
A. {(1, 2), (2, 1), (3, 3)}
B. {(1, 2), (2, 1), (2, 3)}
C. {(1, 2), (2, 2), (3, 3)}
D. {(1, 1), (2, 1), (3, 3)}

4. The number of subsets of the set A = {a_1, a_2, ..., a_n} which contain even number of elements is:
A. $2^n - 1$ B. 2^{n-1}
C. 2^{n-2} D. 2^n

5. Using mathematical induction, the value of 2 + 5 + 8 + ... (3n – 1) comes out to be:
A. $\dfrac{n(3n+1)}{2}$ B. $\dfrac{n(2n+1)}{3}$
C. $\dfrac{n(n+2)}{2}$ D. $\dfrac{n(3n-1)}{2}$

6. Let ℘(A) be the power set of a set A{1, 2, ..., 5}. The number of distinct elements of the sub-collection of ℘(A), where each element of that subcollection consists of 1 and 2 other elements of A, is:
A. 5 B. 4
C. 6 D. 8

7. Let R = {(1, 1), (1, 2), (1, 3), (2, 4), (3, 2)} and S = {(1, 3), (1, 4), (2, 3), (3, 1), (4, 1)} be the relations on a set A = {1, 2, 3, 4}. The composition SoR of R and S is:
A. {(1, 1), (1, 3), (1, 2), (2, 1), (3, 3)}
B. {(1, 2), (1, 3), (1, 4), (2, 1), (3, 3)}
C. {(1, 1), (1, 2), (1, 4), (2, 1), (3, 3)}
D. {(1, 1), (1, 3), (1, 4), (2, 1), (3, 3)}

8. If A and B are finite sets, then (A ∪ B) and (A ∩ B) are finite and (A ∪ B) is equal to:
A. n(A) – n(B)
B. n(A) + n(B)
C. n(A) + n(B) – n(A ∩ B)
D. n(A ∩ B) – n(A) + n(B)

9. The powet set of a set A having four distinct elements is:
A. 16 B. 8
C. 14 D. 32

10. Let U = {1, 2, ..., 9} be the universal set. Let A = {1, 2, 5, 6}, B = {2, 5, 7} and C = {1, 3, 5, 7, 9}, then $\left(\dfrac{B \oplus C}{A}\right)$ = ?
A. {1, 6} B. {3, 9}
C. {2, 3, 6, 7, 9} D. {1, 6, 7}

11. Let R be a relation on a set A = {2, 3, 4, 6}, defined as "x divides y". Then a set of ordered pairs is of the form:
A. {(2, 4), (2, 6), (3, 6), (4, 6)}
B. {(2, 2), (2, 4), (2, 6), (3, 3), (3, 6), (4, 4), (6, 6)}
C. {(2, 4), (2, 6), (3, 6), (4, 2), (4, 6), (6, 2), (6, 3)}
D. {(2, 4), (2, 6), (3, 3), (3, 6), (4, 6)}

12. The possible number of relation from a set A = {u, v, w} to a set B = {x, y} is:

* Exam held on 03/07/2018

A. 64 B. 6
C. 32 D. 16

13. Let A = Z\{0} denote the set of all NON-zero integers. Let ≈ be the relation on A × A defined by $(a, b) \approx (c, d)$ if $ad = bc$. Then ≈ is:
A. reflexive, symmetric but not transitive
B. an equivalence relation
C. reflexive, antisymmetric and transitive
D. reflexive, transitive but not symmetric

14. The formula $\left(\frac{A}{B}\right) = A \cap B^C$ represents the difference operation in terms of the operations of intersection and complement. Then the formula for the union A ∪ B in terms of the operations of intersection and complement is:
A. $A^C \cap B^C$ B. $A^C \cap B$
C. $(A \cap B^C)^C$ D. $(A^C \cap B^C)^C$

15. The relation between the sets A = {2, 3, 4, 5} and B = {1, 2, 3, ..., 9} is:
A. A ∩ B = B B. A ⊂ B
C. A ⊃ B D. A ∪ B = A

16. When $n(A) = 3$ and $n(B) = 5$, then the number of injection functions that can be defined from A to B is:
A. 120 B. 60
C. 40 D. 30

17. Consider $n(U) = 80$, $n(A) = 40$, $n(B) = 55$ and $n(A \cap B) = 20$. Then the value of $n(A \oplus B)$ is:
A. 25 B. 55
C. 45 D. 35

18. If A and B are nonempty sets, then $\frac{(A \cup B)}{(A \cap B)}$ is equal to:
A. $\left(\frac{A}{B}\right) \cup \left(\frac{B}{A}\right)$ B. $((A \cap B) \cup B)$
C. $\left(\frac{A}{B}\right) \cap \left(\frac{B}{A}\right)$ D. $((A \cup B) \cap A)$

19. If f is a function satisfying $2f(x) - 3f\left(\frac{1}{x}\right) = x^2$ for any non-zero value of x, then the value of $f(2)$ is equal to:
A. $\frac{-7}{4}$ B. 4
C. –2 D. $\frac{-7}{8}$

20. If set A has m elements and set B has n elements, then the possible number of distinct functions from A to B is:
A. n^m B. mn
C. 2^{mn} D. m^n

21. If $\left(\frac{1-i}{1+i}\right)^n = 1$, then the smallest positive integer n is:
A. 4 B. 1
C. 2 D. 3

22. The modulus of the complex number $(1 - \cos\alpha) + i\sin\alpha$ is:
A. $\sin\left(\frac{\alpha}{2}\right)$ B. $2\sin\alpha$
C. $2\sin\left(\frac{\alpha}{2}\right)$ D. $\cos\left(\frac{\alpha}{2}\right)$

23. How do we express $\frac{(1+2i)^3}{(1+i)(2-i)}$ in the form of a complex number $a + ib$?
A. $\left(\frac{7}{2}\right) + i\left(\frac{1}{2}\right)$ B. $\left(\frac{-7}{2}\right) + i\left(\frac{1}{2}\right)$
C. $\left(\frac{7}{2}\right) - i\left(\frac{1}{2}\right)$ D. $\left(\frac{-7}{2}\right) - i\left(\frac{1}{2}\right)$

24. The rectangular form of $10\angle -30°$ is given by:
A. $-5\sqrt{3} - 5i$ B. $5\sqrt{3} - 5i$
C. $-5\sqrt{3} + 5i$ D. $5\sqrt{3} + 5i$

25. In how many ways can 7 gentlemen and 7 ladies sit down at a round table, NO 2 ladies being together?
A. 6! × 7! ways B. 7! × 7! ways
C. 6! × 6! ways D. 6! ways

26. The number of positive integers not exceeding 1,000, which are divisible by 7 or 11, is:

A. 220 B. 120
C. 210 D. 240

27. The number of words that can be formed by using the letters of the words "MATHEMATICS" that start as well as end with T is:
A. 90,720 B. 20,860
C. 80,720 D. 37,528

28. In an Argand diagram, one vertex of an equilateral triangle is $(1+i\sqrt{3})$, and assume that the origin is the circumcenter of the triangle. Then the complex numbers represented by other vertices are:
A. $\sqrt{3}+i0; 1-i\sqrt{3}$ B. $-2+0i; 1-i\sqrt{3}$
C. $2+i0; \sqrt{3}-i$ D. $0+2i; 1-i\sqrt{3}$

29. If $\arg(z + 2i) = \frac{\pi}{4}$, $\arg(z - 2i) = \frac{3\pi}{4}$, then the value of z is:
A. 2 B. 0
C. –1 D. 1

30. The principal argument of the complex number $\frac{(1+2i)}{[1-(1-i)^2]}$ is:
A. ∞ B. 0
C. 1 D. $-\infty$

31. If ω is a complex cube root of unity, then the value of $(1 - \omega)^6$ is:
A. –9 B. –27
C. 0 D. 6

32. The number of odd three-digit positive integers that have no repeated digits is:
A. 240 B. 320
C. 160 D. 128

33. The number of ways to distribute 20 identical balls in 4 different boxes such that no box remains empty is:
A. 696 B. 323
C. 969 D. 52

34. The number of permutations can be made out of the letters word "COMPUTER" as:
A. 720 B. 10,080
C. 5,040 D. 40,320

35. In how many ways can 12 ballons be distributed at a birthday party of 10 children?
A. 48 ways B. 56 ways
C. 45 ways D. 55 ways

36. If the sum and product of any two distinct complex numbers are 4 and 8 respectively, then the numbers are:
A. $2 + 2i; 2 - 2i$ B. $2 + 3i; 2 - 3i$
C. $3 + 2i; 1 - 2i$ D. $1 + 2i; 3 - 2i$

37. Using mathematical induction, the value of $1^3 + 2^3 + ... n^3$ is:
A. $\frac{n^2(n^2+1)}{4}$ B. $\frac{n(n+1)(2n+1)}{6}$
C. $\frac{n^2(n+1)^2}{4}$ D. $\frac{n(n+2)}{4}$

38. The polar form of the complex number $\left(\frac{2+i}{3-i}\right)^2$ is:
A. $\frac{1}{2}\left(\cos\frac{\pi}{4} - i\sin\frac{\pi}{4}\right)$
B. $\frac{1}{2}\left(\cos\frac{\pi}{2} - i\sin\frac{\pi}{2}\right)$
C. $\frac{1}{2}\left(\cos\frac{\pi}{4} + i\sin\frac{\pi}{4}\right)$
D. $\frac{1}{2}\left(\cos\frac{\pi}{2} + i\sin\frac{\pi}{2}\right)$

39. The number of ways of choosing m objects out of $(3m + 1)$ objects, of which m are identical and $(2m + 1)$ are distinct, is:
A. 2^{2m-1} B. 2^{m+2}
C. 2^{2m} D. $2^{2(m+1)}$

40. How many integer solutions are there for the equation $x + y + z = 15$, where $x \geq 0$, $y \geq 0$, $z \geq 0$?
A. 136 B. 6
C. 15 D. 1

41. The series whose nth term is of the form $\sqrt{(n^3+1)} - \sqrt{n^3}$ is:

A. Convergent
B. Oscillatory
C. Conditionally convergent
D. Divergent

42. The sum of the last 20 coefficients in the Binomial expansion of $(1 + x)^{39}$, when expanded in the ascending powers of x, is:

A. 2^{39} B. 2^{38}
C. 2^{18} D. 2^{17}

43. If $\log\sqrt{5}(x)+\log 3\sqrt{5}(x)\log 4\sqrt{5}(x)+...$ up to 7 terms = 35, then the value of x is:

A. 5 B. 75
C. 25 D. 125

44. Solve the absolute value inequality $3|2x + 6| < 42$.

A. $x \in (-10, 4)$ B. $x \in (5, 2)$
C. $x \in (-10, 2)$ D. $x \in (-5, 4)$

45. Use Cauchy-Schwarz inequality to determine the value of $a^3 + b^3 + c^3$, where $a, b, c > 0$ and $a + b + c = 3$.

A. less than 2
B. greater than 4
C. greater than or equal to 3
D. less than or equal to 4

46. The possible solution of the inequality $|x + 1| + |x| > 3$ is:

A. $x \in (-\infty, -1), \cup (1, \infty)$
B. $x \notin (1, \infty)$
C. $x \notin (-\infty, -2)$
D. $x \in (-\infty, -2) \cup (1, \infty)$

47. The series $x-\frac{x^2}{2}+\frac{x^3}{3}-\frac{x^4}{4}+\frac{x^5}{5}+...$ converges in:

A. $2 < x < \infty$ B. $|x| > 1$
C. $-1 < x \leq 1$ D. $x < -1$

48. If the 6th term in the Binomial expansion of $\left(\frac{1}{x^{\frac{8}{3}}}+x^2\log_{10}x\right)^8$ is 5,600, then the value of x is:

A. 10 B. $\sqrt{2}$
C. 5 D. $\sqrt{5}$

49. The sum of the series $\cos x+\frac{1}{3}\cos^3 x+\frac{1}{5}\cos^5 x + ... \infty$, where x is real, is equal to:

A. $\ln\left(\tan\left(\frac{x}{2}\right)\right)$ B. $\ln(1 + \cos x)$
C. $\ln(1 - \cos x)$ D. $\ln\left(\cot\left(\frac{x}{2}\right)\right)$

50. The number of rational and irrational terms in the Binomial expansion of $\left(5^{\frac{1}{6}}+2^{\frac{1}{8}}\right)$ are respectively.

A. 8, 93 B. 15, 86
C. 4, 97 D. 6, 95

51. If A_1 and A_2 are two Arithmetic means, and G_1 and G_2 are two Geometric means between two positive numbers a and b, then $\frac{A_1+A_2}{G_1G_2}$ is equal to:

A. $\frac{a+b}{ab}$ B. $\frac{a+b}{2ab}$
C. $\frac{ab}{a+b}$ D. $\frac{2ab}{a+b}$

52. The sum of the series $1+\frac{3}{1!}+\frac{5}{2!}+\frac{7}{3!}+...\infty$ is:

A. $2e$ B. $3e$
C. $\frac{e}{2}$ D. $e - 1$

53. Which is true with regard to the system of inequalities $\frac{x}{2x+1}\geq 0.25;\ \frac{6x}{4x-1}<0.5$?

A. $x \in (-0.5, 0.5)$
B. There is no solution
C. $x \in (-0.125, 0.25)$
D. $x < -0.5$ or $x \geq 0.5$

54. The sum of the 24 terms of the series $\sqrt{2}+\sqrt{8}+\sqrt{18}+\sqrt{32}+...$ is:

A. $500\sqrt{2}$ B. $100\sqrt{2}$

C. $200\sqrt{2}$ D. $300\sqrt{2}$

55. When 2^{2000} is divided by 17, then the remainder is:

A. 9 B. 2

C. 5 D. 1

56. If a is sufficiently large when compare with b, and $\sqrt{\left(\frac{a}{a-b}\right)}+\sqrt{\left(\frac{a}{a+b}\right)}=2+k\left(\frac{b}{a}\right)^2$, then the value of '$k$' is:

A. $\frac{2}{3}$ B. $\frac{3}{4}$

C. $\frac{4}{5}$ D. $\frac{5}{6}$

57. The sum of the series $\frac{1}{2}-\frac{1}{2}\cdot\frac{1}{2^2}+\frac{1}{3}\cdot\frac{1}{2^3}-\frac{1}{4}\cdot\frac{1}{2^4}+...$ is equal to:

A. $\ln\left(\frac{1}{2}\right)$ B. ln 2

C. $\ln\left(\frac{2}{3}\right)$ D. $\ln\left(\frac{3}{2}\right)$

58. The largest term in the Binomial expansion of $(3 + 2x)^{50}$, when $x = \frac{1}{5}$, is:

A. 3rd term B. 8th term

C. 6th term D. 5th term

59. Suppose that a, b, c are in A.P. and a^2, b^2, c^2 are in G.P. If $a < b < c$ and $a + b + c = \frac{3}{2}$, then the value of a is given by:

A. $\frac{1}{2}(1-\sqrt{2})$ B. $\frac{1}{2}-\frac{1}{\sqrt{3}}$

C. $\frac{1}{2\sqrt{2}}$ D. $\frac{1}{2\sqrt{3}}$

60. The solution of polynomial inequality $f(x) = (x + 1)(x - 2)^2(x + 3) \le 0$ is:

A. $x \in (3, \infty)$ B. $x \in (-\infty, -3)$

C. $x \in [-3, -1]$ D. $x \in (0, 2)$

61. If a, b and c any three complex numbers such that $a^2 + b^2 + c^2 = 0$ and

$$\begin{vmatrix} b^2+c^2 & ab & ca \\ ab & c^2+a^2 & bc \\ ca & bc & a^2+b^2 \end{vmatrix} = k(abc)^2,$$ then the value of k is:

A. 4 B. −2

C. 3 D. 1

62. The number of real values of x satisfying the equation $2\left(x^2+\frac{1}{x^2}\right)-9\left(x+\frac{1}{x}\right)+14=0$ is given by:

A. 3 B. 4

C. 2 D. 1

63. When $a + b + c = 0$, then the quadratic equation $3ax^2 + 2bx + c = 0$ has:

A. Imaginary roots

B. At least one root in [0, 1]

C. One root in [−2, −1] and other root in [2, 3]

D. One root in [−2, −1] and other root in [1, 2]

64. The positive value of

$x = \sqrt{12+\sqrt{12+\sqrt{12+... \text{up to } \infty}}}$ is

A. 4 B. 2

C. 1 D. 3

65. The prime factorization of 42833 is given by:

A. 7.21.291 B. 7.21.299

C. 7.21.219 D. 7.29.211

66. Every prime divisor of the Fermat number $F_n = 2^{2^n}+1$ is of the form:

A. $2^{2n+1}k + 1$ B. $2^{n+1}k + 1$

C. $2^{2n}k + 1$ D. $2^{n+2}k + 1$

67. Let a, b and c be real numbers such that a and b are distinct. Then the roots of the equation $2(a - b)x^2 - 11(a + b + c)x - 3(a - b) = 0$ are:

A. Real and equal

B. Purely imaginary

C. Real and unequal

D. Both real and imaginary

68. If a, b and c are real numbers, then both the roots of the equation $(x - a)(x - b) + (x - b)(x - c) + (x - c)(x - a) = 0$.

A. Are negative B. Do not exist
C. Are positive D. Are real

69. The number of real solutions of the equation $\sqrt{x+9}+\sqrt{4+x}=5$ is:

A. 3 B. 1
C. 2 D. 0

70. What is the maximum number of divisions used by Euclidean algorithm to find the greatest common divisor of two positive integers 252 and 198?

A. 36 B. 12
C. 4 D. 16

71. The number of real roots of the equation $(7+4\sqrt{3})^{|x|-6}+(7-4\sqrt{3})^{|x|-6}=14$ is

A. 4 B. 3
C. 2 D. 1

72. The number of real solutions of the equation

$$\frac{1}{x+1}-\frac{1}{x+2}=\frac{1}{x+4}-\frac{1}{x+5}$$ is:

A. 4 B. 1
C. 3 D. 2

73. When the quadratic equations $x^2 - 7x + k = 0$ and $x^2 - 11x + 2k = 0$ have a common root, then the value of k is:

A. 1, –12 B. 0, 14
C. 12, –1 D. 0, 12

74. Let a and b be the roots of the equation $x^2 + px + 1 = 0$. Let c and d be the roots of the equation $x^2 + qx + 1 = 0$. Then the value of $(a - c)(b - c)(a + d)(b + d)$ is equal to:

A. $-p^2 + q^2$ B. $p^2 - q^2$
C. $-p^2 - q^2$ D. $p^2 + q^2$

75. The greatest common divisor of three integers 105, 140 and 350 is:

A. 5 B. 70
C. 15 D. 35

76. The sum of the positive integer divisors of 200 and the number of positive integer divisors of 200, respectively, are:

A. 456, 12 B. 435, 21
C. 455, 21 D. 465, 21

77. If c and d are integers and $c = dq + r$, then:

A. $(c, d) = (d, r)$ B. $(c, q) = (d, r)$
C. $(c, r) = (d, r)$ D. $(c, d) = (d, q)$

78. The solutions of the linear congruence $7x \equiv 22 \pmod{31}$ is:

A. $x \equiv 21 \pmod{31}$ B. $x \equiv 12 \pmod{31}$
C. $x \equiv 196$ D. $x \equiv 12 \pmod{21}$

79. If α, β and γ are the roots of the equation $x^3 + px^2 + q = 0$, where $q \neq 0$, then the value of

$$\begin{vmatrix} \frac{1}{\alpha} & \frac{1}{\beta} & \frac{1}{\gamma} \\ \frac{1}{\beta} & \frac{1}{\gamma} & \frac{1}{\alpha} \\ \frac{1}{\gamma} & \frac{1}{\alpha} & \frac{1}{\beta} \end{vmatrix}$$ is equal to:

A. $\frac{p}{q}$ B. 0
C. $\frac{1}{p}$ D. $\frac{1}{q}$

80. The product of the roots of the equation $x^2 - 3kx + 2e^{4\ln(k)} = 1$ is 31. Then the sum of the root is:

A. 6 B. 2
C. 5 D. 4

81. For what value of k, does the straight line $y = x + k$ touches the ellipse $\left(\frac{x}{4}\right)^2+\left(\frac{y}{3}\right)^2=1$?

A. 7 B. ±5
C. 2 D. ±6

82. Two vertices of a triangle are (0, 5) and (6, 3). When its centroid is (1, –2), then the third vertex is:

A. (–3, –14) B. (–3, 14)
C. (3, 14) D. (3, –14)

83. Which of the following statements is not true?

A. if det(A) = 0, then adj (det(A)) = 0
B. adj(AB) = adj(A) adj(B)
C. Adjoint of a diagonal matrix of order 3 × 3 is a diagonal matrix
D. The product of upper triangular matrices is an upper triangular matrix

84. If A = $\begin{bmatrix} i & -i \\ -i & i \end{bmatrix}$ and B = $\begin{bmatrix} 1 & -1 \\ -1 & 1 \end{bmatrix}$, then A^8 equals:

A. 16B B. 64B
C. 32B D. 128B

85. All the four entries of the 2 × 2 matrix A = $\begin{bmatrix} a_{11} & a_{12} \\ a_{21} & a_{22} \end{bmatrix}$ are NON-zero, and one of its eigen values is zero. Which of the following statements is true?

A. $a_{11}a_{22} - a_{12}a_{21} = 0$
B. $a_{11}a_{22} - a_{12}a_{21} = 1$
C. $a_{11}a_{22} - a_{12}a_{21} = -1$
D. $a_{11}a_{22} + a_{12}a_{21} = 0$

86. The equation of the straight line that is equidistant from the lines $x = -3.5$ and $x = 7.5$ is:

A. $x = 2$ B. $x = -2$
C. $x = 1$ D. $x = -1$

87. If A, B and C are the angles of a triangle ABC, then the value of $\begin{vmatrix} \sin^2 A & \cot A & 1 \\ \sin^2 B & \cot B & 1 \\ \sin^2 C & \cot C & 1 \end{vmatrix}$ is:

A. 8 sin A sin B sin C
B. –4 sin A sin B sin C
C. 0
D. 1 + 4 cos A cos B cos C

88. For which value of k, the points $(k, 2 - 2k)$, $(-k + 1, 2k)$ and $(-4 - k, 6 - 2k)$ are collinear?

A. 2 B. 0.5
C. –1 D. 1

89. The equation of the straight line passing through the point of intersection of the lines $x + 5y + 7 = 0$, $3x + 2y - 5 = 0$ and parallel the line $7x + 2y - 5 = 0$ is:

A. $7x + 2y - 17 = 0$ B. $2x + 7y + 20 = 0$
C. $7x + 2y - 20 = 0$ D. $2x - 7y + 17 = 0$

90. If a system of equations $\lambda x + y + z = 1, x + \lambda y + z = 1$ and $x + y + \lambda z = 1$ is consistent, then λ can have value as:

A. 1 B. –2
C. –1 D. 2

91. The value of tan θ tan(60° + θ) tan(60° – θ) is:

A. $\left(\frac{1}{4}\right)\sin 3\theta$ B. 3 tan θ
C. tan 3θ D. $\left(\frac{1}{4}\right)\cos 3\theta$

92. If $x = \sin^2\theta + \cos^4\theta$, then for all values of θ:

A. $1 \le x \le 2x$ B. $1 \le x \le 3$
C. $0.75 \le x \le 1$ D. $0.5 \le x \le 1.5$

93. One radian is equal to:

A. $\frac{3\pi}{2}$ B. 57°17′45″
C. 360° D. 180°

94. If (1.5, 0), (1.5, 6) and (–1, 6) are the midpoints of the sides of a triangle, then the in-centre of the triangle is at coordinates:

A. (1, 2) B. (3, 1)
C. (2, 4) D. (2, 3)

95. The equation of the straight line that passes through the point (3, 4) and has intercepts on the axes equal in magnitude but opposite in sign is:

A. $x - y = 1$ B. $x - y = -1$
C. $x + y = 2$ D. $x + y = 1$

96. If a system of equations $x + y = 3$, $(1 + k)x + (2 + k)y = 8$ and $x - (1 + k)y + (2 + k) = 0$ is consistent, then the values of k are:

A. $1, \frac{-5}{3}$ B. $-1, \frac{1}{3}$
C. $\frac{2}{3}, -1$ D. 0, 1

97. The orthocentre of the triangle ABC, whose angular points are A(1, 2), B(2, 3) and C(4, 3), is of the form:

A. (1, 4) B. (2, 1)
C. (2, 5) D. (1, 6)

98. When m is a variable, then the equation of a family of lines making a constant intercept c on the y-axis is:

A. $y = mx \pm c$

B. $y = \left(\frac{x}{2}\right) - c$

C. $m(x + y) = c$

D. $x = my \pm c$

99. The equation of the locus of a point which moves such that its difference of distances from the points (3, 0) and (–3, 0) is 4 units, is given by:

A. $\frac{x^2}{5} - \frac{y^2}{6} = 1$

B. $\frac{x^2}{4} - \frac{y^2}{5} = 1$

C. $\frac{x^2}{5} + \frac{y^2}{6} = 1$

D. $\frac{x^2}{4} + \frac{y^2}{5} = 1$

100. The distance between two parallel lines $5x - 12y + 2 = 0$ and $5x - 12y - 3 = 0$ is given by:

A. $\frac{1}{17}$

B. $\frac{5}{14}$

C. $\frac{1}{13}$

D. $\frac{5}{13}$

101. When we use Mean Value theorem for $f(x) = x(x - 1)(x - 2)$, then the value of c between 0 and $\frac{1}{2}$ is:

A. 0.138

B. 0.236

C. 1.764

D. 0.317

102. The slope of the circle $x^2 + y^2 = 25$ at the point (3, –4) is:

A. 0.25

B. 0.75

C. 1

D. 0.5

103. If $A = \tan^{-1}\left(\frac{1}{7}\right)$ and $B = \tan^{-1}\left(\frac{1}{3}\right)$ then:

A. cos 2A = sin 4B

B. sin 2A = cos 2B

C. sin 4A = cos 2B

D. sin 2B = cos 2A

104. If $\sin^{-1}(x) + \sin^{-1}(y) + \sin^{-1}(z) = \frac{3\pi}{2}$, then the value of $((x)^{100} + (y)^{100} + (z)^{100}) - \left(\frac{9}{(x)^{101} + (y)^{101} + (z)^{101}}\right)$ is:

A. 0

B. 3

C. 2

D. –1

105. A tree is broken by wind, its upper part touching the ground at a point 16 m from the foot of the tree and making an angle of 45° with the ground. The entire length of the tree is:

A. $16\sqrt{2}$ m

B. $(4\sqrt{2} + 1)$ m

C. $4(1 + \sqrt{2})$ m

D. $4^2(1 + \sqrt{2})$ m

106. When we use Rolle's theorem for $f(x) = x^{2m-1}(a - x)^{2n}$, then the value of x between 0 and a is:

A. $\frac{(2m-1)a}{2m+2n-1}$

B. $\frac{(2m+1)a}{2m-2n+1}$

C. $\frac{(m-1)a}{m+n-1}$

D. $\frac{(m+1)a}{m+n+1}$

107. The function $f(x) = (x^2 - 1)|x^2 - 3x + 2| + \cos|x|$ is not differentiable at the point:

A. $x = 2$

B. $x = 0$

C. $x = -1$

D. $x = 1$

108. If the median of the triangle ABC through A is perpendicular to AB, then the value of tan A + 2 tan B is:

A. 0

B. sin C

C. cos C

D. tan C

109. The possible solution(s) of the equation $\tan x + \frac{1}{\cos x} = 2\cos x$, lying in the interval $0 \le x \le 2\pi$, are:

A. 3

B. 2

C. 1

D. 4

110. An aeroplane flying at a height of 3,000 m above the ground, passes vertically above another plane at an instant, when the angles of elevation of the two planes from the same point on the ground are 60° and 45° respectively. The height of the lower plane from the ground is:

A. $100\sqrt{300}$ m

B. $100\sqrt{30}$ m

C. $300\sqrt{10}$ m

D. $\frac{100}{\sqrt{30}}$ m

111. If $f(x) = \begin{cases} \frac{1}{x^3}[x(1+a\cos x)-b\sin x] & \text{if } x \neq 0 \\ 1 & \text{if } x = 0 \end{cases}$

is a continuous function, then the values of a and b, respectively, are:

A. $\frac{-5}{2}, \frac{3}{2}$ B. $\frac{1}{3}, \frac{1}{5}$

C. $\frac{-5}{2}, \frac{-3}{2}$ D. $\frac{5}{2}, \frac{-3}{2}$

112. Let f be a continuous function on [1, 3]. If f takes only rational values for all x and $f(2) = 10$, then $f(1.5)$ is equal to:

A. 20 B. 8

C. 10 D. $\left(\frac{1}{3}\right)[f(1)+f(3)]$

113. When $\tan^{-1}(x) = \cos^{-1}(x)$, then the value of $\sin(\cos^{-1}(x))$ is:

A. x^{-2} B. x^{-1}

C. x^2 D. $2x$

114. Does $\lim_{x\to 0} \frac{\tan x - x}{x^2 \tan x}$ exist? If it does, then the value of this limit is:

A. $\frac{1}{3}$

B. Such value does not exist

C. 1

D. $\frac{1}{2}$

115. If the two sides of a triangle are the roots of the equation $4x^2 - (2\sqrt{6})x + 1 = 0$ and they include an angle 60°, then third side of the triangle is:

A. $\sqrt{3}$ B. $\frac{1}{2}$

C. $\frac{\sqrt{3}}{2}$ D. $\frac{2}{\sqrt{3}}$

116. The first derivative of $y = \frac{(x-1)(x^2-2x)}{x^4}$ with respect of x, is:

A. $2x^{-2} + 5x^{-3} - 6x^{-4}$

B. $-x^{-2} + 6x^{-3} - 6x^{-4}$

C. $x^{-2} - 6x^{-3} + 6x^{-4}$

D. $x^{-2} + 6x^{-3} - 2x^{-4}$

117. If $\sin^{-1}(x) + \sin^{-1}(-x) + \cos^{-1}(1 - x) = 0$, then x satisfies the equation:

A. $2x^2 - 5x + 2 = 0$ B. $2x^2 + x - 2 = 0$

C. $2x^2 - 5x = 0$ D. $2x^2 - x + 1 = 0$

118. The distance of a point on the curve $y = x(x^3 + 3x + 2)$ which is nearest to the line $y = 2x - 1$ is:

A. $\frac{4}{\sqrt{5}}$ B. $\frac{1}{\sqrt{5}}$

C. $\frac{2}{\sqrt{5}}$ D. $\frac{3}{\sqrt{5}}$

119. In a triangle ABC, if $a + b - 3c = 0$, then cos A + cos B is equal to:

A. 3(1 – cos C) B. 3 cos C

C. 3 sin C D. 3 cos (A – B)

120. The possible extreme point of a function $f(x, y) = x^2 + y^2 + \left(\frac{2}{x}\right) + \left(\frac{2}{y}\right)$ is:

A. (1, 1) B. $\left(\frac{1}{3}\right), \left(\frac{1}{3}\right)$

C. (–1, –1) D. (0, 0)

121. If $f(x) = \frac{\sqrt{\tan x}}{(\sin x \cos x)}$, and F($x$) is its antiderivative such that $F\left(\frac{\pi}{4}\right) = 6$, then F($x$) is of the form:

A. $2\sqrt{\tan x} + 4$ B. $2\sqrt{\tan x} + 2$

C. $2\sqrt{\tan x} + 1$ D. $2\sqrt{\tan x} + 3$

122. If $(\vec{a}\times\vec{b})\times\vec{c} = \vec{a}\times(\vec{b}\times\vec{c})$, where, $\vec{a} = 2\hat{i} + \hat{j} + \lambda\hat{k}$, $\vec{b} = \hat{i} - \hat{j}$, $\vec{c} = 4\hat{i} + \mu\hat{j} + 2\hat{k}$, then the value of λ and μ are respectively:

A. 1, 4 B. 1, 2

C. 2, 3 D. 4, 2

123. The solution of the differential equation $\frac{dy}{dx}=\frac{(ax+b)}{(cx+d)}$ represents a parabola if:

A. Both a and c are 1
B. Both a and c are 0
C. c is zero and a is non-zero
D. a = 1 and b = 2

124. If $f(x) = 2x + 3^x \log_e(3)$, and F($x$) is its antiderivative such that F(2) = 7, then the value of x for which the curve F(x), cut the abscissa axis is:

A. $x = 1$ B. $x = 3$
C. $x = 0$ D. $x = 2$

125. The general solution of the equation $\frac{dy}{dx}=\left(\frac{y}{x}\right)+\phi\left(\frac{x}{y}\right)$ is given by $y \ln |Cx| = x$.

Then $\phi\left(\frac{x}{y}\right)$ is:

A. $\left(-\frac{x}{y}\right)^2$ B. $\left(\frac{y}{x}\right)^2$
C. $\left(-\frac{y}{x}\right)^2$ D. $\left(\frac{x}{y}\right)^2$

126. The value of the integral $\int\frac{\cos 4x-1}{\cot x-\tan x}dx$ is:

A. $\frac{1}{2}in|\cos(2x)|+C$
B. $\frac{1}{2}in|\cos(2x)|-\frac{1}{4}\cos^2(2x)+C$
C. $\frac{1}{2}\cos(4x)+C$
D. $\frac{1}{4}\cos(4x)+C$

127. Let $\vec{a}$ be any non-zero vector, whereas $\vec{b}$ and $\vec{c}$ be unit vectors. Then the value of $\{[(\vec{a}+\vec{b})\times(\vec{a}+\vec{c})]\times(\vec{b}\times\vec{c})\}\bullet(\vec{b}+\vec{c})$ is:

A. $3|\vec{a}|^2$ B. $|\vec{a}|^2$
C. 0   D. $2|\vec{a}|^2$

128. The solution of the differential equation $2y \sin x\left(\frac{dy}{dx}\right) = \sin 2x - y^2 \cos x$ with $y\left(\frac{\pi}{2}\right) = 1$ is:

A. $y^2 = \sin x$ B. $x^2 = \sin y$
C. $y = \sin^2 x$ D. $y^2 = 1 + \cos x$

129. The particular solution of the differential equation $\frac{dy}{dx}=e^{(3x+4y)}, y(0)=0$ is:

A. $4e^{3x} + 3e^{-4y} = 7$ B. $e^{3x} + 3e^{-4y} = 4$
C. $4e^{3x} + 3e^{4y} = 7$ D. $4e^{3x} - e^{-4y} = 3$

130. The possible number of solutions of the equation $k^{f(x)} + g(x) = 0$, where $k > 0$, $g(x) \neq 0$ and $g(x)$ has minimum value of 0.5, is/are:

A. Infinitely many   B. Zero
C. One   D. Two

131. The degree of the differential equation $\left(\frac{d^2y}{dx^2}\right)^{\frac{2}{2}}-\left(\frac{dy}{dx}\right)^{\frac{1}{2}}-4=0$ is:

A. 6   B. 3
C. 4   D. 2

132. Let, $\vec{a}, \vec{b}$ and $\vec{c}$ be any three vectors such that $|\vec{a}|=1, |\vec{b}|=4, |\vec{c}|=8$ and $\vec{a}\cdot(\vec{b}+\vec{c})=\vec{b}\cdot(\vec{c}+\vec{a})$ $=\vec{c}\cdot(\vec{a}+\vec{b}) = 0$, then $|\vec{a}+\vec{b}+\vec{c}|$ is equal to:

A. 9   B. 12
C. 8   D. 7

133. The distance between a point whose position is $5\hat{i}+\hat{j}+3\hat{k}$ and the line $\hat{r}=(3\hat{i}+7\hat{j}+\hat{k}+t(\hat{j}+\hat{k}))$ is given by:

A. 3   B. 6
C. 4   D. 5

134. The solution of the linear differential equation $\frac{dy}{dx}=1\left(\frac{2x}{y^2}\right)$ is given by:

A. $y=Ce^{-2x}+\left(\frac{1}{4}\right)[x^2+2x+1]$

B. $x=Ce^{2y}+\left(\frac{1}{4}\right)[y^2+2y+1]$

C. $x = Ce^{2y} + \left(\frac{1}{2}\right)[y^2 + y + 1]$

D. $x = Ce^{2y} + \left(\frac{1}{4}\right)[2y^2 + 2y + 1]$

135. The general solution of the differential equation $\frac{dy}{dx} + \sin\left(\frac{x+y}{2}\right) = \sin\frac{(x-y)}{2}$ = is:

A. $\ln\left|\tan\left(\frac{y}{2}\right)\right| = C + 2\sin\left(\frac{x}{2}\right)$

B. $\ln\left|\tan\left(\frac{y}{4}\right)\right| = C - 2\sin\left(\frac{x}{2}\right)$

C. $\ln\left|\tan\left(\frac{y}{2}\right)\right| = C - 2\sin(x)$

D. $\ln\left|\tan\left(\frac{y}{2}\right)\right| = C - 2\sin\left(\frac{x}{4}\right)$

136. The coordinates of the point on the parabola $y^2 = 8x$, which is at a minimum distance from the circle $[x - 0]^2 + [y - (-6)]^2 = 1$, are given by:

A. (–2, 4) B. (–1, 2)
C. (2, –4) D. (1, –2)

137. The unit vector in the direction of the vector $2\hat{i} - \hat{j} - 2\hat{k}$ is:

A. $\left(\frac{1}{9}\right)(2\hat{i} + \hat{j} - 2\hat{k})$ B. $3(2\hat{i} + \hat{j} - 2\hat{k})$

C. $9(2\hat{i} + \hat{j} - 2\hat{k})$ D. $\left(\frac{1}{3}\right)(2\hat{i} - \hat{j} - 2\hat{k})$

138. Let $f(x) = \int_0^{\sin^2 x} \sin^{-1}\sqrt{u}\, du$ and $g(x) = \int_0^{\cos^2 x} \cos^{-1}\sqrt{u}\, du$.

Then the value of $f(x) + g(x)$ is equal to:

A. $\frac{2\pi}{3}$ B. $\frac{\pi}{3}$

C. $\frac{\pi}{4}$ D. $\frac{\pi}{2}$

139. The value of the integral $\int_0^{\infty} \frac{x\ln(x)}{(1+x^2)^2} dx$ is:

A. 2 ln(5) B. 13
C. 5 ln(2) D. 0

140. The value of the integral $\int \frac{\sin x}{\sqrt{1+\cos x}} dx$ is:

A. $-\sqrt{8}\cos\left(\frac{x}{2}\right) + C$ B. $\sqrt{2}\cos\left(\frac{x}{2}\right) + C$

C. $-\sqrt{2}\cos\left(\frac{x}{2}\right) + C$ D. $\sqrt{8}\cos\left(\frac{x}{2}\right) + C$

141. If A and B are mutually exclusive events such that $P(A) = 0.29$ and $P(B) = 0.43$, then $P(A \cap \overline{B})$ is equal to:

A. 0.29 B. 0.85
C. 0.50 D. 0.37

142. When the mode is ill-defined, then the Empirical mode formula is of the form:

A. 3 Median – Mode = 2 Mean
B. Mean – Mode = 2[Mean – Median]
C. Mean – Mode = 3[Median – Mean]
D. Mean – Median = 3[Mean – Mode]

143. The relation between mean deviation (M.D.) and standard deviation (S.D.) is:

A. 5 M.D. = 4 S.D. B. 3 M.D. = 4 S.D.
C. 4 M.D. = 3 S.D. D. 4 M.D. = 5 S.D.

144. The straight lines are coplanar if:

A. A line is perpendicular to each of them
B. A line is parallel to each other
C. They are concurrent
D. They are concurrent and a line is perpendicular to each of them

145. The co-ordinate of the point the divides the line joining the points P(2, 3, 1) and Q(5, 0, 4) in the ratio 1 : 2 are:

A. (3, 2, 2) B. (3, 1, 1)

C. (4, 1, 3) D. $\left(\frac{7}{3}, 1, \frac{5}{3}\right)$

146. The mean deviation about the mean and the standard deviation of the set of numbers 3, 5, 6, 7, 10, 12, 15, 18, respectively, are:

A. 4.25, 4.875 B. 3.75, 2.575
C. 4.15, 4.825 D. 4.1, 4.5

147. The angle θ between the line $\frac{x+1}{2} = \frac{y-0}{3} = \frac{z-3}{6}$ and the plane $3x + y + z = 7$ is:

A. $\cos^{-1}\left(\frac{2}{\sqrt{13}}\right)$ B. $\sin^{-1}\left(\frac{5}{7\sqrt{11}}\right)$

C. $\sin^{-1}\left(\frac{15}{7\sqrt{11}}\right)$ D. $\cos^{-1}\left(\frac{5}{7\sqrt{11}}\right)$

148. If a straight line makes angle α, β, γ with the axes of coordinates, then cos 2α + cos 2β + cos 2γ is equal to:

A. 2 B. 1
C. –1 D. –2

149. The mean and variance of a group of 100 observations are 6.5 and 3 respectively. 55 of these observations have the mean 6.6 and standard deviation 1.5. Then the mean and the standard deviation of the remaining 45 observations, respecitvely, are:

A. 6.25, 1.89 B. 6.83, 1.78
C. 6.38, 1.97 D. 8.36, 1.91

150. The median of the numbers 20, 18, 22, 27, 25, 12, 15 is:

A. 20 B. 22
C. 19.8 D. 19.9

151. It at least one child in a family with 2 children is a boy, then the probability that both children are boys is:

A. $\frac{1}{4}$ B. $\frac{3}{4}$

C. $\frac{1}{3}$ D. $\frac{2}{3}$

152. The mean and standard deviation of 20 numbers are found to be 10 and 2 respectively. At the time of checking, it is found that one value was wrongly taken as 8, which should have been ideally 12. If the wrong value is replaced by the correct one, then the correct mean and standard deviation, respectively, are:

A. 10.11, 1.997 B. 10.01, 1.097
C. 10.2, 1.99 D. 10.01, 1.917

153. When the spheres $x^2 + y^2 + z^2 = 25$ and $x^2 + y^2 + z^2 - 18x - 24y - 40z + 225 = 0$ touch externally, then the point of contact of the spheres is:

A. (9, 12, 20) B. $\left(\frac{9}{5}, \frac{12}{5}, \frac{20}{5}\right)$

C. $\left(\frac{2}{5}, \frac{3}{5}, \frac{-1}{5}\right)$ D. $\left(\frac{3}{7}, \frac{5}{7}, \frac{-2}{7}\right)$

154. The distance of the point of intersection of the line $\frac{x-2}{3} = \frac{y+1}{4} = \frac{z-2}{12}$ and the plane $x - y + z = 5$, from the point (–1, –5, –10), is:

A. 9 B. 2
C. 10 D. 13

155. The equation of the sphere on the join of (2, –3, 1) and (1, –2, –1) as diameter is:

A. $x^2 + y^2 + z^2 + 3x - 5y - 7 = 0$
B. $x^2 + y^2 + z^2 - 3x + 5y + 7 = 0$
C. $x^2 + y^2 + z^2 + 3x + 5y + 7 = 0$
D. $x^2 + y^2 + z^2 + 3x - 5y + 7 = 0$

156. The length of the shortest distance between the lines $\frac{x-1}{2} = \frac{y-2}{3} = \frac{z-3}{4}$ and $\frac{x-2}{3} = \frac{y-4}{4} = \frac{z-5}{5}$ is:

A. $\frac{2}{3\sqrt{6}}$ B. $\frac{1}{\sqrt{6}}$

C. $3\sqrt{30}$ D. $13\sqrt{66}$

157. The arithmetic mean of the data (x; f) : (8, 5), (10, 8), (15, 8), (20, 4) is:

A. 12.5 B. 25
C. 12.4 D. 12.8

158. The mode of the numbers 25, 15, 23, 40, 27, 25, 23, 25, 20 is:

A. 13 B. 24.8
C. 24.7 D. 25

159. Which of the following triplets gives the direction cosine of a straight line?

A. 1, –1, 1 B. 1, 1, –1

C. $\frac{1}{\sqrt{3}}, \frac{1}{\sqrt{3}}, \frac{1}{\sqrt{3}}$ D. 1, 1, 1

160. The point of contact of the plane $2x - 2y + z + 12 = 0$ touches the sphere $x^2 + y^2 + z^2 - 2x - 4y + 2z - 3 = 0$ is:

A. (2, 1, 4) B. (1, 4, 2)
C. (–1, 4, –2) D. (4, 1, 2)

161. A box contains 20 electric bulbs, out of which 4 are defective. Two bulbs are chosen at random from this box. The probability that at least one of these is defective is:

A. $\frac{12}{19}$ B. $\frac{4}{19}$
C. $\frac{7}{19}$ D. $\frac{21}{95}$

162. The radius of convergence of the series $\sum_{n=1}^{\infty} \frac{(z+2)^{n-1}}{(n+1)^2 4^n}$ is:

A. 2 B. 4
C. 1 D. –2

163. Identify which one of the following matrices is similar to a diagonal matrix.

A. $\begin{bmatrix} 2 & 1 & 0 \\ 0 & 2 & 1 \\ 0 & 0 & 2 \end{bmatrix}$ B. $\begin{bmatrix} 3 & 1 & 1 \\ 2 & 4 & 2 \\ 1 & 1 & 3 \end{bmatrix}$

C. $\begin{bmatrix} 3 & 10 & 5 \\ -2 & -3 & -4 \\ 3 & 5 & 7 \end{bmatrix}$ D. $\begin{bmatrix} 2 & 3 & 4 \\ 0 & 2 & -1 \\ 0 & 0 & 1 \end{bmatrix}$

164. Let $W = \{(a, b, 0); a, b \in R\}$ be a subset of R^3. Then which of the following is true?

A. W is a subspace of R^3
B. W is not closed under vector addition and multiplication
C. W= ∅
D. W is not a subspace of R^3

165. If $f(z) = (x^2 + axy + by^2) + i(cx^2 + dxy + y^2)$ is an analytic function of z, then the values of a, b, c and d are:

A. $a = 2, b = -1, c = -1, d = 4$
B. $a = -2, b = 1, c = -1, d = 2$
C. $a = 2, b = 1, c = -1, d = -2$
D. $a = 2, b = -1, c = -1, d = 2$

166. If the probability density function of a continuous random variable X is defined by $f(x) = kx(2 - x), 0 < x < 2$, then the value of 'k' is:

A. $\frac{3}{4}$ B. $\frac{1}{2}$
C. $\frac{3}{8}$ D. $\frac{1}{4}$

167. The probability density function $f(x)$ of a continuous random variable X is given by $f(x) = \begin{cases} k(x)^{-3} & \text{if } 5 \le x \le 10 \\ 0 & \text{otherwise} \end{cases}$. Then the value of 'k' is:

A. $\frac{200}{3}$ B. $\frac{3}{200}$
C. 200 D. 40

168. The eigen vectors corresponding to distinct eigen values of a real symmetric matrix are:

A. Invertible B. Symmetry
C. Orthogonal D. Distinct

169. If F(s) is the Fourier transform of a function $f(x)$, then the Fourier transform of $f(2x)$ is given by:

A. e^{2is} F(s) B. $\frac{1}{2}F\left(\frac{2}{s}\right)$
C. F(s – 2) D. $\frac{1}{2}F\left(\frac{s}{2}\right)$

170. The norm of $v = (3, 4) \in R^2$, with respect to the usual inner product, is given by:

A. 5 B. 25
C. 9 D. 16

171. The function $f(x, y) = x^3 + y^3 - 63(x + y) + 12xy$ attains minimum at the point:

A. (–7, –7) B. (–1, 5)
C. (3, 3) D. (5, –1)

172. A bag contains 4 white, 5 red and 6 blue balls. Three balls are drawn at random from the bag. The probability that all of them are red is:

A. $\frac{2}{91}$ B. $\frac{2}{77}$
C. $\frac{1}{22}$ D. $\frac{3}{22}$

173. Which of the following vectors form a basis for the vector space R^3?
A. (1, 2, 3), (1, 0, –1), (3, –1, 4) and (2, 1, 1)
B. (2, 4, –3), (0, 1, 1) and (0, 1, –1)
C. (1, 2, –1) and (1, –1, 5)
D. (1, 3, –4), (1, 4, –3) and (2, 3, –11)

174. Let f be a function such that $f(x) = f(1 - x)$, for all $x \in R$. If f is differentiable everywhere, then $f'(0)$ is equal to:
A. $f(0)$ B. $f(1)$
C. $-f'(1)$ D. $-f(0)$

175. Let T be linear transformation of R^3 into R^2 defined by $T(x, y, z) = (2x + y - z, 3x - 2y + 4z)$ for all $(x, y, z) \in R^3$. Then the matrix of T relative to the bases $\beta = \{\varepsilon_1 = (1, 1, 1), \varepsilon_2 = (1, 1, 0)\}; \varepsilon_3 = (1, 0, 0)\}$ and $\delta = \{\eta_1 = (1, 3), \eta_2 = (1, 4)\}$ is:

A. $\begin{bmatrix} 3 & 11 & 5 \\ -1 & -8 & -3 \end{bmatrix}$ B. $\begin{bmatrix} 3 & 11 & -5 \\ 1 & -8 & 3 \end{bmatrix}$

C. $\begin{bmatrix} -3 & 11 & 5 \\ 1 & 8 & 3 \end{bmatrix}$ D. $\begin{bmatrix} 3 & -11 & 5 \\ -1 & 8 & 3 \end{bmatrix}$

176. If the Laplace transform of a function $f(t)$ is $\frac{1}{s(s+a)}$, then $f(t)$ is equal to:

A. $\frac{1}{a}(1-e^{-at})$ B. $(1 - e^{-at})$

C. $\frac{1}{a}e^{-at}$ D. ae^{-at}

177. If the mean of a Poisson distribution is 0.5, then the ratio of $P(x = 3)$ to $P(x = 2)$ is:
A. 1 : 2 B. 1 : 8
C. 1 : 6 D. 1 : 4

178. Suppose U and W are distinct 4-dimensional subspaces of a vector space V of dimension 6. The possible dimension of $U \cap W$ is:
A. 5 or 6 B. 1 or 4
C. 4 or 6 D. 2 or 3

179. Suppose $M = \begin{pmatrix} A_1 & B \\ 0 & A_2 \end{pmatrix}$, where A_1 and A_2 are square matrices. The characteristic polynomial of M is _____ to/of the characteristic polynomials of A_1 and A_2.
A. The quotient B. The product
C. The sum D. equal

180. In a plane triangle ABC, the maximum value of cos A cos B cos C is:
A. $\frac{1}{4}$ B. $\frac{1}{8}$
C. $\frac{1}{2}$ D. $\frac{3}{4}$

181. Which of these is NOT a part of social science?
A. Biology B. Anthropology
C. Statistics D. Sociology

182. Which of these factors does NOT affect the emotionality of a person?
A. Child B is exhausted after travelling for 4 hours in the car
B. Child C is happily sleeping at night undisturbed for 8 hours
C. Child D is suffereing from disease due to malnutrition
D. Child A is too much excited at the thought of an ice cream

183. Which is these is NOT an assessment method?
A. Homework exercises
B. Presentations
C. Simulations
D. Students watching an audiovisual

184. The ability to perceive existing gender differences and issues and to incorporate these into strategies and actions is known as:
A. gender equality B. gender parity
C. gender equity D. gender sensitivity

185. The assessment that expands the findings of an assessment with analysis of abilities and potentials with a further dimension is known as:
A. summative assessment
B. prognostic assessment
C. formative assessment
D. diagnostic assessment

186. Which of these is NOT a correct statement of the CAI?
A. It facilitates reteaching and reinforcing
B. It can help teachers to improve their role in education process
C. It can create simulations in the learner
D. CAI can give a human touch better than traditional teaching

187. When knowledge is acquired through religious texts, it is known as ____.
A. authority B. reason
C. testimony D. revelation

188. Which of these is NOT a correct statement on the guiding principles of constructivism?
A. Learning requires standing wholes as well as parts and parts must be understood in the context of wholes
B. Learning must start with the issues around which students are actively trying to construct meaning
C. The learning process focuses on isolated facts, not on primary concepts
D. The purpose of learning is for an individual to construct his or her own meaning, not just to memorise the "right" answers

189. Identify the correct statement on role play from the given options?
A. Low level of learner involvement
B. Effective while addressing issues in the affective domain
C. Introverts enjoy Role plays
D. All kinds of learners are proactive to take up role plays

190. ____ is/are mandated to provide academic and technical resource support to adult and continuing education through development and production of material and training modules. In addition to this, it/they would be required to conduct motivational and environmental building, action research and evaluation and monitoring.
A. The State Resource Centre(s)
B. Rashtriya Madhyamik Shiksha Abhiyan
C. Jan Shikshan Sansthans
D. Sarva Shiksha Abhiyan

191. Which of these is NOT a correct statement on including inclusive education in India?
A. Children with special needs cannot be made a part of regular school.
B. It is an opportunity to form friendships with other children.
C. It develops the tolerance and appreciation of normal children for differently abled students.
D. Giving all the normal and differently abled children equal opportunities to learn and get equal treatment as others.

192. When a learner performs a skill according to the instruction rather than the observation, he is known to be at the ____ level of psycho-motor domain.
A. 'Articulates' B. 'Imitates'
C. 'Manipulates' D. 'Naturalises'

193. Which of these is NOT a 2D art, method or technique to use while teaching a subject?
A. Rangoli B. Installation
C. Collage making D. Mandna

194. Identify the learning style from the given description:

Sonu likes to have a hands-on experience in anything he learns. He enjoys field trips to experience the physical proximity of the target knowledge. He makes his own notes on whatever he learns.
A. Tactile Learning style
B. Auditory Learning style
C. Visual/Verbal Learning style
D. Visual/Non-verbal Learning style

195. Which of these skills is a receptive skill?
A. Speaking B. Listening
C. Writing D. Language

196. ____ is a development disability significantly affecting verbal and non-verbal communication and social interaction, generally evident before age three and characterised by engaging in repetitive activities and stereotyped movements.
A. Autism B. Dyslexia
C. ADHD D. Dysgraphia

197. Which of these is NOT a good aspect relating to reading a newspaper?
A. Latest update on the current happenings
B. Exaggerated or underplayed news of the real situation
C. Increased vocabulary
D. Knowledge on antisocial elements in the society

198. What should be the objective of teaching science at higher secondary school level?
A. To develop economic efficiency and capacity to earn a livelihood
B. To get the knowledge about the society and natural environment
C. To develop the observation skills
D. Develop the quantitative sense to solve the problems

199. Which of these is NOT a blog tool?
A. Trackback
B. Blogger
C. WordPress
D. Edublog

200. In a particular Mathematics class, a student can draw geometrical figures and graphs. Which stage of cognitive domain is the student exhibiting?
A. Application B. Skill
C. Knowledge D. Understanding

ANSWER

1	2	3	4	5	6	7	8	9	10
B	D	A	B	A	C	D	C	A	B
11	**12**	**13**	**14**	**15**	**16**	**17**	**18**	**19**	**20**
B	A	B	D	B	B	B	A	A	A
21	**22**	**23**	**24**	**25**	**26**	**27**	**28**	**29**	**30**
A	C	B	B	A	A	A	B	A	B
31	**32**	**33**	**34**	**35**	**36**	**37**	**38**	**39**	**40**
B	B	C	D	D	A	C	D	C	A
41	**42**	**43**	**44**	**45**	**46**	**47**	**48**	**49**	**50**
A	B	A	A	C	D	C	A	D	C
51	**52**	**53**	**54**	**55**	**56**	**57**	**58**	**59**	**60**
A	B	B	D	D	B	D	C	A	C
61	**62**	**63**	**64**	**65**	**66**	**67**	**68**	**69**	**70**
A	A	B	A	D	D	C	D	B	C
71	**72**	**73**	**74**	**75**	**76**	**77**	**78**	**79**	**80**
A	B	D	A	D	D	C	B	B	A
81	**82**	**83**	**84**	**85**	**86**	**87**	**88**	**89**	**90**
B	A	B	D	A	A	C	C	A	B
91	**92**	**93**	**94**	**95**	**96**	**97**	**98**	**99**	**100**
C	C	B	A	B	A	D	A	B	D
101	**102**	**103**	**104**	**105**	**106**	**107**	**108**	**109**	**110**
B	B	A	A	D	A	A	A	B	A
111	**112**	**113**	**114**	**115**	**116**	**117**	**118**	**119**	**120**
C	C	C	A	C	B	C	B	A	A
121	**122**	**123**	**124**	**125**	**126**	**127**	**128**	**129**	**130**
A	B	C	A	C	B	C	A	A	B
131	**132**	**133**	**134**	**135**	**136**	**137**	**138**	**139**	**140**
A	A	B	D	B	C	D	C	D	A
141	**142**	**143**	**144**	**145**	**146**	**147**	**148**	**149**	**150**
A	A	A	D	A	A	C	C	C	A
151	**152**	**153**	**154**	**155**	**156**	**157**	**158**	**159**	**160**
C	C	B	D	B	B	D	D	C	C
161	**162**	**163**	**164**	**165**	**166**	**167**	**168**	**169**	**170**
C	B	B	A	D	A	A	C	D	A
171	**172**	**173**	**174**	**175**	**176**	**177**	**178**	**179**	**180**
C	A	B	C	A	A	C	D	B	B
181	**182**	**183**	**184**	**185**	**186**	**187**	**188**	**189**	**190**
A	B	D	D	B	D	D	C	B	A
191	**192**	**193**	**194**	**195**	**196**	**197**	**198**	**199**	**200**
A	B	B	A	B	A	B	A	A	B

EXPLANATORY ANSWERS

1. We have, A = {1, 2, 3, 4} to a set B = {u, v, w, x} defined by R = {(1, v), (1, u), (3, v), (3, x), (4, v)}

∴ The domain of R = The set of all first components or cordinates of the ordered pairs belonging to R = {1, 3, 4}

and, the range of R = the set of all second compound belonging to R = {u, v, x}

Hence, the domain of R and Range of R are {1, 3, 4}, {u, v, x} respectively.

3. Clearly $f(1) = 2$, $f(2) = 1$ and $f(3) = 3$

∴ $f = \{(1, 2), (2, 1), (3, 3)\}$

which is clearly a bijection. On interchaning the components of ordered pairs in f, we obtain,

$$f^{-1} = \{(2, 1), (1, 2), (3, 3)\}$$
$$= \{(1, 2), (2, 1), (3, 3)\}$$

5. $2 + 5 + 8 + ... + (3n - 1)$

$$= \Sigma(3n - 1) = 3\Sigma n - \Sigma 1$$
$$= \frac{3n(n+1)}{2} - n = \frac{3n^2 + 3n - 2n}{2}$$
$$= \frac{3n^2 + n}{2} = \frac{n(3n+1)}{2}$$

Hence, the value of $2 + 5 + 8 + ... + (3n - 1)$ comes out to be $\frac{n(3n+1)}{2}$

8. Given, A and B are finite sets, then (A ∪ B) and (A ∩ B) are finite sets

∴ $n(A \cup B) = n(A) + n(B) - n(A \cap B)$

9. The power set of a set A having for distinct elements. We know that, a set having n elements has 2^n subsets

therefore, A is finite set having n elements then P(A) has 2^n elements

∴ P(A) has 2^4 elements

∴ P(A) has 16 elements.

10. Given, U = {1, 2, ..., 9} A = {1, 2, 5, 6}, B = {2, 5, 7} and C = {1, 3, 5, 7, 9}

$$\therefore \left(\frac{B \oplus C}{A}\right) = (B \oplus C) \cap A'$$
$$= \{(B \cup C) - (B \cap C)\} \cap \{U - A\}$$
$$= [\{1, 2, 3, 5, 7, 9\} - \{5, 7\}] \cap \{3, 4, 7, 8, 9\}$$
$$= \{1, 2, 3, 9\}\ \{3, 4, 7, 8, 9\} = \{3, 9\}$$

12. A = {u, v, w}, B = {x, y}

If A and B are finite sets having m and n elements respectively.

Then 2^{mn} relation can be defined from A to B

That is $2^{mn} = 2^{3\times2} = 2^6 = 6^4$ [$m = 3$, $n = 2$]

Hence, the possible number of relations from set A to a set B is 64.

15. A = {2, 3, 4, 5} and B = {1, 2, 3, ..., 9}

Here, as every element of A is an element of B. So, A is subset of B that is A ⊂ B.

17. $n(U) = 80$, $n(A) = 40$, $n(B) = 55$ and $n(A \cap B) = 20$

$$\therefore n(A \oplus B) = n(A) + n(B) - 2n(A \cap B)$$
$$= 40 + 55 - 2 \times 20$$
$$= \cancel{40} + 55 - \cancel{40} = 55$$

∴ $n(A \oplus B) = 55$

21. Given, $\left(\frac{1-i}{1+i}\right)^n = 1$

$$\therefore \frac{1-i}{1+i} = \frac{1-i}{1+i} \times \frac{1-i}{1-i} = \frac{(1-i)^2}{1^2 - i^2}$$
$$= \frac{1^2 + i^2 - 2i}{1+1}, [i^2 = -1]$$
$$= \frac{1-1-2i}{2} = -\frac{\cancel{2}i}{\cancel{2}} = -i$$

Now, $\left(\frac{1-i}{1+i}\right)^n = (-i)^n = (-i)^4 = (i)^4$

$$= (i^2)^2 = (-1)^2 = 1$$

∴ Smallest positive integer, $n = 4$

22. Let $Z = (1 - \cos\alpha) + i \sin\alpha$

Then, Modulus = $|Z| = \sqrt{(1-\cos\alpha)^2 + \sin^2\alpha}$

$= \sqrt{1+\cos^2\alpha - 2\cos\alpha + \sin^2\alpha}$

$= \sqrt{1+(\cos^2\alpha+\sin^2\alpha) - 2\cos\alpha}$

$= \sqrt{1+1-2\cos\alpha} = \sqrt{2-2\cos\alpha}$

$= \sqrt{2(1-\cos\alpha)} = \sqrt{2\cdot 2\sin^2\frac{\alpha}{2}}$

$= \sqrt{4\sin^2\frac{\alpha}{2}} = 2\sin\frac{\alpha}{2}$

23. Let $Z = \frac{(1+2i)^3}{(1+i)(2-i)}$

$= \frac{1^3+3(1)^2(2i)+3(1)(2i)^2+(2i)^3}{2-i+2i-i^2}$

$= \frac{1+6i+3(4i^2)+8i^3}{2+i-(-1)}$

$[i^2 = -1,\ i^3 = -i]$

$= \frac{1+6i+3(-4)+8(-i)}{2+i+1}$

$= \frac{1+6i-12-8i}{3+i}$

$= \frac{-11-2i}{3+i} = \frac{-(11+2i)}{3+i}\times\frac{3-i}{3-i}$

$= \frac{-(33-11i+6i-2i^2)}{3^2-i^2}$

$= \frac{-[33-5i-2(-1)]}{9+1}$

$= \frac{-(33-5i+2)}{10} = \frac{-(35-5i)}{10}$

$= \frac{-5(7-i)}{10}$

$= \frac{-(7-i)}{2} = \left(-\frac{7}{2}\right)+i\left(\frac{1}{2}\right)$

then, $Z = \left(-\frac{7}{2}\right)+i\left(\frac{1}{2}\right)$

Hence, Z is the form of $a + ib$.

24. The rectangular form of $10\angle -30°$ is

$= 10[\cos(-30°) + i\sin(-30°)]$

$= 10[\cos 30° - i\sin 30°]$

$= 10\left[\frac{\sqrt{3}}{2} - i\frac{1}{2}\right] = 10\left(\frac{\sqrt{3}-i}{2}\right)$

$= 5(\sqrt{3}-i) = 5\sqrt{3}-5i$

27. 'MATHEMATICS'

words that can be formed. Start from M and end with T

$\therefore$ In MATHEMAICST, number of letters between M and T = 9

But there is 2M's and 2T's

$\therefore$ Total no. of words that can be formed

$= \frac{\lfloor 9}{\lfloor 2 \lfloor 2} = \frac{9\cdot 8\cdot 7\cdot 6\cdot 5\cdot \cancel{4}\cdot 3\cdot 2\cdot 1}{\cancel{2}\cdot\cancel{2}}$

$= 72 \times 7 \times 180$

$= 504 \times 180 = 90720$

31. Given, ω is a complex cube root of unity

$\therefore 1 + \omega + \omega^2 = 0$ and $\omega^3 = 1$

$\therefore (1-\omega)^6 = [(1-\omega)^2]^3$

$= (1 - 2\omega + \omega^2)^3$

$= (1-2\omega)^3 + 3(1-2\omega)^2\cdot\omega^2 + 3(1-2\omega)\cdot\omega^4 + \omega^6$

$= 1^3 - 3\cdot 1^2\cdot 2\omega + 3\cdot 1\times 4\omega^2 - 8\omega^3 + 3\omega^2(1^2 - 4\omega + 4\omega^2) + 3\omega^4(1-2\omega) + \omega^6$

$= 1 - 6\omega + 12\omega^2 - 8\omega^3 + 3\omega^2 - 12\omega^3 + 12\omega^4 + 3\omega^4 - 6\omega^5 + \omega^6$

$= 1 - 6\omega + 12\omega^2 - 8\cdot 1 + 3\omega^2 - 12\cdot 1 + 12\omega\cdot\omega^3 + 3\omega\cdot\omega^3 - 6\omega^2\cdot\omega^3 + (\omega^3)^2$

$= 1 - 6\omega + 12\omega^2 - 8 + 3\omega^2 - 12 + 12\cdot\omega\cdot 1 + 3\omega\cdot 1 - 6\omega^2\cdot 1 + 1^2$

$= 1 - 8 - 12 + 1 + 9\omega + 9\omega^2$

$= 2 - 20 + 9(\omega + \omega^2)$

$= -18 + 9(-1) = -18 - 9 = -27$

33. Number of combinations with n different things taken r at a time $= {}^{n-1}C_{r-1}$

Here, $n = 20$, $r = 4$

$\therefore$ The number of ways to distribute 20 identical balls in 4 different boxes

$= {}^{20-1}C_{4-1} = {}^{19}C_3 = \frac{\lfloor 19}{\lfloor 3 \lfloor 19-3}$

$= \frac{\lfloor 19}{\lfloor 3 \lfloor 16} = \frac{19 \cdot \overset{3}{\cancel{18}} \cdot 17 \cancel{\lfloor 16}}{\cancel{6} \cancel{\lfloor 16}}$

$= 57 \cdot 17 = 969$

34. Given, word "COMPUTER"

There are 8 letters in word

$\therefore$ The number of permutation $= {}^8P_8$

$= \frac{\lfloor 8}{\lfloor 8-8} = \frac{\lfloor 8}{\lfloor 0} = \frac{\lfloor 8}{1} = \lfloor 8$

$= 8 \cdot 7 \cdot 6 \cdot 5 \cdot 4 \cdot 3 \cdot 2 \cdot 1$

$= 56 \cdot 720 = 40{,}320$

35. Here, $n = 12$, $c = 10$

$\therefore$ Number of ways can be distributed $= {}^{n-1}C_{r-1}$

$= {}^{12-1}C_{10-1} = {}^{11}C_9$

$= \frac{\lfloor 11}{\lfloor 9 \lfloor 11-9} = \frac{\lfloor 11}{\lfloor 9 \lfloor 2} = \frac{11 \cdot \overset{5}{\cancel{10}} \cdot \cancel{\lfloor 9}}{2 \cancel{\lfloor 9}}$

$= 11 \cdot 5 = 55$

37. $1^3 + 2^3 + \ldots n^3$

by Mathematical induction

$1^3 + 2^3 + \ldots + n^3 = \left[\frac{n(n+1)}{2}\right]^2 = \frac{n^2(n+1)^2}{4}$

38. Let $Z = \left(\frac{2+i}{3-i}\right)^2 = \left(\frac{2+i}{3-i} \times \frac{3+i}{3+i}\right)^2$

$= \left(\frac{6+2i+3i+i^2}{9-i^2}\right)^2$

$= \left(\frac{6+5i-1}{9+1}\right)^2$

$= \left(\frac{5+5i}{10}\right)^2 = \left[\frac{5(1+i)}{10}\right]^2$

$= \left[\frac{1}{2}(1+i)\right]^2 = \frac{1}{4}(1+i)^2$

$= \frac{1}{4}(1+2i+i^2) = \frac{1}{4}(i+2i-1)$

$= \frac{1}{4}(2i) = \frac{1}{2}i$

Then, $r = |Z| = \sqrt{0^2 + \left(\frac{1}{2}\right)^2} = \sqrt{\frac{1}{4}} = \frac{1}{2}$

Let θ be the acute angle given by $\tan\theta = \left|\frac{\text{Im}(z)}{\text{Re}(z)}\right|$

Then, $\tan\theta = \left|\frac{1/2}{0}\right| = \alpha \Rightarrow \theta = \frac{\pi}{2}$

The point $\left(0, \frac{1}{2}\right)$ representing z lies in first quadrant

$\therefore$ The argument of Z is $\theta = \frac{\pi}{2}$

Hence, the polar form of $Z = \left(\frac{2+i}{3-i}\right)^2$ is

$Z = r(\cos\theta + i\sin\theta) = \frac{1}{2}\left(\cos\frac{\pi}{2} + i\sin\frac{\pi}{2}\right)$

44. $3|2x + 6| < 42$

or, $|2x + 6| < 14$

or, $-14 < |2x + 6| < 14$

or, $-14 < 2x + 6 < 14$

or, $-14 - 6 < 2x < 14 - 6$

or, $-20 < 2x < 8$

or, $-10 < x < 4$

$\therefore x \in (-10, 4)$

46. $|x + 1| + |x| > 3$

or, $-(x + 1) - x > 3$

or, $-2x - 1 > 3$

or, $-2x > 4$

or, $x < -2$

that is, $x \in (-\infty, -2)$

and, $|x + 1| + |x| > 3$

or, $x + 1 + x > 3$

or, $2x + 1 > 3$

or, $2x > 3 - 1$

or, $2x > 2$

or, $x > 1$

$\therefore x \in (1, \infty)$, Hence, $x \in (-\infty, -2) \cup (1, \infty)$

48. Given, expansion $= \left(\frac{1}{x^{\frac{8}{3}}} + x^2 \log_{10} x\right)^8$

general term in $(a + x)^n$ is

$$t_{r+1} = {}^nC_r\, a^{n-r}\, x^r$$

$\therefore$ 6th term in given expansion is

$$t_{5+1} = {}^8C_5 \left(\frac{1}{x^{\frac{8}{3}}}\right)^{8-5} (x^2 \log_{10} x)^5$$

$$= \frac{\lfloor 8}{\lfloor 5 \lfloor 3}\left(x^{-\frac{8}{3}}\right)^3 \cdot x^{10} (\log_{10} x)^5$$

$$= \frac{8\cdot 7\cdot 6 \lfloor \not{5}}{\lfloor \not{5} \lfloor 3} \cdot x^{-8} \cdot x^{10} (\log_{10} x)^5$$

$$= \frac{8\cdot 7\cdot \not{6}}{\not{6}} x^2 (\log_{10} x)^5$$

$$= 56\ x^2(\log_{10} x)^5$$

$$= 5600 = 56x^2(\log_{10} x)^5$$

or, $\quad 100 = x^2(\log_{10} x)^5$

R.H.S. $= x^2(\log_{10} x)^5$, when $x = 10$

$= 10^2(\log_{10} 10)^5 \quad [\log_{10} 10 = 1]$

$= 10^2(1)^5 = 10^2(1)^5 = 100$

Hence, $\quad x = 10$

51. Given, A_1, A_2 be 2 A.M's between a and b then, a, A_1, A_2, b are in A.P.

whose common difference d is given by

$$d = \frac{b-a}{2+1} = \frac{b-a}{3}$$

$$\therefore \quad A_1 = a + d = a + \frac{b-a}{3} = \frac{2a+b}{3}$$

$$A_2 = a + 2d = a + \frac{2(b-a)}{3}$$

$$= \frac{3a+2b-2a}{3} = \frac{a+2b}{3}$$

$$\therefore A_1 + A_2 = \frac{2a+b}{3} + \frac{a+2b}{3}$$

and, G_1G_2 be 2 G.M.'s between a and b then a, G_1, G_2, b is a G.P., r is the common ratio

$$\therefore \quad r = \left(\frac{b}{a}\right)^{\frac{1}{2+1}} = \left(\frac{b}{a}\right)^{\frac{1}{3}}$$

$$\therefore G_1 = ar = a\left(\frac{b}{a}\right)^{\frac{1}{3}}, G_2 = ar^2 = a\left(\frac{b}{a}\right)^{\frac{2}{3}}$$

$$\therefore G_1 \cdot G_2 = a\left(\frac{b}{a}\right)^{\frac{1}{3}} \cdot a\left(\frac{b}{a}\right)^{\frac{2}{3}}$$

$$\therefore \frac{A_1 + A_2}{G_1G_2} = \frac{\frac{2a+b}{3} + \frac{a+2b}{3}}{a\left(\frac{b}{a}\right)^{\frac{1}{3}} \cdot a\left(\frac{b}{a}\right)^{\frac{2}{3}}}$$

$$= \frac{\frac{2a+b+a+2b}{3}}{a^2\left(\frac{b}{a}\right)^{\frac{1}{3}+\frac{2}{3}}}$$

$$= \frac{\frac{3a+3b}{3}}{a^2\left(\frac{b}{a}\right)^1} = \frac{\frac{\not{3}(a+b)}{\not{3}}}{a^{\not{2}} \frac{b}{\not{a}}} = \frac{a+b}{ab}$$

53. Given, the equation

$$\frac{x}{2x+1} \geq 0.25$$

or, $\quad \frac{x}{2x+1} \geq \frac{1}{4}$

or, $\quad 4x \geq 2x+1$

or, $\quad 2x \geq 1$

or, $\quad x \geq \frac{1}{2}$

And, $\quad \frac{6x}{4x-1} < 0.5$

or, $\quad \frac{6x}{4x-1} < \frac{1}{2}$

or, $\quad 12x < 4x - 1$ or, $8x < -1$

or, $\quad x < -\frac{1}{8}$

As $\quad x \geq \frac{1}{2}$ and $x < -\frac{1}{8}$

So, there is no solution.

54. The sum of the 24 terms of the series

$$\sqrt{2}+\sqrt{8}+\sqrt{18}+\sqrt{32}+....$$

$$= \sqrt{2}+2\sqrt{2}+3\sqrt{2}+4\sqrt{2}+...+24\sqrt{2}$$

$$= \sqrt{2}[1+2+3+4+...+24]$$

$$= \sqrt{2}\left[\frac{24}{2}(2\cdot1+(24-1)\cdot1)\right]$$

$$= \sqrt{2}[12(2+23)] = \sqrt{2}[12(25)]$$

$$= \sqrt{2}(300) = 300\sqrt{2}$$

55. $2^{2000} = (2^8)^{250} = (256)^{250}$

when 2^{2000} is divided by 17,

$$\therefore \quad \frac{2^{2000}}{17} = \frac{(256)^{250}}{17}$$

$$\Rightarrow \quad \frac{256}{17} = 17 \times 15 + 1$$

$\therefore$ Remainder = 1

61. Let $\quad \Delta = \begin{vmatrix} b^2+c^2 & ab & ca \\ ab & c^2+a^2 & bc \\ ca & bc & a^2+b^2 \end{vmatrix}$

Multiplying R_1, R_2 and R_3 by a, b and c respectively, we get

$$\Rightarrow \Delta \frac{1}{abc} = \begin{vmatrix} 2(b^2+c^2) & a^2b & a^2c \\ b^2a & b(c^2+a^2) & b^2c \\ c^2a & c^2b & c(a^2+b^2) \end{vmatrix}$$

(taking a, b and c common from c_1, c_2 and c_3 respectively)

$$\Rightarrow \Delta = \frac{abc}{abc}\begin{vmatrix} b^2+c^2 & a^2 & a^2 \\ b^2 & c^2+a^2 & b^2 \\ c^2 & c^2 & a^2+b^2 \end{vmatrix}$$

(Applying $R_1 \to R_1 + R_2 + R_3$)

$$\Rightarrow \Delta = \begin{vmatrix} 2(b^2+c^2) & 2(a^2+c^2) & 2(a^2+b^2) \\ b^2 & c^2+a^2 & b^2 \\ c^2 & c^2 & a^2+b^2 \end{vmatrix}$$

(taking 2 common from R_1)

$$\Rightarrow \quad \Delta = 2\begin{vmatrix} b^2+c^2 & a^2+c^2 & a^2+b^2 \\ b^2 & c^2+a^2 & b^2 \\ c^2 & c^2 & a^2+b^2 \end{vmatrix}$$

Applying $R_2 \to R_2 - R_1$ and $R_3 \to R_3 - R_1$

$$\Rightarrow \quad \Delta = 2\begin{vmatrix} b^2+c^2 & c^2+a^2 & a^2+b^2 \\ -c^2 & 0 & -a^2 \\ -b^2 & -a^2 & 0 \end{vmatrix}$$

Applying $R_1 \to R_1 + R_2 + R_3$

$$\Rightarrow \quad \Delta = \begin{vmatrix} 0 & c^2 & b^2 \\ -c^2 & 0 & -a^2 \\ -b^2 & -a^2 & 0 \end{vmatrix}$$

Expanding along R_1

$$\Rightarrow \Delta = 2\left\{-c^2\begin{vmatrix} -c^2 & -a^2 \\ -b^2 & 0 \end{vmatrix} + b^2\begin{vmatrix} -c^2 & 0 \\ -b^2 & -a^2 \end{vmatrix}\right\}$$

$$\Rightarrow \Delta = 2(a^2b^2c^2 + a^2b^2c^2) = 4a^2b^2c^2 = 4(abc)^2$$

Given, $\quad \Delta = k(abc)^2$

$$\therefore 4\cancel{(abc)^2} = k\cancel{(abc)^2}$$

$$\therefore \quad k = 4$$

64. $x = \sqrt{12+\sqrt{12+\sqrt{12+...}}}$ up to ∞

$$\Rightarrow \quad x = \sqrt{12+x}$$

Squaring both sides, we get

$$x^2 = 12 + x$$

$$\Rightarrow x^2 - x - 12 = 0$$

$$\Rightarrow x^2 - 4x + 3x - 12 = 0$$

$$\Rightarrow x(x-4) + 3(x-4) = 0$$

$$\Rightarrow (x-4)(x+3) = 0$$

either $x - 4 = 0$ or, $x + 3 = 0$

$$\therefore \quad x = 4$$

$\left\{\begin{matrix} x=-3 \\ x=-3 \end{matrix}\right.$ is ignored because of –ve value}

65.

7	42833
29	6119
	211

$\therefore \quad 42833 = 7 \times 29 \times 211$

Hence, the prime factorization of 42833 is 7.29.211

75. $\because$ $105 = 3 \times 35,$

$140 = 4 \times 35,$

$350 = 10 \times 35$

$\therefore$ The greatest common divisor of three integers 105, 140 and 350 is 35.

76. The positive integer divisors of 200 are,

1, 2, 4, 5, 8, 10, 20, 25, 40, 50, 100, 200

Sum = 1 + 2 + 4 + 5 + 8 + 10 + 20 + 25 + 40 + 50 + 100 + 200 = 465

and, Number of integers = 12.

82. Given, two vertices of triangle are (0, 5) and (6, 3) when its centroid is (1, –2)

Let the third vertex is (x_1, y_1)

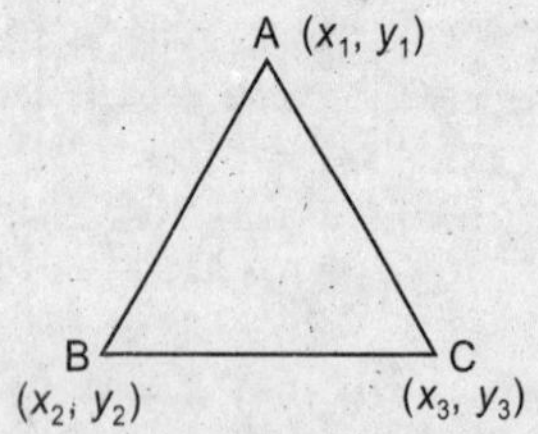

The co-ordinates of the centroid

$$= \left(\frac{x_1 + x_2 + x_3}{3}, \frac{y_1 + y_2 + y_3}{3}\right)$$

Then, centroid is

$$\left(\frac{x_1 + 0 + 6}{3}, \frac{y_1 + 5 + 3}{3}\right) = (1, -2)$$

$\Rightarrow \quad \frac{x_1 + 6}{3} = 1$ and $\frac{y_1 + 8}{3} = -2$

$\Rightarrow \quad x_1 = 3 - 6$ and $y_1 = -6 - 8$

$\Rightarrow \quad x_1 = -3$ and $y_1 = -14$

Hence, third vertex is $(x_1, y_1) = (-3, -14)$

85. $\because$ $A = \begin{bmatrix} a_{11} & a_{12} \\ a_{21} & a_{22} \end{bmatrix}$ is a square matrix of order 2.

Then, |A| is the product of the diagonal elements minus the product of off-diagonal elements.

$$= a_{11}a_{22} - a_{12}a_{21}$$

As, A are non-zero and one of its eigen value is zero

So, $a_{11}a_{22} - a_{12}a_{21} = 0$

88. Let A(k, 2 – 2k), B(–k + 1, 2k) and C(–4 – k, 6 – 2k) be three points

Then A, B, C are collinear

$\Rightarrow$ Area of triangle ABC = 0

$$\Rightarrow \frac{1}{2}\begin{vmatrix} k & 2-2k & 1 \\ -k+1 & 2k & 1 \\ -4-k & 6-2k & 1 \end{vmatrix} = 0$$

$$\Rightarrow \frac{1}{2}[k(2k - 6 + 2k) - (2 - 2k)(-k + 1 + 4 + k) + \{(-k + 1)(6 - 2k) - 2k(-4 - k)\}] = 0$$

$$\Rightarrow k(4k - 6) + (2k - 2)(5) + 6 - \cancel{2k} - \cancel{6k} + 2k^2 + \cancel{8k} + 2k^2 = 0$$

$\Rightarrow 4k^2 - 6k + 10k - 10 + 6 + 4k^2 = 0$

$\Rightarrow 8k^2 + 4k - 4 = 0$

$\Rightarrow 2k^2 + k - 1 = 0$

$\Rightarrow 2k^2 + 2k - k - 1 = 0$

$\Rightarrow 2k(k + 1) - 1(k + 1) = 0$

$\Rightarrow (k + 1)(2k - 1) = 0$

either $k + 1 = 0$ or $2k - 1 = 0$

$\therefore \quad k = -1$ or $k = \frac{1}{2}$

89. The eqn. of the straight line passing through the intersection of the line $x + 5y + 7 = 0$ and $3x + 2y - 5 = 0$ is

$(x + 5y + 7) + \lambda(3x + 2y - 5) = 0$

or, $(1 + 3\lambda)x + (5 + 2\lambda)y + 7 - 5\lambda = 0$ ...(i)

The line in (i) is parallel to the line $7x + 2y - 5 = 0$

Therefore, their slopes are equal

So, slope of line in equation (i) is same as that of the line $7x + 2y - 5 = 0$

i.e., $-\frac{(1 + 3\lambda)}{5 + 2\lambda} = -\frac{7}{2}$

$\Rightarrow \quad 2 + 6\lambda = 35 + 14\lambda$

$\Rightarrow \quad 2 - 35 = -6\lambda + 14\lambda$

$\Rightarrow \quad -33 = 8\lambda \therefore \lambda = -\frac{33}{8}$

putting the value of $\lambda = -\frac{33}{8}$ in (*i*), we get

$(x+5y+7)+-\frac{33}{8}(3x+2y-5) = 0$

$\Rightarrow 8(x + 5y + 7) - 99x - 66y + 165 = 0$

$\Rightarrow 8x + 40y + 56 - 99x - 66y + 165 = 0$

$\Rightarrow -91x - 26y + 221 = 0$

$\Rightarrow -7x - 2y + 17 = 0$

$\Rightarrow 7x + 2y - 17 = 0$

which is required line.

91. $\tan\theta \tan(60° + \theta) \tan(60° - \theta)$

$= \tan\theta\left[\frac{\tan 60° + \tan\theta}{1-\tan 60° \tan\theta}\right]\left[\frac{\tan 60° \tan\theta}{1+\tan 60° \tan\theta}\right]$

$= \tan\theta\left[\frac{\sqrt{3}+\tan\theta}{1-\sqrt{3}\tan\theta}\right]\left[\frac{\sqrt{3}-\tan\theta}{1+\sqrt{3}\tan\theta}\right]$

$= \tan\theta\left[\frac{(\sqrt{3})^3-\tan^2\theta}{1^2-(\sqrt{3}\tan\theta)^2}\right]$

$= \tan\theta\left[\frac{3-\tan^2\theta}{1-3\tan^2\theta}\right]$

$= \frac{3\tan\theta-\tan^3\theta}{1-3\tan^2\theta} = \tan 3\theta$

$[\tan (A \pm B) = \frac{\tan A \pm \tan B}{1 \mp \tan A \tan B};$

$(\tan 60° = \sqrt{3})]$

94. Let P(1.5, 0), Q(1.5, 6) and R(−1, 6) be the mid-point of sides AB, BC and CA respectively of triangle ABC.

Let $A(x_1, y_1)$, $B(x_2, y_2)$ and $C(x_3, y_3)$ be the vertices of triangle ABC. Then, P is the mid-point of AB.

$\therefore \frac{x_1+x_2}{2} = 1.5, \frac{y_1+y_2}{2} = 0$

$\Rightarrow x_1 + x_2 = 3$ and $y_1 + y_2 = 0$ ...(i)

Q is the mid-point of BC

$\frac{x_2+x_3}{2} = 1.5, \frac{y_2+y_3}{2} = 6$

$\Rightarrow x_2 + x_3 = 3$ and $y_2 + y_3 = 12$ ...(ii)

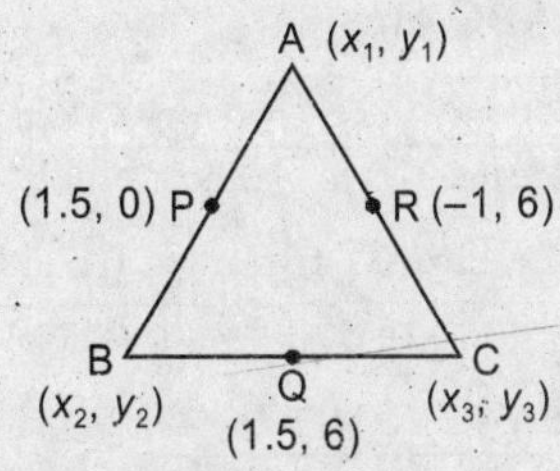

R is the mid-point of AC

$\frac{x_1+x_3}{2} = -1, \frac{y_1+y_3}{2} = 6$

$\Rightarrow x_1 + x_3 = -2$ and $y_1 + y_3 = 12$ ...(iii)

from (i), (ii) and (iii), we get

$x_1 + x_2 + x_2 + x_3 + x_1 + x_3 = 3 + 3 - 2$ and $y_1 + y_2 + y_2 + y_3 + y_1 + y_3 = 0 + 12 + 12$

$\Rightarrow x_1 + x_2 + x_3 = 2$ and $y_1 + y_2 + y_3 = 12$ (iv)

From (i) and (iv), we get

$x_3 + 3 = 2$ and $0 + y_3 = 12$

$\Rightarrow \quad x_3 = -1, y_3 = 12$

So, the co-ordinates of C are (−1, 12).

From (ii) and (iv), we get

$x_1 + 3 = 2$ and $y_1 + 12 = 12$

$\Rightarrow \quad x_1 = -1$ and $y_1 = 0$

So, co-ordinate at A are (−1, 0)

From (iii) and (iv), we get

$x_2 + (-2) = 2$ and $y_2 + 12 = 12$

$\Rightarrow \quad x_2 = 4$ and $y_2 = 0$

So, co-ordinate of B are (4, 0)

Now, $a = BC = \sqrt{(-1-4)^2+(12-0)^2}$

$= \sqrt{25+144} = \sqrt{169} = 13$

$b = AC = \sqrt{(-1+1)^2+(12-0)^2}$

$= \sqrt{0+12^2} = 12$

and, $c = AB = \sqrt{(-1-4)^2+(0-0)^2}$

$= \sqrt{5^2} = 5$

The co-ordinates of the in-centre of the triangle ABC are

$$\left(\frac{ax_1+bx_2+cx_3}{a+b+c+}, \frac{ay_1+by_2+cy_3}{a+b+c}\right)$$

or, $\left(\frac{13\times-1+12\times4+5\times-1}{13+12+5}, \frac{13\times0+12\times0+5\times12}{13+12+5}\right)$

or, $\left(\frac{-13+48-5}{30}, \frac{0+0+60}{30}\right)$

or, $\left(\frac{30}{30}, \frac{60}{30}\right)$

or, (1, 2)

97. Given, A(1, 2), B(2, 3), C(4, 3) be the vertices of triangle ABC

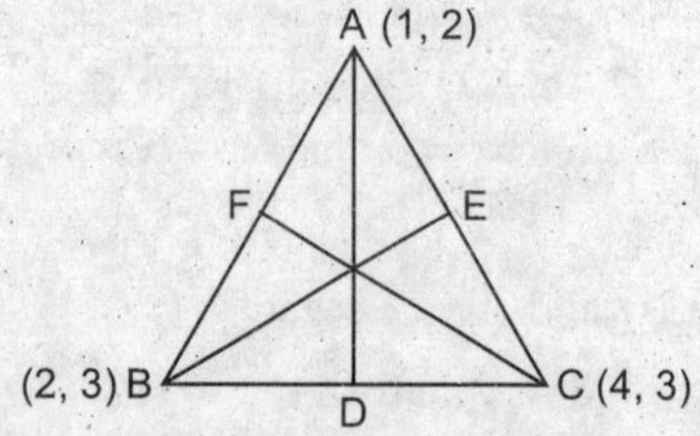

Let AD, BE and CF be three altitude of ΔABC.
Clearly AD $\perp$ BC, BE $\perp$ CA and CF $\perp$ AB.
We have,

Slope of BC $= \frac{3-3}{4-2} = \frac{0}{2} = 0$

$\therefore$ Slope of AD = 0
Since, AD passes through A(1, 2).
Therefore, equation of AD is

$$y - 2 = 0(x - 1) \Rightarrow y - 2 = 0 \quad \text{...(i)}$$

Slope of AC $= \frac{2-3}{1-4} = \frac{-1}{-3} = \frac{1}{3}$

$\therefore$ Slope of BE = –3
Clearly, BE passes through B(2, 3) and has slope –3.
So, the equation of BE is

$$y - 3 = -3(x - 2) \Rightarrow y - 3 = -3x + 6$$

$\Rightarrow 3x + y - 9 = 0$ ...(ii)

Slope of AB $= \frac{2-3}{1-2} = \frac{-1}{-1} = 1$

$\Rightarrow$ Slope of CF = –1

Clearly, CF passes through C(4, 3) and has slope –1.
So, the equation of CF is

$$y - 3 = -1(x - 4)$$
$$\Rightarrow y - 3 = -x + 4$$

$\Rightarrow x + y - 7 = 0$ ...(iii)

Thus, the altitudes of ΔABC are
$y - 2 = 0$, $3x + y - 9 = 0$ and $x + y = 7 = 0$
The orthocentre of ΔABC is the point of intersection of its altitudes,
Solving (ii) and (iii), we get

$$9 - 3x = 7 - x$$
$$\Rightarrow 9 - 7 = 3x - x$$
$$\Rightarrow 2 = 2x$$
$$\Rightarrow x = 1$$

and, $y = 9 - 3x = 9 - 3(1) = 9 - 3 = 6$

$\Rightarrow y = 6$

Hence, required orthocenter is (1, 6).

100. Given lines are
$5x - 12y + 2 = 0$ ...(i)
and, $5x - 12y - 3 = 0$ ...(ii)
Given: $ax + by + c_1 = 0$
$ax + by + c_2 = 0$

$\therefore$ distance $= d = \frac{|c_1 - c_2|}{\sqrt{a^2+b^2}}$

$\therefore$ Required distance $= \frac{|2-(-3)|}{\sqrt{5^2+(-12)^2}}$

$$= \frac{|2+3|}{\sqrt{25+144}} = \frac{5}{\sqrt{169}} = \frac{5}{13}$$

101. We have, $f(x) = x(x-1)(x-2) = x^3 - 3x^2 + 2x$
Since, $f(x)$ is a polynomial function and a polynomial function is everywhere continuous and differentiable. Therefore, $f(x)$ is continuous on $\left[0, \frac{1}{2}\right]$ and differentiable on $\left(0, \frac{1}{2}\right)$.
Thus, both the conditions of Lagrange's mean value theorem are satisfied.
So, there must exist at least one real number $c \in \left(0, \frac{1}{2}\right)$ such that

$$f'(c) = \frac{f\left(\frac{1}{2}\right) - f(0)}{\frac{1}{2} - 0}$$

Now, $f(x) = x^3 - 3x^2 + 2x$

$\Rightarrow f'(x) = 3x^2 - 6x + 2,\ f(0) = 0$

and $f\left(\frac{1}{2}\right) = \frac{1}{8} - \frac{3}{4} + 1 = \frac{3}{8}$

$$\therefore \quad f'(x) = \frac{f\left(\frac{1}{2}\right) - f(0)}{\left(\frac{1}{2}\right) - 0}$$

$$\Rightarrow 3x^2 - 6x + 2 = \frac{\frac{3}{8} - 0}{\frac{1}{2} - 0}$$

$$\Rightarrow 3x^2 - 6x + 2 = \frac{3}{4} \Rightarrow 12x^2 - 24x + 5 = 0$$

$$\Rightarrow \quad x = \frac{24 \pm \sqrt{336}}{24} = 1 \pm \frac{\sqrt{21}}{6}$$

$$= 1 \pm \frac{4.58}{6} = 1 \pm 0.764$$

Since, $c = 1 - \frac{\sqrt{21}}{6} = 1 - 0.764 = 0.236$

So, $c \in \left(0, \frac{1}{2}\right)$, such that $f'(c) = \frac{f\left(\frac{1}{2}\right) - f(0)}{\left(\frac{1}{2}\right) - 0}$

Hence, mean value theorem used.

103. Given, $A = \tan^{-1}\left(\frac{1}{7}\right)$ and $B = \tan^{-1}\left(\frac{1}{3}\right)$

$\Rightarrow \quad \tan A = \frac{1}{7}$ and $\tan B = \frac{1}{3}$

We know that,

$\sin 2\theta = \frac{2\tan\theta}{1+\tan^2\theta}$ and $\cos 2\theta = \frac{1-\tan^2\theta}{1+\tan^2\theta}$

$\therefore$ In option

$$\cos 2A = \frac{1-\tan^2 A}{1+\tan^2 A} = \frac{1-\left(\frac{1}{7}\right)^2}{1+\left(\frac{1}{7}\right)^2}$$

$$= \frac{1-\frac{1}{49}}{1+\frac{1}{49}} = \frac{\frac{49-1}{49}}{\frac{49+1}{49}}$$

$$= \frac{\frac{48}{49}}{\frac{50}{49}} = \frac{48}{\cancel{49}} \times \frac{\cancel{49}}{50} = \frac{48}{50} = \frac{24}{25}$$

and $\sin 4B = 2\sin 2B \cos 2B$

$$= 2\frac{2\tan B}{1+\tan^2 B} \times \frac{1-\tan^2 B}{1+\tan^2 B}$$

$$= 4 \times \frac{\frac{1}{3}}{1+\frac{1}{9}} \times \frac{1-\frac{1}{9}}{1+\frac{1}{9}} = 4 \times \frac{\frac{1}{3}}{\frac{10}{9}} \times \frac{\frac{8}{9}}{\frac{10}{9}}$$

$$= \overset{2}{\cancel{4}} \times \frac{1}{\cancel{3}} \times \frac{9}{\underset{5}{\cancel{10}}} \times \frac{8}{\cancel{9}} \times \frac{\cancel{9}}{\underset{5}{\cancel{10}}} = \frac{24}{25}$$

Hence, $\cos 2A = \sin 4B$

104. We have,

$$\sin^{-1}(x) + \sin^{-1}(y) + \sin^{-1}(z) = \frac{3\pi}{2}$$

$$\Rightarrow \sin^{-1}(x) + \sin^{-1}(y) + \sin^{-1}(z) = \frac{\pi}{2} + \frac{\pi}{2} + \frac{\pi}{2}$$

$$\Rightarrow \sin^{-1}(x) = \frac{\pi}{2},\ \sin^{-1}(y) = \frac{\pi}{2},\ \sin^{-1}(z) = \frac{\pi}{2}$$

$$\Rightarrow x = \sin\frac{\pi}{2},\ y = \sin\frac{\pi}{2},\ z = \sin\frac{\pi}{2}$$

$$\Rightarrow \quad x = 1,\ y = 1,\ z = 1$$

Therefore,

$$(x)^{100} + (y)^{100} + (z)^{100} - \left(\frac{9}{(x)^{100} + (y)^{100} + (z)^{100}}\right)$$

$$= (1)^{100} + (1)^{100} + (1)^{100} - \left(\frac{9}{(1)^{100} + (1)^{100} + (1)^{100}}\right)$$

$$= 1+1+1-\left(\frac{9}{1+1+1}\right)$$

$$= 3 - 3 = 0$$

105. Let AC is the upper part of a tree, touching the ground at a point 16 m from the foot of the tree and making an angle of 45° with the ground.

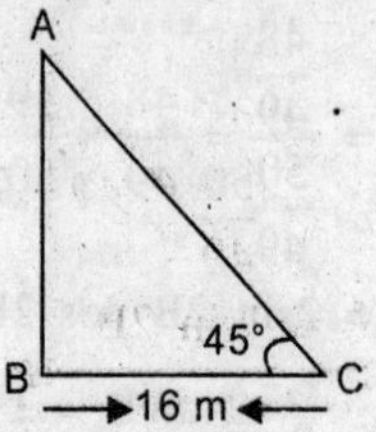

Then $\angle ACB = 45°$, BC = 16 m

Length of tree = AB + AC

In ΔABC

$$\tan 45° = \frac{AB}{BC}$$

$$\Rightarrow \quad 1 = \frac{AB}{16} \Rightarrow AB = 16 \text{ m}$$

Again, In ΔABC

$$\cos 45° = \frac{BC}{AC}$$

$$\Rightarrow \quad \frac{1}{\sqrt{2}} = \frac{16}{AC} \Rightarrow AC = 16\sqrt{2}$$

$\therefore$ Length of the tree

$$= AB + AC = (16+16\sqrt{2}) \text{ m}$$

$$= 16(1+\sqrt{2}) \text{ m} = 4^2(1+\sqrt{2}) \text{ m}$$

106. We have, $f(x) = x^{2m-1}(a-x)^{2n}$

Since, a polynomial function is every where differentiable and so continuous also.

Therefore, $f(x)$ is continuous on $[0, a]$ and derivable on $(0, a)$

Also, $f(0) = f(a) = 0$

Thus, all the three conditions of Rolle's theorem are satisfied.

Now, we have to show that $c \in (0, a)$ such that $f'(c) = 0$

We have, $f(x) = x^{2m-1} \times (a-x)^{2n}$

$$\Rightarrow \quad f'(x) = x^{2m-1} \times 2n(a-x)^{2n-1} \times (0-1) + (a-x)^{2n} \times (2m-1)x^{2m-2}$$

$$= -2n \times x^{2m-1} \times (a-x)^{2n-1} + (2m-1)(a-x)^{2n} \times x^{2m-2}$$

$\therefore \quad f'(x) = 0$

$$\Rightarrow -2n \times x^{2m-1} \times (a-x)^{2n-1} + (2m-1)(a-x)^{2n} \times x^{2m-2} = 0$$

$$\Rightarrow 2n \times x^{2m-1} \times (a-x)^{2n-1} = (2m-1)(a-x)^{2n} \times x^{2m-2}$$

$$\Rightarrow \frac{(a-x)^{2n-1}}{(a-x)^{2n}} = \frac{(2m-1)x^{2m-2}}{2n \times x^{2m-1}}$$

$$\Rightarrow (a-x)^{-1} = \frac{2m-1}{2n} \times x^{2m-2-2m+1}$$

$$\Rightarrow (a-x)^{-1} = \frac{2m-1}{2n} \times x^{-1}$$

$$\Rightarrow \quad \frac{1}{a-x} = \frac{2m-1}{2n} \times \frac{1}{x} \Rightarrow a-x = \frac{2nx}{2m-1}$$

$$\Rightarrow \quad a - x = \frac{2nx}{2m-1}$$

$$\Rightarrow \quad a = x + \frac{2nx}{2m-1} \Rightarrow a = x\left[1+\frac{2n}{2m-1}\right]$$

$$\Rightarrow \quad a = x\left[\frac{2m+2n-1}{2m-1}\right]$$

$$\therefore \quad x = \frac{a(2m-1)}{2m+2n-1}$$

Thus, $c = \dfrac{a(2m-1)}{2m+2n-1} \in (0, a)$ such that $f'(c) = 0$

Hence, Rolle's theorem is verified.

110. Let A be an aeroplane flying at a height of 3000 m above the ground, and D passes vertically above another plane at an instant. The angle of elevation of A and D from the same point at C on the ground are 60° and 45° respectively.

Then, the height of the lower plane = h = ?

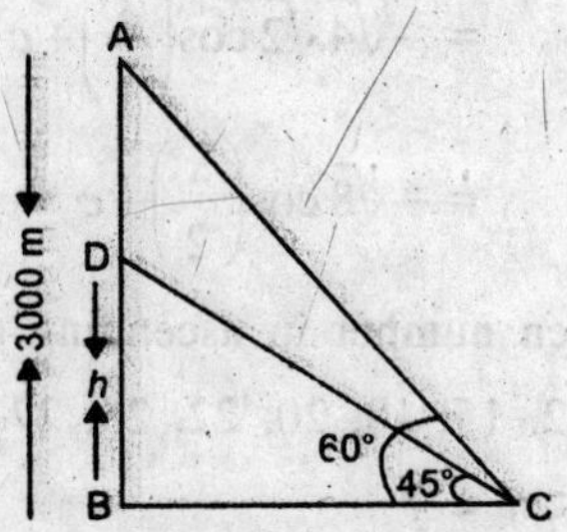

In ΔABC,

$$\tan 60° = \frac{AB}{BC}$$

$$\Rightarrow \quad \sqrt{3} = \frac{3000 \text{ m}}{BC}$$

$$\Rightarrow \quad BC = \frac{3000}{\sqrt{3}} = \frac{1000 \times 3}{\sqrt{3}} = 1000\sqrt{3} \text{ m}$$

and, In ΔDBC

$$\tan 45° = \frac{DB}{BC}$$

$$\Rightarrow \quad 1 = \frac{h}{BC} \Rightarrow h = BC$$

$$\Rightarrow \quad h = 1000\sqrt{3} \text{ m}$$

$$= 100 \times 10\sqrt{3} \text{ m}$$

$$= 100 \times 1\sqrt{00} \times \sqrt{3} \text{ m}$$

$$= 100\sqrt{300} \text{ m}$$

Hence, the height of the lower plane

$$h = 100\sqrt{300} \text{ m}$$

116. Given $\quad y = \dfrac{(x-1)(x^2-2x)}{x^4}$

$$\therefore \quad \frac{dy}{dx} = \frac{x^4 \dfrac{d\{(x-1)(x^2-2x)\}}{dx} - (x-1)(x^2-2x)\dfrac{d(x^4)}{dx}}{(x^4)^2}$$

$$\Rightarrow \quad \frac{dy}{dx} = \frac{x^4\left[(x-1)\dfrac{d(x^2-2x)}{dx} + (x^2-2x)\dfrac{d(x-1)}{dx}\right] - (x-1)(x^2-2m)\times 4x^3}{x^8}$$

$$\Rightarrow \quad \frac{dy}{dx} = \frac{x^4[(x-1)(2x-2)+(x^2-2x)(1-0)] - 4x^3(x-1)(x^2-2x)}{x^8}$$

$$\Rightarrow \quad \frac{dy}{dx} = \frac{x^4[2x^2-2x-2x+2+x^2-2x] - 4x^3(x^3-2x^2-x^2+2x)}{x^8}$$

$$\Rightarrow \quad \frac{dy}{dx} = \frac{x^4[3x^2-6x+2] - 4x^3(x^3-3x^2+2x)}{x^8}$$

$$\Rightarrow \quad \frac{dy}{dx} = \frac{3x^6-6x^5+2x^4-4x^6+12x^5-8x^4}{x^8}$$

$$\Rightarrow \quad \frac{dy}{dx} = \frac{-x^6+6x^5-6x^4}{x^8} \Rightarrow \frac{dy}{dx} = \frac{-x^6}{x^8} + \frac{6x^5}{x^8} - \frac{6x^4}{x^8}$$

$$\Rightarrow \quad \frac{dy}{dx} = -x^{-2} + 6x^{-3} - 6x^{-4}$$

Hence, the first derivative of y with respect to x is

$$\frac{dy}{dx} = -x^{-2} + 6x^{-3} - 6x^{-4}$$

137. Let $\vec{a} = 2\hat{i} - \hat{j} - 2\hat{k}$

Then, $|\vec{a}| = \sqrt{(2)^2 + (-1)^2 + (-2)^2}$

$= \sqrt{4+1+4} = \sqrt{9} = 3$

$\therefore$ The unit vector in the direction of $\vec{a}$

$= \hat{a} = \dfrac{\vec{a}}{|\vec{a}|} = \dfrac{2\hat{i} - \hat{j} - 2\hat{k}}{3}$

$= \dfrac{1}{3}(2\hat{i} - \hat{j} - 2\hat{k})$

140. Let $I = \int \dfrac{\sin x}{\sqrt{1+\cos x}}\,dx$

$$= \int \frac{2\sin\left(\frac{x}{2}\right)\cos\left(\frac{x}{2}\right)dx}{\sqrt{2\cos^2\left(\frac{x}{2}\right)}}$$

$$= \int \frac{2\sin\frac{x}{2}\cos\left(\frac{x}{2}\right)}{\sqrt{2}\times\cos\left(\frac{x}{2}\right)}dx$$

$$\left[\sin\theta = 2\sin\frac{\theta}{2}\cos\frac{\theta}{2}, 1+\cos\theta = 2\cos^2\frac{\theta}{2}\right]$$

$$= \int\sqrt{2}\sin\left(\frac{x}{2}\right)dx$$

$$= \sqrt{2}\int\sin\left(\frac{x}{2}\right)dx$$

$$= \sqrt{2}\times -\frac{\cos\left(\frac{x}{2}\right)}{\frac{1}{2}} + c$$

$$= -2\sqrt{2}\cos\left(\frac{x}{2}\right) + c$$

$$= -\sqrt{4}\sqrt{2}\cos\left(\frac{x}{2}\right) + c$$

$$= -\sqrt{8}\cos\left(\frac{x}{2}\right) + c$$

150. The given number in ascending order

12, 15, 18, 20, 22, 25, 27

Here, $n = 7$

$\therefore$ Median $= \dfrac{n+1}{2}th$ term

$= \dfrac{7+1}{2} = 4th$

$\therefore$ Median = 20

172. Total number of balls = 4 + 5 + 6 = 15

the number of red balls = 5

As three balls are drawn at random

$\therefore \quad n(S) = {}^{15}C_3 = \dfrac{\lfloor 15}{\lfloor 3 \lfloor 15-3} = \dfrac{\lfloor 15}{\lfloor 3 \lfloor 12}$

$= \dfrac{15 \times 14 \times 13 \lfloor 12}{3 \times 2 \times 1 \lfloor 12}$

$= 5 \times 7 \times 13$

and three red balls are drawn

$\therefore \quad n(E) = {}^{5}C_3 = \dfrac{\lfloor 5}{\lfloor 3 \lfloor 5-3} = \dfrac{\lfloor 5}{\lfloor 3 \lfloor 2}$

$= \dfrac{5 \times 4 \times 3 \times 2 \times 1}{3 \times 2 \times 1 \times 2} = 10$

$\therefore$ The probability all of them are red

$= \dfrac{n(E)}{n(S)} = \dfrac{10}{5 \times 7 \times 13} = \dfrac{2}{91}$

Previous Paper (Solved)

DSSSB—TEACHERS PGT MATHS EXAM, 2015*

1. If a and b are positive integers such that $a^2 - b^2$ is a prime number, then $a^2 - b^2$ is equal to:
(*a*) $a - b$ (*b*) $a + b$
(*c*) $(a + b)(a - b)$ (*d*) None of these

2. The remainder when 0! + 1! + 2! + ... +99! + 100! divided by 12 is:
(*a*) 6 (*b*) 5
(*c*) 11 (*d*) 10

3. The value of x satisfying $3x = 4 \pmod 5$ is:
(*a*) 3 (*b*) 1
(*c*) 2 (*d*) 5

4. The last digit of 6^{500} is:
(*a*) 5 (*b*) 7
(*c*) 6 (*d*) 4

5. The domain of the function $f: R \to R$ defined by $f(x) = \sqrt{x^2 - 3x + 2}$ is:
(*a*) $(-\infty, \infty)$
(*b*) $(1, 2)$
(*c*) $(-\infty, 1) \cup (2, \infty)$
(*d*) None of these

6. Let, $f: R \to R$ be the function defined by $f(x) = \dfrac{1}{2 - \cos x}$ for all $x \in R$. Then the range of f is:
(*a*) $[-1, 1]$ (*b*) $\left[\dfrac{1}{3}, 1\right]$
(*c*) $(-\infty, \infty)$ (*d*) $\dfrac{R}{\{0\}}$

7. Let, $f: [0, 1] \to [0, 1]$ be defined by
$$f(x) = \begin{cases} x, & \text{if } x \text{ is rational} \\ 1 - x, & \text{if } x \text{ is irrational} \end{cases}$$
then $(f\,.\,f)(x)$ is:
(*a*) Constant (*b*) $1 + x$
(*c*) x (*d*) None of these

8. Let, $f: R \to R$ be defined by
$$f(x) = \begin{cases} 2x & \text{if } x > 3 \\ x^2 & \text{if } 1 < x \le 3 \\ 3x & \text{if } x \le 1 \end{cases}$$
then, $f(-1) + f(2) + f(4)$ is:
(*a*) 14 (*b*) 5
(*c*) 8 (*d*) 9

9. Let, $f: R \to R$ be defined by $f(x) = x^2 + 1$. Then, pre-image of 17 is:
(*a*) $(4, -4)$ (*b*) $(3, -3)$
(*c*) $(2, -2)$ (*d*) None of these

10. If $\sin\theta$ and $\cos\theta$ are the roots of the equation $ax^2 - bx + c = 0$, then a, b and c satisfy the relation:
(*a*) $a^2 + b^2 + 2ac = 0$ (*b*) $a^2 - b^2 + 2ac = 0$
(*c*) $a^2 + c^2 + 2ab = 0$ (*d*) $a^2 - b^2 - 2ac = 0$

11. If $\sin\theta + \cos\theta = 1$, then the value of $\sin 2\theta$ is equal to:
(*a*) 1 (*b*) $\dfrac{1}{2}$
(*c*) 0 (*d*) -1

12. The value of $\cos^{-1}\left(\cos\dfrac{3\pi}{2}\right)$ is equal to:
(*a*) $\dfrac{\pi}{2}$ (*b*) $\dfrac{3\pi}{2}$
(*c*) $\dfrac{5\pi}{2}$ (*d*) $\dfrac{7\pi}{2}$

13. The value of $\cot(\sin^{-1} x)$ is:
(*a*) $\dfrac{\sqrt{1+x^2}}{x}$ (*b*) $\dfrac{x}{\sqrt{1+x^2}}$
(*c*) $\dfrac{1}{x}$ (*d*) $\dfrac{\sqrt{1-x^2}}{x}$

* Tier-I Exam

14. The order and degree of the differential equation $\left[1+\left(\frac{dy}{dx}\right)^2\right]^2 = \frac{d^2y}{dx^2}$ respectively are:

(*a*) 1, 2 (*b*) 2, 2
(*c*) 2, 1 (*d*) 4, 2

15. The integrating factor of the differential equation $\frac{dy}{dx}(x\log x) + y = 2\log x$ is:

(*a*) e^x (*b*) $\log x$
(*c*) $\log(\log x)$ (*d*) x

16. Solution of differential equation $xdy - ydx = 0$ represents:

(*a*) A rectangular hyperbola
(*b*) Parabola whose vertex is at origin
(*c*) Straight line passing through origin
(*d*) A circle whose centre is at origin

17. If $y = e^{-x}$ (A cos x + B sin x), then y is a solution of:

(*a*) $\frac{d^2y}{dx^2} + 2\frac{dy}{dx} = 0$

(*b*) $\frac{d^2y}{dx^2} - 2\frac{dy}{dx} + 2y = 0$

(*c*) $\frac{d^2y}{dx^2} + 2\frac{dy}{dx} + 2y = 0$

(*d*) $\frac{d^2y}{dx^2} + 2y = 0$

18. The differential equation of the family of curves $x^2 + y^2 - 2ay = 0$, where a is arbitrary constant, is:

(*a*) $(x^2 - y^2)\frac{dy}{dx} = 2xy$

(*b*) $2(x^2 + y^2)\frac{dy}{dx} = xy$

(*c*) $2(x^2 - y^2)\frac{dy}{dx} = xy$

(*d*) $(x^2 + y^2)\frac{dy}{dx} = 2xy$

19. Two finite sets have m and n elements respectively. The total number of subsets of first set is 56 more than the total number of the second set. The values of m and n respectively are:

(*a*) 7, 6 (*b*) 5, 1
(*c*) 6, 3 (*d*) 8, 7

20. Let, F_1 be the set of parallelograms, F_2 the set of rectangles, F_3 the set of rhombuses, F_4 the set of squares and F_5 the set of trapeziums in a plane. Then, F_1 may be equal to:

(*a*) $F_2 \cap F_3$
(*b*) $F_3 \cap F_4$
(*c*) $F_2 \cup F_5$
(*d*) $F_2 \cup F_3 \cup F_4 \cup F_1$

21. Let, x and y be real numbers and

$A = \{(x, y) | y = \frac{1}{x}, x \neq 0\}$, $B = \{(x, y) | y = -x\}$

be two sets. Then:

(*a*) $A \cap B = A$ (*b*) $A \cap B = \phi$
(*c*) $A \cap B = B$ (*d*) $A \cup B = A$

22. In a town of 840 persons, 450 persons read Hindi, 300 read English and 200 read both. Then, the number of persons who read neither is:

(*a*) 210 (*b*) 180
(*c*) 260 (*d*) 290

23. Let, $n(A) = m$ and $n(B) = n$. Then, the total number of non-empty relations that can be defined from A to B is:

(*a*) m^n (*b*) $n^m - 1$
(*c*) $mn - 1$ (*d*) $2^{mn} - 1$

24. If $[x]^2 - 5[x] + 6 = 0$, where [.] denote the greatest integer function, then:

(*a*) $x \in [3, 4]$ (*b*) $x \in (2, 3]$
(*c*) $x \in [2, 4)$ (*d*) $x \in [2, 3]$

25. If $x^n - 1$ is divisible by $x - K$, then the least positive integral value of K is:

(*a*) 1 (*b*) 2
(*c*) 3 (*d*) 4

26. If $f = \{(-1, -5), (1, -1), (3, 3)\}$ is a function described by $f(x) = ax + b$, then the values of a and b are:

(*a*) −3, −1 (*b*) 2, −3
(*c*) 0, 2 (*d*) 2, 3

27. The value of $^{10}C_1 + ^{10}C_2 + ^{10}C_3 + ... + ^{10}C_9$ is:

(*a*) 2^{10} (*b*) 2^{11}
(*c*) $2^{10} - 2$ (*d*) $2^{10} - 1$

28. Everybody in a room shakes hands with everybody else. The total number of handshakes is 66. The total number of persons in the room is:

(*a*) 11 (*b*) 12
(*c*) 13 (*d*) 14

29. The total number of 9 digit numbers which have all different digits is:

(*a*) 10! (*b*) 9!
(*c*) 9 × 9! (*d*) 10 × 10!

30. The sum $^nC_r + ^nC_{r-1}$ is equal to:

(*a*) $^{n+1}C_r$ (*b*) $^nC_{r+1}$
(*c*) $^{n+1}C_{r+1}$ (*d*) None of these

31. The total number of terms in the expansion of $(x + a)^{51} - (x - a)^{51}$ after simplification is:

(*a*) 102 (*b*) 25
(*c*) 26 (*d*) None of these

32. The 10th common term between the series 3 + 7 + 11 + ... and 1 + 6 + 11 + ... is:

(*a*) 191 (*b*) 193
(*c*) 211 (*d*) None of these

33. If $|x + 3| \geq 10$, then

(*a*) $x \in (-13, 7]$
(*b*) $x \in (-13, 10]$
(*c*) $x \in (-\infty, -13] \cup (7, \infty]$
(*d*) $x \in (-7, 7]$

34. Let A = $\{x \in R \,|\, x^2 > x \div 6\}$ and B = $\{x \in R \,|\, x > 3\}$. Which of the following is true?

(*a*) $A \subseteq B$ (*b*) $B \subseteq A$
(*c*) A = B (*d*) $A \cap B = \phi$

35. Number of solutions of the equation $Z^2 + |Z|^2 = 0$ is

(*a*) 1 (*b*) 2
(*c*) 3 (*d*) infinitely many

36. If $a + ib = c + id$, then

(*a*) $a^2 + c^2 = 0$ (*b*) $b^2 + c^2 = 0$
(*c*) $b^2 + d^2 = 0$ (*d*) $a^2 + b^2 = c^2 + d^2$

37. If $|Z^2 - 1| = |Z|^2 + 1$, then Z lies on

(*a*) Circle (*b*) Real axis
(*c*) Imaginary axis (*d*) Ellipse

38. The value of $\dfrac{i^{4n+1} - i^{4n-1}}{2}$, where $i = \sqrt{-1}$, is

(*a*) 1 (*b*) i
(*c*) $-i$ (*d*) None of these

39. If ω is a cube root of unity then ω is equal to

(*a*) 3 (*b*) $\dfrac{1 - i\sqrt{3}}{2}$
(*c*) $\dfrac{1 + i\sqrt{3}}{2}$ (*d*) $\dfrac{-1 + i\sqrt{3}}{2}$

40. If $|Z + 4| = 3$ then the maximum value $|Z + 1|$ is

(*a*) 10 (*b*) 4
(*c*) 0 (*d*) 6

41. The locus of a point for which $x = 0$ is

(*a*) xy – plane (*b*) yz – plane
(*c*) zx – plane (*d*) None of these

42. The perpendicular distance of the point P(6, 7, 8) from xy – plane is

(*a*) 8 (*b*) 7
(*c*) 6 (*d*) None of these

43. If α, β, γ are the angles that a line makes with the positive direction of x, y, z axis respectively, then the direction cosine of the lines are

(*a*) sin α, sin β, sin γ
(*b*) cos α, cos β, cos γ
(*c*) tan α, tan β, tan γ
(*d*) $\cos^2 \alpha, \cos^2 \beta, \cos^2 \gamma$

44. The reflection of the point (α, β, γ) in the xy–plane is

(*a*) (α, β, 0) (*b*) (0, 0, γ)
(*c*) (–α, –β, γ) (*d*) (α, β, –γ)

45. If $\hat{i}, \hat{j}$ and $\hat{k}$ are unit vectors. The value of $\hat{i}.(\hat{j} \times \hat{k}) + \hat{j}.(\hat{i} \times \hat{k}) + \hat{k}.(\hat{i} \times \hat{j})$ is

(*a*) 0 (*b*) –1
(*c*) 1 (*d*) 3

46. If θ is the angle between any two vectors $\vec{a}$ and $\vec{b}$, then $|\vec{a}.\vec{b}| = |\vec{a} \times \vec{b}|$ when θ is equal to

(a) 0 (b) $\frac{\pi}{4}$

(c) $\frac{\pi}{2}$ (d) π

47. The point (4, 1) undergoes the following two successive transformations

(i) Reflection about the line $y = x$

(ii) Translation through a distance 2 units along the positive x-axis

Then the final coordinates of the point are

(a) (4, 3) (b) (3, 4)

(c) (1, 4) (d) $\left(\frac{1}{2}, \frac{7}{2}\right)$

48. A point equidistant from the lines $4x + 3y + 10 = 0$, $5x - 12y + 26 = 0$ and $7x + 24y - 50 = 0$ is

(a) (1, –1) (b) (1, 1)

(c) (0, 0) (d) (0, 1)

49. The area of the circle centred at (1, 2) and passing through (4, 6) is

(a) 5 π (b) 10 π

(c) 25 π (d) None of these

50. The function $f(x) = [x]$, where [.] denotes the greatest integer function, is continuous at

(a) 4 (b) –2

(c) 1 (d) 1.5

51. The function $f(x) = \frac{4-x^2}{4x-x^3}$ is discontinuous at

(a) Only one point

(b) Exactly two points

(c) Exactly three points

(d) None of these

52. The maximum value of $\sin x + \cos x$ is

(a) 2 (b) 1

(c) $\sqrt{2}$ (d) 0

53. Which of the following function is decreasing on $\left(0, \frac{\pi}{2}\right)$?

(a) $\sin 2x$ (b) $\tan x$

(c) $\cos x$ (d) $\cos 3x$

54. The two curves $x^3 - 3xy^2 + 2 = 0$ and $3x^2y - y^3 = 2$

(a) touch each other

(b) cut at right angle

(c) cut at an angle $\frac{\pi}{3}$

(d) cut at an angle $\frac{\pi}{4}$

55. If x is real, the minimum value of $x^2 - 8x + 17$ is

(a) –1 (b) 0

(c) 1 (d) 2

56. The function $f(x) = 2x^3 - 3x^2 - 12x + 4$, has

(a) two points of local maximum

(b) two points of local minimum

(c) one maxima and one minima

(d) no maxima or minima

57. If $\int_0^1 \frac{e^t}{1+t} dt = a$, then $\int_0^1 \frac{e^t}{1+t^2} dt$ is equal to

(a) $a-1+\frac{e}{2}$ (b) $a+1-\frac{e}{2}$

(c) $a-1-\frac{e}{2}$ (d) $a+1+\frac{e}{2}$

58. The area of the region bounded by the curve $y = x^2$ and the line $y = 4$ is

(a) $\frac{32}{3}$ (b) $\frac{64}{3}$

(c) $\frac{256}{3}$ (d) $\frac{128}{3}$

59. If A and B are matrices of same order, then $(AB^T - BA^T)$ is a

(a) skew symmetric matrix

(b) null matrix

(c) symmetric matrix

(d) unit matrix

60. If A and B are square matrices of the same order, then (A + B) (A –B) is equal to

(a) $A^2 - B^2$

(b) $A^2 - BA - AB - B^2$

(c) $A^2 - B^2 + BA - AB$

(d) $A^2 - BA + B^2 + AB$

61. If matrix $A = [a_{ij}]_{3\times3}$ where $a_{ij} = \begin{matrix} 1 & \text{if } i \neq j \\ 0 & \text{if } i = j \end{matrix}$

then A^2 is equal to

(*a*) *i* (*b*) A

(*c*) O (*d*) None of these

62. If A is skew symmetric matrix, then A^2 is a

(*a*) null matrix

(*b*) unitary matrix

(*c*) skew symmetric matrix

(*d*) symmetric matrix

63. If A and B are invertible matrices, then which of the following is not correct?

(*a*) adj A = |A| . A^{-1}

(*b*) det $(A)^{-1} = [\det(A)]^{-1}$

(*c*) $(AB)^{-1} = B^{-1}A^{-1}$

(*d*) $(A + B)^{-1} = B^{-1} + A^{-1}$

64. If A, B and C are angles of a triangle, then the determinant $\begin{vmatrix} -1 & \cos C & \cos B \\ \cos C & -1 & \cos A \\ \cos B & \cos A & -1 \end{vmatrix}$ is equal to

(*a*) 1 (*b*) 0

(*c*) –1 (*d*) None of these

65. If A is a square matrix such that $A^2 = 1$, then $(A - 1)^3 + (A + 1)^3 - 7A$ is

(*a*) A (*b*) 1 – A

(*c*) 1 + A (*d*) 3A

66. $\lim\limits_{x\to0} \frac{|x|}{x}$ is equal to

(*a*) 1 (*b*) –1

(*c*) 0 (*d*) Does not exists

67. $\lim\limits_{n\to\infty} \frac{1+2+3+...+n}{n^2}$, $n \in N$ is equal to

(*a*) 0 (*b*) 1

(*c*) $\frac{1}{2}$ (*d*) $\frac{1}{4}$

68. Value of the $\lim\limits_{x\to0} x \sin\frac{1}{x}$ is equal to

(*a*) 1 (*b*) 0

(*c*) Not defined (*d*) None of these

69. The radius of convergence R of the series $\sum_{n=0}^{\infty}(n+1)x^n$ is

(*a*) infinite radius (*b*) 1

(*c*) 0 (*d*) None of these

70. Which of the following is not an indeterminate form?

(*a*) $\infty + \infty$ (*b*) $\infty - \infty$

(*c*) ∞ / ∞ (*d*) $0 \times \infty$

71. Value of the integral $\int_1^2\int_0^x (x+2y)dy\,dx$ is

(*a*) $\frac{14}{3}$ (*b*) $\frac{12}{5}$

(*c*) $\frac{8}{3}$ (*d*) $\frac{3}{14}$

72. If $f(z) = u(x, y) + iv(x, y)$, then Cauchy-Riemann equations are

(*a*) $\frac{\partial u}{\partial x} = \frac{\partial u}{\partial y}$ and $\frac{\partial v}{\partial x} = \frac{-\partial v}{\partial y}$

(*b*) $\frac{\partial u}{\partial x} = \frac{\partial v}{\partial y}$ and $\frac{\partial u}{\partial y} = \frac{-\partial v}{\partial x}$

(*c*) $\frac{\partial u}{\partial x} = \frac{\partial v}{\partial x}$ and $\frac{\partial u}{\partial y} = \frac{-\partial v}{\partial y}$

(*d*) None of these

73. Laplace transform of the function $f(t) = e^{2t} + \cos^{3t}$ is

(*a*) $\frac{1}{s+2} + \frac{3}{s^2+9}$ (*b*) $\frac{1}{s-2} + \frac{s}{s^2+9}$

(*c*) $\frac{1}{s+2} + \frac{s}{s^2-3}$ (*d*) None of these

74. A real valued bounded function $f(x)$ is Riemann integrable on $[a, b]$, then

(*a*) $\int_{-a}^{b} f(x)dx$ and $\int_{a}^{-b} f(x)dx$ exist

(*b*) $\int_{-a}^{b} f(x)dx \neq \int_{a}^{-b} f(x)dx$

(c) $\int_{-a}^{b} f(x)dx = \int_{a}^{-b} f(x)dx$

(d) None of these

75. The rank of a matrix $\begin{bmatrix} 1 & 2 & 3 \\ 2 & 4 & 7 \\ 3 & 6 & 10 \end{bmatrix}$ is

(a) 1 (b) 2
(c) 3 (d) None of these

76. The dimension of the vector space of all 3×3 real matrices is

(a) 3 (b) 9
(c) 6 (d) 4

77. Let V be the vector space of functions on the interval [0, 1]. Then the functions x^3, sin x and cos x are

(a) Linearly dependent
(b) Linearly independent
(c) Data are insufficient
(d) None of these

78. If S = {(1, 1, 0), (2, 1, 3)} is a subset of $\mathbb{R}^3$ then which one of the following vectors of $\mathbb{R}^3$ is not in the linear span of S?

(a) (0, 0, 0) (b) (3, 2, 3)
(c) (1, 2, 3) (d) $\left(\frac{4}{3}, 1, 1\right)$

79. Let T : $\mathbb{R}^3 \to \mathbb{R}^2$ be a linear transformation defined by T(x, y, z) = ($x + y$, $y + z$). Then dimension of nullspace of T is

(a) 1 (b) 2
(c) 0 (d) None of these

80. Dimension of a subspace W = $\{(a, b, c) \mid a + b + c = 0\}$ of $\mathbb{R}^3$ is

(a) 4 (b) 3
(c) 1 (d) 2

81. Which of the following is uniformly continuous in $(0, \infty)$?

(a) $f(x) = \sin\frac{1}{x}$ (b) $f(x) = \frac{1}{x}$
(c) $f(x) = \frac{1}{x^2}$ (d) None of these

82. Standard deviations for first 10 natural numbers is

(a) 5.5 (b) 3.87
(c) 2.97 (d) 2.87

83. Mean of five observations is 4 and their variance is 5.2. If three of them are 1, 2, 6 then other two are

(a) 2, 9 (b) 5, 6
(c) 2, 10 (d) 4, 7

84. The mean of 100 observations is 30. If two observations were wrongly taken as 32 and 12 instead of 23 and 11, then the correct mean is

(a) 29.9 (b) 28.9
(c) 25 (d) None of these

85. In a leap year the probability of having 53 Sundays or 53 Mondays is

(a) $\frac{2}{7}$ (b) $\frac{3}{7}$
(c) $\frac{4}{7}$ (d) $\frac{5}{7}$

86. The probability that in a family of 5 members, exactly two members have birthday on Sunday, is

(a) $\frac{12 \times 5^3}{7^5}$ (b) $\frac{10 \times 6^2}{7^5}$
(c) $\frac{2}{5}$ (d) $\frac{10 \times 6^3}{7^5}$

87. A coin is tossed 3 times. The probability of getting head and tail alternatively is

(a) $\frac{1}{4}$ (b) $\frac{1}{8}$
(c) $\frac{1}{2}$ (d) $\frac{3}{8}$

88. If the events A and B are independent, then $P(A \cap B)$ is equal to

(a) $P(A) + P(B)$ (b) $P(A) - P(B)$
(c) $P(A) . P(B)$ (d) $P(A) \mid P(B)$

89. A bag contains 5 red and 3 blue balls. If 3 balls are drawn at random without replacement. The probability of getting exactly one red ball is

(a) $\frac{45}{196}$ (b) $\frac{135}{392}$
(c) $\frac{15}{56}$ (d) $\frac{15}{29}$

90. In a frequency distribution, the mean and median are 21 and 22 respectively, then its mode is approximately

(a) 20.5 (b) 25.5
(c) 24 (d) 22

91. How many terms of the G.P. $3, \frac{3}{2}, \frac{3}{4}, \ldots,$ are needed to give the sum $\frac{3069}{512}$?

(a) 8 (b) 10
(c) 9 (d) None of these

92. Number of subsets of a finite set with n elements are

(a) 2^n (b) $n!$
(c) n^2 (d) n^n

93. If $f(x)$ is an even function, then $f'(x)$ is

(a) an odd function
(b) an even function
(c) may be even or may be odd
(d) None of these

94. The remainder when $10^{10}.(10^{10} + 1)(10^{10} + 2)$ is divided by 6 is

(a) 2 (b) 4
(c) 0 (d) 6

95. The power series $\sum_{n=0}^{\infty} \frac{[2+(-1)^n]^n}{3^n} x^n$ converges

(a) only for $x = 0$
(b) for all $x \in \mathbb{R}$
(c) only for $-1 < x < 1$
(d) only for $-1 < x \leq 1$

96. Let $T : \mathbb{R}^n \to \mathbb{R}^n$ be a linear transformation. Which of the following statements implies that T is bijective?

(a) Nullity (T) = n
(b) Rank (T) = Nullity (T) = n
(c) Rank (T) + Nullity (T) = n
(d) Rank (T) – Nullity (T) = n

97. A linear transformation T rotates each vector in $\mathbb{R}^2$ clockwise through 90°. The matrix T relative to the standard ordered basis $\left(\begin{bmatrix}1\\0\end{bmatrix}, \begin{bmatrix}0\\1\end{bmatrix}\right)$ is

(a) $\begin{bmatrix}0 & -1\\-1 & 0\end{bmatrix}$ (b) $\begin{bmatrix}0 & 1\\-1 & 0\end{bmatrix}$
(c) $\begin{bmatrix}0 & 1\\1 & 0\end{bmatrix}$ (d) $\begin{bmatrix}0 & -1\\1 & 0\end{bmatrix}$

98. The limit of the sequence 0.5, 0.55, 0.555, ..., is

(a) $\frac{5}{9}$ (b) 5
(c) $\frac{9}{5}$ (d) None of these

99. Value of the $\lim_{n\to\infty} n[\log(n+1) - \log n]$ is

(a) e (b) 1
(c) 0 (d) None of these

100. A line makes equal angles with co-ordinate axis. Direction cosines of this line are

(a) $\pm(1, 1, 1)$
(b) $\pm\left(\frac{1}{\sqrt{3}}, \frac{1}{\sqrt{3}}, \frac{1}{\sqrt{3}}\right)$
(c) $\pm\left(\frac{1}{3}, \frac{1}{3}, \frac{1}{3}\right)$
(d) $\pm\left(\frac{1}{\sqrt{3}}, \frac{-1}{\sqrt{3}}, \frac{-1}{\sqrt{3}}\right)$

ANSWERS

1	2	3	4	5	6	7	8	9	10
(*b*)	(*d*)	(*a*)	(*c*)	(*c*)	(*b*)	(*c*)	(*d*)	(*a*)	(*b*)
11	**12**	**13**	**14**	**15**	**16**	**17**	**18**	**19**	**20**
(*c*)	(*a*)	(*d*)	(*c*)	(*b*)	(*c*)	(*c*)	(*a*)	(*c*)	(*d*)
21	**22**	**23**	**24**	**25**	**26**	**27**	**28**	**29**	**30**
(*b*)	(*d*)	(*d*)	(*c*)	(*a*)	(*b*)	(*c*)	(*b*)	(*c*)	(*a*)
31	**32**	**33**	**34**	**35**	**36**	**37**	**38**	**39**	**40**
(*c*)	(*a*)	(*c*)	(*b*)	(*d*)	(*d*)	(*c*)	(*b*)	(*d*)	(*d*)
41	**42**	**43**	**44**	**45**	**46**	**47**	**48**	**49**	**50**
(*b*)	(*a*)	(*b*)	(*d*)	(*c*)	(*b*)	(*b*)	(*c*)	(*c*)	(*d*)
51	**52**	**53**	**54**	**55**	**56**	**57**	**58**	**59**	**60**
(*c*)	(*c*)	(*c*)	(*b*)	(*c*)	(*c*)	(*b*)	(*a*)	(*a*)	(*c*)
61	**62**	**63**	**64**	**65**	**66**	**67**	**68**	**69**	**70**
(*a*)	(*d*)	(*d*)	(*b*)	(*a*)	(*d*)	(*c*)	(*b*)	(*b*)	(*a*)
71	**72**	**73**	**74**	**75**	**76**	**77**	**78**	**79**	**80**
(*a*)	(*b*)	(*b*)	(*c*)	(*b*)	(*b*)	(*b*)	(*c*)	(*a*)	(*d*)
81	**82**	**83**	**84**	**85**	**86**	**87**	**88**	**89**	**90**
(*c*)	(*d*)	(*d*)	(*a*)	(*b*)	(*d*)	(*a*)	(*c*)	(*c*)	(*c*)
91	**92**	**93**	**94**	**95**	**96**	**97**	**98**	**99**	**100**
(*b*)	(*a*)	(*a*)	(*c*)	(*c*)	(*d*)	(*b*)	(*a*)	(*b*)	(*b*)

SOME SELECTED EXPLANATORY ANSWERS

1. Let $a = 3$ and $b = 2$

$\therefore$

$$a^2 - b^2 = (3)^2 - (2)^2 = 9 - 4 = 5 \quad ...(i)$$

$$a + b = 3 + 2 = 5 \quad ...(ii)$$

Hence, $a^2 - b^2 = a + b$.

2. $\lfloor 0 + \lfloor 1 + \lfloor 2 + \lfloor 3 + \lfloor 4$

$= 1 + 1 + 2 + 6 + 24 = 34$

$34 \div 12$ gives remainder $= 10$

$\lfloor 0 + \lfloor 1 + \lfloor 2 + \lfloor 3 + \lfloor 4 + \lfloor 5 = 34 + 120 = 154$

$154 \div 12$ gives remainder $= 10$

$\lfloor 0 + \lfloor 1 + \lfloor 2 + \lfloor 3 + \lfloor 4 + \lfloor 5 + \lfloor 6 = 154 + 720 = 874$

$874 \div 12$ gives remainder $= 10$

Similarly,

$\lfloor 0 + \lfloor 1 + \lfloor 2 + \lfloor 3 + \lfloor 4 + ... \lfloor 99 + \lfloor 100$ is divided by 12 gives remainder = 10.

4. Digit at unit place

$6^1 = 6$

$6^2 = 36$

$6^3 = 216$

....

$6^{500} = ...6$

Hence, last digit of 6^{500} is 6.

5. Domain of function f,

$x^2 - 3x + 2 \geq 0$

$(x - 2)(x - 1) \geq 0$

$x \in (-\infty, -1] \cup [2, \infty)$.

6. Range of function $f(x)$:

We know that

$-1 \le \cos x \le 1$

For $\cos x = 1$

$$f(x) = \frac{1}{2-1} = 1$$

For $\cos x = -1$

$$f(x) = \frac{1}{2-(-1)} = \frac{1}{3}$$

$$\frac{1}{3} \le \frac{1}{2-\cos x} \le 1$$

Hence, range of $f(x) = \left[\frac{1}{3}, 1\right]$.

7. When x is rational

$$(fof)(x) = f(f(x)) = f(x) = x$$

when x is irrational,

$$(fof)(x) = f(f(x)) = f(1-x) = 1-(1-x) = x$$

8. For $x = -1$, $f(x) = 3x$

$f(-1) = 3 \times (-1) = -3$

for $x = 2$, $f(x) = x^2$

$f(2) = (2)^2 = 4$

for $x = 4$, $f(x) = 2x$

$f(4) = 2 \times 4 = 8$

$\therefore\ f(-1) + f(2) + f(4) = -3 + 4 + 8 = 9.$

9. Pre-image = 17

$$x^2 + 1 = 17$$
$$x^2 = 16$$
$$x = \sqrt{16}$$
$$x = -4 \text{ or } 4.$$

10. Sum of roots

$$\sin\theta + \cos\theta = \frac{b}{a} \quad ...(i)$$

$$\sin\theta \,.\, \cos\theta = \frac{c}{a} \quad ...(ii)$$

from (*i*) and (*ii*)

$$(\sin\theta + \cos\theta)^2 = \left(\frac{b}{a}\right)^2$$

$$\sin^2\theta + \cos^2\theta + 2\sin\theta \,.\, \cos\theta = \frac{b^2}{a^2}$$

$$1 + \frac{2c}{a} = \frac{b^2}{a^2}$$

$$1 + \frac{2c}{a} - \frac{b^2}{a^2} = 0$$

$$a^2 - b^2 + 2ac = 0.$$

11. $\because \sin\theta + \cos\theta = 1$

$\therefore \sin 2\theta = 2\sin\theta \,.\, \cos\theta$

$(\sin\theta + \cos\theta)^2 = (1)^2$

$\Rightarrow \sin^2\theta + \cos^2\theta + 2\sin\theta \,.\, \cos\theta = 1$

$\Rightarrow 2\sin\theta \,.\, \cos\theta = 1 - 1 = 0$

$\Rightarrow \sin 2\theta = 0.$

12. $\cos^{-1}\cos\left(2\pi - \frac{\pi}{2}\right)$

$$\cos^{-1}.\cos\frac{\pi}{2} = \frac{\pi}{2}.$$

13. Let $\sin^{-1} x = \theta$

$\therefore \sin\theta = x$

$\cot(\sin^{-1} x) = \cot\theta$

Now, $\cot\theta = \dfrac{\cos\theta}{\sin\theta} = \dfrac{\sqrt{1-\sin^2\theta}}{\sin\theta}$

$$= \frac{\sqrt{1-x^2}}{x}.$$

22. $n(U) = 840$, $n(H) = 450$,

$n(E) = 300$, $n(H \cap E) = 200$

Required number

$= 840 - n(H \cup E)$

$= 840 - \{n(H) + n(E) - n(H \cap E)$

$= 840 - \{450 + 300 - 200\}$

$= 840 - 550$

$= 290.$

27. $^{10}C_1 + {}^{10}C_2 + {}^{10}C_3 + ... + {}^{10}C_9$

$= 10 + 45 + 120 + 210 + 252 + 210 + 120 + 45 + 10$

$= 2(10) + 2(45) + 2(120) + 2(210) + 252$

$= 20 + 90 + 240 + 420 + 252$

$= 110 + 660 + 252 = 1022 = 2^{10} - 2.$

28. Let n be the number of persons.

$\therefore$ Total number of hand shakes $= {}^nC_2$

By hypothesis,

$$\frac{n(n-1)}{2} = 66$$

$\Rightarrow \quad n^2 - n - 132 = 0$

$\Rightarrow \quad (n - 12)(n + 11) = 0$

$\Rightarrow \quad n = 12$

or $\quad n = -11$

$\therefore \quad n = 12$

Hence, number of persons = 12.

30. Let n and r be non-negative integers such that $r \leq n$.

Then, ${}^nC_r + {}^nC_{r-1}$

$$= \frac{n!}{r!(n-r)!} + \frac{n!}{(r-1)!(n+1-r)!}$$

$$= \frac{n!}{(r-1)!(n-r)!}\left[\frac{1}{r} + \frac{1}{(n+1-r)}\right]$$

$$= \frac{n!}{(r-1)!(n-r)!}\left[\frac{n+1-r+r}{r.(n+1-r)}\right]$$

$$= \frac{n!.(n+1)}{r.(r-1)!(n+1-r).(n-r)!}$$

$$= \frac{(n+1)!}{r!(n+1-r)!} = {}^{n+1}C_r.$$

31. $(x + a)^{51} - (x - a)^{51}$

$\because n = 51$ which is odd

$\therefore$ Total no. of terms in $(x + a)^{51} - (x - a)^{51}$

$$= \left(\frac{n+1}{2}\right) = \left(\frac{51+1}{2}\right) = 26.$$

32. $3 + 7 + 11 + 15 + 19 + 23 + 27 + 31 + ...$

$1 + 6 + 11 + 16 + 21 + 26 + 31 + ...$

First common term = 11

2nd common term = 31

3rd common term = 51

....

....

10th common term = 191.

39. $x^3 - 1 = 0 \quad \Rightarrow (x - 1)(x^2 + x + 1) = 0$

$x^2 + x + 1 = 0$

$$x = \frac{-b \pm \sqrt{D}}{2a}$$

$$= \frac{-1 \pm \sqrt{1-4}}{2}$$

$$= \frac{-1 \pm \sqrt{3}i}{2}$$

$$\omega = \frac{-1 + i\sqrt{3}}{2}$$

[Where ω = cube root of unity]

40. We have,

$\because |z + 4| = 3$

Now, $|z + 1| = |z + 4 - 3| = |z + 4| + |-3|$

$= 3 + 3 = 6.$

49. Area of circle $= \pi r^2$

where r is the distance between (1, 2) and (4, 6)

$$r = \sqrt{(4-1)^2 + (6-2)^2}$$

$$= \sqrt{9+16} = 5$$

$\therefore$ Required area of circle $= \pi(5)^2 = 25\,\pi.$

51. Here $f(x) = \dfrac{4-x^2}{x(4-x^2)}$

Since $f(x)$ does not exist at $x = 0, 2, -2$

$\therefore$ There are three points of discontinuity.

52. $\sin x + \cos x = \sqrt{2}\left(\frac{1}{\sqrt{2}}\sin x + \frac{1}{\sqrt{2}}\cos x\right)$

$= \sqrt{2}(\cos 45° \times \sin x + \sin 45° \times \cos x)$

$= \sqrt{2}[\sin(x+45°)]$ ...(*i*)

Since $-1 \leq \sin A \leq 1$

$\therefore -1 \leq \sin(x + 45°) \leq 1$

and $-\sqrt{2} \leq \sqrt{2}[\sin(x+45°)] \leq \sqrt{2}$

Thus least value of $\sin x + \cos x = -\sqrt{2}$

and greatest value of $\sin x + \cos x = \sqrt{2}$

Hence, the maximum value of $\sin x + \cos x$ $= \sqrt{2}$.

59. We have,

$$\begin{aligned}(AB - BA)^T &= (AB)^T - (BA)^T \\ &= B^TA^T - A^TB^T \\ &= BA - AB \quad [\because A^T = A, B^T = B], \\ &= -(AB - BA)\end{aligned}$$

So, AB – BA is Skew Symmetric matrix.

66. $\lim_{x\to 0} \frac{|x|}{x}$

$\text{LHL} = \lim_{h\to 0} \frac{|0-h|}{(0-h)} = \lim_{h\to 0} \frac{h}{-h} = -1$

$\text{RHL} = \lim_{h\to 0} \frac{|0+h|}{(0+h)} = \lim_{h\to 0} \frac{h}{h} = 1$

$\because$ LHL $\neq$ RHL

So, it does not exist.

67. $\lim_{n\to\infty} \frac{1+2+3+...+n}{n^2}$

$= \lim_{n\to\infty} \frac{n(n+1)}{2n^2} = \lim_{n\to\infty} \frac{n^2+n}{2n^2}$

$= \lim_{n\to\infty} \left(\frac{n^2}{2n^2} + \frac{n}{2n^2}\right)$

$= \left(\frac{1}{2} + 0\right) = \frac{1}{2}$.

82. Sum of first 10 natural numbers

$= 1 + 2 + 3 + 4 + 5 + 6 + 7 + 8 + 9 + 10 = 55$

$\bar{x} = \frac{1+2+3+4+5+6+7+8+9+10}{10}$

$= \frac{55}{10} = 5.5.$

x_i	$(x_i - \bar{x})$	$(x_i - \bar{x})^2$
1	1 – 5.5 = –4.5	20.25
2	2 – 5.5 = –3.5	12.25
3	3 – 5.5 = –2.5	6.25
4	4 – 5.5 = –1.5	2.25
5	5 – 5.5 = –.5	.25
6	6 – 5.5 = .5	.25
7	7 – 5.5 = 1.5	2.25
8	8 – 5.5 = 2.5	6.25
9	9 – 5.5 = 3.5	12.25
10	10 – 5.5 = 4.5	20.25
		82.50

Here, $n = 10$, $\sum(x_i - \bar{x})^2 = 82.50$

$\text{Variance} = \frac{82.50}{10} = 8.25$

$\text{SD} = \sqrt{8.25} = 2.87.$

83. Mean of 5 observation = 4

$\therefore$ Total number = 5 × 4 = 20

Let other two numbers are 4 and 7

$\bar{x} = \frac{1+2+6+4+7}{5} = \frac{20}{5} = 4$

$\text{Variance} = \frac{\sum(x_i - \bar{x})^2}{5}$

$\Rightarrow \quad 5.2 \times 5 = \sum(x_i - \bar{x})^2$

$= (1-4)^2 + (2-4)^2 + (6-4)^2 + (4-4)^2 + (7-4)^2$

$26 = 9 + 4 + 4 + 0 + 9 = 26$

Hence, other two numbers are 4 and 7.

84. Sum of 100 observations = 100 × 30 = 3000

Decrease number = (32 – 23) + (12 – 11)

= 9 + 1 = 10

New total number = 3000 – 10 = 2990

New mean = $\frac{2990}{100}$ = 29.9.

85. The leap year consists of 366 days and there are 52 complete weeks and 2 days over. These two days may have the following 7 pairs:

1. Monday and Tuesday
2. Tuesday and Wednesday
3. Wednesday and Thursday
4. Thursday and Friday
5. Friday and Saturday
6. Saturday and Sunday
7. Sunday and Monday

∵ 53 Sunday or 53 Monday are in 3 ways.

Hence, required probability = $\frac{3}{7}$.

87. Probability of head = probability of tail = $\frac{1}{2}$

$\therefore \quad P(HTH \text{ or } THT) = P(HTH) + P(THT)$

$= \frac{1}{2}\times\frac{1}{2}\times\frac{1}{2}+\frac{1}{2}\times\frac{1}{2}\times\frac{1}{2}$

$= \frac{2}{8}=\frac{1}{4}.$

90. Mode = 3 median – 2 mean

= 3 × 22 – 2 × 21

= 66 – 42

= 24.

91. $\because 3, \frac{3}{2}, \frac{3}{4}, \ldots$ are in G.P.

Here, $a = 3$, $r = \frac{1}{2}$, $S_n = \frac{3069}{512}$

$$S_n = a\left(\frac{1-r^n}{1-r}\right)$$

$$\Rightarrow \quad \frac{3069}{512} = \frac{3\left[1-\left(\frac{1}{2}\right)^n\right]}{1-\frac{1}{2}} = \frac{3\left[1-\left(\frac{1}{2}\right)^n\right]}{\frac{1}{2}}$$

$$\Rightarrow \quad \frac{3069}{512} = 3\times 2\left[1-\left(\frac{1}{2}\right)^n\right]$$

$$\Rightarrow \quad \frac{3069}{6\times 512} = 1-\left(\frac{1}{2}\right)^n$$

$$\Rightarrow \quad \frac{1023}{1024} = 1-\left(\frac{1}{2}\right)^n$$

$$\Rightarrow \quad \left(\frac{1}{2}\right)^n = 1-\frac{1023}{1024}$$

$$= \frac{1}{1024} = \left(\frac{1}{2}\right)^{10}$$

$$\Rightarrow \quad n = 10.$$

94. $\because 10^1(10^1 + 1)(10^1 + 2)$

= 10 × 11 × 12 = 1320

1320 is divided by 6 gives remainder = 0

$10^2(10^2 + 1)(10^2 + 2)$

= 100(101)(102) = 1030200

1030200 is divided by 6 gives remainder = 0

$10^3(10^3 + 1)(10^3 + 2)$ = 1003002000

1003002000 is divided by 6 gives remainder = 0

....

....

Hence, when $10^{10}(10^{10} + 1)(10^2 + 2)$ is divided by 6 then remainder = 0.

MATHEMATICS

1. SETS

1. Set : According to G. Cantor, a German mathematician in the last part of the nineteenth century "A set is a well-defined collection of distinct objects of our perception or of our thought to be conceived as a whole."

Commonly we use capital letters A,B, C, ... to denote sets and small letters a, b, c, ... to denote objects (or elements) of a set.

2. Types of Sets

(i) Singleton Set : If a set consists of only one element, it is called an singleton set.

e.g. $\{a\}$, $\{b\}$, $\{c\}$ are singleton set.

(ii) Finite Set : A set consisting of a finite number of elements, is called a finite set.

(iii) Infinite Set : A set containing infinitely many elements is called an infinite set.

(iv) Equal Set : Two sets A and B are called equal sets if each element of set A in an element of B.

(v) Empty Set : If a set consists of no elements, it is called the empty set. The empty set is represented by the symbol ϕ. An empty set is also called null set or void set.

(vi) Equivalent Set : Two finite sets A and B are equivalent if their cardinal numbers are same *i.e.*, $n(\text{A}) = n(\text{B})$.

3. Subset : Let A be a set. A set B is said to be a subset of A if $x \in \text{B} \Rightarrow x \in \text{A}$. Therefore, B is a subset of A if each element of B is an element of A. This is expressed symbolically by $\text{B} \subset \text{A}$, signifying that B is contained in A.

Properties

(i) Every set is a subset of itself.

(ii) The empty set is a subset of every set.

(iii) The total number of subsets of a finite set containing n elements is 2^n.

4. Proper Subset : Set A is called a proper subset of set B if B has at least one element more, than that of A and all elements of A are contained in B. It is denoted by $\text{A} \subset \text{B}$.

If a set A has n elements, then total number of proper subsets of A is $2^n - 1$.

5. Power Set : We have defined a set as a collection of its elements. If the elements be sets themselves, then we have a family of sets or a set of sets. This set is said to be the power set of S and is denoted by P(S). If S contains n elements, then P(S) contains 2^n subsets, because a subset of P(S) is either ϕ or a subset containing relements of S, $r = 1, 2, ..., n$.

6. Universal Set : A set which is such that all the sets under consideration are its subsets is called the universal set. It is denoted by U. Set of natural numbers is a universal set for all the finite sets of natural numbers.

7. Complement of a Set : Complement of set A is the set which contains all those elements of the universal set which are not in A. It is denoted by A' or A^c

Thus $\text{A}^c = \{x : x \in \text{U}; x \notin \text{A}\}$.

Important Results

(i) $\text{U}' = \{x \in \text{U}; x \notin \text{U}\} = \phi$

(ii) $\phi' = \text{U}$

(iii) $(\text{A}')' = \text{A}$

8. Venn Diagram : The idea of sets when represented diagrammatically is called venn diagram. In venn diagrams universal set U is usually shown by a rectangular region and the sets of U by circular regions inside it.

9. Algebraic Operations on Sets : Let A, B, C, ... be subsets of a universal set S.

(i) **Union :** Union (or join) of two subsets A and B

is a subset denoted by $A \cup B$ and is defined by $A \cup B = \{x | x \in A \text{ or } x \in B\}$. Therefore, $A \cup B$ is the set of all those elements which either belong to A or B or both. It follows that $A \subset A \cup B$, $B \subset A \cup B$.

(ii) **Intersection :** Intersection (or meet) of two subsets A and B is a subset denoted by $A \cap B$ and is defined by $A \cap B = \{x | x \in A \text{ and } x \in B\}$. Therefore, $A \cap B$ is the set of those elements which belong to both A and B. It follows that $A \cap B \subset A$, $A \cap B \subset B$.

Note : Two subset A and B are said to be **disjoint** if $A \cap B = \phi$.

10. Properties of Set Operations

(a) Consistency Properties : The three properties $B \subset A$, $A \cup B = A$ and $A \cap B = B$ are mutually equivalent *i.e.,* one implies the other two. The following properties can be easily deduced from the consistency property.

(i) $A \cup \phi = A$, $A \cap \phi = \phi$, follows from relation $\phi \subset A$.

(ii) $A \cup S = S$, $A \cap S = A$, follows from relation $A \subset S$ (universal set).

(iii) $A \cup A = A$, $A \cap A = A$ (Idempotent property), follows from $A \subset A$.

(iv) $A \cup (A \cap B) = A$, $A \cap (A \cup B) = A$ (Absorptive property), follows from $A \cap B \subset A \cup B$.

(b) Commutative property : $A \cup B = B \cup A$, $A \cap B = B \cap A$.

(c) Associative property : $A \cup (B \cup C) = (A \cup B) \cup C$, $A \cap (B \cap C) = (A \cap B) \cap C$.

(d) Distributive property : $A \cup (B \cap C) = (A \cup B) \cap (A \cup C)$, $A \cap (B \cup C) = (A \cap B) \cup (A \cap C)$.

11. Difference : Difference of two subsets A and B is a subset of A, denoted by $A - B$ and is defined by $A - B = \{x \in A \mid x \notin B\}$. Thus $A - B$ is the set of those elements of A which are not elements of B. In particular $A - B = \phi$ if $A \subset B$ and $A - B = A$ if $A \cap B = \phi$. The subset $A - B$ is also called the complement of B relative to A.

12. De Morgan's Laws

(i) $(A \cup B)' = A' \cap B'$

(ii) $(A \cap B)' = A' \cup B'$.

13. If A and B are any two sets, then,

(i) $A - B = A \cap B' = B' - A'$

(ii) $B - A = B \cap A' = A' - B'$

(iii) $A - B = A$ if*f* $A \cap B = \phi$

(iv) $(A - B) \cup B = A \cup B$

(v) $(A - B) \cap B = \phi$

(vi) $A \subseteq B$ if $B' \subseteq A'$

(vii) $(A - B) \cup (B - A) = (A \cup B) - (A \cap B) = A \Delta B$

$\because$ $A \Delta B$ is called symmetric difference of A and B.

(viii) *(a)* $A \Delta \phi = A$

(b) $A \Delta A = \phi$

(c) $A \Delta B = B \Delta A$

(d) $A \Delta B = \phi$ if $A = B$

(e) $A \Delta B = A \cup B$ if*f* $A \cap B = \phi$

14. If A, B and C are any three sets, then

(i) $A - (B \cap C) = (A - B) \cup (A - C)$

(ii) $A - (B \cup C) = (A - B) \cap (A - C)$

(iii) $A \cap (B - C) = (A \cap B) - (A \cap C)$

(iv) $A \cap (B \Delta C) = (A \cap B) \Delta (A \cap C)$

15. If A, B, C are finite sets

(i) $n(A \cup B) = n(A) + n(B) - n(A \cap B)$

(ii) $n(A \cup B) = n(A) + n(B)$, if A and B are disjoint and non-empty set.

(iii) $n(A - B) = n(A) - n(A \cap B)$ as $n(A - B) + n(A \cap B) = n(A)$

(iv) $n(A \Delta B) = n\{(A - B) \cup (B - A)\}$

$= n(A - B) + n(B - A)$

[$\because$ $(A - B)$ and $(B - A)$ are disjoint]

$= n(A) + n(B) - 2n(A \cap B)$.

Where $n(A \Delta B)$ = No. of elements belongs to exactly one of A or B.

(v) $n(A \cup B \cup C) = n(A) + n(B) + n(C) - n(A \cap B) - n(B \cap C) - n(A \cap C) + n(A \cap B \cap C)$.

(vi) No. of elements in exactly two of the sets A, B, C $= n(A \cap B) + n(B \cap C) + n(C \cap A) - 3n(A \cap B \cap C)$

(vii) No. of elements in exactly one of the sets A, B, C

$= n(A) + n(B) + n(C) - 2n(A \cap B) - 2n(B \cap C) - 2n(A \cap C) + 3n(A \cap B \cap C)$.

16. Ordered Pair : By an ordered pair of elements we mean a pair (a, b) where $a \in A$ and $b \in B$. $(a, b), (b, a)$ are different unless $a = b$. In other words two ordered pairs (a_1, b_1) and (a_2, b_2) are equal if $a_1 = a_2$ and $b_1 = b_2$.

17. Cartesian Product of Sets : Let A, B be two non-empty sets. The cartesian product of A and B, denoted by A × B, is the set defined by $A \times B = \{(a, b) \mid a \in A \text{ and } b \in B\}$. Thus A × B is the set of all ordered pairs (a, b), the first element of the pair is an element of A and the second is an element of B.

For example let $A = \{a, b\}, B = \{c, d, e\}$, then $A \times B = \{(a, c), (a, d), (a, e), (b, c), (b, d), (b, e)\}$.

Here A × B has 2 × 3 *i.e.*, 6 elements.

EXERCISE

Mark the correct alternative(s) in each of the following :

1. If sets A and B are defined as

$A = \{(x, y) \mid y = e^x, x \in R\}$

$B = \{(x, y) \mid y = e^{-x}, x \in R\}$, then

(a) $A \cap B = \phi$ *(b)* $A \cup B = R^2$

(c) $A \cap B \neq \phi$ *(d)* None of these

2. If A = {2, 5, 7, 11, 13, 17, 19} and B = {1, 2, 3, 4, 5, 6, 7, 8, 9}, then $(A - B) \cap (B - A)$ equals to

(a) {11, 13, 17, 19}

(b) {1, 3, 6, 8, 9}

(c) {1, 3, 3, 6, 8, 9, 11, 13, 17, 19}

(d) ϕ

3. If A contains n elements, then number of elements in power set of A is

(a) n^2 *(b)* $n!$

(c) $2n$ *(d)* 2^n

4. The number of elements in the power set P(S) of the set $= \{2, \{1, 4\}\}$ is

(a) 2 *(b)* 4

(c) 8 *(d)* None of these

[J.N.U. M.C.A.]

5. If A and B have n elements in common, then the number of elements common to (A × B) and (B × A) is

(a) n *(b)* $n!$

(c) n^2 *(d)* $n^2/2$

6. If $aN = \{a x \mid x \in N\}$ and $bN \cap cN = dN$, where $b, c \in N$ are relatively prime, then

(a) $d = bc$ *(b)* $c = bd$

(c) $b = cd$ *(d)* None of these

7. The number of non-empty subset of a set consisting of 6 elements is

(a) 64 *(b)* 63

(c) 65 *(d)* None of these

8. If $(A - B) \subset (B - A)$, then

(a) $A - B = B - A$ *(b)* $B \subset A$

(c) $A \subset B$ *(d)* $A \cup B = A$

[D.U. M.C.A.]

9. Let A and B be two sets having 7 common elements. The number of elements common to A × B and B × A is

(a) 0 *(b)* 48

(c) 2^7 *(d)* 49

10. If $A = \{\phi, \{\phi\}\}$, then the power set of A is

(a) A *(b)* $\{\phi, \{\phi\}, A\}$

(c) $\{\phi, \{\phi\}, \{\{\phi\}\}, A\}$ *(d)* None of these

11. Let A and B have 3 and 6 elements respectively. What can be the maxium and minimum number of elements in $A \cup B$?

(a) 9 and 6 *(b)* 6 and 13

(c) 9 and 3 *(d)* 6 and 12

12. If A, B and C are three sets and U is the universal set such that

$n(U) = 700$, $n(A) = 200$, $n(B) = 300$ and

$n(A \cap B) = 100$. Then $n(A' \cap B')$ equals to

(a) 200 (b) 300
(c) 500 (d) None of these

13. A survey shows that 63% of the Britishers like cheese 7 whereas 76% like apples. If x% of the Britishers like both cheese and apples, then the value of x

(a) $40 \le x \le 60$ (b) $35 \le x \le 65$
(c) $39 \le x \le 63$ (d) None of these

14. If $A \subset B$, then $A' \cup B'$ equals

(a) A' (b) B'
(c) $A' \cap B'$ (d) None of these

15. A question and two statements labelled (I) and (II) containing some data are given as follows : How many of the 50 members of a club could speak neither Hindi nor English?

(I) Out of 50 members, exactly 50 per cent could speak Hindi and exactly 20 per cent could speak English.
(II) Of the 50 members, exactly 10 per cent could speak both Hindi and English.

Which one among the following is correct with respect to above?

(a) Statement (II) alone is sufficient but statement (I) alone is not sufficient to answer the question asked.
(b) Statement (I) and (II) together are not sufficient to answer the question and additional data required.
(c) Statement (I) alone is sufficient to answer the question but statement (II) alone is not sufficient.
(d) Both statement (I) and (II) together are sufficient to answer the question but neither statement alone is sufficient.

[J.N.U. M.C.A.]

16. A and B are two finite sets. Then $(A \cup B) - C$ is equal to

(a) $(A - C) \cap (B - C)$ (b) $(A - C) \cup (B - C)$
(c) $(C - A) \cup (C - B)$ (d) $A \cap B \cap C$

17. On a set of n elements, a boolean algebra is defined. Then n can be

(a) 5 (b) 6 (c) 7 (d) 8

18. If the symmetric difference $A \nabla B$ is an empty set then

(a) $A \subset B$ (b) $A = B$
(c) $B \subset A$ (d) $A \cap B = \phi$

19. If $A = \{1, 2\}, B = \{2, 5\}, C = \{5, 7\}$, then $(A \times B) \cap (A \times C)$ is equal to

(a) $\{(2, 7), (1, 5)\}$ (b) $\{(5, 7), (2, 1)\}$
(c) $\{(2, 5), (1, 5)\}$ (d) None of these

20. Let A, B be two non-empty sets. If A_1 and A_2 are subsets of A and B_1 and B_2 subsets of B, then $(A_1 \times B_1) - (A_2 \times B_2)$ is equal to

(a) $(A_1 - A_2) \times (B_1 - B_2) \cup (A_1 \cap A_2) \times (B_1 - B_2) \cup (A_1 - A_2) \times (B_1 \cap B_2)$
(b) $(A_1 - A_2) \times (B_1 - B_2) \cap (A_1 \cap A_2) \times (B_1 - B_2) \cap (A_1 - A_2) \times (B_1 \cap B_2)$
(c) $(A_1 - A_2) \times (B_1 - B_2) \cup (A_1 \cup A_2) \times (B_1 - B_2) \cup (A_1 - A_2) \times (B_1 \cup B_2)$
(d) None of these [J.N.U. M.C.A.]

21. The expressions $A \times (B \cup C)$ is the same as

(a) $(A \times C) \cup (B \times C)$ (b) $(A \times C) \cap (B \times C)$
(c) $(A \times C) \cup (A \times C)$ (d) $(A \times C) \cap (A \times C)$

[J.N.U. M.C.A.]

22. In a dinner attended by 432 people, 300 choose non-vegetarian and 132 choose vegetarian dishes. If 20 choose both, then how many choose exactly one kind of food?

(a) 412 (b) 392 (c) 402 (d) 372

[J.N.U. M.C.A.]

ANSWERS

1	2	3	4	5	6	7	8	9	10
(c)	(d)	(d)	(b)	(c)	(a)	(b)	(c)	(d)	(c)
11	**12**	**13**	**14**	**15**	**16**	**17**	**18**	**19**	**20**
(a)	(b)	(c)	(a)	(d)	(b)	(a)	(b)	(c)	(a)
21	**22**								
(c)	(a)								

SOME SELECTED EXPLANATORY ANSWERS

1. Set A consists of all points which satisfies equation $y = e^x$.
Set B consists of all points which satisfies equation $y = e^{-x}$.
These two curve intersect at point (0, 1)
$\therefore A \cap B \neq \phi$.

2. Given $A = \{2,5,7,11,13,17,19\}$
$B = \{1,2,3,4,5,6,7,8,9\}$
$\therefore A - B = \{11,13,17,19\}$
$B - A = \{1,3,4,6,8,9\}$.
$\therefore (A-B) \cap (B-A) = \phi$.

4. Number of elements in the power set P(S) where S contains n elements is 2^n.
Here S contains 2 elements; 2 and (1, 4)
$\therefore P(S) = 2^2 = 4$.

5. If A and B have n elements in common, then $(A \times B)$ and $(B \times A)$ have n^2 elements in common.

6. Here
$bN = \{bx \mid x \in N\}$ = Set of positive integers which are integral multiple of b.
$cN = \{cx \mid x \in N\}$ = Set of positive integers which are integral multiple of c.
$\therefore bN \cap cN$ = Set of positive integral multiples of be
$= bcN$. $[\because b \text{ and } c \text{ are prime}]$
Thus $d = bc$.

7. Number of non-empty subset of a set consisting of n elements is $2^n - 1$.
Here $n = 6$
$\therefore$ Required number $= 2^6 - 1 = 63$.

9. If A and B be two sets having n common elements, then the number of elements common to $A \times B$ and $B \times A$ is $n \times n = n^2$.
Here $n = 7$
$\therefore$ Required number $= 7 \times 7 = 49$.

12. We know that $A' \cap B' = (A \cup B)'$
$\Rightarrow n(A' \cap B') = n(A \cup B)'$
$= n(U) - n(A \cup B)$
$= n(U) - [n(A) + n(B) - n(A \cap B)]$
$= 700 - (200 + 300 - 100) = 300$.

13. Set A denotes Britishers, who like cheese.
Set B denotes Britishers, who like apples.
Let the population of Britishers be 100.
The $n(A) = 63$, $n(B) = 76$.
Now $n(A \cup B) = n(A) + n(B) - n(A \cap B)$
$\Rightarrow n(A \cup B) = 63 + 76 - n(A \cap B)$
$\Rightarrow n(A \cup B) + n(A \cap B) = 139$
$\Rightarrow n(A \cap B) = 139 - n(A \cup B)$ ...(i)
But $n(A \cup B) \leq 100$
$\Rightarrow -n(A \cup B) \geq -100$
$\Rightarrow 139 - n(A \cup B) \geq 139 - 100$
$\Rightarrow n(A \cup B) \geq 39$ (from (i)) ...(ii)
Now $A \cap B \subseteq A$ and $A \cap B \subseteq B$
$\Rightarrow n(A \cap B) \leq n(A)$ and $n(A \cap B) \leq n(B)$
$\Rightarrow n(A \cap B) \leq 63$ and $n(A \cap B) \leq 76$
$\Rightarrow n(A \cap B) \leq 63$ ...(iii)
From (ii) and (iii) we have
$39 \leq n(A \cap B) \leq 63$
$\Rightarrow 39 \leq x \leq 63$.

14. $A \subset B \Rightarrow A' \subset B' \Rightarrow A' \cup B' = A'$.

15. Let $n(U)$ = Total member of a club = 50
$n(H)$ = Member who can speak in Hindi
$= 50\%$ of $50 = 25$
$n(E)$ = Member who can speak in English
$= 20\%$ of $50 = 10$
$n(E \cap H)$ = Member who can speak both Hindi and English = 10% of $50 = 5$.
$n(E \cup H)'$ = Member who can speak neither Hindi nor English
$= n(U) - \{n(H) + n(E) - (H \cap E)\}$
$= 50 - \{25 + 10 - 5\}$
$= 50 - 30 = 20$.

17. A Boolean algebra can be defined only if n is a power of 2 i.e. $n = 2^k$ for some $k \in N$.
$\therefore n$ should be equal to 8.

18. $A \nabla B = (A-B) \cup (B-A)$

If $A \nabla B = \phi$, then $(A-B) \cup (B-A) = \phi$

$\Rightarrow A - B = \phi$ or $A \cap B' = \phi \Rightarrow A \subset B$

Similarly $B - A = \phi \Rightarrow B \subset A$.

They together implies A = B.

19. Given $A = \{1, 2\}, B = \{2, 5\}, C = \{5, 7\}$

$\therefore A \times B = \{(1,2), (2,2), (1,5), (2,5)\}$

$A \times C = \{(1,5), (2,5), (1,7), (2,7)\}$

$\therefore (A \times B) \cap (A \times C) = \{(2,5), (1,5)\}$.

21. Let (a, b) be an arbitrary element of $A \times (B \cup C)$

Then $(a, b) \in A \times (B \cup C)$

$\Rightarrow a \in A$ and $b \in B \cup C$

$\Rightarrow a \in A$ and $(b \in B$ or $b \in C)$

$\Rightarrow (a \in A$ and $b \in B)$ or $(a \in A$ and $b \in C)$

$\Rightarrow (a, b) \in A \times B$ or $(a, b) \in A \times C$

$\Rightarrow (a, b) \in (A \times B) \cup (A \times C)$ ...*(i)*

Again, let (x, y) be an arbitrary element of $(A \times B) \cup (A \times C)$

Then $(x, y) \in (A \times B) \cup (A \times C)$

$\Rightarrow (x, y) \in A \times B$ or $(x, y) \in A \times C$

$\Rightarrow (x \in A$ and $y \in B)$ or $(x \in A$ and $y \in C)$

$\Rightarrow x \in A$ and $(y \in B$ or $y \in C)$

$\Rightarrow x \in A$ and $y \in (B \cup C)$

$\Rightarrow (x, y) \in A \times (B \cup C)$

$\therefore (A \times B) \cup (A \times C) \subseteq A \times (B \cup C)$ ...*(ii)*

From *(i)* and *(ii)*, we have

$A \times (B \cup C) = (A \times B) \cup (A \times C)$.

22. Let $n(A)$ = people who choose non-vege = 300

$n(B)$ = people who choose vege = 132

$n(A \cap B)$ = people who choose both = 20.

$n(A \cup B)$ = people who chose exactly one kind of food.

We know that

$n(A \cup B) = n(A) + n(B) - n(A \cap B)$

$= 300 + 132 - 20 = 412.$

2. RELATION AND FUNCTIONS

1. Relation : Let A, B be two non-empty sets. A binary relation ρ between A and B is a rule that associates some or all elements of A with some or all elements of B. For example, let L be the set of all lines on a plane π and $\rho = \{(l, m) \in L \times L \mid l \text{ is parallel to } m\}$. Then ρ is a relation on L defined by '$l \rho m$ if l, m are lines on the plane π and l is parallel to m'.

2. Domain and Range of a Relation : Let R be a relation from A to B, that is, let $R \subseteq A \times B$. Then ***Domain*** **R** = $\{a : a \in A. (a, b) \in R \text{ for some } b \in B\}$, *i.e.*, dom. R in the set of all the first elements of the ordered pairs which belong to R.

Also ***Range*** R = $\{b : b \in B, (a, b) \in R \text{ for some } a \in A\}$, *i.e.*, range R is the set of all the second elements of the ordered pairs which belong to R. Thus domain $R \subseteq A$, range $R \subseteq B$.

3. Inverse Relation : Let A, B be two sets and ρ, be a relation from a set A to set B. Then the inverse of ρ, denoted by ρ^{-1}, is a relation from B to A and is defined by $\rho^{-1} = \{(b, a; (a, b) \in \rho\}$.

Here Dom (ρ) = Range (ρ^{-1}) and Range (ρ) = Dom (ρ^{-1}).

4. Types of Relation

(i) **Void Relation :** Let A be a set. Then $\phi \subseteq A \times A$ *i.e.,* it is relation on A. This relation is called void or empty relation.

(ii) **Universal Relation :** Let A be a set. In particular, if $\rho = A \times A$, then $a \rho a$ holds for all a in A. Here ρ is said to be the universal relation on A.

(iii) **Identity Relation :** Let A be a set. Then the relation $I_A = \{(a, a) : a \in A\}$ on A is called identity relation on A. For example let A = {2, 3, 5}. Then $I_A = \{(2,2), (3,3), (5,5)\}$.

(iv) **Reflexive Relation :** Let ρ be a binary relation on a set A. The relation ρ is said to be reflexive if $(a, a) \in \rho$ for all a in A *i.e.,* $a \rho a$ holds for all a in A.

(v) **Symmetric Relation :** Let ρ be a binary relation on a set A. The relation ρ is said to be symmetric if for any two elements $a, b \in A$, $(a, b) \in \rho \Rightarrow (b, a) \in \rho$ *i.e.,* $a \rho b \Rightarrow b \rho a$.

(vi) **Transitive Relation :** Let ρ be a binary relation on a set A. The relation ρ is said to be transitive if for any three elements $a, b, c \in A$, $(a, b) \in \rho$ and $(b, c) \in \rho \Rightarrow (a, c) \in \rho$ *i.e.,* $a \rho b$ and $b \rho c \Rightarrow a \rho c$.

(vii) **Equivalence Relation :** A binary relation ρ on a set A is said to be an equivalence relation or an RST relation, if ρ is reflexive, symmetric and transitive.

(viii) **Anti-symmetric Relation :** Let A be any set. A relation ρ on set A is said to be an anti-symmetric relation if $(a, b) \in \rho$ and $(b, a) \in \rho \Rightarrow a = b$ for all $a, b \in A$.

5. Congruence Modulo *m* : Let m be an arbitrary but fixed integer. Two integers a and b are said to be congruence modulo m if $a - b$ is divisible by m and we write $a \equiv b \pmod{m}$.

So $a \equiv b \pmod{m}$ if $a - b$ is divisible by m.

6. Mapping : Let A, B be two non-empty sets. A relation f between A and B is said to be a mapping (or a function, or a map) from A to B if for each x in A there is related exactly one y in B.

In other words, a mapping from A to B is a rule that assigns to each element x of A, a definite element y in B.

A is said to be domain of f and B is said to be the co-domain of f. A Mapping f having the domain A and co-domain B is expressed by the symbol $f : A \to B$.

We can imagine f as a kind of agent that carries (or transforms or maps) each elements x of A to a definite element y in B. y is called f-image of x and is denoted by $f(x)$.

7. Into Mapping : A mapping $f : A \to B$ is said to be an into mapping if $f(A)$ is a proper subset of B i.e. if f there is at least one element in B which is not the f-image of any element in A. In this case we say that f maps A into B.

8. Onto Mapping (Surjective) : A mapping $f: A \rightarrow B$ is said to be an onto mapping if $f(A) = B$ *i.e.,* if f every elements in B is the f-image of at least one element in A.

9. One-one Mapping (Injection) : A mapping $f: A \rightarrow B$ is said to be injective (one-to-one) if for each pair of distinct elements of A, their f-images are distinct.

10. One-one-onto Mapping (Bijection) : A mapping $f: A \rightarrow B$ is said to be bijective if f is both injective and surjective.

11. Constant Mapping : A mapping $f: A \rightarrow B$ is said to be a constant mapping (a constant function) if f maps each element of A to one and the same element of B, *i.e.,* $f(A)$ is singleton set.

12. Identity Mapping : A mapping $f: A \rightarrow A$ is said to be the identity mapping on A if $f(x) = x \ \forall\ x \in A$. The identity mapping on A is denoted by I_A.

13. Number of Injective Mappings : Number of injective mapping from A to B is the number of arrangements of n items by taking m at a time *i.e.,*

$$^nP_m = \begin{cases} ^nP_m, \text{ if } n \geq m \\ 0, \text{ if } n < m \end{cases}$$

Where A and B are finite sets having m and n elements.

14. Number of Surjective Mappings: The number of surjective mapping from A to B is

$$\sum_{r=1}^{n} (-1)^{n-r}\ {}^nC_r . r^m$$

where A and B are finite sets having m and n elements such that $1 \leq n \leq m$.

15. Number of Bijective Mapping : Let A and B are finite sets and $f: A \rightarrow B$ is a bijecting mapping. Then A and B have the same number of elements. If A has n elements then the number of bijections from A to B is the total number of arrangements of n elements taken all at a time *i.e., n!.*

16. Composite Mapping : Let $f: A \rightarrow B$ and $g: C \rightarrow D$ be two mapping such that $f(A)$ is a subset of C. Let $x \in A$. Then f maps x to an element y in B and since $y \in C$, g maps y to an element z in D. We can conceive of a mapping $h: A \rightarrow D$ defined by $h(x) = g[f(x)], x \in A$. The mapping $h: A \rightarrow D$ is said to be the **composite** of f and g, and is denoted by gof (or by gf). Then $gof(x) = g[f(x)], x \in A$.

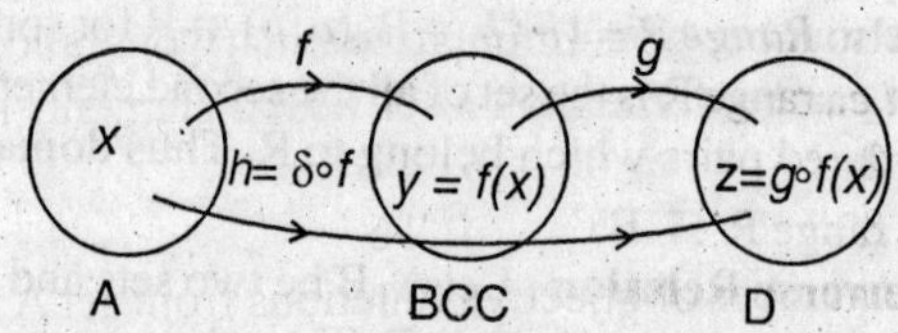

Properties of Composite Function

(i) Composite mapping is not commutative *i.e.,* $fog \neq gof$

(ii) Composite mapping is associative *i.e.,* if f, g, h are three functions then $(fog)\, oh = fo\,(goh)$.

(iii) Composition of two bijective mapping is also a bijective mapping. *i.e.,* if f and g are two bijections then gof is also a bijection.

(iv) The composition of any function with the identity function is the function itself.

EXERCISE

Mark the correct alternative(s) of each of the following :

1. If R is a relation from a finite set A having m elements to a finite set B having n elements, then the number of relations from A to B is
   (a) 2^{mn} *(b)* $2^{mn} - 1$
   (c) $2mn$ *(d)* m^n
2. Let the set A contains m elements and the set B, n elements. The number of distinct functions that can be defined from A to B is
   (a) n *(b)* $m + n$
   (c) n^m *(d)* m^n
3. If S contains n elements, then the number of distinct relations that can be defined on S is
   (a) 2^{n^2} *(b)* n^2
   (c) 2^n *(d)* 2^{2n}
4. If S contains n elements, then the number of distinct binary operations that can be defined

on S is

(a) n^2 (b) n^{n^2}

(c) 2^n (d) 2^{2n}

5. Let b be a finite set containing n elements. Then the total number of commulative binary operation on b is

(a) $n^{\frac{n(n+1)}{2}}$ (b) $n^{\frac{n(n-1)}{2}}$

(c) n^{n^2} (d) 2^{n^2}

6. The number of equivalence relations that can be defined on a set with two elements is

(a) 0 (b) 1

(c) 2 (d) 3

7. The number of equivalence relations that can be defined on a set with three elements is

(a) 3 (b) 4

(c) 5 (d) 6

8. The number of commutative binary operations that can be defined on a set with 2 elements is

(a) 2 (b) 4

(c) 8 (d) 16

9. The number of bijective functions from set A to itself when A contains 100 elements is

(a) 50! (b) 100!

(c) 50^2 (d) 100^2

10. The number of injective functions that can be defined from a set with 4 elements is

(a) 6 (b) 12

(c) 24 (d) 36

11. A set A contains m elements and a Set B contain n $(n > m)$ elements. The number of injective functions that can be defined from A to B is

(a) $n!$ (b) $\frac{n!}{m!}$

(c) $\frac{n!}{(n-m)!}$ (d) $(n-m)!$

12. The number of surjective functions that can be defined from a set with 5 elements to a set with 3 elements is,

(a) 150 (b) 75

(c) 25 (d) 15

13. Let $P = \{(x, y) \mid x^2 + y^2 = 1, x, y \in R\}$. Then P is

(a) reflexive (b) symmetric

(c) transitive (d) anti-symmetric

14. In the set A = {1, 2, 3, 4, 5}, a relation R is defined by

$R = \{(x, y) \mid x, y \in A \text{ and } x < y\}$. The R is

(a) reflexive (b) symmetric

(c) transitive (d) None of these

15. Let R be a relation on the set N be defined by $\{(x, y) \mid x, y \in N, 2x + y = 41\}$. Then R is

(a) reflexive (b) symmetric

(c) transitive (d) None of these

16. For real numbers x and y, we write $x \, R \, y \Leftrightarrow x - y + \sqrt{2}$ is an irrational number. Then the relation R is

(a) reflexive (b) symmetric

(c) transitive (d) None of these

17. Let L denote the set of all straight lines in a plane. Let a relation R be defined by $\alpha \, R \, \beta \Leftrightarrow \alpha \perp \beta, \alpha \, \beta, \in L$. Then R is

(a) reflexive (b) symmetric

(c) transitive (d) None of these

18. The function $f : C \to R : f(z) = |z|$ is

(a) many-one, into (b) many-one, onto

(c) one-one, into (d) one-one, onto

19. The range of $f(x) = 1 - |x|$ is

(a) $]-\infty, 1]$ (b) $[-1, 1]$

(c) $[1, \infty[$ (d) $]-\infty, -1]$

20. The range of $f(x) = x - [x]$ is

(a) $]0, 1[$ (b) $[0, 1[$

(c) $[0, 1]$ (d) $\{0, 1\}$

21. The domain of $f(x) = \cos^{-1}\left(\frac{2-|x|}{4}\right) + [\log(3-x)]^{-1}$ is

(a) $[-2, 6]$ (b) $[(-6, 2) \cup (2, 3)]$

(c) $[-6, 2]$ (d) $[-2, 2] \cup (2, 3)$

22. The domain of the function $f(x) = \sqrt{\log\left(\frac{1}{|\sin x|}\right)}$ is

(a) $R - \{-\pi, \pi\}$ (b) $R - \{n\pi \mid n \in z\}$

(c) $R - \{2n\pi \mid n \in z\}$ (d) $(-\infty, \infty)$

23. The domain of definition of

$f(x) = \sqrt{\log(\log x) - \log(4 - \log x) - \log 3}$ is

(a) $(10^3, 10^4)$ (b) $[10^3, 10^4]$

(c) $[10^3, 10^4)$ (d) $(10^3, 10^4]$

24. If $f(x) = \cos(\log x)$, then $f(x) f(y) - \frac{1}{2}\left\{f\left(\frac{x}{y}\right) + f(xy)\right\}$ has the value

(a) – 1 (b) 1/2

(c) – 2 (d) None of these

[J.N.U. M.C.A.]

25. Let $f(x) = |x - 1|$. Then

(a) $f(x^2) = \{f(x)\}^2$ (b) $f(x + y) = f(x) + f(y)$

(c) $f(|x|) = |f(x)|$ (d) None of these

26. If $f(x)$ is a polynomial satisfying $f(x) f\left(\frac{1}{x}\right) = f(x) + f\left(\frac{1}{x}\right)$ and $f(3) = 10$, then $f(5)$ equals to

(a) 126 (b) – 125

(c) 26 (d) None of these

27. The domain of $f(x) = \log_2 \log_3 \log_{4/\pi} (\cot^{-1} x)^{-1}$ is

(a) R (b) $\left(\frac{4}{\pi}, \infty\right)$

(c) $(1, \infty)$ (d) None of these

28. The domain of $f(x) = \log_2 \log_3 \log_{4/\pi} (\tan^{-1} x)^{-1}$ is

(a) R (b) $\left(\frac{4}{\pi}, \infty\right)$

(c) $(0, 1)$ (d) None of these

29. The domain of $f(x) = 3^{-x^2} + \cos^{-1}\left(\frac{x}{2} - 1\right) + \log \cos x$

(a) $\left(-\frac{\pi}{4}, \frac{\pi}{4}\right)$ (b) $\left[0, \frac{\pi}{2}\right]$

(c) $\left[0, \frac{\pi}{2}\right)$ (d) None of these

30. If $f(x)$ is a polynomial of degree 8 and $f(x) f\left(\frac{1}{x}\right) = f(x) + f\left(\frac{1}{x}\right)$ then $f(x)$ is

(a) an odd function

(b) an even function

(c) neither even nor odd

(d) None of these

31. If $f(x)$ is a polynomial of degree 5 and $f(x) f\left(\frac{1}{x}\right) = f(x) + f\left(\frac{1}{x}\right)$ then $f(x)$ is

(a) an odd function

(b) an even function

(c) neither even nor odd

(d) None of these

32. If $\left[x + \frac{1}{2}\right] + \left[x - \frac{1}{2}\right] = [2x]$, then

(a) $x - [x] < \frac{1}{2}$ (b) $x - [x] \geq \frac{1}{2}$

(c) $x - [x] \leq \frac{1}{4}$ (d) None of these

[D.U. M.C.A.]

33. If the function

$f(x) = \frac{x}{x-1}$, express $f(3x)$ in terms of $f(x)$

(a) $\frac{3f(x)}{3f(x)-1}$ (b) $\frac{3f(x)}{3f(x)-3}$

(c) $\frac{3f(x)}{2f(x)+1}$ (d) $3f(x) - 1$

[J.N.U. M.C.A.]

34. If $f(x) = \tan x$, then the value of $f(x) + f(-x)$ is equal to

(a) $2 \tan x$ (b) $-2 \tan x$

(c) ∞ (d) 0

[D.U. M.C.A.]

35. If $f(x) = 5^{-x}$, then which of the following false?

(a) $f(x)$ is strictly increasing in $[0, \infty)$

(b) $f(x)$ is strictly decreasing in $[0, \infty]$

(c) $f(x)$ is strictly increasing in $(-\infty, 0]$

(d) $D(f) = R$ (real numbers), $R(F) = (0, \infty)$.

[D.U. M.C.A.]

36. $f(x) = \frac{x-1}{x+1}$, then $f(2x)$ is

(a) $\frac{f(x)+1}{f(x)+3}$ (b) $\frac{3f(x)+1}{f(x)+3}$

(c) $\frac{f(x)+3}{f(x)+1}$ (d) $\frac{f(x)+3}{3f(x)+1}$

37. Given $f(x) = \log\left(\frac{1+x}{1-x}\right)$ and $g(x) = \frac{3x+x^3}{1+3x^2}$, then $fog(x)$ equals

(a) $-f(x)$ (b) $3f(x)$

(c) $[f(x)]^3$ (d) None of these

38. Let $f(x) = \frac{ax+b}{cx+d}$. Then $fof(x) = x$ provided that

(a) $d = -a$ (b) $d = a$

(c) $a = b = c = d = 1$ (d) $a = b = 1$

39. If $f(x) = \frac{x+1}{x}$, $x \neq 0$ and if $f[g(x)] = x$, then $g(x)=$

(a) $\frac{x^2}{x+1}$ (b) $\frac{x}{x-1}$

(c) $\frac{1}{1-x}$ (d) $\frac{1}{x-1}$

40. If $f(x) = \frac{1}{1-x}$, then $(fofof)(x) =$

(a) x (b) $\frac{1}{1-3x}$

(c) $\frac{x}{1-3x}$ (d) None of these

ANSWERS

1	2	3	4	5	6	7	8	9	10
(a)	(c)	(a)	(b)	(a)	(c)	(c)	(c)	(b)	(c)
11	12	13	14	15	16	17	18	19	20
(c)	(a)	(b)	(c)	(d)	(a)	(b)	(a)	(a)	(b)
21	22	23	24	25	26	27	28	29	30
(b)	(b)	(c)	(d)	(a)	(c)	(c)	(c)	(c)	(b)
31	32	33	34	35	36	37	38	39	40
(c)	(b)	(c)	(d)	(a)	(b)	(b)	(a)	(d)	(a)

SOME SELECTED EXPLANATORY ANSWERS

1. Set A contains m elements and set B contains n elements.

∴ The cartesian product (A × B) contains mn elements.

A relation (or a being relation) from A to B is a subset of A × B. Hence the number of relations is equal to the number of subsets of (A × B) which is equal to 2^{mn}.

3. The cartesian product (S × S) contains $n \times n = n^2$ elements.

A relation (or a binary relation) S to S is a subset of S × S. Hence the number of relations is equal to the number of subsets of (S × S) which is equal to 2^{n^2}.

4. A binary operation on S is a function from S into S × S. Now S × S has n^2 elements.

Hence the number of binary operations

= number of functions from $S \to S \times S = n^{n^2}$.

5. In the previous solution we have seen the number of elements of A × A = n^2.

Since $a*b$ and $b*a$ are to be counted as one binary image only, to calculate the number of distinct images in A × A, we have to subtract the number of elements like $a*a$ which are n in number. Hence the number of distinct elements in A × A, not counting $a*b, b*a$ as two is

$$\frac{n^2-n}{2} + n = \frac{n^2+n}{2} = \frac{n(n+1)}{2}.$$

∴ Number of commutative binary operation on

$$A = n^{\frac{n(n+1)}{2}}$$

8. Total number of commutative binary operation for n elements $= n^{\frac{n(n+1)}{2}}$

∴ For 2 elements it is $2^{\frac{2(2+1)}{2}} = 2^3 = 8$.

9. Total number of bijections from a set containing n elements to itself is n!.

∴ For $n = 100$, required number = 100!.

10. Total number of injective mappings from a set with m elements to a set with n elements, $m \le n$, is $\frac{n!}{(n-m)!}$.

Here $m = n = 4$.

∴ Required number $= \frac{4!}{(4-4)!} = \frac{4!}{0!} = 4! = 24.$

11. Let $A = \{a_1, a_2, ..., a_m\}$.

Now a_1 can be mapped on to any one of the n elements of B.

Hence a_1 can be mapped in n ways. Next a_2 can be mapped to the remaining $(n - 1)$ elements of B. Thus a_2 can be mapped in $(n - 1)$ ways and so on.

Hence total number of mapping

$= n(n-1)(n-2)$....m factors

$= n(n-1)(n-2)....(n-m+1)$

$= \frac{n!}{(n-m)!}$ ways.

12.

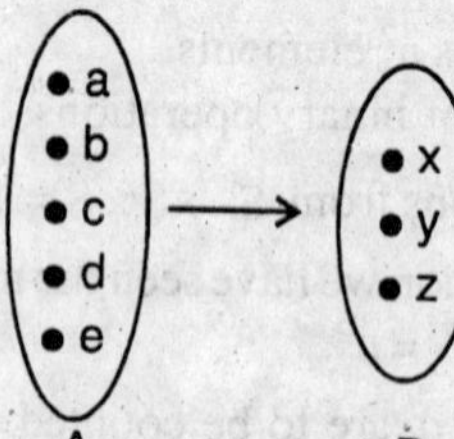

Required number of functions possible

$= {}^5C_2 \times {}^3C_2 \times 1 \times 3 + {}^5C_3 \times {}^2C_1 \times 3$

$= 90 + 60 = 150.$

Because

(i) As there are only 3 elements in set B, so possible association are $\left.\begin{matrix}2\\2\\1\end{matrix}\right\}$ in A with x, y, z associated with the 3 units.

(ii) or $\left.\begin{matrix}3\\1\\1\end{matrix}\right\}$ in A with the same condition.

13. Relation is not reflexive and transitive but it is symmetric, because $x^2 + y^2 = 1 \Rightarrow y^2 + x^2 = 1$.

14. As $x \nless x$, so R is not reflexive

Also $x < y$ does not imply that $y < x$, so R is symmetric

Now let xRy and yRz. Then $x < y$ and $y < z \Rightarrow x < z$ i.e. xRz.

∴ R is transitive.

15. All the ordered pair which satisfies the relation $\{(x, y) | x, y \in N, 2x + y = 41\}$

are R = $\{(1, 39), (2, 37), (3, 35), (4, 33), (5, 31), (6, 29), (7, 27), (8, 25), (9, 23), (10, 21), (11, 19), (12, 17), (13, 15), (14, 13), (15, 11), (16, 9), (17, 7), (18, 5), (19, 3), (20, 1)$

(i) $(1, 39) \in R$ but $(39, 1) \notin R$, therefore R is not symmetric

(ii) clearly R is not reflexive as $(x, x) \in R \ \forall \ x \in N$.

(iii) Now $(14, 13) \in R$ and $(13, 15) \in R$ but $(14, 15) \notin R$. So R is not transitive.

16. Give relation is for $x, y \in R$,

xR$y \Leftrightarrow x - y + \sqrt{2}$ is an irrational number.

(i) For $x \in R$, xR$x \Leftrightarrow x - x + \sqrt{2} = \sqrt{2}$ is an irrational number

∴ R is reflexive.

(ii) R is not symmetric because $1R\sqrt{2}$, but $\sqrt{2}R1$.

(iii) R is not transitive also because $\sqrt{2}R1$ and $1R2\sqrt{2}$ but $\sqrt{2}R2\sqrt{2}$.

17. Let L be the set of all lines in a plane.

Given $\alpha R \beta \Leftrightarrow \alpha \perp \beta$ for all $\alpha, \beta \in L$.

(i) R is not reflexive because a line cannot be perpendicular to itself i.e. $\alpha \perp \alpha$.

(ii) Let $\alpha, \beta \in L$ such that $\alpha R \beta$.

Then $\alpha R \beta \Rightarrow \alpha \perp \beta \Rightarrow \beta \perp \alpha \Rightarrow \beta R \alpha$.

So R is symmetric on L.

(iii) R is not transitive, because $\alpha \perp \beta$ and $\beta \perp \gamma$ does not imply $\alpha \perp \gamma$.

18. I. Given function is $f: C \to R: f(z) = |z|$.
Let $z_1 = x + iy$ and $z_2 = x - iy$.

$$\therefore \quad f(z_1) = |z_1| = \sqrt{x^2 + y^2} \quad ...(i)$$

$$f(z_2) = |z_2| = \sqrt{x^2 + y^2} \quad ...(ii)$$

(i) and *(ii)* implies $f(x + iy) = f(x - iy)$.
So *f* is many-one functon.
II. Since the modulus of a Comlex number can never be negative, so range $(f) \neq R$.
$\therefore$ *f* is into.

19. We know that $|x|$ is always greater than equals to zero i.e. $|x| \geq 0$.
$\therefore -|x| \leq 0$.
Thus, Range $(f) = \{y \in R : y \leq 1\} =]-\infty, 1[$.

20. Let $\quad y = x - [x]$

Then, $y = \begin{cases} 0, & \text{when } x \text{ is an integer} \\ < 1, & \text{when } x \text{ is not an integer} \end{cases}$

$\therefore$ Range $(f) = [0, 1[$.

21. I. $\cos^{-1}\left[\dfrac{2-|x|}{4}\right]$ exists if

$$-1 \leq \frac{2-|x|}{4} \leq 1$$

$\Rightarrow -6 \leq -|x| \leq 2$
$\Rightarrow -2 \leq |x| \leq 6$
$\Rightarrow |x| \leq 6$
$\Rightarrow -6 \leq x \leq 6$.

II. The function $[\log(3-x)]^{-1} = \dfrac{1}{\log(3-x)}$ exists if $3 - x > 0$ and $x \neq 2$ i.e. if $x \neq 2$ and $x < 3$.
From I and II we get domain of the function as

$$\{x \mid -6 \leq x \leq 6\} \cap \{x \mid x \neq 2, x < 3\}$$

$$= [-6, 2) \cup (2, 3).$$

22. $f(x) \in R$ if $\log\left\{\dfrac{1}{|\sin x|}\right\} \geq 0$

$\Rightarrow \dfrac{1}{|\sin x|} \geq 1$ and $|\sin x| \neq 0$

$\Rightarrow |\sin x| \neq 0 \quad \left[\because \dfrac{1}{|\sin x|} \geq 1 \text{ for all } x\right]$

$\Rightarrow x \neq n\pi, n \in Z$.

$\therefore$ Domain of $f(x) = R - \{n\pi : n \in Z\}$.

23. Given function is

$$f(x) = \sqrt{\log(\log x) - \log(4 - \log x) - \log 3}$$

$$= \sqrt{\log\left\{\frac{\log x}{(12 - 3\log x)}\right\}}$$

$f(x) \in R$ if

$$\log\left\{\frac{\log x}{(12 - 3\log x)}\right\} \geq 0$$

$\Rightarrow \dfrac{\log x}{(12 - 3\log x)} \geq 1$ and $12 - 3\log x > 0$

$\Rightarrow \log x \geq 3$ and $\log x < 4$
$\Rightarrow x \geq 10^3$ and $x < 10^4$

($\because$ Logarithmic base is 10)

$\Rightarrow x \in [10^3, 10^4)$.

24. Given $\quad f(x) = \cos(\log x)$

$\Rightarrow \quad f(y) = \cos(\log y)$

$\Rightarrow \quad f\left(\dfrac{x}{y}\right) = \cos\left[\log\left(\dfrac{x}{y}\right)\right]$

$= \cos[\log x - \log y]$

$\Rightarrow \quad f(xy) = \cos[\log(xy)]$

$= \cos[\log x + \log y]$

$\therefore \; f(x)f(y) - \dfrac{1}{2}\left\{f\left(\dfrac{x}{y}\right) + f(xy)\right\}$

$= \cos(\log x).\cos(\log x)$

$-\dfrac{1}{2}[\cos(\log x - \log y) + \cos(\log x + \log y)]$

$= \cos(\log x).\cos(\log y)$

$-\dfrac{1}{2}[2\cos(\log x)\cos(\log y)]$

$= \cos(\log x).\cos(\log y) - \cos(\log x)\cos(\log y)$
$= 0$.

25. Given function is $f(x) = |x - 1|$

$\Rightarrow \quad f(x^2) = |x^2 - 1| = |(x-1)(x+1)|$

$\neq |x-1|^2$

$= [f(x)]^2$

$\Rightarrow \quad f(|x|) = ||x| - 1| \neq ||x-1|| = |f(x)|$

$\Rightarrow \quad f(x+y) = |x+y-1| \neq |x-1| + |y-1|$

$= f(x) + f(y).$

Hence none of the above as given.

26. $f(x)$, is polynomial satisfying relation

$$f(x) f\left(\frac{1}{x}\right) = f(x) + f\left(\frac{1}{x}\right)$$

Let

$f(x) = a_0x^n + a_1x^{n-1} + a_2x^{n-2} + \dots + a_{n-1}x + a_n.$

Then

$$f\left(\frac{1}{x}\right) = \frac{a_0}{x^n} + \frac{a_1}{x^{n-1}} + \frac{a_2}{x^{n-2}} + \dots + \frac{a_{n-1}}{x} + a_n$$

$$\therefore \quad f(x) f\left(\frac{1}{x}\right) = f(x) + f\left(\frac{1}{x}\right)$$

$$\Rightarrow \left(a_0x^n + a_1x^{n-1} + \dots + a_{n-1}x + a_n\right)\left(\frac{a_0}{x^n} + \frac{a_1}{x^{n-1}} + \dots + \frac{a_{n-1}}{x} + a_n\right)$$

$$= \left(a_0x^n + a_1x^{n-1} + \dots + a_{n-1}x + a_n\right) + \left(\frac{a_0}{x^n} + \frac{a_1}{x^{n-1}} + \dots + \frac{a_{n-1}}{x} + a_n\right)$$

on compairing the coefficients of like powers of x on both sides, we get

$a_0 = \pm 1, a_n = 1, a_1 = a_2 = \dots = a_{n-1} = 0$

$\therefore f(x) = x^n + 1$ on $f(x) = -x^n + 1$

If $f(x) = -x^n + 1$, then $f(3) = -3^n + 1 \neq 10$

$[\because f(3) = 10]$

So $\quad f(x) = x^n + 1$

$\Rightarrow \quad f(3) = 3^n + 1$

$\Rightarrow \quad 10 = 3^n + 1$

$\Rightarrow \quad 3^n = 10 - 1 = 9 = 3^2$

$\Rightarrow \quad n = 2.$

Thus $\quad f(x) = x^2 + 1$

$\Rightarrow \quad f(5) = 5^2 + 1 = 25 + 1 = 26.$

30. $f(x)$ is a polynomial of degree 8.

Let $\quad f(x) = a_0x^8 + a_1x^7 + \dots + a_7x + a_8.$

$$\Rightarrow \quad f\left(\frac{1}{x}\right) = \frac{a_0}{x^8} + \frac{a_1}{x^7} + \dots + \frac{a_7}{x} + a_8.$$

Now $f(x) f\left(\frac{1}{x}\right) = f(x) + f\left(\frac{1}{x}\right)$

$$\Rightarrow \left(a_0x^8 + a_1x^7 + \dots + a_7x + a_8\right)\left(\frac{a_0}{x^8} + \frac{a_1}{x^7} + \dots + \frac{a_7}{x} + a_8\right)$$

$$= \left(a_0x^8 + a_1x^7 + \dots + a_7x + a_8\right) + \left(\frac{a_0}{x^8} + \frac{a_1}{x^7} + \dots + \frac{a_7}{x} + a_8\right)$$

Compairing the coefficient of like powers of x on both sides, we get

$a_0 = \pm 1, a_8 = 1, a_1 = a_2 = \dots = a_7 = 0$

$\therefore f(x) = \pm x^8 + 1 \Rightarrow f(-x) = \pm x^8 + 1$

$\therefore$ Function $f(x)$ is even function.

31. By similar procedure as above we get

$f(x) = \pm x^5 + 1$

$\Rightarrow f(-x) = \mp x^5 + 1 \neq -[\pm x^5 + 1] = -f(x).$

$\therefore$ Function $f(x)$ is neither even nor odd function.

32. Given relation

$\left[x + \frac{1}{2}\right] + \left[x - \frac{1}{2}\right] = [2x]$ is true only when

$\frac{1}{2}(2n-1) \leq x < n,$ where n is an integer.

Then $\quad \frac{-3}{2} \leq x < -1, -\frac{1}{2} \leq x < 0, \quad \frac{1}{2} \leq x < 1,$

$\frac{3}{2} \leq x < 2 \dots$ for different values of n

$\therefore \; x - [x] \geq \frac{1}{2}$ satisfies the given relation.

33. Let $\quad f(x) = y = \dfrac{x}{x-1} \quad$ ...(i)

$\Rightarrow \quad x = \dfrac{y}{y-1} \quad$ ...(ii)

Now $\quad f(3x) = \dfrac{3x}{3x-1}$

$$= \frac{3\frac{y}{y-1}}{\frac{3y}{y-1}-1} \text{ (from } (ii))$$

$$= \frac{\frac{3y}{y-1}}{\frac{2y+1}{y-1}} = \frac{3y}{2y+1}$$

$$= \frac{3f(x)}{2f(x)+1} \qquad \text{[from } (i)]$$

34. Given function is $f(x) = \tan x$.

$\Rightarrow f(-x) = \tan(-x) = -\tan x$

($\because$ $\tan x$ is an odd function)

$\therefore f(x) + f(-x) = \tan x - \tan x = 0.$

37. Given $f(x) = \log\left(\frac{1+x}{1-x}\right)$ and $g(x) = \frac{3x+x^3}{1+3x^2}$

Now $fog(x) = f[g(x)]$

$$= \log\left[\frac{1+g(x)}{1-g(x)}\right] = \log\left[\frac{1+\frac{3x+x^3}{1+3x^2}}{1-\frac{3x+x^3}{1+3x^2}}\right]$$

$$= \log\left[\frac{1+3x^2+3x+x^3}{1+3x^2-3x-x^3}\right]$$

$$= \log\left[\frac{(1+x)(1-x+x^2)+3x(x+1)}{(1-x)(1+x+x^2)-3x(1-x)}\right]$$

$$= \log\left[\frac{(1+x)(1+2x+x^2)}{(1-x)(1-2x+x^2)}\right]$$

$$= \log\left\{\frac{(1+x)^3}{(1-x)^3}\right\} = 3\log\left(\frac{1+x}{1-x}\right) = 3f(x).$$

38. Given $\quad f(x) = \frac{ax+b}{cx+d}$

$$fof(x) = f[f(x)] = \frac{af(x)+b}{cf(x)+d}$$

$$= \frac{a\left\{\frac{ax+b}{cx+d}\right\}+b}{c\left\{\frac{ax+b}{cx+d}\right\}+d}$$

$$= \frac{x(a^2+bc)+ab+bd}{x(ac+cd)+bc+d^2} \quad ...(i)$$

For function $fof(x)$ to become x we must have

$ab + bd = 0$

$ac + cd = 0$

and $\quad bc + d^2 = a^2 + bc$

they together give $d = -a$.

39. Given $\quad f(x) = \frac{x+1}{x}, x \neq 0.$

$$f[g(x)] = \frac{g(x)+1}{g(x)} = x \text{ (given)}$$

$\Rightarrow \quad g(x) + 1 = x.g(x)$

$\Rightarrow \quad g(x)(1-x) = -1 \Rightarrow g(x) = \frac{1}{x-1}.$

40. Given $\quad f(x) = \frac{1}{1-x}$

$$\therefore \quad f[f(x)] = \frac{1}{1-f(x)} = \frac{1}{1-\frac{1}{1-x}}$$

$$= \frac{1-x}{-x} = \frac{x-1}{x}$$

$$\therefore f[f(f(x))] = \frac{1}{1-f[f(x)]} = \frac{1}{1-\frac{x-1}{x}} = x.$$

3. PERMUTATION AND COMBINATION

Sum Rule : Suppose A and B are two disjoint events that is they never occur together. Further suppose that A occurs in m ways and B in n ways. Then A or B (at least one of them occur) can occur in $(m + n)$ ways.

Note : This rule can be applied to more than two mutually exclusive events.

Product Rule : Suppose that an event X can be decomposed into two stages, A and B. Let stage A occur in m ways and suppose that these stages are unrelated in the sense that stage B occur in n ways regardless of the outcome of stage A. Then event X occurs in $m \times n$ ways. Then event X occurs in $m \times n$ ways. This rule is applicable even if event X can be decomposed in more than two stages.

Permutations : Each of the arrangements which can be made by taking some or all of a number of things is called a permutations. If the arrangement is in a line, then it is a linear permutation, if it is a circle, then it is a circular permutation.

Note : Order of arrangement in permutation is important. If the order is changed, a different permutation is obtained.

Some Important Theorem :

1. If r and n be positive integers such that $1 \le r \le n$, then the number of all permutations of n distinct things taken r at a time is given by

$$P(n, r) = {}^nP_r = n(n-1)(n-2) \ldots [n-(r-1)]$$

2. $P(n, r) = \dfrac{n!}{(n-r)!}$.

3. The number of all permutations of n distinct things taken all at a time is $n!$.

4. Number of all permutations of n different objects taken r at a time, when a particular object is to be always included in each arrangement is $r\ {}^{n-1}P_{r-1}$.

5. Number of permutations of n distinct objects taken r at a time, when a particular object is never taken in each arrangement is ${}^{n-1}P_r$.

6. Number of permutations of n different objects taken r at a time in which two specified objects always occur together is $2!\ (r-1)\ {}^{n-2}P_{r-2}$.

7. The number of mutually distinguishable permutations of n things, taken all at a time, of which p are alike of one kind, q alike of second such that $p + q = n$ is

$$\frac{n!}{p!q!}.$$

Note :

(i) The number of permutations of n things, of which p_1 are alike of one kind; p_2 are alike of second kind; p_3 are alike of third kind; .... p_r are alike of rth kind such that $p_1 + p_2 + \ldots + p_r = n$, is

$$\frac{n!}{p_1!p_2!p_3!\cdots p_r!}.$$

(ii) The number of permutations of n things of which p are alike of one kind, q are alike of second kind and remaining all are distinct, is

$$\frac{n!}{p!q!}.$$

(iii) Let there be r things to be arranged, allowing repetitions. Let further $p_1, p_2, \ldots, p_r$ be the integers such that first object occurs exactly p_1 times, the second occurs exactly p_2 times, etc. Then the total number of permutations of these r objects to the above condition is

$$\frac{(p_1 + p_2 + \ldots + p_r)!}{p_1!p_2!\cdots p_r!}.$$

8. The number of permutations of n different things, taken r at a time, when each may be repeated once, twice, ... upto r times in each arrangement is n^r.

Circular Permutations

9. The number of circular permutations of n distinct objects is $(n-1)!$.

Note : In the above theorem anti-clockwise and clockwise order of arrangements are considered as distinct permuations.

Difference between clockwise and anti-clockwise arrangements :

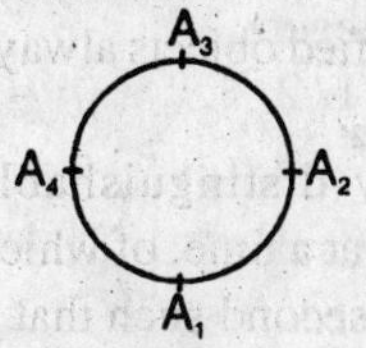

Fig-1

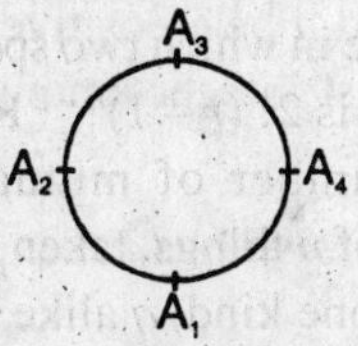

Fig-2

In both the figure the order of circular arrangement is A_1, A_2, A_3, A_4. In Fig-1 the order is anti-clockwise, whereas in Fig-2 the order is clockwise. Thus, the number of circular permutation of n things in which clockwise and anticlockwise arrangements give rise to different permuations is $(n-1)!$.

If anti-clockwise and clockwise order of arrangements are not distinct e.g. arrangements of flowers in a garland, then the number of circular permutations of n distinct items is $\frac{1}{2}(n-1)!$.

Combinations : Each of the different selections made by taking some or all or a number of objects, irrespective of their arrangements is called a combinations.

Theorem for combinations of n different things taken r at a time :

The number of all combinations of n distinct objects, taken r at a time is given by

$$^nC_r = \frac{n!}{(n-r)!r!}$$

Properties of ^nC_r :

1. $^nC_r = {}^nC_{r-1}$ for $0 \le r \le n$.
2. $^nC_r + {}^nC_{r-1} = {}^{n+1}C_r$ for $r \le n$.
3. $^nC_r = \frac{n}{r}\, {}^{n-1}C_{r-1}$.
4. $n.{}^{n-1}C_{r-1} = (n-r+1)\,{}^nC_{r-1}$ for $1 \le r \le n$.
5. $^nC_x = {}^nC_y \Rightarrow x = y$ or $x + y = n$.
6. If n is even, then the greatest value of ^nC_r is $^nC_{r/2}$ for $0 \le r \le n$.
7. If n is odd, then the greatest value of ^nC_r is $^nC_{(n-1)/2}$ or $^nC_{(n-1)/2}$ for $0 \le r \le n$.

Selection of one or more items :

1. The number of ways of selecting one or more items from a group of n distinct items is $2^n - 1$.
2. The number of ways of selecting r items out of n identical items is 1.
3. The total number of ways of selecting zero or more i.e. at least one item from a group of n identical items is $(n + 1)$.
4. The total number of selection of some or all out of $p + q + r$ items where p are alike of one kind, q are alike of second kind and rest are alike of third kind is $[(p+1)(q+1)(r+1)]-1$.
5. The total number of ways of selecting one or more items from p identical items of one kind; q identical items of second kind; r identical items of third kind and n different items is
$$(p+1)(q+1)(r+1)2^n - 1.$$

Division of items into groups :

1. Number of ways in which $(m + n)$ items can be divided into two groups containing m and n items is
$$\frac{(m+n)!}{m!n!}.$$

Note : *(i)* The number of ways in which $(m + n + p)$ items can be divided into three groups containing m, n, p items is
$$^{m+n+p}C_m \cdot {}^{n+p}C_n = \frac{(m+n+p)!}{m!n!p!}.$$

(ii) The number of ways to distribute $(m + n + p)$ items among 3 persons in the groups containing m, n and p items is
$$\frac{(m+n+p)!}{m!n!p!} \times 3!$$

2. The number of ways in which mn different items can be divided equally into m groups, each containing n objects and the groups is not important is
$$\left(\frac{(mn)!}{(n!)^m}\right)\frac{1}{m!}.$$

3. The number of ways in which mn different items can be divided equally into m group, each containing n objects and the order of groups is important is

$$\left(\frac{(mn)!}{(n!)^m}\times\frac{1}{m!}\right)m!=\frac{(mn)!}{(n!)^m}.$$

Division of identical objects into Groups :

1. The total number of ways of dividing n identical items among r persons, each one of whom, 0, 1, 2 or more items ($\le n$) is ${}^{n+r-1}C_{r-1}$.

Alternate form : The total number of ways of dividing n identical objects into r groups, if blank groups are allowed is ${}^{n+r-1}C_{r-1}$.

2. The total number of ways of dividing n identical items among r persons, each one of whom, receives at least one items is ${}^{n-1}C_{r-1}$.

Alternate form : The number of ways in which n identical items can be divided into r groups such that blank groups are not allowed is ${}^{n-1}C_{r-1}$.

3. The number of ways in which n identical items can be divided into r groups so that no group contains less than m items and more than k ($m < k$) is

coefficient of x^n in the expansion

$$\left(x^m + x^{m+1} + ... + x^k\right)^r.$$

Derangements : If n things form an arrangement in a row, the number of ways which they can be rearranged so that no one of them occupies its original place is

$$n!\left(1-\frac{1}{1!}+\frac{1}{2!}-\frac{1}{3!}+....+(-1)^n\frac{1}{n!}\right).$$

Some important resutls : If there are p_1 items of one kind, p_2 items of second kind, ..., p_n items of nth kind then the number of ways of choosing r items out of these $(p_1 + p_2 + ... + p_n)$ items is

coefficients of x^r in

$$(1+x+....+x^{p_1})(1+x+....+x^{p_2})....(1+x+....+x^{p_n})$$

If there are p_1 items of one kind, p_2 items of second kind, ...p_n items of nth kind then the number of ways of choosing r items out of these $(p_1 + p_2 + ... + p_n)$ items such that at least one item of each kind is included in every selection is

coefficient of x^r in

$$(x+x^2+....+x^{p_1})(x+x^2+....+x^{p_2})....(x+x^2+....+x^{p_n}).$$

Exponent of prime p in $n!$: Let p be the prime number and n be a positive integer.

The last integer amongst 1, 2, 3, ..., $(n - 1)$, n which is divisible by p is $\left[\frac{n}{p}\right]p$, where $\left[\frac{n}{p}\right]$ denotes the greatest integer less than or equal to $\frac{n}{p}$.

Let $E_p(m)$ denote the exponent of the prime p in the positive integer m. Then

$$E_p(n!) = E_p[1.2.3....(n-1)n]$$

$$= E_p\left(p.2p.3p....\left[\frac{n}{p}\right]p\right)$$

$\because$ Remaining integers between 1 and n are not divisible by p.

Again last integer among 1, 2, 3, ... $\left[\frac{n}{p}\right]$ which is divisible by p is

$$\left[\frac{n/p}{p}\right]p=\left[\frac{n}{p^2}\right]p.$$

$$\therefore\quad E_p(n!)=\left[\frac{n}{p}\right]+E_p\left(p.2p.3p....\left[\frac{n}{p^2}\right]p\right)$$

$\because$ Remaining integers between 1 and $\left[\frac{n}{p}\right]$ are not divisible by p.

$$=\left[\frac{n}{p}\right]+\left[\frac{n}{p^2}\right]+E_p\left(1.2.3....\left[\frac{n}{p^2}\right]\right)$$

Proceeding in the same manner we have

$$E_p(n!)=\left[\frac{n}{p}\right]+\left[\frac{n}{p^2}\right]+\left[\frac{n}{p^3}\right]+....+\left[\frac{n}{p^r}\right]$$

where $p^r \le n \le p^{r+1}$.

EXERCISE

Mark the correct alternatives of each of the following:

1. If $^{56}P_{r+6} : {^{54}P_{r+3}} = 30800 : 1$, then r equals

(a) 14 (b) 15
(c) 41 (d) 51

2. If $^{2n}C_3 : {^nC_2} = 44 : 3$, then n equals

(a) 4 (b) 5
(c) 6 (d) 7

3. If $^{28}C_r : {^{24}C_{2r-4}} = 225 : 11$, then r equals

(a) 4 (b) 5
(c) 6 (d) 7

4. The number of arrangements that can be made out of the letters of the word DRAUGHT, where the vowels never being separated is

(a) 144 (b) 440
(c) 441 (d) 1440

5. From 3 capitals, 5 consonants and 4 vowels, number of words that can be made, each containing 3 consonants and 2 vowels and beginning with a capital is

(a) 21600 (b) 12600
(c) 21605 (d) 25016

6. The number of ways 10 examination papers be arranged so that the best and worst papers never come together is

(a) 2803040 (b) 2903040
(c) 2003040 (d) 2703040

7. A five digit number divisible by 3 is to be formed using the numerals 0, 1, 2, 3, 4 and 5, without repetition. The total number of ways this can be done is

(a) 216 (b) 240
(c) 600 (d) 201

8. A set contains $(2n + 1)$ elements. The number of subsets of the set which contain at most n elements is

(a) 2^n (b) 2^{n+1}
(c) 2^{n-1} (d) 2^{2n}

9. The sum of all the five digit number that can be formed using the digits 1, 2, 3, 4 and 5 (repetition of digits not allowed) is

(a) 360000 (b) 660000
(c) 366000 (d) None of these

10. Ten different letters of an alphabet are given. Words with five letters are formed from given letters. The number of words which have at least one letter repeated is

(a) 30240 (b) 66790
(c) 69760 (d) 99748

[J.N.U. M.C.A.]

11. The total number of ways of arranging the letters AAABBBCCDEF in row such that letters C are separated from one another is

(a) 2772000 (b) 1386000
(c) 2836000 (d) None of these

12. Using 7 consonants and 5 vowels, how many words consisting of 4 consonants and 3 vowels can be formed?

(a) $\binom{7}{4}\binom{5}{3}$ (b) $\binom{7}{4}\binom{5}{3}(3!)$
(c) $\binom{7}{4}\binom{5}{3}(7!)$ (d) None of these

[J.N.U. M.C.A.]

13. Numbers greater than a million can be formed with the digits 2, 3, 0, 3, 4, 2, 3 is

(a) 180 (b) 360
(c) 260 (d) 520

14. Number of arrangements which can be made out of the letters of the word ALGEBRA, without altering the relative positions of vowels and consonants is

(a) 72 (b) 5040
(c) 35 (d) None of these

15. Number of ways five things can be divided between two persons is

(a) 32 (b) 30
(c) 36 (d) None of these

16. How many numbers less than 1000 can be made with the eight digits 1, 2, 3, 0, 4, 5, 6, 7?

(a) 3548 (b) 4095
(c) 4580 (d) 3584

17. The number of four digits decimal numbers (< 1) in which no digit is repeated, is
(a) 5040 (b) 4536
(c) 10^4 (d) 3024

18. The number of natural numbers smaller than 10^4, in the decimal notation of which all the digits are different is
(a) 5274 (b) 5265
(c) 4676 (d) None of these

19. A number of five digits has the sum of digits equal to 20. The number of such numbers is
(a) $^{28}C_4$ (b) $^{27}C_4$
(c) $^{24}C_4 - 5\,^{14}C_4 + 10$ (d) None of these

20. Sum of all four digit numbers that can be formed with the digits 2, 3, 4, 5 with no repetition allowed is
(a) 90024 (b) 84
(c) 93324 (d) 84432

21. The number of times the digit 3 will be written when listing the integers from 1 to 1000 is
(a) 291 (b) 250
(c) 300 (d) 350

22. The total number of natural numbers of six digits that can be made with digits 1, 2, 3, 4 if all digits are to be appear in the same number at least once is
(a) 1040 (b) 1540
(c) 1560 (d) 1450

23. The total number of numbers greater than 1000, but not greater than 4000, that can be formed with the digits 0, 1, 2, 3, 4 when the repetition of digits allowed is
(a) 371 (b) 373
(c) 375 (d) None of these

24. The number of six digit numbers that can be formed from the digits 1, 2, 3, 4, 5, 6 and 7 so that the digits do not repeat and the terminal digits are even is
(a) 270 (b) 702
(c) 720 (d) None of these

25. All possible two factors product are formed from the numbers 1, 2, 3, 4, ..., 200. The number factors out of the total obtained which are multiples of 5 is
(a) 6180 (b) 5180
(c) 8180 (d) 7180

26. How many 10 digits numbers can be written by using the digits 1 and 2.
(a) $^{10}C_1 + {}^{10}C_2$ (b) 2^{10}
(c) $^{10}C_2$ (d) 10!

27. How many numbers can be formed with the digits 1, 2, 3, 4, 3, 2, 1, so that odd digits always occupy the odd places?
(a) 22 (b) 18
(c) 32 (d) 14

28. There are n straight lines in a plane, no two of which are parallel and no three pass through the same point. There points of intersection are joined. Then the number of fresh limes thus obtained is
(a) $\dfrac{n(n-1)(n-2)}{8}$
(b) $\dfrac{n(n-1)(n-2)(n-3)}{6}$
(c) $\dfrac{n(n-1)(n-2)(n-3)}{8}$
(d) None of these

29. The number of triangles whose vertices are at the vertices of an octagon but none of whose sides happen to come from the sides of the octagon is
(a) 16 (b) 36
(c) 54 (d) 27
[J.N.U. M.C.A]

30. If 5 points out of 11 are in the same straight line, then the number of triangles formed is
(a) 150 (b) 155
(c) 160 (d) 165

31. x parallel lines in a plane are intersected by a family of y parallel lines. The total number of parallelograms so formed is
(a) $\dfrac{xy(x-1)(y-1)}{4}$ (b) $\dfrac{(x^2-1)(y^2-1)}{4}$
(c) $\dfrac{x(x-1)(y-1)}{4}$ (d) $\dfrac{(x-1)y(y-1)}{4}$

32. A parallelogram is cut by two sets of m lines parallel to its sides. The number of parallelograms thus formed is
(a) $\left({}^{m}C_2\right)^2$ (b) $\left({}^{m+1}C_2\right)^2$
(c) $\left({}^{m+2}C_2\right)^2$ (d) None of these

33. The greatest possible number of points of intersection of 8 straight lines and 4 circles is
(a) 101 *(b)* 102
(c) 103 *(d)* 104

34. Number of diagonals that can be drawn by joining the vertices of an octagon is
(a) 28 *(b)* 48
(c) 20 *(d)* None of these

35. The numbers of odd integers between 1000 and 9999 with no digit repeated is
(a) 3333 *(b)* 2120
(c) 2240 *(d)* 3331 *[J.N.U. M.C.A.]*

36. There are 12 points in a plane, no three of which are in the same straight line with the exception of 6, which are all in the same straight line. Then the number of triangles which result from joining them is
(a) 200 *(b)* 220
(c) 240 *(d)* 260

37. There are 15 points in space, no four of which are in the same plane with the exception of 5, which are all in the same plane. Then how many planes are there each containing three of the points?
(a) 445 *(b)* 446
(c) 447 *(d)* 448

38. Sum of all numbers greater than 10000 formed by using the digits 0, 2, 4, 6, 8, where no digit being repeated in any number is
(a) 6190005 *(b)* 59100060
(c) 5199960 *(d)* 519960

39. The number of different seven digit numbers that can be written using only the three digits 1, 2 and 3 with the condition that the digit 2 occurs twice in each number is
(a) ${}^7P_2.2^5$ *(b)* ${}^7C_2.2^5$
(c) ${}^7C_2.5^2$ *(d)* None of these
[J.N.U. M.C.A.]

40. A polygon has 77 diagonals, the number of its sides is
(a) 10 *(b)* 12
(c) 14 *(d)* 16

ANSWERS

1	2	3	4	5	6	7	8	9	10
(c)	(c)	(d)	(d)	(a)	(b)	(a)	(d)	(d)	(c)
11	**12**	**13**	**14**	**15**	**16**	**17**	**18**	**19**	**20**
(b)	(c)	(b)	(a)	(b)	(d)	(c)	(a)	(d)	(c)
21	**22**	**23**	**24**	**25**	**26**	**27**	**28**	**29**	**30**
(a)	(c)	(c)	(d)	(b)	(b)	(b)	(c)	(a)	(b)
31	**32**	**33**	**34**	**35**	**36**	**37**	**38**	**39**	**40**
(a)	(a)	(d)	(c)	(c)	(a)	(b)	(c)	(b)	(c)

SOME SELECTED EXPLANTORY ANSWERS

1. ${}^{56}P_{r+6} : {}^{54}P_{r+3} = 30800 : 1$

or $\dfrac{{}^{56}C_{r+6}}{{}^{54}C_{r+3}} = \dfrac{30800}{1}$

or $\dfrac{56!\,(51-r)!}{(50-r)! \times 54!} = 30800$

or $\dfrac{56 \times 55 \times 54! \times (50-r)! \times (51-r)}{(50-r)! \times 54!} = 30800$

or $(51 - r) = 10$

$\therefore$ $r = 41.$

2. ${}^{2n}C_3 : {}^nC_2 = 44 : 3$

or $\dfrac{{}^{2n}C_3}{{}^nC_2} = \dfrac{44}{3}$

or $\dfrac{(2n)!}{3! \times (2n-3)!} \times \dfrac{2! \times (n-2)!}{n!} = \dfrac{44}{3}$

or $\frac{(2n)(2n-1)(2n-2)(2n-3)!}{3\times2\times1\times(2n-3)!}\times$

$$\frac{2\times1\times(n-2)!}{n(n-1)(n-2)!}=\frac{44}{3}$$

or $2(2n-1)\times2=44$

or $2n-1=11$

or $n=6.$

3. ${}^{28}C_{2r} : {}^{24}C_{2r-4} = 225 : 11$

or $\frac{{}^{28}C_{2r}}{{}^{24}C_{2r-4}}=\frac{225}{11}$

or $\frac{(28)!\times(28-2r)!\,(2r-4)!}{(2r)!\times(28-2r)!\times24!}=\frac{225}{11}$

or $\frac{28\times27\times26\times25}{2r(2r-1)(2r-2)(2r-3)}=\frac{225}{11}$

or $2r(2r-1)(2r-2)(2r-3)=11\times28\times3\times26$

or $2r(2r-1)(2r-2)(2r-3)=14\times13\times12\times11$

or $r=7$

4. There are 7 letters in the word "DRAUGHT", the two vowels are 'A' and 'U'. Since the vowels are not to be separated so 'AU' may be considered as one letter. Therefore the number of letters will be 6 instead of 7.

The arrangement can be in ${}^6P_6$ ways.

But as the arrangement of the two vowels can be either 'UA' or 'AU' so the required number of arrangements will be $2\times{}^6P_6=2\times720=1440.$

5. Each word is of 6 letters. Capital letter in the beginning and 3 consonants and two vowels in each word can be selected in ${}^3C_1\times{}^5C_3\times{}^4C_2$ combined ways. Further besides the capital letter, remaining 5 letters can be arranged among themselves in 5! ways.

Hence, the required number of words

$$={}^3C_1\times{}^5C_3\times{}^4C_2\times5!$$
$$=21600.$$

6. 10 examination papers can be arranged in 10! = 3628800 ways.

These arrangements include those cases also when the worst and the best paper come together. It can be so in 9! = 362880 ways.

Position of two papers among themselves can be arranged in 2! ways.

∴ Combined number such that best and worst papers come together

$$=2\times362880=725760.$$

∴ Required number of ways

$$=3628800-725760=2903040.$$

7. If a number is divisible by 3, the sum of the digits in it must be a multiple of 3. The sum of the given six numerals is $0+1+2+3+4+5=15$. So to make a five digit numbers divisible by 3 we can either exclude 0 or 3. If 0 is left out, then 5! = 120 number of possible ways. If 3 is left out, then the number of ways of making a five digit number is $4\times4!=96$, as 0 cannot be placed in the first place from left, as it will give a number of four digits.

Thus, the required number of ways $=120+96=216$.

8. The number of subsets of the set which contain at most n elements is

${}^{2n+1}C_0+{}^{2n+1}C_1+{}^{2n+1}C_2+....+{}^{2n+1}C_n=N$ (say).

Thus we have

$$2N=2\left({}^{2n+1}C_0+{}^{2n+1}C_1+{}^{2n+1}C_2+....+{}^{2n+1}C_n\right)$$

$$=\left[{}^{2n+1}C_0+{}^{2n+1}C_1+{}^{2n+1}C_2+....+\left({}^{2n+1}C_n+{}^{2n+1}C_{n+1}\right)\right]$$

$$[\because {}^nC_r={}^nC_{n-r}]$$

$$={}^{2n+1}C_0+{}^{2n+1}C_1+{}^{2n+1}C_2+....+{}^{2n+1}C_{2n+1}$$
$$=2^{2n+1}$$

$$\therefore N=\frac{2^{2n+1}}{2}=2^n.$$

9. Total number of 5 digit numbers that can be formed using the digits 1, 2, 3, 4 and 5 is 5! = 120.

If 5 occurs at the units place, then the remaining digits can be arranged in ${}^4P_4=4!=24$ ways. Similarly 4 can occur at the unit place in ${}^4P_4=24$ ways, and so on.

Thus the sum due to the units place of all the 120 numbers is

$24(1+2+3+4+5)$ units $=24\times15$ units $=360$ units.

Next 5 can occur at the tens place in 24 ways. The same is true of the remaining digits.

Thus, the sum due to the tens place of all the 120 numbers is

24 (1 + 2 + 3 + 4 + 5) tens = 360 tens.

Sum of the remaining places are obtained similarly.

Hence, the sum of all the 120 numbers is given by

360 (1 + 10 + 100 + 1000 + 10000)

$= 360 \times 11111 = 3999960.$

10. Total number of words consists of five letters each can be formed using 10 letters where repetition is allowed is $10 \times 10 \times 10 \times 10 \times 10 = 10^5$.

When the repetition is not allowed, first place can be occupied in 10 ways, second in 9 ways, third in 8 ways, fourth in 7 ways and fifth in 6 ways out of 10 available letters.

Thus total number of words without repetition is $= 10 \times 9 \times 8 \times 7 \times 6 = 30240$.

$\therefore$ The number of words which have at least one letter repeated is

$= 100000 - 30240 = 69760.$

11. We have 12 letters including 2C's. Let us ignore 2C's and thus have 10 letters (4A's, 3B's, 1D, 1E, 1F) and these 10 letters can be arranged in $\frac{10!}{4!3!}$ ways. Now after arranging these 10 letters there will be 11 gaps in which 2 different letters can be arranged in ${}^{11}P_2$ ways. But since 2C's are alike, the number of arrangements will be $\frac{1}{2!}\,{}^{11}P_2 = \frac{11!}{9!2!}$.

$\therefore$ The total number of ways in which C's are separated from one another is

$\frac{10!}{4!3!}\cdot\frac{11!}{9!2!} = 1386000.$

12. Out of 7 consonants, 4 consonants can be choosen in ${}^7C_4$ ways.

Similarly out of 5 vowels, 3 vowels can be choosen in ${}^5C_3$ ways.

Now, these 7 letters can be arranged in 7! ways among themselves.

$\therefore$ Total number of ways in which words consisting of 9 consonants and 3 vowels can be formed is ${}^7C_4 \times {}^5C_3 \times 7!$ i.e. $\binom{7}{4}\binom{5}{3}(7!)$.

13. 2, 3, 0, 3, 4, 2, 3 are 7 figures of which two are 2, three are 3, one 4 and one 0.

Then total number of arrangements

$$= \frac{7!}{2!3!} = 420.$$

This number 420 includes those cases also in which zero would be at the ten lak's place. Hence, these number must be subtracted from the total number of arrangements.

These arrangements are $\frac{6!}{2! \times 3!} = 60$ in number.

$\therefore$ Required number of arrangemnts

$= 420 - 60 = 360.$

14. In the word 'ALGEBRA' we have three vowels and four consonants.

The three vowels (two 'A's and one 'E') can be arranged in three ways and the four consonants in 4! ways as the relative positions of vowels and consonants are not to be changed.

$\therefore$ Required arrangements

$= 3 \times 4! = 3 \times 3 \times 4 \times 2 = 72.$

15. Any one of the things can be given in 2 ways. Also any one of the remaining in two ways. Thus, two things can be arranged in $2 \times 2 = 2^2$ ways. Similarly three things in 2^3 ways and so on. Hence, 5 things will be arranged in 2^5 ways. It includes those very two classes in which either may receive none.

$\therefore$ Required number $= 2^5 - 2 = 32 - 2 = 30$.

16. Any 7 number can fill one thousands place in ${}^7C_1 = 7$ ways. In hundreds place for every number it can be filled in 8 ways.

$\therefore$ Total no. of filling's 100's place

$= 7 \times 8 = 56$ ways.

Total no. of filling's 10's place

$= 7 \times 8 \times 8 = 448$ ways.

Total no. of filling's unit's place

$= 7 \times 8 \times 8 \times 8 = 3584$ ways.

$\therefore$ Total number of ways required

$= 7 + 56 + 448 + 3584$

$= 4095$ ways.

17. In four digits decimal number, the first place after decimal (i.e.) can be filled in 10 ways. As no digits is repeated, second place is occupied in 9 ways, third in 8 ways and fourth in 7 ways.

$\therefore$ Total number of four digit decimal numbers (< 1)

$= 10 \times 9 \times 8 \times 7 = 5040.$

18. The required natural numbers consists of 4 digits, 3 digits and one digit so that their number is equal to
$9.9.8.7 + 9.9.8 + 9.9 + 9 = 5274$.

19. Required number= Coefficient of x^{20} in $\left(1 + x + ... + x^9\right)^5$.
= Coefficient of x^{20} in $(1 - x^{10})(1 - x)^5$
= Coefficieint of x^{20} in
$(1 - 5x^{10} + 10x^{20} + ...)(1 - x)^5$
$= {}^{24}C_4 - 5.{}^{14}C_4 + 10$.
From this we have to exclude numbers like 02567 which are of four digits. Such numbers are equal to $({}^{23}C_3 - 4.{}^{13}C_4 + 6)$.
Hence, the total number
$= \left({}^{24}C_4 - 5.{}^{14}C_4 + 10\right) - \left({}^{23}C_3 - 4.{}^{13}C_3 + 6\right)$

20. Total number of 4 digit numbers that can be formed using the digits 2, 3, 4 and 5 is $4! = 24$.
If 5 occurs at the units place, then the remaining digits can be arranged in ${}^3P_3 = 3! = 6$ ways.
Similarly 4 can occur at the unit place in ${}^3P_3 = 6$ ways and soon. Thus, the sun due to the unit place of all the 24 numbers is
$6(2 + 3 + 4 + 5)$ units = 84 units.
Next 5 can occur at the tens place in 6 ways. The same is true of the remaining digits.
Thus, the sum due to the tens place of all the 24 numbers is
$6(2 + 3 + 4 + 5)$ tens = 84 tens.
Sum of the remaining places are obtained similarly.
Hence, the sum of all the 24 numbers is given by $84(1 + 10 + 10^2 + 10^3) = 93324$.

21. 3 does not occur in the number 1000. So we are to count the number of times 3 occurs between integers 1 and 999. Any number between 1 and 999 is of the form where $0 \le a, b, c \le 9$.
Number of times 3 occurs
= Number of times 3 occurs in 3 digit numbers
+ Number of times 3 occurs in 2 digit numbers
+ Number of times 3 occurs in 1 digit numbers.
(i) Number of times 3 occurs in 3 digit numbers
$= {}^3C_1 \times 9 \times 9 + {}^3C_2 \times 9 + {}^3C_3$
$= 243 + 27 + 1 = 271$
(ii) Number of times 3 occurs in 2 digit numbers
$= {}^2C_1 \times 9 + {}^2C_2$
$= 18 + 1 = 19$
(iii) Number of times 3 occurs in 1 digit numbers
$= {}^1C_1 = 1$
$\therefore$ Total number of times 3 occurs $= 271 + 19 + 1 = 291$.

22. There are two ways where it appears at least once.
(i) Out of the given digits any one of them repeats thrice and the remaining only once.
It can be done in ${}^4C_1 \times \frac{6!}{3!} = 480$
(ii) Out of the given digits any two of them repeats twice and the remaining two only once. It can be done in ${}^4C_2 \times \frac{6!}{2!2!} = 1080$.
$\therefore$ Total number of ways $= 480 + 1080 = 1560$.

23. Numbers greater than 1000 and less than or equal to 4000, consists of four digit numbers. As repetition is allowed, so numbers having 1 in first place from left side can be arranged in $5 \times 5 \times 5 = 125$ ways.
It includes the number 1000 which is to be excluded. Thus, there are 124 ways where 1 is in first place.
Similarly the number of ways where 2 or 3 appears in first place is 125 each.
There is only one number i.e. 4000 which starts with the number 4 in first place.
Thus, total number of required ways = 124 + 125 + 125 + 1 = 375.

24. Terminal digits are the digits at the first and the last place.
There are total 3 even numbers and 4 odd numbers.
Thus the number of six digit numbers that can be formed so that digits do not repeat and the terminal digits are even is
$\left\{{}^3C_2 \times (2!)\right\} \times \left\{{}^5C_4 \times (4!)\right\} = 720$.

25. Total number of two factor products formed from the numbers 1, 2, 3, ..., 200 is ${}^{200}C_2 = 19900$.
The number of numbers from 1 to 200 which are divisible by 5 is
(i) Three digit numbers starts with 1 and ends with 0 or 5 is $1 \times 10 \times 2 = 20$.
It also include the number 200. Thus total number of ways = 21.

(ii) Two digit numbers ends with 0 or 5 is $9 \times 2 = 18$.

(iii) One digit number divisible by 5 is only 1 i.e. 5.

$\therefore$ Total number of ways $= 21 + 18 + 1 = 40$.

Thus number of numbers from 1 to 200 which are not divisible by 5 is $200 - 40 = 160$.

Therefore total number of two factor products which are not multiple of 5 is $^{160}C_2 = 12720$.

Hence, the required number of factors $= 19900 - 12720 = 7180$.

26. Since each place of the 10 digit numbers taken by either 1 or 2, then the total number of required ten digit numbers $= 2 \times 2 \times ....$ 10 times $= 2^{10}$.

27. Seven digit numbers to be formed, out of which there are four odd places and three even places.

(i) The number of ways four odd places occupied by odd numbers 1, 3, 3, 1 is

$$^4C_4 \times \frac{4!}{2! \times 2!} = 6 \text{ ways.}$$

(ii) The number of ways three even places occupied by even numbers 2, 4, 2 is

$$^3C_3 \times \frac{3!}{2!} = 3 \text{ ways.}$$

$\therefore$ Total number of required numbers are

$$6 \times 3 = 18.$$

28. Since no two lines are parallel and no three are concurrent, therefore n straight lines intersect at $^nC_2 = N$ (say) points.

Since two points are required to determine a straight line, therefore the total number of lines obtained by joining N points is $^NC_2$. But in this, each odd line has been counted $^{n-1}C_2$ times, since on each old line there will be $(n-1)$ points of intersection made by remaining $(n-1)$ lines.

Hence required number of fresh lines is

$$^NC_2 - n.^{n-1}C_2$$

$$= \frac{N(N-1)}{2} - \frac{n(n-1)(n-2)}{2}$$

$$= \frac{^nC_2(^nC_2 - 1)}{2} - \frac{n(n-1)(n-2)}{2}$$

$$= \frac{n(n-1)(n-2)(n-3)}{8}$$

29. In a octagon there are total eight vertices. Three vertices needed to form a triangle.

(i) Total number of triangles formed from the vertices of octagon is $^8C_3 = 56$.

(ii) Out of the total triangles formed, number of triangles with one common side with that of the octagon is $^8C_1 \times {^4C_1} = 32$.

(iii) Out of the total triangles formed, number of traingles with two common sides with that of the octagon is $2 \times {^4C_1} = 8$.

$\therefore$ Required number is *(i)* – *(ii)* – *(iii)*

$$= 56 - 32 - 8 = 16.$$

Note :

1. $^4C_1$ is taken because four furthest points from the two vertices of the side can only form triangle with that side.
2. $2 \times {^4C_1}$ is taken because two adjacent sides are taken as one and each side is taken twice.

30. Number of ways in which we can select 3 points out of 11 points is $^{11}C_3$.

Also the number of ways of selecting 3 points on the same straight line is $^5C_3$.

Therefore, the number of triangle formed equals to

$^{11}C_3 - {^5C_3} = 165 - 10 = 155$.

31. Out of four lines in a parallelogram opposite sides are parallel to each other.

Thus, we are to choose two parallel lines each from two sets of parallel lines which intersect each other.

This can be done in $^xC_2 \times {^yC_2}$

$$= \frac{xy(x-1)(y-1)}{4}.$$

32. Each set is having m parallel lines and each parallelogram is formed by choosing two straight lines from the first set and two straight line from the two sets.

Two straight line from the first set can be chosen in $^mC_2$ ways and two straight lines from the second set can be chosen in $^mC_2$ ways.

Hence total number of parallelograms formed

$$= {^mC_2}.{^mC_2} = \left(^mC_2\right)^2.$$

33. *(i)* Number of points we get from the intersection of 8 straight line with each other is $^8C_2$ as intersection of two straight lines give one point.

(*ii*) Number of points we get the intersection of 4 circles with each other is $^4C_2 \times 2$ as we get two point for two circles intersection.

(*iii*) Number of points we get from the intersection on of 8 straight line and 4 circles is $2 \times \left({}^8C_1 \times {}^4C_1\right)$

2 is multiplies because intersection of line and circle gives two points for maximum points.

Thus, total number of points equals to

$$^8C_2 + 2 \times {}^4C_2 + 2 \times \left({}^8C_1 \times {}^4C_1\right)$$

$$= 28 + 12 + 64 = 104.$$

34. For a diagonal we need two points. Thus, total number of lines obtained by joining 8 vertices of octagon is $^8C_2 = 28$.

Out of these, 8 lines are sides and remaining are diagonal.

∴ Required number of diagonals = 28 – 8 = 20.

35. All the digits that will be formed are 4 digit numbers.

There are all together five odd numbers which can occupy the last digit to form an odd number. As soon as we place an odd number in the last place we are left with 9 numbers. But 0 cannot occupy the first place as it reduce into 3 digit number. So, first place is occupied by 8 numbers. Second place with 8 numbers as 0 can be included. Third place with remaining 7 numbers as repetition is not allowed.

Thus required number of odd numbers = 8 × 8 × 7 × 5 = 2240.

36. If there had been no three points in one straight line, we would have obtained triangles

$$^{12}C_3 = \frac{12 \times 11 \times 10}{3 \times 2} = 220.$$

But as 6 points are in one straight line, so the number of cases where there will be no triangle is

$$^6C_3 = \frac{6 \times 5 \times 4}{3 \times 2} = 20.$$

Hence, required number of triangles equals to 220 – 20 = 200.

37. Number of planes each containing three points out of 15 will be

$$^{15}C_3 = \frac{15 \times 14 \times 13}{3 \times 2} = 455.$$

Since 5 points are in one plane, so the planes $^5C_3 = 10$ can be obtained by joining any three points. It gives only one plane.

∴ Required number of planes = 455 – 10 + 1 = 446.

38. Since all the numbers formed are greater than 10000, so zero can not occur at ten thousand's place. All the numbers required consists of 5 digits.

Sum of all the numbers occurring at units place is

$4! \times 0 + (4! - 3!)\,(2 + 4 + 6 + 8) = 360.$

Similar for the sum of the numbers at tenth, hundreth and thousand place.

Sum of numbers occurring at ten thousands place is

$4!\,(2 + 4 + 6 + 8) = 480.$

∴ Required sum of numbers = 360 + 3600 + 36000 + 480000 = 5199960.

39. Seven digit number consist of seven places which are to be filled by numbers 1, 2, 3.

Any two places can be taken by digit 2 in $^7C_2$ ways.

Since the digit can be repeated, remaining five places can be taken by 1 or 3 in $2 \times 2 \times 2 \times 2 \times 2 = 2^5$ ways.

∴ Required number of seven digit numbers = $^7C_2 \times 2^5$.

40. Let the polygon consists of n sides. Then the number of diagonals which can be formed equals to $^nC_2 - n$. Here we have subtracted all the sides which are not its diagonals.

Thus, according to the problem

$$^nC_2 - n = 77$$

or $\quad \dfrac{n\,(n-1)}{2} - n = 77$

or $\quad n^2 - 3n = 154$

or $\quad n^2 - 3n - 154 = 0$

or $(n - 14)\,(n + 11) = 0$

or $n = 14$ or -11.

As diagonals can not be negative we have $n = 14$.

4. COMPLEX NUMBER

1. Definition : Any ordered pair of real number, x, y written as (x, y) is called a complex number. Thus the complex number $z = x + iy$ is defined as the ordered pair (x, y) of real number x and y usually written as $z = (x, y)$.

The real numbers x and y are called the real and imaginary part of z. It is customary to write Re $(z) = x$, Im $(z) = y$, where Re (z) stands for the real part of z and Im (z) stands for the imaginary part of z.

A complex number z is purely real if its imaginary part is zero *i.e.,* Im $(z) = 0$ and purely imaginary if its real part is zero *i.e.,* Re $(z) = 0$.

Set of complex number is denoted by C.

$\therefore$ $C = \{(x + iy) : x, y \in R \text{ and } i = \sqrt{-1}\}$.

2. Integral Power of *i* : Euler was first to introduce the symbol i for $\sqrt{-1}$ with the property $i^2 = -1$. Thus $i^3 = i^2.i = (-1).i = -i$, $i^4 = (i^2)^2 = (-1)^2 = 1$, etc.

3. Equality of Complex Numbers : Two complex numbers are equal if real part of the one is equal to the real part of the other and imaginary part of one is equal to the imaginary part of the other. Two complex numbers $z_1 = x_1 + iy_1$ and and $z_2 = x_2 + iy_2$ are equal if $x_1 = x_2$ and $y_1 = y_2$ *i.e.,* Re (z_1) = Re(z_2) and Im (z_1) = Im (z_2).

Note : The phrases "greater than" or "less than" have no meaning in relations of two complex numbers. Inequalities can occur only in relations between the moduli of complex numbers.

4. Fundamental Operations : If $z_1 = (x_1 + iy_1)$ and $z_2 = (x_2 + iy_2)$

We have the following definitions of the addition, substraction and multiplication of z_1 and z_2.

(i) **Addition :** $z_1 + z_2 = (x_1 + iy_1) + (x_2 + iy_2) = (x_1 + x_2) + i\,(y_1 + y_2)$

(ii) **Subtraction :** $z_1 - z_2 = (x_1 - iy_1) + (x_2 - iy_2) = (x_1 - x_2) + i\,(y_1 - y_2)$

(iii) **Multiplication :** $z_1 z_2 = (x_1 + iy_1)(x_2 + iy_2) = (x_1 x_2 - y_1 y_2) + i\,(x_1 y_2 - x_2 y_1)$ $[\because i^2 = 1]$

5. Properties

(a) **For Addition**

(i) The Commutative law : $z_1 + z_2 = z_2 + z_1$

(ii) The Associative law : $z_1 + (z_2 + z_3) = (z_1 + z_2) + z_3$

(iii) Additive identity exit : $z_1 + 0 = 0 + z_1$

(iv) Additive inverse exist : $z_1 + (-z_1) = 0 = (-z_1) + z_1$

(v) Closure law : $z_1 + z_2 = (x_1 + iy_1) + (x_2 + iy_2) = (x_1 + x_2) + i\,(y_1 + y_2) \in C$

(b) **For Multiplication**

(i) Closure law : $z_1.z_2 = (x_1 x_2 - y_1 y_2) + i\,(x_1 y_2 + x_2 y_1) \in C$

(ii) The Commutative law : $z_1.z_2 = z_2.z_1$

(iii) The Associative law : $z_1.(z_2.z_3) = (z_1.z_2).z_3$

(iv) Multiplicative identity exist : $z_1.(1 + i.0) = (x_1 + iy_1).(1 + i.0) = x_1 + iy_1 = z_1$
($\because$ $1 + i.0$ is the multiplicative inverse).

(v) Multiplicative inverse exist : If $z_1 = x_1 + iy_1 \neq 0$, then

$$z_1 \cdot \left(\frac{x_1}{x_1^2 + y_1^2} - \frac{iy_1}{x_1^2 + y_1^2}\right) = (x_1 + iy_1).\frac{(x_1 - iy_1)}{x_1^2 + y_1^2}$$

$$= \frac{x_1^2 + y_1^2}{x_1^2 + y_1^2} = 1 = 1 + i.0$$

(vi) Distributive law : $z_1.(z_2 + z_3) = z_1.z_2 + z_1.z_3$
(Left distributive law)

$(z_2 + z_3).z_1 = z_2.z_1 + z_3.z_1$
(Right distributive law)

Multiplicative Inverse : Multiplicative inverse of a non-zero complex number z_1, denoted by z^{-1}, is defined to be a complex number z_2 such that $z_1.z_2 = 1$.

Multiplicative inverse of the zero complex is not defined.

Let $z_1 = (x_1 + iy_1), z_2 = (x_2 + iy_2)$

Then $z_1.z_2 = (x_1x_2 - y_1y_2) + i(x_1y_2 + x_2y_1)$

$= (1 + i.0)$

$\Rightarrow x_1x_2 - y_1y_2 = 1$

$x_1y_2 - x_2y_2 = 0$

$\therefore x_2 = \dfrac{x_1}{x_1^2 + y_1^2}$ and $y_2 = \dfrac{-y_1}{x_1^2 + y_1^2}$

Since $(x_1, y_1) \neq (0, 0)$, x_2, y_2 both exists

$$\therefore z_2 = z_1^{-1} = \frac{x_1}{x_1^2 + y_1^2} + i\frac{(-y_1)}{x_1^2 + y_1^2} = \frac{x_1 - iy_1}{x_1^2 + y_1^2}$$

7. Division of Complex Numbers : Let z_1, z_2 be two complex numbers where z_2 is non-zero. The division of a complex number z_1 by a non-zero complex number z_2 is defined as the multiplication of z_1 by the multiplicative inverse of z_2 and is denoted by $\dfrac{z_1}{z_2}$.

Let $z_1 = x_1 + iy_1$ and $z_2 = x_2 + iy_2$

$$\text{Then } \frac{z_1}{z_2} = \frac{(x_1 + iy_1)}{(x_2 + iy_2)}$$

$$= \frac{(x_1 + iy_1)(x_2 - iy_2)}{(x_2 + iy_2)(x_2 - iy_2)}$$

$$= \frac{(x_1x_2 + y_1y_2) + (-x_1y_2 + x_2y_1)}{x_2^2 + y_2^2}$$

$$= \frac{x_1x_2 + y_1y_2}{x_2^2 + y_2^2} + i\frac{x_2y_1 - x_1y_2}{x_2^2 + y_2^2}$$

8. Conjugate of a Complex Number : Let $z = x + iy \in C$. We define the complex conjugate (or simply conjugate) of z to be the complex number $\bar{z}$ (call it z bar) and is given by $\bar{z} = x - iy$ where $\text{Re}(\bar{z}) = x = \text{Re}(z)$ and $\text{Im}(\bar{z}) = -y = -\text{Im}(z)$.

Properties : If z, z_1, z_2 are complex numbers, then

(i) $z + \bar{z} = (x + iy) + (x - iy) = 2x$ = purely real number.

(ii) $z - \bar{z} = (x + iy) - (x - iy) = 2iy$ = purely imaginary number.

(iii) $z = \bar{z} \Rightarrow z$ is purely real.

(iv) $z + \bar{z} = 0 \Rightarrow z$ is purely imaginary.

(v) $\overline{(\bar{z})} = \overline{(x + iy)} = \overline{(x - iy)} = (x + iy) = z.$

(vi) $z.\bar{z} = (x + iy)(x - iy) = x_2 + y_2$ = purely real number.

(vii) $\overline{z_1 + z_2} = \bar{z}_1 + \bar{z}_2$

(viii) $\overline{z_1 - z_2} = \bar{z}_1 - \bar{z}_2$

(ix) $\overline{z_1 . z_2} = \bar{z}_1 . \bar{z}_2$

(x) $\overline{\left(\dfrac{z_1}{z_2}\right)} = \dfrac{\bar{z}_1}{\bar{z}_2}$, provided $z_2 \neq 0$.

9. Modulus and Agrument of Complex Numbers: Let $z = x + iy$ be any complex number.

If $x = r\cos\theta$, $y = r\sin\theta$, then $r = +\sqrt{x^2 + y^2}$ $= \sqrt{\{\text{Re}(z)\}^2 + \{\text{Im}(z)\}^2}$ is called the modulus of the complex number z written as $|z|$ and $\theta = \tan^{-1}\dfrac{y}{x}$ is called the argument or amplitude of z written as *argz*.

Properties : If z, z_1, z_2 are complex numbers, then

(i) $|z| = 0 \Rightarrow z = 0$ *i.e.*, $\text{Re}(z) = \text{Im}(z) = 0$

(ii) $|z| = |\bar{z}| = |-z|$

(iii) $-|z| \le \text{Re}(z) \le |z|$; $-|z| \le \text{Im}(z) \le |z|$

(iv) $z\bar{z} = |z|^2$

(v) $|z_1z_2| = |z_1||z_2|$

(vi) $\left|\dfrac{z_1}{z_2}\right| = \dfrac{|z_1|}{|z_2|}$; $z \neq 0$

(vii) $|z_1 + z_2|^2 = |z_1|^2 + |z_2|^2 + 2\,\text{Re}(z_1\bar{z}_2)$

(viii) $|z_1 + z_2| \le |z_1| + |z_2|$

(ix) $|z_1 - z_2|^2 = |z_1|^2 - |z_2|^2 - 2\,\text{Re}(z_1\bar{z}_2)$

(x) $|z_1 - z_2| \ge \big||z_1| - |z_2|\big|$

(xi) $|z_1 + z_2|^2 + |z_1 - z_2|^2 = \left(|z_1|^2 + |z_2|^2\right)$

(xii) $\arg(z_1.z_2) = \arg z_1 + \arg z_2$

(xiii) $\arg\left(\dfrac{z_1}{z_2}\right) = \arg z_1 - \arg z_2$

(xiv) $\arg(\bar{z}) = -\arg(z)$

(xv) $\arg(z_1.\bar{z}_2) = \arg z_1 - \arg z_2$

10. Square Root of a Complex Number : Let $a + ib$ be a non-zero complex number and $x + iy$ be its square root, then

$$\sqrt{a+ib} = x + iy$$

$$\Rightarrow \quad a + ib = (x + iy)^2 = (x^2 - y^2) + 2ixy$$

Equating real and imaginary parts, we get

$$x^2 - y^2 = a \qquad ...(i)$$

and $$2xy = b \qquad ...(ii)$$

But we know that

$$(x^2 + y^2)^2 = (x^2 - y^2)^2 + 4x^2y^2 = a^2 + b^2$$

$$\therefore \quad x^2 + y^2 = \sqrt{a^2 + b^2} \qquad ...(iii)$$

From *(i)* and *(iii)* we get

$$2x^2 = \sqrt{a^2 + b^2} + a$$

$$2y^2 = \sqrt{a^2 + b^2} - a$$

$$\therefore \quad x = \pm\sqrt{\frac{1}{2}\left[\sqrt{a^2 + b^2} + a\right]}$$

and $$y = \pm\sqrt{\frac{1}{2}\left[\sqrt{a^2 + b^2} - a\right]} \qquad ...(iv)$$

From *(ii)* if b is +ve, then x and y are either both +ve or both –ve and therefore the square roots of $a + ib$ are

$$\pm\left\{\sqrt{\frac{1}{2}\left\{\sqrt{a^2+b^2}+a\right\}} + i\left\{\sqrt{\frac{1}{2}\left\{\sqrt{a^2+b^2}-a\right\}}\right\}\right\}$$

If b is –ve, then either x is +ve and y is –ve or x is –ve and y is +ve

$\therefore$ Square roots of $a + ib$ are

$$\pm\left\{\sqrt{\frac{1}{2}\left\{\sqrt{a^2+b^2}+a\right\}} - i\left\{\sqrt{\frac{1}{2}\left\{\sqrt{a^2+b^2}-a\right\}}\right\}\right\}$$

11. Geometrical Representation of a Complex Number : A complex number $z = x + iy$ can be represented by a point (x, y) on the plane known as Argand plane, Complex plane or Gaussian plane.

Length of the line segment OP, shown below is called the modulus of z and is denoted by $|z|$.

From Fig. we have

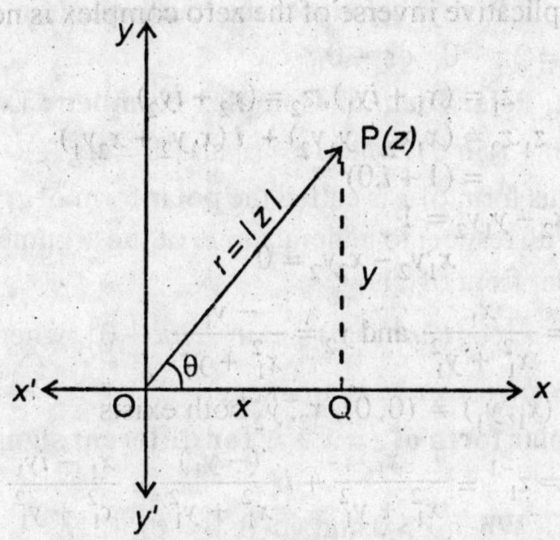

$$OP^2 = OQ^2 + QP^2$$

or $OP^2 = x^2 + y^2$

or $OP = \sqrt{x^2 + y^2}$

so, $|z| = \sqrt{x^2 + y^2} = \sqrt{\{Re\,(z)\}^2 + \{Im\,(z)\}^2}$

OP makes angle θ with x-axis along anticlockwise direction and is called argument or amplitude of z.

Thus $\tan\theta = \dfrac{PQ}{OQ} = \dfrac{y}{x} = \dfrac{Im\,(z)}{Re\,(z)}$

$$\Rightarrow \quad \theta = \tan^{-1}\left\{\frac{Im\,(z)}{Re\,(z)}\right\}.$$

θ is defined for each non-zero complex number. For a non-zero complex number z, θ has infinitely many values differing one another by a multiple of 2π. The argument θ which satisfies the ineqality $-\pi < \theta \leq \pi$ is known as principal argument of z.

Steps for Finding Argument of $z = x + iy$

I. Find the value of $\tan^{-1}\left(\dfrac{y}{x}\right)$ lying in the 1st quadrant. Denote it by θ_0.

II. Sort out the quadrant in which P(x, y) belongs

(i) If P (x, y) belongs to the first quadrant, then arg $(z) = \theta_0$

(ii) If P (x, y) belongs to the second quadrant, then arg $(z) = \pi - \theta_0$

(iii) If P (x, y) belongs to the third quadrant, then arg $(z) = \pi + \theta_0$

(iv) If P (x, y) belongs to the fourth quadrant, then $\arg(z) = 2\pi - \theta_0$ or $-\theta_0$.

12. Polar form of Complex Number : Let $z = r(\cos\theta + i\sin\theta)$, where $r = |z|$ and $\theta = \arg(z)$.

This form of z is called the polar form of z.

With respect to general value of the argument θ, the polar from of z is

$z = r[\cos(2n\pi + \theta) + i\sin(2n\pi + \theta]$, where $r = |z|$, $\theta = \arg(z)$ and n is an integer.

Polar form of $z = x + iy$ for different signs of x and y :

(i) When $x > 0$ and $y > 0$; $\theta = \theta_0$

So polar form of $z = x + iy$ is

$r(\cos\theta_0 + i\sin\theta_0)$.

(ii) When $x < 0$ and $y > 0$; $\theta = \pi - \theta_0$

So polar form of z is

$r[\cos(\pi - \theta_0) + i\sin(\pi - \theta_0)]$

or $r[-\cos\theta_0 + i\sin\theta_0]$

(iii) When $x < 0$ and $y < 0$; $\theta = -(\pi - \theta_0)$.

So polar form of z is

$r[\cos(\pi - \theta_0) - i\sin(\pi - \theta_0)]$

or $r(-\cos\theta_0 - i\sin\theta_0)$

(iv) When $x > 0$ and $y < 0$; $\theta = -\alpha$.

So polar form of z is

$r[\cos(-\theta_0) + i\sin(-\theta_0)]$

or $r(\cos\theta_0 - i\sin\theta_0)$

13. Euler's Theorem

$$e^{i\theta} = \cos\theta + i\sin\theta$$

$$e^{-i\theta} = \cos\theta - i\sin\theta$$

Polar form of Eular's notation is $z = r(\cos\theta + i\sin\theta)$

Using Euler's notation, we have $z = r\,e^{i\theta}$, known as Eulerian form.

14. Modulus and Argument of Multiplication of Two Complex Numbers : Let $z_1 = r_1(\cos\theta_1 + i\sin\theta_1)$ and $z_2 = r_2(\cos\theta_2 + i\sin\theta_2)$

Then $z_1 z_2 = r_1 r_2\{\cos(\theta_1 + \theta_2) + i\sin(\theta_1 + \theta_2)\}$

$\Rightarrow$ *(i)* Modulus $= |z_1 z_2| = r_1 r_2$

(ii) $\arg(z_1 z_2) = \theta_1 + \theta_2 = \arg z_1 + \arg z_2$

Note : For principal argument $\arg(z_1 z_2) \neq \arg(z_1) + \arg(z_2)$

Thus in general if $z_1, z_2, z_3, \ldots\ldots, z_n$ are complex numbers, then

(i) $|z_1, z_2, z_3 \ldots\ldots z_n| = |z_1||z_2||z_3|, \ldots\ldots |z_n|$

(ii) $\arg(z_1, z_2, z_3, \ldots\ldots z_n) = \arg(z_1) + \arg(z_2) + \ldots\ldots + \arg(z_n)$.

15. Modulus and Argument of Division of Two Complex Numbers : Let $z_1 = r_1(\cos\theta_1 + i\sin\theta_1)$ and $z_2 = r_2(\cos\theta_2 + i\sin\theta_2)$

Then $\dfrac{z_1}{z_2} = \dfrac{r_1}{r_2}[\cos(\theta_1 - \theta_2) + i\sin\theta(\theta_1 - \theta_2)]$

$\Rightarrow$ *(i)* Modulus $= \left|\dfrac{z_1}{z_2}\right| = \dfrac{r_1}{r_2} = \dfrac{|z_1|}{|z_2|}$

(ii) $\arg\left(\dfrac{z_1}{z_2}\right) = \theta_1 - \theta_2 = \arg(z_1) - \arg(z_2)$

Note : For principal argument, $\arg\left(\dfrac{z_1}{z_2}\right) \neq \arg(z_1) - \arg(z_2)$.

16. Distance Between Two Points : Let P and Q be two points in the argand plane which represents z_1 and z_2. Let $z_1 = x_1 + iy_1$ and $z_2 = x_2 + iy_2$. Then co-ordinates of P and Q are (x_1, y_1) and (x_2, y_3) respectively.

By distance formula

$$PQ = \sqrt{(x_2 - x_1)^2 + (y_2 - y_1)^2} \quad \ldots(i)$$

But $z_2 - z_1 = (x_2 + iy_2) - (x_1 + iy_1) = (x_2 - x_1) + i(y_2 - y_1)$

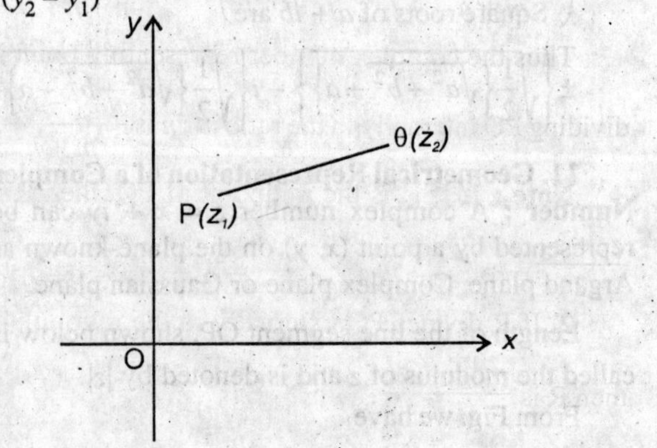

$\therefore |z_2 - z_1| = \sqrt{(x_2 - x_1)^2 + (y_2 - y_1)^2}$ ...(ii)

Thus from (i) and (ii)

$PQ = |z_2 - z_1|$

So distance between two points P and Q is $PQ = |z_2 - z_1|$.

17. Point Representing a Complex Number Dividing the Line Segment Joining z_1 and z_2 :

Let $z_1 = x_1 + iy_1$ and $z_2 = x_2 + iy_2$.

So co-ordinates of P and Q are (x_1, y_1) and (x_2, y_2).

Co-ordinate of point R dividing point P and Q in the ratio $m : n$ is

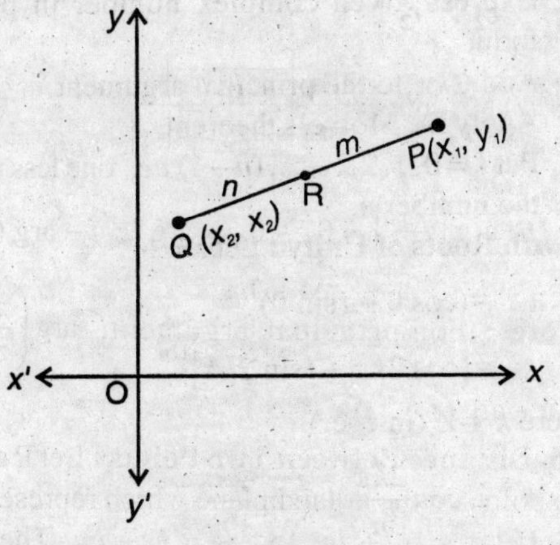

$$\left(\frac{mx_2 + nx_1}{m+n}, \frac{my_2 + ny_1}{m+n}\right)$$

So the complex number which represent point R is

$$\left(\frac{mx_2 + nx_1}{m+n}\right) + \left(\frac{my_2 + ny_1}{m+n}\right)i = \frac{mz_2 + nz_1}{m+n}.$$

Thus the complex number representing point R dividing PQ internally in the ratio $m : n$ is $\frac{mz_2 + nz_1}{m+n}$.

Note : 1. If R is the midpoint of PQ, then R is $\frac{z_1 + z_2}{2}$.

2. If R divides PQ externally in the ratio $m : n$, then R is $\frac{mz_2 - nz_1}{m-n}$.

18. Equation of a Circle : The equation of a circle with centre at C representing complex number z_0 and radius r is $|z - z_0| = r$, where

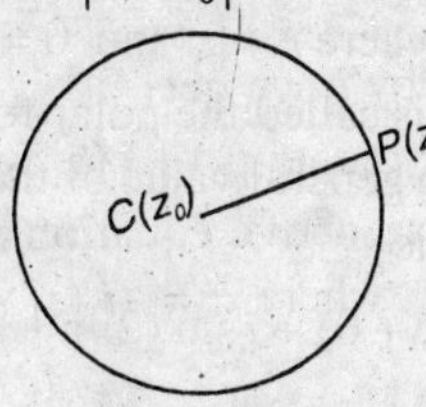

$CP = |z - z_0| = r$ (constant).

Note : 1. If the centre is at the origin and its radius is r, then equation of the circle is $|z| = r$.

2. $|z - z_0| < r$, represents interior of the circle and $|z - z_0| \geq r$ represents set of all point outside the circle, including the points on the circle.

General equation of a circle having centre at z_0 and radius r is $|z - z_0| = r$

$$\Rightarrow |z - z_0|^2 = r^2$$

$$\Rightarrow (z - z_0)\overline{(z - z_0)} = r^2$$

$$\Rightarrow (z - z_0)(\bar{z} - \bar{z}_0) = r^2$$

$$\Rightarrow z\bar{z} - z_0\bar{z} - \bar{z}_0\bar{z} + z_0\bar{z}_0 = r^2$$

$$\Rightarrow z\bar{z} + (-z_0)\bar{z} + (-\bar{z}_0)z + |z_0|^2 - r^2 = 0$$

$\Rightarrow z\bar{z} + b\bar{z} + \bar{b}z + c = 0$, where $b = -z_0$ and $c = |z_0|^2 - r^2$.

$\Rightarrow z\bar{z} + b\bar{z} + \bar{b}z + c = 0$ where $c \in R$, represents a circle having centre at $-b$ and radius $= \sqrt{|b|^2 - c}$.

19. Equation of a Straight Line :

1. Parametric Form : Equation of a straight line joining the points representing complex numbers z_1 and z_2 is $z = tz_1 + (1 - t)z_2$, $t \in R$

2. Non-Parametric Form : Equation of a straight line joining the points representing complex numbers z_1 and z_2 is

$$\begin{vmatrix} z & \bar{z} & 1 \\ z_1 & \bar{z}_1 & 1 \\ z_2 & \bar{z}_2 & 1 \end{vmatrix} = 0$$

or $z(\bar{z}_1 - \bar{z}_2) - \bar{z}(z_1 - z_2) + z\bar{z}_2 - \bar{z}_1 z_2 = 0$

3. General Equation of a Straight Line : The equation of a straight line passing through points z_1 and z_2 is given by

$$z(\bar{z}_1 - \bar{z}_2) - \bar{z}(z_1 - z_2) + z_1\bar{z}_2 - \bar{z}_1 z_2 = 0 \quad ...(i)$$

Multiplying *(i)* by *i*, we get

$$z\,i(\bar{z}_1 - \bar{z}_2) - \bar{z}\,i(z_1 - z_2) + i(z_1\bar{z}_2 - \bar{z}_1 z_2) = 0$$

on simplification, above equation reduces to

$a\bar{z} + \bar{a}z + b = 0$, where $a = -i(z_1 - z_2)$, $b = \text{Re}(z_1\bar{z}_2)$

Thus general equation of a straight line is of the from $a\bar{z} + \bar{a}z + b = 0$ where $b \in R$.

4. Slope of the Line Segment Joining Two Points: If P and Q represent complex number z_1 and z_2 in the Argand plane, the slope of PQ is $\frac{z_1 - z_2}{\bar{z}_1 - \bar{z}_2}$.

5. Slope of the Line $a\bar{z} + \bar{a}z + b = 0$: Let P and Q represents two points on the line $a\bar{z} + \bar{a}z + b = 0$, then $a\bar{z}_1 + \bar{a}z_1 + b = 0$ and $a\bar{z}_2 + \bar{a}z_2 + b = 0$

$\therefore\ a(\bar{z}_1 - \bar{z}_2) + \bar{a}(z_1 - z_2) = 0$

or $\frac{z_1 - z_2}{\bar{z}_1 - \bar{z}_2} = \frac{-a}{\bar{a}}$ or slope of PQ $= \frac{-a}{\bar{a}} = -\frac{\text{coeff. of } \bar{z}}{\text{coeff. of } z}$.

6. Length of the Perpendicular from a Point on a Line: The length of the perpendicular from a point z_1 to the line $a\bar{z} + \bar{a}z + b = 0$ is given by $\frac{a\bar{z}_1 + \bar{a}z_1 + b}{2|a|}$.

20. De-Moiver's Theorem

(i) When *n* is an integer, positive or negative and θ is a real number, then

$$(\cos\theta + i\sin\theta)^n = \cos n\theta + i\sin\theta$$

(ii) When *n* is a fraction, positive or negative and θ is a real number $(\cos n\theta + i\sin n\theta)$ is one of value of $(\cos\theta + i\sin\theta)^n$.

21. Roots of a Complex Number : If *z* be a non-zero complex number and *n* be a positive integer, then there are *n* distinct values of $z^{n/1}$.

Let $z = r(\cos\theta + i\sin\theta)$, where $r > 0, -\pi < \theta \le \pi$

Then $z^{1/n} = r^{1/n}(\cos\theta + i\sin\theta)^{1/n}$

$= r^{1/n}[\cos(2k\pi + \theta) + i\sin(2k\pi + \theta)]^{1/n}$, where $k = 0, 1, 2, \ldots (n-1)$

$$= r^{1/n}\left[\cos\frac{2k\pi + \theta}{n} + i\sin\frac{2k\pi + \theta}{n}\right]$$

All these roots are distinct and if it takes move, then there must be some roots within them, identical to the distinct roots.

Note : Geometrically, they (*i.e.*, all *n* roots) lie on a circle of radius $\sqrt[n]{r}$ and are equally spaced on it.

Steps for Finding nth Roots of a Given Complex Numbers :

I. Express given complex number in polar form.

II. Add $2k\pi$ to the principal argument.

III. Apply De Moive's theorem

IV. Put $k = 0, 1, 2, \ldots, (n-1)$ *i.e.*, one less than the number *n*.

22. *n*th Roots of Unity : Let $z = 1^{1/n}$

Then $z = (\cos 0 + i\sin 0)^{1/n}$

$= [\cos 2k\pi + i\sin 2k\pi]^{1/n}$, where $k \in Z$ (integer).

$= \cos\frac{2k\pi}{n} + i\sin\frac{2k\pi}{n}$, where $k = 0, 1, 2, \ldots, (n-1)$

(By De Moiver's theorem)

$= e^{i2k\pi/n}$, where $k = 0, 1, 2, \ldots, (n-1)$

(By Euler's theorem)

$= \left\{e^{i2\pi/n}\right\}^k$, where $k = 0, 1, 2, \ldots, (n-1)$

$= \beta^k$, where $\beta = e^{i2\pi/n}$.

Thus *n*th roots of unity are $\beta^0 = 1, \beta, \beta^2, \beta^3, \ldots, \beta^{n-1}$.

Properties of nth Roots of Unity

(i) The *n*th roots of unity form a G.P. with common ratio $e^{i2\pi/n}$.

(ii) Sum of the *n*th roots of unity is always zero *i.e.*, $1 + \beta + \beta^2 + \ldots + \beta^{n-1} = 0$.

(iii) Product of *n*th roots of unity is $(-1)^{n-1}$.

(iv) nth roots of unity lie on the unit circle $|z| = 1$ and divide its circumference into n equal parts.

23. Square Roots of Unity : nth roots of unity are $1, \beta, \beta^2, \ldots, \beta^{n-1}$, where $\beta = e^{i2\pi/n}$.

For square roots of unity, we have $n = 2$.

$\therefore\ \beta = e^{i\pi} = \cos\pi + i\sin\pi = -1.$

Thus, square roots of unity are 1, – 1.

24. Cube Roots of Unity : For cube roots of unity, we have $n = 3$

$\therefore\ \beta = e^{i2\pi/3}.$

So, cube roots of unity are $1, \beta, \beta^2$ or $1, e^{i2\pi/3}$ and $e^{i4\pi/3}$.

We denote $e^{i2\pi/3}$ by ω *i.e.,*

$$\omega = \cos\frac{2\pi}{3} + i\sin\frac{2\pi}{3} = -\frac{1}{2} + i\frac{\sqrt{3}}{2}.$$

Thus cube roots of unity are $1, \omega, \omega^2$

where $\omega = -\frac{1}{2} + i\frac{\sqrt{3}}{2}$ and $\omega^2 = -\frac{1}{2} - \frac{\sqrt{3}}{2}$.

Some Results Related to Cube Roots

(i) $\arg(\omega) = \frac{2\pi}{3}$ and $\arg(\omega^2) = \frac{4\pi}{3}$

(ii) $z^3 - 1 = (z-1)(z-\omega)(z-\omega^2)$.

(iii) ω and ω^2 are the roots of the equation $z^2 + z + 1 = 0$

(iv) $1 + \omega^n + \omega^{2n} = \begin{cases} 0, \text{if } n \text{ is not a multiple of 3} \\ 3, \text{if } n \text{ is a multiple of 3} \end{cases}$

(v) $a^2 + b^2 - ab = (a\omega + b\omega^2)(a\omega^2 + b\omega)$

(vi) $a^3 + b^3 = (a+b)(a\omega + b\omega^2)(a\omega^2 + b\omega)$

(vii) $a^2 + b^2 + ab = (a\omega - b\omega^2)(a\omega^2 - b\omega)$

(viii) $a^3 - b^3 = (a-b)(a\omega - b\omega^2)(a\omega^2 - b\omega)$

(ix) $a^2 + b^2 + c^2 - ab - bc - ca = (a + b\omega + c\omega^2)(a + b\omega^2 + c\omega)$

(x) $a^3 + b^3 + c^3 - 3abc = (a+b+c)(a + b\omega + c\omega^2)(a + b\omega^2 + c\omega)$.

25. Logarithm of a Complex Number

Logarithm of a complex number z is written as

$\text{Log}(z) = \log|z| + i\ \text{amp}(z)$

where $|z|$ is the modulus of the complex number z.

EXERCISE

Mark the correct alternative(s) of each of the following :

1. If $x + iy = \left(1 - i\sqrt{3}\right)^{100}$, where x and y are reals, then the ordered pair (x, y) is given by

(a) $\left(2^{99}, 2^{99}\sqrt{3}\right)$ (b) $\left(2^{99}, -2^{99}\sqrt{3}\right)$

(c) $\left(-2^{99}, 2^{99}\sqrt{3}\right)$ (d) None of these

2. In a geometrical progression first term and common ratio are both $\frac{1}{2}\left(\sqrt{3} + i\right)$. Then the absolute value of the nth term of the progression is

(a) 2^n (b) 4^n

(c) 1 (d) none of these

3. The value of

$$\sum_{n=1}^{10}\left(\sin\frac{2n\pi}{11} - i\cos\frac{2n\pi}{11}\right) \text{ is}$$

(a) 1 (b) 0 (c) $-i$ (d) i

4. The value of

$$\sum_{k=0}^{14}\left\{\cos\frac{(2k+1)\pi}{15} - i\sin\frac{(2k+1)\pi}{15}\right\} \text{ is}$$

(a) 1 (b) 0 (c) i (d) $-i$

5. The value of $\sum_{n=1}^{13}(i^n + i^{n-1})$, where $i = \sqrt{-1}$, equals to

(a) $i - 1$ (b) $i + 1$

(c) i (d) None of these

6. The value of

$$\sum_{k=1}^{6}\left(\sin\frac{2\pi k}{7}-i\cos\frac{2\pi k}{7}\right), \text{ equals to}$$

(a) 0 (b) 1 (c) i (d) $-i$

7. If the area of the triangle on the complex plane formed by the points z, iz, and $z + iz$ is 50 square unit, then $|z|$ is

(a) 6 (b) 8 (c) 10 (d) 12

8. The equation $|z-1|^2 + |z+1|^2 = 2$ represents

(a) circle of radius one unit
(b) a straight line
(c) the ordered pair (0, 0)
(d) None of these

9. If $1, \alpha_1, \alpha_2, \alpha_3, \ldots, \alpha_{n-1}$ are the nth roots of unity and n is an odd natural number, then $(1+\alpha_1)(1+\alpha_2)(1+\alpha_3)\ldots(1+\alpha_{n-1})$ equals

(a) n (b) 0
(c) 1 (d) None of these

10. If $1, \alpha_1, \alpha_2, \ldots, \alpha_{n-1}$ are the nth roots of unity and n is an even natural number, then $(1+\alpha_1)(1+\alpha_2)(1+\alpha_3)\ldots(1+\alpha_{n-1})$ equals

(a) 0 (b) 1
(c) n (d) None of these

11. If α is an nth root of unity, then $1 + 2\alpha + 3\alpha^2 + \ldots + n.\alpha^{n-1}$ equals

(a) $n(1-\alpha)$ (b) $\dfrac{n}{1-\alpha}$

(c) $-\dfrac{n}{(1-\alpha)}$ (d) None of these

12. If $1, \alpha, \alpha^2, \ldots + \alpha^{n-1}$ are the nth roots of a polynomial. Then the value of $(3-\alpha)(3-\alpha^2)\ldots(3-\alpha^{n-1})$ is

(a) $\dfrac{3^n-1}{2}$ (b) $\dfrac{3^n+1}{2}$

(c) $n\,3^{n-1}$ (d) None of these

13. If $1, a_1, a_2, a_3, \ldots, a_{n-1}$ are the nth roots of unity, then $(1-a_1)(1-a_2)(1-a_3)\ldots(1-a_{n-1})$ is equal to

(a) $-n$ (b) n (c) 1 (d) 0

14. If α is the nth root of unity other than unity itself, then the value of $1+\alpha+\alpha^2+\ldots+\alpha^{n-1}$ is

(a) 1 (b) n (c) $-n$ (d) 0

15. The product of n, nth roots of unity is

(a) 1 (b) $(-1)^{n-1}$
(c) 0 (d) None of these.

16. The locus of point z satisfying $\text{Re}\left(\dfrac{1}{2}\right) = k$, where k is a non-zero real number, is

(a) straight line (b) a circle
(c) an ellipse (d) a hyperbolic

17. If the complex numbers z_1, z_2, z_3 are in A.P., then they lie on a

(a) circle (b) parabola
(c) line (d) ellipse

18. The cube roots of unity

(a) are collinear
(b) lie on a circle of radius $\sqrt{3}$
(c) form a equilateral triangle
(d) None of these

19. If the roots of $(z-1)^n = i(z+1)^n$ are plotted in the Argand plane, they are

(a) on a parabola
(b) concyclic
(c) collinear
(d) The vertices of a triangle

20. If $z = x + iy$ and $w = \dfrac{1-iz}{z-i}$, then $|w| = 1$ implies that in the complex plane

(a) z lies on the real axis
(b) z lies on the imaginary axis
(c) z lies on the unit circle
(d) None of these

[J.N.U. M.C.A.]

21. If $z^2 + z|z| + |z|^2 = 0$, then the locus of z is

(a) circle
(b) straight line
(c) a pair of straight line
(d) None of these

22. If z_1, z_2, z_3, z_4 are the affixes of the vertices of a parallelogram taken in order in Argand plane, then

(a) $z_1 + z_3 = z_2 + z_4$ (b) $z_1 + z_2 = z_3 + z_4$
(c) $z_1 - z_3 = z_2 - z_4$ (d) None of these

[J.N.U. M.C.A.]

23. The points representing the numbers $a + b\omega$, $a + b\omega^2$, $a + b$ where w is an imaginary root of unity

(a) are the vertices of an isosceles triangle
(b) are the vertices of an right-angled triangle
(c) are the vertices of an equilateral triangle
(d) lie on a straight line

24. The complex numbers z_1, z_2, z_3 are the vertices A, B, C of a parallelogram ABCD then the fourth vertex D is

(a) $\frac{1}{2}(z_1 + z_2)$ *(b)* $\frac{1}{4}(z_1 + z_2 + z_3 + z_4)$

(c) $\frac{1}{2}(z_1 + z_2 + z_3)$ *(d)* $z_1 + z_2 - z_3$

25. If the points z_1, z_2, z_3 are the vertices of an equilateral triangle in the argand plane, then

(a) $\frac{1}{z_1 - z_2} + \frac{1}{z_2 - z_3} + \frac{1}{z_3 - z_1} = 0$

(b) $z_1^2 + z_2^2 + z_3^2 = z_1z_2 + z_2z_3 + z_3z_1$

(c) $(z_1 - z_2)^2 + (z_2 - z_3)^2 + (z_3 - z_1)^2 = 0$

(d) All of these

26. If $\left(\frac{\frac{\sqrt{3}}{2} + \left(\frac{1}{2}\right)i}{\frac{\sqrt{3}}{2} - \left(\frac{1}{2}\right)i}\right)^{120} = p + iq$, then

(a) $p = \cos 20°$, $q = \sin 20°$
(b) $p = -\cos 20°$, $q = -\sin 20°$
(c) $p = \cos 20°$, $q = -\sin 20°$
(d) $p = 1$, $q = 0$

27. If $u_{n+1} = i\,u_n + 1$, where $u_1 = i + 1$ and $i = \sqrt{-1}$, then U_{27} is

(a) i *(b)* 1 *(c)* $i + 1$ *(d)* 0

28. For any complex number z, the minimum value of $|z| + |z - 1|$ is

(a) 1 *(b)* 0 *(c)* $\frac{1}{2}$ *(d)* $\frac{3}{2}$

29. The centre of a regular polygon of n sides is located at the point $z = 0$ and one of its vertex z is known. If z_2 be the vertex adjacent to z_1, then z_2 is equal to

(a) $z_1\left(\cos\frac{2\pi}{n} \pm i\sin\frac{2\pi}{n}\right)$

(b) $z_1\left(\cos\frac{\pi}{n} \pm i\sin\frac{\pi}{n}\right)$

(c) $z_1\left(\cos\frac{\pi}{2n} \pm i\sin\frac{\pi}{2n}\right)$

(d) None of these

30. If $x^2 + x + 1 = 0$, then the value of

$$\left(x + \frac{1}{x}\right) + \left(x^2 + \frac{1}{x^2}\right) + \left(x^3 + \frac{1}{x^3}\right) + \ldots\ldots + \left(x^{27} + \frac{1}{x^{27}}\right)$$ is

(a) 54 *(b)* 27 *(c)* 72 *(d)* 45

31. The value of the expression

$1.(2 - \omega)(2 - \omega^2) + 2.(3 - \omega)(3 - \omega^2) + \ldots\ldots + (n - 1)(n - \omega)(n - \omega^2)$, where ω is an imaginary cube root of unity is

(a) $\left\{\frac{n(n+1)}{2}\right\}^2$ *(b)* $\left\{\frac{n(n+1)}{2}\right\}^2 - n$

(c) $\left\{\frac{n(n+1)}{2}\right\}^2 + n$ *(d)* None of these

32. The value of the expression

$2.(1 + \omega)(1 + \omega^2) + 3.(2 + \omega)(2 + \omega^2) + 4(3 + \omega)(3 + \omega^2) + \ldots\ldots + (n + 1)(n + \omega)(n + \omega^2)$, where ω is an imaginary cube root of unity is

(a) $\left\{\frac{n(n+1)}{2}\right\}^2$ *(b)* $\left\{\frac{n(n+1)}{2}\right\}^2 - n$

(c) $\left\{\frac{n(n+1)}{2}\right\}^2 + n$ *(d)* None of these

33. The value of the expression

$\left(1 + \frac{1}{\omega}\right)\left(1 + \frac{1}{\omega^2}\right) + \left(2 + \frac{1}{\omega}\right)\left(2 + \frac{1}{\omega^2}\right) + \ldots\ldots + \left(n + \frac{1}{\omega}\right)\left(n + \frac{1}{\omega^2}\right)$, where ω is an imaginary cube root of unity is

(a) $\frac{n(n^2+2)}{3}$ (b) $\frac{n(n^2-2)}{3}$

(c) $\frac{n(n^2+1)}{3}$ (d) None of these

34. If $1, \omega, \omega^2, \ldots\ldots \omega^{n-1}$ are the n roots of unity, then $(1-\omega)(1-\omega^2)\ldots\ldots(1-\omega^{n-1})$ equals

(a) 0 (b) 1 (c) n (d) n^2

35. If $1, \omega, \omega^2$ are the three cube roots of unity, then $(1-\omega+\omega^2)(1-\omega^2+\omega^4)(1-\omega^4+\omega^8)\ldots$ to $2n$ factors equals to

(a) 2^{2n} (b) 2^n

(c) 2^{2n-1} (d) 2^{n-1}

36. If $z_r = \cos\frac{\pi}{3^r} + i\sin\frac{\pi}{3^r}, r = 1, 2, 3, \ldots\ldots$ then $z_1, z_2, z_3 \ldots\ldots \infty$ equal to

(a) 0 (b) 1 (c) i (d) $-i$

37. If $x^2 - 2x\cos\theta + 1 = 0$, then $x^{2n} - 2x^n \cos n\theta + 1$ equals to

(a) 0 (b) 1 (c) i (d) $-i$

38. Let the complex number z_1, z_2 and z_3 be the vertices of an equilateral triangle. Let z_0 be the circumcentre of the triangle. Then

(a) $z_1^3 + z_2^3 + z_3^3 = 3z_0^3$

(b) $z_1^2 + z_2^2 + z_3^2 = 3z_0^2$

(c) $z_1 + z_2 + z_3 = 3z_0$

(d) None of these

39. The value of z satisfying the equation $\log z + \log z^2 + \ldots\ldots + \log z^n = 0$ is

(a) $\cos\frac{4m\pi}{n(n+1)} + i\sin\frac{4m\pi}{n(n+1)}, m = 1, 2, 3, \ldots\ldots$

(b) $\cos\frac{4m\pi}{n(n+1)} - i\sin\frac{4m\pi}{n(n+1)}, m = 1, 2, 3, \ldots\ldots$

(c) $\sin\frac{4m\pi}{n} - i\cos\frac{4m\pi}{n}, m = 1, 2, 3, \ldots\ldots$

(d) None of these

40. If $z = i\log(2-\sqrt{3})$, then $\cos z$ is

(a) i (b) $2i$

(c) 1 (d) 2

ANSWERS

1	2	3	4	5	6	7	8	9	10
(c)	(c)	(d)	(b)	(a)	(c)	(c)	(c)	(c)	(a)
11	**12**	**13**	**14**	**15**	**16**	**17**	**18**	**19**	**20**
(c)	(a)	(b)	(d)	(b)	(b)	(c)	(c)	(b)	(a)
21	**22**	**23**	**24**	**25**	**26**	**27**	**28**	**29**	**30**
(c)	(a)	(d)	(d)	(a)	(d)	(d)	(a)	(a)	(a)
31	**32**	**33**	**34**	**35**	**36**	**37**	**38**	**39**	**40**
(b)	(c)	(a)	(c)	(a)	(c)	(a)	(b)	(a)	(d)

SOME SELECTED EXPLANATORY ANSWERS

1. Given $x + iy = (1 - i\sqrt{3})^{100}$

$$\Rightarrow \quad x + iy = 2^{100}\left(\frac{1}{2} - i\frac{\sqrt{3}}{2}\right)^{100}$$

$$= 2^{100}\left(\cos\frac{5\pi}{3} + i\sin\frac{5\pi}{3}\right)^{100}$$

$$= 2^{100}\left(\cos\frac{500\pi}{3} + i\sin\frac{500\pi}{3}\right)$$

($\because$ By De-Moiver's Theorem)

$$= 2^{100}\left\{\cos\left(167\pi - \frac{\pi}{3}\right) + i\sin\left(167\pi - \frac{\pi}{3}\right)\right\}$$

$$= 2^{100}\left\{\cos\left(334.\frac{\pi}{2} - \frac{\pi}{3}\right) + i\sin\left(334.\frac{\pi}{2} - \frac{\pi}{3}\right)\right\}$$

$$= 2^{100}\left\{-\cos\frac{\pi}{3} + i\sin\frac{\pi}{3}\right\} = 2^{100}\left\{-\frac{1}{2} + i\frac{\sqrt{3}}{2}\right\}$$

$$= \left(-2^{99} + i.2^{99}.\sqrt{3}\right)$$

$\therefore$ Ordered pair $(x, y) = \left\{-2^{99}, 2^{990}\sqrt{3}\right\}$.

Alternate Methode

Given $\quad x + iy = \left(1 - i\sqrt{3}\right)^{100}$

$\Rightarrow \quad x + iy = 2^{100}\left(\frac{1}{2} - i\frac{\sqrt{3}}{2}\right)^{100}$

$$= 2^{100}(-\omega)^{100}$$

$$\left(\because \omega = -\frac{1}{2} + i\frac{\sqrt{3}}{2}\right)$$

$$= 2^{100}\omega^{100} = 2^{100}\omega \quad (\because \omega^3 = 1)$$

$$= 2^{100}\left(-\frac{1}{2} + i\frac{\sqrt{3}}{2}\right)$$

$$= \left(-2^{99} + i2^{99}\sqrt{3}\right)$$

$\therefore$ Ordered pair $(x, y) = \left\{-2^{99}, 2^{99}\sqrt{3}\right\}$.

2. Given $a = \frac{1}{2}\left(\sqrt{3} + i\right)$ and $r = \frac{1}{2}\left(\sqrt{3} + i\right)$ where a and r represents first term and common ratio of the geometric progression.

Now the nth term of the geometric progression

i.e. $T_n = a\, r^{n-1} = \left[\frac{1}{2}\left(\sqrt{3} + i\right)\right]^n$.

Let $\frac{\sqrt{3}}{2} = r\cos\theta,\ \frac{1}{2} = r\sin\theta$; then we get

$r = 1$ and $\theta = \frac{\pi}{6}$.

$\therefore \quad T_n = \left[r(\cos\theta + i\sin\theta)\right]^n$

$$= \left(\cos\frac{\pi}{6} + i\sin\frac{\pi}{6}\right)^n$$

$$= \cos\frac{n\pi}{6} + i\sin\frac{n\pi}{6}$$

$\therefore$ Absolute value of nth term i.e.

$$|T_n| = \sqrt{\left\{\cos^2\frac{n\pi}{6} + \sin^2\frac{n\pi}{6}\right\}} = 1.$$

3. $\displaystyle\sum_{n=1}^{10}\left\{\sin\frac{2n\pi}{11} - i\cos\frac{2n\pi}{11}\right\}$

$$= -i\sum_{n=1}^{10}\left\{\cos\frac{2n\pi}{11} + i\sin\frac{2n\pi}{11}\right\}$$

$$= -i\sum_{n=1}^{10} e^{i2n\pi/11} = -i\sum_{n=1}^{10}\left(e^{i2\pi/11}\right)^n$$

$$= -i\left(\sum_{n=1}^{10}\alpha^n\right), \text{ where } \alpha = e^{i2\pi/11}$$

$$= -i\left(\alpha + \alpha^2 + \ldots + \alpha^{10}\right)$$

$$= -i\left\{\frac{\alpha(1-\alpha^{10})}{1-\alpha}\right\} = -i\left\{\frac{\alpha - \alpha^{11}}{1-\alpha}\right\}$$

$$= -i\left\{\frac{\alpha - 1}{1-\alpha}\right\}$$

$$\left(\because \alpha = e^{i2\pi/11}, \text{so that } \alpha^{11} = e^{i2\pi} = 1\right)$$

$= i.$

4. $\displaystyle\sum_{k=0}^{14}\left\{\cos\frac{(2k+1)\pi}{15} + i\sin\frac{(2k+1)\pi}{15}\right\}$

$$= \sum_{k=0}^{14} e^{i(2k+1)\pi/15} = \sum_{k=0}^{14}\alpha^{2k+1}$$

where $\alpha = e^{i\pi/15}$

$$= \left(\alpha + \alpha^3 + \alpha^5 + \ldots + \alpha^{29}\right)$$

$$= \alpha\left\{\frac{1 - (\alpha^2)^{15}}{1-\alpha^2}\right\} = \alpha\left\{\frac{1-\alpha^{30}}{1-\alpha^2}\right\}$$

$$= \alpha\left\{\frac{1-1}{1-\alpha^2}\right\} \quad \left(\because \alpha^{30} = e^{i2\pi} = 1\right)$$

$= 0.$

5. $\sum_{n=1}^{13}(i^n + i^{n-1})$

$= (i + i^2 + ... + i^{13}) + (1 + i + i^2 + ... + i^{12})$

$= 1 + 2(i + i^2 + ... + i^{12}) + i^{13}$

$= 1 + 2i(1 + i + ... + i^{11}) + i^{13}$

$= 1 + 2i8\frac{1-i^{12}}{1-i} + i^{13}$

$= 1 + i^{13}$ ($\because i^{12} = 1$) $= 1 + i$

7. Here $iz = ze^{i\pi/2}$. This implies that iz is the vector obtained by rotating vectors z in anticlockwise direction through 90°. Therefore, $OA \perp AB$.

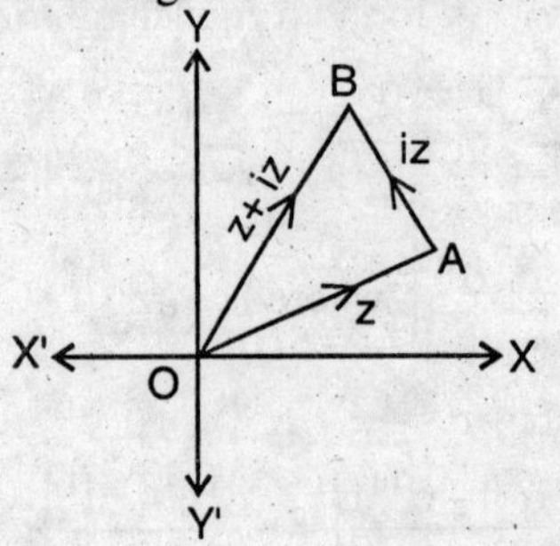

$\therefore$ Area of $\Delta OAB = \frac{1}{2} OA \times OB$

$= \frac{1}{2}|z||iz| = \frac{1}{2}|z|^2$.

Thus $\frac{1}{2}|z|^2 = 50 \Rightarrow |z| = 10$.

8. Given $|z-1|^2 + |z+1|^2 = 2$

$\Rightarrow |(x-1)+iy|^2 + |(x+1)^2 + iy|^2 = 2$

$\Rightarrow (x-1)^2 + y^2 + (x+1)^2 + y^2 = 2$

$\Rightarrow x^2 + y^2 = 0$

It is possible only when $x = y = 0$ where $x, y \in R$.

Thus the order pair i.e. $(x, y) = (0, 0)$.

9. Given $1, \alpha_1, \alpha_2, \alpha_3, ..., \alpha_{n-1}$ are the roots of the equation $x^n - 1 = 0$.

$\therefore x^n - 1 = (x-1)(x-\alpha_1)(x-\alpha_2)(x-\alpha_3)... (x-\alpha_{n-1})$

or $\frac{x^n-1}{x-1} = (x-\alpha_1)(x-\alpha_2)(x-\alpha_3)... (x-\alpha_{n-1})$

or $(x-\alpha_1)(x-\alpha_2)(x-\alpha_3)... (x-\alpha_{n-1}) = \frac{x^n-1}{x-1}$

or $(x-\alpha_1)(x-\alpha_2)(x-\alpha_3)... (x-\alpha_{n-1})$

$= x^{n-1} + x^{n-2} + ... + x^2 + x + 1$.

Putting $x = -1$, in the above equation we get

$(-1-\alpha_1)(-1-\alpha_2)(-1-\alpha_3)... (-1-\alpha_{n-1})$

$= (-1)^{n-1} + (-1)^{n-2} + ... + (-1) + (-1)^0$.

$\Rightarrow (-1)^n (1+\alpha_1)(1+\alpha_2)(1+\alpha_3)... (1+\alpha_{n-1}) = (-1)^{n-1} + (-1)^{n-2} + ... + (-1) + (-1)^0$.

If n is odd then in the LHS $(n-1)$ is even, so that $(-1)^n$ is 1. Simultaneously RHS contains odd number of terms with alternately positive and negative terms.

Thus RHS = 1.

$\therefore (1+\alpha_1)(1+\alpha_2)(1+\alpha_3)... (1+\alpha_{n-1}) = 1$.

10. Proceed Similar to solution of Q.No. 9.

If n is even, then RHS will be zero.

So, $(1+\alpha_1)(1+\alpha_2)(1+\alpha_3)...(1+\alpha_{n-1}) = 0$.

11. Let $S = 1 + 2\alpha + 3\alpha^2 + ... + n.\alpha^{n-1}$

Then

$\alpha S = \alpha + 2\alpha^2 + 3\alpha^3 + ... + (n-1).\alpha^{n-1} + n.\alpha^n$

$\therefore S - \alpha S = (1 + \alpha + \alpha^2 + ... + \alpha^{n-1}) - n.\alpha^n$

or $S(1-\alpha) = \frac{\alpha^2 - 1}{\alpha - 1} - n\alpha^n$

or $S(1-\alpha) = \frac{1-1}{\alpha-1} - n\alpha^n \quad [\because \alpha^n = 1]$

or $S = -\frac{n}{\alpha - 1} \quad [\because \alpha^n = 1]$

12. $1, \alpha, \alpha^2, ..., \alpha^{n-1}$ the nth roots of unity.

$\therefore x^{n-1} = (x-1)(x-\alpha_1)(x-\alpha_2)(x-\alpha_3)... (x-\alpha_{n-1})$

or $\frac{x^n-1}{x-1} = (x-\alpha_1)(x-\alpha_2)(x-\alpha_3)... (x-\alpha_{n-1})$

or $(x-\alpha_1)(x-\alpha_2)(x-\alpha_3)...$

$$(x-\alpha_{n-1}) = \frac{x^n-1}{x-1}$$

Putting $n = 3$, we get

$(3-\alpha_1)(3-\alpha_2)\ldots(3-\alpha_{n-1})$

$$= \frac{3^n-1}{3-1} = \frac{3^n-1}{2}.$$

13. Similar as previous problem

$$(x-a_1)(x-a_2)\ldots(x-a_{n-1}) = \frac{x^n-1}{x-1}$$

or $(x-a_1)(x-a_2)\ldots(x-a_{n-1})$

$$= 1+x+x^2+\ldots+x^{n-1}$$

Putting $x = 1$, we get

or $(1-a_1)(1-a_2)\ldots(1-a_{n-1})$

$$= 1+1+1+\ldots n \text{ times} = n.$$

14. Similar as previous problem

$$1+x+x^2+\ldots+x^{n-1} = \frac{x^n-1}{x-1}$$

Putting $x=\alpha$ we get

$$1+\alpha+\alpha^2+\ldots+\alpha^{n-1} = \frac{\alpha^n-1}{\alpha-1}$$

$$= \frac{e^{i2\pi}-1}{e^{i2\pi/n}-1}\left[\because \alpha = e^{i2\pi/n}\right]$$

$$= 0.$$

15. n, nth roots of unity are $1, \alpha, \alpha^2, \ldots, \alpha^{n-1}$

$\therefore$ Product $= 1.\alpha.\alpha^2\ldots\alpha^{n-1}$

$$= \alpha^{1+2+3+\ldots+n-1}$$

$$= \alpha^{n(n-1)/2} = \left(\alpha^{n/2}\right)^{n-1}$$

$$= \left(e^{i\pi}\right)^{n-1}\left[\because \alpha = e^{i2\pi/n}\right]$$

$$= (\cos\pi + i\sin\pi)^{n-1} = (-1)^{n-1}$$

16. Let $z = x + iy$

Then $\text{Re}\left(\frac{1}{z}\right) = k \Rightarrow \text{Re}\left(\frac{1}{x+iy}\right) = k$

$$\Rightarrow \text{Re}\left(\frac{x}{x^2+y^2} - i\frac{y}{x^2+y^2}\right) = k$$

$$\Rightarrow \frac{x}{x^2+y^2} = k \Rightarrow x^2+y^2-\frac{1}{k}x = 0$$

which represents a circle.

17. Let z_1, z_2, z_3 be affixes of points A, B, C respectively.

z_1, z_2, z_3 are in A.P., therefore

$$2z_2 = z_1 + z_3$$

or $$z_2 = \frac{z_1+z_3}{2}$$

$\Rightarrow$ B is the midpoint of the line AC. Thus A, B, C are collinear and z_1, z_2, z_3 lie on a line.

18. $1, \omega, \omega^2$ are cube roots of unity, where

$$\omega = \frac{-1+i\sqrt{3}}{2},\ \omega^2 = \frac{-1-i\sqrt{3}}{2}$$

Now

$$|1-\omega|^2 = \left(\frac{3}{2}\right)^2 + \left(\frac{\sqrt{3}}{2}\right)^2 = 3$$

$$\Rightarrow \quad |1-\omega| = \sqrt{3}$$

Similarly $|\omega-\omega^2| = \sqrt{3}$ and $|1-\omega^2| = \sqrt{3}$.

$\therefore$ $1, \omega, \omega^2$ form an equilateral triangle.

20. Given $|\omega| = 1$

$$\Rightarrow \left|\frac{1-iz}{z-i}\right| = 1$$

$$\Rightarrow |1-iz| = |z-i|$$

$$\Rightarrow |1-iz|^2 = |z-i|^2$$

$$\Rightarrow (1-iz)\overline{(1-iz)} = (z-i)\overline{(z-i)}$$

$$(\because |z|^2 = z\bar{z})$$

$$\Rightarrow (1-iz)(1+i\bar{z}) = (z-i)(\bar{z}+i)$$

$$\left(\because \overline{z_1+z_2} = \bar{z}_1+\bar{z}_2 \text{ and } \overline{iz} = -i\bar{z}\right)$$

$$\Rightarrow 1+i\bar{z}-iz+z\bar{z} = z\bar{z}+iz-i\bar{z}+1$$

$$\Rightarrow 2i(z-\bar{z}) = 0$$

$$\Rightarrow 2i(2iy) = 0$$

$$\Rightarrow y = 0.$$

Thus z lies on the real axis.

21. Given $z^2 + z|z| + |z|^2 = 0$

or $$\left(\frac{z}{|z|}\right)^2 + \left(\frac{z}{|z|}\right) + 1 = 0$$

$\Rightarrow \omega = \frac{z}{|z|}$ and $\omega^2 = \frac{z}{|z|}$ ($\because x^2+x+1=0$ has two roots ω and ω^2)

or $z = \omega|z|$ or $z = \omega^2|z|$

$\Rightarrow$ z lies on a pair of straight lines.

22. Diagonals of a parallelogram bisect each other, so affix of the midpoint of AC is same as the affix of the midpoint of BD.

Thus $\dfrac{z_1+z_3}{2} = \dfrac{z_2+z_4}{2} \Rightarrow z_1+z_3 = z_2+z_4$.

25. AC is obtained by rotating $\vec{AB}$ through $\dfrac{\pi}{3}$ in anticlockwise direction.

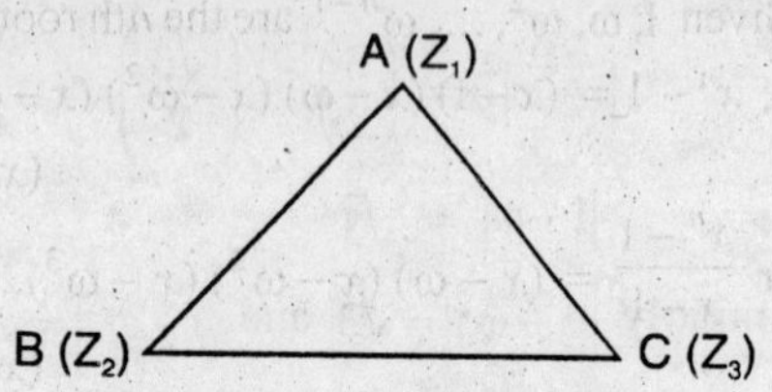

$\therefore \quad \vec{AC} = \vec{AB}.e^{i\pi/3}$

$\Rightarrow \quad z_3 - z_1 = (z_2 - z_1)\, e^{i\pi/3}$ ...(i)

Similarly, $\vec{BA} = \vec{BC}.e^{i\pi/3}$

$\Rightarrow \quad z_1 - z_2 = (z_3 - z_2)\, e^{i\pi/3}$ ...(ii)

from (i) and (ii), we get

$$\frac{z_3-z_2}{z_1-z_2} = \frac{z_2-z_1}{z_3-z_2}$$

$\Rightarrow z_3^2 - z_1z_3 - z_2z_3 + z_1z_2$

$= z_1z_2 - z_1^2 - z_2^2 + z_1z_2$

$\Rightarrow z_1^2 + z_2^2 + z_3^2 = z_1z_2 + z_2z_3 + z_3z_1$.

26. Given $\left\{\dfrac{\dfrac{\sqrt{3}}{2}+i\dfrac{1}{2}}{\dfrac{\sqrt{3}}{2}-i\dfrac{1}{2}}\right\}^{120} = \left\{\dfrac{\dfrac{1}{2}-i\dfrac{\sqrt{3}}{2}}{-\dfrac{1}{2}-i\dfrac{\sqrt{3}}{2}}\right\}^{120}$

$= \left\{\dfrac{-\omega}{\omega^2}\right\}^{120}$ where ω, ω^2 are cube roots of unity.

$= \left(-\omega^2\right)^{120} \left(\because \omega^3 = 1\right) = \omega^{240} = 1 + 0i.$

Thus $p = 1$ and $q = 0$.

27. Given $\quad u_{n+1} = iu_n + 1$ ...(i)

and $\quad u_1 = i + 1$ ...(ii)

Putting $n = 1$ in (i) we get

$u_2 = i\,u_1 + 1$

$= i\,(i+1) + 1$ [from (ii)]

$= i$

Similarly putting $n = 2, 3, 4$ we get

$u_3 = iu_2 + 1$

$= i(i) + 1 = 0$

$u_4 = iu_3 + 1 = 0$

$u_5 = iu_4 + 1 = i + 1$

$\therefore \quad u_1 = u_5.$

Similarly $u_1 = u_5 = u_9 = \ldots = u_{25} = i + 1$

$\therefore \quad u_{27} = iu_{26} + 1$

$= i\,(iu_{25} + 1) + 1$

$= -u_{25} + i + 1$

$= -(i+1) + (i+1)$

$= 0$

28. $|z_1 - z_2| \geq |z_1| - |z_2|$ ($\because$ Triangle Inequality)

$\Rightarrow |z-1| \geq 1 - |z| \qquad (\because z_1 = 1, z_2 = z)$

$\Rightarrow |z| + |z-1| \geq 1$ for all complex numbers z.

$\therefore$ Minimum value of $|z| + |z-1|$ is 1.

29. In the given problem it is not clearly mentioned how to reach z_2 from z_1 *i.e.* clockwise or anti-clockwise. Thus it may be

$\pm\dfrac{2\pi}{n}$

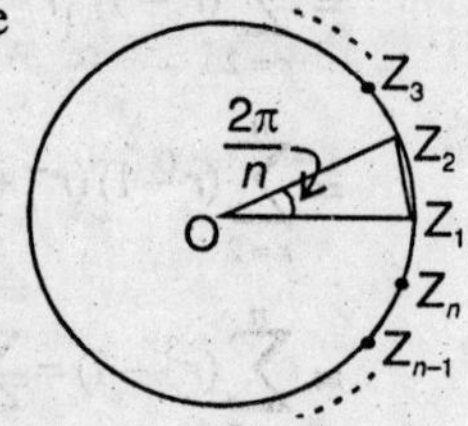

$\therefore z_2 = z_1\, e^{\pm i\,2\pi/n}$

$= z_1\left(\cos\dfrac{2\pi}{n} \pm i\sin\dfrac{2\pi}{n}\right)$

30. Equation $x^2 + x + 1 = 0$ gives two roots i.e ω and ω^2.

Let $x = \omega$. Then

$$x + \frac{1}{x} = \omega + \frac{1}{\omega} = \omega + \omega^2 = -1$$

$$(\because \omega^3 = 1)$$

$$x^2 + \frac{1}{x^2} = \omega^2 + \frac{1}{\omega^2} = \omega^2 + \omega = -1$$

$$x^3 + \frac{1}{x^3} = \omega^3 + \frac{1}{\omega^3} = 2$$

$$x^4 + \frac{1}{x^4} = \omega^4 + \frac{1}{\omega^4} = \omega + \omega^2 = -1 \text{ etc.}$$

$$\therefore \left(x+\frac{1}{x}\right)^2 + \left(x^2+\frac{1}{x^2}\right)^2 + \left(x^3+\frac{1}{x^3}\right)^2 + \ldots + \left(x^{27}+\frac{1}{x^{27}}\right)^2$$

$$= \left[\left(x+\frac{1}{x}\right)^2 + \left(x^2+\frac{1}{x^2}\right)^2 + \left(x^4+\frac{1}{x^4}\right)^2 + \ldots\right.$$

$$+\left(x^{26}+\frac{1}{x^{26}}\right)^2\Bigg]+\left[\left(x^3+\frac{1}{x^3}\right)^2+\left(x^6+\frac{1}{x^6}\right)^2+\dots\right.$$

$$\left.+\left(x^{27}+\frac{1}{x^{27}}\right)^2\right]$$

$$=\left[(-1)^2+(-1)^2+\dots+18\text{ times}\right]+\left[2^2+2^2+\dots+9\text{ times}\right]$$

$$=18+36=54.$$

31. $1.(2-\omega)(2-\omega^2)+2.(3-\omega)(3-\omega^2)+\dots+(n-1)(n-\omega)(n-\omega^2)$

$$=\sum_{r=2}^{n}(r-1)(r-\omega)(r-\omega^2)$$

$$=\sum_{r=2}^{n}(r-1)\{r^2-r(\omega+\omega^2)+\omega^3\}$$

$$=\sum_{r=2}^{n}(r-1)(r^2+r+1)$$

$$=\sum_{r=2}^{n}(r^3-1)=\sum_{r=2}^{n}r^3-\sum_{r=2}^{n}1$$

$$=(2^3+3^3+\dots+n^3)-(n-1)$$

$$=(1^3+2^3+3^3+\dots+n^3)-1-(n-1)$$

$$=\left\{\frac{n(n+1)}{2}\right\}^2-n.$$

33. $\left(1+\frac{1}{\omega}\right)\left(1+\frac{1}{\omega^2}\right)+\left(2+\frac{1}{\omega}\right)\left(2+\frac{1}{\omega^2}\right)+\dots+\left(n+\frac{1}{\omega}\right)\left(n+\frac{1}{\omega^2}\right)$

$$=(1+\omega^2)(1+\omega)+(2+\omega^2)(2+\omega)+\dots+(n+\omega^2)(n+\omega)$$

$$=\sum_{r=1}^{n}(r+\omega)(r+\omega)$$

$$=\sum_{r=1}^{n}\{r^2-r+1\}$$

$$=\sum_{r=1}^{n}r^2-\sum_{r=1}^{n}r+\sum_{r=1}^{n}1$$

$$=\frac{n(n+1)(2n+1)}{6}-\frac{n(n+1)}{2}+n$$

$$=n\left\{\frac{(n+1)(2n+1)}{6}-\frac{n+1}{2}+1\right\}$$

$$=\frac{n(n^2+2)}{3}.$$

34. Given $1,\omega,\omega^2,\dots,\omega^{n-1}$ are the nth root of unity.

$$\therefore x^n-1=(x-1)(x-\omega)(x-\omega^2)(x-\omega^3)\dots(x-\omega^{n-1})$$

or $$\frac{x^n-1}{x-1}=(x-\omega)(x-\omega^2)(x-\omega^3)\dots(x-\omega^{n-1})$$

or $$1+x+x^2+\dots+x^{n-1}=(x-\omega)(x-\omega^2)(x-\omega^3)\dots(x-\omega^{n-1})$$

Putting $x=1$, we get

$$n=(1-\omega)(1-\omega^2)(1-\omega^3)\dots(1-\omega^{n-1}).$$

35. $(1-\omega+\omega^2)(1-\omega^2+\omega^4)(1-\omega^4+\omega^8)\dots$

$$=(-2\omega)(-2\omega^2)(-2\omega)(-2\omega^2)\dots 2n\text{ times}$$

$$=\left[(-2\omega)(-2\omega)\dots n\text{ times}\right]\left[(-2\omega^2)(-2\omega^2)\dots n\text{ times}\right]$$

$$=(-1)^{2n}.2^{2n}.\omega^n.\omega^{2n}=2^{2n}.(\omega^3)^n=2^{2n}.$$

36. $z_r=\cos\frac{\pi}{3^r}+i\sin\frac{\pi}{3^r}$, where $r=1,2,3,\dots$

$$\therefore\quad z_1=\cos\frac{\pi}{3}+i\sin\frac{\pi}{3}$$

$$z_2=\cos\frac{\pi}{3^2}+i\sin\frac{\pi}{3^2}$$

....

$\therefore z_1z_2z_3\dots\infty=$

$$\left(\cos\frac{\pi}{3}+i\sin\frac{\pi}{3}\right)\left(\cos\frac{\pi}{3^2}+i\sin\frac{\pi}{3^2}\right)\dots$$

$$=\cos\left(\frac{\pi}{3}+\frac{\pi}{3^2}+\dots\right)+i\sin\left(\frac{\pi}{3}+\frac{\pi}{3^2}+\dots\right)$$

$$=\cos\left(\frac{\pi/3}{1-1/3}\right)+i\sin\left(\frac{\pi/3}{1-1/3}\right)$$

$$=\cos\frac{\pi}{2}+i\sin\frac{\pi}{3}=0+i=i.$$

37. Given $x^2 - 2x\cos\theta + 1 = 0$

$$\Rightarrow \quad x = \cos\theta \pm i\sin\theta$$

$$\Rightarrow \quad x^{2n} = \cos 2n\theta \pm i\sin 2n\theta$$

(By De Moiver's Theorem)

$$\Rightarrow \quad x^n = \cos n\theta \pm i\sin n\theta$$

$$\therefore \; x^{2n} - 2x^n\cos n\theta + 1$$

$$= (\cos 2n\theta \pm i\sin 2n\theta)$$

$$-2(\cos n\theta \pm i\sin n\theta)\cos n\theta + 1$$

$$= \cos 2n\theta \pm i\sin 2n\theta - 2\cos^2 n\theta \mp i\sin 2n\theta + 1$$

$$= \cos 2n\theta - 2\cos^2 n\theta + 1$$

$$= (1 + \cos 2n\theta) - 2\cos^2 n\theta$$

$$= 2\cos^2 n\theta - 2\cos^2 n\theta = 0.$$

38. In an equilateral triangle circumcentre, controid and orthocentre are coincident.

$$\therefore \; z_0 = \frac{z_1 + z_2 + z_3}{3} \Rightarrow z_1 + z_2 + z_3 = 3z_0$$

Given that z_1, z_2, z_3 are the affixes of the vertices of an equilateral triangle.

$$\therefore \; z_1^2 + z_2^2 + z_3^2 = z_1z_2 + z_2z_3 + z_3z_1$$

($\because$ See Q.No. 25)

$$\Rightarrow (z_1 + z_2 + z_3)^2 = 3(z_1z_2 + z_2z_3 + z_3z_1)$$

$$\Rightarrow (3z_0)^2 = 3(z_1z_2 + z_2z_3 + z_3z_1)$$

$$\Rightarrow z_1z_2 + z_2z_3 + z_3z_1 = 3z_0^2$$

$$\Rightarrow z_1^2 + z_2^2 + z_3^2 = 3z_0^2$$

39. Given $\log z + \log z^2 + \ldots + \log z^n = 0$

$$\Rightarrow \log(z^1.z^2.z^3\ldots z^n) = 0$$

$$\Rightarrow z^{\frac{n(n+1)}{2}} = e^0 = 1$$

$$\Rightarrow z = 1^{\frac{2}{n(n+1)}}$$

$$\Rightarrow z = (\cos 0 + i\sin 0)^{\frac{2}{n(n+1)}}$$

$$\Rightarrow z = (\cos 2m\pi + i\sin 2m\pi)^{\frac{2}{n(n+1)}}, \; \forall\, m \in z$$

$$\Rightarrow z = \cos\frac{4m\pi}{n(n+1)} + i\sin\frac{4m\pi}{n(n+1)},$$

$$\forall\, m = 1, 2, 3, \ldots.$$

40. Given $z = i\log\left(2 - \sqrt{3}\right)$

$$\therefore \quad e^{iz} = e^{i^2\log\left(2-\sqrt{3}\right)} = e^{-\log\left(2-\sqrt{3}\right)}$$

$$\text{or} \quad e^{iz} = e^{\log\left(2-\sqrt{3}\right)^{-1}} = e^{\log\left(2+\sqrt{3}\right)} = 2 + \sqrt{3}$$

$$\text{or } \cos z = \frac{e^{iz} + e^{-iz}}{2}$$

$$= \frac{\left(2+\sqrt{3}\right) + \left(2-\sqrt{3}\right)}{2} = 2$$

5. BINOMIAL THEOREM

1. Binomial Theorem for Positive Integral Index : If x and a are real numbers, then for all $n \in \mathrm{N}$,

$(x+a)^n = {}^n\mathrm{C}_0 x^n.a^0 + {}^n\mathrm{C}_1 x^{n-1}.a^1 + {}^n\mathrm{C}_2 x^{n-2}.a^2 + \ldots.. + {}^n\mathrm{C}_r x^{n-r}.a^r + \ldots\ldots + {}^n\mathrm{C}_{n-1} x^1.a^{n-1} + {}^n\mathrm{C}_n x^0.a^n.$

i.e., $(x+a)^n = \sum_{r=0}^{n} {}^nC_r\, x^{n-r}.a^r$.

2. Some Important Conclusions from the Binomial Theorem

(i) The number of terms in each expression is $n+1$

(ii) The sum of the indices of x and a in each term is n

(iii) Since ${}^n\mathrm{C}_r = {}^n\mathrm{C}_{n-r}$, $r = 0, 1, 2, \ldots\ldots, n$.
It shows ${}^n\mathrm{C}_0 = {}^n\mathrm{C}_n$, ${}^n\mathrm{C}_1 = {}^n\mathrm{C}_{n-1}$, ${}^n\mathrm{C}_2 = {}^n\mathrm{C}_{n-2} \ldots.$
Thus, the co-efficients of terms equidistant from the beginning and the end are equal.

(iv) Replacing $-a$ in place of a, we get
$(x-a)^n = {}^n\mathrm{C}_0\, x^n.a^0 + {}^n\mathrm{C}_1\, x^{n-1}.(-a)^1 + {}^n\mathrm{C}_2 x^{n-2}.(-a)^2 + \ldots. + {}^n\mathrm{C}_r x^{n-r}.(-a)^r + \ldots. + {}^n\mathrm{C}_n\, x^0.(-a)^n.$
$= {}^n\mathrm{C}_0 x^n.a^0 - {}^n\mathrm{C}_1 x^{n-1}.a^1 + {}^n\mathrm{C}_2 x^{n-2}.a^2 - {}^n\mathrm{C}_3 x^{n-3}.a^3 + \ldots.. + (-1)^r\, {}^n\mathrm{C}_r x^{n-r}.a^r + \ldots\ldots + (-1)^n\, {}^n\mathrm{C}_n x^0.a^n.$

i.e., $(x-a)^n = \sum_{r=0}^{n} (-1)^r\, {}^n\mathrm{C}_r\, x^{n-r}.a^r$.

(v) Replace $x = 1$ and $a = x$ in the expansion $(x+a)^n$, we get
$(1+x)^n = {}^n\mathrm{C}_0 + {}^n\mathrm{C}_1\, x + {}^n\mathrm{C}_2\, x^2 + \ldots\ldots + {}^n\mathrm{C}_r\, x^r + \ldots.. + {}^n\mathrm{C}_n\, x^n$

i.e., $(1+x)^n = \sum_{r=0}^{n} {}^nC_r\, x^r$.

Expansion of $(1+x)^n$ is in ascending powers of x.

(vi) Replace $x = 1$ and $a = -x$ in the expansion $(x+a)^n$, we get
$(1-x)^n = {}^n\mathrm{C}_0 - {}^n\mathrm{C}_1\, x + {}^n\mathrm{C}_2\, x^2 - {}^n\mathrm{C}_3\, x^3 + \ldots. + (-1)^r\, {}^n\mathrm{C}_r x^r + \ldots. + (-1)^n\, {}^n\mathrm{C}_n x^n.$

i.e., $(1-x)^n = \sum_{r=0}^{n} (-1)^r\, {}^n\mathrm{C}_r\, x^r$.

(vi) Replace $a = 1$ in the expansion of $(x+a)^n$, we get
$(x+1)^n = {}^n\mathrm{C}_0 x^n + {}^n\mathrm{C}_1 x^{n-1} + {}^n\mathrm{C}_2 x^{n-2} + \ldots. + {}^n\mathrm{C}_r x^{n-r} + \ldots\ldots + {}^n\mathrm{C}_{n-1}\, x + {}^n\mathrm{C}_n.$

i.e., $(x+1)^n = \sum_{r=0}^{n} {}^nC_r\, x^{n-r}$

Expansion of $(x+1)^n$ is in descending powers of x.

(vii) $(x+a)^n + (x-a)^n = 2\,[{}^n\mathrm{C}_0 x^n.a^0 + {}^n\mathrm{C}_2 x^{n-2}.a^2 + {}^n\mathrm{C}_4 x^{n-4}.a^4 + \ldots.]$

(viii) $(x+a)^n - (x-a)^n = 2\,[{}^n\mathrm{C}_1\, x^{n-1}.a^1 + {}^n\mathrm{C}_3\, x^{n-3}.a^3 + \ldots..]$

3. General Term : T_{r+1} i.e., the $(r+1)$th term is called the general term, because by giving different values to r we can determine all terms of the expansion.

(i) $\mathrm{T}_{r+1} = {}^n\mathrm{C}_r\, x^{n-r}.\, a^r$ for $(x+a)^n$
(ii) $\mathrm{T}_{r+1} = (-1)^r\, {}^n\mathrm{C}_r\, x^{n-r}.\, a^r$ for $(x-a)^n$
(iii) $\mathrm{T}_{r+1} = {}^n\mathrm{C}_r\, x^r$ for $(1+x)^n$
(iv) $\mathrm{T}_{r+1} = (-1)^r\, {}^n\mathrm{C}_r\, x^r$ for $(1-x)^n$

4. Multinomial Theorem

$(x_1 + x_2 + x_3 + \ldots. + x_m)^n$

$$= \sum_{r_1+r_2+\ldots+r_m = n} \frac{n!}{r_1!\,r_2!\,r_3!\ldots.r_m!} \times x_1^{r_1}.\,x_2^{r_2}\ldots..x_m^{r_m}$$

The general term in the expansion is

$$\frac{n!}{r_1!\,r_2!\,r_3!\ldots.\,r_m!} \times x_1^{r_1}.\,x_2^{r_2}\ldots..x_m^{r_m}$$

Where $r_1, r_2, \ldots.\, r_m$ have all possible set of values which can be chosen from the numbers $0, 1, 2, \ldots..\, n$ such that $r_1 + r_2 + \ldots.. + r_m = n$.

5. Middle Term : The number of terms in the expansion $(x + a)^n$ is $n + 1$.

(i) If n is **even** there will be only one middle term, *i.e.*, $\left(\frac{n}{2}+1\right)$th

(ii) If n is **odd** then there will be two middle terms, *i.e.*, $\left(\frac{n+1}{2}\right)$th and $\left(\frac{x+3}{2}\right)$th.

6. Greatest Term in the Expansion of $(x + a)^n$

$T_{r+1} = {}^nC_r x^{n-r} a^r$ and $T_r = {}^nC_{r-1} x^{n-r+1} a^{r-1}$

$$\therefore \frac{T_{r+1}}{T_r} = \frac{{}^nC_r x^{n-r} . a^r}{{}^nC_{r-1} x^{n-r+1} . a^{r-1}} = \frac{n-r+1}{r} . \frac{a}{x}.$$

For a given value of x we find as to when $\frac{T_{r+1}}{T_r} \geq 1$ or $T_{r+1} \geq T_r$ where r is to be a positive integer. This inequality will reduce either to the form $r \leq m + k$ or $r \leq m$.

Where m is +ve integer and $0 \leq k < 1$.

In the first case T_{m+1} is the greatest term and in the second case both T_m and T_{m+1} are numerically greatest terms.

7. Independent Term : Let T_{r+1} be the term independent of x in $(x + a)^n$, equate to zero the index of x and find the value of n.

8. Properties of the Binomial Co-efficients

(i) ${}^nC_0 + {}^nC_1 + {}^nC_2 + \ldots\ldots + {}^nC_n = 2^n$

or $\sum_{r=0}^{n} {}^nC_r = 2^n$

(ii) ${}^nC_0 + {}^nC_2 + {}^nC_4 + \ldots\ldots = {}^nC_1 + {}^nC_3 + {}^nC_5 + \ldots\ldots = 2^{n-1}$.

(iii) ${}^nC_0 - {}^nC_1 + {}^nC_2 - {}^nC_3 + \ldots\ldots + (-1)^n C_n = 0$.

9. For a rational number n and a real number x, such that $|x| < 1$,

$$(1+x)^n = 1 + nx + \frac{n(n-1)}{2!}x^2 + \frac{n(n-1)(n-2)}{3!}x^3 + \ldots\ldots + \frac{n(n-1)(n-2)\ldots(n-r+1)}{r!}x^r + \ldots\infty.$$

10. Expansion of $(x + a)^n$ for any Rational Index

(i) When $x > a$, *i.e.*, $\frac{a}{x} < 1$

$$(x+a)^n = x^n \left\{1 + n.\frac{a}{x} + \frac{n(n-1)}{2!}\left(\frac{a}{x}\right)^2 + \frac{n(n-1)(n-2)}{3!}\left(\frac{a}{x}\right)^3 + \ldots\right\}$$

(ii) When $x < a$, *i.e.*, $\frac{x}{a} < 1$

$$(x+a)^n = a^n \left\{1 + n.\frac{x}{a} + \frac{n(n-1)}{2!}\left(\frac{x}{a}\right)^2 + \frac{n(n-1)(n-2)}{3!}\left(\frac{x}{a}\right)^3 + \ldots\right\}.$$

11. Some Important Inference of the Binomial Expansion

(i) $$(1+x)^{-n} = 1 - nx + \frac{n(n+1)}{2!}x^2 - \frac{n(n+1)(n+2)}{3!}x^3 + \ldots\ldots + (-1)^r \frac{n(n+1)(n+2)\ldots(n+r-1)}{r!}x^r + \ldots\ldots$$

(ii) $$(1-x)^{-n} = 1 + nx + \frac{n(n+1)}{2!}x^2 + \frac{n(n+1)(n+2)}{3!}x^3 + \ldots\ldots + \frac{n(n+1)(n+2)\ldots(n+r-1)}{r!}x^r + \ldots\ldots$$

(iii) $$(1-x)^n = 1 - nx + \frac{n(n-1)}{2!}x^2 - \frac{n(n-1)(n-2)}{3!}x^3 + \ldots\ldots + (-1)^r \frac{n(n-1)(n-2)\ldots(n-r+1)}{r!}x^r + \ldots\ldots$$

12. Putting $n = 1, 2, 3, 4$ in the expansion of $(1 + x)^{-n}$ we get

(i) $(1+x)^{-1} = 1 - x + x^2 - x^3 + x^4 + \ldots\ldots + (-1)^r x^r + \ldots\ldots$

(ii) $(1+x)^{-2} = 1 - 2x + 3x^2 - 4x^3 + 5x^4 + \ldots + (-1)^r (r+1) x^r + \ldots$

(iii) $(1+x)^{-3} = 1 - 3x + 6x^2 - 10x^3 + \ldots + (-1)^r \dfrac{(r+1)(r+2)}{2} x^r + \ldots$

(iv) $(1+x)^{-4} = 1 - 8x + 20x^2 - 40x^3 + \ldots + (-1)^r \dfrac{(r+1)(r+2)(r+3)}{3} x^r + \ldots$

Replacing x by $-x$ in all the above expression we get

(v) $(1-x)^{-1} = 1 + x + x^2 + x^3 + \ldots + x^r + \ldots$

(vi) $(1-x)^{-2} = 1 + 2x + 3x^2 + 4x^3 + \ldots + (r+1) x^r + \ldots$

(vii) $(1-x)^{-3} = 1 + 3x + 6x^2 + \ldots + \dfrac{(r+1)(r+2)}{2} x^r + \ldots$

(viii) $(1-x)^{-4} = 1 + 8x + 20x^2 + 40x^3 + \ldots + \dfrac{(r+1)(r+2)(r+3)}{3} x^r + \ldots$

EXERCISE

Mark the correct alternative(s) of each of the following :

1. The number of integral terms in the expression of $\left(5^{\frac{1}{2}} + 7^{\frac{1}{8}}\right)^{1024}$ is

(a) 127 (b) 129 (c) 131 (d) 133

2. If the sum of the co-efficients in the expansion of $(a+b)^n$ is 1024, then the greatest co-efficient in the expansion is

(a) 252 (b) 352 (c) 452 (d) 552

3. If the sum of the co-efficients in the expansion of $(1+2x)^n$ is 6561, the greatest term in the expansion for $x = \frac{1}{2}$ is

(a) 3rd (b) 4th
(c) 5th (d) None of these

4. The positive integer just greater than $(1+0.0001)^{1000}$ is

(a) 2 (b) 3
(c) 4 (d) None of these

5. The number $101^{100} - 1$ is divisible by

(a) 100 (b) 1000
(c) 10000 (d) All of them

6. The remainder when 2^{2003} is divisible 17 is

(a) 1 (b) 2
(c) 8 (d) None of these

7. The digit at unit's place in the number $17^{1995} + 11^{1995} - 7^{1995}$ is

(a) 0 (b) 1 (c) 2 (d) 3

J.N.U. M.C.A.

8. The sum to $(n+1)$ terms of the series $\dfrac{C_0}{2} - \dfrac{C_1}{3} + \dfrac{C_2}{4} - \dfrac{C_3}{5} + \ldots$ is

(a) $\dfrac{1}{n+1}$ (b) $\dfrac{1}{n+2}$

(c) $\dfrac{1}{n(n+1)}$ (d) $\dfrac{1}{(n+1)(n+2)}$

9. If $|x| = 1$, then the co-efficient of x^n in the expansion of $(1 + x + x^2 + \ldots)^2$ is

(a) n (b) $n-1$
(c) $n+2$ (d) $n+1$

10. If a_1, a_2, a_3, a_4 are the co-efficients of any four consecutive terms in the expansion of $(1+x)^n$, then $\dfrac{a_1}{a_1 + a_2} + \dfrac{a_2}{a_3 + a_4}$ is equal to

(a) $\dfrac{a_2}{a_2 + a_3}$ (b) $\dfrac{1}{2} \cdot \dfrac{a_2}{a_2 + a_3}$

(c) $\dfrac{2a_2}{a_2 + a_3}$ (d) $\dfrac{2a_3}{a_2 + a_3}$

11. The remainder when 5^{99} is divided by 13 is

(a) 6 (b) 8 (c) 9 (d) 10

12. If the co-efficient of x^7 and x^8 in $\left[2 + \dfrac{x}{3}\right]^n$ are equal then n is

(a) 15 (b) 25 (c) 45 (d) 55

[J.N.U. M.C.A.]

13. If ${}^8C_r - {}^7C_3 = {}^7C_2$, then the value(s) of n is/are

(a) 2 (b) 3
(c) 1 (d) None of these

[J.N.U. M.C.A.]

14. What is the remainder when $(14)^{251}$ is divided by 100?

(a) 12 (b) 46 (c) 24 (d) 64

[J.N.U. M.C.A.]

15. If C_1 stands for ${}^nC_r$ then the sum of the series

$$\frac{2\left[\frac{n}{2}\right]!\left[\frac{n}{2}\right]!}{n!}\left(C_0^2 - 2C_1^2 + 3C_2^2 - \ldots + (-1)^n (n+1) C_n^2\right)$$ is equal to

(a) 0 (b) $(-1)^n (n+2)$
(c) $(-1)^n n$ (d) None of these

[J.N.U. M.C.A.]

16. The last term in $\left(2^{\frac{1}{3}} + 2^{-\frac{1}{2}}\right)^n$ is $\left(\frac{1}{3(9)^{\frac{1}{2}}}\right)^{\log_3 8}$,

then the fifth term is

(a) 210 (b) 120
(c) 102 (d) None of these

17. If the third term in the expansion of $\left(\frac{1}{x} + x^{\log_{10} x}\right)^5$ is 1000, then the value of x is

(a) 10 (b) 100
(c) 1 (d) None of these

18. The number of positive integers satisfying the inequality ${}^{(n+1)}C_{n-2} - {}^{(n+1)}C_{n-1} \leq 100$ is

(a) 0 (b) 5
(c) 8 (d) None of these

[J.N.U. M.C.A.]

19. The number of terms which are free from radical signs in the expansion of $\left(x^{\frac{1}{5}} + y^{\frac{1}{10}}\right)^{55}$ is

(a) 5 (b) 6 (c) 11 (d) 9

20. The total number of terms in the expansion of $(x+y)^{100} + (x-y)^{100}$ after simplification is

(a) 101 (b) 50
(c) 51 (d) 102

21. The sum of the series

$$1 + \frac{1}{3^2} + \frac{1.4}{1.2}\cdot\frac{1}{3^4} + \frac{1.4.7}{1.2.3}\cdot\frac{1}{3^6} + \ldots$$ is

(a) $\sqrt{\frac{3}{2}}$ (b) $\left(\frac{3}{2}\right)^{\frac{1}{3}}$
(c) $\sqrt{\frac{1}{3}}$ (d) $\left(\frac{1}{3}\right)^{\frac{1}{3}}$

22. For every integer $n \geq 2$, the sum of the expression

$$1 - \binom{n}{1} + \binom{n}{2} + \ldots + (-1)^n \binom{n}{n}$$ is

(a) 0 (b) $n.2^{n-1}$
(c) $n(n-1)2^{n-2}$ (d) $\binom{2n}{n}^2$

[J.N.U. M.C.A.]

23. The value of $\frac{1}{n!} + \frac{1}{2!(n-2)!} + \frac{1}{4!(n-4)!} + \ldots$

(a) $\frac{2^{n-1}}{(n-1)!}$ (b) $\frac{2^{n-1}}{n!}$
(c) $\frac{2^n}{n!}$ (d) None of these

24. The approximate value of $(7.995)^{\frac{1}{3}}$ correct to four decimal places is

(a) 1.9995 (b) 1.9996
(c) 1.9990 (d) 1.9991

25. The co-efficient of the term independent of x in the expansion of

$$\left(\frac{x+1}{x^{\frac{2}{3}} - x^{\frac{1}{3}} + 1} - \frac{x-1}{x - x^{\frac{1}{2}}}\right)^{10}$$ is

(a) 210 (b) 105
(c) 70 (d) 112

ANSWERS

1	2	3	4	5	6	7	8	9	10
(b)	(a)	(c)	(b)	(d)	(c)	(b)	(c)	(d)	(c)
11	**12**	**13**	**14**	**15**	**16**	**17**	**18**	**19**	**20**
(b)	(d)	(b)	(d)	(d)	(a)	(b)	(d)	(b)	(c)
21	**22**	**23**	**24**	**25**					
(b)	(a)	(b)	(b)	(a)					

SOME SELECTED EXPLANATORY ANSWERS

1. General term in the expansion of $\left(5^{1/2}+7^{1/8}\right)^{1024}$

is $\quad T_{r+1} = {}^{1024}C_r\left(5^{1/2}\right)^{1024-r}.\left(7^{1/8}\right)^r$

$= {}^{1024}C_r.5^{512-r/2}.7^{r/8}$

$= {}^{1024}C_r.5^{512-r}.5^{r/2}.7^{r/8}$

$= {}^{1024}C_r.5^{512-r}.\left(5^4.7\right)^{r/8}.$

Now T_{r+1} will be an integer, iff $r/8$ is an integer such that $0\le r\le 1024$.

$\therefore$ possible values of r are multiple of 8 lying between $0\le r\le 1024$.

$\therefore r = 0, 8, 16, ..., 1024.$

$\therefore$ Total number of integral term is $(n-1)\,8 = 1024 \Rightarrow n = 128+1 = 129.$

2. Sum of the coefficients in any binomial expansion is obtained by replacing such variable by unit i.e. 1.

$\therefore$ Sum of coefficients in

$(a+b)^n = (1+1)^n = 2^n.$

$\therefore \quad 2^n = 1024$

$\Rightarrow \quad 2^n = 2^{10} \Rightarrow n = 10.$

As n is even, so the greatest coefficient is ${}^nC_{n/2} = {}^{10}C_5 =$

3. Given sum of the coefficients in the expansion $(1+2x)^n$ is 6561.

$\Rightarrow (1+2.1)^n = 6561$ for $x = 1$

$\Rightarrow \quad 3^n = 6561$

$\Rightarrow \quad 3^n = 3^8$

$\Rightarrow \quad n = 8.$

Now $\quad \dfrac{T_{r+1}}{T_r} = \dfrac{{}^8C_r\,(2x)^r}{{}^8C_{r-1}\,(2x)^{r-1}} = \dfrac{9-r}{r}\times 2x$

$\Rightarrow \quad \dfrac{T_{r+1}}{T_r} = \dfrac{9-r}{r} \quad \left(\because x = \dfrac{1}{2}\right)$

For greatest term we must have

$\dfrac{T_{r+1}}{T_r} > 1 \Rightarrow \dfrac{9-r}{r} > 1 \Rightarrow r < 4\dfrac{1}{2}.$

$\therefore$ 5th term is the greatest term.

4. We know that for any $x \in N$,

$$\left(1+\frac{1}{n}\right)^n = 1+n.\frac{1}{n}+\frac{n(n-1)}{2!}.\left(\frac{1}{2}\right)^2 + \frac{n(n-1)(n-2)}{3!}.\left(\frac{1}{3}\right)^2 + ...$$

$$= 1+1+\frac{1}{2!}\left(1-\frac{1}{n}\right)+\frac{1}{3!}\left(1-\frac{1}{n}\right)\left(1-\frac{2}{n}\right)+....$$

$$= 2+\frac{1}{2!}\left(1-\frac{1}{n}\right)+\frac{1}{3!}\left(1-\frac{1}{n}\right)\left(1-\frac{2}{n}\right)+....$$

$$\therefore \left(1+\frac{1}{n}\right)^n > 2 \text{ for } \forall\, n \in N. \qquad ...(i)$$

Also we know that

$$\lim_{n\to\infty}\left(1+\frac{1}{n}\right)^n = e \approx 2.71 \qquad ...(ii)$$

$\therefore$ From *(i)* and *(ii)* we get

$$2 < \left(1+\frac{1}{n}\right)^n < 3 \text{ for } \forall\, n \in N.$$

Hence greatest integer just greater than $(1+0.0001)^{10000}$ is 3.

5. Now $101^{100} - 1 = (1 + 100)^{100} - 1$

$= \left[{}^{100}C_0 + {}^{100}C_1.(100) + {}^{100}C_2.(100)^2 + ... + {}^{100}C_{100}.(100)^{100}\right] - 1$

$= {}^{100}C_1.(100) + {}^{100}C_2.(100)^2 + ... + {}^{100}C_{100}$

$\left(\because {}^{100}C_0 = 1\right)$

$= (100)^2\left[1 + {}^{100}C_2 + {}^{100}C_3.(100) + ... + {}^{100}C_{100}.(100)^{98}\right]$

$\left(\because {}^{100}C_1 = 100\right)$

$\therefore$ $101^{100}-1$ is divisible by 100, 1000 and 10000.

6. We have $2^{2000} = \left(2^4\right)^{500} = (17 - 1)^{500}$

$= {}^{500}C_0.17^{500} - {}^{500}C_1 17^{499} + ... - {}^{500}C_{499}.17 + (-1)^{500}$.

$= 17m + 1$ where m is some positive integer.

$\therefore\quad 2^{2003} = 8\,(2^{2000}) = 8\,(17m+8)$

$= 17\,(8m) + 8$

$\therefore$ Required remainder is 8.

7. Given $17^{1995} + 11^{1995} - 7^{1995}$

$= (7 + 10)^{1995} + (1 + 10)^{1995} - 7^{1995}$

$= \left[{}^{1995}C_0.7^{1995} + {}^{1995}C_1.7^{1994}.(10)^1 + {}^{1995}C_2.7^{1993}(10)^2 + ... + {}^{1995}C_{1995}.(10)^{1995}\right]$

$+\left[{}^{1995}C_0 + {}^{1995}C_1.(10)^1 + {}^{1995}C_2.(10)^2 + ... + {}^{1995}C_{1995}.(10)^{1995}\right] - 7^{1995}$

$= \left[{}^{1995}C_1.7^{1994}.10^1 + {}^{1995}C_2.10^2 + ... + 10^{1995}\right]$

$+\left[{}^{1995}C_1.10^1 + {}^{1995}C_2.10^2 + ... + 10^{1995}\right] + 1$

= integral multiple of 10 + 1.

$\therefore$ Digit at the unit place is 1.

8. We have

$(1 - x)^n = C_0 - C_1x + C_2x^2 - C_3x^3 + ...$

$\Rightarrow x\,(1 - x)^2 = C_0x - C_1x^2 + C_2x^3 - C_3x^4 + ...$

$\Rightarrow \int_0^1 x\,(1 - x)^n dx = \int_0^1 \left(C_0x - C_1x^2 + C_2x^3 - ....\right)dx$

Now L.H.S. $= \int_0^1 x\,(1 - x)^n\, dx$

$= \int_0^1 (1 - t)\,t^n.(-1)\,dt \quad (\because 1 - x = t)$

$= \int_0^1 (t^n - t^{n+1})\,dt = \left[\frac{t^{n+1}}{n+1} - \frac{t^{n+2}}{n+2}\right]_0^1$

$= \frac{1}{n+1} - \frac{1}{n+2} = \frac{1}{(n+1)(n+2)}$ ...(i)

R.H.S. $= \int_0^1 \left(C_0x - C_1x^2 + C_2x^3 - ....\right)dx$

$= \left[\frac{C_0x^2}{2} - \frac{C_1x^3}{3} + \frac{C_2x^4}{4} - ....\right]_0^1$

$= \frac{C_0}{2} - \frac{C_1}{3} + \frac{C_2}{4} - ....$ ...(ii)

$\therefore$ Fom *(i)* and *(ii)* we get

$\frac{C_0}{2} - \frac{C_1}{3} + \frac{C_2}{4} - .... = \frac{1}{(n+1)(n+2)}$.

9. Given $\left(1 + x + x^2 + ...\right)^2$

$= \left\{(1 - x)^{-1}\right\}^2 = (1 - x)^{-2}$

Now coefficient of x^n in $(1 - x)^{-r}$ is ${}^{n+r-1}C_{r-1}$

$\therefore$ Coefficient of x^n in $(1 - x)^{-2}$ is ${}^{n+2-1}C_{2-1}$

$= {}^{n+1}C_1 = n + 1$.

10. Let us suppose that a_1, a_2, a_3, a_4 be the consecutive coefficients of $(r + 1)$th, $(r + 2)$th, $(r + 3)$th and $(r + 4)$th terms in the expansion of $(1 + x)^n$.

$\therefore\ a_1 = {}^nC_r,\ a_2 = {}^nC_{r+1},\ a_3 = {}^nC_{r+2},\ a_4 = {}^nC_{r+3}$.

$\therefore\ \frac{a_1}{a_1 + a_2} + \frac{a_3}{a_3 + a_4}$

$= \frac{{}^nC_r}{{}^nC_r + {}^nC_{r+1}} + \frac{{}^nC_{r+2}}{{}^nC_{r+2} + {}^nC_{r+3}}$

$= \frac{{}^nC_r}{{}^{n+1}C_{r+1}} + \frac{{}^nC_{r+2}}{{}^{n+1}C_{r+3}}$

$\left(\because {}^nC_r + {}^nC_{r+1} = {}^{n+1}C_{r+1}\right)$

$= \frac{{}^nC_r}{\frac{(n+1)}{(r+1)}.{}^nC_r} + \frac{{}^nC_{r+2}}{\frac{(n+1)}{(r+3)}.{}^nC_{r+2}}$

$$\left(\because \frac{{}^{n+1}C_{r+1}}{{}^{n}C_r} = \frac{n+1}{r+1}\right)$$

$$= \frac{r+1}{n+1} + \frac{r+3}{n+1}$$

$$= \frac{2(r+2)}{n+1} = \frac{2.{}^{n}C_{r+1}}{\frac{(n+1)}{(r+2)}.{}^{n}C_{r+1}}$$

$$= 2.\frac{{}^{n}C_{r+1}}{{}^{n+1}C_{r+2}} = 2.\frac{{}^{n}C_{r+1}}{{}^{n}C_{r+1} + {}^{n}C_{r+2}} = \frac{2a_2}{a_2 + a_3}.$$

11. Given $\quad 5^{99} = 5^1.5^{98} = 5^1.\left(5^2\right)^{49}$

$= 5\left[(2 \times 13 - 1)\right]^{49}$

$= 5\left[{}^{49}C_0.26^{49} + {}^{49}C_1.26^{48}.(-1)^1 + {}^{49}C_2.26^{47}.(-1)^2 + ... + {}^{49}C_{49}.(-1)^{49}\right]$

$= 5\left[{}^{49}C_0.26^{49} + {}^{49}C_1.26^{48}.(-1)^1 + ... + {}^{49}C_{48}.26^1.(-1)^{48}\right] - 5$

$= 13 \times$ an integer $- 5$

$= 13 \times$ an integer $- 13 + (13 - 5)$

$= 13 \times$ an integer $+ 8$

$\therefore$ Remainder = 8.

12. $(r + 1)$th term of the binomial expansion $\left(2 + \frac{x}{3}\right)^x$

is ${}^{n}C_r.(2)^{n-r}.\left(\frac{x}{3}\right)^r$ i.e. ${}^{n}C_r.2^{n-r}.\left(\frac{1}{3}\right)^r.x^r.$

$\therefore$ Co-efficient of x^7 i.e. coefficient of T_8 = ${}^{n}C_7.2^{n-7}.\left(\frac{1}{3}\right)^7.$

Also co-efficient of x^8 i.e. coefficient of $T_9 = {}^{n}C_8.2^{n-8}.\left(\frac{1}{3}\right)^8.$

Given that both the coefficient are equal

$$\therefore \ {}^{n}C_7.2^{n-7}.\left(\frac{1}{3}\right)^7 = {}^{n}C_8.2^{n-8}.\left(\frac{1}{3}\right)^8$$

$$\Rightarrow \frac{n!}{(n-7)!7!}.2 = \frac{n!}{(n-8)!8!}.\frac{1}{3}$$

$$\Rightarrow \frac{2}{n-7} = \frac{1}{24}$$

$$\Rightarrow \quad n = 55.$$

13. Given $\ {}^{8}C_r - {}^{7}C_3 = {}^{7}C_2$

$\Rightarrow \quad {}^{8}C_r = {}^{7}C_2 + {}^{7}C_3$

$\Rightarrow \quad {}^{8}C_r = {}^{8}C_3$

$\Rightarrow \quad r = 3.$

14. Given $(14)^{251} = (10 + 4)^{251}$

$= {}^{251}C_0.10^{251} + {}^{251}C_1.10^{250}.(4)^1 + ... + {}^{251}C_{250}.10^1.(4)^{250} + {}^{251}C_{251}.(4)^{251}.$

$= 10^2\left[{}^{251}C_0.10^{249} + {}^{251}C_1.10^{248}.(4)^1 + ...\right] + {}^{251}C_{250}.10^1.(4)^{250} + {}^{251}C_{251}.(4)^{251}.$

= Integral multiple of $100 + 2510 \times 4^{250} + 4^{251}$ ...(i)

Now $2510 \times 4^{250} + 4^{251}$

$= 4^{250}(2510 + 4) = 2514 \times 4^{250}$

$= 2500 \times 4^{250} + 14 \times 4^{250}$

= Integral multiple of $100 + 14 \times 4^{250}$ ...(ii)

Next 14×4^{250}

$= 14 \times 16^{125} = 14 \times (10 + 6)^{125}$

$= 14\left[{}^{125}C_0.10^{125} + {}^{125}C_1.10^{124}.(6)^1 + ... + {}^{125}C_{124}.10^1.(6)^{124} + {}^{125}C_{125}.(6)^{125}\right]$

$= 14\left[{}^{125}C_0.10^{125} + {}^{125}C_1.10^{124}.(6)^1 + ...\right] + 14\left[{}^{125}C_{124}.10^1.(6)^{124} + {}^{125}C_{125}.(6)^{125}\right]$

$= 10^2 \times 14 \times \left[{}^{125}C_0.10^{123} + {}^{125}C_1.10^{122}.(6)^1 + ...\right] + 14 \times (1250 \times 6^{124} + 6^{125})$

$= 10^2 \times 14 \times \left[{}^{125}C_0.10^{123} + {}^{125}C_1.10^{122}.(6)^1 + ...\right] + 7 \times 2500 \times 6^{124} + 14 \times 6^{125}$

= Integral multiple of $100 + 14 \times 6^{125}$ ...(iii)

Again $14 \times 6^{125} = 14 \times 6 \times 6^{124}$

$= 14 \times 6 \times (5 + 1)^{124}$

$= 14 \times 6 \times \left[{}^{124}C_0.5^{124} + {}^{124}C_1.5^{123} + ... + {}^{124}C_{123}.5^1 + {}^{124}C_{124}.1\right]$

$= 14 \times 6 \times \left[{}^{124}C_0.5^{124} + {}^{124}C_1.5^{123} + ...\right] + 14 \times 6 \times (124 \times 5 + 1)$

$= 21 \times 2^2 \times 5^2\left[{}^{124}C_0.5^{122} + {}^{124}C_1.5^{121} + ...\right] + 84 \times (620 + 1)$

= Integral multiple of $100 + 84 \times 600 + 84 \times 21$

= Integral multiple of 100 + 1764
= Integral multiple of 100 + 1700 + 64
= Integral multiple of 100 + 64 ...*(iv)*
From *(i)*, *(ii)*, *(iii)* and *(iv)* be conclude that remainder of $(14)^{251}$ is 64.

15. Here

$$C_0^2 - 2C_1^2 + 3C_2^2 - 4C_3^2 + ... + (-1)^n (n+1) C_n^2$$

$$= \left[C_0^2 - C_1^2 + C_2^2 - C_3^2 + ... + (-1)^n C_n^2\right]$$

$$- \left[C_1^2 - 2C_2^2 + 3C_3^2 - .... + (-1)^n .n.C_n^2\right]$$

$$= (-1)^{n/2} \frac{n!}{\left(\frac{n}{2}\right)!\left(\frac{n}{2}\right)!} - (-1)^{n/2-1} \frac{n}{2}\, {}^nC_{n/2}$$

$$= (-1)^{n/2} \frac{n!}{\left(\frac{n}{2}\right)!\left(\frac{n}{2}\right)!}\left(1+\frac{n}{2}\right)$$

$$= \frac{1}{2}(-1)^{n/2} \frac{n!}{\left(\frac{n}{2}\right)!\left(\frac{n}{2}\right)!}(n+2)$$

$$\therefore\ 2\frac{\left(\frac{n}{2}\right)!\left(\frac{n}{2}\right)!}{n!}\left[C_0^2 - 2C_1^2 + 3C_2^2 - .... + (-1)^n (n+1) C_n^2\right]$$

$$= (-1)^{n/2} (n+2).$$

16. Given that last term in $\left(2^{1/3} + 2^{-1/2}\right)^n$ is $\left[\frac{1}{3(9)^{1/3}}\right]^{\log_3 8}$

$$\Rightarrow\ {}^nC_n.\left(2^{1/3}\right)^0.\left(2^{-1/2}\right)^n = \left[\frac{1}{3(9)^{1/3}}\right]^{\log_3 8}$$

$$\Rightarrow\ 2^{-n/2} = \left(3^{-5/3}\right)^{2\log_3 2}$$

$$\Rightarrow\ 2^{-n/2} = \left(3^{-5}\right)^{\log_3 2}$$

$$\Rightarrow\ 2^{n/2} = 3^{5\log_3 2}$$

$$\Rightarrow\ \frac{n}{2}.\log_e 2 = 5\log_3 2.\log_e 3$$

$$\Rightarrow\ \frac{n}{2} = 5\log_3 2.\log_2 3$$

$$\Rightarrow\ \frac{n}{2} = 5$$

$$\Rightarrow\ n = 10.$$

$$\therefore \text{ Fifth term} = T_5 = {}^{10}C_4.\left(2^{1/3}\right)^6.\left(2^{-1/2}\right)^4$$

$$= \frac{10!}{6!4!} \times 2^2 \times 2^{-2}$$

$$= \frac{10\times 9\times 8\times 7}{4\times 3\times 2\times 1} = 210.$$

17. Third term of the expansion $\left(\frac{1}{x} + x^{\log_{10} x}\right)^5$ is

$$T_3 = {}^5C_2.\left(\frac{1}{x}\right)^3.\left(x^{\log_{10} x}\right)^2$$

$$= 10 \times x^{2\log_{10} x - 3}.$$

$\therefore$ From given condition we get

$$10 \times x^{2\log_{10} x - 3} = 1000$$

$$\Rightarrow\ x^{2\log_{10} x - 3} = 10^2$$

$$\Rightarrow\ 2\log_{10} x - 3 = 2\log_x 10$$

$(\because a^x = y \Rightarrow \log_a y = x)$

$$\Rightarrow\ 2\log_{10} x - 3 = \frac{2}{\log_{10} x}$$

$$\Rightarrow\ 2z - 3 = \frac{2}{z} \text{ where } z = \log_{10} x.$$

$$\Rightarrow\ 2z^2 - 3z = 2$$

$$\Rightarrow\ 2z^2 - 3z - 2 = 0$$

$$\Rightarrow (z-2)(2z+1) = 0$$

$$\Rightarrow\ z = 2, -\frac{1}{2}$$

$$\Rightarrow\ \log_{10} x = 2 \text{ or } \log_{10} x = -\frac{1}{2}$$

$$\Rightarrow x = 10^2 \text{ or } x = 10^{-1/2}$$

$\therefore$ 100 is the required value of x.

18. Given ${}^{(n+1)}C_{(n-2)} - {}^{(n+1)}C_{n-1} \le 100$

$$\Rightarrow\ \frac{(n+1)!}{(n-2)!3!} - \frac{(n+1)!}{(n-1)!2!} \le 100$$

$$\Rightarrow\ \frac{(n+1)\,n\,(n-1)}{3!} - \frac{(n+1)\,n}{2!} \le 100$$

$$\Rightarrow\ n(n+1)\left[\frac{n-1}{6} - \frac{1}{2}\right] \le 100$$

$$\Rightarrow n(n+1)(n-4) \le 600$$

It is satisfied for numbers $n = 1, 2, 3, 4, 5, 6, 7, 8, 9$.

19. General term $T_{r+1} = {}^{55}C_r.\left(x^{1/5}\right)^{55-r}.y^{r/10}$.

$= {}^{55}C_r.x^{(55-r)/5}.y^{r/10}$.

To get the terms radical free, r should be multiple of 10.

$\therefore$ Possible values of r = 0, 10, 20, 30, 40, 50

$\therefore$ There will be total 6 terms.

20. Given $(x + y)^{100} + (x - y)^{100}$

$$= \left({}^{100}C_0.x^{100} + {}^{100}C_1.x^{99}.y + {}^{100}C_2x^{98}.y^2 + \ldots + {}^{100}C_{100}.y^{100}\right)$$

$$+ \left({}^{100}C_0.x^{100} - {}^{100}C_1.x^{99}.y + {}^{100}C_2x^{98}.y^2 - \ldots + {}^{100}C_{100}.y^{100}\right)$$

$$= 2\left({}^{100}C_0.x^{100} + {}^{100}C_2.x^{98}.y^2 + \ldots + {}^{100}C_{100}.y^{100}\right)$$

$\therefore$ Total number of terms = 51.

21. The given series is

$$1 + \frac{1}{3^2} + \frac{1.4}{1.2}.\frac{1}{3^4} + \frac{1.4.7}{1.2.3}.\frac{1}{3^6} + \ldots$$

Let the given series above be compaired with the series

$(1 + x)^n =$

$$1 + nx + \frac{n(n-1)}{2!}x^2 + \frac{n(n-1)(n-2)}{3!}x^3 + \ldots$$

We get $\quad nx = \dfrac{1}{9} \quad$ ...*(i)*

and $\quad \dfrac{n(n-1)x^2}{2} = \dfrac{4}{162} \quad$ ...*(ii)*

Squaring *(i)* and dividing it by *(ii)* we get

$\dfrac{n-1}{2n} = 2 \Rightarrow n = -\dfrac{1}{3} \quad$ ...*(iii)*

From *(i)* and *(iii)* we get $x = -\dfrac{1}{3}$.

$\therefore$ Sum of the series $= \left(1 - \dfrac{1}{3}\right)^{-1/3} = \left(\dfrac{3}{2}\right)^{1/3}$.

22. From binomial theorem we know that

$(1 + x)^n = {}^nC_0 + {}^nC_1 x + {}^nC_2 x^2 + \ldots + {}^nC_n x^n$.

$$= 1 + \binom{n}{1}x + \binom{n}{2}x^2 + \ldots + \binom{n}{n}x^n.$$

Putting $x = -1$, we get

$$1 - \binom{n}{1} + \binom{n}{2} + \ldots + (-1)^n\binom{n}{n} = 0.$$

23. Given $\dfrac{1}{n!} + \dfrac{1}{2!(n-2)!} + \dfrac{1}{4!(n-4)!} + \ldots$

$$= \frac{1}{n!}\left[\frac{n!}{n!} + \frac{n!}{2!(n-2)!} + \frac{n!}{4!(n-4)!} + \ldots\right]$$

$$= \frac{1}{n!}\left({}^nC_0 + {}^nC_2 + {}^nC_4 + \ldots\right) = \frac{2^{n-1}}{n!}.$$

24. Given $(7.995)^{1/3} = (8 - 0.005)^{1/3}$

$$= 8^{1/3}\left(1 - \frac{0.005}{8}\right)^{1/3}$$

$$= 2\left[1 - \frac{1}{3} \times \frac{0.005}{8} + \frac{\frac{1}{3}\left(\frac{1}{3} - 1\right)}{2!}\left(\frac{0.005}{8}\right)^2 + \ldots\right]$$

$= 2.\ [1 - 0.00208] = 1.9958 \approx 1.9996.$

25. Given $\dfrac{x+1}{x^{2/3} - x^{1/3} + 1} - \dfrac{x-1}{x - x^{1/2}}$

$$= \frac{\left(x^{1/3}+1\right)\left(x^{2/3} - x^{1/3} + 1\right)}{\left(x^{2/3} - x^{1/3} + 1\right)} - \frac{\left(x^{1/2}-1\right)\left(x^{1/2}+1\right)}{x^{1/2}\left(x^{1/2}-1\right)}$$

$$= \left(x^{1/3} + 1\right) - \left(1 + x^{-1/2}\right) = x^{1/3} - x^{-1/2}.$$

$$\therefore \left[\frac{x+1}{x^{2/3} - x^{1/3} + 1} - \frac{x-1}{x - x^{1/2}}\right]^{10} = \left(x^{1/3} - x^{-1/2}\right)^{10}.$$

Now general term i.e. T_{r+1} for the expansion $\left(x^{1/3} - x^{-1/2}\right)^{10}$

is $T_{r+1} = {}^{10}C_r\left(x^{1/3}\right)^{10-r}.\left(x^{-1/2}\right)^r$.

For the terms to be independent of x, we must have

$$\frac{10-r}{3} - \frac{r}{2} = 0$$

$\Rightarrow \quad 20 - 2r - 3r = 0$

$\Rightarrow \quad 5r = 20$

$\Rightarrow \quad r = 4.$

$\therefore$ Co-efficient of the term independent of x = ${}^{10}C_4 = 210$.

6. SEQUENCE AND SERIES

1. Sequence which follows a certain pattern are called progression. Three common progression are

(i) Arithmetic Progression (A.P.)

(ii) Geometric Progression (G.P.)

(iii) Harmonic Progression (H.P).

2. Arithmetic Progression (A.P.) : A finite or infinite sequence $a_1, a_2, ..., a_n$ or $a_1, a_2, ..., a_n, ...$ is said to be an arithmetic progression if $a_k - a_{k-1} = d$, a constant independent of k, for $k = 2, 3, ...n$ or $k = 2, 3 .....$ as the case be be. In other way the difference between any two consecutive terms is a constant. Here common difference is a constant, d. Now $a_2 - a_1 = d$ or $a_2 = a_1 + d$, $a_3 - a_2 = d$ or $a_3 = a_2 + d = a_1 + d + d = a_1 + 2d$.

Similarly, $a_k = a_1 + (k-1)\,d$, where $k = 1, 2, ...n$ or $k = 1, 2, ...$ as the case may be. The sequence being an A.P.

$a_{k+1} - a_k = d$ or $a_{k+1} = a_k + d$

or $a_{k+1} = a_1 + (k-1)\,d + d = a_1 + kd$.

The expression for a_k holds for a_{k+1} also if it holds for a_k. Thus, by induction, the expression holds for relevant k since it holds for a_1.

Thus in an A.P. whose first term is a_1 and common difference is d, the formula for ***n*th term** is

$a_n = a_1 + (n-1)\,d$

3. Selection of Terms in an A.P.

No. of terms	*Terms*	*Common difference*
3	$a-d, a, a+d$	d
4	$a-3d, a-d, a+d, a+3d$	$2d$
5	$a-2d, a-d, a, a+d, a+2d$	d
6	$a-5d, a-3d, a-d, a+d, a+3d, a+5d$	$2d$

4. Sum of *n* Terms of an A.P. : The sum S_n of n terms of an A.P. with first term 'a' and common difference 'd' is

$$S_n = \frac{n}{2}[2a + (n-1)\,d]$$

or $S_n = \frac{n}{2}[a + l]$ where l = last term = $a + (n-1)d$.

5. Arithmetic Mean (A.M.) : Let A be the arithmetic mean of a and b. Then a, A, b are in A.P.

$$\therefore\ A - a = b - A \Rightarrow 2A = a + b \Rightarrow A = \frac{a+b}{2}.$$

6. Insertion of *n* Arithmetic Means Between *a* and *b* : Let $A_1, A_2, ..., A_n$ be n arithmetic mean between a and b. Then $a, A_1, A_2, ..., A_n, b$ are in A.P.

Let d, be the common difference. Thus $b = a + (n+1)\,d$, as it is the $(n+2)$th term of the series.

$$\therefore\quad d = \frac{b-a}{n+1}$$

Now $\quad A_1 = a + d = a + \dfrac{b-a}{n+1}$

$$A_2 = a + 2d = a + \frac{2(b-a)}{n+1}$$

....

$$A_n = a + nd = a + \frac{n(b-a)}{n+1}$$

7. Geometric Progression (G.P.) : Let $a_1, a_2, ..., a_n, ...$ be respectively a finite or an infinite sequence. None of the a_n's is zero and $\frac{a_{k+1}}{a_k} = r$, a constant (*i.e.*, independent of k) for $k = 1, 2, ..., n$ or $k = 1, 2, ...,$ as the case may be. We call $\{a_k\}_{k=1}^{n}$ or $\{a_k\}_{k=1}^{\infty}$ as the case may be, a geometric progression. The constant ratio r is called common ratio. If a is the first term and r is the common ratio of a G.P., then G.P. can be written as $a, ar, ar^2, ar^3, ..., ar^{n-1}, ...$ The nth term of a G.P. is denoted by T_n and $T_n = ar^{n-1}$.

8. Selection of Terms in G.P.

No. of Terms	*Terms*	*Common Ratio*
3	$\frac{a}{r}, a, ar$	r
4	$\frac{a}{r^3}, \frac{a}{r}, ar, ar^3$	r^2
5	$\frac{a}{r^2}, \frac{a}{r}, a, ar, \frac{a}{r^2}$	r
6	$\frac{a}{r^5}, \frac{a}{r^3}, \frac{a}{r}, ar, ar^3, ar^5$	r^2

9. Sum of n Terms of an G.P. : Let S_n denote, sum of n terms of G.P. with first term 'a' and common ration r.

Now $S_n = a + ar + ar^2 + \ldots\ldots + ar^{n-1}$

and $r.S_n = ar + ar^2 + \ldots\ldots\ldots + ar^{n-1} + ar^n$

If $r = 1$, the sequence reduces to a constant sequence a, a, ... Hence we assume $r \neq 1$. Now subtracting the second sum from the first, we get

$(1 - r)\, S_n = a - ar^n$.

$$\text{or } S_n = \frac{a(1-r^n)}{1-r} = \frac{a_1 - r.a_n}{1-r}.$$

Where a, is the first term, a_n is the nth term and r is common ratio.

10. Sum of Infinity of a G.P. : Let us consider an infinite G.P. with first term a and common ration r, where $|r| < 1$ *i.e.*, $-1 < r < 1$.

Sum of n terms of G.P. is

$$S_n = a\left(\frac{1-r^n}{1-r}\right) = \frac{a}{1-r} - \frac{ar^n}{1-r}$$

Since $|r| < 1$, therefore r^n decreases as n increases and tends to zero as n comes closer to infinity *i.e.*, $r^n \to 0$ as $n \to \infty$.

$$\therefore \frac{ar^n}{1-r} \to 0 \text{ as } n \to \infty.$$

Thus sum of an infinite G.P. is given by

$$S = \lim_{n\to\infty} S_n = \lim_{n\to 0}\left\{\frac{a}{1-r} - \frac{ar^n}{1-r}\right\} = \frac{a}{1-r}.$$

11. Geometric Mean (G.M.) : Let G be geometric mean between a and b *i.e.*, a, G, b. Then $\frac{G}{a} = \frac{b}{G}$

or $G^2 = ab$ *i.e.*, $G = \sqrt{ab}$.

12. Insertion of n Geometric Means Between Two Given Numbers a and b : Let $G_1, G_2, G_3, \ldots\ldots, G_n$ be n geometric means between two given numbers a and b. Then $a, G_1, G_2, \ldots\ldots, G_n, b$ is a G.P.

Let r be the common ratio of this G.P. Then

$b = (n + 2)$th term $= ar^{n+1}$ or $\frac{b}{a} = r^{n+1}$ or

$$r = \left(\frac{b}{a}\right)^{\frac{1}{n+1}}.$$

$$\therefore G_1 = ar = a\left(\frac{b}{a}\right)^{\frac{1}{n+1}}, G_2 = ar^2 = a\left(\frac{b}{a}\right)^{\frac{2}{n+1}},$$

$$\ldots\ldots G_n = ar^n = a\left(\frac{b}{a}\right)^{\frac{n}{n+1}}.$$

13. The product of the n geometric means is the nth power of the single geometric mean between two numbers a and b.

i.e., $G_1.G_2 \ldots\ldots G_n = \left(\sqrt{ab}\right)^n = G^n$ where $G = \sqrt{ab}$ is the single geometric mean between a and b.

14. Properties of A.M. and G.M. Between Two Given Quantities

(i) If A and G are respectively arithmetic and Geometric means between a and b, where a, b are positive numbers, then A > G.

(ii) If A and G lies between two positive quantities a and b, then the quadratic equation having a, b as its roots is $x^2 - 2Ax + G^2 = 0$.

(iii) If A and G lies between two positive numbers, then the numbers are $A \pm \sqrt{A^2 + G^2}$.

15. Arithmetico-Geometric Sequence: Arithmetic progression is

$a, a + d, a + 2d, \ldots\ldots$

Geometric progression is

$a, ar, ar^2, \ldots\ldots\ldots$

A typical arithmetico-geometric sequence is

$a, (a + d)\, r, (a + 2d)\, r^2, (a + 3d)\, r^3, \ldots\ldots$

The **nth term** of this sequence is $(a + \overline{n-1}\, d) r^{n-1}$.

Let S_n denote the sum of n terms of the given sequence.

Then $S_n = a + (a + d)r + (a + 2d)r^2 + \ldots\ldots$ $+ (a + \overline{n-1}\,d)\,r^{n-1}$

$\Rightarrow r.S_n = ar + (a + d)r^2 + (a + 2d)r^3 + \ldots\ldots$ $+ (a + \overline{n-2}\,d)\,r^{n-1} + (a + \overline{n-1}\,d)\,r^n$

Subtracting we get

$(1 - r)\,S_n = a + dr + dr^2 + \ldots + dr^{n-1}$ $- (a + \overline{n-1}\,d)\,r^n$

$$i.e.,\ S_n = \frac{a}{1-r} + dr\frac{1-r^{n-1}}{(1-r)^2} - \frac{(a+\overline{n-1}\,d)}{1-r}r^n.$$

When $|r| < 1$, $S = \lim_{n\to 0} S_n = \frac{a}{1-r} + \frac{dr}{(1-r)^2}$ as $r^{n-1}, r^n \to 0$

16. ***(i)* Sum of first *n* natural terms :**

$$S_n = 1 + 2 + 3 + \ldots\ldots + n = \sum_{k=1}^{n} k = \frac{n(n+1)}{2}.$$

***(ii)* Sum of Squares of first *n* natural numbers :**

$S_n = 1^2 + 2^2 + 3^2 + \ldots + n^2$

$$= \sum_{k=1}^{n} k^2 = \frac{n(n+1)(2n+1)}{6}$$

***(iii)* Sum of Cubes of first n natural numbers :**

$$S_n = 1^3 + 2^3 + 3^3 + \ldots + n^3 = \sum_{k=1}^{n} k^3 = \left\{\frac{n(n+1)}{2}\right\}^2$$

17. Harmonic Progression : A sequence $a_1, a_2, a_3, \ldots\ldots, a_n$ of non-zero numbers is said to be in harmonic progression if its reciprocal $\frac{1}{a_1}, \frac{1}{a_2}, \ldots, \frac{1}{a_n}, \ldots$ is in arithmetic progression.

18. Harmonic Mean (H.M.) : Let H be the harmonic mean between two non-zero number *a*, *b*. Then *a*, H, *b* is a harmonic progression.

So $\frac{1}{a}, \frac{1}{H}, \frac{1}{b}$ is a arithmetic progression.

Thus $\frac{1}{H} - \frac{1}{a} = \frac{1}{b} - \frac{1}{H}$ or $\frac{2}{H} = \frac{1}{a} + \frac{1}{b}$ or

$$H = \frac{2ab}{a+b}.$$

19. Insertion of *n* Harmonic Means Between Two Given Numbers : Let $H_1, H_2, \ldots, H_n$ be *n* numbers inserted between two given numbers *a* and *b* such that the sequence $a, H_1, H_2, \ldots\ldots, H_n, b$ is an harmonic progression, then $H_1, H_2, \ldots, H_n$ are called *n* harmonic means.

Now $a, H_1, H_2, \ldots\ldots, b$ are in H.P.

So $\frac{1}{a}, \frac{1}{H_1}, \frac{1}{H_2}, \ldots\ldots, \frac{1}{b}$, are in A.P.

Let *d* be the common diff of this A.P.

Then $\frac{1}{b} = \frac{1}{a} + (n+1)\,d$ or $d = \frac{a-b}{(n+1)\,ab}$ where $\frac{1}{b}$ is the $(n+2)^{th}$ term.

$$\text{Thus } \frac{1}{H_1} = \frac{1}{a} + d = \frac{1}{a} + \frac{a-b}{(n+1)\,ab},$$

$$\frac{1}{H_2} = \frac{1}{a} + 2d = \frac{1}{a} + \frac{2(a-b)}{(n+1)\,ab}, \ldots,$$

$\frac{1}{H_n} = \frac{1}{a} + nd = \frac{1}{a} + \frac{n(a-b)}{(n+1)\,ab}$. So we can find out $H_1, H_2, \ldots\ldots, H_n$.

20. Properties of A.M., G.M. and H.M. Between Two Given Numbers : Let A, G and H are the arithmetic, geometric and harmonic mean between two numbers *a* and *b*. Then

$$A = \frac{a+b}{2},\ G = \sqrt{ab} \text{ and } H = \frac{2ab}{a+b}.$$

(i) $A \geq G \geq H$

(ii) A, G, H form a G.P. such that $G^2 = AH$.

21. If A, G, H are arithmetic, geometric and harmonic means between three given numbers *a*, *b* and *c*, then the equation having *a*, *b*, *c* as its roots is

$$x^3 - 3Ax^2 + \frac{3G^3}{H}x - G^3 = 0$$

Where $A = \frac{a+b+c}{3}$,

$$G = \sqrt[3]{(abc)},\ H = \frac{\frac{1}{a} + \frac{1}{b} + \frac{1}{c}}{3}.$$

22. The number e

$$e = 1 + \frac{1}{1!} + \frac{1}{2!} + \frac{1}{3!} + \ldots\ldots + \infty$$

$$= \lim_{n \to \infty} \left(1 + \frac{1}{n}\right)^n.$$

23. *e* **is a finite irrational number and its value lies between 2 and 3. Its value is approximately 2.7183.**

24. Exponential Series

$$e^x = 1 + \frac{x}{1!} + \frac{x^2}{2!} + \frac{x^3}{3!} + \ldots\ldots + \infty$$

$$= \lim_{n \to \infty} \left[\left(1 + \frac{1}{n}\right)^n\right]^x.$$

25. Important Deductions from Exponential Series

(i) $e^{-x} = 1 - \frac{x}{1!} + \frac{x^2}{2!} - \frac{x^3}{3!} + \ldots + \frac{(-x)^n}{n!} x^n +$

$$\ldots\ldots \infty = \sum_{n=0}^{\infty} (-1)^n \frac{x^n}{n!}$$

(ii) $e^{-1} = 1 - \frac{1}{1!} + \frac{1}{2!} - \frac{1}{3!} + \ldots\ldots \infty$

$$= \sum_{n=0}^{\infty} \frac{(-1)^n}{n!}$$

(iii) $\frac{e^x + e^{-x}}{2} = 1 + \frac{x^2}{2!} + \frac{x^4}{4!} + \frac{x^6}{6!} + \ldots\ldots \infty$

$$= \sum_{n=0}^{\infty} \frac{x^{2n}}{(2n)!}$$

(iv) $\frac{e^x - e^{-x}}{2} = x + \frac{x^3}{3!} + \frac{x^5}{5!} + \ldots\ldots\ldots \infty$

$$= \sum_{n=0}^{\infty} \frac{x^{2n+1}}{(2n+1)!}$$

(v) $\frac{e + e^{-1}}{2} = 1 + \frac{1}{2!} + \frac{1}{4!} + \ldots\ldots\ldots \infty$

$$= \sum_{n=0}^{\infty} \frac{1}{(2n)!}$$

(vi) $\frac{e - e^{-1}}{2} = 1 + \frac{1}{3!} + \frac{1}{5!} + \ldots\ldots\ldots \infty$

$$= \sum_{n=0}^{\infty} \frac{1}{(2n+1)!}$$

(vii) $\sum_{n=0}^{\infty} \frac{1}{(n+1)!} = \frac{1}{1!} + \frac{1}{2!} + \frac{1}{3!} + \ldots\infty = e - 1$

(viii) $\sum_{n=0}^{\infty} \frac{1}{(n+2)!} = \frac{1}{2!} + \frac{1}{3!} + \frac{1}{4!} + \ldots\infty = e - 2$

(ix) $e^{ax} = 1 + \frac{(ax)}{1!} + \frac{(ax)^2}{2!} + \frac{(ax)^3}{3!} + \ldots\ldots$

$$+ \frac{(ax)^n}{n!} + \ldots\ldots\ldots \infty$$

(x) $a^y = e^{y \log a} = 1 + y(\log_e a) + \frac{y^2}{2!}(\log_e a)^2$

$$+ \frac{y^3}{3!}(\log_e a)^3 + \ldots\ldots\ldots \infty$$

26. Logarithmic Series

$$\log_e (1 + x) = x - \frac{x^2}{2} + \frac{x^3}{3} - \frac{x^4}{4} \ldots\ldots\ldots \infty$$

$$= \sum_{n=1}^{\infty} (-1)^{n-1} \cdot \frac{x^n}{n!}.$$

27. Some Important Deduction from Logarithmic Series

(i) $\log_e (1 - x)$

$$= - x - \frac{x^2}{2} - \frac{x^3}{3} - \frac{x^4}{4} + \ldots\ldots\ldots \infty$$

$$= -\left\{x + \frac{x^2}{2} + \frac{x^3}{3} + \frac{x^4}{4} + \ldots\ldots\ldots \infty\right\}$$

$$\text{or } -\log_e (1 - x) = x + \frac{x^2}{2} + \frac{x^3}{3} + \frac{x^4}{4} + \ldots\ldots\ldots \infty$$

(ii) $\log(1 + x) - \log(1 - x)$

$$= 2\left\{x + \frac{x^3}{3} + \frac{x^5}{5} + \ldots\ldots\ldots \infty\right\}$$

$$\text{or } \log\left\{\frac{1 + x}{1 - x}\right\} = 2\left\{x + \frac{x^3}{3} + \frac{x^5}{5} + \ldots\ldots \infty\right\}$$

(iii) $\log_e 2 = 1 - \frac{1}{2} + \frac{1}{3} - \frac{1}{4} + \frac{1}{5} \ldots\ldots \infty$

(iv) $\log(1+x)(1-x)$

$$= -2\left\{\frac{x^2}{2} + \frac{x^4}{4} + \frac{x^6}{6} + \ldots\ldots \infty\right\}$$

28. Some Important Formulae for Logarithm:

(i) If $a^x = y$, then $x = \log_a y$

(ii) $\log_a a = \log_b b = 1$

(iii) $\log_a 1 = 0, \log_b 1 = 0$

(iv) $\log_b a . \log_a b = 1$ or $\log_b a = \frac{1}{\log_a b}$

(v) $\log_b a = \log_c a . \log_b c = \frac{\log_c a}{\log_c b}$

(vi) $\log_a mn = \log_a m + \log_a n$

(vii) $\log_a \frac{m}{n} = \log_a m - \log_a n$

(viii) $\log_a m^n = n \log_a m$

(ix) $a^{\log_a n} = n$

(x) $\log_a a^n = n.$

EXERCISE

Mark the correct alternative(s) of each of the following :

1. If the non-zero numbers *x, y, z* are in A.P. and $\tan^{-1}x, \tan^{-1}y, \tan^{-1}z$, are also in A.P., then

(a) $x = y = z$ *(b)* $xy = yz$
(c) $x^2 = yz$ *(d)* $z^2 = xy$

2. If the expression

$\exp\{(1 + |\cos x| + \cos^2 x + |\cos^3 x| + \cos^4 x + \ldots + \infty) \log_e 4\}$ satisfies the equation $y^2 - 20y + 64 = 0$ for $0 < x < \pi$, then the set of values of *x* is

(a) $\left\{\frac{\pi}{3}, \frac{2\pi}{3}\right\}$ *(b)* $\left\{\frac{\pi}{2}, \frac{\pi}{3}\right\}$

(c) $\left\{\frac{\pi}{2}, 0, \frac{\pi}{3}\right\}$ *(d)* $\left\{\frac{\pi}{2}, \frac{\pi}{3}, \frac{2\pi}{3}\right\}$

3. $\tan^{-1}\left(\frac{1}{2}\right) + \tan^{-1}\left(\frac{2}{11}\right) + \tan^{-1}\left(\frac{3}{46}\right) + \tan^{-1}\left(\frac{4}{137}\right) + \ldots\ldots$ up to infinity, equals to

(a) $\frac{\pi}{3}$ *(b)* $\frac{\pi}{4}$

(c) $\frac{\pi}{6}$ *(d)* $\frac{\pi}{2}$

4. The interior angles of a polygon are in arithmetic progression. The smallest angle is 120° and the common difference is 5°. The number of sides of the polygon are

(a) 6 *(b)* 16 *(c)* 9 *(d)* 12

5. If the sides of a triangle are in A.P. and greatest angle of the triangle is double the smallest angle, the ratio of the sides of the triangle is

(a) 3 : 4 : 5 *(b)* 4 : 5 : 6
(c) 5 : 6 : 7 *(d)* 7 : 8 : 9

6. The value of $0.2^{\log_{\sqrt{5}}\left(\frac{1}{4}+\frac{1}{8}+\frac{1}{16}+\ldots\ldots\right)}$ is

(a) 4 *(b)* log 4
(c) 2 *(d)* None of these

7. If $x > 1, y > 1, z > 1$ are in G.P., then $\frac{1}{1+\ln x}, \frac{1}{1+\ln y}, \frac{1}{1+\ln z}$ are in

(a) A.P. *(b)* H.P.
(c) G.P. *(d)* None of these

8. Let $a_1, a_2, \ldots, a_{10}$ be in A.P. and $h_1, h_2, \ldots, h_{10}$ are in H.P. If $a_1 = h_1 = 2$ and $a_{10} = h_{10} = 3$, then $a_4 h_7$ is

(a) 2 *(b)* 3 *(c)* 5 *(d)* 6

9. The natural number *a* for which $\sum_{k=1}^{n} f(a+k) = 16(2^n - 1)$ where the function *f* satisfies $f(x+y) = f(x)f(y)$ for all natural number *x, y* and further $f(1) = 2$, is

(a) 2 *(b)* 3
(c) 4 *(d)* None of these

10. Let $S_1, S_2, \ldots$ be squares such that for each $n \geq 1$, the length of *a* side of S_n equal the length of a diagonal of S_{n+1}. If the length of a side of S_1 is 10 cm, then for which of the following values of *n* the area of S_n is less than 1 sq. cm?
(a) 10 *(b)* 8
(c) 9 *(d)* All of them

11. If $H_1, H_2, H_3, \ldots, H_n$ are *n*-harmonic means lying between *a* and *b* then $\frac{H_1 + a}{H_1 - a} + \frac{H_n + b}{H_n - b}$ equal to
(a) n *(b)* $2n$ *(c)* $n+1$ *(d)* $n+2$

12. If $(1 - p)(1 + 2x + 4x^2 + 8x^3 + 16x^4 + 32x^5) = 1 - p^6$ $(p \neq 1)$, then a value of $\frac{p}{x}$ is
(a) $\frac{1}{2}$ *(b)* 2 *(c)* $\frac{1}{4}$ *(d)* 4

13. Sum of integers from 1 to 100 which are divisible by 2 or 5 is
(a) 3000 *(b)* 3010
(c) 3150 *(d)* 3050

14. The co-efficient of x^{99} in the expansion of $(x-1)(x-2)\ldots(x-100)$ is
(a) 5050 *(b)* 5000
(c) – 5050 *(d)* – 5000

[J.N.U. M.C.A.]

15. If $x^a = x^{\frac{b}{2}} z^{\frac{b}{2}} = z^c$, then *a, b, c* are in
(a) A.P. *(b)* G.P.
(c) H.P. *(d)* None of these

16. Divide 28 into 4 parts in A.P. such that the ratio of product of first and third with the product of second and fourth is 8 : 15. The required numbers are
(a) 4, 6, 8, 10 *(b)* 4, 7, 10, 13
(c) 7, 9, 11, 13 *(d)* None of these

[J.N.U. M.C.A.]

17. The natural numbers are divided into groups as (1), (2, 3), (4, 5, 6), (7, 8, 9, 10), ... and so on. The sum of the numbers in the 50th group is
(a) 1225 *(b)* 24505
(c) 62525 *(d)* None of these

[J.N.U. M.C.A.]

18. Sum of *n* terms of a G.P. is S, their product P and sum of their reciprocal is R, then
(a) $P^2 = \frac{R}{S}$ *(b)* $P^2 = \frac{S}{R}$
(c) $P^2 = \left(\frac{R}{S}\right)^n$ *(d)* $P^2 = \left(\frac{S}{R}\right)^n$

[J.N.U. M.C.A.]

19. The sides *a, b, c* of ΔABC are in G.P., where $\log a - \log 2b, \log 2b - \log 3c, \log 3c - \log a$ are in A.P., then $\angle A$ in the ΔABC is
(a) acute angle *(b)* obtuse angled
(c) right angled *(d)* None of these

20. The sum of $i - 2 - 3i + 4 + \ldots$ up to 100 terms, where $i = \sqrt{-1}$ is
(a) $50(1 - i)$ *(b)* $25i$
(c) $25(1 + i)$ *(d)* $100(1 + i)$

21. $3\log_e 2 + \frac{1}{4} - \frac{1}{2}\cdot\frac{1}{4^3} + \frac{1}{3}\cdot\frac{1}{4^3} - \frac{1}{4}\cdot\frac{1}{4^3} + \ldots$ equals to
(a) $5\log_e 10$ *(b)* $\log_{10} e$
(c) $\log_e 10$ *(d)* None of these

22. $1 + \frac{1}{3.2^2} + \frac{1}{5.2^4} + \frac{1}{7.2^6} + \ldots$ equals to
(a) $\log_e 3$ *(b)* $\log_e 5$
(c) $1 + \log_e 3$ *(d)* None of these

23. $\frac{4}{1!} + \frac{11}{2!} + \frac{22}{3!} + \frac{37}{4!} + \ldots$ equals to
(a) $4e - 1$ *(b)* $6e - 1$
(c) $6e + 1$ *(d)* $4e + 1$

24. $\frac{1^2}{3!} + \frac{2^2}{4!} + \frac{3^2}{5!} + \ldots$ equals to
(a) $2e - 5$ *(b)* $2e + 5$
(c) $3e - 5$ *(d)* $5e - 3$

25. $\frac{1}{1.2.3} + \frac{1}{3.4.5} + \frac{1}{5.6.7} + \ldots$ equals to
(a) $\log_e 3 - \frac{1}{3}$ *(b)* $\log_e 2 - \frac{1}{2}$
(c) $2\log_e 2 - \frac{1}{4}$ *(d)* None of these

26. $1+\frac{2^2}{2!}+\frac{3^2}{3!}+\frac{4^2}{4!}+\ldots\ldots$ equals to

(a) $3e$ (b) $5e$
(c) $2e$ (d) None of these

27. $\frac{2}{1!}+\frac{12}{2!}+\frac{28}{3!}+\ldots+\frac{3n^2+n-2}{n!}+\ldots$ equals to

(a) $5e+2$ (b) $2e+5$
(c) $3e+2$ (d) None of these

28. $\frac{2}{3!}+\frac{4}{5!}+\frac{6}{7!}+\ldots$ will be equal to

(a) $2e^{-2}$ (b) e^{-1}
(c) $2e^{-1}$ (d) e

29. $1+\frac{1+2}{2!}+\frac{1+2+2^2}{3!}+\frac{1+2+2^2+2^3}{4!}+\ldots$ equals to

(a) e^2+e (b) e^2-2e
(c) e^2-e (d) None of these

30. $1+\frac{1^2+2^2}{2!}+\frac{1^2+2^2+3^2}{3!}+\frac{1^2+2^2+3^2+4^2}{4!}$ $+\ldots\ldots$ equals to

(a) $\frac{19e}{6}$ (b) $\frac{15e}{6}$
(c) $\frac{17e}{6}$ (d) None of these

31. $\frac{(1+3)}{1!}\log_e 3+\frac{(1+3^2)}{2!}(\log_e 3)^2$ $+\frac{(1+3^3)}{3!}(\log_e 3)^3+\ldots\ldots$ equals to

(a) 23 (b) 25 (c) 27 (d) 28

32. $\frac{1}{1.2}-\frac{1}{2.3}+\frac{1}{3.4}-\frac{1}{4.5}+\ldots\ldots$ equals to

(a) $\log_e 4-1$ (b) $2\log_e 2+1$
(c) $\log_e 5-1$ (d) None of these

33. $\log_3\left(1+\frac{1}{3}\right)+\log_3\left(1+\frac{1}{4}\right)+\log_3\left(1+\frac{1}{5}\right)+\ldots+\log_3\left(1+\frac{1}{242}\right)$ equals to

(a) 1 (b) 2 (c) 3 (d) 4

34. $\frac{2}{1.2.3}+\frac{3}{3.4.5}+\frac{4}{5.6.7}+\ldots\ldots$ equals to

(a) $2\log_e 2+\frac{1}{4}$ (b) $2\log_e 2-\frac{1}{4}$
(c) $\log_e 2+\frac{1}{4}$ (d) None of these

35. $1+\left(\frac{1}{2}+\frac{1}{3}\right)\frac{1}{4}+\left(\frac{1}{4}+\frac{1}{5}\right)\frac{1}{4^2}+\left(\frac{1}{6}+\frac{1}{7}\right)\frac{1}{4^2}+\ldots\ldots$ equals to

(a) $\log_e 2\sqrt{3}$ (b) $\log_e 3\sqrt{2}$
(c) $\log_e 5\sqrt{2}$ (d) None of these

36. If $x\neq 0$, $1+\frac{x}{2!}+\frac{2x^2}{3!}+\frac{3x^3}{4!}+\ldots$ equals to

(a) $\frac{e^x(x+1)+1+x}{x}$
(b) $\frac{e^x(x+1)+1-x}{x}$
(c) $\frac{e^x(x-1)+1+x}{x}$
(d) None of these

37. $\log_4 2-\log_8 2+\log_{16} 2-\log_{32} 2+\ldots$ equals to

(a) $1-2\log_e 2$ (b) $1+2\log_e 2$
(c) $1+\log_e 2$ (d) $1-\log_e 2$

38. If $S=\frac{1}{1.2}-\frac{1}{2.3}+\frac{1}{3.4}-\frac{1}{4.5}+\ldots\ldots$ then e^S equals to

(a) $\frac{4}{e}$ (b) $\log_e\left(\frac{4}{e}\right)$
(c) $\frac{e}{4}$ (d) None of these

39. $\frac{1}{1.2}+\frac{1.3}{1.2.3.4}+\frac{1.3.5}{1.2.3.4.5.6}+\ldots\ldots$ equals to

(a) $e^{\frac{1}{2}}-1$ (b) $e^{\frac{1}{2}}+1$
(c) $e^{\frac{1}{3}}+1$ (d) $e^{\frac{1}{3}}-1$

40. $\frac{1}{2}\left(\frac{1}{2}+\frac{1}{3}\right)-\frac{1}{4}\left(\frac{1}{2^2}+\frac{1}{3^2}\right)+\frac{1}{6}\left(\frac{1}{2^3}+\frac{1}{3^2}\right)-\ldots$ equals to

(a) 0 (b) $\log_e\sqrt{2}$
(c) $\log_e\sqrt{3}$ (d) $2\log_e\sqrt{2}$

ANSWERS

1	2	3	4	5	6	7	8	9	10
(a)	(d)	(b)	(c)	(b)	(a)	(b)	(d)	(b)	(b)
11	**12**	**13**	**14**	**15**	**16**	**17**	**18**	**19**	**20**
(b)	(b)	(d)	(c)	(c)	(a)	(c)	(d)	(b)	(a)
21	**22**	**23**	**24**	**25**	**26**	**27**	**28**	**29**	**30**
(c)	(a)	(b)	(a)	(b)	(c)	(a)	(b)	(c)	(c)
31	**32**	**33**	**34**	**35**	**36**	**37**	**38**	**39**	**40**
(d)	(a)	(d)	(b)	(a)	(c)	(d)	(a)	(a)	(b)

SOME SELECTED EXPLANATORY ANSWERS

1. Given x, y, z are in AP.

$\therefore \quad 2y = x + z \quad ...(i)$

Also given $\tan^{-1} x, \tan^{-1} y, \tan^{-1} z$ are in AP.

$\therefore \quad 2\tan^{-1} y = \tan^{-1} x + \tan^{-1} z$

$$\Rightarrow \tan^{-1}\frac{2y}{1-y^2} = \tan^{-1}\left(\frac{x+z}{1-xz}\right)$$

$$\Rightarrow \frac{2y}{1-y^2} = \frac{x+z}{1-xz}$$

$\Rightarrow \quad 1 - y^2 = 1 - xz \quad$ [from (i)]

$\Rightarrow \quad y^2 = xz$

$\Rightarrow x, y, z$ are in GP. $\quad ...(ii)$

Conditions *(i)* and *(ii)* satisfies simulta-neously only if $x = y = z$.

2. Here

$$1 + |\cos x| + \cos^2 x + |\cos^3 x| + ...$$

$$= \frac{1}{1-|\cos x|} = \lambda \text{ (say) } (\because -1 < \cos x < 1)$$

$$\therefore \exp\left\{\left(1 + |\cos x| + \cos^2 x + |\cos^3 x| + ...\infty\right)\log_e 4\right\}$$

$$= \exp\{\lambda.\log_e 4\} = \exp\left(\log_e 4^{\lambda}\right) = 4^{\lambda}.$$

Now, $y^2 - 20y + 64 = 0$

$\Rightarrow (y-4)(y-16) = 0$

$\Rightarrow y = 4$ or 16.

As the given expression satisfies the given equation, therefore

$$4^{\lambda} = 4 \text{ or } 16$$

$$\Rightarrow \quad \lambda = 1 \text{ or } 2$$

$$\Rightarrow \quad \frac{1}{1-|\cos x|} = 1 \text{ or } 2$$

$$\Rightarrow \quad |\cos x| = 0 \text{ or } \frac{1}{2}$$

$$\Rightarrow x = \frac{\pi}{2} \text{ or } \lambda = \frac{\pi}{3}, \frac{2\pi}{3}.$$

3. Given $\tan^{-1}\left(\frac{1}{2}\right) + \tan^{-1}\left(\frac{2}{11}\right) + \tan^{-1}\left(\frac{3}{46}\right) + \tan^{-1}\left(\frac{4}{137}\right) + ...$ upto infinity

$$= \sum_{k=1}^{\infty} \tan^{-1}\left[\frac{2k}{2+k^2+k^4}\right]$$

$$= \sum_{k=1}^{\infty} \tan^{-1}\left[\frac{(k^2+k+1)-(k^2-k+1)}{1+(k^2+k+1)(k^2-k+1)}\right]$$

$$= \sum_{k=1}^{\infty}\left[\tan^{-1}(k^2+k+1) - \tan^{-1}(k^2-k+1)\right]$$

$$= (\tan^{-1} 3 - \tan^{-1} 1) + (\tan^{-1} 7 - \tan^{-1} 3) + (\tan^{-1} 13 - \tan^{-1} 7) + ... + \left[\tan^{-1}(n^2+n+1) - \tan^{-1}(n^2-n+1)\right] + ...$$

(for $k = 1, 2, 3, ..., n, ...$)

Taking limit as n tends to inifinity we get

$$\lim_{n\to\infty}\left[\tan^{-1}(n^2+n+1)-\tan^{-1}1\right]$$

$$=\tan^{-1}\infty-\frac{\pi}{4}=\frac{\pi}{2}-\frac{\pi}{4}=\frac{\pi}{4}.$$

4. Let the number of sides of the polygon be n. Sum of the interior angles of the polygon $= (n-2)\,\pi = (n-2)180°$.

Given that first term of AP i.e. $a = 120°$ and common difference $= d = 5°$.

$\therefore$ Sum of all the interior angles is

$$=\frac{n}{2}[2\times 120°+(n-1)5°]$$

$$\therefore\ \frac{n}{2}[240°+(n-1)5°]=(n-1)180°$$

$$\Rightarrow n(48+n-1)=(n-2).72$$

$$n^2-25n+144=0$$

$$\Rightarrow n=9 \text{ or } 16.$$

For $n = 16$, the largest angle $= 120° + 15 \times 5° = 195°$.

This is not possible as an interior angle of a polygon can not be greater than 180°. Hence $n = 9$.

5. Being in AP, let the sides of the triangle be $a-d$, a and $a+d$, with $a > d > 0$.

$\therefore$ $a-d$ is the smallest and $a+d$ is the largest side.

So A is the smallest angle and C is the largest angle. Then $C = 2A$.

$\therefore$ Angles of the triangle are A, 2A and $\pi - 3A$.

Applying the law of sines, we have

$$\frac{a-d}{\sin A}=\frac{a}{\sin(\pi-3A)}=\frac{a+d}{\sin 2A}$$

$$\Rightarrow \frac{a-d}{\sin A}=\frac{a}{\sin 3A}=\frac{a+d}{\sin 2A}$$

$$\Rightarrow \frac{a-d}{\sin A}=\frac{a}{3\sin A-4\sin^3 A}$$

$$=\frac{a+d}{2\sin A\cos A}$$

$$\Rightarrow \frac{a-d}{1}=\frac{a}{3-4\sin^2 A}=\frac{a+d}{2\cos A}\quad (\because \sin A\neq 0)$$

$$\Rightarrow 3-4\sin^2 A=\frac{a}{a-d} \text{ and } 2\cos A=\frac{a+d}{a-d}$$

$$4\cos^2 A-1=\frac{a}{a-d} \text{ and } 2\cos A=\frac{a+d}{a-d}$$

$$\Rightarrow \left(\frac{a+d}{a-d}\right)^2=1+\frac{a}{a-d}$$

$$\Rightarrow \quad a=5d.$$

$\therefore$ Sides of the triangle are $a-d$, a, $a+d$ i.e. $4d$, $5d$, $6d$.

$\therefore$ Ratio of the sides of the triangle is $4d : 5d : 6d$ i.e. $4 : 5 : 6$.

6. The given series $\frac{1}{4}+\frac{1}{8}+\frac{1}{16}+....$ is in G.P. with $a=\frac{1}{4}$ and $r=\frac{1}{2}$.

$$\therefore \quad \text{Its sum} = \frac{1/4}{1-1/2}=\frac{1}{2}\quad\left(\because S=\frac{a}{1-r}\right)$$

$$\text{Let} \quad y=0.2^{\log_{\sqrt{5}}\left(\frac{1}{4}+\frac{1}{8}+\frac{1}{16}+....\right)}$$

$$=0.2^{\log_{\sqrt{5}}\left(\frac{1}{2}\right)}$$

Taking log we get

$$\log y=\log_{\sqrt{5}}\left(\frac{1}{2}\right)\times\log(0.2)$$

$$\Rightarrow \quad \log y=\frac{\log(1/2)}{\log\sqrt{5}}\times\log\left(\frac{1}{5}\right)$$

$$\Rightarrow \quad \log y=\frac{\log 2\times\log 5}{\frac{1}{2}\log 5}=2\log 2$$

$$\Rightarrow \quad \log y=\log 2^2$$

$\Rightarrow \quad y = 4$, which is the required value.

7. Given x, y, z are in GP.

$$\therefore \quad y^2 = xz$$

$$\Rightarrow \quad 2\ln y=\ln x+\ln y$$

$$\Rightarrow 2+2\ln y=(1+\ln x)+(1+\ln y)$$

$$\Rightarrow 2(1+\ln y) = (1+\ln x)+(1+\ln y)$$

$\Rightarrow$ $1+\ln x$, $1+\ln y$, $1+\ln z$ are in AP.

$\therefore$ $\frac{1}{1+\ln x},\frac{1}{1+\ln y},\frac{1}{1+\ln z}$ are in HP.

8. Given $a_1, a_2, a_3, ..., a_{10}$ are in AP.
Also given $a_{10} = 3 \Rightarrow a_1 + 9d = 3$, where d is the common difference.

$\Rightarrow \quad 2 + 9d = 3 \qquad (\because a_1 = 2)$

$\Rightarrow \quad d = \frac{1}{9}.$

$\therefore a_4 = a_1 + 3d = 2 + 3.\frac{1}{9} = \frac{7}{3}.$

Given $h_1, h_2, h_3, ..., h_{10}$ are in HP.

$\therefore \frac{1}{h_1}, \frac{1}{h_2}, \frac{1}{h_2}, ..., \frac{1}{h_{10}}$ are is AP.

Now given $h_{10} = 3 \Rightarrow \frac{1}{h_{10}} = \frac{1}{3}.$

$\Rightarrow \frac{1}{h_1} + 9\lambda = \frac{1}{3},$

where λ is the common difference.

$\Rightarrow \quad 9\lambda = \frac{1}{3} - \frac{1}{2} \quad (\because h_1 = 2)$

$\Rightarrow \quad \lambda = -\frac{1}{54}.$

$\therefore \quad \frac{1}{h_7} = \frac{1}{h_1} + 6\lambda = \frac{1}{2} - 6 \times \frac{1}{54}$

$= \frac{1}{2} - \frac{1}{9} = \frac{7}{18}.$

$\Rightarrow \quad h_7 = \frac{18}{7}.$

$\therefore \quad a_4 h_7 = \frac{7}{3} \times \frac{18}{7} = 6,$

which is the required value.

9. Given $f(x + y) = f(x) f(y)$ and $f(1) = 2$

$\Rightarrow f(2) = f(1 + 1) = f(1).f(1) = 2 \times 2 = 2^2.$

$\Rightarrow f(3) = f(1 + 2) = f(1).f(2) = 2 \times 2^2 = 2^3.$

....

$\Rightarrow \quad f(k) = 2^k$ and $f(a) = 2^a.$

$$\therefore \sum_{k=1}^{n} f(a+k) = \sum_{k=1}^{n} f(a)f(k)$$

$$= f(a)\sum_{k=1}^{n} f(k) = f(a)\sum_{k=1}^{n} 2^k$$

$$= f(a)\left[2^1 + 2^2 + 2^3 + ... + 2^n\right]$$

$$= f(a).\frac{2(2^n - 1)}{2-1} \quad \left(\because S = \frac{a(r^n - 1)}{r-1}\right)$$

$= 2^a.2\,(2^n - 1)$

$\Rightarrow 16\,(2^n - 1) = 2^a.2\,(2^n - 1)$ ($\because$ Given)

$\Rightarrow \quad 2^a = 8 = 2^3 \qquad (\because 2^n - 1 \neq 0)$

$\Rightarrow \quad a = 3$

10. Given
Length of a side of S_n = Length of a diagonal of S_{n+1}.

$\Rightarrow$ Length of a side of $S_n = \sqrt{2}$ (Length of a side of S_{n+1}).

$$\Rightarrow \frac{\text{Length of a side of } S_n}{\text{Length of a side of } S_{n+1}} = \sqrt{2} \text{ for } n \geq 1$$

$$\Rightarrow \frac{\text{Length of a side of } S_{n+1}}{\text{Length of a side of } S_n} = \frac{1}{\sqrt{2}}$$

$\therefore$ Sides of $S_1, S_2, ..., S_n$ form GP with common ratio $\frac{1}{\sqrt{2}}$, with first term 10. (Given).

$\therefore$ Side of nth side i.e.

$$S_n = 10\left(\frac{1}{\sqrt{2}}\right)^{n-1} = \frac{10}{2^{(n-1)/2}}$$

$$\therefore n\text{th Area} = (S_n)^2 = \left[\frac{10}{2^{(n-1)/2}}\right]^2 = \frac{100}{2^{n-1}}.$$

Now, area of $S_n < 1$ (given)

$\Rightarrow \frac{100}{2^{n-1}} < 1 \Rightarrow 2^{n-1} > 100$

$\Rightarrow n - 1 \geq 7 \Rightarrow n \geq 8.$

11. Given $a, H_1, H_2, H_3, ..., H_n, b$ are in H.P.

$\therefore \frac{1}{a}, \frac{1}{H_1}, \frac{1}{H_2}, \frac{1}{H_3}, ..., \frac{1}{H_n}, \frac{1}{b}$ are in AP.

Let d be the common difference.

$\therefore \frac{1}{b} = \frac{1}{a} + (n+2-1)\,d$

($\because$ Total $n + 2$ terms)

$\Rightarrow d = \frac{a-b}{ab\,(n+1)}.$

Now $\frac{1}{H_1} = \frac{1}{a} + d = \frac{1}{a} + \frac{a-b}{ab(n+1)}$

$\Rightarrow \frac{1}{H_1} = \frac{bn+a}{ab(n+1)}$

$\Rightarrow \frac{a}{H_1} = \frac{bn+a}{b(n+1)}$

Using Componendo and dividendo rule, we get

$$\frac{H_1+a}{H_1-a} = \frac{2bn+(a+b)}{b-a} \quad ...(i)$$

Again $\frac{1}{H_n} = \frac{1}{b} - d = \frac{1}{b} - \frac{a-b}{ab(n+1)}$

$\Rightarrow \frac{1}{H_n} = \frac{an+b}{ab(n+1)}$

$\Rightarrow \frac{b}{H_n} = \frac{an+b}{a(n+1)}$

Again using Componendo and dividendo rule, we get

$$\frac{H_n+b}{H_n-b} = \frac{2an+(a+b)}{a-b} \quad ...(ii)$$

From *(i)* and *(ii)* we get

$$\frac{H_1+a}{H_1-a} + \frac{H_n+b}{H_n-b}$$

$$= \frac{2bn+(a+b)}{b-a} + \frac{2an+(a+b)}{a-b}$$

$$= \frac{2(b-a)n}{(b-a)} = 2n.$$

12. Given $(1-p)(1+2x+4x^2+8x^3+16x^4+32x^5) = 1-p^6$ $(\because p \neq 1)$

$\Rightarrow 1+2x+4x^2+8x^3+16x^4+32x^5 = \frac{1-p^6}{1-p}$

$\Rightarrow \frac{1-(2x)^6}{1-2x} = \frac{1-p^6}{1-p}$

$\Rightarrow p = 2x \Rightarrow \frac{p}{x} = 2$, which is the required value.

13. Sum of integers from 1 to 100 which are divisible by 2 or 5 is

$= (2+4+6+8+ .... +98+100) + (5+15+25+ .... +85+95)$

$= 2(1+2+3+4+ .... +49+50) + 5(1+3+5+ .... +17+19)$

$= 2\times\frac{50\times 51}{2} + 5\times\frac{10}{2}\times(1+19)$

$= 2550 + 500 = 3050.$

14. The expression $(x-1)(x-2)(x-3) .... (x-100)$

$= x^{100} - (1+2+3+ .... +100)x^{99} + ...$

$\therefore$ Coefficient of $x^{99} = -(1+2+3+ .... +100)$

$$= -\frac{100}{2}\times 101 = -5050.$$

15. Let $x^a = x^{b/2}z^{b/2} = z^c = \lambda$

$\Rightarrow x = \lambda^{1/a},\ z = \lambda^{1/c},\ xz = \lambda^{2/b}$

$\Rightarrow \frac{1}{a} + \frac{1}{c} = \frac{2}{b}$

$\Rightarrow$ *a, b, c* are in HP.

16. Let the four parts which are in AP whose sum is 28 be

$a-3d, a-d, a+d, a+3d.$

$\therefore$ Sum $= a-3d+a-d+a+d+a+3d = 28$

$\Rightarrow 4a = 28$

$\Rightarrow a = 7.$

Also given $\frac{(a-3d)(a+d)}{(a-d)(a+3d)} = \frac{8}{15}$

$\Rightarrow \frac{(7-3d)(7+d)}{(7-d)(7+3d)} = \frac{8}{15}$

$\Rightarrow \frac{49-14d-3d^2}{49+14d-3d^2} = \frac{8}{15}$

$\Rightarrow 21d^2 + 322d - 343 = 0$

$\Rightarrow (d-1)(21d+343) = 0$

$\Rightarrow d = 1, -\frac{343}{21}$

$\therefore$ Required numbers are $7-3, 7-1, 7+1, 7+3$ i.e. 4, 6, 8, 10.

17. Frist term of the *n*th group of the series is $\{1+2+3+ .... +(n-1)\}+1$

$$= \frac{n(n-1)}{2} + 1.$$

$\therefore$ Frist term of the 50th term.

$$= \frac{50\times 49}{2} + 1 = 1226$$

$\therefore$ Sum of the numbers in the 50th group is
$=1226 + 1227 + ... +$ up to 50th term.

$$= \frac{50}{2}[2\times1226+49\times1]$$

$$\left[\because S=\frac{n}{2}\{2a+(n-1)d\}\right]$$

$= 62525.$

18. Let S be the sum, with a the first term and r the common ratio of the G.P.
Then $S = a + ar + ar^2 + ... + ar^{n-1}$

$$= a\left(\frac{r^n-1}{r-1}\right) \quad ...(i)$$

P is the product of n term in GP

$$\therefore \quad P = a.ar.ar^2....ar^{n-1}$$
$$= a^n.r^{1+2+3+....+(n-1)}$$
$$= a^n.r^{n(n-1)/2} \quad ...(ii)$$

Also R is the sum of the reciprocal of n terms which are in G.P.

$$\therefore \quad R = \frac{1}{a}+\frac{1}{ar}+\frac{1}{ar^2}+....+\frac{1}{ar^{n-1}}$$

$$= \frac{1}{a}.\frac{\left(1-\frac{1}{r^n}\right)}{1-\frac{1}{r}} = \frac{1}{ar^{n-1}}.\frac{r^n-1}{r-1} \quad ...(iii)$$

Squaring equation *(ii)* we get

$$p^2 = a^{2n}.r^{n(n-1)} \quad ...(iv)$$

From *(i)* and *(iii)* we get

$$\frac{S}{R} = a^2.r^{n-1}$$

Raising the power of the equation to n both the sides we get

$$\left(\frac{S}{R}\right)^n = a^{2n}.r^{n(n-1)} \quad ...(v)$$

$\therefore$ From *(iv)* and *(v)* we conclude that

$$p^2 = \left(\frac{S}{R}\right)^n$$

which is the required solution.

19. Given a, b, c of ΔABC are in GP

$$\therefore \quad b^2 = ac \quad ...(i)$$

Also given $\log a - \log 2b$, $\log 2b - \log 3c$, $\log 3c - \log a$ are in AP

$\therefore 2(\log 2b - \log 3c) = \log a - \log 2b + \log 3c - \log a$

$\Rightarrow 2\log 2b - 2\log 3c = \log 3c - \log 2b$

$\Rightarrow \log 2b = \log 3c$

$\Rightarrow 2b = 3c \quad ...(ii)$

Eliminating b from *(i)* and *(ii)* we get

$$4ac = 9c^2 \Rightarrow a = \frac{9c}{3}$$

$$\therefore a:b:c = \frac{9}{4}:\frac{3}{2}:1 = 9:6:4$$

But $\cos A = \dfrac{b^2+c^2-a^2}{2bc} = \dfrac{36+16-81}{48} < 0$

$\therefore \angle A$ is obtuse angle.

20. Let the given sum be denoted by S.

$\therefore S = i - 2 - 3i + 4 + ...$
$= i + 2i^2 + 3i^3 + 4i^4 + 5i^5 + ... + 100i^{100} \quad ...(i)$

Multiplying both sides of equation *(i)* by i we get

$iS = i^2 + 2i^3 + 3i^4 + ... + 99i^{100} + 100i^{101} \quad ...(ii)$

Subtracting *(ii)* from *(i)* we get

$S - iS = i + (i^2 + i^3 + i^4 + ... + i^{100}) - 100i^{101}$

$$= i + i^2.\frac{(1-i^{99})}{1-i} - 100.i^{101}$$

$$= i - \frac{\left[1-\left(i^2\right)^{49}\right]}{1-i} - 100.i^{101}$$

$$= i - \frac{1+i}{1-i} - 100.i^{101}$$

$= i - i - 100.i^{101} = -100.i^{100}$

$$\Rightarrow S = -\frac{100.i^{101}}{(1-i)}$$

$= -50i(1+i) = -50(i-1) = 50(1-i)$

23. 4, 11, 22, 37, 56...... are such that the successive differences, 7, 11, 15, 19 etc., are in A.P.

$S = 4 + 11 + 22 + 37 + ... + t_n \quad ...(i)$

$S = 4 + 11 + 22 + ... + t_{n-1} + t_n \quad ...(ii)$

Subtracting *(ii)* from *(i)* we get

$0 = 4 + 7 + 11 + 15 + ... + (t_n - t_{n-1}) - t_n$

or $t_n = 4 + \{7 + 11 + 15 + ... + (n-1) \text{ term}\}$

$$= 4 + \left[\frac{n-1}{2}\{14+(n-2).4\}\right]$$

$= 4 + (n-1)(2n+3) = 2n^2 + n + 1$

$$\therefore\ T_n = \frac{2n^2+n+1}{n!} = \frac{2n(n-1)+3n+1}{n!}$$

$$= \frac{2}{(n-2)!} + \frac{3}{(n-1)!} + \frac{1}{n!}$$

$$T_1 = \frac{2}{(-1)!} + \frac{3}{0!} + \frac{1}{1!}$$

$$T_2 = \frac{2}{0!} + \frac{3}{1!} + \frac{1}{2!}$$

$$T_3 = \frac{2}{1!} + \frac{3}{2!} + \frac{1}{3!}$$

....

Adding all the terms we get the series as a whole as

$$2\left(1+\frac{1}{1!}+\frac{1}{2!}+\ldots\right)+3\left(1+\frac{1}{1!}+\frac{1}{2!}+\ldots\right)$$

$$+\left(\frac{1}{1!}+\frac{1}{2!}+\frac{1}{3!}\ldots\ldots\right)$$

$$= 2e + 3e + e - 1 = 6e - 1.$$

25. $$T_n = \frac{1}{(2n-1)\,2n\,(2n+1)}$$

$$= \frac{1}{2}\left(\frac{1}{2n-1} - \frac{1}{2n}\right) - \frac{1}{2}\left(\frac{1}{2n} - \frac{1}{2n+1}\right)$$

$$T_1 = \frac{1}{2}\left(\frac{1}{1}-\frac{1}{2}\right) - \frac{1}{2}\left(\frac{1}{2}-\frac{1}{3}\right)$$

$$T_2 = \frac{1}{2}\left(\frac{1}{3}-\frac{1}{4}\right) - \frac{1}{2}\left(\frac{1}{4}-\frac{1}{5}\right)$$

$$T_3 = \frac{1}{2}\left(\frac{1}{5}-\frac{1}{6}\right) - \frac{1}{2}\left(\frac{1}{6}-\frac{1}{7}\right)$$

Adding all the terms we get the series as

$$S = \frac{1}{2}\left(\frac{1}{1}-\frac{1}{2}+\frac{1}{3}-\frac{1}{4}+\frac{1}{5}-\frac{1}{6}+\ldots\right)$$

$$-\frac{1}{2}\left(\frac{1}{2}-\frac{1}{3}+\frac{1}{4}-\frac{1}{5}+\frac{1}{6}-\frac{1}{7}+\ldots\right)$$

$$= \frac{1}{2}\log_e 2 + \frac{1}{2}(\log_e 2 - 1)$$

$$= \log_e 2 - \frac{1}{2}.$$

26. $$T_n = \frac{n^2}{n!} = \frac{1}{(n-2)!} + \frac{1}{(n-1)!}$$

$$T_1 = \frac{1}{(-1)!} + \frac{1}{0!}$$

$$T_2 = \frac{1}{0!} + \frac{1}{1!}$$

$$T_3 = \frac{1}{1!} + \frac{1}{2!}$$

....

Adding all the terms we get the series as

$$S = 2\left(1+\frac{1}{1!}+\frac{1}{2!}+\ldots\ldots\right) = 2e.$$

30. $$T_n = \frac{1^2+2^2+\ldots+n^2}{n!}$$

$$= \frac{n(n+1)(2n+1)}{6.n!}$$

$$= \frac{1}{6}\left[2.\frac{n^3}{n!} + 3.\frac{n^2}{n!} + \frac{n}{n!}\right]$$

$$= \frac{1}{6}[2.5e + 3.2e + e] = \frac{17e}{6}.$$

31. $$\frac{(1+3)}{1!}\log_e 3 + \frac{(1+3^2)}{2!}(\log_e 3)^2 + \ldots\ldots$$

$$= \left(\frac{1}{1!}\log_e 3 + \frac{1}{2!}(\log_e 3)^2 + \ldots\ldots\right)$$

$$+\left\{\frac{3\log_e 3}{1!} + \frac{(3\log_e 3)^2}{2!} + \ldots\ldots\right\}$$

$$= \left(e^{\log_e 3} - 1\right) + \left(e^{3\log_e 3} - 1\right)$$

$$= (3-1) + (27-1) = 28.$$

32. $$\left(\frac{1}{1.2}-\frac{1}{2.3}\right)+\left(\frac{1}{3.4}-\frac{1}{4.5}\right)+\ldots = \frac{3-1}{1.2.3}+\frac{5-3}{3.4.5}+\ldots$$

$$= 2\left(\frac{1}{1.2.3}+\frac{1}{3.4.5}+\ldots\right) = 2\left(\log_e 2 - \frac{1}{2}\right)$$

[See solution 25]

$$= \log_e 4 - 1$$

33. $\log_3\left(1+\frac{1}{3}\right)+\log_3\left(1+\frac{1}{4}\right)+....+\log_3\left(1+\frac{1}{242}\right)$

$= \log_3 \frac{4}{3} + \log_3 \frac{5}{4} + ... + \log_3 \frac{243}{242}$

$= (\log_3 4 - \log_3 3) + (\log_3 5 - \log_3 4) + ...$
$+ (\log_3 243 - \log_3 242)$

$= \log_3 243 - \log_3 3 = \log_3 81 = 4$

34. $T_n = \frac{(n+1)}{(2n-1)\,2n\,(2n+1)}$

$= \frac{3}{4(2n-1)} - \frac{1}{2n} + \frac{1}{4(2n+1)}$

[∵ By partial fraction]

$= \frac{3}{4}\left(\frac{1}{2n-1} - \frac{1}{2n}\right) - \frac{1}{4}\left(\frac{1}{2n} - \frac{1}{2n+2}\right)$

$T_1 = \frac{3}{4}\left(\frac{1}{1} - \frac{1}{2}\right) - \frac{1}{4}\left(\frac{1}{2} - \frac{1}{3}\right)$

$T_2 = \frac{3}{4}\left(\frac{1}{3} - \frac{1}{4}\right) - \frac{1}{4}\left(\frac{1}{4} - \frac{1}{5}\right)$

$T_3 = \frac{3}{4}\left(\frac{1}{5} - \frac{1}{6}\right) - \frac{1}{4}\left(\frac{1}{6} - \frac{1}{7}\right)$

....

Adding all the terms we get

$S = \frac{3}{4}\left(1 - \frac{1}{2} + \frac{1}{3} - \frac{1}{4} + \frac{1}{5} - \frac{1}{6} + ...\right)$

$- \frac{3}{4}\left(\frac{1}{2} - \frac{1}{3} + \frac{1}{4} - \frac{1}{5} + ...\right)$

$= \frac{3}{4}\log_e 2 - \frac{1}{4}\{-(\log_e 2 - 1)\}$

$= \frac{3}{4}\log_e 2 + \frac{1}{4}(\log_e 2 - 1) = \log_e 2 - \frac{1}{4}.$

35. $1+\left(\frac{1}{2}+\frac{1}{3}\right)\frac{1}{4}+\left(\frac{1}{4}+\frac{1}{5}\right)\frac{1}{4^2}+\left(\frac{1}{6}+\frac{1}{7}\right)\frac{1}{4^3}+....$

$= \frac{1}{2}\left(\frac{1}{4} + \frac{1}{2}.\frac{1}{4^2} + \frac{1}{3}.\frac{1}{4^3} + ...\right)$

$+\left(1 + \frac{1}{3}.\frac{1}{4} + \frac{1}{5}.\frac{1}{4^2} + ...\right)$

$= -\frac{1}{2}\log_e\left(1 - \frac{1}{4}\right)$

$+ 2\left(\frac{1}{2} + \frac{1}{3}.\frac{1}{2^3} + \frac{1}{5}.\frac{1}{2^5} + ...\right)$

$= -\frac{1}{2}\log_e\frac{3}{4} + \log\frac{\left(1+\frac{1}{2}\right)}{\left(1-\frac{1}{2}\right)}$

$= -\frac{1}{2}\log_e\frac{3}{4} + \log_e 3$

$= \frac{1}{2}\log_e 3 + \frac{1}{2}\log_e 4 = \log_e 2\sqrt{3}$

36. Let $S = \frac{x}{2!} + \frac{2x^2}{3!} + \frac{3x^3}{4!} + ...$

then $T_n = \frac{nx^n}{(n+1)!} = \left[\frac{1}{n!} - \frac{1}{(n+1)!}\right]x^n$

$T_1 = \left[\frac{1}{1!} - \frac{1}{2!}\right]x$

$T_2 = \left[\frac{1}{2!} - \frac{1}{3!}\right]x^2$

$T_3 = \left[\frac{1}{3!} - \frac{1}{4!}\right]x^3$

....

Adding all the terms we get

$S = \left(\frac{x}{1!} + \frac{x^2}{2!} + \frac{x^3}{3!} + ...\right) - \left(\frac{x}{2!} + \frac{x^2}{3!} + \frac{x^3}{4!} + ...\right)$

$= \left(\frac{x}{1!} + \frac{x^2}{2!} + \frac{x^3}{3!} + ...\right) - \frac{1}{x}\left(\frac{x^2}{2!} + \frac{x^3}{3!} + \frac{x^4}{4!} + ...\right)$

$= (e^x - 1) - \frac{1}{x}(e^x - 1 - x)$

Thus the series is 1 + S

$= 1 + (e^x - 1) - \frac{1}{x}(e^x - 1 - x)$

$= \frac{e^x(x-1) + 1 + x}{x}$

37. $\log_4 2 - \log_8 2 + \log_{16} 2 - \log_{32} 2 + ...$

$= \frac{1}{\log_2 4} - \frac{1}{\log_2 8} + \frac{1}{\log_2 16} - \frac{1}{\log_2 32} + ...$

$$= \frac{1}{2} - \frac{1}{3} + \frac{1}{4} - \frac{1}{5} + \ldots$$

$$= 1 - \left(1 - \frac{1}{2} + \frac{1}{3} - \frac{1}{4} + \frac{1}{5} - \ldots\right) = 1 - \log_e 2$$

38. $T_n = \dfrac{1}{n(n+1)} = \left(\dfrac{1}{n} - \dfrac{1}{n+1}\right)$

$$\therefore \quad S = T_1 - T_2 + T_3 - T_4 + \ldots$$

$$= \left(\frac{1}{1} - \frac{1}{2}\right) - \left(\frac{1}{2} - \frac{1}{3}\right) + \left(\frac{1}{3} - \frac{1}{4}\right) + \ldots$$

$$= 2\left(1 - \frac{1}{2} + \frac{1}{3} - \frac{1}{4} + \ldots\right) - 1$$

$$= 2\log(1+1) - \log_e e = \log_e\left(\frac{4}{e}\right)$$

$$\therefore \quad e^S = e^{\log_e\left(\frac{4}{e}\right)} = \frac{4}{e}.$$

39. $T_n = \dfrac{1.3.5.7\ldots(2n-1)}{1.2.3.4.5\ldots(2n)}$

$$= \frac{1}{2.4.6.8\ldots(2n-2)(2n)}$$

$$= \frac{1}{2^n n!} = \frac{\left(\frac{1}{2}\right)^n}{n!}$$

$$T_1 = \frac{\left(\frac{1}{2}\right)}{1!};\; T_2 = \frac{\left(\frac{1}{2}\right)^2}{2!};\; T_3 = \frac{\left(\frac{1}{2}\right)^3}{3!}$$

....

Adding all the terms we get

$$S = \frac{\left(\frac{1}{2}\right)}{1!} + \frac{\left(\frac{1}{2}\right)^2}{2!} + \frac{\left(\frac{1}{2}\right)^3}{3!} + \ldots$$

$$= \left[1 + \frac{\left(\frac{1}{2}\right)}{1!} + \frac{\left(\frac{1}{2}\right)^2}{2!} + \frac{\left(\frac{1}{2}\right)^3}{3!} + \ldots\right] - 1$$

$$= e^{\frac{1}{2}} - 1.$$

40. $\dfrac{1}{2}\left(\dfrac{1}{2} + \dfrac{1}{3}\right) - \dfrac{1}{4}\left(\dfrac{1}{2^2} + \dfrac{1}{3^2}\right) + \dfrac{1}{6}\left(\dfrac{1}{2^3} + \dfrac{1}{3^3}\right) + \ldots$

$$= \frac{1}{2}\left(\frac{1}{2} - \frac{1}{2}.\frac{1}{2^2} + \frac{1}{3}.\frac{1}{2^3} - \ldots\right)$$

$$+ \frac{1}{2}\left(\frac{1}{3} - \frac{1}{2}.\frac{1}{3^2} + \frac{1}{3}.\frac{1}{3^3} - \ldots\right)$$

$$= \frac{1}{2}\log_e\left(1 + \frac{1}{2}\right) + \frac{1}{2}\log\left(1 + \frac{1}{3}\right) = \log_e \sqrt{2}$$

7. ELEMENTARY NUMBER THEORY

1. Number of Divisors of a Positive Integer

(i) If $n = p_1^{\alpha_1} p_2^{\alpha_2}, \ldots\ldots p_r^{\alpha_r}$, where p's are positive primes and $\alpha_1, \alpha_2, \ldots\ldots \alpha_r$ are positive integers, then the number of distinct positive integral divisors of $n = (1+\alpha_1)(1+\alpha_2), \ldots\ldots (1+\alpha_r)$, since each term of the product $(1 + p_1 + p_1^2 + \ldots\ldots + p_1^{\alpha_1})$ $(1 + p_2 + p_2^2 + \ldots\ldots + p_2^{\alpha_2}), \ldots\ldots\ldots (1 + p_r + p_r^r + \ldots\ldots + p_r^{\alpha_r})$ is a divisor. This include the two trivial divisors, namely 1 and the number itself.

(ii) Also the sum of all distinct positive integral divisors of n = the sum of terms in the product

$$(1 + p_1 + p_2^2 + \ldots + p_1^{\alpha_1}) \quad (1 + p_2 + p_2^2 + \ldots + p_2^{\alpha_2})$$

$$\ldots\ldots = \left(\frac{p_1^{\alpha_1+1} - 1}{p_1 - 1}\right)\left(\frac{p_2^{\alpha_2+1} - 1}{p_2 - 1}\right), \ldots \left(\frac{p_r^{\alpha_r+1} - 1}{p_r - 1}\right)$$

2. Assume that $n = p_1^{\alpha_1} p_2^{\alpha_2}, \ldots\ldots p_r^{\alpha_r}$ is a composite number, where p_i $(i = 1, 2, \ldots\ldots, r)$ are distinct primes and exponents $\alpha_1, \ldots\ldots \alpha_r$ are positive integers. Then

(i) The number of ways in which n may be resolved into two factors if $\frac{1}{2}(\alpha_1 + 1)(\alpha_2 + 1) \ldots\ldots (\alpha_r + 1)$ in case n is not a perfect square.

(ii) But if n is perfect square, then the number of ways in which n may be resolved into two factors is $\frac{1}{2}\left[(\alpha_1 + 1)(\alpha_2 + 1), \ldots\ldots (\alpha_r + 1) + 1\right]$.

3. If p is a positive prime and $a, b \in Z$ then $(a + b)^p = a^p + b^p + M(p)$, where $M(p)$ stands for an integral multiple of p.

Note : If p is a positive prime and $a_1, a_2, \ldots\ldots a_n \in Z$, then $(a_1 + a_2 + \ldots\ldots + a_n)^p = a_1^p + a_2^p + \ldots\ldots + a_n^p + M(p)$.

4. The highest power of a prime numbere 'p' which is contained in $n!$ is

$$\left[\frac{n}{p}\right] + \left[\frac{n}{p^2}\right] + \left[\frac{n}{p^3}\right] + \ldots\ldots$$

Where $[x]$ stands for greatest integer less than or equal to x.

5. Mersenne Number : The numbers of the form $M_n = 2^n - 1$, where n is a prime, are known as Mersenne numbers. All Mersenne numbers are not prime $M_n = 2^{11} - 1 = 2047$ is composite because 23 is a divisor of 2047.

6. Euler's ϕ-functions : The Euler ϕ-function is the function $\phi : Z^+ \to Z^+$ defined as follows

(i) $\phi(1) = 1$ and

(ii) for $n (> 1) \in Z^+, \phi(n)$ = the number of positive integers less than n and relatively prime to n.

Case I : If m and n are relatively prime positive integers *i.e.*, $(m, n) = 1$, then $\phi(mn) = \phi(m).\phi(n)$.

Case II : If p is a positive prime, then

$$\phi(p^n) = p^n - p^{n-1} = p^n\left(1 - \frac{1}{p}\right) \text{ for every}$$

positive integer n.

Case III : If $n > 1$ and $p_1, p_2, \ldots\ldots, p_m$ are distinct prime factors of n, then

$$\phi(n) = n\left(1 - \frac{1}{p_1}\right)\left(1 - \frac{1}{p_2}\right) \ldots\ldots \left(1 - \frac{1}{p_m}\right).$$

Case IV : If $d_1, d_2, \ldots\ldots\ldots d_r$ be the distinct positive divisors of a positive integer n, then $\phi(d_1) + \phi(d_2) + \ldots\ldots + \phi(d_r) = n$.

Case V : If $n > 1$, the sum of all positive integers which are less than n and prime to n is $\frac{1}{2} n\,\phi(n)$.

7. Fermat's Theorem : If p is a positive prime and a is any integer such that p is not a divisor of a so that $(a, p) = 1$, then $a^{p-1} \equiv 1 \pmod p$ or $a^{p-1} - 1$ is a multiple of p.

8. Euler's Theorem : If m is a positive integer and a is any integer such that $(a, m) = 1$, then $a^{\phi(m)} \equiv 1 \pmod m$.

9. Wilson's Theorem : If p is a positive prime, then

$(p-1)! + 1 \equiv 0 \pmod p$ *i.e.,* $(p-1)! + 1$ is a multiple of p.

10. Lagrange's Theorem : If p is a positive prime and q is a positive integer $< p - 1$, then the sum of the products of the numbers $1, 2, 3, \ldots, p-1$, taken q at a time, is divisible by p.

11. Congruences : Two integers a and b are called congruent with respect to the modulus m if an integer r exists such that $a - b = rm$, r may be positive, negative or zero.

$a \equiv b \pmod m$ or $a - b \equiv 0 \pmod m$.

Properties of Congruences with Same Modulii :

(*i*) If $a \equiv b \pmod m$ and $c \equiv d \pmod m$ and if x and y are integers, then
$xa + yc \equiv xb + yd \pmod m$
Gives $a + c \equiv b + d \pmod m$
$a - c \equiv b - d \pmod m$.

(*ii*) If $a \equiv b \pmod m$ and $c \equiv d \pmod m$, then $ac \equiv bd \pmod m$.

(*iii*) If $a \equiv b \pmod m$, then $a^n = b^n \pmod m$

(*iv*) If $a \equiv b \pmod m$, then $f(a) \equiv f(b) \pmod m$ where $f(x)$ is a polynomial in x.

(*v*) If $a \equiv b \pmod {m_1}$, $a \equiv b \pmod {m_2}$, $a \equiv b \pmod {m_3}$, then $a \equiv b \pmod m$ where m is the least common multiple of m_1, m_2, m_3.

12. (*i*) A number n divisible by 3, if and only if the sum of the digits is divisible by 3.

(*ii*) A number N is divisible by 9, if and only if the sum of the digits is divisible by 9.

(*iii*) A number n = abcd....... is divisible by 11 if and only if the alternate sum $a - b + c - d + \ldots\ldots$ of the digits is divisible by 11, *i.e.,* the Sum of odd integers = Sum of the even digits.

EXERCISE

1. In how many ways can the number 7056 be resolved into two factors
(*a*) 20 (*b*) 21 (*c*) 22 (*d*) 23

2. The number of ways in which N = 2,778,300 can be resolved into the two factors prime to each other
(*a*) 7 (*b*) 8 (*c*) 9 (*d*) 10

3. What is the highest power of 3 contained in 100!
(*a*) 46 (*b*) 47 (*c*) 48 (*d*) 49

4. The number zeros at the end, if 100! is fully expanded and written out is
(*a*) 23 (*b*) 24 (*c*) 26 (*d*) 25

5. The least positive integer having remainders 2, 3, 2 when divided by 3, 5, 7 respectively is
(*a*) 23 (*b*) 24 (*c*) 25 (*d*) 27

6. What is the number of zeros at the end when 50! is expanded and written as a number?
(*a*) 10 (*b*) 12 (*c*) 20 (*d*) 25

7. The sum of the divisors of 630 is
(*a*) 809 (*b*) 1439 (*c*) 1872 (*d*) 1579
(*e*) None of these

8. If n is positive odd integer, then $n^3 - n$ is divisible by
(*a*) 15 (*b*) 18 (*c*) 24 (*d*) 32

9. When $(1234)^4$ is divisible by 5 the remainder is
(*a*) 1 (*b*) 2 (*c*) 3 (*d*) 4

10. The remainder when 2^{1000} is divided by 17 is
(*a*) 1 (*b*) 2 (*c*) 3 (*d*) 4

11. The sum of all the divisors of 5544 is
(*a*) 18720 (*b*) 13176
(*c*) 13175 (*d*) 18719

12. Cube of a positive integer has the form
(*a*) $7p$ (*b*) $7p \pm 1$
(*c*) $7p \pm 2$ (*d*) $7p \pm 3$

13. Which of the following forms a square integer has?
(a) $5m$ (b) $5m \pm 1$
(c) $5m \pm 2$ (d) $5m \pm 3$

14. For all integral values of n, $13^{2n+1} + 9^{2n+1}$ is divisible by
(a) 31 (b) 35 (c) 22 (d) 48

15. $3^{2n} - 8n - 1$ is divisible by
(a) 65 (b) 67 (c) 71 (d) 64

16. For all positive integral values of n, $49^n + 16n - 1$ is a multiple of
(a) 64 (b) 96 (c) 128 (d) 144

17. If x and y are two numbers, then $[x + y]$ can be
(a) equal to $[x] + [y]$ (b) greater then $[x] + [y]$
(c) less than $[x] + [y]$ (d) None of these

18. Remainder when $1! + 2! + 3! + \ldots\ldots + 50!$ is divided by 15 is
(a) 1 (b) 2 (c) 3 (d) 4

19. The remainder when 2^{50} is divided by 7 is
(a) 1 (b) 2 (c) 3 (d) 4

20. The remainder obtained by dividing $1! + 2! + 3! + 4! + \ldots\ldots + 100!$ by 12 is
(a) 7 (b) 8 (c) 9 (d) 6

21. The number of distinct positive integral divisors of the number 56700 is
(a) 70 (b) 80 (c) 90 (d) 100

22. Reference to Q. 21, the sum of all the distinct positive integral divisors of 56700 is
(a) 210000 (b) 210056
(c) 220000 (d) None of these

23. If $n > 2$, then $n^5 - 5n^3 + 4n$ is divisible by
(a) 100 (b) 110
(c) 120 (d) None of these

24. $n(n + 1)(n + 5)$ is a multiple of
(a) 5 (b) 6
(c) 7 (d) None of these

25. Find the digit in the unit's position of the integere denoting the sum $1! + 2! + 3! + \ldots + 99!$
(a) 1 (b) 2
(c) 3 (d) 5

26. $N = p^a q^b r^c$ where p, q, r are primes and a, b, c are positive integers. The number of divisors of N excluding 1 and itself is
(a) $(a + 1)(b + 1)(c + 1)$
(b) $(a - 1)(b - 1)(c - 1) - 1$
(c) $(a + 1)(b + 1)(c + 1) - 2$
(d) $abc - 2$

27. Sum of all the divisors of 360 excluding 1 and itself is
(a) 1170 (b) 924 (c) 809 (d) 723

28. The smallest number with 16 divisors excluding 1 and itself is
(a) 180 (b) 192 (c) 240 (d) 360

29. Sum of the integers less than N and prime to it including unity is
(a) $\frac{1}{2}\phi$ (b) $\frac{1}{2}N\phi$
(c) $\phi(N)$ (d) None of these

30. a, b, c are three consecutive integers. Then $(a + b + c)^3 - 3a^3 - 3b^3 - 3c^3$ is divisible by
(a) 126 (b) 72 (c) 90 (d) 108

31. The sum of the cubes of three consecutive integers is divisible by
(a) 9 (b) 12 (c) 18 (d) 36

32. $2^{2^n} + 1$ where n is a positive integer greater than one ends in
(a) 5 (b) 7
(c) 9 (d) any number

33. If $d_1, d_2, \ldots\ldots, d_r$ (including 1 and N) are the divisors of N, then
$\phi(d_1) + \phi(d_2) + \ldots\ldots + \phi(d_r)$ is equal to
(a) N (b) N^2 (c) 2N (d) $\frac{N}{2}$

34. The number of integers less than 720 and prime to it
(a) 36 (b) 144 (c) 192 (d) 216

35. If N has n divisors including itself and 1, then their continued product is
(a) $N^{n/2}$ (b) N^n
(c) N^{2n} (d) None of thesee

36. If $2^n - 1$ is a prime, then sum of all the divisors including 1 and itself of $2^{n-1}(2^n - 1)$ is
(a) $2^n(2^n - 1)$ (b) $2^{n-1}(2^n - 1)$
(c) $2^{n+1}(2^n - 1)$ (d) $2^n(2^n - 1)^2$

37. When $2^n - 1$ is a prime number, then the sum of the reciprocals of all the divisors of the number $2^n(2^n - 1)$ is
(a) $\frac{1}{2^n}$ (b) $\frac{1}{2^{n+1}}$ (c) $\frac{1}{2}$ (d) 2

38. The number of positive integer less than 3600 that are relatively prime to 3600 is
(a) 900 *(b)* 950 *(c)* 960 *(d)* 970

39. $n^5 - n$ is divisible by
(a) 20 *(b)* 30
(c) 50 *(d)* None of these

40. If *m, n* are primes then $m^{n-1} + n^{m-1} - 1$ is a multiple of
(a) $m + n$ *(b)* $m - n$ *(c)* $\frac{m}{n}$ *(d)* mn

41. 16! + 86 is divisible by
(a) 320 *(b)* 323
(c) 232 *(d)* None of these

42. If *p* is a prime, then $2(p-3)! + 1$ is a multiple of
(a) p *(b)* $p + 1$
(c) $p - 1$ *(d)* None of thse

43. If $(n, 7) = 1$ *i.e.,* if *n* is prime to 7, then $n^{12} - 1$ is divisible by
(a) 3 *(b)* 5 *(c)* 7 *(d)* 9

44. $n^7 - n$ is divisible by
(a) 40 *(b)* 42 *(c)* 45 *(d)* 50

45. 18! + 1 is divisible by
(a) 19 *(b)* 23
(c) 19 and 23 *(d)* None of these

46. 10! – 32 is divisible by
(a) 11 *(b)* 13
(c) 11 and 13 *(d)* None of these

47. 28! + 233 is divisible by
(a) 900 *(b)* 899
(c) 888 *(d)* None of these

ANSWERS

1	2	3	4	5	6	7	8	9	10
(d)	(b)	(c)	(b)	(a)	(b)	(b)	(c)	(a)	(a)
11	**12**	**13**	**14**	**15**	**16**	**17**	**18**	**19**	**20**
(a)	(c)	(a)	(b)	(d)	(d)	(b)	(c)	(d)	(c)
21	**22**	**23**	**24**	**25**	**26**	**27**	**28**	**29**	**30**
(c)	(b)	(c)	(b)	(c)	(c)	(c)	(d)	(b)	(a)
31	**32**	**33**	**34**	**35**	**36**	**37**	**38**	**39**	**40**
(a)	(b)	(a)	(c)	(a)	(a)	(d)	(c)	(b)	(d)
41	**42**	**43**	**44**	**45**	**46**	**47**			
(b)	(a)	(c)	(b)	(c)	(c)	(b)			

SOME SELECTED EXPLANATORY ANSWERS

1. $n = 7056 = 7^2 \times 3^2 \times 2^4 = 7^{\alpha_1} \times 3^{\alpha_2} \times 2^{\alpha_3}$

Here *n* is a perfect square. Thus the number of ways in which *n* may be resolved into two factors

is $\frac{1}{2}[(\alpha_1 + 1)(\alpha_2 + 1)\ldots\ldots(\alpha_r + 1) + 1]$

$= \frac{1}{2}[(2 + 1)(2 + 1)(4 + 1) + 1]$

$= \frac{1}{2} \times 46 = 23.$

2. $n = 2{,}778{,}300 = 7^3 \times 5^2 \times 3^4 \times 2^2.$

The number of ways of resolving *n* into two factors prime to each other is

$= \frac{1}{2}(1 + 1)(1 + 1)\ldots\ldots = 2^{p-1}$, where *p* is the number of different prime factors of *n*.

Here $p = 4$. Thus the number of ways $= 2^{p-1} = 2^{4-1} = 2^3 = 8.$

3. Highest power of 3 contained in 100!

$= \mathrm{I}\left(\frac{100}{3}\right) + \mathrm{I}\left(\frac{100}{3^2}\right) + \mathrm{I}\left(\frac{100}{3^3}\right) + \ldots\ldots$

$= 33 + 11 + 3 + 1 + 0 + 0 + \ldots\ldots = 48.$

4. Highest power of 2 in 100! is 97
Similarly power of 5 in 100! is 24.
Each pair of 5 and 2 will give rise to a 10 or a zero at the end.

Hence the number of zero in 100! is equal to 24.

5. $\left.\begin{array}{l} N \equiv 2 \pmod 3 \\ N \equiv 2 \pmod 7 \end{array}\right\} \Rightarrow N \equiv 2 \pmod{21}$

$\Rightarrow N = 21p + 2 = (5 \times 4p + p) + 2$

$= \quad (p + 2) \pmod 5$

$\therefore\ p + 2 \equiv 3 \pmod 5 \ \Rightarrow p = 1$

$\therefore$ Least number satisfying the given criteria = 23.

$(\because N = 21p + 2)$.

7. $630 = 2^1 \times 3^2 \times 5^1 \times 7^1$

Sum of all the divisors

$= (1 + 2)(1 + 3 + 3^2)(1 + 5)(1 + 7)$

$= 3 \times 13 \times 6 \times 8 = 1872.$

8. $n^3 - n = (n - 1)\ n\ (n + 1)$ = product of three consecutive positive integers and is divisible by $3! = 6$.

Also $(n - 1)$ and $(n + 1)$ are consecutive even integers and their product is divisible by 4.

Hence $n^3 - n$ is divisible by $6 \times 4 = 24$ if n is positive odd.

10. $16 = 2^4 \equiv -1 \pmod{17}$

$\therefore\ \left(2^4\right)^{250} \equiv (-1)^{250} \pmod{17}$

i.e., $2^{100} \equiv 1 \pmod{17}$

Thus remainder = 1

15. We use the principle of induction to prove the statement

Let $f(n) = 3^{2n} - 8n - 1$

Step 1 : $f(1) = 9 - 8 - 1 = 0$. $f(1)$ is divisible by 64.

Therefore the statement is true for $n = 1$.

Step 2 : $f(k + 1) - f(k) = \{3^{2k+2} - 8(k + 1) - 1\} - \{3^{2k} - 8k - 1\}$

$= 8(3^{2k} - 1) = 8(9^k - 1)$

$= 8.8(9^{k-1} + 9^{k-2} + \ldots\ldots + 1)$

$= 64p$ where p is an integer.

$\therefore\ f(k + 1)$ is divisible by 64 if $f(k)$ is so.

This proves the statement.

18. $5! \equiv 0 \pmod{15}$ and for any positive integer n, $(5 + n)! \equiv 0 \pmod{15}$

$\therefore\ 1! + 2! + 3! + \ldots\ldots + 50! = (1! + 2! + 3! + 4!) \pmod{15}$

Now $1! + 2! + 3! + 4! = 33 = 15.2 + 3$

$\therefore\ 33 \equiv 3 \pmod{15}$ and therefore

$1! + 2! + 3! + \ldots\ldots + 50! \equiv 3 \pmod{15}$.

20. For $n \geq 4$, $n!$ is a multiple of 12 i.e. $n \equiv 0 \pmod{12}$ for $n \geq 4$.

$\Rightarrow 4! + 5! + \ldots\ldots + 100! \equiv \quad 0 \pmod{12}$

Now $1! + 2! + 3! = 1 + 2 + 6 = 9 \equiv 9 \pmod{12}$

Thus

$1! + 2! + 3! + \ldots\ldots + 100! \equiv 0 + 9 \pmod{12} = 9 \pmod{12}$

Hence 9 is the required remainder.

23. We have $n^5 - 5n^3 + 4n = n(n^4 - 5n^2 + 4)$

$= n(n^2 - 1)(n^2 - 4)$

$= n(n - 1)(n + 1)(n - 2)(n + 2)$

$= (n - 2)(n - 1)\ n\ (n + 1)(n + 2)$

Thus if $n > 2$, then $n^5 - 5n^3 + 4n$ has been expressed as a product of five consecutive natural numbers and so it is divisible by 5! *i.e.,* 120.

24. We have

$n(n + 1)(n + 5) = n(n + 1)[(n + 2) + 3]$

$= n(n + 1)(n + 2) + 3n(n + 1)$

Now $n(n + 1)(n + 2)$ is a product of three consecutive natural numbers and so it is divisible by 3! *i.e.,* 6.

Again $n(n + 1)$ is a product of two consecutive natural numbers and so it is divisible by 2! *i.e.,* consequently $3.n(n + 1)$ is divisible by 6.

Thus $n(n + 1)(n + 5)$ is divisible by 6.

27. $N = 360 = 2^3 \times 3^2 \times 5^1 = p_1^{\alpha_1} . p_2^{\alpha_2} . p_3^{\alpha_3}$

The sum of all the distinct positive integral divisor of 360

$$= \left(\frac{p_1^{\alpha_1+1} - 1}{p_1 - 1}\right)\left(\frac{p_2^{\alpha_2+1} - 1}{p_2 - 1}\right)\left(\frac{p_3^{\alpha_3+1} - 1}{p_3 - 1}\right)$$

$$= \frac{2^4 - 1}{2 - 1} . \frac{3^3 - 1}{3 - 1} . \frac{5^2 - 1}{5 - 1}$$

$$= \frac{15}{1} . \frac{26}{2} . \frac{24}{4} = 1170.$$

This include 1 and the number 360. Thus sum of all the divisors of 360 excluding 1 and itself is $1170 - 361 = 809$.

29. Let x be any positive integer less than n and prime to n *i.e.,* $1 \leq x < n$ and $(x, n) = 1$.

Then $1 \leq n - x < n$ and $(n - x, n) = 1$

[Note : $(a, b) = 1 \Rightarrow (b - a, b) = 1$]

Let $1, a_1, a_2, a_3, \ldots, n-1$ be the $\phi(n)$ positive integers which are less than n prime to n and S be their sum.

We have

$S = 1 + a_1 + a_2 + a_3 + \ldots + (n-a_2) + (n-a_1) + (n-1)$ ...(i)

Writing the terms in the sum S in the reverse order, we have

$S = (n-1) + (n-a_1) + (n-a_2) + \ldots + a_2 + a_1 + 1$ ...(ii)

Adding (i) and (ii), we have

$2S = [1+(n-1)] + [a_1 + (n-a_1)] + [a_2 + (n-a_2)] + \ldots$ upto $\phi(n)$ terms

$= n + n + n \ldots$ upto $\phi(n)$ terms

$= n.\phi(n)$

$\therefore S = \frac{1}{2} n.\phi(n).$

31. Try by trial method.

$$\left.\begin{aligned} 1^3 + 2^3 + 3^3 &= 36 \\ 2^3 + 3^3 + 4^3 &= 36 \\ 3^3 + 4^3 + 5^3 &= 36 \end{aligned}\right\}$$ All these numbers are divisible by 9.

32. For $2^{2^n} + 1$ for $n > 1$

$2^{2^2} + 1 = 2^4 + 1 = 17$ for $n = 2$

$2^{2^3} + 1 = 2^8 + 1 = 257$ for $n = 3$

$2^{2^4} + 1 = 2^{16} + 1 = 56537$ for $n = 4$

and so on.

We observe that it ends with 7.

33. $\phi(d_1) + \phi(d_2) + \ldots + \phi(d_r) = n$

If $n = 1$, then 1 is the only positive divisor of 1 and we have $\phi(1) = 1$.

Thus the result is true for $n = 1$.

Now let $n > 1$. Then by fundamental theorem of arithmatic, on being expressed in canonical form,

we have $n = p_1^{\alpha_1} p_2^{\alpha_2} \ldots p_m^{\alpha_m}$

Where $p_1, p_2 \ldots p_m$ are positive primes and $\alpha_1, \alpha_2, \ldots \alpha_m$ are positive integers. Any positive divisor d of n is of the form $p_1^{\beta_1} p_2^{\beta_2} \ldots p_m^{\beta_m}$.

Where $0 \le \beta_1 \le \alpha_1$, $0 \le \beta_2 \le \alpha_2$, ... $0 \le \beta_m \le \alpha_m$.

Consider the product

$$P = \left[1 + \phi(p_1) + \phi(p_1^2) + \ldots + \phi(p_1^{\alpha_1})\right] \left[1 + \phi(p_2) + \phi(p_2^2) + \ldots + \phi(p_2^{\alpha_2})\right] \ldots \left[1 + \phi(p_m) + \phi(p_m^2) + \ldots + \phi(p_m^{\alpha_m})\right]$$

General term in the product P

$= \phi(p_1^{\beta_1}).\phi(p_2^{\beta_2}) \ldots \phi(p_m^{\beta_m})$

$= \phi(p_1^{\beta_1}.p_2^{\beta_2} \ldots p_m^{\beta_m}) = \phi(d)$

Thus if d is any positive divisor of n, then $\phi(d)$ is equal to the value of one and only one term in the product P.

$\therefore d_1, d_2, \ldots, d_r$ be the positive distinct divisor of n, then

$\Sigma\phi(d) = \phi(d_1) + \phi(d_2) + \ldots + \phi(d_r)$

= Sum of all the terms in the product P

= P

But $1 + \phi(p_1) + \phi(p_1^2) + \ldots + \phi(p_1^{\alpha_1}) = p_1^{\alpha_1}$

$1 + \phi(p_2) + \phi(p_2^2) + \ldots + \phi(p_2^{\alpha_2}) = p_2^{\alpha_2}$

and

$\therefore \Sigma\phi(d) = P = p_1^{\alpha_1} p_2^{\alpha_2} \ldots p_m^{\alpha_m} = n.$

34. We have to find $\phi(720)$.

We shall first express 720 in canonical form

we have $720 = 2^4 \times 3^2 \times 5^1$

$\therefore \quad \phi(720) = \phi(2^4 \times 3^2 \times 5^1)$

$= \phi(2^4).\phi(3^2).\phi(5^1)$

$= 2^4\left(1-\frac{1}{2}\right).3^2\left(1-\frac{1}{3}\right).5^1\left(1-\frac{1}{5}\right)$

$= 2^4.3^2.5^1\left(1-\frac{1}{2}\right)\left(1-\frac{1}{3}\right)\left(1-\frac{1}{5}\right)$

$= 720 \times \frac{1}{2} \times \frac{2}{3} \times \frac{4}{5} = 192$

36. Here $\alpha_1 = n-1, \alpha_2 = 1$

$p_1 = 2, p_2 = (2^n - 1)$

Sum of all the distinct positive divisiors including 1 and itself of $2^{n-1}.(2^n - 1)$ is

$$= \frac{(p_1^{\alpha+1}-1)}{(p_1-1)} \cdot \frac{(p_2^{\alpha_2+1}-1)}{(p_2-1)}$$

$$= \frac{2^{n-1+1}-1}{2-1} \cdot \frac{(2^n-1)^{1+1}-1}{2^n-1-1}$$

$$= \frac{(2^n-1)}{1} \cdot \frac{(2^n-1)^2-1}{(2^n-2)}$$

$$= (2^n-1) \cdot \frac{(2^n-1-1)(2^n-1+1)}{(2^n-2)}$$

$$= (2^n-1) \cdot \frac{(2^n-2)\,2^n}{(2^n-2)} = 2^n(2^n-1).$$

37. Sum of the reciprocals of all the divisors of the number $2^n(2^n-1)$

$$= \frac{\text{Sum of all divisors including 1 and itself of } 2^{n-1}(2^n-1)}{2^{n-1}.(2^n-1)}$$

$$= \frac{2^n.(2^n-1)}{2^{n-1}.(2^n-1)} = 2.$$

40. We have $m \mid m^{n-1}$ *i.e.,* m is a divisor of m^{n-1} ...*(i)*

Since m and n are primes, therefore $(m, n) = 1$.

So by Fermat's theorem

$n^{m-1} \equiv 1 \pmod m$ *i.e.,* $m \mid (n^{m-1}-1)$ ...*(ii)*

From *(i)* and *(ii)*, we have

$m \mid (m^{n-1} + n^{m-1} - 1)$ ...*(iii)*

Again $n \mid n^{m-1}$. Also by Fermat's theorem

$m^{n-1} \equiv 1 \pmod n$ *i.e.,* $n \mid (m^{n-1}-1)$

$\therefore n \mid (n^{m-1} + m^{n+1} - 1)$ ...*(iv)*

From *(iii)* and *(iv)*,

$m^{n-1} + n^{m-1} - 1 \equiv 0 \pmod m$

and $m^{n-1} + n^{m-1} - 1 \equiv 0 \pmod n$

$\therefore m^{n-1} + n^{m-1} - 1 \equiv 0$ (mod L.C.M. of m and n)

$\equiv 0 \pmod{mn}$

Thus, $mn \mid (m^{n-1} + n^{m-1} - 1)$

Hence, $m^{n-1} + n^{m-1} - 1$ is a multiple of mn.

41. We have $323 = 17 \times 19$ where 17 and 19 are primes.

Since 17 is prime, therefore by Wilson's theorem

$(17-1)! + 1 \equiv 0 \pmod{17}$

$\Rightarrow 16! + 86 - 85 \equiv 0 \pmod{17}$

$\Rightarrow 16! + 86 \equiv 0 \pmod{17}$ ...*(i)*

$[\because 85 \equiv 0 \pmod{17}]$

Again 19 is a prime, so by Wilson's theorem

$(19-1)! + 1 \equiv 0 \pmod{19}$

$\Rightarrow 18! + 1 \equiv 0 \pmod{19}$

$\Rightarrow [(19-1)(19-2)]\,.\,16! + 1 \equiv 0 \pmod{19}$

$\Rightarrow (19^2 - 3 \times 19 + 2)\,.\,16! + 1 \equiv 0 \pmod{19}$

$\Rightarrow (19^2 - 3 \times 19)\,.\,16! + 2(16!) + 1 \equiv 0 \pmod{19}$

$\Rightarrow 2(16!) + 1 \equiv 0 \pmod{19}$ ...*(ii)*

$[\because (19^2 - 3 \times 19).16! \equiv 0 \pmod{19}]$

Also $171 \equiv 0 \pmod{19}$ ...*(iii)*

Adding congruence *(ii)* and *(iii)*, we have

$2(16!) + 172 \equiv 0 \pmod{19}$

$\Rightarrow 16! + 86 \equiv 0 \pmod{19}$ ...*(iv)*

Thus from (i) and (iv), we have

$16! + 86 \equiv 0 \pmod{17}$ and $16! + 86 \equiv 0 \pmod{19}$

$\Rightarrow 16! + 86 \equiv 0$ (mod L.C.M. of 17 and 19)

$\Rightarrow 16! + 86 \equiv 0 \pmod{17 \times 19}$

$\Rightarrow 16! + 86 \equiv 0 \pmod{323}$

42. Since p is prime, by Wilson's theorem, we have

$(p-1)! + 1 \equiv 0 \pmod p$

$\Rightarrow (p-1)(p-2)(p-3)! + 1 \equiv 0 \pmod p$

$\Rightarrow (p^2 - 3p + 2)(p-3)! + 1 \equiv 0 \pmod p$

$\Rightarrow 2(p-3)! + 1 + (p^2 - 3p)(p-3)! \equiv 0 \pmod p$

$\Rightarrow 2(p-3)! + 1 \equiv 0 \pmod p$

$[\because (p^2 - 3p)(p-3) \equiv 0 \pmod p]$

Thus $2(p-3)! + 1$ is a multiple of p.

43. Since 7 is prime, $(n, 7) = 1$, therefore by Fermat's theorem,

we have

$n^{7-1} \equiv 1 \pmod 7$

$\Rightarrow n^6 \equiv 1 \pmod 7$

$\Rightarrow (n^6)^2 \equiv 1^2 \pmod 7$

$\Rightarrow n^{12} \equiv 1 \pmod 7$

$\Rightarrow 7 \mid (n^2 - 1)$

44. Since 7 is prime, therefore by Fermat's theorem, we have

$n^7 \equiv n \pmod 7$

i.e., $7 \mid (n^7 - n)$ ...(1)

Also $n^7 - n = n(n^6 - 1) = n(n^3 - 1)(n^3 - 1)$

$= n(n-1)(n^2+n+1)(n+1)(n^2-n+1)$

$= (n-1)\,n\,(n+1)(n^2+n+1)(n^2-n+1)$

Now $(n - 1)\, n\, (n + 1)$ is a product of three consecutive integers and so it is divisible by 3! *i.e.,* 6.

Thus $6 \mid (n^7 - n)$ ...(ii)

Since $(6, 7) = 1$ *i.e.,* 6 and 7 are relatively prime, therefore from (i) and (ii),

we have $(6.7) \mid (n^7 - n) \Rightarrow 42 \mid (n^7 - n)$.

Note : if $a \mid m$, $b \mid m$ and $(a, b) = 1$, then $ab \mid m$.

45. Since 19 is prime, therefore by Wilson's theorem, we have

$(19 - 1)! + 1 \equiv 0 \pmod{19}$

$\Rightarrow 18! + 1 \equiv 0 \pmod{19}$ ...*(i)*

Again 23 is prime, therefore by Wilson's theorem, we have

$(23 - 1)! + 1 \equiv 0 \pmod{23}$

$\Rightarrow \quad 22! + 1 \equiv 0 \pmod{23}$

$\Rightarrow 22.21.19.18! + 1 \equiv 0 \pmod{23}$

$\Rightarrow (23 - 1)(23 - 2)(23 - 3)(23 - 4).18! + 1$

$\equiv 0 \pmod{23}$

$\Rightarrow (-1)(-2)(-3)(-4).18! + 1 \equiv 0 \pmod{23}$

$\Rightarrow 24.18! + 1 \equiv 0 \pmod{23}$

$\Rightarrow (23 + 1).18! + 1 \equiv 0 \pmod{23}$

$\Rightarrow 18! + 1 \equiv 0 \pmod{23}$ ...*(ii)*

(i) and *(ii)* proves that $18! + 1$ is divisible by both 19 and 23.

8. QUADRATIC EQUATIONS

1. Polynomials : An expression of the form

$a_0x^n + a_1x^{n-1} + \ldots\ldots + a_{n-1} + a_n$

where $a_0, a_1, \ldots\ldots, a_n$ are given numbers (real or complex), n is a non-negative integer and x is a variable called polynomial in x or rational integral function of x. $a_0, a_1, \ldots\ldots, a_n$ are called coefficients and $a_0x^n, a_1x^{n-1}, \ldots\ldots, a_n$ are called terms of the polynomial. If $a_0 \neq 0$, the polynomial is said to be of degree n and the term a_0x^n is called the leading term.

2. Polynomial Equation : When a polynomial is equated to zero, then it is called a polynomial equation. The general form of an algebraic polynomial equation of degree n is

$a_0x^n + a_1x^{n-1} + \ldots\ldots + a_{n-1}x + a_n = 0$, where $a_0, a_1, \ldots, a_n$ are real or complex numbers and $a_0 \neq 0$.

If α be a value of x for which $f(x)$ becomes zero, *i.e.*, $f(\alpha) = 0$, then α is said to be a root of the equation $f(x) = 0$. Every algebraic equation has a root, real or complex.

3. Some Important Properties of Polynomial Roots

(i) A polynomial equation of degree n has n roots and no more.

(ii) If a equation with **real coefficients** has a complex root $\alpha + i\beta$ then it has also the conjugate complex root $\alpha - i\beta$. In other words, in an equation with real coefficients imaginary roots occur in conjugate pairs.

(iii) If an polynomial equation with **rational co-efficients** has a surd root $\alpha + \sqrt{\beta}$, where α, β are rational and β is not a perfect square, then it has also the conjugate root $\alpha - \sqrt{\beta}$. In other words, in an equation, with rational co-efficients, surd roots occur in conjugate pairs.

(iv) Let $f(x)$ be a polynomial with real co-efficients. If α, β be two distinct real numbers such that $f(\alpha)$ and $f(\beta)$ are of opposite signs then the equation $f(x) = 0$ has at least one real root between α and β.

(v) Let $f(x)$ be a polynomial with real co-efficients and α, β be two distinct real numbers. If $f(\alpha)$ and $f(\beta)$ are of opposite signs then the equation $f(x) = 0$ has an odd number of real roots between α and β.

If $f(\alpha)$ and $f(\beta)$ are of same sign then $f(x) = 0$ has either no real root or even number of seal roots between α and β.

4. Descarte's Rule of Signs : Two number of positive roots of an equation $f(x) = 0$ with real coefficients does not exceed the number of variations of signs in the sequence of the co-efficient of $f(x)$ and if less it is less by an even number.

Example: Let $f(x) = x^6 + x^4 + x^2 + x + 3$

Then $f(-x) = x^6 + x^4 + x^2 - x + 3$

The signs in the sequence of co-efficients of $f(x)$ are

$+ + + + +$

There is no variation of signs. Therefore the equation has no positive root. The signs in the sequence of co-efficients of $f(-x)$ are

$+ + + - +$

There are two variations of signs. Therefore the number of negative roots of $f(x) = 0$ is either 2 or 0.

The equation being of degree 6 has 6 roots. Therefore the number of complex roots is either 4 or 6.

5. Relation Between Roots and Co-efficients

Let $f(x) = a_0x^n + a_1x^{n-1} + \ldots\ldots + a_n$ be a polynomial of degree n with co-efficients real or complex. Then $a_0 \neq 0$. Let $\alpha_1, \alpha_2, \ldots\ldots, \alpha_n$ be the roots of the equation $f(x) = 0$. Then

$a_0x^n + a_1x^{n-1} + \ldots + a_n = a_0(x - \alpha_1)(x - \alpha_2)\ldots(x - \alpha_n)$

$$= a_0\left[x^n - \sum \alpha_1 x^{n-1} + \sum \alpha_1\alpha_2 x^{n-2} - \ldots\right.$$

$$\left. + (-1)^n (\alpha_1\alpha_2 \ldots \alpha_n)\right]$$

where, $\sum \alpha_1$ = Sum of the roots

$\sum \alpha_1\alpha_2$ = Sum of the product of the roots taken two at a time.

....

$\sum \alpha_1\alpha_2 \ldots \alpha_n$ = Sum of the product of the roots taken n at a time.

From the equality of polynomials, it follows that

$$a_1 = a_0\left(-\sum \alpha_1\right);\ a_2 = a_0\left(\sum \alpha_1\alpha_2\right)$$

$$a_3 = a_0\left(-\sum \alpha_1\alpha_2\alpha_3\right)$$

....

$$a_n = a_0 (-1)^n \alpha_1\alpha_2 \ldots \alpha_n.$$

$$\therefore \sum \alpha_1 = -\frac{a_1}{a_0} = -\frac{\text{Co-efficient of } x^{n-1}}{\text{Co-efficient of } x^n}$$

$$\sum \alpha_1\alpha_2 = -\frac{a_2}{a_0} = (-1)^2 \frac{\text{Co-efficient of } x^{n-2}}{\text{Co-efficient of } x^n}$$

....

$$\sum \alpha_1\alpha_2 \ldots \alpha_n = (-1)^n \frac{\text{Constant term}}{\text{Co-efficient of } x^n}$$

Particular Cases :

(i) If α, β be the roots of the quadratic equation $a_0x^2 + a_1x + a_2 = 0$, then

$$\sum \alpha = \alpha + \beta = -\frac{a_1}{a_0},\ \sum \alpha\beta = \alpha\beta = \frac{a_2}{a_0}$$

(ii) If α, β, γ be the roots of the cubic equation $a_0x^3 + a_1x^2 + a_2x + a_3 = 0$

then $\sum \alpha = \alpha + \beta + \gamma = -\dfrac{a_1}{a_0}$,

$$\sum \alpha\beta = \alpha\beta + \beta\gamma + \gamma\alpha = \frac{a_2}{a_0},$$

$$\sum \alpha\beta\gamma = \alpha\beta\gamma = -\frac{a_3}{a_0}.$$

(iii) If $\alpha, \beta, \gamma, \delta$ be the roots of biquadratic equation

$$a_0x^4 + a_1x^3 + a_2x^2 + a_3x + a_4 = 0$$

then $\sum \alpha = \alpha + \beta + \gamma + \delta = -\dfrac{a_1}{a_0}$,

$$\sum \alpha\beta = \alpha\beta + \beta\gamma + \gamma\delta + \delta\alpha + \beta\delta + \alpha\gamma = \frac{a_2}{a_0}$$

$$\sum \alpha\beta\gamma = \alpha\beta\gamma + \beta\gamma\delta + \gamma\delta\alpha + \alpha\beta\delta = -\frac{a_3}{a_0},$$

$$\alpha\beta\gamma\delta = \frac{a_4}{a_0}.$$

6. Symmetric Function of Roots : A function f of two or more variables is said to be a symmetric function if f remains unaltered by an interchange of any two of its variables.

$f(x, y, z) = x^2y^2 + y^2z^2 + z^2x^2$ is a symmetric function of x, y, z.

$f(x, y, z) = xy + yz$ is not symmetric in x, y, z because f does not remain unaltered if x and y are interchanged.

A symmetric function of the roots of an equation is an expression that involves all the roots alike and the expression remains unaltered if any two of the roots be interchanged.

If α, β, γ be the roots of a cubic equation, $\alpha^2 + \beta^2 + \gamma^2$ is a symmetric function of the roots, while $\alpha^2\beta + \beta^2\gamma + \gamma^2\alpha$ is not a symmetric function.

7. Transformation of Equations : The methode of finding new equation whose roots are related to the previous roots of the old equation, without knowing its individual roots is known as transformation. Such a transformation sometimes helps us to study the nature of the roots of the given equation which would have been otherwise a difficult job.

8. To Transform an Equation into one whose Roots are Reciprocal of the Roots of the Equation

Let the given equation be

$$a_0x^n + a_1x^{n-1} + a_2x^{n-2} + \ldots\ldots + a_{n-1}x + a_n = 0$$

and let the roots be $\alpha_1, \alpha_2, \ldots\ldots, \alpha_n$.

It is assumed that none of the roots is zero.

Let $y = \dfrac{1}{\alpha_1}$. Thus $\alpha_1 = \dfrac{1}{y}$.

Since α_1 is a root, $a_0\alpha_1^n + a_1\alpha_1^{n-1} + a_2\alpha_1^{n-2} + \ldots$
$+ a_{n-1}\alpha_1 + a_n = 0$

So $a_0\left(\frac{1}{y}\right)^n + a_1\left(\frac{1}{y}\right)^{n-1} + a_2\left(\frac{1}{y}\right)^{n-2} + \ldots$

$a_{n-1}\left(\frac{1}{y}\right) + a_n = 0$

or $a_n y^n + a_{n-1} y^{n-1} + \ldots\ldots\ldots + a_1 y + a_0 = 0$

This is the transformed equation.

9. To Find the Equation whose Roots are $\alpha_1 - h, \alpha_2 - h, \ldots\ldots, \alpha_n - h$ where h is a Constant and $\alpha_1, \alpha_2, \ldots\ldots, \alpha_n$ Roots of the Equation $f(x) = a_0x^n + a_1x^{n-1} + \ldots\ldots\ldots + a_n = 0$

Let $y = \alpha_1 - h$. Then $\alpha_1 = y + h$

Since α_1 is a root, $a_0\alpha_1^n + a_1\alpha_1^{n-1} + \ldots + a_n = 0$

$\therefore a_0 (y+h)^n + a_1 (y+h)^{n-1} + \ldots + a_n = 0$

This can be expressed as

$A_0x^n + A_1x^{n-1} + \ldots + A_n = 0$, where

A_n is the remainder when $f(x)$ is divided by $x - h$ and let $q_1(x)$ be the quotient; A_{n-1} is the remainder when the quotient $q_1(x)$ is divided by $x - h$ and so on.

10. Roots of a Quadratic Equation having Real Co-efficients : $a_0x^2 + a_1x + a_2 = 0$ is a quadratic equation where $a_0 \neq 0$, $a_0, a_1, a_2 \in R$. The quantity $D = a_1^2 - 4a_0a_2$ is known as discriminant and its roots are given by

$$\alpha = \frac{-a_1 + \sqrt{a_1^2 - 4a_0a_2}}{2a_0} \text{ and}$$

$$\beta = \frac{-a_1 - \sqrt{a_1^2 - 4a_0a_2}}{2a_0}.$$

Properties

(i) Roots are real and distinct if $D > 0$.

(ii) Roots are real and equal if $D = 0$.

(iii) Roots are complex with non-zero imaginary part if $D < 0$.

(iv) Roots are of the form $a + \sqrt{b}$ $(a, b \in Q)$ if a_0, a_1, a_2 are rational and D is not a perfect square.

11. Graph of Quadratic Expression : Let the quadratic equation be expressed as a quadratic polynomial in the form

$f(x) = y = a_0x^2 + a_1x + a_2$

We shall prove that the graph of the quadratic polynomial is actually a parabola

$$y = a_0x^2 + a_1x + a_2, \text{ where } a_0 \neq 0$$

or $y = a_0\left(x^2 + \frac{a_1}{a_0}x + \frac{a_2}{a_0}\right)$

or $y = a_0\left[\left(x + \frac{a_1}{2a_0}\right)^2 + \frac{4a_0a_2 - a_1^2}{4a_0^2}\right]$

or $\left[y + \frac{a_1^2 - 4a_0a_2}{4a_0}\right] = a_0\left(x + \frac{a_1}{2a_0}\right)^2$

or $\left(y + \frac{D}{4a_0}\right) = a_0\left(x + \frac{a_1}{2a_0}\right)^2$,

where D = discriminant.

Shifting the origin to the point $\left(-\frac{a_1}{2a_0}, -\frac{D}{4a_0}\right)$.

we have $Y = a_0x^2$

where $x = X - \frac{a_1}{2a_0}$ and $y = Y - \frac{D}{2a_0}$

Above equation represents equation of a parabola with vertex at $\left(-\frac{a_1}{2a_0}, -\frac{D}{4a_0}\right)$

Parabola opens upwards or downwards according as $a_0 > 0$ or $a_0 < 0$ as shown below

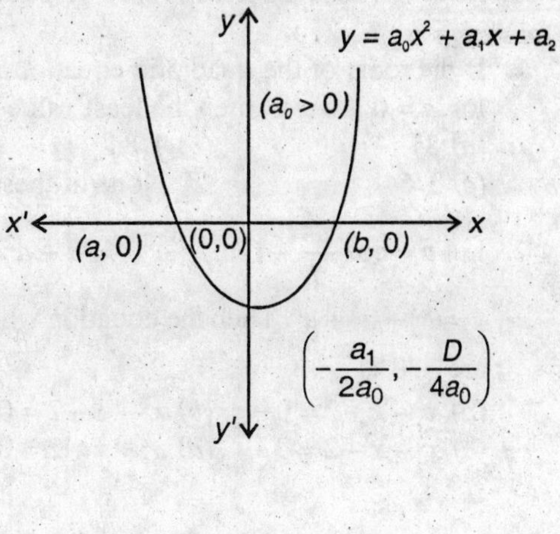

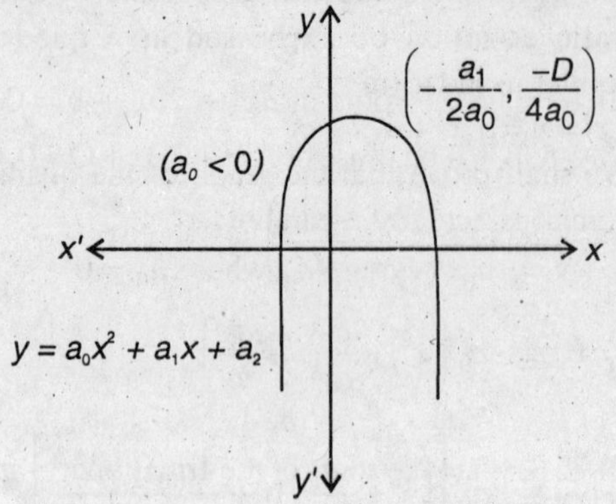

For $a_0 > 0$ Parabola $y = a_0x^2 + a_1x + a_2$ opens upwards

$$y_{\min} = -\frac{D}{4a_0} \text{ when } x = -\frac{a_1}{2a_0} \text{ and } y_{\max} \to -\infty.$$

For $a_0 < 0$ Parabola $y = a_0x^2 + a_1x + a_2$ opens downwards

$$y_{\max} = \frac{-D}{4a_0} \text{ when } x = \frac{-a_1}{2a_0} \text{ and } y_{\min} \to \infty.$$

Conclusion from the Graph

(i) parabola intersect x-axis in two points if $D > 0$.

(ii) parabola touches the x-axis in one point if $D = 0$.

(iii) parabola will not intersect x-axis if $D < 0$.

12. The General Solution of a Cubic (Cardan's Method Equation) : Let the cubic equation be

$a_0x^3 + 3a_1x^2 + 3a_2x + a_3 = 0$

In standard form it is written as

$Z^3 + 3HZ + G = 0$, where $Z = a_0x + a_1$,

$H = a_0a_2 - a_1^2$, and $G = a_0^2a_3 - 3a_0a_1a_2 + 2a_1^3$.

Here the values of Z are $p - \frac{H}{p}$, $\omega p - \frac{\omega^2 H}{p}$, $\omega^2 p - \frac{\omega H}{p}$ and three values of x are $\frac{1}{a_0}\left(p - \frac{H}{p} - a_1\right)$, $\frac{1}{a_0}\left(\omega p - \frac{\omega^2 H}{p} - a_1\right)$ and $\frac{1}{a_0}\left(\omega^2 p - \frac{\omega H}{p} - a_1\right)$

where p is any three values of

$$\left\{\frac{1}{2}\left(-G + \sqrt{G^2 + 4H^3}\right)\right\}^{1/3}$$

The quantity $G^2 + 4H^3$ is the discriminant of the given cubic equation.

Nature of Cubic Equation

(i) When $G^2 + 4H^3 < 0$, then the roots are all real and distinct.

(ii) When $G^2 + 4H^3 > 0$, then the roots are one real and two complex conjugate.

(iii) When $G^2 + 4H^3 = 0$, then the roots are all real and two of them are equal.

(iv) When $G^2 + 4H^3 < 0$ and $G = 0$, then the roots are real and equal.

EXERCISE

Mark the correct alternative(s) of each of the following :

1. If the roots of the quadratic equation $x^2 - 4x - \log_3 a = 0$ are real, then the least value of a is

(a) 81 *(b)* 1/81
(c) 1/64 *(d)* None of these

2. Let $a = \cos\frac{2\pi}{7} + i\sin\frac{2\pi}{7}$, $\alpha = a + a^2 + b^4$ and $\beta = a^3 + a^5 + a^6$. Then the equation whose roots are α, β is

(a) $x^2 - x + 2 = 0$ *(b)* $x^2 + x - 2 = 0$
(c) $x^2 - x - 2 = 0$ *(d)* $x^2 + x + 2 = 0$

3. The least integral value of a for which the equation
$x^2 - 2(a - 1)x + (2a + 1) = 0$ has both the roots positive, is

(a) 3 *(b)* 4 *(c)* 1 *(d)* 5

4. The number of solutions of the equation $9x^2 - 18|x| + 5 = 0$ belonging to the domain of definition of $\log_e |(x + 1)(x + 2)|$ is

(a) 1 *(b)* 2 *(c)* 3 *(d)* 4

5. The number of real roots of $(6 - x)^4 + (8 - x)^4 = 16$ is

(a) 0 *(b)* 2
(c) 4 *(d)* None of these

6. If $x \in R$, the least value of the expression $\frac{x^2 - 6x + 5}{x^2 + 2x + 1}$ is

(a) -1 (b) $-\frac{1}{2}$

(c) $-\frac{1}{3}$ (d) None of these

7. Let $\frac{\alpha}{\beta}, \frac{\beta}{\alpha}$ be two roots of $(x + 1)^n + x^n + 1 = 0$ where α, β are roots of $x^2 + px + q = 0$. If α, β are also roots of $x^{2n} + p^n x^n + q^n = 0$, then n must be

(a) even integer (b) odd integer

(c) integer (d) None of these

8. The constant m so that '1' lies between the roots of the quadratic equation $(2m + 1)x^2 - mx + m - 2 = 0$ is

(a) $-1 < m < 1$ (b) $-\frac{1}{2} < m < \frac{1}{2}$

(c) $-\frac{1}{3} < m < \frac{1}{3}$ (d) None of these

9. The number of real roots of the equation $x^3 + x^2 + 2x + \sin x = 0$ in $[-2\pi, 2\pi]$ is

(a) 1 (b) 2 (c) 3 (d) 4

10. If $x^2 + px + 1$ is a factor of $2\cos^2\theta\, x^3 + 2x + \sin 2\theta$, then

(a) $\theta = n\pi, n \in I$ (b) $\theta = n\pi + \frac{\pi}{2}, n \in I$

(c) $\theta = 2n\pi, n \in I$ (d) $\theta = \frac{n\pi}{2}, n \in I$

11. If α, β be roots of $x^2 - x - 1 = 0$ and $A_n = \alpha^n + \beta^n$ then AM of A_{n-1} and A_n is

(a) $2A_{n+1}$ (b) $\frac{1}{2}A_{n+1}$

(c) $2A_{n-2}$ (d) None of these

12. If $y = 2[x] + 3 = 3[x - 2] + 5$, then $[x + y]$ is

(a) 10 (b) 15

(c) 12 (d) None of these

13. Suppose $f(x)$ is such a quadratic expression that it is positive for all real x. If $g(x) = f(x) + f'(x) + f''(x)$, then for any real x

(a) $g(x) > 0$ (b) $g(x) < 0$

(c) $g(x) = 0$ (d) $g(x) \geq 0$

14. If α, β be the roots of $ax^2 + 2bx + c = 0$ and $\alpha + \delta, \beta + \delta$ be those of $Ax^2 + 2Bx + C = 0$, then the value of $\left(\frac{b^2 - ac}{B^2 - AC}\right)$ is

(a) $\frac{a^2}{A^2}$ (b) $\frac{A^2}{a^2}$

(c) 0 (d) 1

15. If α, β, γ are the roots of the equation $x^3 - px^2 + qx - r = 0$, then $(\alpha + \beta)(\beta + \gamma)(\gamma + \alpha)$ is equal to

(a) $pq - r$ (b) $p - qr$

(c) $p(q + r)$ (d) None of these

16. If $\sqrt{a} + \sqrt{b}$ be one of the roots of the given equation (a and b are not perfect squares) with rational co-efficients, then the lowest degree of such an equation must be

(a) 2 (b) 3 (c) 4 (d) 6

[J.N.U. M.C.A.]

17. The difference between the larger root and the smaller root of

$$x^2 - px + \frac{p^2 - 1}{4} = 0 \text{ is}$$

(a) 0 (b) 1 (c) $-p$ (d) $-p + 1$

[J.N.U. M.C.A.]

18. If $a \in R$ and $a_1, a_2, a_3, \ldots\ldots a_n \in R$ then $(x - a_1)^2 + (x - a_2)^2 + \ldots\ldots + (x - a_n)^2$ assumes its least value at $x =$.

(a) $a_1 + a_2 + \ldots + a_n$

(b) $2(a_1 + a_2 + a_3 + \ldots + a_n)$

(c) $n(a_1 + a_2 + \ldots + a_n)$

(d) None of these

19. If α is root of the equation $4x^2 + 2x - 1 = 0$ then other root of the equation is given by

(a) $3\alpha^2 + 4\alpha$ (b) $3\alpha^2 - 4\alpha$

(c) $4\alpha^2 - 3\alpha$ (d) None of these

[J.N.U. M.C.A.]

20. If the roots of the equation $\frac{a}{x + a + k} + \frac{b}{x + b + k} = 1$ are equal in magnitude but opposite in sign, then the value of k is

(a) 0 (b) 1
(c) 2 (d) None of these

[J.N.U. M.C.A.]

21. For the equation $|x|^2 + |x| - 6 = 0$
(a) There is only one root
(b) The sum of the roots is + 1
(c) The sum of roots is 0
(d) The product of roots is + 4.

[J.N.U. M.C.A.]

22. The equation
$(x-a)^3 + (x-b)^3 + (x-c)^3 = 0$, has
(a) all the roots real
(b) one real and two imaginary roots
(c) three real roots namely $x = a, x = b, x = c$
(d) None of these

23. The roots of $x^2 + bx + c = 0$ are both real and greater than 1. Let $S = b + c + 1$ then S is
(a) may be less than zero
(b) may be equal to zero
(c) must be greater than zero
(d) must be less than zero

[J.N.U. M.C.A.]

24. If $1, \alpha_1, \alpha_2, \ldots\ldots, \alpha_{n-1}$ be the roots of the equation $x^n - 1 = 0$, then the value of $(1-\alpha_1)(1-\alpha_2)\ldots\ldots(1-\alpha_{n-1})$ is.
(a) 0 (b) n (c) 1 (d) n^2

25. If $\alpha_1, \alpha_2, \ldots\ldots, \alpha_n$ are the roots of the equation $x^n - nax - b = 0$ and $(\alpha_1 - \alpha_2)(\alpha_1 - \alpha_3)\ldots$ $(\alpha_1 - \alpha_n) = A$, the value of $A - n\alpha_1^{n-1}$ is
(a) na (b) $-na$ (c) a (d) $-a$

[J.N.U. M.C.A.]

26. If $\alpha_1, \alpha_2, \ldots\ldots, \alpha_n$ are the roots of the equation $x^n - nax - b = 0$ and $(\alpha_1 - \alpha_2)(\alpha_1 - \alpha_3)\ldots$ $(\alpha_1 - \alpha_n)$ is equal to
(a) $n\alpha_1^{n-1} + a$ (b) $n(\alpha_1^{n-1} + a)$
(c) $\alpha_1^{n-1}.na$ (d) $n\alpha$

27. If $\alpha_1, \alpha_2, \ldots\ldots, \alpha_n$ be the roots of the equation $x^n + p_1x^{n-1} + p_2x^{n-2} + \ldots\ldots + p_{n-1}x + p_n = 0$, then $\sum \dfrac{\alpha_1^2 + \alpha_2^2}{\alpha_1\alpha_2}$ is equal to
(a) $\dfrac{p_1 p_{n-1}}{p_n}$ (b) $\dfrac{p_1 p_{n-1}}{p_n} - 1$
(c) $\dfrac{p_{n-1}}{p_1 p_n} - n$ (d) $\dfrac{p_1 p_{n-1}}{p_n} - n$

28. If $\alpha_1, \alpha_2, \ldots\ldots, \alpha_n$ are the roots of the equation $x^n - a_1x^{n-1} + a_2x^{n-2} + \ldots\ldots + (-1)^n a_n = 0$, then the value of $(1+\alpha_1)(1+\alpha_2)\ldots\ (1+\alpha_n) = 0$ is given by
(a) $1 + a_n$
(b) $1 - a_1 + a_2 - a_3 + \ldots\ldots + (-1)^n a_n$
(c) $1 + a_1 + a_2 + \ldots\ldots + a_n$
(d) $1 - a_1 - a_2 \ldots\ldots - a_n$

29. If the sum of the squares of the roots of $x^2 - (a-2)x - a + 1 = 0$ is a minimum than the value of a is
(a) 0 (b) 1 (c) 2 (d) 3

30. If $x + y + z = 13$, $xy + yz + zx = 69$ and $x^3 + y^3 + z^3 = 352$ then the value of xyz is
(a) 483 (b) 397 (c) 282 (d) 274

31. If $x = 2 + 2^{\frac{2}{3}} + 2^{\frac{1}{3}}$, then $x^2 - 6x^2 + 6x$ is
(a) 3 (b) 2 (c) 1 (d) 0

32. If $(1 + k)\tan^2 x - 4\tan x - 1 = 0$ has real roots, then
(a) $k^2 \le 5$ (b) $\tan(x_1 + x_2) = 2$
(c) for $k = 2$, $x_1 = \dfrac{\pi}{4}$ (d) All of them

33. The number of real solutions of the equation $\left(5+2\sqrt{6}\right)^{x^2-3} + \left(5-2\sqrt{6}\right)^{x^2-3} = 10$ is
(a) 2 (b) 4
(c) 6 (d) None of these

34. For $a > 0$, the roots of the equation $\log_{ax} a + \log_x a^2 + \log_{a^2x} a^3 = 0$ are given by
(a) $a^{\frac{-4}{3}}, a^{\frac{1}{2}}$ (b) $a^{\frac{-3}{4}}, a^{\frac{-1}{2}}$
(c) $a^{\frac{-4}{3}}, a^{\frac{-1}{2}}$ (d) None of these

35. The real value of $\left(27+\sqrt{756}\right)^{\frac{1}{3}} + \left(27-\sqrt{756}\right)^{\frac{1}{3}}$ is
(a) 3 (b) 54 (c) 9 (d) 27

[J.N.U. M.C.A.]

36. The number of real roots of the equation $x^6 + x^4 + x^2 - 1 = 0$ is
(a) 0 (b) 6 (c) 2 (d) 4
[J.N.U. M.C.A.]

37. The least possible number of positive roots of the equation $2x^7 - x^4 + 4x^3 - 5 = 0$ is
(a) 2 (b) 3
(c) 6 (d) None of these
[J.N.U. M.C.A.]

38. The condition that the roots of the equation $x^3 - px^2 + qx - r = 0$ may be in arithmetical progression is
(a) $p^3 - 9pq - 27r = 0$
(b) $2p^3 - 9pq - 27r = 0$
(c) $2p^3 - 9pq + 27r = 0$
(d) None of these

39. The condition that the roots of the equation $x^3 - px^2 + qx - r = 0$ may be in geometrical progression is
(a) $p^3 - rq^3 = 0$ (b) $p^3 + rq^3 = 0$
(c) $p^3r + q^3 = 0$ (d) $p^3r - q^3 = 0$

40. The condition that the roots of the equation $x^3 - px^2 + qx - r = 0$ may be in harmonic progression is
(a) $9r^2 - 27pqr + 2q^3$
(b) $27r^2 - 9pqr + 2q^3 = 0$
(c) $r^2 - 9pqr + 2q^3$
(d) None of these

ANSWERS

1	2	3	4	5	6	7	8	9	10
(b)	(d)	(b)	(c)	(b)	(c)	(a)	(b)	(a)	(a)
11	12	13	14	15	16	17	18	19	20
(b)	(b)	(b)	(a)	(a)	(c)	(b)	(d)	(d)	(a)
21	22	23	24	25	26	27	28	29	30
(c)	(b)	(c)	(b)	(b)	(b)	(d)	(c)	(b)	(c)
31	32	33	34	35	36	37	38	39	40
(b)	(d)	(b)	(b)	(a)	(c)	(d)	(c)	(d)	(b)

SOME SELECTED EXPLANATORY ANSWERS

1. Roots of the given equation are real

$\therefore$ Discriminant > 0

$\Rightarrow (4)^2 + 4\log_3 a > 0 \; (\because b^2 - 4ac > 0)$

$\Rightarrow 16 + 4\log_3 a > 0 \Rightarrow \log_3 a \geq -4$

$\Rightarrow a \geq 3^{-4} \Rightarrow a \geq \dfrac{1}{81}.$

2. Given $\quad a = \cos\dfrac{2\pi}{7} + i\sin\dfrac{2\pi}{7}.$

$\therefore \quad a^7 = \cos 2\pi + i\sin 2\pi = 1 + 0i = 1.$

Now $\quad \alpha + \beta = a + a^2 + a^3 + a^4 + a^5 + a^6.$

$= a\left\{\dfrac{1-a^6}{1-a}\right\} = \dfrac{a-a^7}{1-a} = \dfrac{a-1}{1-a}$

$= -1 \; (\because a^7 = 1)$

and $\quad \alpha\beta = (a + a^2 + a^4)(a^3 + a^5 + a^6)$

$= a^4(1 + a + a^3)(1 + a^2 + a^3)$

$= a^4(1 + a^2 + a^3 + a + a^3 + a^4 + a^3 + a^5 + a^6)$

$= a^4(1 + a + a^2 + 3a^3 + a^4 + a^5 + a^6)$

$= (a^4 + a^5 + a^6 + 3a^7 + a^8 + a^9 + a^{10})$

$= 3 + a + a^2 + a^3 + a^4 + a^5 + a^6 \; (\because a^7 = 1)$

$= 3 + a\left\{\dfrac{1-a^6}{1-a}\right\}$

$= 3 + \dfrac{a-a^7}{1-a} = 3 - 1 = 2.$

$\therefore$ Required equation is

$x^2 - (\alpha + \beta)x + \alpha\beta = 0$

i.e. $x^2 + x + 2 = 0.$

3. Let $f(x) = x^2 - 2(a-1)x + (2a+1) = 0$

Then $f(x) = 0$ will have both roots positive if

I. Discriminant > 0

$\Rightarrow 4(a-1)^2 - 4(2a+1) \geq 0$

$\Rightarrow a^2 - 4a \geq 0 \Rightarrow a \geq 0 \text{ or } a \geq 4$ ...(i)

II. Sum of the roots > 0 $\Rightarrow 2(a-0) > 0$

$\Rightarrow a > 1$ ...(ii)

III. $f(0) > 0 \Rightarrow 2a + 1 > 0$

$\Rightarrow a > -\dfrac{1}{2}$ ...(iii)

From (i), (ii) and (iii) we get $a \geq 4$.

4. Given $9x^2 - 18|x| + 5 = 0$

$\Rightarrow 9|x|^2 - 18|x| + 5 = 0$

$\Rightarrow (3|x| - 1)(3|x| - 5) = 0$

$\Rightarrow |x| = \dfrac{1}{3} \text{ or } |x| = \dfrac{5}{3}$

$\Rightarrow x = \pm\dfrac{1}{3} \text{ or } x = \pm\dfrac{5}{3}$

Now $\log_e\{(x+1)(x+2)\}$ exists if

$(x+1)(x+2) > 0 \Rightarrow x < -2 \text{ or } x > -1$

Thus other then $x = \dfrac{-5}{3}$, all other values of x satisfies the given conditions. Hence number of solutions is 3.

5. Let $y = 7 - x$. Then the given equation becomes

$(y+1)^4 + (y-1)^4 = 16$

$\Rightarrow y^4 + 6y^4 - 7 = 0$

$\Rightarrow (y^2 - 1)(y^2 + 7) = 0$

$\Rightarrow y^2 = 1 \ (\because y^2 + 7 \neq 0)$

$\Rightarrow y = \pm 1$

$\Rightarrow 7 - x = \pm 1$

$\Rightarrow x = 6, 8.$

Thus number of real roots are 2.

6. Let $y = \dfrac{x^2 - 6x + 5}{x^2 + 2x + 1} \quad \forall x \neq -1$

Then $x^2(y-1) + 2(y+3)x + y - 5 = 0$

Since $x \in R$, the discriminant of the above quadratic in x must be non-negative.

i.e. $4(y+3)^2 - 4(y-1)(y-5) \geq 0$

or $(y^2 + 6y + 9) - (y^2 - 6y + 5) \geq 0$

or $y \geq -\dfrac{1}{3}$.

Thus for $y = -\dfrac{1}{3}$, the given expression assumes its least value.

$\therefore$ Corresponding value of x is given by

$\dfrac{x^2 - 6x + 5}{x^2 + 2x + 1} = -\dfrac{1}{3}$

$\Rightarrow x^2 + 4x + 4 = 0$

$\Rightarrow (x-2)^2 = 0 \Rightarrow x = 2.$

7. As $\dfrac{\alpha}{\beta}$ is a root of $(x+1)^n + x^n + 1 = 0$

so $\left(\dfrac{\alpha}{\beta} + 1\right)^n + \left(\dfrac{\alpha}{\beta}\right)^n + 1 = 0$

or $(\alpha + \beta)^n + \alpha^n + \beta^n = 0$ ...(i)

But α, β are roots of $x^2 + px + q = 0$

$\therefore (\alpha + \beta) = -p; \ \alpha\beta = q$

$\therefore$ From (i), $(-p)^n + \alpha^n + \beta^n = 0$ ...(ii)

As α, β are roots of $x^{2n} + p^n x^n + q^n = 0$; we get

$\alpha^{2n} + p^n \alpha^n + q^n = 0$

and $\beta^{2n} + p^n \beta^n + q^n = 0$

Subtracting, we get

$\alpha^{2n} - \beta^{2n} + p^n(\alpha^n - \beta^n) = 0$

or $(\alpha^n - \beta^n)(\alpha^n + \beta^n + p^n) = 0$

$\therefore$ Either $\alpha^n + \beta^n + p^n = 0$ or $\alpha^n - \beta^n = 0$

Case I : When $\alpha^n + \beta^n + p^n = 0$ ...(iii)

From (ii)-(iii) $(-p)^n - p^n = 0$

$\therefore (-p)^n = p^n \Rightarrow n$ is an even number.

Case II : When $\alpha^n - \beta^n = 0$ i.e. $\alpha^n = \beta^n$ ...(iv)

From (ii) and (iv) we get

$(-p)^n + 2\alpha^n = 0$ or $\alpha^n = -\dfrac{(-p)^n}{2}$ ...(v)

Also $\alpha\beta = q \Rightarrow \alpha^n\beta^n = q^n \Rightarrow \alpha^{2n} = q^n$

$(\because \alpha^n = \beta^n)$ ...(vi)

From (v) and (vi)

$q^n = \left\{\dfrac{-(-p)^n}{2}\right\}^2 = \dfrac{(-p)^{2n}}{4} = \dfrac{p^{2n}}{4}$ ...(vii)

Now $\alpha^{2n} + p^n\alpha^n + q^n = 0$

$$\Rightarrow \left\{-\frac{(-p)^n}{2}\right\}^2 + p^n\left\{-\frac{(-p)^n}{2}\right\} + \frac{p^{2n}}{4} = 0$$

$$\Rightarrow \frac{p^{2n}}{4} - (-1)^n \frac{p^{2n}}{2} + \frac{p^{2n}}{4} = 0$$

$$\Rightarrow \frac{p^{2n}}{2} - (-1)^n \frac{p^{2n}}{2} = 0$$

$\Rightarrow 1 - (-1)^n = 0$ ($\because p \neq 0$)

$\Rightarrow$ n is an even integer.

Thus from both the cases it follows that n must be an even integer.

8. Given $(2m + 1)x^2 - mx + (m - 2) = 0$

$$\Rightarrow x^2 - \frac{m}{(2m+1)}x + \frac{(m-2)}{(2m+1)} = 0 \quad \left(m \neq -\frac{1}{2}\right)$$

It is said that 1 lies between the roots.

$\Rightarrow$ the roots are real and distinct.

$$\therefore \left(-\frac{m}{2m+1}\right)^2 - 4\left(\frac{m-2}{2m+1}\right) > 0$$

i.e. $m^2 - 4(m-2)(2m+1) > 0$

i.e. $\frac{6-2\sqrt{33}}{7} < m < \frac{6+2\sqrt{33}}{7}$ ...(i)

Further let roots are α and β such that $\alpha < \beta$.

Then $\alpha < 1, \beta > 1$ or $(\alpha - 1)(\beta - 1) < 0$

$\Rightarrow \alpha\beta - (\alpha + \beta) + 1 < 0$

$$\Rightarrow \frac{(m-2)}{(2m+1)} - \frac{m}{(2m+1)} + 1 < 0$$

$$\Rightarrow \frac{2m-1}{2m+1} < 0 \Rightarrow (2m+1)(2m-1) < 0$$

$\Rightarrow -\frac{1}{2} < m < \frac{1}{2}$ ...(ii)

From (i) and (ii) it follows that $-\frac{1}{2} < m < \frac{1}{2}$.

11. α, β are roots of $x^2 - x - 1 = 0$

$\therefore \alpha^2 - \alpha - 1 = 0$ ...(i)

$\beta^2 - \beta - 1 = 0$ ...(ii)

Given $A_n = \alpha^n + \beta^n$

$\therefore A_{n-1} = \alpha^{n-1} + \beta^{n-1}$

AM of A_{n-1} and A_n is $\frac{A_{n-1} + A_n}{2}$

$$= \frac{\alpha^{n-1} + \beta^{n-1} + \alpha^n + \beta^n}{2}$$

$$= \frac{\alpha^{n-1}(\alpha+1) + \beta^{n-1}(\beta+1)}{2}$$

$$= \frac{\alpha^{n-1}.\alpha^2 + \beta^{n-1}\beta^2}{2} \quad (\because \text{from (i) and (ii)})$$

$$= \frac{\alpha^{n+1} + \beta^{n+1}}{2} = \frac{1}{2}A_{n+1}.$$

13. Let the function be $f(x) = ax^2 + c$, which is positive for all real x.

Then $f'(x) = 2ax$ and $f''(x) = 2a$.

But
$$\begin{aligned} g(x) &= f(x) + f'(x) + f''(x) \\ &= ax^2 + c + 2ax + 2a \\ &= a(x^2 + 2x + 2) + c \\ &= a\left[(x+1)^2 + 1\right] + c \\ &= a(x+1)^2 + D \end{aligned}$$

$\therefore g(x) > 0$ for any value of x.

14. α, β be the roots of $ax^2 + 2bx + c = 0$

$\therefore \alpha + \beta = -\frac{2b}{a}$ and $\alpha\beta = \frac{c}{a}$.

Also let α', β' be the roots of

$Ax^2 + 2Bx + C = 0$

$\therefore \alpha' + \beta' = -\frac{2B}{A}$ and $\alpha'\beta' = \frac{C}{A}$

$\therefore \alpha' - \beta' = (\alpha + \delta) - (\beta + \delta) = (\alpha - \beta)$

$\Rightarrow (\alpha' + \beta')^2 - 4\alpha'\beta' = (\alpha - \beta)^2 - 4\alpha\beta$

$$\Rightarrow \frac{4B^2}{A^2} - \frac{4C}{A} = \frac{4b^2}{a^2} - \frac{4c}{a}$$

$$\Rightarrow \frac{B^2 - AC}{A^2} = \frac{b^2 - ac}{a^2}$$

$$\Rightarrow \frac{b^2 - ac}{B^2 - AC} = \frac{a^2}{A^2}.$$

15. Given $x^3 - px^2 + qx - r = 0$

$\therefore \alpha + \beta + \gamma = -\frac{(-p)}{1} = p$ ...(i)

$\alpha\beta + \beta\gamma + \gamma\alpha = q$ ...(ii)

$\alpha\beta\gamma = r$ ...(iii)

$\therefore (\alpha + \beta)(\beta + \gamma)(\gamma + \alpha)$

$= (p-\gamma)(p-\alpha)(p-\beta)$ [from (i)]
$= p^3 - p^2(\alpha+\beta+\gamma) + p(\alpha\beta+\beta\gamma+\gamma\alpha) - \alpha\beta\gamma$
$= p^3 - p^2(p) + p(q) - r$ [from (i), (ii) and (iii)]
$= p^3 - p^3 + pq - r = pq - r.$

16. Irrational roots occur in pairs

$\therefore$ If one root is $\sqrt{a}+\sqrt{b}$ then other roots are

$\sqrt{a}-\sqrt{b}, -\sqrt{a}+\sqrt{b}$ and $-\sqrt{a}-\sqrt{b}$

$\therefore$ Number of roots $= 4$
$\therefore$ Equation will be of degree 4.

17. Let α and β are the bigger and smaller roots of the given equation

$\therefore\ \alpha+\beta = p$ and $\alpha\beta = \dfrac{p^2-1}{4}$

Thus difference : $\alpha-\beta = \sqrt{(\alpha+\beta)^2 - 4\alpha\beta}$

$$= \sqrt{p^2 - 4\left(\frac{p^2-1}{4}\right)} = 1.$$

18. $(x-a_1)^2 + (x-a_2)^2 + \dots + (x-a_n)^2$
$= nx^2 - 2x(a_1+a_2+\dots+a_n)$
$+ \left(a_1^2 + a_2^2 + a_3^2 + \dots + a_n^2\right)$

Denoting the above function by y we have
$y = nx^2 - 2x(a_1+a_2+\dots+a_n)$
$+ \left(a_1^2 + a_2^2 + a_3^2 + \dots + a_n^2\right)$

represents a parabola which opens upward. So it attains its minimum value at the vertex i.e. at

$$x = \frac{2(a_1+a_2+\dots+a_n)}{2n}$$

$$= \frac{a_1+a_2+\dots+a_n}{n} \quad \left(\because x = -\frac{b}{2a}\right)$$

19. Let the other root be β.

As α, β are the roots of $4x^2+2x-1=0$

Then $\alpha+\beta = -\dfrac{1}{2}$ ...(i)

As α is one of the roots of the given equation, so

$4\alpha^2 + 2\alpha - 1 = 0$ ...(ii)

$\therefore$ From (i) we have $\beta = -\dfrac{1}{2} - \alpha$

$= -\dfrac{1}{2}(1+2\alpha)$

$= -\dfrac{1}{2}\left[(2\alpha+4\alpha^2)+2\alpha\right]$ (from (ii))

$= -2\alpha^2 - 2\alpha = \alpha(1-2\alpha) - 3\alpha$

$= \alpha(4\alpha^2) - 3\alpha$ (from (ii))

$= 4\alpha^3 - 3\alpha$

$\therefore$ The other root is $4\alpha^3 - 3\alpha$

20. Given equation is

$$\frac{a}{x+a+k} + \frac{b}{x+b+k} = 1$$

$\Rightarrow x^2 + 2kx + k^2 - ab = 0$

Let the roots of this equation be α and $-\alpha$

$\therefore$ Sum of roots $= \alpha + (-\alpha) = -2k \Rightarrow k = 0$

21. Given equation is $|x|^2 + |x| - 6 = 0$

Case I : When $x \geq 0$, above equation reduces to
$x^2 + x - 6 = 0$
$\Rightarrow (x+3)(x-2) = 0 \Rightarrow x = -3, 2.$
But $x \geq 0$, therefore $x = 2$ is the only root.

Case II : When $x < 0$, above equation reduces to
$x^2 - x - 6 = 0$
$\Rightarrow (x-3)(x+2) = 0 \Rightarrow x = 3, -2.$
But $x < 0$, therefore $x = -2$ is the only root.
$\therefore$ The sum of the roots $= 2 + (-2) = 0.$

22. Let $f(x) = (x-a)^3 + (x-b)^3 + (x-c)^3$
Then $f'(x) = 3\left[(x-a)^2 + (x-b)^2 + (x-c)^2\right]$
$\Rightarrow f'(x) > 0$ for all x.
So, $f'(x) = 0$ has no real roots. So $f(x) = 0$ has two imaginary and one real root.

23. Given $S = b + c + 1$
Given equation is $x^2 + bx + c = 0$
$\Rightarrow x^2 + (S - c - 1)x + c = 0$
Let the two roots be α and β both greater than 1
$\therefore\ \alpha+\beta > 2$ and $\alpha\beta > 1$.
But $\alpha+\beta = -(S-c-1)$ and $\alpha\beta = c$.
$\therefore (S-c-1) < -2$ and $c > 1$.
$\Rightarrow S < c - 1$
$\Rightarrow S > 0\ (\because c > 1)$
Thus, S must be greater than zero.

25. Let $f(x) = x^n - nax - b$ ...(i)
If $\alpha_1, \alpha_2, \dots, \alpha_n$ are the roots of the equation
$x^n - nax - b = 0$

Then $f(x) = (x-\alpha_1)(x-\alpha_2)....(x-\alpha_n)$

$$\therefore \quad f'(x) = (x-\alpha_2)(x-\alpha_3)....(x-\alpha_n) + (x-\alpha_1)(x-\alpha_3)....(x-\alpha_n)+.... + (x-\alpha_1)(x-\alpha_2)....(x-\alpha_{n-1})$$

Thus $f'(\alpha_1) = (\alpha_1-\alpha_2)(\alpha_1-\alpha_3)...$

$(\alpha_1-\alpha_n) = \text{A (given)}$ ...(ii)

Differentiating equation (i), we get

$$f'(x) = n\,x^{n-1} - na$$

$$\Rightarrow \quad f'(\alpha_1) = n\alpha_1^{n-1} - na \quad ...(iii)$$

From equation (ii) and (iii), we get

$$A = n\alpha_1^{n-1} - na$$

or $A - n\alpha_1^{n-1} = -na$

which is the required value.

26. As $\alpha_1, \alpha_2, ..., \alpha_n$ are the roots of the equation $x^n + nax - b = 0$

$$\therefore (x-\alpha_1)(x-\alpha_2)...(x-\alpha_n) = x^n + nax - b$$

Differentiating both the sides w.r.t. x we get

$$(x-\alpha_2)(x-\alpha_3)...(x-\alpha_n) + (x-\alpha_1)(x-\alpha_3)...(x-\alpha_n) + ... + (x-\alpha_1)(x-\alpha_2)...(x-\alpha_{n-1}) = n\,x^{n-1} + na.$$

Putting $x = \alpha_1$, we get

$$(\alpha_1-\alpha_2)(\alpha_1-\alpha_3)...(\alpha_1-\alpha_n) = n\alpha_1^{n-1} + na.$$

27. Given $\sum\left(\frac{\alpha_1^2+\alpha_2^2}{\alpha_1\alpha_2}\right) = \sum\left(\frac{\alpha_1}{\alpha_2}+\frac{\alpha_2}{\alpha_1}\right)$

$$= \alpha_1\left(\frac{1}{\alpha_1}+\frac{1}{\alpha_2}+...+\frac{1}{\alpha_n}\right) - 1 + \alpha_2\left(\frac{1}{\alpha_1}+\frac{1}{\alpha_2}+...+\frac{1}{\alpha_n}\right) - 1 + ... + \alpha_n\left(\frac{1}{\alpha_1}+\frac{1}{\alpha_2}+....+\frac{1}{\alpha_n}\right) - 1.$$

Adding, we get the value of the given Sigma as

$$\sum\alpha_1.\sum\frac{1}{\alpha_1} - n = (-p_1)\left(\frac{-p_{n-1}}{p_n}\right) - n = \frac{p_1\,p_{n-1}}{p_n} - n.$$

28. $\alpha_1, \alpha_2, ..., \alpha_n$ are the roots of the equation $x^n - a_1x^{n-1} + a_2x^{n-2} + ... + (-1)^n a_n = 0$,

so $(x-\alpha_1)(x-\alpha_2)...(x-\alpha_n) = x^n - a_1x^{n-1} + a_2x^{n-2} + ... + (-1)^n a_n$.

Putting $x = -1$, we get

$$(-1-\alpha_1)(-1-\alpha_2)...(-1-\alpha_n) = (-1)^n - a_1(-1)^{n-1} + a_2(-1)^{n-2} + ... + (-1)^n a_n.$$

or $(-1)^n\left[(1+\alpha_1)(1+\alpha_2)...(1+\alpha_n)\right] = (-1)^n[1 + a_1 + a_2 + ... + a_n]$

or $(1+\alpha_1)(1+\alpha_2)...(1+\alpha_n) = 1 + a_1 + a_2 + ... + a_n$.

29. Given equation is $x^2 - (a-2)x - a + 1 = 0$.

$$\therefore \quad \alpha+\beta = a-2 \text{ and } \alpha\beta = (1-a)$$

$$\therefore \quad S = \alpha^2+\beta^2 = (\alpha+\beta)^2 - 2\alpha\beta = (a-2)^2 - 2(1-a) = a^2 - 2a + 2.$$

S is minimum if $\frac{ds}{da} = 0$

i.e., $2a - 2 = 0 \Rightarrow a = 1$

30. We know that $(x+y+z)^3 = x^3 + y^3 + z^3 + 3(x+y)(y+z)(z+x)$

or $13^3 = 352 + 3(13-z)(13-x)(13-y)$
$= 352 + 3[13^3 - 13^2(x+y+z) + 13(xy+yz+zx) - xyz]$

or $13^3 = 352 + 3[13 \times 69 - xyz]$

or $xyz = 282$.

31. Given $x = 2 + 2^{2/3} + 2^{1/3}$

or $(x-2) = 2^{2/3} + 2^{1/3}$

Cubing both the sides we get

$$(x-2)^3 = \left(2^{2/3}+2^{1/3}\right)^3$$

or $x^3 - 6x^2 + 12x - 8 = 2^2 + 2 + 3(2)(x-2)$

or $x^3 - 6x^2 + 6x = 2$.

$\therefore$ Required value = 2.

32. Let $\tan x_1$ and $\tan x_2$ be the two roots of the given equation,

$(1+k)\tan^2 x - 4\tan x + (k-1) = 0$

$\therefore \tan x_1 + \tan x_2 = \frac{4}{1+k}$ and

$\tan x_1 \tan x_2 = \frac{k-1}{k+1}$.

For $k = 2$, the equation reduces to

$3\tan^2 x - 4\tan x + 1 = 0$

or $(\tan x - 1)(3\tan x - 1) = 0$

or $\tan x = 1 \text{ or } \frac{1}{3}$

or $x = \frac{\pi}{4} \text{ or } \tan^{-1}\left(\frac{1}{3}\right)$

For $k = 1$, the equation reduces to

$2\tan^2 x - 4\tan x = 0$

$\Rightarrow \tan x = 0$ or $\tan x = 2$.

$\Rightarrow x_1 = 0$ or $x_2 = \tan^{-1} 2$.

Since the equation has real roots, therefore

Discriminant ≥ 0

$\Rightarrow 16 - 4(k^2 - 1) \geq 0 \Rightarrow k^2 \geq 5.$

33. Given equation is

$$\left(5+2\sqrt{6}\right)^{x^2-3} + \left(5-2\sqrt{6}\right)^{x^2-3} = 10$$

or $\left(5+2\sqrt{6}\right)^{x^2-3} + \frac{1}{\left(5+2\sqrt{6}\right)^{x^2-3}} = 10$

or $y + \frac{1}{y} = 10$

where $y = \left(5+2\sqrt{6}\right)^{x^2-3}$

or $y^2 - 10y + 1 = 0$ or $y = 5 \pm 2\sqrt{6}$

Case I : $y = 5 + 2\sqrt{6}$

$\Rightarrow \left(5+2\sqrt{6}\right)^{x^2-3} = 5 + 2\sqrt{6}$

$\Rightarrow x^2 - 3 = 1$

$\Rightarrow x = \pm 2$

Case II : $y = 5 - 2\sqrt{6}$

$\left(5+2\sqrt{6}\right)^{x^2-3} = \left(5+2\sqrt{6}\right)^{-1}$

$\Rightarrow x^2 - 3 = -1$

$\Rightarrow x^2 = 2$

$\Rightarrow x^2 = \pm\sqrt{2}$

Thus there are four real solutions.

34. Given $\log_{ax} a + \log_x a^2 + \log_{a^2x} a^3 = 0$

$$\Rightarrow \frac{1}{\log_a ax} + \frac{2}{\log_a x} + \frac{3}{\log_a a^2 x} = 0$$

$$\Rightarrow \frac{1}{1+\log_a 2} + \frac{2}{\log_a x} + \frac{3}{2+\log_a x} = 0$$

$$\Rightarrow \frac{1}{1+y} + \frac{2}{y} + \frac{3}{2+y} = 0 \quad (\because \log_a x = y)$$

$\Rightarrow y^2 + 2y + 2y^2 + 6y + 4 + 3y^2 + 3y = 0$

$\Rightarrow 6y^2 + 11y + 4 = 0$

$\Rightarrow y = -\frac{4}{3} \text{ or } -\frac{1}{2} \Rightarrow \log_a x = -\frac{4}{3} \text{ or } -\frac{1}{2}$

$\Rightarrow x = a^{-4/3} \text{ or } a^{-1/2}.$

35. Let $\left(27+\sqrt{756}\right)^{1/3} + \left(27-\sqrt{756}\right)^{1/3} = y$

Cubing both the sides we get

$$\left(27+\sqrt{756}\right) + \left(27-\sqrt{756}\right) + 3\left(27+\sqrt{756}\right)^{1/3} + \left(27-\sqrt{756}\right)^{1/3}$$
$$\left\{\left(27+\sqrt{756}\right)^{1/3} + \left(27-\sqrt{756}\right)^{1/3}\right\} = x^3.$$

or $54 + 3(729 - 756)^{1/3} x = x^3$

or $54 + 3(-27)^{1/3} x = x^3$

or $54 + 3(-3)x = x^3$

or $x^3 + 9x - 54 = 0$

or $(x - 3)(x^2 + 3x + 18) = 0$

or $x = 3, \frac{-3 \pm i3\sqrt{7}}{2}$

$\therefore$ Required real value is 3.

36. Let $f(x) = x^6 + x^4 + x^2 - 1$

Then $f(-x) = x^6 + x^4 + x^2 - 1$

The signs in the sequence of co-efficients of $f(x)$ are

+ + + −

There is only one variation of signs and therefore the number of positive roots of $f(x) = 0$ is exactly 1.

The signs in the sequence of co-efficients of $f(-x)$ are

+ + + −

There is only one variation of signs and therefore the number of negative roots of $f(x) = 0$ is exactly 1.

Thus total number of variation is 2.

$\therefore$ Number of real roots is 2.

37. Let $f(x) = 2x^7 - x^4 + 4x^3 - 5$

Then $f(-x) = -2x^7 - x^4 + 4x^3 - 5.$

The signs in the sequence of co-efficients of $f(x)$ are

$+ \quad - \quad + \quad -$

There are three variations of signs and therefore the number of positive roots of $f(x) = 0$ is exactly 3.

The signs in the sequence of $f(-x)$ are

$- \quad - \quad - \quad -$

There is no variation of signs and therefore the number of negative roots of $f(x) = 0$ is zero.

So total number of variation is 3.

$\therefore$ Maximum number of positive real roots is 3 and minimum number of complex roots are 4. Complex roots occurs in pair. So minimum number of positive roots is $(3 - 2) = 1$.

38. Let the roots of the given equation be $a - d$, a, $a + d$, being in A.P.

$\therefore$ Summation of Roots i.e. $\sum \alpha = a - d + a + a + d = p$ or $3a = p$ or $a = \frac{p}{3}$.

But a is a root of the given equation and as such it will satisfy it

$$\therefore \left(\frac{p}{3}\right)^3 - p\left(\frac{p}{3}\right)^2 + q\left(\frac{p}{3}\right) - r = 0$$

or $2p^3 - 9pq + 27r = 0$ is the required condition.

39. Let the roots of the given equation be $ar, a, \frac{a}{r}$ in G.P.

Then $\sum \alpha\beta\gamma = \alpha\beta\gamma = ar.a.\frac{a}{r}$ or $a^3 = r$.

But a is a root of the given equation such that

$$a^3 - pa^2 + qa - r = 0$$

or $\quad -pa^2 + qa = 0 \qquad (\because a^3 = r)$

or $\quad pa = q$

or $\quad p^3a^3 = q^3$

or $\quad p^3r = q^3$

or $p^3r - q^3 = 0$, is the required equation.

40. Let the roots be α, β, γ which are in H.P. and hence $\frac{1}{\alpha}, \frac{1}{\beta}, \frac{1}{\gamma}$ are in A.P.

$$\therefore \quad \frac{1}{\alpha} + \frac{1}{\beta} = \frac{2}{\beta}$$

or $\quad \beta\gamma + \alpha\beta = 2\gamma\alpha$

Adding $\gamma\alpha$ to both sides, we get

$$\alpha\beta + \beta\gamma + \gamma\alpha = 3\gamma\alpha$$

or $q = 3\gamma\alpha$ $\left(\because \sum \alpha\beta = \text{Third Co-efficient of the given equation}\right)$

or $\quad \gamma\alpha = \frac{q}{3}$.

Again $\alpha\beta\gamma = r$ or $\left(\frac{q}{3}\right)\beta = r$ or $\beta = \frac{3r}{q}$.

But as β is a root of the given equation, so

$$\left(\frac{3r}{q}\right)^3 - p\left(\frac{3r}{q}\right)^2 + q\left(\frac{3r}{q}\right) - r = 0$$

or $27r^3 - 9pqr + 2p^3 = 0$ is the required condition.

9. MATRICES & DETERMINANTS

1. Definition : A rectangular array of *mn* elements a_{ij} into *m* rows and *n* columns, where the elements a_{ij} belong to a field F, is said to be a matrix of order $m \times n$ (or an $m \times n$ matrix) over a field F.

An $m \times n$ matrix is exhibited in the form

$$\begin{pmatrix} a_{11}\ a_{12} \ldots\ldots a_{1n} \\ a_{21}\ a_{22} \ldots\ldots a_{2n} \\ \ldots\ldots \quad \ldots\ldots \\ a_{m1}\ a_{m2} \ldots\ldots a_{mn} \end{pmatrix} \text{ or in the form }$$

$$\begin{bmatrix} a_{11}\ a_{12} \ldots\ldots a_{1n} \\ a_{21}\ a_{22} \ldots\ldots a_{2n} \\ \ldots\ldots \quad \ldots\ldots \\ a_{m1}\ a_{m2} \ldots\ldots a_{mn} \end{bmatrix}$$

F is said to be the field of scalars. If, in particular, F be the field of real (complex) numbers, the matrix is said to be a real (complex) matrix. The matrix is denoted by the symbol $(a_{ij})_{mn}$. Where $1 \le i \le m$, $1 \le j \le n$ and a_{ij} is the element of *i*th row and *j*th column.

2. Types of Matrices

(i) **Row Matrix :** If in an $m \times n$ matrix, $m = 1$, the matrix is said to be a row matrix. In other words a matrix having only one row is called a row matrix.

(ii) **Column Matrix :** If in an $m \times n$ matrix, $n = 1$, the matrix is said to be a column matrix. In other words a matrix having only one column is called a column matrix.

(iii) **Square Matrix :** If in an $m \times n$ matrix, $m = n$; the matrix is said to be a square matrix. In other words in a square matrix the number of rows is equal to the number of columns. A square matrix of order *n* is represented by $(a_{ij})_{n \times n}$. The elements a_{ij} of a square matrix for which $i = j$ *i.e.*, the elements $a_{11}, a_{22}, \ldots ; a_{nn}$ are called the diagonal elements and the line along which they lie is called the principal diagonal or leading diagonal of a matrix.

(iv) **Diagonal Matrix :** A square matrix is said to be a diagonal matrix if the elements other than the diagonal elements be all zero. In other words at square matrix $(a_{ij})_{n \times n}$ is called a diagonal matrix if

$a_{ij} = 0$ for all $i \ne j$.

A diagonal matrix of order $n \times n$ having $d_1, d_2, \ldots, d_n$ as diagonal elements is denoted by diag $[d_1, d_2, \ldots, d_n]$.

(v) **Scalar Matrix :** A diagonal matrix is said to be a scalar matrix if all the diagonal elements be the same scalar.

In other words a square matrix $(a_{ij})_{n \times n}$ is called scalar matrix if

(i) $a_{ij} = 0$ for all $i \ne j$ and

(ii) $a_{ii} = k$ for all *i*, where $k \ne 0$.

(vii) **Identity (or Unit) Matrix :** A scalar matrix whose diagonal elements are all equal to 1, the identity element of the ground field F, is called identity (or unit) matrix.

In other words, a square matrix $(a_{ij})_{m \times n}$ is called an indentity (or unit) matrix if

(i) $a_{ij} = 0$ for all $i \ne j$ and

(ii) $a_{ij} = 1$ for all $i = j$.

(viii) **Null (or Zero) Matrix :** If each element of an $m \times n$ matrix be zero *i.e.*, 0, the null element of F, the matrix is said to be the null matrix or the zero matrix of order $m \times n$, denoted $O_{m \times n}$. It is also denoted by O, when no confusion regarding its order arises.

(ix) **Upper Triangular Matrix :** A square matrix $(a_{ij})_{n \times n}$ is called an upper triangular matrix when $a_{ij} = 0$ for $i > j$. Thus, in an upper triangular matrix all the elements below the principal diagonal are zero.

For example : $\begin{pmatrix} a_{11} & a_{12} & a_{13} & \ldots\ldots & a_{1n} \\ 0 & a_{22} & a_{23} & \ldots\ldots & a_{2n} \\ 0 & 0 & a_{33} & \ldots\ldots & a_{3n} \\ \ldots\ldots & & & & \ldots\ldots \\ 0 & 0 & 0 & \ldots\ldots & a_{nn} \end{pmatrix}_{n \times n}$

is an upper triangular matrix of type $n \times n$.

(ix) **Lower Triangular Matrix :** A square matrix $(a_{ij})_{n \times n}$ is called a lower triangular matrix when $a_{ij} = 0$ for $i < j$.

Thus, in a lower trinagular matrix all elements above the principal diagonal are zero.

For example : $\begin{pmatrix} a_{11} & 0 & 0 & \ldots\ldots & 0 \\ a_{21} & a_{22} & 0 & \ldots\ldots & 0 \\ a_{31} & a_{32} & a_{33} & \ldots\ldots & 0 \\ \ldots\ldots & & & & \ldots\ldots \\ a_{n1} & a_{n2} & a_{n3} & \ldots\ldots & a_{nn} \end{pmatrix}_{n \times n}$

is a lower triangular matrix of the size $n \times n$.

3. Equality of Matrices : Two matrices A and B are said to be equal if A and B have the same order and their corresponding elements be equal. Thus if $A = (a_{ij})_{m \times n}$ and $B = (b_{ij})_{m \times n}$, then A = B if $fa_{ij} = b_{ij}$ for $i = 1, 2, \ldots\ldots n$.

Algebraic Operation on Matrices

4. Multiplication by a Scalar : The product of an $m \times n$ matrix $A = (a_{ij})_{m \times n}$ by a scalar k where $k \in F$, the field of scalars, is a matrix $B = (b_{ij})_{m \times n}$ defined by $b_{ij} = k\,a_{ij}$, $i = 1, 2, \ldots m; j = 1, 2, \ldots n$ and is written as $B = kA$.

Properties of Scalar Multiplication : Let A and B be two $m \times n$ matrices and k_1, k_2 are scalars. Then

(i) $k_1(k_2A) = (k_1k_2)A$

(ii) $OA = O_{m \times n}$

(iii) $k_1O_{m \times n} = O_{m \times n}$

(iv) $k_1I_n = \begin{pmatrix} k_1 & 0 & \ldots\ldots & 0 \\ 0 & k_1 & \ldots\ldots & 0 \\ \ldots\ldots & & & \ldots\ldots \\ 0 & 0 & \ldots\ldots & k_1 \end{pmatrix}$

(v) $(k_1 + k_2)A = k_1A + k_2A$

(vi) $k_1(A + B) = k_1A + k_1B$.

5. Addition of Matrices : Two matrices A and B are said to be conformable for addition if they have the same order.

If $A = (a_{ij})_{m \times n}$ and $B = (b_{ij})_{m \times n}$, then their sum $A + B$ is the matrix $C = (c_{ij})_{m \times n}$ where $c_{ij} = a_{ij} + b_{ij}$, $i = 1, 2, \ldots\ldots m, j = 1, 2, \ldots\ldots n$.

If A, B be matrices of different orders, then A + B is not defined.

Properties of Addition : Let A, B and C be three matrices of same order $m \times n$. Then

(i) $A + B$ is also a matrix of order $m \times n$.

(ii) $A + B = B + A$ (commutative)

(iii) $A + (B + C) = (A + B) + C$ (associative)

(iv) $A + O = A = O + A$ ('O' is additive identity) where 'O' is a $m \times n$ null matrix.

(v) $A + (-A) = O = (-A) + A$ ($\because -A$ is the additive inverse of A).

(vi) $A + B = A + C \Rightarrow B = C$ (Left cancellation law)

$B + A = C + A \Rightarrow B = C$ (Right cancellation law).

6. Multiplication of Matrices : Two matrices A and B are said to be conformable for the product AB if the number of columns of A be equal to the number of rows of B. If $A = (a_{ij})_{m \times n}$ and $B = (b_{ij})_{n \times p}$, then the product AB is a matrix of order $m \times p$ and $AB = C = (c_{ij})_{m \times p}$ is defined by

$$c_{ij} = \sum_{k=1}^{n} a_{ik}b_{kj} = a_{i1}b_{1j} + a_{i2}b_{2j} + \ldots + a_{in}b_{nj}$$

$$= [a_{i1}\ a_{i2} \ldots\ldots a_{in}] \begin{bmatrix} b_{1j} \\ b_{2j} \\ \vdots \\ b_{nj} \end{bmatrix}$$

= (ith row of A) (jth column of B).

$i = 1, 2, \ldots, m$ and $j = 1, 2, \ldots, p$.

Now let $A = [a_1 a_2 \ldots \ldots a_n]$ be a row matrix and

$$B = \begin{bmatrix} b_1 \\ b_2 \\ \vdots \\ b_n \end{bmatrix}$$ be a column matrix.

Then $AB = a_1 b_1 + a_2 b_2 + \ldots\ldots + a_n b_n$.

Properties of Matrix Multiplication

(i) Matrix multiplication is not commutative in general.

(ii) Matrix multiplication is associative *i.e.*, if A, B, C be $m \times n$, $n \times p$, $p \times q$ matrices, then (AB) C = A (BC).

(iii) Matrix multiplication is distributive with respect to matrix addition *i.e.*, if A, B, C be $m \times n$, $n \times p$, $n \times p$ matrices respectively, then

$A . (B + C) = AB + AC$.

(iv) If A is an $m \times n$ matrix, then $I_m A = A = A I_m$.

(v) The product of two matrices can be the null matrix without any matrix being null matrix.

7. Trace of a Matrix : Let A be a square matrix of order n. The sum of the elements of A lying along the principal diagonal is called the trace of A. It is denoted by tr A.

$$\text{If } A = (a_{ij})_{n \times n}, \text{ tr } A = \sum_{i=1}^{n} a_{ii} = a_{11} + a_{22} + \ldots + a_{nn}.$$

Properties of Trace : Let A and B be two square matrices of order n and λ a scalar. Then

(i) $\text{tr}(\lambda A) = \lambda \text{ tr } A$

(ii) $\text{tr}(A + B) = \text{tr } A + \text{tr } B$

(iii) $\text{tr}(AB) = \text{tr}(BA)$

8. Positive Integral Powers of A Square Matrix

Let A be a square matrix. Then

(i) $A^m . A^n = A^{m+n}$

(ii) $(A^m)^n = A^{mn}$ for all $m, n \in N$.

9. Transpose of a Matrix : Let A be an $m \times n$ matrix. Then $n \times m$ matrix obtained by interchanging rows and columns of A is said to be the transpose of A and is denoted by A' (or A^T).

Thus if $A = (a_{ij})_{m \times n}$, then $A' = B = (b_{ij})_{n \times m}$ where $b_{ij} = a_{ji}$, $i = 1, 2, \ldots, n$, $j = 1, 2, \ldots, m$.

Properties of Transpose : Let A and B be two matrices. Then

(i) $(A')' = A$

(ii) $(A + B)' = A' + B'$, where A and B are of same order.

(iii) If K be a scalar, $(KA)' = KA'$

(iv) If A and B be two matrices such that AB is defined, then $(AB)' = B'A'$.

10. Conjugate of a Matrix : Over a complex field, the matrix obtained from any given matrix A by replacing its elements by the corresponding conjugate complex numbers is called the conjugate of A and is denoted by $\overline{A}$.

If $A = (a_{ij})_{m \times n}$, then $\overline{A} = (\overline{a}_{ij})_{m \times n}$, where $\overline{a}_{ij}$ denotes then conjugate complex of a_{ij}.

Properties of Conjugate Matrix : If $\overline{A}$ and $\overline{B}$ be the conjugates of A and B respectively, then

(i) $\overline{(\overline{A})} = A$

(ii) $\overline{(A + B)} = \overline{A} + \overline{B}$, where A and B are of same order.

(iii) $\overline{(KA)} = \overline{K}\,\overline{A}$, where K is any complex number.

(iv) If multiplication AB is possible, then $\overline{AB} = \overline{A}\,\overline{B}$.

11. Transposed Conjugate of a Matrix : The transpose of the conjugate of a matrix A is called transposed conjugate of A and is denoted by A^θ or by A^*. Thus $\left(\overline{A'}\right) = \left(\overline{A}\right)' = A^\theta$.

If $A = (a_{ij})_{m \times n}$, then $A^\theta = (b_{ji})_{n \times m}$ where $b_{ji} = \overline{a}_{ij}$.

Properties of Transposed Conjugate : If A^θ and B^θ be the transposed conjugate of A and B respectively, then

(i) $(A^\theta)^\theta = A$

(ii) $(A + B)^\theta = A^\theta + B^\theta$, where A and B are of same order

(iii) $(KA)^\theta = \overline{K} A^\theta$, K is any complex number.

(iv) $(AB)^\theta = B^\theta A^\theta$, where A and B are comfortable to multiplication

12. Symmetric Matrices : A square matrix A is said to be symmetric if $A = A'$. Therefore $A = (a_{ij})$ is symmetric if $a_{ij} = a_{ji}$.

Skew-Symmetric Matrix : A square matrix A is said to be skew symmetric if $A = -A'$. Therefore $A = (a_{ij})$ is skew symmetric if $a_{ij} = -a_{ji}$

Properties of Symmetric and Skew-Symmetric Matrix

(i) If A, B be two symmetric matrices of the same order then A + B is symmetric.

(ii) If A, B be two symmetric matrices of the same order then AB is symmetric if and only if AB = BA.

(iii) If A be an $m \times n$ matrix, then AA', $A'A$ are both symmetric.

(iv) The diagonal elements of a skew-symmetric matrix are all zero, provided the ground field F is of characteristic $\neq 2$.

(v) If A be a square matrix, then $A + A'$ is symmetric and $A - A'$ is skew symmetric.

(vi) A real (or complex) square matrix can be uniquely expressed as the sum of a symmetric and a skew-symmetric matrix.

i.e., $A = P + Q$ where $P = \frac{1}{2}(A + A')$ and $Q = \frac{1}{2}(A - A')$.

This theorem hold good if the ground field F be of characteristic 2.

13. Hermitian Matrix : A square matrix A is said to be a hermitian matrix if the transpose of the conjugate matrix is equal to the matrix itself.

i.e., if $A^{\theta} = A \Rightarrow \overline{a}_{ij} = a_{ji}$ where $A = (a_{ij})_{n \times n}$.

In a hermitian matrix, the elements on the principal diagonal must be all real number *i.e.,* $\overline{a}_{ii} = a_{ii}$.

Skew-Hermitian Matrix : A square matrix $A = (a_{ij})_{n \times n}$ is said to be skew-hermitian, if $A^{\theta} = -A$ *i.e.,* if $\overline{a}_{ij} = -a_{ij}$.

Thus if $(a_{ij})_{n \times n}$ is a Skew-Hermitian matrix, then $a_{ii} = -\overline{a}_{ii}$, by definition. $a_{ii} + \overline{a}_{ii} = 0$

i.e., a_{ii} must be either pure imaginary or must be zero. Thus the diagonal elements of a Skew-Hermitian matrix must be pure imaginary numbers or zero.

Properties of Hermitian and Skew-Hermitian Matrix

(i) If A is a Hermitian matrix, then *i*A is Skew-Hermitian.

(ii) If A and B are Hermitian, then AB + BA is Hermitian and AB – BA is Skew-Hermitian.

(iii) If A be any square matrix, then $A + A^{\theta}$, AA^{θ}, $A^{\theta}A$ are all Hermitian and $A - A^{\theta}$ is Skew-Hermitian.

(iv) If A and B are conformable to multiplication then $(AB)^{\theta} = B^{\theta}A^{\theta}$.

(v) Every square matrix A can be uniquely expressed as P + *i*Q where P and Q are Hermitian matrices.

(vi) Every hermitian matrix A can be written as A = B + *i*C, where B is real and, symmetric and C is real and skew-symmetric.

14. Idempotent Matrix : A square matrix A is called an idempotent matrix if $A^2 = A$.

15. Nilpotent Matrix : If A is a square matrix and $A^m = O$, where *m* is a positive integer then A is called a niepotent matrix of index *m*.

16. Involutory Matrix : If in a $n \times n$ square matrix A, $A^2 = I_n$, then A is called an involutory matrix.

17. Orthogonal Matrix : An $n \times n$ matrix A is said to be orthogonal if $AA' = I_n = A'A$.

Properties of Orthogonal Matrix

(i) If A be an orthogonal matrix, A is non-singular and det $A = \pm 1$.

(ii) If A, B be two orthogonal matrices of the same order, AB is orthogonal.

(iii) If A be an orthogonal matrix, A^{-1} is orthogonal.

(iv) If A be an orthogonal matrix, $A^{-1} = A'$.

(v) If A be an orthogonal matrix, A' is also orthogonal.

18. Unitary Matrix : A complex $n \times n$ matrix A is said to be unitary if $A^{\theta}A = I_n$. If A be a unitary matrix then $|\det A| = 1$.

19. Adjoint of a Square Matrix : Let (a_{ij}) be a square matrix. Let A_{ij} be the co-factor of a_{ij} in determinant A.

The transpose of the matrix (A_{ij}) is said to be the adjoint (or adjugate) of A and is denoted by adj A.

Some Important Properties

(i) If A be a square matrix of order *n*, then A. adj A = adj A.A = det A.I_n

(ii) If A be a non-singular square matrix of order *n*, then

$|\text{adj A}| = |A|^{n-1}$

(iii) If A and B are non-singular square matrices of same order, then adj AB = (adj B) (adj A)

(iv) If A is a non-singular square matrix, then

adj (adj A) $= |A|^{n-2}.A$

20. Singular Matrix : A square matrix A is said to be singular if its determinant is zero and non-singular if it is a non-zero.

21. Inverse of a Matrix : A square matrix A of order *n* is said to be invertible if there exists a matrix B such that AB = BA = I_n. B is said to be an inverse of A we write B = A^{-1}.

Important Properties

(i) Every invertible matrix posses a unique inverse.

(ii) A square matrix is invertible if *f* it is non-singular.

(iii) If A and B are invertible matrices of the same order, then AB is invertible and $(AB)^{-1} = B^{-1}A^{-1}$.

(iv) If A be an invertible matrix, A^{-1} is invertible and $(A^{-1})^{-1} = A$.

(v) If A be an invertible matrix, A' is invertible and $(A')^{-1} = (A^{-1})'$.

(vi) If A, B be two square matrices of the same order and A is a non-singular, the matrix equation AX = B has the unique solution X = $A^{-1}B$, and the equation YA = B has the unique solution Y = BA^{-1}.

(vii) If A is a non-singular matrix, then $(\det A)^{-1} = \det(A^{-1})$.

22. Solution of a System of Linear Equation by Matrix Method : Let the system of *n* linear equations in *n* unknown be

$$\begin{aligned} a_{11}x_1 + a_{12}x_2 + \ldots + a_{1n}x_n &= b_1 \\ a_{21}x_1 + a_{22}x_2 + \ldots + a_{2n}x_n &= b_2 \\ \ldots \quad \ldots \quad &\ldots \\ a_{n1}x_1 + a_{n2}x_2 + \ldots + a_{nn}x_n &= b_n \end{aligned}$$

where $\det\left(a_{ij}\right)_{n \times n} \neq 0$

Let $A = \left(a_{ij}\right)_{n\times n}$, $X = \begin{pmatrix} x_1 \\ x_2 \\ \vdots \\ x_n \end{pmatrix}$, $B = \begin{pmatrix} b_1 \\ b_2 \\ \vdots \\ b_n \end{pmatrix}$.

Then the above system of equation can be expressed as AX = B.

Since det A $\neq 0$, A^{-1} exists. Therefore the equation AX = B has the unique solution X = $A^{-1}B$.

23. Rank of a Matrix : Let A be a non-zero matrix of order $m \times n$. Rank of A is defined to be the greatest positive integer *r* such that A has at least one non-zero minor of order *r*. Rank of zero matrix is defined to be zero. If I_n is a unit matrix of order *n*, then its rank is *n*.

If rank of A be *r*, every minor of order $r + 1$ is zero. Therefore, every minor of order $r + 2$ is also zero. Similarly it can be proved that every minor of order greater than *r* is zero.

For a non-zero $m \times n$ matrix A, 0 < rank A $\leq$ min (m, n).

For a square matrix A of order *n*, rank A $\leq n$ according as A is singular or non-singular.

Important Properties

(i) Elementary operations do not change the rank of matrix.

(ii) It A' is a transpose of A, then rank (A') = rank (A).

(iii) If A^θ is the transpose conjugate of A, then rank (A^θ) = rank (A).

(iv) If A and B are matrices of same order, then rank (A + B) $\leq$ rank (A) + rank (B).

(v) If A and B be conformable to multiplication, then rank (AB) $\leq$ min {rank (A), rank (B)}.

24. Elementary Operation : An elementary operation on a matrix A over a field F is an operation of the following three types:

(i) Interchange of two rows (or columns) of A.

(ii) Multiplication of a row (or column) by a non-zero scalar k in F.

(iii) Addition of a scalar multiple of one row (or column) to another row (or column) when applied to rows, the elementary operations are said to be **elementary row operations**. When applied to columns they are said to be **elementary columns operations**.

25. Elementary Matrices : An elementary matrix of order n is an $n \times n$ matrix obtained by applying a single elementary row operation on I_n. There are three types of elementary matrices.

(i) The elementary matrix obtained by applying R_{ij} on In is denoted by E_{ij}.

(ii) The elementary matrix obtained by applying kR_i on I_n is denoted by $E_i(k)$.

(iii) The elementary matrix obtained by applying $R_i + kR_i$ on I_n is denoted by $E_{ij}(k)$.

Solution of a System of Linear Equation : Let the system of m equations be

$$\begin{array}{l} a_{11}x_1 + a_{12}x_2 + \ldots + a_{1n}x_n = b_1 \\ a_{21}x_1 + a_{22}x_2 + \ldots + a_{2n}x_n = b_2 \\ \ldots \quad \ldots \quad \ldots \quad \ldots \\ a_{m1}x_1 + a_{m2}x_2 + \ldots + a_{mn}x_n = b_m. \end{array} \qquad ...(i)$$

in the unknowns $x_1, x_2, \ldots, x_n$.

The matrix

$$\begin{pmatrix} a_{11} & a_{12} & \ldots & a_{1n} \\ a_{21} & a_{22} & \ldots & a_{2n} \\ \ldots & \ldots & \ldots & \ldots \\ a_{m1} & a_{m2} & \ldots & a_{mn} \end{pmatrix}$$

whose elements are the co-efficients of n unknowns $x_1, x_2, \ldots, x_n$ in the given equations is called the co-efficient matrix of the given system.

Let it be denoted by A of $m \times n$ matrix. Also let the matrices $\begin{pmatrix} x_1 \\ x_2 \\ \vdots \\ x_n \end{pmatrix}$ and $\begin{pmatrix} b_1 \\ b_2 \\ \vdots \\ b_m \end{pmatrix}$ be denoted by X and B respectively.

The given system can now be written as AX = B. ...*(ii)*

If matrix B is a zero-matrix, we say that the set of equation *(ii)* is a system of **linear homogeneous equations.**

If the set of numbers $b_1, b_2, \ldots, b_m$ are not all zero, then the given set of equation *(ii)* is said to be a linear **non-homogenous system**. A system of conditions is said to be **consistent** if it has a solution, and is said to be **inconsistent** if it does not have a solution. A system of homogeneous equations is always consistent because it always has at least one solution, namely the solution $x_1 = x_2 = \ldots = x_n = 0$. The solution $x_1 = x_2 = \ldots = x_n = 0$ is often called **zero solution** or **trivial solution.**

Existence and Nature of Solutions

(i) If A be a non-singular matrix of order n, then the system of equations AX = B in n variables has the unique solution $X = A^{-1}B$.

(ii) If A be a non-singular matrix of order n, the system of homogeneous equations AX = O has the trivial solution X = O as the only solution.

(iii) If A be an $m \times n$ matrix of rank $r < n$, then the system of homogeneous equations AX = O has non-trivial solutions as well.

(iv) If A be an $m \times n$ matrix of rank $r < n$, the system of equations AX = B is consistent if and only if the matrix [A, B] is of rank r.

Characteristic Equation : Let $A = (a_{ij})_{n \times n}$ be an $n \times n$ matrix. The matrix $A - \lambda I$ is called the characteristic matrix of A. The determinant $|A - \lambda I|$ is a non-null polynomial of degree n in λ and is called the **characteristic polynomial** of A. The equation $|A - \lambda I| = 0$ is called the **characteristic equation** of A and its roots are called **characteristic roots** or **latent roots** or **eigenvalues** of A.

Cayley Hamilton Theorem : Every square matrix satisfies its own characteristic equation *i.e.*, if for a square matrix A of order n.

$$|A - \lambda I| = (-1)^n \left[\lambda^n + a_1\lambda^{n-1} + a_2\lambda^{n-2} + \ldots + a_n\right]$$

Then the matrix equation

$$X^n + a_1X^{n-1} + a_2X^{n-2} + \ldots + a_nI = O$$

is satisfied by X = A

i.e., $A^n + a_1A^{n-1} + a_2A^{n-2} + \ldots + a_nI = O$

26. Determinant : A determinant function $f : S \to F$ is a scalar function on the set S of all $n \times n$ matrices over the field F such that if $A = (a_{ij})_{n \times n} \in S$, then $f(A)$ or det A or det (a_{ij}) is a scalar belonging to F and is given by

$$\det A = \det(a_{ij}) = \sum_{\phi} \text{Sgn}\ \phi\ a_{1\phi(1)}\ a_{2\phi(2)} \ldots a_{n\phi(n)},$$

where ϕ is a permutation $\begin{pmatrix} 1 & 2 & \ldots\ldots & n \\ \phi(1) & \phi(2) & \ldots\ldots & \phi(n) \end{pmatrix}$

and Sgn $\phi = \pm 1$ according as ϕ is an even or an odd permutation. det A is said to be a determinant of order n and is denoted by the symbol

$$\begin{vmatrix} a_{11} & a_{12} & \ldots a_{1n} \\ a_{21} & a_{22} & \ldots a_{2n} \\ \ldots & \ldots & \ldots \\ a_{n1} & a_{n2} & \ldots a_{nn} \end{vmatrix} \text{ or shortly by } |a_{ij}|_{n \times n}$$

27. Minor : The minor of an element a_{ij} in det A of order $n \times n$ is the value of the determinant of order $(n-1) \times (n-1)$ obtained by deleting the ith row and jth column of det A, denoted by M_{ij}.

28. Cofactor : The cofactor of an element a_{ij} of a det A is equal to $(-1)^{i+j}$ times its minor. The cofactor of a_{ij} is denoted by C_{ij}.

$$C_{ij} = (-1)^{i+j}.M_{ij}$$

29. Value of a Determinant : The value of a determinant is the sum of the products of elements of any row or column with their corresponding co-factors.

30. Determinants of Order n : A determinant of order n rows and n columns. It has $n \times n$ elements. It is represented by

$$\Delta = \begin{vmatrix} a_{11} & a_{12} & \ldots a_{1n} \\ a_{21} & a_{22} & \ldots a_{2n} \\ \ldots & \ldots & \ldots \\ a_{n1} & a_{n2} & \ldots a_{nn} \end{vmatrix}$$

i.e., $\Delta = a_{i1}C_{i1} + a_{i2}C_{i2} + \ldots + a_{in}C_{in}$ $(i = 1, 2, \ldots n)$

or $\Delta = a_{1j}C_{1j} + a_{2j}C_{2j} + \ldots + a_{nj}C_{nj}$ $(j = 1, 2, \ldots n)$

31. Determinant of Order 3 : A determinant of order 3 has 3rows and 3 columns. It has 3 ×3 = 9 elements. It is represented by

$$\Delta = \begin{vmatrix} a_{11} & a_{12} & a_{13} \\ a_{21} & a_{22} & a_{23} \\ a_{31} & a_{32} & a_{33} \end{vmatrix}$$

i.e., $\Delta = a_{11}C_{11} + a_{12}C_{12} + a_{13}C_{13}$ (by row operations)

$= a_{11}.(-1)^{1+1}.M_{11} + a_{12}.(-1)^{1+2}.M_{12} + a_{13}.(-1)^{1+3}.M_{13}$

$= a_{11}M_{11} - a_{12}M_{12} + a_{13}M_{13}$

$= a_{11}.\begin{vmatrix} a_{22} & a_{23} \\ a_{32} & a_{33} \end{vmatrix} - a_{12}.\begin{vmatrix} a_{21} & a_{23} \\ a_{31} & a_{33} \end{vmatrix} + a_{13}.\begin{vmatrix} a_{21} & a_{22} \\ a_{31} & a_{32} \end{vmatrix}$

$= a_{11}(a_{22}a_{33} - a_{32}a_{23}) - a_{12}(a_{21}a_{33} - a_{31}a_{23}) + a_{13}(a_{21}a_{32} - a_{31}a_{22})$

$= a_{11}(a_{22}a_{33} - a_{32}a_{23}) - a_{21}(a_{12}a_{33} - a_{32}a_{13}) + a_{31}(a_{12}a_{23} - a_{22}a_{13})$

$= a_{11}M_{11} - a_{21}M_{21} + a_{31}M_{31}$

$= a_{11}(-1)^{1+1} + a_{21}(-1)^{2+1}M_{21} + a_{31}(-1)^{3+1}.M_{31}$

$= a_{11}C_{11} + a_{21}C_{21} + a_{31}C_{31}$

(by column operation).

Note : While finding the value of a determinant it does not matter whether we find it by row operation or column operation.

32. Properties of Determinant

(i) In an $n \times n$ matrix A if a row (column) be multiplied by a scalar k then det A is multiplied by k.

(ii) In an $n \times n$ matrix (a_{ij}) if each element in a particular row, say the rth, be expressed as the sum of two terms as $a_{rj} = a'_{rj} + a''_{rj}$ then

det (a_{ij}) = det (b_{ij}) + det (c_{ij}) where

$b_{ij} = a_{ij},\ i \neq r$ and $c_{ij} = a_{ij},\ i \neq r$

$b_{rj} = a'_{rj}$ $\qquad c_{rj} = a''_{rj}$.

(iii) In an $n \times n$ matrix A if a scalar multiple of one row (column) be added to another row (column), then det A remains unchanged.

(iv) In an $n \times n$ matrix A, if one row (column) be expressed as a linear combination of the remaining rows (columns) then det A = 0.

(v) The sum of the products of the elements of one row (column) of A and the cofactors in det A of the corresponding elements of another row (column) is zero.

$$a_{i1}C_{k1} + a_{i2}C_{k2} + \ldots\ldots + a_{in}C_{kn} = 0 \quad i \neq k$$

$$a_{1j}C_{1j} + a_{2j}C_{2j} + \ldots\ldots + a_{nj}C_{nj} = 0 \quad j \neq k.$$

(vi) By interchanging rows and columns of a determinant the value of the determinant remains unchanged. Thus for any square matrix A, we have $|A'| = |A|$.

(vii) If any two adjacent rows or columns of a determinant are interchanged, the numerical value of the determinant remains the same but its sign is changed.

(viii) If two rows (or two columns) of a determinant are identical or their elements are proportional, the value of the determinant is zero.

33. Multiplication of Determinant : If A and B be square matrices of the same order, then det (AB) = det A.det B.

Let $A = (a_{ij})$, $B = (b_{ij})$ be $n \times n$ matrices.

Then det A.det B = det (AB) = det (c_{ij}).

Where $c_{ij} = \sum_{k=1}^{n} a_{ik} b_{kj}$.

For example : Let $\det A = \begin{vmatrix} a_{11} & a_{12} & a_{13} \\ a_{21} & a_{22} & a_{23} \\ a_{31} & a_{32} & a_{33} \end{vmatrix}$,

$\det B = \begin{vmatrix} b_{11} & b_{12} & b_{13} \\ b_{21} & b_{22} & b_{23} \\ b_{31} & b_{32} & b_{33} \end{vmatrix}$,

Then det (AB) = det A.det B.

$$= \begin{vmatrix} a_{11} & a_{12} & a_{13} \\ a_{21} & a_{22} & a_{23} \\ a_{31} & a_{32} & a_{33} \end{vmatrix} \cdot \begin{vmatrix} b_{11} & b_{12} & b_{13} \\ b_{21} & b_{22} & b_{23} \\ b_{31} & b_{32} & b_{33} \end{vmatrix}$$

$$= \begin{vmatrix} a_{11}b_{11}+a_{12}b_{21}+a_{13}b_{31} & a_{11}b_{12}+a_{12}b_{22}+a_{13}b_{32} & a_{11}b_{13}+a_{12}b_{23}+a_{13}b_{33} \\ a_{21}b_{11}+a_{22}b_{21}+a_{23}b_{31} & a_{21}b_{12}+a_{22}b_{22}+a_{23}b_{32} & a_{21}b_{13}+a_{22}b_{23}+a_{23}b_{33} \\ a_{31}b_{11}+a_{32}b_{21}+a_{33}b_{31} & a_{31}b_{12}+a_{32}b_{22}+a_{33}b_{32} & a_{31}b_{13}+a_{32}b_{23}+a_{33}b_{33} \end{vmatrix}$$

34. Solution of System of Linear Equations in n-variables by Cramer's Rule : Let there be a system of n simultaneous linear equations with n unknowns given by

$$\begin{aligned} a_{11}x_1 + a_{12}x_2 + \dots + a_{1n}x_n &= b_1 \\ a_{21}x_1 + a_{22}x_2 + \dots + a_{2n}x_n &= b_2 \\ \dots \quad \dots \quad & \dots \quad \dots \\ a_{n1}x_1 + a_{n2}x_2 + \dots + a_{nn}x_n &= b_n. \end{aligned}$$

$$\text{Let } D = \begin{vmatrix} a_{11} & a_{12} & \dots a_{1n} \\ a_{21} & a_{22} & \dots a_{2n} \\ \dots & \dots & \dots \\ a_{n1} & a_{n2} & \dots a_{nn} \end{vmatrix}$$

and let D_j be the determinant from D after replacing the jth column by $\begin{vmatrix} b_1 \\ b_2 \\ \vdots \\ b_n \end{vmatrix}$

Then $x_1 = \frac{D_1}{D}, x_2 = \frac{D_2}{D}, \dots, x_n = \frac{D_n}{D}$, provided $D \neq 0$.

35. Solution of System of Linear Equations in Three variables by Cramers Rule : Solution of three linear equations in three unknown

$$\begin{aligned} a_1x_1 + b_1x_2 + c_1x_3 &= d_1 \\ a_2x_1 + b_2x_2 + c_2x_3 &= d_2 \\ a_3x_1 + b_3x_2 + c_3x_3 &= d_3 \end{aligned}$$

is given by $x_1 = \frac{D_1}{D}$, $x_2 = \frac{D_2}{D}$ and $x_3 = \frac{D_3}{D}$.

Where $D = \begin{vmatrix} a_1 & b_1 & c_1 \\ a_2 & b_2 & c_2 \\ a_3 & b_3 & c_3 \end{vmatrix}$, $D_1 = \begin{vmatrix} d_1 & b_1 & c_1 \\ d_2 & b_2 & c_2 \\ d_3 & b_3 & c_3 \end{vmatrix}$,

$D_2 = \begin{vmatrix} a_1 & d_1 & c_1 \\ a_2 & d_2 & c_2 \\ a_3 & d_3 & c_3 \end{vmatrix}$ and $D_3 = \begin{vmatrix} a_1 & b_1 & d_1 \\ a_2 & b_2 & d_2 \\ a_3 & b_3 & d_3 \end{vmatrix}$, provided that $D \neq 0$.

Conditions for Consistency and Inconsistency

(i) If $D \neq 0$ and out of D_1, D_2, D_3 at least one is $\neq 0$, then the system of equation is consistent and has a unique solution.

(ii) If D = 0 and also $D_1 = D_2 = D_3 = 0$, then the given system of equation is consistent and has infinite number of solutions.

(iii) If D = 0 and at least one of D_1, D_2, D_3 is non-zero, then the given system of equation is inconsistent.

36. Symmetric and Skew-Symmetric Determinants : If A be a symmetric matrix, det A is said to be a symmetric determinant.

If A be a Skew-Symmetric matrix, det A is said to be a Skew-Symmetric determinant.

Properties

(i) Adjoint of a Symmetric determinant is a symmatric determinant.

(ii) Adjoint of a Skew-Symmetric determinant of order n is symmetric if n be odd and Skew-Symmetric if n be even.

(iii) A Skew-Symmetric determinant of odd order is zero.

(iv) A Skew-Symmetric determinant of even order is the square of a polynomial function of its elements.

EXERCISE

Mark the correct alternatives of each of the following:

1. If $M(\theta) = \begin{bmatrix} \cos\theta & \sin\theta \\ -\sin\theta & \cos\theta \end{bmatrix}$, then $M(\alpha)\, M(\beta)$ is equal to
   (a) M(0) (b) $M(\alpha\beta)$
   (c) $M(\alpha + \beta)$ (d) $M(\alpha - \beta)$

2. If the product of matrices
   $$A = \begin{bmatrix} \cos^2\theta & \cos\theta\sin\theta \\ \cos\theta\sin\theta & \sin^2\theta \end{bmatrix}$$
   $$B = \begin{bmatrix} \cos^2\phi & \cos\phi\sin\phi \\ \cos\phi\sin\phi & \sin^2\phi \end{bmatrix}$$
   is a null matrix, then θ and ϕ differ by
   (a) an odd multiple of π
   (b) an even multiple of π
   (c) an odd multiple of $\frac{\pi}{2}$
   (d) an even multiple of $\frac{\pi}{2}$

3. If $A = \begin{bmatrix} 0 & -\tan(\alpha/2) \\ \tan(\alpha/2) & 0 \end{bmatrix}$
   then $(I - A)\begin{bmatrix} \cos\alpha & -\sin\alpha \\ \sin\alpha & \cos\alpha \end{bmatrix}$ is equal to
   (a) I + A (b) I − A
   (c) I + 2A (d) I − 2A

4. If $A_\alpha = \begin{bmatrix} \cos\alpha & \sin\alpha \\ -\sin\alpha & \cos\alpha \end{bmatrix}$, then which of the following statement is correct
   (a) $A_\alpha . A_\beta = A_{\alpha\beta}$ (b) $A_\alpha . A_\beta = A_{(\alpha+\beta)}$
   (c) $A_\alpha . A_\beta = A_{(\alpha-\beta)}$ (d) None of these

5. If $D = \text{diag}\,(d_1, d_2, d_3, \ldots, d_n)$, where $d_i \neq 0$ for all $i = 1, 2, \ldots, n$ then D^{-1} is equal to
   (a) D
   (b) $\text{diag}\left(d_1^{-1}, d_2^{-1}, \ldots, d_n^{-1}\right)$
   (c) I_n
   (d) None of these

6. If $X = \begin{bmatrix} 3 & -4 \\ 1 & -1 \end{bmatrix}$, the value of X^n is
   (a) $\begin{bmatrix} 3n & -4n \\ n & -n \end{bmatrix}$ (b) $\begin{bmatrix} 2+n & 5-n \\ n & -n \end{bmatrix}$
   (c) $\begin{bmatrix} 3^n & (-4)^n \\ 1^n & (-1)^n \end{bmatrix}$ (d) None of these

7. The matrix, $A = \begin{bmatrix} 2 & -2 & -4 \\ -1 & 3 & 4 \\ 1 & -2 & -3 \end{bmatrix}$ is
   (a) non-singular (b) idempotent
   (c) nilpotent (d) orthogonal

8. If A is a square martix such that $A^k = O$, then $(I + A + A^2 + \ldots + A^{k-1})$ is equal to
   (a) (I − A) (b) (I + A)
   (c) $(I - A)^{-1}$ (d) $(I + A)^{-1}$

9. If $A = \begin{bmatrix} 1 & -1 \\ 2 & -1 \end{bmatrix}$, $B = \begin{bmatrix} a & 1 \\ b & -1 \end{bmatrix}$, and $(A + B)^2 = A^2 + B^2$, then the values of a and b are respectively
   (a) 2, 2 (b) 3, −2
   (c) 1, 4 (d) −4, 7

10. If $A = \begin{bmatrix} 1 & 0 \\ 0 & 1 \end{bmatrix}$, $B = \begin{bmatrix} 0 & 1 \\ -1 & 0 \end{bmatrix}$ and $C = \begin{bmatrix} \cos\theta & \sin\theta \\ -\sin\theta & \cos\theta \end{bmatrix}$ then which of the following is true?
    (a) $C = A\cos\theta - B\sin\theta$
    (b) $C = A\sin\theta + B\cos\theta$
    (c) $C = A\sin\theta - B\cos\theta$
    (d) $C = A\cos\theta + B\sin\theta$
    [D.U. M.C.A.]

11. If a be a nilpotent of order 2, then $A(I \pm A)^n$ equal to
    (a) O (b) A
    (c) nA (d) A^n

12. The inverse of the matrix

$$\begin{bmatrix} 2 & -5 & 1 \\ 8 & 6 & 7 \\ \lambda & -10 & 2 \end{bmatrix}$$ does not exist if λ equals to

(a) 0 (b) 2 (c) 4 (d) 5

13. The characteristic roots of the matrix

$$A = \begin{bmatrix} 8 & -6 & 2 \\ -6 & 7 & -4 \\ 2 & -4 & 3 \end{bmatrix}$$ are

(a) 0, 3, 15 (b) 0, – 3, – 15
(c) 0, 3, – 15 (d) 0, – 3, 15

14. The rank of

$$A = \begin{bmatrix} 6 & 1 & 3 & 8 \\ 4 & 2 & 6 & -1 \\ 10 & 3 & 9 & 7 \\ 16 & 4 & 12 & 15 \end{bmatrix}$$ is

(a) 4 (b) 3 (c) 2 (d) 1

15. The transformation matrix $\begin{bmatrix} 1 & 0 & 0 \\ 0 & 0 & 1 \\ 0 & 1 & 0 \end{bmatrix}$ represents

(a) Rotation about x-axis by 90°
(b) Reflection about $y = z$
(c) Reflexion about x-axis
(d) None of these

16. The matrix $\begin{bmatrix} 1 & 5-i & 3 \\ 5+i & 2 & 3i \\ 3 & -3i & 0 \end{bmatrix}$ is

(a) Symmetric (b) Skew-Symmetric
(c) Hermitian (d) Skew-Hermitian

17. Caley-Hamilton theorem gives A $(A^2 - I)$ equals to

(a) O (b) $A^2 + I$
(c) $A^2 - I$ (d) $A - I$

18. The characteristic equation of the following matrix is $\begin{bmatrix} 2 & -1 & 1 \\ -1 & 2 & -1 \\ 1 & -1 & 2 \end{bmatrix}$

(a) $8x^3 - 6x^2 - 9x + 81 = 0$
(b) $-x^3 + 6x^2 - 9x + 4 = 0$
(c) $x^3 + 6x^2 + 9x + 4 = 0$
(d) $8x^3 - 6x^2 + 9x - 81 = 0$

19. If $U = \begin{bmatrix} 0 & 1 & 0 & 0 \\ 0 & 0 & 1 & 0 \\ 0 & 0 & 0 & 1 \\ 0 & 0 & 0 & 0 \end{bmatrix}$, the rank of U^4 is

(a) 1 (b) 2 (c) 3 (d) 0

20. The rank of the martix $\begin{bmatrix} 2 & 2 & 2 & 2 \\ 3 & 3 & 3 & 3 \\ 4 & 4 & 4 & 4 \\ 5 & 5 & 5 & 5 \end{bmatrix}$ is

(a) 4 (b) 3 (c) 2 (d) 1

[J.N.U. M.C.A.]

21. Given that $b^2 - ac < 0$, $a > 0$ the value of

$$\begin{vmatrix} a & b & ax+by \\ b & c & bx+cy \\ ax+by & bx+cy & 0 \end{vmatrix}$$ is

(a) Zero (b) Positive
(c) Negative (d) None of these

22. Given that $xyz = -1$, the value of the determinant

$$\begin{vmatrix} x & x^2 & 1+x^3 \\ y & y^2 & 1+y^3 \\ z & z^2 & 1+z^3 \end{vmatrix}$$ is

(a) 0 (b) Positive
(c) Negative (d) None of these

23. If the value of the determinant $\begin{vmatrix} a & 1 & 1 \\ 1 & b & 1 \\ 1 & 1 & c \end{vmatrix}$ is positive, then

(a) $abc > 1$ (b) $abc > -8$
(c) $abc < -8$ (d) $abc > -2$

[J.N.U. M.C.A.]

24. If ω is an imaginary cube root of unity, then one of the factors of

$$\begin{vmatrix} a & b & c \\ b & c & a \\ c & a & b \end{vmatrix}$$ is

(a) $(a + b\omega^2 + c\omega)$ (b) $(a + b\omega + c\omega^2)$

(c) $(a\omega + b + c\omega^2)$ (d) None of these

25. If $\omega = \dfrac{(-1+\sqrt{3}i)}{2}$, then the value of

$$\begin{vmatrix} 1 & 1 & 1 \\ 1 & \omega & \omega^2 \\ 1 & \omega^2 & \omega \end{vmatrix} \text{ is}$$

(a) $3\sqrt{3}i$ (b) $-3\sqrt{3}i$

(c) $-\sqrt{3}i$ (d) $\sqrt{3}i$

26. If ω is an imaginary cube root of unity, then the value of $\begin{vmatrix} 1 & \omega & \omega^2 \\ \omega & \omega^2 & 1 \\ \omega^2 & 1 & \omega \end{vmatrix}$ is

(a) 1 (b) ω

(c) ω^2 (d) 0

27. If *a, b, c* be positive real numbers, then the value of $\begin{vmatrix} a & b & c \\ b & c & a \\ c & a & b \end{vmatrix}$ is

(a) 0 (b) positive

(c) negative (d) a perfect square

28. If $\Delta = \begin{vmatrix} \cos\alpha & -\sin\alpha & 1 \\ \sin\alpha & \cos\alpha & 1 \\ \cos(\alpha+\beta) & -\sin(\alpha+\beta) & 1 \end{vmatrix}$, then

(a) $\Delta \in [1-\sqrt{2}, 1+\sqrt{2}]$

(b) $\Delta \in [-1, 1]$

(c) $\Delta \in [-\sqrt{2}, \sqrt{2}]$

(d) None of these

29. If $1, \omega, \omega^2$ are the cube roots of unity, then value

$$\begin{vmatrix} 1 & \omega^n & \omega^{2n} \\ \omega^{2n} & 1 & \omega^n \\ \omega^n & \omega^{2n} & 1 \end{vmatrix} \text{ is}$$

(a) 0 (b) 1

(c) ω (d) ω^2

30. Let $D_r = \begin{vmatrix} a & 2^r & 2^{16}-1 \\ b & 3(4^r) & 2(4^{16}-1) \\ c & 7(8^r) & 4(8^{16}-1) \end{vmatrix}$, then the value of $\sum_{k=1}^{16} D_k$ is

(a) 0 (b) $a + b + c$

(c) $ab + bc + ca$ (d) None of these

[J.N.U. M.C.A.]

31. If $d(r) = \begin{vmatrix} 2^{r-1} & 2(3^{r-1}) & 4(5^{r-1}) \\ x & y & z \\ 2^{n-1} & 3^{n-1} & 5^{n-1} \end{vmatrix}$

Then $\sum_{r=1}^{n} d(r)$ is equal to

(a) -1 (b) 0

(c) 1 (d) None of these

[J.N.U. M.C.A.]

32. If $\begin{vmatrix} x^n & x^{n+2} & x^{n+3} \\ y^n & y^{n+2} & y^{n+3} \\ z^n & z^{n+2} & z^{n+3} \end{vmatrix} = (x-y)(y-z)(z-x)$

$\left(\dfrac{1}{x} + \dfrac{1}{y} + \dfrac{1}{z}\right)$, then *n* equals

(a) 1 (b) -1 (c) 2 (d) -2

33. If $a_1, a_2, a_3, \ldots, a_m, \ldots$ are in G.P., then the determinant

$$\Delta = \begin{vmatrix} \log a_n & \log a_{n+1} & \log a_{n+2} \\ \log a_{n+3} & \log a_{n+4} & \log a_{n+5} \\ \log a_{n+6} & \log a_{n+7} & \log a_{n+8} \end{vmatrix} \text{ is equal to}$$

(a) 0 (b) 1

(c) 2 (d) None of these

34. Value of $\begin{vmatrix} 1 & 1 & 1 \\ a & b & c \\ a^3 & b^3 & c^3 \end{vmatrix}$ is

(a) $(a + b + c)^2 (a^2 + b^2 + c^2)$

(b) $a^2b^2 + b^2c^2 + c^2a^2$

(c) $(a + b + c)(a - b)(b - c)(c - a)$

(d) $(a + b + c)(a + b)(b + c)(c + a)$

[J.N.U. M.C.A.]

35. If a, b, c are non-zero real numbers, then $\begin{vmatrix} bc & ca & ab \\ ca & ab & bc \\ ab & bc & ca \end{vmatrix}$ vanishes, when

(a) $\frac{1}{a}+\frac{1}{b}+\frac{1}{c}=0$ (b) $\frac{1}{a}-\frac{1}{b}-\frac{1}{c}=0$

(c) $\frac{1}{b}+\frac{1}{c}-\frac{1}{a}=0$ (d) $\frac{1}{b}-\frac{1}{c}-\frac{1}{a}=0$

36. If $\Delta_1 = \begin{vmatrix} x & b & b \\ a & x & b \\ a & a & x \end{vmatrix}$ and $\Delta_2 = \begin{vmatrix} x & b \\ a & x \end{vmatrix}$, then

(a) $\Delta_1 = 3(\Delta_2)^2$ (b) $\frac{d}{dx}(\Delta_1) = 3\Delta_2$

(c) $\frac{d}{dx}(\Delta_1) = 3\Delta_2^2$ (d) $\Delta_1 = 3(\Delta_2)^{3/2}$

37. For positive number x, y, z the numerical value of

$\begin{vmatrix} 1 & \log_x y & \log_x z \\ \log_y x & 1 & \log_y z \\ \log_z x & \log_z y & 1 \end{vmatrix}$ is

(a) 0
(b) 1
(c) $\log x + \log y + \log z$
(d) $\log (x + y + z)$

38. If $a + b + c = 0$, then one root of $\begin{vmatrix} a-x & c & b \\ c & b-x & a \\ b & a & c-x \end{vmatrix} = 0$, is

(a) $x = 1$ (b) $x = 2$
(c) $x = a^2 + b^2 + c^2$ (d) $x = 0$

39. If $2s = a + b + c$, then the value of the determinant

$\begin{vmatrix} a^2 & (s-a)^2 & (s-a)^2 \\ (s-b)^2 & b^2 & (s-b)^2 \\ (s-c)^2 & (s-c)^2 & c^2 \end{vmatrix}$ is

(a) $\sqrt{s(s-a)(s-b)(s-c)}$
(b) $2s(s-a)(s-b)(s-c)$
(c) $2s^2(s-a)(s-b)(s-c)$
(d) $2s^3(s-a)(s-b)(s-c)$

40. If a, b, c are all different from zero and

$\Delta = \begin{vmatrix} 1+a & 1 & 1 \\ 1 & 1+b & 1 \\ 1 & 1 & 1+c \end{vmatrix} = 0$, then

$\left(1+\frac{1}{a}+\frac{1}{b}+\frac{1}{c}\right)$ is equal to

(a) abc (b) $\frac{1}{abc}$

(c) $\frac{1}{a+b+c}$ (d) None of these

ANSWERS

1	2	3	4	5	6	7	8	9	10
(c)	(c)	(a)	(b)	(b)	(d)	(b)	(c)	(c)	(d)
11	**12**	**13**	**14**	**15**	**16**	**17**	**18**	**19**	**20**
(b)	(c)	(a)	(a)	(b)	(c)	(c)	(b)	(d)	(d)
21	**22**	**23**	**24**	**25**	**26**	**27**	**28**	**29**	**30**
(c)	(a)	(b)	(b)	(b)	(d)	(c)	(a)	(a)	(a)
31	**32**	**33**	**34**	**35**	**36**	**37**	**38**	**39**	**40**
(a)	(b)	(a)	(c)	(a)	(b)	(a)	(d)	(d)	(d)

SOME SELECTED EXPLANATORY ANSWERS

1. Given $M(\theta) = \begin{bmatrix} \cos\theta & \sin\theta \\ -\sin\theta & \cos\theta \end{bmatrix}$

$\therefore \quad M(\alpha) = \begin{bmatrix} \cos\alpha & \sin\alpha \\ -\sin\alpha & \cos\alpha \end{bmatrix}$

and $\quad M(\beta) = \begin{bmatrix} \cos\beta & \sin\beta \\ -\sin\beta & \cos\beta \end{bmatrix}$

$$\therefore M(\alpha)M(\beta) = \begin{bmatrix} \cos\alpha & \sin\alpha \\ -\sin\alpha & \cos\alpha \end{bmatrix} \begin{bmatrix} \cos\beta & \sin\beta \\ -\sin\beta & \cos\beta \end{bmatrix}$$

$$= \begin{bmatrix} \cos(\alpha+\beta) & \sin(\alpha+\beta) \\ -\sin(\alpha+\beta) & \cos(\alpha+\beta) \end{bmatrix} = M(\alpha+\beta).$$

2. Product of two matrices

$$AB = \begin{bmatrix} \cos^2\theta & \cos\theta\sin\theta \\ \cos\theta\sin\theta & \sin^2\theta \end{bmatrix} \begin{bmatrix} \cos^2\phi & \cos\phi\sin\phi \\ \cos\phi\sin\phi & \sin^2\phi \end{bmatrix}$$

$$= \begin{bmatrix} \cos\theta\cos\phi\cos(\theta-\phi) & \cos\theta\sin\phi\cos(\theta-\phi) \\ \cos\phi\sin\theta\cos(\theta-\phi) & \sin\theta\sin\phi\cos(\theta-\phi) \end{bmatrix}.$$

= A null matrix if $\cos(\theta-\phi) = 0$

Now $\cos(\theta-\phi) = 0 \Rightarrow (\theta-\phi)$ is an odd multiple of $\frac{\pi}{2}$.

3. Let $\tan\left(\frac{\alpha}{2}\right) = z$

$$\Rightarrow \cos\alpha = \frac{1-\tan^2\left(\frac{\alpha}{2}\right)}{1+\tan^2\left(\frac{\alpha}{2}\right)} = \frac{1-z^2}{1+z^2}$$

$$\text{and } \sin\alpha = \frac{2\tan\left(\frac{\alpha}{2}\right)}{1+\tan^2\left(\frac{\alpha}{2}\right)} = \frac{2z}{1+z^2}$$

$$\therefore (I-A)\begin{bmatrix} \cos\alpha & -\sin\alpha \\ \sin\alpha & \cos\alpha \end{bmatrix}$$

$$= \begin{bmatrix} 1 & z \\ -z & 1 \end{bmatrix} \begin{bmatrix} \frac{1-z^2}{1+z^2} & \frac{-2z}{1+z^2} \\ \frac{2z}{1+z^2} & \frac{1-z^2}{1+z^2} \end{bmatrix}$$

$$= \begin{bmatrix} 1 & -z \\ z & 1 \end{bmatrix} = \begin{bmatrix} 1 & -\tan(\alpha/2) \\ \tan(\alpha/2) & 1 \end{bmatrix}$$

$= (I + A)$

5. Given $D = \text{diag}(d_1, d_2, d_3, ..., d_n)$

$$\Rightarrow D = \begin{bmatrix} d_1 & 0 & 0 & ....0 \\ 0 & d_2 & 0 & ....0 \\ \vdots & \vdots & \vdots & \vdots \\ 0 & 0 & 0 & ......d_n \end{bmatrix}$$

$\Rightarrow |D| = d_1 d_2 .... d_n.$

Cofactor of $D_{11} = d_2 d_3 .... d_n$.

Cofactor of $D_{22} = d_1 d_3 .... d_n$.

....

Cofactor of $D_{nn} = d_1 d_3 .... d_{n-1}$.

and Cofactor of $D_{ij} = 0$, when $i \neq j$.

Now $D^{-1} = \frac{1}{|D|} \text{adj } D$

$$= \frac{1}{d_1 d_2 .... d_n} \times \begin{bmatrix} d_1d_2....d_n & 0 & 0 & ....0 \\ 0 & d_2d_3....d_n & 0 & ....0 \\ \vdots & \vdots & \vdots & \vdots \\ 0 & 0 & 0 & ......d_1d_2....d_{n-1} \end{bmatrix}$$

$$= \begin{bmatrix} \frac{1}{d_1} & 0 & 0 & ...0 \\ 0 & \frac{1}{d_2} & 0 & ...0 \\ \vdots & \vdots & \vdots & \vdots \\ 0 & 0 & 0 & ...\frac{1}{d_n} \end{bmatrix}$$

$= \text{diag}\left(d_1^{-1} d_2^{-1} .... d_n^{-1}\right).$

6. Given $X=\begin{bmatrix}3 & -4\\1 & -1\end{bmatrix}$

$$\Rightarrow \quad X^2=\begin{bmatrix}3 & -4\\1 & -1\end{bmatrix}\begin{bmatrix}3 & -4\\1 & -1\end{bmatrix}$$

$$=\begin{bmatrix}5 & -8\\2 & -3\end{bmatrix}$$

Putting $n = 2$ in all the given option i.e. *(a)*, *(b)* and *(c)*, it is seen that none of them talies. Thus *(d)* is the required choice.

7. Given $A=\begin{bmatrix}2 & -2 & -4\\-1 & 3 & 4\\1 & -2 & 3\end{bmatrix}$

$$\Rightarrow \quad A^2=\begin{bmatrix}2 & -2 & -4\\-1 & 3 & 4\\1 & -2 & 3\end{bmatrix}\begin{bmatrix}2 & -2 & -4\\-1 & 3 & 4\\1 & -2 & 3\end{bmatrix}$$

$$\Rightarrow \quad A^2=\begin{bmatrix}2 & -2 & -4\\-1 & 3 & 4\\1 & -2 & -3\end{bmatrix}=A$$

Hence, A is idempotent.

8. We know that

$$I+A+A^2+....+A^{k-1}=\frac{I-A^k}{I-A}$$

$$=\frac{I}{I-A} \quad (\because A^k=O)$$

$$=I.(I-A)^{-1}=(I-A)^{-1}.$$

9. Given $A=\begin{bmatrix}1 & -1\\2 & -1\end{bmatrix}, B=\begin{bmatrix}a & 1\\b & -1\end{bmatrix}$

$$\therefore \quad A+B=\begin{bmatrix}1+a & 0\\2+b & -2\end{bmatrix}$$

$$\Rightarrow (A+B)^2=\begin{bmatrix}a^2+2a+1 & 0\\ab+2a-b-2 & 4\end{bmatrix}$$

Also $A^2=\begin{bmatrix}-1 & 0\\0 & -1\end{bmatrix}$ and $B^2=\begin{bmatrix}a^2+b-1 & a-1\\ab-b & b\end{bmatrix}$

$(A+B)^2=A^2+B^2$ (given)

$$\Rightarrow \begin{bmatrix}a^2+2a+1 & 0\\ab+2a-b-2 & 4\end{bmatrix}=\begin{bmatrix}a^2+b-1 & a-1\\ab-b & b\end{bmatrix}$$

$\Rightarrow a-1=0$ and $b=4$

$\Rightarrow a=1$ and $b=4$.

10. By closely inspecting $A=\begin{bmatrix}1 & 0\\0 & 1\end{bmatrix}$ and $B=\begin{bmatrix}0 & 1\\-1 & 0\end{bmatrix}$ w.r.t. $\cos\theta$ and $\sin\theta$ we conclude that

$$A\cos\theta+B\sin\theta=\begin{bmatrix}1 & 0\\0 & 1\end{bmatrix}\cos+\begin{bmatrix}0 & 1\\-1 & 0\end{bmatrix}\sin\theta$$

$$=\begin{bmatrix}\cos\theta & \sin\theta\\-\sin\theta & \cos\theta\end{bmatrix}=C$$

11. Since A is nilpotent of index 2, we have $A^2=O$.

$\Rightarrow A^3=A^2A=OA=O$

Similarly $A^4=A^5=....=A^n=O$

Again I and A commute i.e. IA = AI = A and hence by Binomial Theorem

$$A(I\pm A)^n=A(I\pm nA+O+O+....)$$

$$=A\pm nA^2+O+....$$

$$=A\pm n.O=A.$$

12. Inverse of a matrix does not exist if its determinant is zero.

i.e. $\begin{vmatrix}2 & -5 & 1\\8 & 6 & 7\\\lambda & -10 & 2\end{vmatrix}=0$

$$\Rightarrow 2\begin{vmatrix}6 & 7\\-10 & 2\end{vmatrix}+5\begin{vmatrix}8 & 7\\\lambda & 2\end{vmatrix}+\begin{vmatrix}8 & 6\\\lambda & -10\end{vmatrix}=0$$

$\Rightarrow 2(12+70)+5(16-7\lambda)-(80+6\lambda)=0$

$\Rightarrow 164+80-35\lambda-80-6\lambda=0$

$\Rightarrow 164-41\lambda=0$

$\Rightarrow \lambda=4.$

13. Characteristic roots of the given matrix is given by the equation

$|A-\lambda I|=0$

$$\Rightarrow \begin{vmatrix}8-\lambda & -6 & 2\\-6 & 7-\lambda & -4\\2 & -4 & 3-\lambda\end{vmatrix}=0$$

$$\Rightarrow (8-\lambda)\begin{vmatrix}7-\lambda & -4\\-4 & 3-\lambda\end{vmatrix}+6\begin{vmatrix}-6 & -4\\2 & 3-\lambda\end{vmatrix}+2\begin{vmatrix}-6 & 7-\lambda\\2 & -4\end{vmatrix}=0$$

$$\Rightarrow (8-\lambda)\{(7-\lambda)(3-\lambda)-16\}+6\{6(\lambda-3)+8\}+2\{24-2(7-\lambda)\}=0$$

$$\Rightarrow (8-\lambda)(\lambda^2-10\lambda+5)+6(6\lambda-10)+2(10+2\lambda)=0$$

$$\Rightarrow -\lambda^3+18\lambda^2-85\lambda+40+36\lambda-60+20+4\lambda=0$$

$$\Rightarrow -\lambda^3+18\lambda^2-45\lambda=0$$

$$\Rightarrow \lambda^3-18\lambda^2+45\lambda=0$$

$$\Rightarrow \lambda(\lambda-3)(\lambda-15)=0$$

$$\Rightarrow \lambda=0, 3, 15.$$

$\therefore$ Required characteristic roots of the given matrix are 0, 3, 15.

14. Given matrix is

$$(\because R_3 \to R_3-(R_1+R_2)\quad R_4 \to R_4-(R_1+R_3))$$

$$A=\begin{bmatrix} 6 & 1 & 3 & 8 \\ 4 & 2 & 6 & -1 \\ 10 & 3 & 9 & 7 \\ 16 & 4 & 12 & 15 \end{bmatrix}=\begin{bmatrix} 6 & 1 & 3 & 8 \\ 4 & 2 & 6 & -1 \\ 0 & 0 & 0 & 0 \\ 0 & 0 & 0 & 0 \end{bmatrix}$$

Hence Rank of the matrix i.e. Rank A = the number of non-zero rows in this matrix = 2.

15. Transformation matrix is $\begin{bmatrix} 1 & 0 & 0 \\ 0 & 0 & 1 \\ 0 & 1 & 0 \end{bmatrix}$

$$\begin{bmatrix} 1 & 0 & 0 \\ 0 & 0 & 1 \\ 0 & 1 & 0 \end{bmatrix}\begin{bmatrix} x \\ y \\ z \end{bmatrix}=\begin{bmatrix} x \\ z \\ y \end{bmatrix}$$

Since y and z co-ordinates get interchanged, this matrix represents a reflection about the plane $y = z$.

16. All the elements of the given matrix are of the form $a_{ji}=\bar{a}_{ij}$.

17. Characteristic equation of A is

$$\begin{vmatrix} 1-\lambda & 0 & 0 \\ 1 & -\lambda & 1 \\ 0 & 1 & -\lambda \end{vmatrix}=0$$

$\Rightarrow \lambda^3-\lambda^2-\lambda+1=0$, since the matrix satisfies the characteristic equation we have $A^3-A^2-A+I=0$ or $A^2(A-I)=A^2-I$.

18. Let $A=\begin{bmatrix} 2 & -1 & 1 \\ -1 & 2 & -1 \\ 1 & -1 & 2 \end{bmatrix}$

Characteristic equation is given by the equation $|A-\lambda I|=0$

$$\text{Now } |A-\lambda I|=\begin{vmatrix} 2-x & -1 & 1 \\ -1 & 2-x & -1 \\ 1 & -1 & 2-x \end{vmatrix}=0$$

$$\Rightarrow -x^3+6x^2-9x+4=0.$$

19. Given $U=\begin{bmatrix} 0 & 1 & 0 & 0 \\ 0 & 0 & 1 & 0 \\ 0 & 0 & 0 & 1 \\ 0 & 0 & 0 & 0 \end{bmatrix}$

$$\Rightarrow \quad U^2=\begin{bmatrix} 0 & 0 & 1 & 0 \\ 0 & 0 & 0 & 1 \\ 0 & 0 & 0 & 0 \\ 0 & 0 & 0 & 0 \end{bmatrix}$$

$$\Rightarrow \quad U^4=\begin{bmatrix} 0 & 0 & 0 & 0 \\ 0 & 0 & 0 & 0 \\ 0 & 0 & 0 & 0 \\ 0 & 0 & 0 & 0 \end{bmatrix}$$

Now Rank of matrix is the number of non-zero rows.

Thus Rank of the given matrix is zero.

20. Given matrix is

$$A=\begin{bmatrix} 2 & 2 & 2 & 2 \\ 3 & 3 & 3 & 3 \\ 4 & 4 & 4 & 4 \\ 5 & 5 & 5 & 5 \end{bmatrix}=\begin{bmatrix} 2 & 0 & 0 & 0 \\ 3 & 0 & 0 & 0 \\ 4 & 0 & 0 & 0 \\ 5 & 0 & 0 & 0 \end{bmatrix}$$

$$(\because C_2 \to C_2-C_1, C_3 \to C_3-C_1, C_4 \to C_4-C_1)$$

Rank of the given matrix is the number of non zero column. Thus Rank of the given matrix is 1.

21. L $\Delta = \begin{vmatrix} a & b & ax+by \\ b & c & bx+cy \\ ax+by & bx+cy & 0 \end{vmatrix}$

$= \begin{vmatrix} a & b & ax+by \\ b & c & bx+cy \\ 0 & 0 & -(ax^2+2bxy+cy^2) \end{vmatrix}$

$(\because R_3 \to R_3 - xR_1 - yR_2)$

$= (b^2 - ac)(ax^2 + 2bxy + cy^2)$

Now, $b^2 - ac < 0$ and $a > 0$

$\Rightarrow$ Discriminant of $ax^2 + 2bxy + cy^2$ is negative and $a > 0$

$\Rightarrow ax^2 + 2bxy + cy^2 > 0$ for all $x, y \in R$.

$\therefore \Delta = (b^2 - ac)(ax^2 + 2bxy + cy^2) < 0$.

22. Let $\Delta = \begin{vmatrix} x & x^2 & 1+x^3 \\ y & y^2 & 1+y^3 \\ z & z^2 & 1+z^3 \end{vmatrix}$

$= \begin{vmatrix} x & x^2 & 1 \\ y & y^2 & 1 \\ z & z^2 & 1 \end{vmatrix} + \begin{vmatrix} x & x^2 & x^3 \\ y & y^2 & y^3 \\ z & z^2 & z^3 \end{vmatrix}$

$= \begin{vmatrix} x & x^2 & 1 \\ y & y^2 & 1 \\ z & z^2 & 1 \end{vmatrix} + xyz \begin{vmatrix} 1 & x & x^2 \\ 1 & y & y^2 \\ 1 & z & z^2 \end{vmatrix}$

($\because$ *x, y, z* are taken common from C_1, C_2, and C_3)

$= \begin{vmatrix} 1 & x & x^2 \\ 1 & y & y^2 \\ 1 & z & z^2 \end{vmatrix} + xyz \begin{vmatrix} 1 & x & x^2 \\ 1 & y & y^2 \\ 1 & z & z^2 \end{vmatrix}$

$= (1+xyz) \begin{vmatrix} 1 & x & x^2 \\ 1 & y & y^2 \\ 1 & z & z^2 \end{vmatrix}$

$= (1+xyz) \begin{vmatrix} 1 & x & x^2 \\ 0 & 1 & y+x \\ 0 & 1 & z+x \end{vmatrix}$ $\left(\because \begin{matrix} R_2 \to R_2 - R_1 \\ R_3 \to R_3 - R_1 \end{matrix}\right)$

$= (y-x)(z-3) \begin{vmatrix} 1 & x & x^2 \\ 0 & 1 & y+x \\ 0 & 1 & z+x \end{vmatrix} (1+xyz)$

$= (y-x)(z-x) \begin{vmatrix} 1 & y+x \\ 1 & z+x \end{vmatrix} (1+xyz)$

($\because$ Expanding along C_1)

$= (y-x)(z-x)(z-y)(1+xyz)$

$= (x-y)(y-z)(z-x)(1+xyz)$.

Given $xyz = -1$; so $\Delta = 0$.

23. Let $\Delta = \begin{vmatrix} a & 1 & 1 \\ 1 & b & 1 \\ 1 & 1 & c \end{vmatrix} = abc - (a+b+c) + 2$.

Given that $\Delta > 0$

$\therefore abc - (a+b+c) + 2 > 0$

or $abc + 2 > (a+b+c)$

or $abc + 2 > 3(abc)^{1/3}$ ($\because$ AM > GM)

or $x^3 + 2 > 3x$, where $x = (abc)^{1/3}$.

or $x^3 - 3x + 2 > 0$

or $(x-1)^2(x+2) > 0$

or $x + 2 > 0$ ($\because (x-1)^2$ is always positive)

or $x > -2$

or $(abc)^{1/3} > -2$

or $abc > -8$.

24. ω is an imaginary cube root of unity.

$\therefore \omega^2 = \dfrac{-1-i\sqrt{3}}{2}$ and $1 + \omega + \omega^2 = 0$

Now $\Delta = \begin{vmatrix} 1 & 1 & 1 \\ 1 & \omega & \omega^2 \\ 1 & \omega^2 & \omega \end{vmatrix}$

$= \begin{vmatrix} 3 & 1+\omega+\omega^2 & 1+\omega+\omega^2 \\ 1 & \omega & \omega^2 \\ 1 & \omega^2 & \omega \end{vmatrix}$

$(\because R_1 \to R_1 + R_2 + R_3)$

$= \begin{vmatrix} 3 & 0 & 0 \\ 1 & \omega & \omega^2 \\ 1 & \omega^2 & \omega \end{vmatrix}$

$= 3(\omega^2 - \omega^4) = 3(\omega^2 - \omega)$

$= 3\left[\frac{-1-i\sqrt{3}}{2} - \frac{-1+i\sqrt{3}}{2}\right]$

$= -3\sqrt{3}i.$

26. Let $\Delta = \begin{vmatrix} 1 & \omega & \omega^2 \\ \omega & \omega^2 & 1 \\ \omega^2 & 1 & \omega \end{vmatrix}$

$= \begin{vmatrix} 1+\omega+\omega^2 & 1+\omega+\omega^2 & 1+\omega+\omega^2 \\ \omega & \omega^2 & 1 \\ \omega^2 & 1 & \omega \end{vmatrix}$

$(\because R_1 \to R_1 + R_2 + R_3)$

$= \begin{vmatrix} 0 & 0 & 0 \\ \omega & \omega^2 & 1 \\ \omega^2 & 1 & \omega \end{vmatrix} = 0$

27. Let $\Delta = \begin{vmatrix} a & b & c \\ b & c & a \\ c & a & b \end{vmatrix}$

$= \begin{vmatrix} a+b+c & a+b+c & a+b+c \\ b & c & a \\ c & a & b \end{vmatrix}$

$(\because R_1 \to R_1 + R_2 + R_3)$

$= (a+b+c)\begin{vmatrix} 1 & 1 & 1 \\ b & c & a \\ c & a & b \end{vmatrix}$

$= (a+b+c)\begin{vmatrix} 1 & 0 & 0 \\ b & c-b & a-b \\ c & a-c & b-c \end{vmatrix}$ $(\because C_2 \to C_2 - C_1, C_3 \to C_3 - C_1)$

$= (a+b+c)[(c-b)(b-c)-(a-b)(a-c)]$

$= -(a+b+c)(a^2+b^2+c^2-ab-bc-ca)$

$= -\frac{1}{2}(a+b+c)[(a-b)^2+(b-c)^2+(c-a)^2]$

< 0 i.e. negative.

28. Here

$\Delta = \begin{vmatrix} \cos\alpha & -\sin\alpha & 1 \\ \sin\alpha & \cos\alpha & 1 \\ \cos(\alpha+\beta) & -\sin(\alpha+\beta) & 1 \end{vmatrix}$

$= \begin{vmatrix} \cos\alpha & -\sin\alpha & 1 \\ \sin\alpha & \cos\alpha & 1 \\ 0 & 0 & 1+\sin\beta-\cos\beta \end{vmatrix}$

$(\because R_3 \to R_3 - R_1(\cos\beta) + R_2(\sin\beta))$

$= (1+\sin\beta-\cos\beta)(\cos^2\alpha+\sin^2\alpha)$

$= 1+\sin\beta-\cos\beta$

$\therefore\ \Delta = 1+\sin\beta-\cos\beta.$

Now $-\sqrt{2} \le \sin\beta-\cos\beta \le \sqrt{2}$

$(\because 2 \le 1-\sin 2\beta \le 0)$

$\Rightarrow 1-\sqrt{2} \le 1+\sin\beta-\cos\beta \le 1+\sqrt{2}$

$\Rightarrow \Delta \in [1-\sqrt{2}, 1+\sqrt{2}]$

29. Let

$\Delta = \begin{vmatrix} 1 & \omega^n & \omega^{2n} \\ \omega^{2n} & 1 & \omega^n \\ \omega^n & \omega^{2n} & 1 \end{vmatrix}$

$= \begin{vmatrix} \omega^{3n} & \omega^n & \omega^{2n} \\ \omega^{2n} & 1 & \omega^n \\ \omega^n & \omega^{2n} & 1 \end{vmatrix}$ $(\because \omega^{3n} = 1)$

$= \omega^n \begin{vmatrix} \omega^{2n} & 1 & \omega^n \\ \omega^{2n} & 1 & \omega^n \\ \omega^n & \omega^{2n} & 1 \end{vmatrix}$

$= 0$ ($\because$ R_1 and R_2 are identical Row)

30. Here

$D_r = \begin{vmatrix} a & 2^r & 2^{16}-1 \\ b & 3(4^r) & 2(14^{16}-1) \\ c & 7(8^r) & 4(8^{16}-1) \end{vmatrix}$

$$\therefore \sum_{k=1}^{16} D_r = \begin{vmatrix} a & \sum_{k=1}^{16} 2^k & 2^{16}-1 \\ b & 3\left(\sum_{k=1}^{16} 4^k\right) & 2(4^{16}-1) \\ c & 7\left(\sum_{k=1}^{16} 8^k\right) & 4(8^{16}-1) \end{vmatrix}$$

$$= \begin{vmatrix} a & 2\left(\frac{2^{16}-1}{2-1}\right) & 2^{16}-1 \\ b & 3\times 4\left(\frac{4^{16}-1}{4-1}\right) & 2(4^{16}-1) \\ c & 7\times 8\left(\frac{8^{16}-1}{8-1}\right) & 4(8^{16}-1) \end{vmatrix}$$

$$= \begin{vmatrix} a & 2(2^{16}-1) & 2^{16}-1 \\ b & 4(4^{16}-1) & 2(1^{16}-1) \\ c & 8(8^{16}-1) & 4(8^{16}-1) \end{vmatrix}$$

$$= 2\begin{vmatrix} a & (2^{16}-1) & 2^{16}-1 \\ b & 2(2^{16}-1) & 2(2^{16}-1) \\ c & 4(8^{16}-1) & 4(8^{16}-1) \end{vmatrix}$$

($\because$ 2 is taken common from C_2)

$= 0$ ($\because$ C_2 and C_3 are identical column)

31. Here

$$d(r) = \begin{vmatrix} 2^{r-1} & 2(3^{r-1}) & 4(5^{r-1}) \\ x & y & z \\ 2^n-1 & 3^n-1 & 5^n-1 \end{vmatrix}$$

$$\therefore \sum_{r=1}^{n} d(r) = \begin{vmatrix} \sum_{r=1}^{n} 2^{r-1} & 2\sum_{r=1}^{n} 3^{r-1} & 4\sum_{r=1}^{n} 5^{r-1} \\ x & y & z \\ 2^n-1 & 3^n-1 & 5^n-1 \end{vmatrix}$$

Now $\sum_{r=1}^{n} 2^{r-1} = 1 + 2 + ... + 2^{n-1}$

$$= \frac{2^{n-1}-1}{2-1} = 2^n - 1.$$

Similarly $\sum_{r=1}^{n} 3^{r-1} = 3^n - 1$ and

$$4\sum_{r=1}^{n} 5^{r-1} = 5^n - 1$$

$$\therefore \sum_{r=1}^{n} d(r) = \begin{vmatrix} 2^n-1 & 3^n-1 & 5^n-1 \\ x & y & z \\ 2^n-1 & 3^n-1 & 5^n-1 \end{vmatrix}$$

$= 0$ ($\because$ R_1 and R_3 are two identical rows).

32. Given

$$\begin{vmatrix} x^n & x^{n+2} & x^{n+3} \\ y^n & y^{n+2} & y^{n+3} \\ z^n & z^{n+2} & z^{n+3} \end{vmatrix} = (x-y)(y-z)(z-x)$$

$$\left(\frac{1}{x} + \frac{1}{y} + \frac{1}{z}\right)$$

Degree of the determinant in the L.H.S. $= n + (n+2) + (n+3) = 3n + 5$

Degree of the expression in the R.H.S. = 2

Equating we get $3n + 5 = 2 \Rightarrow n = -1$

33. Given $a_1, a_2, a_3, ..., a_n, ...$ are in G.P.

and $$\Delta = \begin{vmatrix} \log a_n & \log a_{n+1} & \log a_{n+2} \\ \log a_{n+3} & \log a_{n+4} & \log a_{n+5} \\ \log a_{n+6} & \log a_{n+7} & \log a_{n+8} \end{vmatrix}$$

$\therefore a_n, a_{n+1}, a_{n+2}$ are also in G.P.

So $a_{n+1}^2 = a_n . a_{n+2}$

Taking log both the sides we get

$2 \log a_{n+1} = \log a_n + \log a_{n+2}$

or $2 \log a_{n+1} - \log a_n - \log a_{n+2} = 0$ ...(i)

Similarly

$2 \log a_{n+4} - \log a_{n+3} - \log a_{n+5} = 0$ ...(ii)

and

$2 \log a_{n+7} - \log a_{n+6} - \log a_{n+8} = 0$ ...(iii)

$\therefore \Delta =$

$$\begin{vmatrix} \log a_n + \log a_{n+2} - 2\log a_{n+1} & \log a_{n+1} & \log a_{n+2} \\ \log a_{n+3} + \log a_{n+5} - 2\log a_{n+4} & \log a_{n+4} & \log a_{n+5} \\ \log a_{n+6} + \log a_{n+7} - 2\log a_{n+5} & \log a_{n+7} & \log a_{n+8} \end{vmatrix}$$

$(\because C_1 \to C_1 + C_3 - 2C_2)$

$$= \begin{vmatrix} 0 & \log a_{n+1} & \log a_{n+2} \\ 0 & \log a_{n+4} & \log a_{n+5} \\ 0 & \log a_{n+7} & \log a_{n+8} \end{vmatrix}$$

($\because$ From *(i)*, *(ii)* and *(iii)*)

$= 0.$

34. Given

$$\Delta = \begin{vmatrix} 1 & 1 & 1 \\ a & b & c \\ a^3 & b^3 & c^3 \end{vmatrix} = \begin{vmatrix} 1 & 1 & 1 \\ a & b-a & c-a \\ a^3 & b^3-a^3 & c^3-a^3 \end{vmatrix}$$

$(\because C_2 \to C_2 - C_1 \text{ and } C_3 \to C_3 - C_1)$

$$= (b-a)(c-a) \begin{vmatrix} 1 & 0 & 0 \\ a & 1 & 1 \\ a^3 & (b^2+ab+a^2) & (c^2+ca+a^2) \end{vmatrix}$$

$= (b-a)(c-a)\{(c^2+ca+a^2)-(b^2+ab+a^2)\}$

$= (b-a)(c-a)\{(c^2-b^2)+(ca-ab)\}$

$= (b-a)(c-a)(c-b)(c+b+a)$

$= (a-b)(b-c)(c-a)(a+b+c)$

35. Given

$$\begin{vmatrix} bc & ca & ab \\ ca & ab & bc \\ ab & bc & ca \end{vmatrix} = 0$$

$$\Rightarrow bc\begin{vmatrix} ab & bc \\ bc & ca \end{vmatrix} - ca\begin{vmatrix} ca & bc \\ ab & ca \end{vmatrix} + ab\begin{vmatrix} ca & ab \\ ab & bc \end{vmatrix} = 0$$

$\Rightarrow bc\,(a^2bc - b^2c^2) - ca\,(c^2a^2 - ab^2c) + ab\,(abc^2 - a^2b^2) = 0$

$\Rightarrow a^2b^2c^2 - b^3c^3 - c^3a^3 + a^2b^2c^2 + a^2b^2c^2 - a^3b^3 = 0$

$\Rightarrow (ab)^3 + (bc)^3 + (ca)^3 - 3a^2b^2c^2 = 0$

$\Rightarrow (ab + bc + ca)(a^2b^2 + b^2c^2 + c^2a^2 - ab^2c - bc^2a - ca^2b) = 0$

$\Rightarrow ab + bc + ca = 0$

$$\Rightarrow \frac{1}{a}+\frac{1}{b}+\frac{1}{c}=0$$

36. Given

$$\Delta_1 = \begin{vmatrix} x & b & b \\ a & x & b \\ a & a & x \end{vmatrix} \text{ and } \Delta_2 = \begin{vmatrix} x & 1 \\ a & x \end{vmatrix}$$

Now

$$\frac{d}{dx}(\Delta_1) = \begin{vmatrix} 1 & 0 & 0 \\ a & x & b \\ a & a & x \end{vmatrix} + \begin{vmatrix} x & b & b \\ 0 & 1 & 0 \\ a & a & x \end{vmatrix} + \begin{vmatrix} x & b & b \\ a & x & b \\ 0 & 0 & 1 \end{vmatrix}$$

$$= \begin{vmatrix} x & b \\ a & x \end{vmatrix} + \begin{vmatrix} x & b \\ a & x \end{vmatrix} + \begin{vmatrix} x & b \\ a & x \end{vmatrix} = 3(\Delta_2).$$

37. Let $\Delta = \begin{vmatrix} 1 & \log_x y & \log_x z \\ \log_y x & 1 & \log_y z \\ \log_z x & \log_z y & 1 \end{vmatrix}$

$$= \begin{vmatrix} 1 & \dfrac{\log_e y}{\log_e x} & \dfrac{\log_e z}{\log_e x} \\ \dfrac{\log_e x}{\log_e y} & 1 & \dfrac{\log_e z}{\log_e y} \\ \dfrac{\log_e x}{\log_e z} & \dfrac{\log_e y}{\log_e z} & 1 \end{vmatrix}$$

$$= \begin{vmatrix} \dfrac{\log_e x}{\log_e x} & \dfrac{\log_e y}{\log_e x} & \dfrac{\log_e z}{\log_e x} \\ \dfrac{\log_e x}{\log_e y} & \dfrac{\log_e y}{\log_e y} & \dfrac{\log_e z}{\log_e y} \\ \dfrac{\log_e x}{\log_e z} & \dfrac{\log_e y}{\log_e z} & \dfrac{\log_e z}{\log_e z} \end{vmatrix}$$

$$= \frac{1}{\log_e x \log_e y \log_e z} \begin{vmatrix} \log_e x & \log_e y & \log_e z \\ \log_e x & \log_e y & \log_e z \\ \log_e x & \log_e y & \log_e z \end{vmatrix}$$

$= 0$ ($\because$ All the rows are identical).

38. Given $a + b + c = 0$

and $\begin{vmatrix} a-x & c & b \\ c & b-x & a \\ b & a & c-x \end{vmatrix} = 0$

$$\Rightarrow \begin{vmatrix} a+b+c-x & c & b \\ a+b+c-x & b-x & a \\ b+a+c-x & a & c-x \end{vmatrix} = 0$$

$$\Rightarrow (a+b+c-x)\begin{vmatrix} 1 & c & b \\ 1 & b-x & a \\ 1 & a & c-x \end{vmatrix} = 0$$

$$\Rightarrow -x\begin{vmatrix} 1 & c & b \\ 1 & b-x & a \\ 1 & a & c-x \end{vmatrix} = 0$$

$$\Rightarrow -x\begin{vmatrix} 1 & c & b \\ 0 & b-x-c & a-b \\ 0 & a-c & c-b-x \end{vmatrix} = 0$$

$(\because R_2 \to R_2 - R_1 \text{ and } R_3 \to R_3 - R_1)$

$\Rightarrow -x\,[(b-x-c)(c-b-x)-(a-b)(a-c)] = 0$

$\Rightarrow x\left[x^2-(a^2+b^2+c^2-ab-bc-ca)\right] = 0$

$\Rightarrow x = 0 \text{ or } x^2 = a^2+b^2+c^2-ab-bc-ca$

$\therefore$ Required root is $x = 0$.

39. Let $s-a = A$, $s-b = B$ and $s-c = C$

Then $A+B+C = s$, $B+C = a$, $C+A = b$, $A+B = c$

$$\therefore \Delta = \begin{vmatrix} (B+C)^2 & A^2 & A^2 \\ B^2 & (C+A)^2 & B^2 \\ C^2 & C^2 & (A+B)^2 \end{vmatrix}$$

$= 2\,ABC\,(A+B+C)^3$

$= 2\,s^3\,(s-a)\,(s-b)\,(s-c).$

40. Given

$$\Delta = \begin{vmatrix} 1+a & 1 & 1 \\ 1 & 1+b & 1 \\ 1 & 1 & 1+c \end{vmatrix} = 0$$

$$\Rightarrow abc\begin{vmatrix} \frac{1}{a}+1 & \frac{1}{a} & \frac{1}{a} \\ \frac{1}{b} & \frac{1}{b}+1 & \frac{1}{b} \\ \frac{1}{c} & \frac{1}{c} & \frac{1}{c}+1 \end{vmatrix} = 0$$

$$\Rightarrow abc\begin{vmatrix} 1+\frac{1}{a}+\frac{1}{b}+\frac{1}{c} & 1+\frac{1}{a}+\frac{1}{b}+\frac{1}{c} & 1+\frac{1}{a}+\frac{1}{b}+\frac{1}{c} \\ \frac{1}{b} & \frac{1}{b}+1 & \frac{1}{b} \\ \frac{1}{c} & \frac{1}{c} & \frac{1}{c}+1 \end{vmatrix} = 0$$

$$\Rightarrow (abc)\left(1+\frac{1}{a}+\frac{1}{b}+\frac{1}{c}\right)\begin{vmatrix} 1 & 1 & 1 \\ \frac{1}{b} & \frac{1}{b}+1 & \frac{1}{b} \\ \frac{1}{c} & \frac{1}{c} & \frac{1}{c}+1 \end{vmatrix} = 0$$

$$\Rightarrow (abc)\left(1+\frac{1}{a}+\frac{1}{b}+\frac{1}{c}\right)\begin{vmatrix} 1 & 0 & 0 \\ \frac{1}{b} & 1 & 0 \\ \frac{1}{c} & 0 & 1 \end{vmatrix} = 0$$

$(\because C_2 \to C_2 - C_1;\ C_3 \to C_3 - C_1)$

$\Rightarrow (abc)\left(1+\frac{1}{a}+\frac{1}{b}+\frac{1}{c}\right) = 0$

$\Rightarrow 1+\frac{1}{a}+\frac{1}{b}+\frac{1}{c} = 0$ ($\because$ *a, b, c* are all different form zero).

10. TWO DIMENSIONAL GEOMETRY

1. Distance Formula:

(a) The distance between two points (x_1, y_1) and $(x_2, y_2) = \sqrt{[(x_2 - x_1)^2 + (y_2 - y_1)^2]}$.

(b) The distance of the point (x_1, y_1) from the origin $= \sqrt{(x_1{}^2 + y_1{}^2)}$.

2. Section Formula:

(a) The coordinates of the point P(*x*, *y*), dividing the line joining the points A(x_1, y_1) and B(x_2, y_2) in the ratio *m* : *n* (internally and externally). If P divide AB internally, then

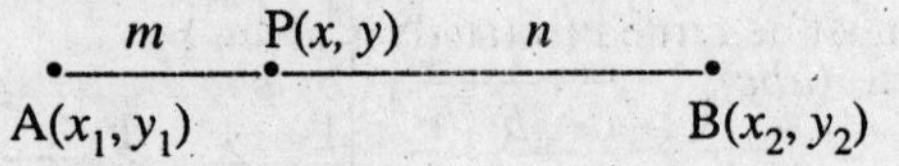

$$x = \frac{mx_2 + nx_1}{m+n}, \qquad y = \frac{my_2 + ny_1}{m+n}$$

If P divide AB externally, then *m* : *n*

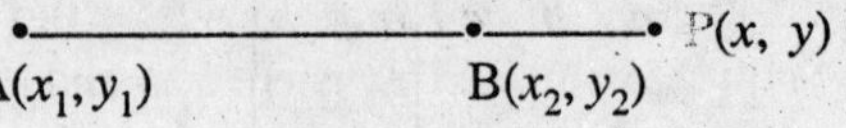

$$x = \frac{mx_2 - nx_1}{m-n}, \qquad y = \frac{my_2 - ny_1}{m-n}$$

(b) The coordinates of the mid-point of line joining A(x_1, y_1) and B(x_2, y_2) are $\left(\frac{x_1 + x_2}{2}, \frac{y_1 + y_2}{2}\right)$

3. Area of a Triangle: The area of a triangle whose vertices are A(x_1, y_1), B(x_2, y_2) and C(z_3, y_3) is

$= \frac{1}{2}\,|(x_1y_2 + x_2y_3 + x_3y_1) - (y_1x_2 + y_2x_3 + y_3x_1)|$

$\Rightarrow \frac{1}{2}\,|x_1(y_2 - y_3) + x_2(y_3 - y_1) + x_3(y_1 - y_2)|$

$$\text{or } \frac{1}{2}\begin{vmatrix} x_1 & y_1 & 1 \\ x_2 & y_2 & 1 \\ x_3 & y_3 & 1 \end{vmatrix}$$

4. Area of a Quadrilateral: The area of a quadrilateral whose vertices are A(x_1, y_1), B(x_2, y_2), C(x_3, y_3) and D(x_4, y_4) is $= \frac{1}{2}\,|(x_1y_2 + x_2y_3 + x_3y_4 + x_4y_1) - (y_1x_2 + y_2x_3 + y_3x_4 + y_4x_1)|$.

5. Centroid of a Triangle: The centroid of a triangle is the point of intersection of its medians (the line joining a vertex to the middle point of the opposite side). The centroid divides the medians in the ratio 2 : 1. If (x_1, y_1), (x_2, y_2) and (x_3, y_3) are the coordinates of the vertices of a triangle, then the coordinates of its centroid are $\left(\frac{x_1 + x_2 + x_3}{3}, \frac{y_1 + y_2 + y_3}{3}\right)$

6. Circumcentre of a Triangle: The point of intersection of the perpendicular bisectors of the sides of a triangle is called its circumcentre. It is the centre of the circle which passes through the vertices of the triangle and so its distance from the vertices of the triangle is the same and this distance is known as the circum-radius of the triangle.

7. In-centre of a Triangle: The centre of the circle which touches the sides of a triangle is called its in-centre. It is the point of intersection of the internal bisectors of the in-centre from the sides of the triangle is the same and this distance is called the in-radius of the triangle. If A(x_1, y_1), B(x_2, y_2) and C(x_3, y_3) are the coordinates of the vertices of a triangle, then the coordinates of its in-centre are $\left(\frac{ax_1 + bx_2 + cx_3}{a+b+c}, \frac{ay_1 + by_2 + cy_3}{a+b+c}\right)$, where BC $= a$, CA $= b$ and AB $= c$.

8. Ortho-centre of a Triangle: The ortho-centre of a triangle is the point of intersection of the lines through the vertices and perpendicular to the opposite sides of the triangle.

9. Collinearity of Three given Points: The three given points A, B, C are collinear, *i.e.*, lie on the same straight line, if

(a) area of ΔABC is zero

(b) slope of AB = slope of AC

(c) any one of the three points (say C) lie on

the straight line joining the other two points (here points A and B).

10. Slope of a Line: The slope of a line joining two points $A(x_1, y_1)$ and $B(x_2, y_2)$ is denoted by m and is given by

$$m = \frac{y_2 - y_1}{x_2 - x_1} = \tan\theta,$$

Where θ is the angle which the line makes with the positive direction of x-axis. This angle θ is taken positive when it is measured in the anticlockwise direction from the positive direction of the axis of x.

11. Locus of a Point: The locus of a moving point is the path traced out by it under some given geometrical condition or conditions.

Method to Find the Locus of a Point: To find the locus of a point proceed as follows:

Let (h, k) be the coordinates of the moving point say P. Now using given geometrical conditions find the relations between h, k and other known and unknown quantities. From these relations eliminate the unknown quantities to get a relation between h, k and the known quantities. Now the locus of $P(h, k)$ is obtained by generalising (h, k), *i.e.*, by putting x for h and y for k.

(a) In a triangle ABC, if AD is the median drawn to BC, then $AB^2 + AC^2 = 2(AD^2 + BD^2)$.

(b) A triangle is isosceles if any two of its medians are equal.

(c) In a right angled triangle, the midpoint of the hypotenuse is equidistant from the vertices.

(d) The diagonals in rhombus, square, rectangle and parallelogram bisect each other.

(e) The figure obtained by joining the middle points of a quadrilateral in order is a parallelogram.

f) If $f(x, y) = 0$ is a curve, then the equation of the curve by shifting the origin at the point (h, k), keeping the axes parallel to original axes, is obtained by replacing x by $X + h$ and y by $Y + k$. Thus the transformed equation of the curve w.r.t. the new origin is

$$f(X + h, Y + k) = 0.$$

(g) If (x, y) are the coordinates of a point P w.r.t. the axes OX and OY and (x', y') its coordinates w.r.t. the axes OX', OY' obtained by rotating the original axes OX, OY through an angle θ in anticlockwise direction, keeping the same origin, then

$$x = x'\cos\theta - y'\sin\theta$$
$$y = x'\sin\theta - y'\cos\theta$$

Thus to find the equation of the curve referred to the turned axes, through angle θ, replace

x by $x'\cos\theta - y'\sin\theta$

and y by $x'\sin\theta + y'\cos\theta$

The relations connecting (x, y) and (x', y') can be written in the following scheme

	x'	y'
x	$\cos\theta$	$-\sin\theta$
y	$\sin\theta$	$\cos\theta$

(h) To remove the term of xy in the equation, $ax^2 + 2hxy + by^2 = 0$, the angle θ through which the axes must be turned (rotated) is given by

$$\theta = \tfrac{1}{2}\tan^{-1}\{2h/(a - b)\}$$

EQUATION OF A LINE IN VARIOUS FORMS

12. Straight Lines: The general form of the equation of a straight line is $ax + by + c = 0$, (the first degree equation in x and y) where a, b and c are real constants not all equal to zero simultaneously.

(i) Lines Parallel to Axes:

(a) The equation of a straight line || to x-axis and at a distance b from it is given by $y = b$.

(b) The equation of the straight line || to y-axis and at a distance a from it is given by $x = a$.

(c) The equations of the straight lines || to x-axis and y-axis respectively and passing through the pt. (a, b) are $y = b$, $x = a$.

(d) Equation of x-axis is $y = 0$ and equation of y-axis is $x = 0$.

(ii) Slope Intercept Form: The equation of a straight line which cuts off an intercept c on y-axis and makes an angle θ (in anticlockwise direction) with the positive direction of x-axis is given by $y = mx + c$, where $m = \tan\theta$. The number $m = \tan\theta$ is called the slope or the gradient of the line. Obviously, $y = mx$ is the equation of the line through the origin.

(iii) Slope Point Form: The equation of a straight line passing through the point $A(x_1, y_1)$ and having slope m is given by $y - y_1 = m(x - x_1)$ .... (1)

This equation can also be written as

$$\frac{x - x_1}{\cos\theta} = \frac{y - y_1}{\sin\theta} = r\,(\text{say}) \quad .... (2)$$

$(m = \tan\theta)$

This form of the line is called parametric form or symmetrical form of the line. The coordinates of any point P on this line are taken as $(x_1 + r\cos\theta, y_1, + r\sin\theta)$

$\therefore$ Distance of point p from A (x_1, y_1)

$= \sqrt{[(x_1 + r\cos\theta - x_1)^2 + (y_1 + r\sin\theta - y_1)^2]} = r$

Thus if the equation of a line through point A(x_1, y_1) is written in the form (2), in which the coefficients of x and y are equal to 1 and the sum of squares of the terms in the denominators is equal to 1 then the coordiantes of a point P on this line at a distance r from from A(x_1, y_1) are $(x_1 + r\cos\theta, y_1 + r\sin\theta)$

(iv) Two Points Form: The equation of a straight line passing through two points A(x_1, y_1) and B(x_2, y_2) is given by $y - y_1 = \frac{y_2 - y_1}{x_2 - x_1}(x - x_1)$ and its

$$\text{slope} = \frac{y_2 - y_1}{x_2 - x_1} = \frac{\text{difference of ordinates}}{\text{difference of abscissae}}$$

(v) Intercept Form: The equation of a straight line making intercepts a and b on the axes of x and y respectively is given by $x/a + y/b = 1$

(vi) Normal (or Perpendicular) Form: The equation of a straight line on which the perpendicular from origin is of length p and makes an angle α with the positive direction of x-axis is given by

$$x\cos\alpha + y\sin\alpha = p.$$

(vii) Slope and Intercepts on Coordinate Axes of the Line Ax + By + C = 0

(a) To find slope of the line: The equation $x + \text{B}y + \text{C} = 0$ .... (1)

can be written as, $y = -(\text{A/B})x - (\text{C/A})$

Comparing with $y = mx + c$, we have $m = -(\text{A/B})$

$$\text{Thus slope of line} = \frac{\text{coefficient of } x}{\text{coefficient of } y}$$

(b) To find intercepts on y-axes: The equation (1) can be written as $\frac{x}{(-\text{C/A})} + \frac{y}{(-\text{C/B})} = 1$

Comparing with $x/a + y/b = 1$, we have

a = intercept on x-axis = – C/A

b = intercept on y-axis = – C/B

ANGLE BETWEEN TWO LINES

13. Angle Between Two Lines: If m_1 and m_2 are the slopes of the two lines, then the angle θ between them is given by

$$\theta = \tan^{-1}\left|\frac{m_1 - m_2}{1 + m_1 m_2}\right|$$

(a) Condition for two lines to be parallel: The two lines whose slopes are m_1 and m_2 are parallel if $\theta = 0°$ or 180°, $\therefore \tan\theta = 0 \Rightarrow m_1 = m_2$. If the two lines are $a_1x + b_1y + c_1 = 0$ and $a_2x + b_2y + c_2 = 0$, then $m_1 = a_1/b_1$ and $m_2 = -a_2/b_2$, *i.e.*, the coefficients of x and y in the two equations are proportional.

(b) Condition for two lines to be perpendicular: The two lines whose slopes are m_1 and m_2 are perpendicular if $\theta = 90°$.

$\therefore \tan\theta = \infty \Rightarrow = 1 + m_1m_2 = 0$ or $m_1m_2 = -1$

If the two lines are $a_1x + b_1y + c_1 = 0$ and $a_2x + b_2y + c_2 = 0$, then the two lines are perpendicular if $m_1m_2 = (-a_1/b_1)(a_2/b_2) = -1$ or $a_1a_2 + b_1b_2 = 0$

i.e., the product of coeffs. of x + product of coeffs. of $y = 0$.

14. Equation of Line Parallel to $ax + by + c = 0$: The equation of the straight line which is parallel to the line $ax + by + c = 0$ is given by $ax + by + \lambda = 0$. Thus to write the equation of any line parallel to a given line, do not change the coefficients of x and y and change the constant term only.

15. Equation of Line Perpendicular to $ax + by + c = 0$: The equation of a straight line which is perpendicular to the line $ax + by + c = 0$ is given by $bx - ay + \lambda = 0$. Thus to write the equation of any line perpendicualr to a given line, interchange the coefficient of x and y in the given equation and change the sign of one of these coefficients and also change the constant term.

16. Point of Intersection of Two Given Lines: Let the two given lines be $a_1x + b_1y + c_1 = 0$ and $a_2x + b_2y + c_2 = 0$. Solving these two equations, the point of intersection of these two lines is given by

$$\left(\frac{b_1c_2 - b_2c_1}{a_1b_2 - a_2b_1}, \frac{c_1a_2 - c_2a_1}{a_1b_2 - a_2b_1}\right).$$

17. Concurrent Lines: Three or more straight lines are said to be concurrent lines if they meet in a point.

Methods to Prove the Three Lines to be Concurrent:

(a) Find the point of intersection of any two lines, and if this point satisfty the equation of the third line, then the three lines are concurrent and this point is the point of intersection of the three lines.

(b) The three lines $a_1x + b_1y + c_1 = 0, a_2x + b_2y + c_2 = 0$ and $a_3x + b_3y + c_3 = 0$ are concurrent if

$$\begin{vmatrix} a_1 & b_1 & c_1 \\ a_2 & b_2 & c_2 \\ a_3 & b_3 & c_3 \end{vmatrix} = 0.$$

(c) Let P = 0, Q = 0 and R = 0 be three given lines. Then these are concurrent if we can find three constants *l, m, n,* not all zero (*i.e.,* at least one of these is not equal to zero) such that $lP + mQ + nR = 0$ takes the form $0.x + 0.y + 0 = 0$.

18. Any Line Through the Point of Intersection of Two Lines: Let P = 0 and Q = 0 be the two given lines. Then the equation of any line passing through the point of intersection of these two lines is $P + \lambda Q = 0$, where λ is any real number. The value of λ will be obtained by the condition given in the question.

DISTANCE OF A POINT FROM A LINE

19. Distance of a Point from a Line: The distance of a point from a line is calculated as the length of perpendicular from a given point (x_1, y_1) to a line. If the equation of line is $ax + by + c = 0$ then distance is $\frac{ax_1 + by_1 + c}{\sqrt{(a^2 + b^2)}}$

(i) Method to find the Perpendicular Distance: Bring all the terms in the equation of the straight line to the L.H.S. so that the R.H.S. of the equation reduces to zero. Then the length of perpendicular from the point (x_1, y_1) to the line is obtained by replacing x and y in the equation by x_1 and y_1 respectively and then dividing it by the square root of the sum of the squares of the coefficients of x and y.

(ii) Distance Between Parallel Lines: Let the two parallel lines be

$$ax + by + c_1 = 0 \text{ and } ax + by + c_2 = 0.$$

To find the distance between these two parallel lines, we proceed as follows.

(a) Find a point on any of the lines. For this put $x = 0$ and find y or put $y = 0$ and find x. Then the disance between the lines is equal to the length of perpendicular from this point on one line to the other line; or

(b) Let P(*h, k*) be a point on one line, say $ax + by + c_1 = 0$, $\therefore ah + bk = -c_1$.

Then distance between lines

= Length of perpendicular from P(*h, k*) to the oher line $ax + by + c_2 = 0$

$$= \left|\frac{ah + bk + c_2}{\sqrt{(a^2 + b^2)}}\right| = \left|\frac{c_2 - c_1}{\sqrt{(a^2 + b^2)}}\right|$$

(c) Find the distance of each line from the origin. If these distances are p_1 and p_2, then

$$p_1 = \frac{c_1}{\sqrt{(a^2 + b^2)}} \text{ and } p_2 = \frac{c_2}{\sqrt{(a^2 + b^2)}}$$ and

retain their signs.

Then the perpendicular distance between lines

$$= |p_2 - p_1| = \left|\frac{c_2 - c_1}{\sqrt{(a^2 + b^2)}}\right|.$$

20. Equation of the Bisectors of the Angles Between Two Lines: Let the two given lines be $a_1x + b_1y + c_1 = 0$ and $a_2x + b_2y + c_2 = 0$. Then the equations of the bisectors of the angles between two lines are

$$\frac{a_1x + b_1y + c_1}{\sqrt{(a_1^2 + b_1^2)}} = \pm \frac{a_2x + b_2y + c_2}{\sqrt{(a_1^2 + b_1^2)}} \quad .... (1)$$

Remember that, every point of the bisectors of angles is equidistant from the given lines.

21. Position of two Points with Respect to a Line: The two points $P(x_1, y_1)$ and $Q(x_2, y_2)$ lie on the same or on the opposite sides of the straight line $ax + by +$

$c = 0$ according as the values of $ax_1 + by_1 + c$ and $ax_2 + by_2 + c$ are of the same sign or of opposite signs. The straight line $ax + by + c = 0$ divides the xy plane into two portions. The (x_1, y_1) and the origin lie in the same or opposite portions of the xy plane divided by the line $ax + by + c = 0$ according as the values of $ax_1 + by_1 + c$ and c are of the same or opposite signs.

CIRCLE

22. Circle: A circle is the locus of a point which moves in a plane in such a manner that its distance from a fixed point in the plane always remains constant. The fixed point is called the centre and the constant distance is called the radius of the circle.

23. Circle with Centre at the Point (h, k) and Radius a: The equation of the circle is

$(x - h)^2 + (y - k)^2$.

Particular Case: The equation of a circle with centre at the origin and radius a is $x^2 + y^2 = a^2$(This is the equation of a circle in ***STANDARD FORM***).

24. Circle with Centre at the Point (h, k) and which Touches the Axis of x: If the circle touches the axis of x, then its radius is equal to the y-coordinate of the centre.

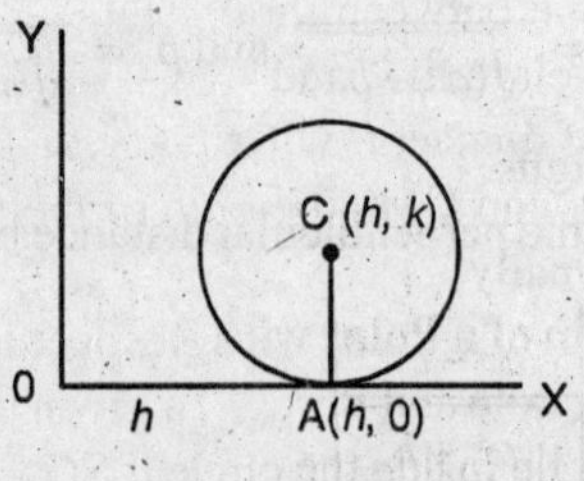

∴ Equation of the circle is $(x - h)^2 + (y - k)^2 = k^2$

or $x^2 + y^2 - 2hx - 2ky + h^2 = 0$ .... *(i)*

This circle meets the x-axis, at the points where $y = 0$.

∴ Putting $y = 0$ in *(i)*, we get $x^2 - 2hx + h^2 = 0$ or $(x - h)^2 = 0$

which gives two identical values of x (= h).

Thus the circle touches the x-axis at the point $(h, 0)$.

Important to Remember: If a circle touches the x-axis at the point $(h, 0)$, then putting $y = 0$, then putting $y = 0$, the equation of the circle will reduce to the form $(x - h)^2 = 0$.

25. Circle with Centre at the Point (h, k) and which Touches the Axis of y: If the circle touches the axis of y, then its radius is equal to the x-coordinate of the centre.

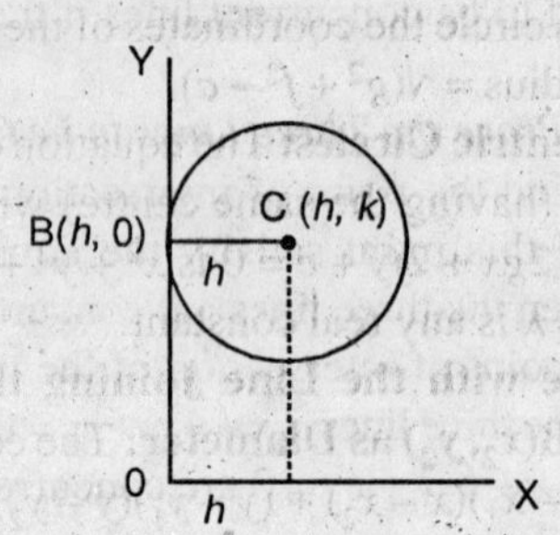

∴ Equation of the circle is given by $(x - h)^2 + (y - k)^2 = h^2$

or $x^2 + y^2 - 2hx - 2ky + k^2 = 0$ .... *(i)*

This circle meets the y-axis at the point where $x = 0$.

∵ Putting $x = 0$ in *(i)* we get $y^2 - 2ky + k^2 = 0$ or $(y - r)^2 = 0$

which gives two identical values of y (= k).

Thus the circle touches the y-axis at the point $(0, k)$.

Important: If a circle touches the y-axis at the point $(0, k)$, then putting $x = 0$, the equation of the circle will reduce to the form $(y - k)^2 = 0$.

26. Circle which Touches both the Coordinate Axes: Let a be the radius of the circle. Since the centre of the circle may be in any of the four quadrants,

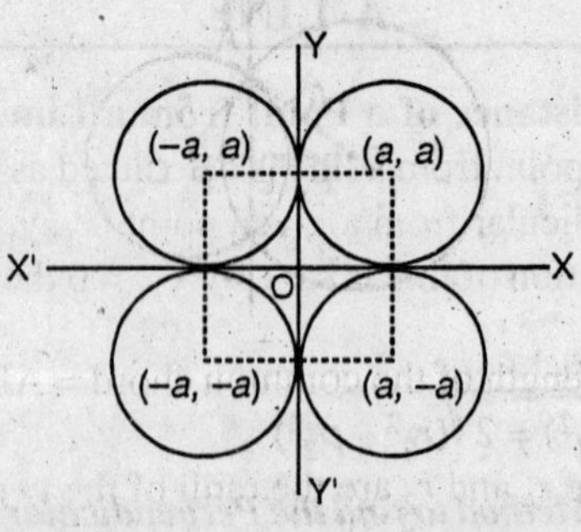

therefore, it will be any one of the four points $(\pm a, \pm a)$. Thus there are four circles of radius a touching both the coordinate axes, and their equations are $(x \pm a)^2 + (y \pm a)^2 = a^2$ or $x^2 + y^2 \pm 2ax \pm 2ay + a^2 = 0$.

27. General Equation of a Circle: The general equation of a circle is

$x^2 + y^2 + 2gx + 2fy + c = 0$, where g, f and c are constants.

For this circle the coordinates of the centre are $(-g, -f)$ and radius $= \sqrt{(g^2 + f^2 - c)}$.

28. Concentric Circles: The equation of any circle concentric (having the same centre) with the circle $x^2 + y^2 + 2gx + 2fy + c = 0$ is $x^2 + y^2 + 2gx + 2fy + \lambda = 0$, where λ is any real constant.

29. Circle with the Line Joining the Points $A(x_1, y_1)$ and $B(x_2, y_2)$ as Diameter: The equation of the circle is $(x - x_1)(x - x_2) + (y - y_1)(y - y_2) = 0$.

30. Parametric Equations of a Circle:

(a) Parametric equations of a circle $x^2 + y^2 = a^2$ are $x = a \cos\theta$ and $y = a \sin\theta$.

(b) The parametric equations of a circle $(x - h)^2 + (y - k)^2 = a^2$ are $x = h + a \cos\theta$ and $y = k + a \sin\theta$ where θ is a parameter.

31. Condition for a Given Line to Touch a Circle: If a line touches a circle, then it will intersect the circle in two coincident points. In this case the length of perpendicular from the centre of the circle on the line will be equal to the radius of the circle.

32. Equation of the Common Chord of Two Circles:

Let $S_1 = 0$ and $S_2 = 0$ be two circle with the coefficients of x^2 and y^2 equal to unity. Then the equation of common chord of these two circles is $S_1 - S_2 = 0$.

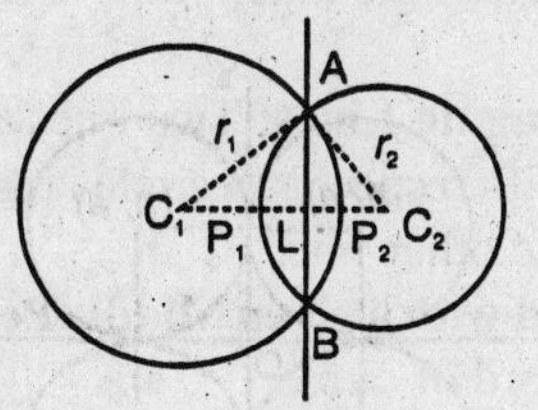

The length of the common chord = AB = 2AL $= 2\sqrt{(r_1^2 - p_1^2)} = 2\sqrt{(r_2^2 - p_2^2)}$

where r_1 and r_2 are the radii of the two circles and

$p_1 = C_1L$ = length of |– from centre C_1 on the common chord AB

$p_2 = C_2L$ = length of |– from centre C_2 on the common chord AB.

The equation of a circle through the points of intersection of a circle S = 0 and a line P = 0, is $S + \lambda P = 0$, where λ is any real number. The equation of a circle through the points of intersection of two circles $S_1 = 0$ and $S_2 = 0$ is $S_1 + \lambda S_2 = 0$ $(\lambda \neq -1)$ where λ is a real number.

33. Condition for the two Circles to Touch:

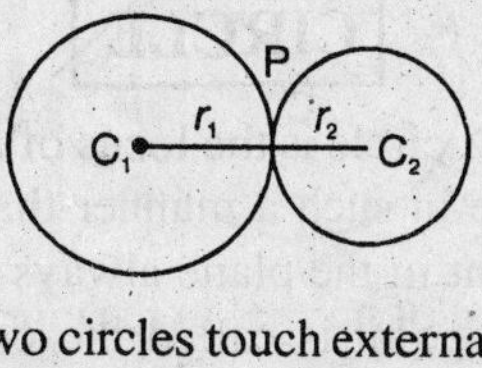

(a) If the two circles touch externally at a point, then the distance between their centres C_1 and C_2 = sum of their radii r_1 and r_2, *i.e.*, $C_1C_2 = r_1 + r_2$ and the point of contact P will divide the line joining their centres C_1 and C_2 in the ratio of their radii, *i.e.*, $r_1 : r_2$, internally.

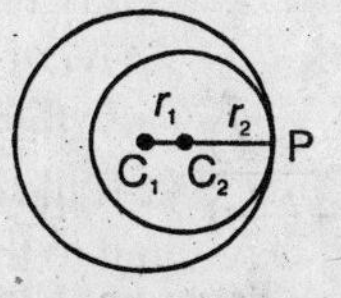

(b) If two circles touch internally at a point, then the distance between their centres C_1 and C_2 = difference of their radii r_1 and r_2, *i.e.*, $C_1C_2 = |r_1 - r_2|$, and the point of contact *P* will divide the line joining their centres C_1 and C_2 in the ratio of their radii, *i.e.*, r_1 and r_2, externally.

34. Position of a Point with Respect to a Circle: Let S = 0 be a circle and $P(x_1, y_1)$ a given point. Then the point P will lie inside the circle if $S(x_1, y_1) < 0$; on the circle if $S(x_1, y_1) = 0$; outside the circle if $S(x_1, y_1) > 0$.

35. Equations of Tangent:

(a) Equation of the tangent of the circle $x^2 + y^2 = a^2$ at the point (x_1, y_1) on it is $xx_1 + yy_1 + a_2$.

(b) Equation of the tangent to the circle $x^2 + y^2 + 2gx + 2fy + c = 0$ at the point (x_1, y_1) on it is $xx_1 + yy_1 + g(x + x_1) + f(y + y_1) + c = 0$

Methods to Write the Equation of the Tangent: To obtain the equation of the tangent to the circle at the point (x_1, y_1) on it, replace x^2 by xx_1, y^2 by yy_1, x by $\frac{1}{2}(x + x_1)$ and y by $\frac{1}{2}(y + y_1)$ in the equation of the circle.

36. Normal: The normal to circle at the point (x_1, y_1) is the line perpendicular to the tangent to the circle at the point (x_1, y_1) and passing through this point. Obviously, the normal to a circle passes through its centre.

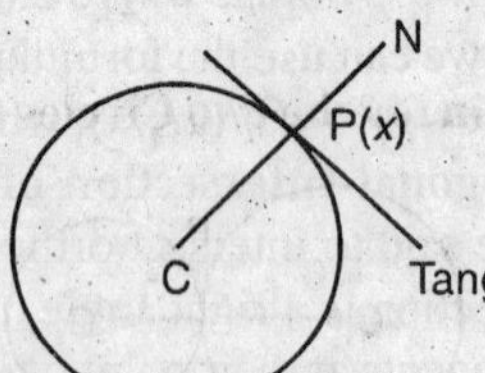

∴ Equation of normal to the circle $x^2 + y^2 = a^2$ at the point (x_1, y_1) on it is

$$y - 0 = \frac{y_1 - 0}{x_1 - 0}(x - 0), \text{ i.e., } \frac{x}{x_1} = \frac{y}{y_1}$$

Also the equation of normal to the circle $x^2 + y^2 + 2gx + 2fy + c = 0$ at the point (x_1, y_1) on it is

$$y - y_1 = \frac{y_1 - (-f)}{x_1 - (-g)}(x - x_1) \text{ i.e., } \frac{x - x_1}{x_1 + g} = \frac{y - y_1}{y_1 + f}$$

37. Tangent in Terms of Slope m: The straight line $y = mx + c$ touches the circle $x^2 + y^2 = a^2$ if $c^2 = a^2(1 + m^2)$, thus the equation of tangent to the circle $x^2 + y^2 = a^2$ in terms of m is $y = mx \pm a\sqrt{(1 + m^2)}$.

38. Chord of Contact: Let $P(x_1, y_1)$ be a point outside the circle and A and B the points of contact of the two tangents drawn to the circle from the point $P(x_1, y_1)$. Then the line AB is called the chord of contact of the tangents drawn from the point P. We also

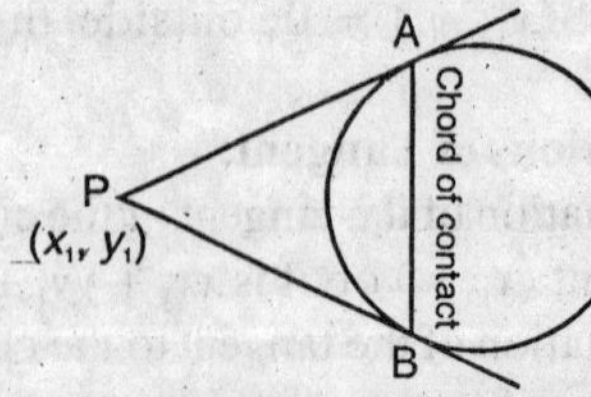

say that AB is the chord of contact of the point P. The equation of the chord of contact of the point $P(x_1, y_1)$ for the circle $x^2 + y^2 = a^2$ is $xx_1 + yy_1 = a^2$ and that for the circle $-x^2 + y^2 + 2gx + 2fy + c = 0$ is $xx_1 + yy_1 + g(x + x_1) + f(y + y_1) + c = 0$.

39. Polar: If P is fixed point and the chords of the circle are drawn through this point, then the locus of the points of intersection of the tangents drawn at the extremities of these chords is called the pole of

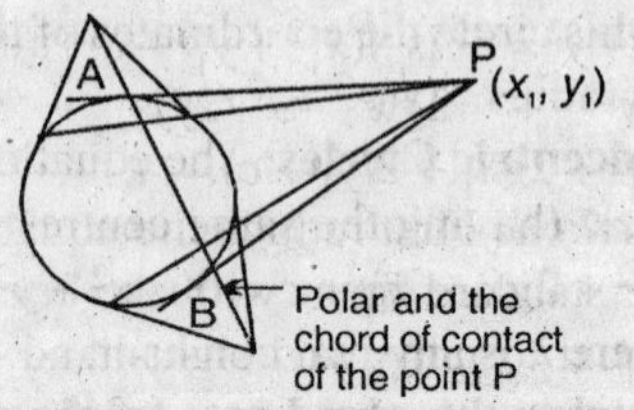

this polar. The equation of the polar of the point $P(x_1, y_1)$ with respect to (w.r.t.) the circle, $x^2 + y^2 = a^2$ is $xx_1 + yy_1 = a_2$; and that w.r.t. to the circle $x^2 + y^2 + 2gx + 2fy + c = 0$ is $xx_1 + yy_1 + g(x + x_1) + f(y + y_1) + c = 0$.

40. To Find the Pole of the Line $lx + my + n = 0$ w.r.t. the Circle $x^2 + y^2 = a^2$:

Let $P(x_1, y_1)$ be the pole of the line

$lx + my + n = 0$ .... (1)

w.r.t. the circle $x^2 + y^2 = a^2$.

Then the equation of the polar of point $P(x_1, y_1)$ w.r.t. this circle is $xx_1 + yy_1 - a^2 = 0$ .... (2)

Obviously, (1) and (2) represent the same line and should be identical.

∴ Comparing (1) and (2), we have

$l/x_1 = m/y_1 = n/(-a^2)$

∴ $x_1 = -a^2l/n$ and $y_1 = -a^2m/n$

Hence the pole of the line is $(-a^2l/n, -a^2m/n)$.

41. Conjugate Points: Two points are called the conjugate points with respect to a circle if each point lies on the polar of the other point with respect to the same circle.

42. Conjugate Lines: Two lines are called conjugate lines with respect to a circle if the pole of each line lies on the other line.

43. Chord with a given Middle Point: The equation of the chord of circle

$S \equiv x^2 + y^2 + 2gx + 2fy + c = 0$ with $P(x_1, y_1)$ as the middle point is $T = S_1$

where $T = xx_1 + yy_1 + g(x + x_1) + f(y + y_1) + c$ which is the expression on the L.H.S. of the equation of tangent to the circle $S = 0$, at the point (x_1, y_1) on it; and $S = x_1{}^2 + y_1{}^2 + 2gx_1 + 2fy_1 + c$, which is the expression obtained by substituting x_1, y_1 for x and y in the L.H.S. of the equation of the circle $S = 0$.

44. Length of the Tangent from a Point: The length of the tangent from the point $P(x_1, y_1)$ to the circle

$x^2 + y^2 = a^2$ is $\sqrt{(x_1^2 + y_1^2 - a^2)}$ and for the circle $x^2 + y^2 + 2gx + 2fy + c = 0$ is $\sqrt{(x_1^2 + y_1^2 + 2gx_1 + 2fy_1 + c)}$.

Method: First reduce the equation of the circle to the standard form with the coefficients of x^2 and y^2 equal to unity and right-hand equal to zero, then substitute the coordinate of the given point in the equation of the circle. The square root of the L.H.S. Thus obtained is the length of the tangent from the given point.

45. Pair of Tangent: From any point outside the circle, two tangents can be drawn to a circle. The equation of the pair of tangent from the point $P(x_1, y_1)$ to the circle $S \equiv x^2 + y^2 + 2gx + 2fy + c = 0$ is $SS_1 = T^2$, where $T = xx_1 + yy_1 + g(x + x_1) + f(y + y_1) + c$ which is the expression on the L.H.S. of the equation of the tangent to the circle $S = 0$, at the point (x_1, y_1) on it; and $S_1 = x_1^2 + y_1^2 + 2gx_1 + 2fy_1 + c$

which is the expression obtained by substituting x_1, y_1 for x and y in the L.H.S. of the equation of the circle $S = 0$.

46. Angle of Intersection of two Circles: The angles of intersection of two circles is the angle between their tangents at their point of intersection which is equal to the angle between the normals to the two circles at their point of intersection.

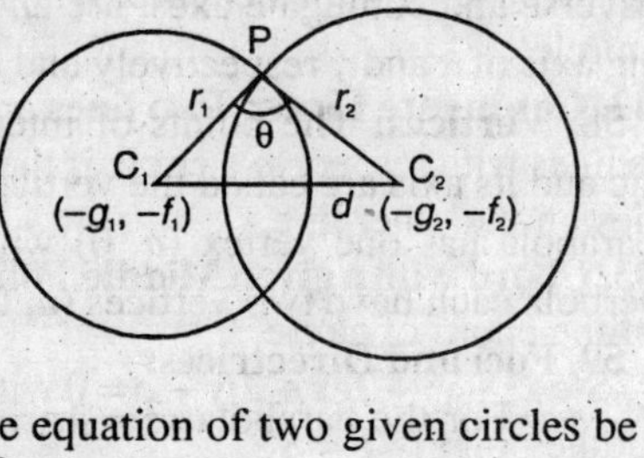

Let the equation of two given circles be

$x^2 + y^2 + 2g_1x + 2f_1y + c_1 = 0$ .... (1)

and $x^2 + y^2 + 2g_2x + 2f_2y + c_2 = 0$ .... (2)

Then for circle (1), the centre is $C_1(-g_1, -f_1)$ and radius $r_1 = \sqrt{(g_1^2 + f_1^2 - c_1)}$; and for circle (2), the centre is $C_2(-g_2, -f_2)$ and radius $r_2 = \sqrt{(g_2^2 + f_2^2 - c_2)}$.

If the two circles intersect at the point P then PC_1 and PC_2 are normals to the two circles at P.

$\therefore$ Angle of intersection of two circles

= Angle between the tangents at P

= Angle between the normals at P = θ, if θ is acute

or = $\pi - \theta$, if θ is obtuse where $\angle C_1PC_2 = \theta$.

To find θ, we can use the formula

$\cos\theta = (r_1^2 + r_2^2 - d^2)/(2r_1r_2)$, where $C_1C_2 = d$.

47. Orthogonal Intersection of Two Circles: Two circles are said to intersect orthogonally if their angle of intersection is a right angle, *i.e.*, if the angle between the tangents at their point of intersection is a right angle. Let the equations of the two circles be $x^2 + y^2 + 2g_1x + 2f_1y + c_1 = 0$ and $x^2 + y^2 + 2g_2x + 2f_2y + c_2 = 0$. The two circles will intersect orthogonally if $2g_1g_2 + 2f_1f_2 = c_1 + c_2$.

48. Radical Axis: The radical axis of two circles is the locus of a point which moves so that the lengthsof the tangents drawn from it to the two circles are equal. Let the equations of two circles be $S_1 \equiv x^2 + y^2 + 2g_1x + 2f_1y + c_1 = 0$ and $S_2 \equiv x^2 + y^2 + 2g_2x + 2f_2y + c_2 = 0$. Then the equation of the radical axis of the two circles is $2(g_1 - g_2)x + 2(f_1 - f_2)y + c_1 - c_2 = 0$ or $S_1 - S_2 = 0$

If the two given circles intersect, then $S_1 - S_2 = 0$ is the equation of their common chord. In case the two circles touch, then the common chord $S_1 - S_2 = 0$ becomes the common tangent at the point of contact. Hence if the two circles intersect, their radical axis is their common chord and if the two circles touch, their radical axis is the common tangent at their point of contact.

49. Radical Centre: The point, at which the radical axes of three circles taken in pairs meet, is called their radical centre.. Obviously the lengths tangents of drawn from the radical centre to the corresponding circles are equal.

50. Coaxal Family of Circle: A family of circles is called a coaxal family of circles if every pair of circles of this family has the same radical axis.

51. Circles Coaxal with Two given Circles: Let $S_1 = 0$ and $S_2 = 0$ be two circles. Then the equation of the family of circles coaxal with these two circles is

$S_1 + \lambda S_2 = 0$ or $S_1 + \mu(S_1 - S_2) = 0$, where λ, μ are parameters.

52. Limiting Points: The point circles of a coaxal system are called the limiting points. Thus the centre of the circle of coaxal system when its radius is equal to zero is the limiting point of the system.

53. Common Tangents to two Circles:

(a) Direct common tangents: The direct common tangents to the two circles meet at a point (say P) which lies on the line joining the centres C_1 and C_2 of the two circles and divide C_1C_2 externally in the ratio of their radii say (r_1 and r_2).

Method to find direct common tangents: First find the coordinates of centres C_1, C_2 and radii r_1, r_2 of two given circles. Then find the coordinates of the point P dividing C_1C_2 in the ratio of $r_1 : r_2$ externally. Then to find the equation of two direct common tangents separately, write the equation of any line through the point P(*h*, *k*),

i.e., $y - k = m(x - h)$ ... (1)

If this line (1) is tangent to the two given circles, then using the fact that the length of $\perp$ on (1) from the centre C_1 of one circles is equal to its radius r_1, find two values of *m*.

Substituting these values of *m* in (1) the equations of two direct common tangents are obtained.

The combined equation of the direct common tangent is obtained by the formula $SS_1 = T^2$, where $S = 0$ is any one of the two given circles and T_1, S_1 have their usual meaning.

(b) Transverse common tangents: The transverse common tangents to the two circles intersect at a point (say Q) which lies on the line joining their centres C_1 and C_2 of the two circles and divide C_1C_2 internally in the ratio of their radii r_1 and r_2.

Method to find transverse common tangents: Find the coordinates of point Q dividing the line joining the centres C_1 and C_2 of the two circles in the ratio of their radii r_1 and r_2 internally. Then proceed as in the case of direct common tangents.

CONIC SECTIONS

4.1.54. Conic Sections: The locus of a point which moves such that its distance from a fixed point bears a constant ratio to its distance from a fixed straight line is called a conic section. The fixed point is called the focus and the fixed line is called the directrix and the constant ratio (say *e*) is called the eccentricity of the conic section. The conic section is called

(a) parabola, if $e = 1$

(b) ellipse, if $e < 1$

(c) hyperbola, if $e > 1$

55. General Equation: The second degree linear equation.

$ax^2 + 2hxy + by^2 + 2gx + 2fy + c = 0$, represents a conic section, which is

(a) parabola, if $h^2 - ab = 0$ and $\Delta \neq 0$

(b) ellipse, if $h^2 - ab < 0$ and $\Delta \neq 0$

(c) hyperbola, if $h^2 - ab > 0$ and $\Delta \neq 0$

56. The Standard Equation: The standard equation of

(a) parabola is $y^2 = 4ax$

(b) ellipse is $x^2/a^2 + y^2/b^2 = 1$

(c) hyperbola is $x^2/a^2 - y^2/b^2 = 1$

57. Axes of a Conic Section: The line (or lines) about which the given conic is symmetrical is (or are) called the axis (or axes) of the conic.

(a) A parabola has one axis.

(b) An ellipse have two axes, called the major and minor axes.

For ellipse $x^2/a^2 + y^2/b^2 = 1$ the length of axes are $2a$ and $2b$ which are major and minor axes if $a > b$ and lie along *x*-axis and *y*-axis respectively and $b^2 = a^2(1 - e^2)$.

(c) A hyperbola have two axes called transverse and conjugate axes.

For hyperbola $x^2/a^2 - y^2/b^2 = 1$, the length of transverse and conjugate axes, are $2a$ and $2b$ and lie along axis of *x* and *y* respectively and $b^2 = a^2(e^2 - 1)$.

58. Vertices: The points of intersection of the conic and its axis are called the vertices of the conic. A parabola has one vertex (*a*, 0) while ellipse and hyperbola each have two vertices (*a*, 0) and (–*a*, 0).

59. Foci and Directrices:

(a) For the parabola $y^2 = 4ax$, focus is (*a*, 0) and the directrix is $x = -a$.

(b) For the ellipse $x^2/b^2 + y^2/b^2 = 1$, the foci are (*ae*, 0) and (–*ae*, 0) and the corresponding directrices are $x = a/e$ and $x = -a/e$ respectively.

(c) For the hyperbola $x^2/a^2 - y^2/b^2 = 1$, the foci are(*ae*, 0) and (–*ae*, 0) and the corresponding directrices are $x = a/e$ and $x = -a/e$ respectively.

60. Focal Property:

(*a*) If P(*x*, *y*) is a point on the parabola $y^2 = 4ax$ and S(*a*, 0) is its focus then PS = *x* + *a*.

(*b*) If P is a point on the ellipse whose foci are S and S' and 2*a*, the length of its major axis, then PS + PS' = 2*a*.

(*c*) If P is a point on the hyperbola whose foci are S and S' and 2a the length of its transverse axis, then |PS – PS'| = 2*a*.

61. Focal Chord: Any chord through the focus of a conic in called its focal chord.

62. Latus Rectum: The cord (or chords) through the focus (or foci) and perpendicular to the major axis (or transverse axis) is called latus rectum. The length of L.R. of

(*a*) parabola is 4*a* (*b*) ellipse is $2b^2/a$

(*c*) hyperbola is $2b^2/a$

63. Tangents: The equation of tangent at the point(x_1, y_1) on the

(*a*) parabola is $yy_1 = 2a(x + x_1)$

(*b*) ellipse is $\frac{xx_1}{a^2} + \frac{yy_1}{b^2} = 1$

(*c*) hyperbola is $\frac{xx_1}{a^2} - \frac{yy_1}{b^2} = 1$

64. Condition for Tangency: The condition that the line *y* = *mx* + *c* is tangent to

(*a*) parabola is *c* = *a*/*m*

(*b*) ellipse is $c^2 = a^2m^2 + b^2$

(*c*) hyperbola is $c^2 = a^2m^2 - b^2$

65. Tangents in Terms of *m*: If *m* is the slope of the tangent, then its equation for

(*a*) parabola is $y = mx + a/m$

(*b*) ellipse are $y = mx \pm \sqrt{(a^2m^2 + b^2)}$

(*c*) hyperbola are $y = mx \pm \sqrt{(a^2m^2 - b^2)}$

66. Equation of Normal: Equation of normal of the parabola $y^2 = 4ax$ is $y = mx - 2am - am^3$

where *m* is the slope of the normal and it is the normal at the point, $(am^2, -2am)$ on the parabola.

67. Chord of Contact: The line joining the points of contact of the tangents from an external points to a conic is called the chord of contact of the point. The equation of chord of contact of the point (x_1, y_1) for

(*a*) parabola is $yy_1 = 2a\,(x + x_1)$

(*b*) ellipse is $\frac{xx_1}{a^2} + \frac{yy_1}{b^2} = 1$

(*c*) hyperbola is $\frac{xx_1}{a^2} - \frac{yy_1}{b^2} = 1$

68. Polar of a Point: The polar of a point is the locus of the points of intersection of the tangents drawn to the conic at the ends of chords passing through the given point. The point is called the pole of the polar. The equation of the polar of the point (x_1, y_1) for

(*a*) parabola is $yy_1 = 2a\,(x + x_1)$

(*b*) ellipse is $\frac{xx_1}{a^2} + \frac{yy_1}{b^2} = 1$

(*c*) hyperbola is $\frac{xx_1}{a^2} - \frac{yy_1}{b^2} = 1$

69. Tangents Through a Point: The equation of the pair of tangents drawn from a point (x_1, y_1) to the conic S = 0 is $SS_1 = T^2$, where

(*a*) for parabola

$y^2 = 4ax$, $S = y^2 - 4ax$, $S_1 = y_1{}^2 - 4ax_1$,

$T = yy_1 - 2a\,(x + x_1)$

(*b*) for ellipse $x^2/a^2 + y^2/b^2 = 1$,

$S = x^2/a^2 + y^2/b^2 - 1$, $S_1 = x_1{}^2/a^2 + y_1{}^2/b^2 - 1$,

$T = xx_1/a^2 + yy_1/b^2 - 1$

(*c*) for hyperbola $x^2/a^2 - y^2/b^2 = 1$,

$S = x^2/a^2 - y^2/b^2 - 1$, $S_1 = x_1{}^2/a^2 - y_1{}^2/b^2 - 1$,

$T = xx_1/a^2 + yy_1/b^2 - 1$.

70. Chord with a given Mid-point: The equation of a chord with $P(x_1, y_1)$ as its middle point is given by

$$T = S_1$$

71. Parametric Equations of Conics:

(*a*) The coordinates of a point on the parabola $y^2 = 4ax$, in terms of parameter *t* are taken as $(at^2, 2at)$. The point is denoted by *t*. Thus parametric equation of parabola are $x = at^2$, $y = 2at$.

(*b*) The coordinates of any point on the ellipse $x^2/a^2 + y^2/b^2 = 1$ are taken as $(a \cos \phi, b \sin \phi)$; ϕ is called the eccentric angle of the point and the point is denoted by ϕ. Thus parametric equations of ellipse are $x = a \cos \phi$, $y = b \sin \phi$.

(c) The coordinates of any point on the hyperbola $x^2/a^2 - y^2/b^2 = 1$ are taken as ($a \sec \phi$, $b \tan \phi$). The point is denoted by ϕ. Thus parametric equations of hyperbola are $x = a \sec \phi$, $y = b \tan \phi$.

72. Equation of Tangent: The equation of tangent at the point

(a) t on $y^2 = 4ax$ is $yt = x + at^2$

(b) ϕ on $x^2/a^2 + y^2/b^2 = 1$ is

$(x/a) \cos \phi + (y/b) \sin \phi = 1$

(c) ϕ on $x^2/a^2 - y^2/b^2 = 1$ is

$(x/a) \sec \phi + (y/b) \tan \phi = 1$.

73. Equation of Normal: The equation of normal at the point

(a) t on $y^2 = 4ax$ is $y = -tx + 2at + at^3$

(b) ϕ on $x^2/a^2 + y^2/b^2 = 1$ is

$ax \sec \phi - by \operatorname{cosec} \phi = a^2 - b^2$

(c) ϕ on $x^2/a^2 - y^2/b^2 = 1$ is

$ax \cos \phi + by \cot \phi = a^2 + b^2$.

74. Director Circle: The locus of the point of intersection of two perpendicular tangents to an ellipse (or hyperbola) is called its director circle. The equation of director circle of

(a) ellipse $x^2/a^2 + y^2/b^2 = 1$ is $x^2 + y^2 = a^2 + b^2$

(b) hyperbola $x^2/a^2 - y^2/b^2 = 1$ is

$x^2 + y^2 = a^2 - b^2$

75. Auxillary Circle: The circle described on the major axis of the ellipse or transverse axis of the hyperbola as diameter is called its auxillary circle. Its equation is $x^2 + y^2 = a^2$.

76. Focal Chord: If PQ is a focal chord of parabola $y^2 = 4ax$ and coordinates of P are $(at^2, 2at)$ then coordinates of Q will be $(a/t^2, -2a/t)$.

77. Point and the Conic: Let S = 0 be a conic section. Then the point $P(x_1, y_1)$ lie

(a) inside the conic if $S(x_1, y_1) < 0$

(b) on the conic if $S(x_1, y_1) = 0$

(c) outside the conic if $S(x_1, y_1) > 0$

78. Conjugate Diameters: Two diameters of an ellipse are said to be conjugate of each bisects the chords parallel to the other.

(a) If $y = m_1x$ and $y = m_2x$ are conjugate diameters of an ellipse $x^2/a^2 + y^2/b^2 = 1$, then

$m_1m_2 = -b^2/a^2$.

(b) If θ and ϕ are the eccentric angles of the points P and Q of the two semi-conjugate diameters CP and CQ of an ellipse, then $\theta \sim \phi = \pi/2$.

79. Asymptotes:

(a) The asymptotes of the hyperbola $x^2/a^2 - y^2/b^2 = 1$ are $y = \pm (b/a)x$.

(b) The equation of the asymptotes differ from that of hyperbola by a constant.

80. Conjugate Hyperbola: The hyperbola whose transverse and conjugate axes are respectively the conjugate and transverse axes of the hyperbola is called the conjugate hyperbola of the given hyperbola. Thus if $x^2/a^2 - y^2/b^2 = 1$ be the given hyperbola, then $y^2/b^2 - x^2/a^2 = 1$ is its conjugate hyperbola. If e and e' are the eccentricities of the two hyperbolas, then $1/e^2 + 1/e'^2 = 1$.

EXERCISE

1. Vertices of a quadrilateral ABCD are A(0, 0), B(3, 4), C(7, 7) and D(4, 3). Then quadrilateral ABCD is

(a) rhombus (b) rectangle
(c) square (d) None of these

2. The triangle joining the points (2, 7), (4, –1), (–2, 6) is

(a) equilateral (b) right angled
(c) isosceles (d) None of these

3. The points (1, 1), (–1, –1) and $(-\sqrt{3}, \sqrt{3})$ are the angular points of a triangle, then the triangle is

(a) right angled (b) isosceles
(c) equilateral (d) None of these

4. The line segment joining the points (–3, –4) and (1, –2) is divided by y-axis in the ratio

(a) 1 : 3 (b) 2 : 3
(c) 3: 1 (d) 3 : 2

5. The straight lines $x + y - 4 = 0$, $3x + y - 4 = 0$, $x + 3y - 4 = 0$ form a triangle which is

(a) isosceles (b) right angled
(c) equilateral (d) None of these

6. If P(1, 2), Q(4, 6), R(5, 7) and S(a, b) are the vertices of a parallelogram PQRS, then

(a) $a = 2, b = 4$ (b) $a = 3, b = 4$
(c) $a = 2, b = 3$ (d) $a = 3, b = 5$

7. The area of the triangle with vertices at the points $(a, b + c)$, $(b, c + a)$, $(c, a + b)$ is

(a) 0 (b) $a + b + c$
(c) $ab + bc + ca$ (d) None of these

8. If A and B are the points (–3, 4) and (2, 1). Then the coordinates of the point C on AB produced such that AC = 2BC are
(a) (2, 4) (b) (3, 7)
(c) (7, –2) (d) (–1/2, 5/2)

9. The extremities of a diagonal of a parallelogram are the points (3, –4) and (–6, 5). If third vertex is (–2, 1) then fourth vertex is
(a) (1, 0) (b) (–1, 0)
(c) (1, 1) (d) None of these

10. The diagonals of a parallelogram PQRS are along the lines $x + 3y = 4$ and $6x - 2y = 7$. Then PQRS must be a
(a) rectangle (b) square
(c) cyclic qudrilateral (d) rhombus

11. If (0, 1), (1, 1) and (1, 0) be the middle points of the sides of a triangle, its incentre is
(a) $(2+\sqrt{2}, 2+\sqrt{2})$ (b) $[2+\sqrt{2}, -(2+\sqrt{2})]$
(c) $(2-\sqrt{2}, 2, -\sqrt{2})$ (d) $[2-\sqrt{2}, -(2-\sqrt{2})]$

12. The coordinates of the points A, B and C are resp. (6, 3)(–3, 5) and (4, –2) and the coordinates of P are (x, y), then Δ PBC/Δ ABC =
(a) $\dfrac{x+y-2}{7}$ (b) $\left|\dfrac{x+y-2}{7}\right|$
(c) $\left|\dfrac{x-y+2}{7}\right|$ (d) None of these

13. If the lines
$3y + 4x = 1$, $y = x + 5$ and $5y + bx = 3$, are concurrent, then the value of b is
(a) 1 (b) 3 (c) 6 (d) 0

14. Given four lines with equations
$x + 2y - 3 = 0$, $3x + 4y - 7 = 0$,
$2x + 3y - 4 = 0$, $4x + 5y - 6 = 0$
then they are
(a) all concurrent
(b) the sides of a quadrilateral
(c) intersect each other
(d) None of these

15. The point $(t^2 + 2t + 5, 2t^2 + t - 2)$ lies on the line $x + y = 2$, for
(a) all real values of t
(b) some real values of t
(c) $t = (-2 \pm \sqrt{3})/6$
(d) None of these

16. If the sum of the distances of a point from two perpendicular lines in a plane is 1, then its locus is
(a) square
(b) circle
(c) straight line
(d) two intersecting lines

17. The locus of the centre of a circle of radius 3 which rolls on the outside of the circle
$x^2 + y^2 + 3x - 6y - 9 = 0$ is
(a) $x^2 + y^2 + 3x - 6y + 5 = 0$
(b) $x^2 + y^2 + 3x - 6y - 31 = 0$
(c) $x^2 + y^2 + 3x - 6y + 29/4 = 0$
(d) None of these

18. The equation of the circle which has two normals $(x - 1)(y - 2) = 0$ and a tangent $3x + 4y = 6$ is
(a) $x^2 + y^2 - 2x - 4y + 4 = 0$
(b) $x^2 + y^2 - 2x - 4y + 5 = 0$
(c) $x^2 + y^2 = 5$
(d) $(x - 3)^2 + (y - 4)^2 = 5$

19. The circles
$x^2 + y^2 - 10x + 16 = 0$ and $x^2 + y^2 = r^2$ intersect each other in two distinct points if
(a) $r < 2$ (b) $r > 8$
(c) $2 < r < 8$ (d) $2 \le r \le 8$

20. A circle is given by $x^2 + y^2 - 6x + 8y - 11 = 0$ and there are two points (0, 0) and (1, 8). These points lie
(a) one outside and one inside the circle
(b) both inside the circle
(c) both outside the circle
(d) one on and the other inside the circle

21. Equation of the circle which passes through the origin and cuts orthogonally each of the circles $x^2+y^2-8y+12=0$ and $x^2+y^2-4x-6y-3=0$ is
(a) $x^2 + y^2 + 6x + 3y = 0$
(b) $x^2 + y^2 + 3x - 6y = 0$
(c) $x^2 + y^2 + 6x - 3y = 0$
(d) $x^2 + y^2 - 3x + 6y = 0$

22. The curve represented by
$x = 3(\cos t + \sin t), y = 4(\cos t - \sin t)$ is
(a) ellipse (b) parabola
(c) hyperbola (d) circle

23. The curve described parametrically by
$x = t^2 + t + 1, y = t^2 - t + 1$ represents
(a) a pair of straight lines (b) an ellipse
(c) a parabola (d) a hyperbola

24. If (2, 0) is the vertex and y-axis the directrix of a parabola, then its focus is
(a) (2, 0) (b) (–2, 0)
(c) (4, 0) (d) (–4, 0)

25. A variable circle is described to pass through $(a, 0)$ and touch the line $x + y = 0$. Let S = 0 represent the locus of the centre of the circle. Then S = 0 represents
(a) a parabola
(b) an ellipse
(c) a hyperbola
(d) pair of parallel straight lines

26. The latus rectum of the ellipse $5x^2 + 9y^2 = 45$ is
(a) 5/3 (b) 10/3 (c) $2\sqrt{5}/3$ (d) $\sqrt{5}/3$

27. The foci of the ellipse $x^2/16 + y^2/b^2 = 1$ and the hyperbola $x^2/144 - y^2/81 = 1/25$ coincide, then the value of b^2 is
(a) 1 (b) 5 (c) 7 (d) 9

28. The equation of hyperbola whose focus is the point (2, 1), the directrix is the straight line $2x + 3y - 1 = 0$ and whose eccentricity is $\sqrt{2}$, is
(a) $5x^2 - 5y^2 + 24xy - 44x - 14y + 63 = 0$
(b) $5x^2 - 5y^2 - 24xy - 44x - 14y + 63 = 0$
(c) $5x^2 + 5y^2 + 24xy - 44x - 14y + 63 = 0$
(d) $5x^2 + 5y^2 + 24xy + 44x - 14y + 63 = 0$

29. The centre of the hyperbola $2x^2 + y^2 - 3xy - 5x + 4y + 6 = 0$ is the point
(a) (1, 2) (b) (2, 1) (c) (1, 1) (d) (2, 2)

30. The centre of the hyperbola $9x^2 - 16y^2 - 18x - 64y - 199 = 0$ is
(a) (1, 2) (b) (1, –2)
(c) (–1, 2) (d) None of these

31. The length of the latus rectum of an ellipse is 1/3 of the major axis. Its eccentricity is
(a) 2/3 (b) $\sqrt{(2/3)}$
(c) $5 \times 4 \times 3/7^3$ (d) $(3/4)^4$

32. The line $y = mx + 1$ is a tangent to the parabola $y^2 = 4x$, if
(a) $m = 1$ (b) $m = 2$ (c) $m = 4$ (d) $m = 3$

33. If a tangent to the parabola $y^2 = ax$ makes an angle 45° with x-axis, its point of contact will be
(a) $(a/2, a/4)$ (b) $(-a/2, a/4)$
(c) $(a/4, a/2)$ (d) $(-a/4, a/2)$

34. Equation of the normal to the parabola $y^2 = 4x$ which is parallel to the line $y = 2x - 5$ is
(a) $y = 2x$ (b) $y = 2x - 12$
(c) $y = 2x - 10$ (d) None of these

35. The equation of the tangent to the parabola $y^2 = 16x$, which is perpendicular to the line $y = 3x + 7$ is
(a) $y - 3x + 4 = 0$ (b) $3y - x + 36 = 0$
(c) $3y + x - 36 = 0$ (d) $3y + x + 36 = 0$

36. The equation of the tangent to the parabola $y^2 = 4x + 5$ which is parallel to the line $y = 2x + 7$ is
(a) $y = 2x + 3$ (b) $y = 2x + 4$
(c) $y = 2x$ (d) None of these

37. If the tangent on the point ($2 \sec \phi$, $3 \tan \phi$) of the hyperbola $x^2/4 - y^2/9 = 1$ is parallel to $3x - y + 4 = 0$, then the value of ϕ is
(a) 45° (b) 60° (c) 30° (d) 75°

38. The number of tangents to the parabola $y^2 = 8x$ through (2, 1) is
(a) 0 (b) 1 (c) 2 (d) 3

39. The equation of the tangents to the ellipse $9x^2 + 16y^2 = 144$ from the point (2, 3) are
(a) $y - 3 = 0, x + y = 5$
(b) $x - 3 = 0, x - y = 5$
(c) $z + y - 3 = 0, x - y + 5 = 0$
(d) None of these

40. The angle between the pair of tangents drawn to the ellipse $3x^2 + 2y^2 = 5$ from the point (1, 2) is
(a) $\tan^{-1}(12/5)$ (b) $\tan^{-1}(6/\sqrt{5})$
(c) $\tan^{-1}(12/\sqrt{5})$ (d) $\tan^{-1}(12/5)$

ANSWERS

1	2	3	4	5	6	7	8	9	10
(a)	(b)	(c)	(c)	(a)	(c)	(a)	(c)	(b)	(d)
11	**12**	**13**	**14**	**15**	**16**	**17**	**18**	**19**	**20**
(c)	(b)	(c)	(c)	(d)	(a)	(d)	(a)	(c)	(a)
21	**22**	**23**	**24**	**25**	**26**	**27**	**28**	**29**	**30**
(c)	(a)	(c)	(c)	(a)	(b)	(c)	(b)	(b)	(b)
31	**32**	**33**	**34**	**35**	**36**	**37**	**38**	**39**	**40**
(b)	(a)	(c)	(b)	(d)	(a)	(c)	(a)	(a)	(c)

SOME SELECTED EXPLANATORY ANSWERS

1. AB = BC = CD = DA = 5 but diagonals AC ≠ BD so it is a rhombus, not a square.
2. If the given points are A, B, C respectively, then AB = √(68), BC = √(85) and CA = √(17) The Δ is right-angled.
3. If the given point are A, B, C respectively, then AB = BC = CA = 2√2
   ∴The triangle is equilateral.
4. If y-axis divide the line segment in the ratio λ : 1 at P, then x coordinate of P
   $= = 0 \Rightarrow \lambda = 3$
   ∴ Required ratio is 3 : 1.
5. Solving for vertices of the Δ, we get A(0, 4), B(1, 1) and C(4, 0).
   Now AB = √(10) = BC. CA = 4√2. Hence the Δ is isosceles.
6. **Hint.** Use slope of PQ = slope of SR and slope of PS = slope of QR.
   Then solve.
7. Area = ½[{$a.(c + a) + b.(a + b) + c.(b + c)$}
   $- \{(b + c).b + (c + a).c + (a + b).a\}] = 0$
8. **Hint.** AC = 2BC where C is on AB produced ⇒ C divides AB externally in the ratio 2 : 1.
9. Let A(3, – 4) and C(–6, 5) be the ends of diagonal of parallelogram ABCD. Let B(– 2, 1) and D be (x, y). Then mid-points of diagonals AC and BD coincide. So
   and
   $\Rightarrow x = -1, y = 0.$
   ∴ Coordinates of D are (– 1, 0).
11. If A(x_1, y_1), B(x_2, y_2), C(x_3, y_3) be the vertices of the triangle and if (0, 1), (1, 1) and (1, 0) are the middle points of AB, BC and CA respectively, then
    $x_1 + x_2 = 0, x_2 + x_3 = 2, x_3 + x_1 = 2,$
    $y_1 + y_2 = 2, y_2 + y_3 = 2, y_3 + y_1 = 0,$
    So, A(0, 0), B(0, 2) and C(2, 0) are the vertices of the Δ ABC.
    Now a = BC = 2√2, b = CA = 2, c = AB = 2.
    ∴ The coordinates (α, β) of the in-centre are given by
    $$\alpha = \frac{ax_1 + bx_2 + cx_3}{a+b+c} = 2 - \sqrt{2},$$
    $$\beta = \frac{ay_1 + by_2 + cy_3}{a+b+c} = 2 - \sqrt{2},$$
    i.e., the in-centre is (2 – √2, 2 – √2).
12. $$\Delta\, PBC = \frac{1}{2}\begin{vmatrix} x & y & 1 \\ -3 & 5 & 1 \\ 4 & -2 & 1 \end{vmatrix}$$
    = ½|7x + 7y – 14|
    and Δ ABC = ½ |42 + 21 – 14| = 49/2
    ∴ Δ PBC/Δ ABC = |$x + y$ – 2|/7.
13. Substituting the coordinates of the point of intersection of first two lines, *i.e.*, (– 2, 3) in the third equation, we have 5.3 – 2b = 3 ⇒ b = 6.
14. The point of intersection of lines $x + 2y - 3 = 0$ and $2x + 3y - 4 = 0$ is (– 1, 2), which satisfy the equation $4x + 5y - 6 = 0$ but not the equation $3x + 4y - 7 = 0$.
    Thus all the four lines are not concurrent. Since three lines meet at a point, so the four points cannot form a quadrilateral.
15. The given point lie on the line
    $x + y = 2$ if $3t^2 + 3t + 1 = 0$.
    Here Δ = 9 – 12 < 0.
    ∴ The value of t is imaginary.
    Thus the given point cannot lie on the line.
16. Considering the two perpendicular lines as axes, sum of the distances of P(x, y) from these lines (axes) is $|x| + |y| = 1$. This gives four lines — $x + y = 1, x - y = 1, -x + y = 1, -x + y = 1, -x - y = 1$ which encloses a square.
17. For the given circle, the centre is (– 3/2, 3) and radius = √(9/4 + 9 + 9) = 9/2.
    Obviously the locus of the centre of the circle which rolls is also a circle having the same centre (– 3/2, 3) and radius = (9/2) + 3 = 15/2.
    Therefore the required locus is
    $(x + 3/2)^2 + (y - 3)^2 = (15/2)^2$
    or $x^2 + y^2 + 3x - 6y - 45 = 0$.

18. Two normals are $x - 1 = 0$ and $y - 2 = 0$.
Their point of intersection (1, 2) is the centre and radius of the circle = perpendicular from centre (1, 2) on tangent $3x + 4y = 6$

$$= \frac{3.1 + 4.2 - 6}{\sqrt{(9+16)}} = 1$$

∴ Equation of the circle is
$(x - 1)^2 + (y - 2)^2 = 1^2$
i.e., $x^2 + y^2 - 2x - 4y + 4 = 0$.

19. Centres of the given circles are $C_1(5, 0)$ and $C_2(0, 0)$ and their radii, $r_1 = 3$ and $r_2 = r$.
We know that the two circles touch externally if $C_1C_2 = r_1 + r_2$ and internally if $C_1C_2 = |r_1 - r_2|$.
Thus the two circles will cut at two distinct points if
$|r_1 - r_2| < C_1C_2 < r_1 + r_2$
or if $r - 3 < 5 < r + 3$
or if $r < 8$ and $r > 2$
or it $2 < r < 8$.

20. Equation of circle is
$S \equiv x^2 + y^2 - 6x + 8y - 11 = 0$
$S(0, 0) = -11 < 0$ so (0, 0) lies inside.
$S(1, 8) = 1 + 64 - 6 + 64 - 11 > 0$ so (1, 8) lies outside the circle.

21. Equation of the circle through the origin can be written as
$x^2 + y^2 + 2gx + 2fy = 0$ .... (1)
It cuts the two given circles orthogonally
so $2.0.g - 2.4.f = 12 + 0$
and $-4g - 6f = -3 + 0$.
Solving $g = 3, f = -3/2$.
The equation of circle is $x^2 + y^2 + 6x - 3y = 0$.

22. From the given relations, we have
$x^2/3^2 + y^2/4^2 = 2$
or $x^2/18 + y^2/32 = 1$, which is an ellipse.

23. $x + y = 2(t^2 + 1), x - y = 2t$.
Eliminating t, we get
$x + y = ½(x - y)^2 + 2$
or $x^2 - 2xy + y^2 - 2x - 2y + 4 = 0$
For which, $D \neq 0$ and $h^2 = ab$
Hence the given curve represent a parabola.

24. Distance between the vertex and the directrix (which is y-axis) = 2 = a (say).
∴ Distance of focus from the y-axis = $2a = 4$ ∴ Coordinates of the focus which is on x-axis are (4, 0).

25. Let P(h, k) be the centre of the circle.
Since it passes through (a, 0), its radius $= \sqrt{[(h - a)^2 + k^2]}$.
Circle touches the line $x + y = 0$, so

$$\frac{h + k}{\sqrt{2}} = \pm \sqrt{[(h - a)^2 + k^2]}.$$

Hence locus of centre P(h, k) is
$S \equiv x^2 + y^2 - 2xy - 4ax + 2a^2 = 0$.
Here $h^2 - ab = 0$ but
$abc + 2fgh - af^2 - bg^2 - ch^2 \neq 0$
So it represents a parabola, not pair of parallel straight lines.

26. The equation of the ellipse can be written as $x^2/9 + y^2/5 = 1$, ∴ $a^2 = 9, b^2 = 5$
∴ L.R. $= 2b^2/a = 10/3$.

27. For the given ellipse, $a^2 = 16, b^2 = b^2$
∴ $e^2 = 1 - b^2/a^2 \Rightarrow e = \sqrt{(16 - b^2)}/4$
Thus the foci of the ellipse are
$(\pm ae, 0)$, *i.e.*, $[\pm \sqrt{(16 - b^2)}, 0]$
The equation of the hyperbola can be written as

$$\frac{x^2}{(12/5)^2} - \frac{y^2}{(9/5)^2} = 1$$

∴ $a = 12/5$ and $b = 9/5$. The centre is (0, 0). ∴ $e^2 = 1 + b^2/a^2 \Rightarrow e = 5/4$.
Thus the foci of the hyperbola are
$(\pm ae, 0)$, *i.e.*, $(\pm 3, 0)$.
Since the foci of ellipse and hyperbola coincide,
∴ $\sqrt{(16 - b^2)} = 3 \Rightarrow b^2 = 7$.

28. If P(x, y) is any point on the hyperbola, then distance of P from (2, 1) = e.
Distance of P from directrix $2x + 3y - 1 = 0$
i.e., $\sqrt{[(x - 2)^2 + (y - 1)^2]} = \sqrt{2}.(2x + 3y - 1)/\sqrt{(4 + 9)}$.
or $13(x^2 + y^2 - 4x - 2y + 5) = 2(2x + 3y - 1)^2$
or $5x^2 - 5y^2 - 24xy - 44x - 14y + 63 = 0$, which is the equation of the hyperbola.

29. The equation of hyperbola is
$f \equiv 2x^2 + y^2 - 3xy - 5x + 4y + 6 = 0$.
The centre is given by

$$\frac{\partial f}{\partial x} = 4x - 3y - 5 = 0$$

and $\dfrac{\partial f}{\partial y} = 2y - 3x + 4 = 0$

Solving, the centre is (2, 1).

30. The equation of the hyperbola can be written as $(x-1)^2/4^2 - (y+2)^2/3^2 = 1$ whose centre is $(1, -2)$.

31. L.R. = (1/3) (Major axis)
$\Rightarrow 2b^2/a = 2a/3$
$\Rightarrow a^2 = 3b^2 = 3a^2(1-e^2) \Rightarrow e = \sqrt{(2/3)}$.

32. Equation of parabola is $y^2 = 4x$
$\therefore \quad a = 1$
The line $y = mx + 1$ will be a tangent to the parabola if
$c = a/m \Rightarrow 1 = 1/m \Rightarrow m = 1$.

33. Let point of contact be $P(x_1, y_1)$, then equation of tangent is
$yy_1 = \frac{1}{2}a(x + x_1)$ .... (1)
Equation of tangent for $m = \tan 45° = 1$ is
$y = x + a/4$ .... (2)
Comparing (1) and (2), $x_1 = a/4, y_1 = a/2$.
$\therefore$ Point of contact is $(a/4, a/2)$.

34. Equation of normal to the parabola $y^2 = 4ax$ in terms of the slope m is
$y = mx - 2am - am^3$.
Here $a = 1, m = 2$, so the equation of normal is $y = 2x - 4 - 8 = 2x - 12$.

35. Equation of tangent to parabola
$y^2 = 4ax$ is $y = mx + a/m$.
Slope of line $y = 3x + 7$ is 3.
Slope of line |– to the line = – 1/3 = m
$\therefore$ Equation of the tangent to parabola
$y^2 = 16x$ |– to the line is
$y = (-1/3)x + 4/(-1/3)$
i.e., $3y + x + 36 = 0$.

36. The equation of parabola is
$y^2 = 4x + 5$ .....(1)
Equation of the line parallel to
$y = 2x + 7$ is $y = 2x + \lambda$ .... (2)
Eliminating x between (1) and (2), we get
$y^2 - 2y + (2\lambda - 5) = 0$ .... (3)
If line (2) is tangent to parabola (1), then (2) will meet (1) at two real coincident points, so the roots of (3) will be real and equal.
$\therefore (-2)^2 - 4(2\lambda - 5) = 0 \Rightarrow \lambda = 3$.
Putting in (2), the equation of tangent is $y = 2x + 3$.

37. Equation of tangent at the point
$(2 \sec \phi, 3 \tan \phi)$
of the hyperbola $x^2/4 - y^2/9 = 1$ is

$$\frac{x.2\sec\phi}{4} - \frac{y.3\tan\phi}{9} = 1$$

whose slope is $\dfrac{3\sec\phi}{2\tan\phi} = 3/(2\sin\phi)$.
Slope of the line $3x - y + 4 = 0$ is 3.
If tangent in || to the line, then
$3/(2\sin\phi) = 3 \Rightarrow \sin\phi = 1/2 \Rightarrow \phi = 30°$.

38. Substituting (2, 1), we get
$S_1 = 1^2 - 8 \times 2 = 15 < 0$.
$\therefore$ The point (2, 1) lies inside the parabola. Hence there is no tangent in this case, *i.e.*, the number of tangents is 0.

39. Equation of the pair of tangents is
$SS_1 = T^2$
$S = 9x^2 + 16y^2 - 114$
$S_1 = 9(2)^2 + 16(3)^2 - 144 = 36$
$T = 9.(2x) + 16.(3y) - 144$
$18x + 48y - 144$
Equation of pair of tangents is
$(9x^2 + 16y^2 - 144)(36) = (18x + 48y - 144)^2$
or $y^2 + xy - 3x - 8y + 15 = 0$
or $y(y + x) - 3(x + y) - 5(y - 3) = 0$
or $(y + x)(y - 3) - 5(y - 3) = 0$
or $(y - 3)(x + y - 5) = 0$
$\therefore$ The tangents are
$y - 3 = 0$ and $x + y = 0$.

40. Equation of the pair of tangents to the ellipse from the point (1, 2) is $SS_1 = T^2$
or $(3x^2 + 2y^2 - 5)(3.1^2 + 2.2^2 - 5)$
$= (3x.1 + 2y.2 - 5)^2$
or $9x^2 - 4y^2 - 24xy + 30x + y - 55 = 0$
$\therefore$ Angle between the tangents

$$\theta = \tan^{-1}\left|\frac{2\sqrt{(h^2 - ab)}}{a+b}\right|$$

$$= \tan^{-1}\left|\frac{2\sqrt{(144+36)}}{9-4}\right|$$

$= \tan^{-1}(12/\sqrt{5})$.

11. TRIGONOMETRIC FUNCTIONS

Literally, the word "trigonometry" means the study of the properties of triangles. This involves the measurement of angles and length. An *angle* is defined as the amount of rotation of a revolving line with respect to a fixed line. If the rotation is in anticlockwise sense, the angle is taken to be positive, otherwise negative.

There are three systems of measuring an angle viz.

(i) Sexagesimal System or English System.

(ii) Circular System.

(iii) French System.

We generally use first two types of system of measure an angle.

In the **Sexagesimal System**, a right angle is divided into 90 parts and each part is called one degree (1°). So, a straight angle is 180° and complete angle is 360°.

Each degree is further divided into 60 equal parts and each part is called one minute (1').

Each minute again has 60 equal parts, each part being called one second (1").

Thus, 1 right angle = 90°

1° = 60'

1' = 60"

In **Circular Systesm**, the unit of measurement is radians. One radian is defined as the angle subtended at the centre of a circle by an arc of length equal to the radius of that circle. It is written as 1^c.

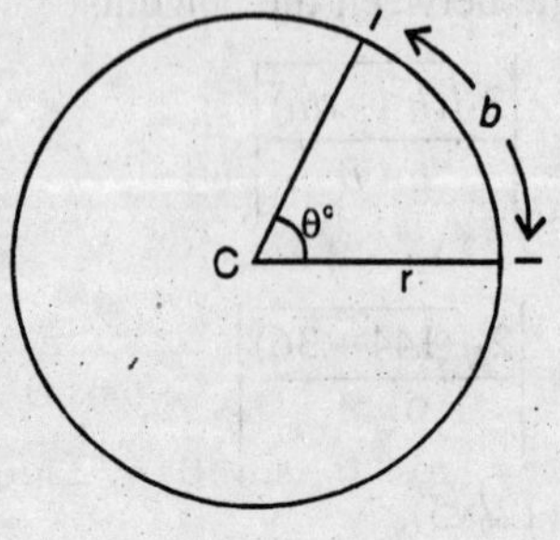

Angle in radians, $\theta^c = \dfrac{S}{r} = \dfrac{\text{Arc}}{\text{Radians}}$

So $\quad 180° = \dfrac{\pi r}{r}$ i.e. π^c

or $\quad 1^c = \dfrac{180°}{\pi} = 57°17'45"$ (approx.)

Basic Trigonometric Functions : Consider a ray OP revolving around the origin. We drop a perpendicular from P on the *x*-axis. Then for ΔOPN, the various trigonometric ratios are defined as

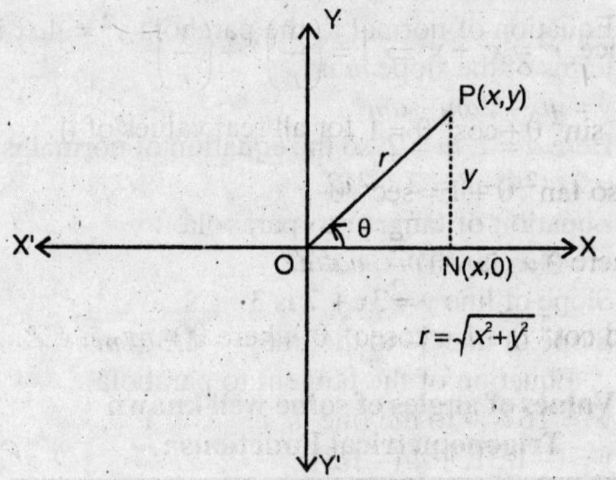

(i) $\sin\theta = \dfrac{PN}{OP} = \dfrac{y}{r}$

(ii) $\cos\theta = \dfrac{ON}{OP} = \dfrac{x}{r}$

(iii) $\tan\theta = \dfrac{PN}{ON} = \dfrac{y}{x} = \dfrac{\sin\theta}{\cos\theta}$

(iv) $\operatorname{cosec}\theta = \dfrac{OP}{PN} = \dfrac{r}{y} = \dfrac{1}{\sin\theta}$

(v) $\sec\theta = \dfrac{OP}{ON} = \dfrac{r}{x} = \dfrac{1}{\cos\theta}$

(vi) $\cot\theta = \dfrac{ON}{PN} = \dfrac{x}{y} = \dfrac{1}{\tan\theta}$

The values of x and y in these definitions are to be put with proper sign based on the quadrant in which P (x, y) lies.

It is easy to observe from the definitions that all trigonometric ratios are positive in Ist quadrant (Q_1) where $0 < \theta < \frac{\pi}{2}$. $\sin\theta$ and $\operatorname{cosec}\theta$ are +ive in Q_2; $\tan\theta$ and $\cot\theta$ are +ive in Q_3 and lastly $\cos\theta$ and $\sec\theta$ are +ive in Q_4.

Also, since $|x| \le r$ and $|y| \le r$

$\Rightarrow |\sin\theta| \le 1$ i.e $-1 \le \sin\theta \le 1$

and $|\operatorname{cosec}\theta| \ge 1$ i.e. $\operatorname{cosec}\theta \le -1$ or $\operatorname{cosec}\theta \ge 1$.

Similarly, $|\cos\theta| \le 1$ and $|\sec\theta| \ge 1$.

$\tan\theta$ and $\cot\theta$ can take any real value.

Since, $r^2 = x^2 + y^2 \Rightarrow 1 = \left(\frac{x}{r}\right)^2 + \left(\frac{y}{r}\right)^2$

$\Rightarrow \sin^2\theta + \cos^2\theta = 1$ for all real values of θ.

Also $\tan^2\theta + 1 = \sec^2\theta$

where $\theta \ne (2n+1)\frac{\pi}{2}, n \in Z$

and $\cot^2\theta + 1 = \operatorname{cosec}^2\theta$ where $\theta \ne n\pi, n \in Z$.

Values of angles of some well known Trigonometrical Functions :

Ratio \ θ	0°	30°	45°	60°	90°
$\sin\theta$	0	$\frac{1}{2}$	$\frac{1}{\sqrt{2}}$	$\frac{\sqrt{3}}{2}$	1
$\operatorname{cosec}\theta$	∞	2	$\sqrt{2}$	$\frac{2}{\sqrt{3}}$	1
$\cos\theta$	1	$\frac{\sqrt{3}}{2}$	$\frac{1}{\sqrt{2}}$	$\frac{1}{2}$	0
$\sec\theta$	1	$\frac{2}{\sqrt{3}}$	$\sqrt{2}$	2	∞
$\tan\theta$	0	$\frac{1}{\sqrt{3}}$	1	$\sqrt{3}$	∞
$\cot\theta$	∞	$\sqrt{3}$	1	$\frac{1}{\sqrt{3}}$	0

Domain and Range of Trigonometrical Functions :

	Domain	*Range*
Sin A	R	$[-1, 1]$
Cos A	R	$[-1, 1]$
tan A	$R - \left\{(2n+1)\frac{\pi}{2} \mid n \in Z\right\}$	$(-\infty, \infty) = R$
cot A	$R - \{n\pi \mid n \in Z\}$	$(-\infty, \infty) = R$
cosec A	$R - \{n\pi \mid n \in Z\}$	$(-\infty, -1] \cup [1, \infty)$
sec A	$R - \left\{(2n+1)\frac{\pi}{2} \mid n \in Z\right\}$	$(-\infty, -1] \cup [1, \infty)$

Thus $|\sin A| \le 1, |\cos A| \le 1, \sec A \ge 1$ $\sec A \le -1$ and $\operatorname{cosec} A \ge 1$ or $\operatorname{cosec} A \le -1$.

Sum and Difference Formulae

(*i*) $\sin(A + B) = \sin A\cos B + \cos A\sin B$.

(*ii*) $\sin(A - B) = \sin A\cos B - \cos A\sin B$.

(*iii*) $\cos(A + B) = \cos A\cos B - \sin A\sin B$.

(*iv*) $\cos(A - B) = \cos A\cos B + \sin A\sin B$.

(*v*) $\sin(A + B)\sin(A - B) = \sin^2 A - \sin^2 B = \cos^2 B - \cos^2 A$.

(*vi*) $\cos(A + B)\cos(A - B) = \cos^2 A - \sin^2 B = \cos^2 B - \sin^2 A$.

(*vii*) $\tan(A + B) = \dfrac{\tan A + \tan B}{1 - \tan A\tan B}$

where $A \ne n\pi + \frac{\pi}{2}$, $B \ne n\pi + \frac{\pi}{2}$

(*viii*) $\tan(A - B) = \dfrac{\tan A - \tan B}{1 + \tan A\tan B}$

and $A \pm B \ne m\pi + \frac{\pi}{2}$

(*ix*) $\cot(A + B) = \dfrac{\cot A\cot B - 1}{\cot A + \cot B}$

where $A \ne n\pi, B \ne n\pi$

(*x*) $\cot(A - B) = \dfrac{\cot A\cot B + 1}{\cot B - \cot A}$ and $A \pm B \ne n\pi$

(*xi*) $\sin 2\theta = 2\sin\theta\cos\theta = \dfrac{2\tan\theta}{1 + \tan^2\theta}$

(*xii*) $\cos 2\theta = \cos^2\theta - \sin^2\theta = 2\cos^2\theta - 1 = 1 - 2\sin^2\theta = \dfrac{1 - \tan^2\theta}{1 + \tan^2\theta}$

(xiii) $1+\cos 2\theta = 2\cos^2\theta$; $1-\cos 2\theta = 2\sin^2\theta$

(xiv) $\tan 2\theta = \dfrac{2\tan\theta}{1-\tan^2\theta}$; where $\theta \neq (2n+1)\dfrac{\pi}{4}$

(xv) $\dfrac{1-\cos\theta}{\sin\theta} = \tan\dfrac{\theta}{2}$; where $\theta \neq (2n+1)\pi$

(xvi) $\dfrac{1+\cos\theta}{\sin\theta} = \cot\dfrac{\theta}{2}$; where $\theta \neq 2n\pi$

(xvii) $\dfrac{1-\cos\theta}{1+\cos\theta} = \tan^2\dfrac{\theta}{2}$; where $\theta \neq (2n+1)\pi$

(xviii) $\dfrac{1+\cos\theta}{1-\cos\theta} = \cot^2\dfrac{\theta}{2}$; where $\theta \neq 2n\pi$

(xix) $\sin 3\theta = 3\sin\theta - 4\sin^3\theta$

(xx) $\cos 3\theta = 4\cos^3\theta - 3\cos\theta$

(xxi) $\cos A \cos 2A \cos 2^2A \ldots \cos 2^{n-1}A = \dfrac{\sin 2^n A}{2^n \sin A}$

Sum and Difference Into Products :

(i) $\sin C + \sin D = 2\sin\left(\dfrac{C+D}{2}\right)\cos\left(\dfrac{C-D}{2}\right)$

(ii) $\sin C - \sin D = 2\cos\left(\dfrac{C+D}{2}\right)\sin\left(\dfrac{C-D}{2}\right)$

(iii) $\cos C + \cos D = 2\cos\left(\dfrac{C+D}{2}\right)\cos\left(\dfrac{C-D}{2}\right)$

(iv) $\cos C - \cos D = 2\sin\left(\dfrac{C+D}{2}\right)\sin\left(\dfrac{D-C}{2}\right)$

(v) $\tan A + \tan B = \dfrac{\sin(A+B)}{\cos A\cos B}$, where $A, B \neq n\pi + \dfrac{\pi}{2}$

(vi) $\tan A - \tan B = \dfrac{\sin(A-B)}{\cos A\cos B}$, $n \in Z$

(vii) $\cot A + \cot B = \dfrac{\sin(A+B)}{\sin A\sin B}$, where $A, B \neq n\pi$, $n \in Z$.

(viii) $\cot A - \cot B = \dfrac{\sin(B-A)}{\sin A\sin B}$, where $A, B \neq n\pi$, $n \in Z$.

Transformation of Products Into Sum or Difference

(i) $2\sin A\cos B = \sin(A+B) + \sin(A-B)$

(ii) $2\cos A\sin B = \sin(A+B) - \sin(A-B)$

(iii) $2\cos A\cos B = \cos(A+B) + \cos(A-B)$

(iv) $2\sin A\sin B = \cos(A-B) - \cos(A+B)$

Sum of Three or More Angles

(i) $\sin(A+B+C) = \sin A\cos B\cos C + \cos A\sin B\cos C + \cos A\cos B\sin C - \sin A\sin B\sin C$

$= \cos A\cos B\cos C(\tan A + \tan B + \tan C - \tan A\tan B\tan C)$

(ii) $\cos(A+B+C) = \cos A\cos B\cos C - \sin A\sin B\cos C - \cos A\cos B\sin C - \cos A\sin B\sin C$

$= \cos A\cos B\cos C(1 - \tan A\tan B - \tan B\tan C - \tan C\tan A)$

(iii) $\tan(A+B+C) = \dfrac{\tan A + \tan B + \tan C - \tan A\tan B\tan C}{1 - \tan A\tan B - \tan B\tan C - \tan C\tan A}$

Trigonometrical Series :

(i) $\sin\alpha + \sin(\alpha+\beta) + \sin(\alpha+2\beta) + \ldots$ upto n terms.

$$= \frac{\sin\left\{\alpha + (n-1)\dfrac{\beta}{2}\right\}}{\sin\left(\dfrac{\beta}{2}\right)}.\sin\left(\frac{n\beta}{2}\right)$$

(ii) $\cos\alpha + \cos(\alpha+\beta) + \cos(\alpha+2\beta) + \ldots$ upto n terms.

$$= \frac{\cos\left\{\alpha + (n-1)\dfrac{\beta}{2}\right\}.\sin\left(\dfrac{n\beta}{2}\right)}{\sin\left(\dfrac{\beta}{2}\right)}$$

Values of Trigonometrical Ratios of Some Important Angles

(i) $\sin 15° = \dfrac{\sqrt{3}-1}{2\sqrt{2}}$

(ii) $\cos 15° = \dfrac{\sqrt{3}+1}{2\sqrt{2}}$

(iii) $\tan 15° = 2 - \sqrt{3} = \cot 75°$

(iv) $\cot 15° = 2 + \sqrt{3} = \tan 75°$

(v) $\sin 22\frac{1}{2}^\circ = \frac{1}{2}\left(\sqrt{2-\sqrt{2}}\right)$

(vi) $\cos 22\frac{1}{2}^\circ = \frac{1}{2}\left(\sqrt{2+\sqrt{2}}\right)$

(vii) $\tan 22\frac{1}{2}^\circ = \sqrt{2} - 1$

(viii) $\cot 22\frac{1}{2}^\circ = \sqrt{2} + 1$

(ix) $\sin 18^\circ = \frac{\sqrt{5}-1}{4} = \cos 72^\circ$

(x) $\cos 18^\circ = \frac{\sqrt{10+2\sqrt{5}}}{4} = \sin 72^\circ$

(xi) $\sin 36^\circ = \frac{\sqrt{10-2\sqrt{5}}}{4} = \cos 54^\circ$

(xii) $\cos 36^\circ = \frac{\sqrt{5}+1}{4} = \sin 54^\circ$

(xiii) $\sin\theta \sin(60^\circ - \theta)\sin(60^\circ + \theta) = \frac{1}{4}\sin 3\theta$

(xiv) $\cos\theta \cos(60^\circ - \theta)\cos(60^\circ + \theta) = \frac{1}{4}\cos 3\theta$

(xv) $\tan\theta \tan(60^\circ - \theta)\tan(60^\circ + \theta) = \tan 3\theta$.

Some Other Useful Results

(i) $\sin\frac{A}{2} + \cos\frac{A}{2} = \pm\sqrt{1+\sin A}$

(ii) $\sin\frac{A}{2} - \cos\frac{A}{2} = \pm\sqrt{1-\sin A}$

(iii) $\sin A \pm \cos A = \sqrt{2}\sin\left(\frac{\pi}{4} \pm A\right)$

$= \sqrt{2}\cos\left(A \mp \frac{\pi}{4}\right)$

(iv) $\cos\alpha + \cos\beta + \cos\gamma + \cos(\alpha+\beta+\gamma)$

$= 4\cos\frac{\alpha+\beta}{2}\cos\frac{\beta+\gamma}{2}\cos\frac{\gamma+\alpha}{2}$

(v) $\sin\alpha + \sin\beta + \sin\gamma - \sin(\alpha+\beta+\gamma)$

$= 4\sin\frac{\alpha+\beta}{2}\sin\frac{\beta+\gamma}{2}\sin\frac{\gamma+\alpha}{2}$.

Maximum and Minimum values of $a\cos\theta + b\sin\theta$: Consider a point *(a, b)* on the cartesian plane. Let its distance from origin be *r* and the line joining the point and the origin make an angle α with the positive direction of *x*-axis.

Then $a = r\cos\alpha$ and $b = r\sin\alpha$.

So, $a\cos\theta + b\sin\theta = r(\cos\alpha\cos\theta + \sin\alpha\cos\theta)$

$= r\cos(\alpha - \theta)$

But $-1 \le \cos(\alpha - \theta) \le 1$

$\Rightarrow -r \le a\cos\theta + b\sin\theta \le r$.

So, the maximum value is $\sqrt{a^2 + b^2}$ and minimum value is $-\sqrt{a^2 + b^2}$.

We can also take $a = r\sin\alpha$ and $b = r\cos\alpha$.

Then,

$a\cos\theta + b\sin\theta = r(\sin\alpha\cos\theta + \cos\alpha\sin\theta)$

$= r\sin(\alpha + \theta)$ which again lies between $-r$ and r.

Properties of Triangles : A triangle has six components; three sides and three angles. Then three angles of a ΔABC are denoted by letters A, B and C and the sides opposite to these angles by letters *a, b* and *c* respectively. Solving a triangle means finding all its components given some components or relations/conditions connecting them.

Following are some well known relations for a triangle (say ΔABC)

(i) $A + B + C = 180^\circ$ (or π)

(ii) $a + b > c$, $b + c > a$ and $c + a > b$

(iii) $|a-b| < c, |b-c| < a$ and $|c-a| < b$.

Some Standard Results :

1. Sine Rule : In any ΔABC

$$\frac{\sin A}{a} = \frac{\sin B}{b} = \frac{\sin C}{c}$$

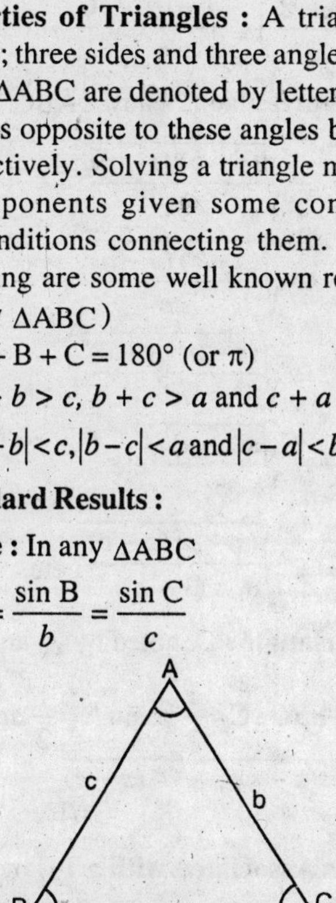

i.e.; sines of the angles are proportional to the length of opposite sides.

2. Cosine Rule : In any ΔABC

(i) $\cos A = \dfrac{b^2 + c^2 - a^2}{2bc}$

(ii) $\cos B = \dfrac{a^2 + c^2 - b^2}{2ac}$

(iii) $\cos C = \dfrac{a^2 + b^2 - c^2}{2ab}$

3. Projection Formulae : In any ΔABC

(i) $a = b\cos C + c\cos B$

(ii) $b = c\cos A + a\cos C$

(iii) $c = a\cos B + b\cos A$

4. Napier's Analogy : In any ΔABC

(i) $\tan\left(\dfrac{B-C}{2}\right) = \dfrac{b-c}{b+c}\cot\dfrac{A}{2}$

(ii) $\tan\left(\dfrac{C-A}{2}\right) = \dfrac{c-a}{c+a}\cot\dfrac{B}{2}$

(iii) $\tan\left(\dfrac{A-B}{2}\right) = \dfrac{a-b}{a+b}\cot\dfrac{C}{2}$

5. Half Angle Formulae : In any ΔABC we have

(i) $\sin\dfrac{A}{2} = \sqrt{\dfrac{(s-b)(s-c)}{bc}}$

$\sin\dfrac{B}{2} = \sqrt{\dfrac{(s-c)(s-a)}{ac}}$

$\sin\dfrac{C}{2} = \sqrt{\dfrac{(s-a)(s-b)}{ab}}$

(ii) $\cos\dfrac{A}{2} = \sqrt{\dfrac{s(s-a)}{bc}}$, etc.

(iii) $\tan\dfrac{A}{2} = \sqrt{\dfrac{(s-b)(s-c)}{s(s-a)}}$, etc.

6. Area of a Triangle : Denoted by Δ and

(i) $\Delta = \dfrac{1}{2}ab\sin C = \dfrac{1}{2}bc\sin A = \dfrac{1}{2}ac\sin B$

(ii) $\Delta = \sqrt{s(s-a)(s-b)(s-c)}$

(Hero's Formula)

7. Some Terms Associated with a Triangle :

(i) Controid (G) : Common point of intersection of medians of a triangle. Divides every median in the ratio 2 : 1. Always lies inside the triangle.

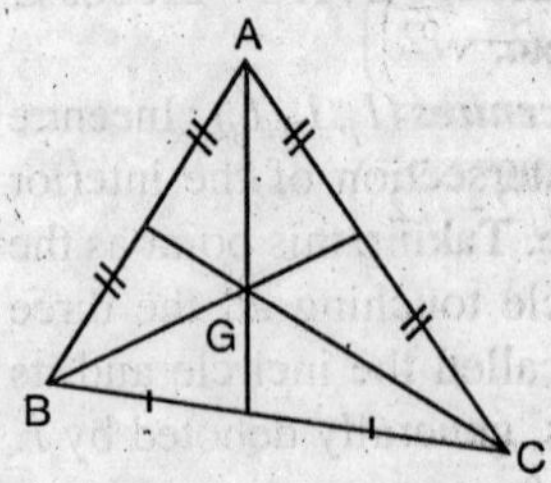

(ii) Circumcentre (O) : Common point of intersection of perpendicular bisectors of the sides of a triangle. It is equidistant from all the vertices of the triangle. Thus, a circle can be drawn passing through all the vertices with centre as this point. This circle is called the circumcircle and its radius is called circumradius generally denoted by R.

It can be proved that

$$\frac{a}{\sin A} = \frac{b}{\sin B} = \frac{c}{\sin C} = 2R.$$

Also, $\qquad R = \dfrac{abc}{4\Delta}$

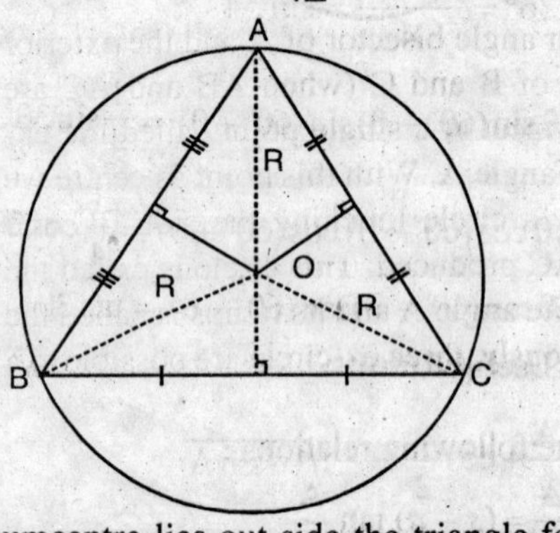

Circumcentre lies out side the triangle for a obtuse angled triangle and on the midpoint of the hypotense for a right angled triangle.

(iii) Orthocentre (H) : Common point of intersection of altitudes of a triangle.

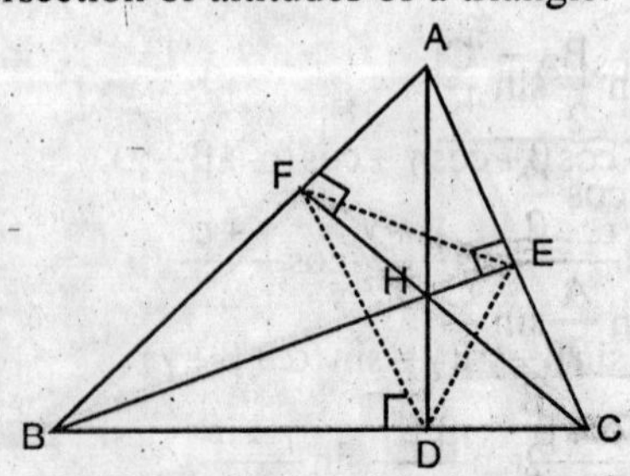

ΔDEF is called pedal triangle of ΔABC.

HA = 2R cos A; HB = 2R cos B; HC = 2R cos C
HD = 2R cos B cos C etc.

(iv) Incentre (I) and Excentres (I_1, I_2, I_3) : Incentre is the common point of intersection of the interior angle bisectors of a triangle. Taking this point as the centre, we can draw a circle touching all the three sides of the triangle. It is called the incircle and its radius is called the inradius, generally denoted by r.

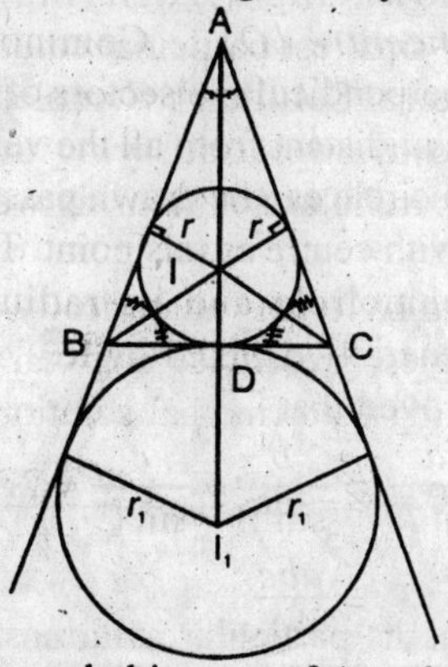

The interior angle bisector of A and the exterior angle bisectors of B and C (when AB and AC are produced) also meet at a single point called the ex-centre opposite angle A. With this point as centre we can again draw a circle touching the side BC and sides AB and AC produced. This circle is called the ex-circle opposite angle A and its radius is called the ex-radius. Obviously, three ex-circle are possible to a triangle.

We have the following relations :

(i) $r = \dfrac{\Delta}{s} = (s-a)\tan\dfrac{A}{2}$

$r = (s-b)\tan\dfrac{B}{2}$

$r = (s-c)\tan\dfrac{C}{2}$

(ii) $r = \dfrac{a\sin\dfrac{B}{2}\sin\dfrac{C}{2}}{\cos\dfrac{A}{2}}$

$r = \dfrac{b\sin\dfrac{A}{2}\sin\dfrac{C}{2}}{\cos\dfrac{B}{2}}$

$r = \dfrac{c\sin\dfrac{B}{2}\sin\dfrac{A}{2}}{\cos\dfrac{C}{2}}$

(iii) $r = 4R\sin\dfrac{A}{2}\sin\dfrac{B}{2}\sin\dfrac{C}{2}$

(iv) $r_1 = \dfrac{\Delta}{s-a} = s\tan\dfrac{A}{2} = a\cos\dfrac{\dfrac{B}{2}\cos\dfrac{C}{2}}{\cos\dfrac{A}{2}}$

$= 4R\sin\dfrac{A}{2}\cos\dfrac{B}{2}\cos\dfrac{C}{2}$

$r_2 = \dfrac{\Delta}{s-b} = s\tan\dfrac{B}{2} = b\cos\dfrac{\dfrac{C}{2}\cos\dfrac{A}{2}}{\cos\dfrac{B}{2}}$

$= 4R\cos\dfrac{A}{2}\sin\dfrac{B}{2}\cos\dfrac{C}{2}$

$r_3 = \dfrac{\Delta}{s-c} = s\tan\dfrac{C}{2} = c\cos\dfrac{\dfrac{A}{2}\cos\dfrac{B}{2}}{\cos\dfrac{C}{2}}$

$= 4R\cos\dfrac{A}{2}\cos\dfrac{B}{2}\sin\dfrac{C}{2}.$

Note : The circumcentre, centroid and ortho-centre all lie on the same line (i.e. they are collinear) and in case of a non-equilateral triangle and centroid divides the line joining the circumcentre and orthocentre in the ratio of 1 : 2. In case of an equilateral triangle, circumcentre, centroid, orthocentre and incentre, all coincide.

8. m – n Theorem

If BD : DC = $m : n$

then $(m+n)\cot\theta = m\cot\alpha - n\cot\beta$
$= n\cot B - m\cot C$

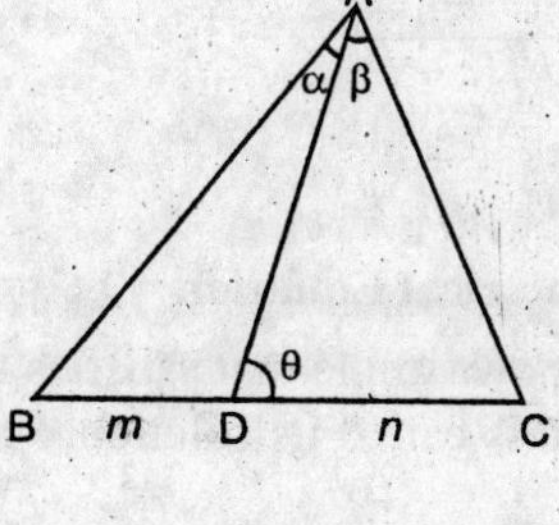

9. Radius of inscribed circle of a regular polygon of n sides

Here the point O is both the incentre and circumcentre of polygon. OB = OC = R, the radius of the circumcircle and OL = r, the radius of the incircle.

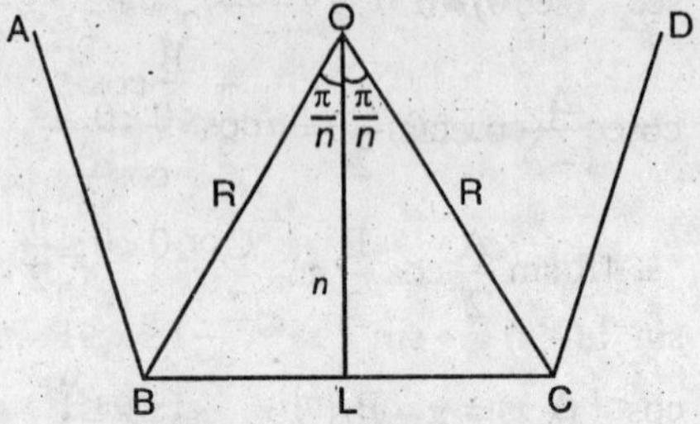

It can be easily seen that

(i) $R = \frac{a}{2}\operatorname{cosec}\left(\frac{\pi}{n}\right)$

(ii) $r = \frac{a}{2}\cot\left(\frac{\pi}{n}\right)$

Where a is the length of a side of the polygon.

10. Area of a regular Polygon :

(i) The area of the polygon = n.Area of ΔOBC

$= n\,(OL)\,(BL)$

$= n\frac{a}{2}\cot\left(\frac{\pi}{n}\right)\cdot\frac{a}{2}$

$= \frac{1}{4}na^2\cot\left(\frac{\pi}{n}\right).$

(ii) The area of the polygon = n (OL) (BL)

$= n\,(OL)\,(OL\tan\angle BOL)$

$= nr^2\tan\left(\frac{\pi}{n}\right).$

(iii) Also the area = n (OL) (BL)

$= nOB\cos\frac{\pi}{n}\;OB\sin\frac{\pi}{n}$

$= \pi R^2\cos\frac{\pi}{n}.\sin\frac{\pi}{n}$

$= \frac{1}{2}nR^2\sin\left(\frac{2\pi}{n}\right).$

Solution of a Trigonometrical Equation

A value of the unknown angle that satisfies the trigonometrical equation is called its solution.

Since all trigonometrical ratios are periodic in nature, generally a trigonometrical equation has more than one solution or an infinite number of solutions.

There are basically three types of solutions :

(i) Particular Solution : A specific value of unknown angle satisfying the equation.

(ii) Principal Solution : Smallest numerical value of the unknown angle satisfying the equation (Numerically smallest particular solution).

(iii) General Solution : Complete set of values of the unknown angle satisfying the equation. It contains all particular solutions as well as principal solution.

When we have two numerically equal smallest unknown angles, preference is given to the positive value in writing the principal solution.

e.g. $\sec\theta = \frac{2}{\sqrt{3}}$ has $\frac{\pi}{6}, -\frac{\pi}{6}, \frac{11\pi}{6}, -\frac{11\pi}{6}, \frac{23\pi}{6}, -\frac{23\pi}{6}$ etc. as its particular solutions. Out of these, the numerically smallest are $\frac{\pi}{6}$ and $-\frac{\pi}{6}$.

But the principal solution is taken as $\theta = \frac{\pi}{6}$.

$\therefore$ The general solution is $\theta = 2k\pi \pm \frac{\pi}{6}$.

General Solution of Some Important Equations :

(i) $\sin\theta = \sin\alpha \Rightarrow \theta = n\pi + (-1)^n\alpha$

(ii) $\cos\theta = \cos\alpha \Rightarrow \theta = 2n\pi \pm \alpha$

(iii) $\tan\theta = \tan\alpha \Rightarrow \theta = n\pi + \alpha$

(iv) $\left.\begin{matrix}\sin^2\theta = \sin^2\alpha\\ \cos^2\theta = \cos^2\alpha\\ \tan^2\theta = \tan^2\alpha\end{matrix}\right\} \Rightarrow \theta = n\pi \pm \alpha$

In all, n is any integer and α may or may not be the principal angle.

General Solution of Some Simple Equations :

(i) $\sin\theta = 0 \Rightarrow \theta = n\pi$

(ii) $\cos\theta = 0 \Rightarrow \theta = (2n+1)\frac{\pi}{2}$

(iii) $\tan\theta = 0 \Rightarrow \theta = n\pi$

(iv) $\cot\theta = 0 \Rightarrow \theta = (2n+1)\frac{\pi}{2}$

(v) $\sin\theta = 1 \Rightarrow \theta = (4n+1)\frac{\pi}{2}$

(vi) $\sin\theta = -1 \Rightarrow \theta = (4n+3)\frac{\pi}{2}$

(vii) $\cos\theta = 1 \Rightarrow \theta = 2n\pi$

(viii) $\cos\theta = -1 \Rightarrow \theta = (2n+1)\pi$

(ix) $\tan\theta = \infty \Rightarrow \theta = (2n+1)\frac{\pi}{2}$

(x) $\cot\theta = \infty \Rightarrow \theta = n\pi$

(xi) $\text{cosec}\,\theta = \infty \Rightarrow \theta = n\pi$

(xii) $\sec\theta = \infty \Rightarrow \theta = (2n+1)\frac{\pi}{2}$.

Inverse Trigonometric Functions

Here is the list given below the definitions of all inverse trigonometric functions with their respective domains and ranges.

Function $y = f(x)$	*Domain (Permitted values of x)*	*Range (Permitted values of y)*
(i) $y = \sin^{-1}x$	$[-1, 1]$	$\left[-\frac{\pi}{2}, \frac{\pi}{2}\right]$
(ii) $y = \cos^{-1}x$	$[-1, 1]$	$[0, \pi]$
(iii) $y = \tan^{-1}x$	$(-\infty, \infty)$	$\left(-\frac{\pi}{2}, \frac{\pi}{2}\right)$
(iv) $y = \cot^{-1}x$	$(-\infty, \infty)$	$(0, \pi)$
(v) $y = \sec^{-1}x$	$(-\infty, -1] \cup [1, \infty)$	$\left[0, \frac{\pi}{2}\right) \cup \left(\frac{\pi}{2}, \pi\right]$
(vi) $y = \text{cosec}^{-1}x$	$(-\infty, -1] \cup [1, \infty)$	$\left[-\frac{\pi}{2}, 0\right) \cup \left(0, \frac{\pi}{2}\right]$

Some Useful Formulae

(i) $\sin(\sin^{-1}x) = x \qquad -1 \le x \le 1$

$\cos(\cos^{-1}x) = x \qquad -1 \le x \le 1$

$\tan(\tan^{-1}x) = x \qquad -\infty < x < \infty$

$\cot(\cot^{-1}x) = x \qquad -\infty < x < \infty$

$\sec(\sec^{-1}x) = x \qquad x \le -1 \text{ or } x \ge 1$

$\text{cosec}(\text{cosec}^{-1}x) = x \qquad x \le -1 \text{ or } x \ge 1$

(ii) $\sin^{-1}(\sin\theta) = \theta$ if $-\frac{\pi}{2} \le \theta \le \frac{\pi}{2}$

$\cos^{-1}(\cos\theta) = \theta$ if $0 \le \theta \le \pi$

$\tan^{-1}(\tan\theta) = \theta$ if $-\frac{\pi}{2} < \theta < \frac{\pi}{2}$

$\cot^{-1}(\cot\theta) = \theta$ if $0 < \theta < \pi$

$\sec^{-1}(\sec\theta) = \theta$ if $0 \le \theta < \frac{\pi}{2}$ or $\frac{\pi}{2} < \theta \le \pi$

$\text{cosec}^{-1}(\text{cosec}\,\theta) = \theta$ it $-\frac{\pi}{2} \le \theta < 0$

or $0 < \theta \le \frac{\pi}{2}$

(iii) $\sin^{-1}(-x) = -\sin^{-1}x \qquad -1 \le x \le 1$

$\cos^{-1}(-x) = \pi - \cos^{-1}x \qquad -1 \le x \le 1$

$\tan^{-1}(-x) = -\tan^{-1}x \qquad -\infty < x < \infty$

$\cot^{-1}(-x) = \pi - \cot^{-1}x \qquad -\infty < x < \infty$

(iv) $\sin^{-1}x = \text{cosec}^{-1}\left(\frac{1}{x}\right) \quad -1 \le x < 0 \text{ or } 0 < x \le 1$

$\cos^{-1}x = \sec^{-1}\left(\frac{1}{x}\right) \quad -1 \le x < 0 \text{ or } 0 < x \le 1$

$\tan^{-1}x = \cot^{-1}\left(\frac{1}{x}\right) \quad x > 0$

If $x < 0$, $\tan^{-1}x = -\pi + \cot^{-1}\left(\frac{1}{x}\right)$

(v) $\sin^{-1}x + \cos^{-1}x = \frac{\pi}{2} \qquad -1 \le x \le 1$

$\tan^{-1}x + \cot^{-1}x = \frac{\pi}{2} \qquad -\infty < x < \infty$

$\sec^{-1}x + \text{cosec}^{-1}x = \frac{\pi}{2} \qquad x \le -1 \text{ or } x \ge 1$

(vi) $\sin^{-1}x = \cos^{-1}\sqrt{1-x^2} = \tan^{-1}\left(\frac{x}{\sqrt{1-x^2}}\right)$

$\cos^{-1}x = \sin^{-1}\sqrt{1-x^2} = \tan^{-1}\left(\frac{\sqrt{1-x^2}}{x}\right)$

$\tan^{-1}x = \sin^{-1}\left(\frac{x}{\sqrt{1+x^2}}\right) = \cos^{-1}\left(\frac{1}{\sqrt{1+x^2}}\right)$

(vi) $\sin^{-1}x+\cos^{-1}x=\dfrac{\pi}{2}\qquad -1\le x\le 1$

$\tan^{-1}x+\cot^{-1}x=\dfrac{\pi}{2}\qquad -\infty<x<\infty$

$\sec^{-1}x+\operatorname{cosec}^{-1}x=\dfrac{\pi}{2}\qquad x\le -1 \text{ or } x\ge 1$

(vii) $\tan^{-1}x+\tan^{-1}y=\tan^{-1}\left(\dfrac{x+y}{1-xy}\right)$

if $x, y, >0$ and $xy<1$

$=\pi+\tan^{-1}\left(\dfrac{x+y}{1-xy}\right)$ if $x, y>0$ and $xy>1$.

$\tan^{-1}x-\tan^{-1}y=\tan^{-1}\left(\dfrac{x-y}{1+xy}\right)$ if $x, y>0$

(viii) $\sin^{-1}x\pm\sin^{-1}y$

$=\sin^{-1}\left(x\sqrt{1-y^2}\pm x\sqrt{1-x^2}\right)$

if $x, y>0,\ x^2+y^2\le 1$

$\sin^{-1}x\ \pm\ \sin^{-1}y$

$=\pi-\sin^{-1}\left(x\sqrt{1-y^2}\pm y\sqrt{1-x^2}\right)$

if $\quad x, y>0, x^2+y^2>1$

(ix) $\cos^{-1}x\pm\cos^{-1}y$

$=\cos^{-1}\left(xy\mp\sqrt{1-x^2}\ \sqrt{1-y^2}\right)$

if $\quad x, y\ge 0$ and $x^2+y^2\le 1$

$\cos^{-1}x\ \pm\ \cos^{-1}y$

$=\pi-\cos^{-1}\left(xy\mp\sqrt{1-x^2}\ \sqrt{1-y^2}\right)$

if $\quad x, y\ge 0$ and $x^2+y^2>1$

(x) $2\sin^{-1}x=\sin^{-1}\left(2x\sqrt{1-x^2}\right)$

$2\cos^{-1}x=\cos^{-1}(2x^2-1)$

$2\tan^{-1}x=\tan^{-1}\left(\dfrac{2x}{1-x^2}\right)=\sin^{-1}\left(\dfrac{2x}{1+x^2}\right)$

$=\cos^{-1}\left(\dfrac{1-x^2}{1+x^2}\right)$

(xi) $3\sin^{-1}x=\sin^{-1}(3x-4x^3)$

$3\cos^{-1}x=\cos^{-1}(4x^3-3x)$

$3\tan^{-1}x=\tan^{-1}\left(\dfrac{3x-x^3}{1-3x^2}\right)$

(xii) $\tan^{-1}x+\tan^{-1}y+\tan^{-1}z$

$=\tan^{-1}\left(\dfrac{x+y+z-xyz}{1-xy-yz-zx}\right)$

Heights and Distances

(i) Angle of Elevation : Consider a point P being observed from a point O (usually called observer) at a lower horizontal leve. We draw a horizontal line OM through O in the direction of P. Then, OP is called the line of sight or observation and ∠POM is called the angle of elevation of point P as seen from O.

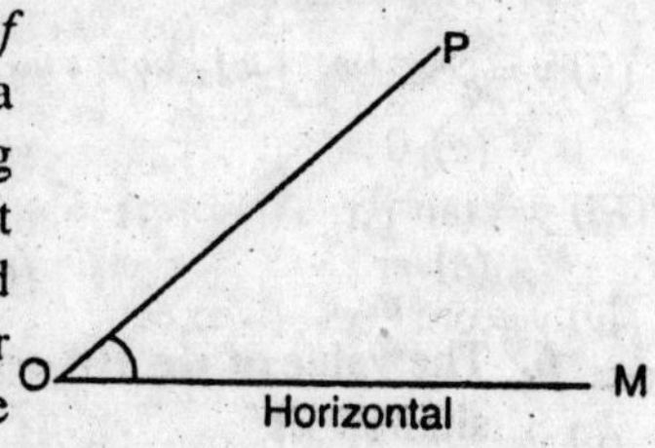

(ii) Angle of Depression : Consider a point P being observed from a point O at a higher horizontal level. ∠POM here is called the angle of depression of the point P as seen O. This is also measured w.r.t. the horozontal at O.

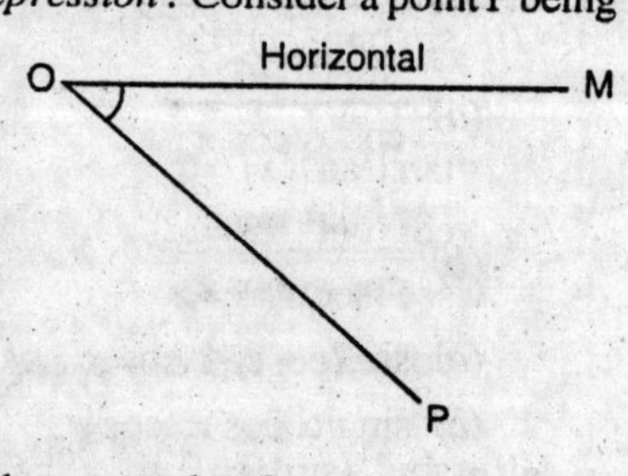

EXERCISE

Mark the correct alternative(s) of each of the following :

1. The value of cos 1° cos 2° cos 3°.... cos 179° is

(a) $\frac{1}{\sqrt{2}}$ (b) 0

(c) 1 (d) None of these

2. The value of tan 1° tan 2° tan 3°.... tan 89° is

(a) 1 (b) 0 (c) ∞ (d) $\frac{1}{2}$

3. The value of log tan 1° + log tan 2° + log tan 3°+ .... + log tan 89° is

(a) 0 (b) 1 (c) – 1 (d) ∞

4. $1 + \sin x + \sin^2 x + \sin^3 x + ... + \infty$ is equal to $4+2\sqrt{3}$, $0<x<\pi$, then x equals to

(a) $\frac{\pi}{6}$ (b) $\frac{\pi}{4}$

(c) $\frac{\pi}{3}$ or $\frac{\pi}{6}$ (d) $\frac{\pi}{3}$ or $\frac{2\pi}{3}$

5. The value of

$e^{\log_{10} \tan 1^\circ + \log_{10} \tan 2^\circ + \log_{10} \tan 3^\circ + ... + \log_{10} \tan 89^\circ}$ is

(a) 0 (b) e

(c) $\frac{1}{e}$ (d) None of these

6. The value of sin 10° + sin 20° + sin 30° + ... + sin 360° is

(a) 1 (b) 0

(c) – 1 (d) None of these

7. The $x_1, x_2, x_3, ..., x_n$ are in A.P., whose common difference is α, then the value of $\sin \alpha$ ($\sec x_1 \sec x_2 + \sec x_2 \sec x_3 + ... + \sec x_{n-1} \sec x_n$) is

(a) $\frac{\sin (n-1)\alpha}{\cos x_1 \cos x_n}$

(b) $\frac{\sin n\alpha}{\cos x_1 \cos x_n}$

(c) $\sin (n-1)\alpha \cos x_1 \cos x_n$

(d) $\sin n\alpha \cos x_1 \cos x_n$

8. In $\sin x + \sin^2 x = 1$, then the value of $\cos^{12} x + 3\cos^{10} x + 3\cos^8 x + \cos^6 x + 2\cos^4 x + \cos^2 x - 2$ is equal to

(a) 0 (b) 1 (c) 2 (d) $\sin^2 x$

9. If $\theta = \frac{\pi}{2^n + 1}$, then

$\cos\theta . \cos 2\theta . 2 \cos 2^2\theta .... \cos 2^{n-1}\theta$ equals to

(a) 0 (b) 1

(c) $\frac{1}{2^n}$ (d) None of these

10. If $\sin^3 x \sin 3x = \sum_{m=0}^{6} c_m \cos mx$

where $c_0, c_1, c_2, ..., c_6$ are constants, then

(a) $c_0 + c_2 + c_4 + c_6 = 0$

(b) $c_1 + c_3 + c_5 = 6$

(c) $2c_2 + 3c_6 = 0$

(d) $c_4 + 2c_6 = 0$

11. If expression $e^{(\sin^2 x + \sin^4 x + \sin^6 x + ... + \infty) \log e^2}$ satisfies the equation $x^2 - 9x + 8 = 0$, then the value of $\frac{\cos x}{\cos x + \sin x}$, $0 < x < \frac{\pi}{2}$ is

(a) $\frac{1}{2}(\sqrt{3}-1)$ (b) $\frac{1}{3}(\sqrt{2}-1)$

(c) $\frac{1}{2}(\sqrt{3}-\sqrt{2})$ (d) None of these

12. Given $A = \sin^2\theta + \cos^4\theta$, then for all real θ

(a) $1 \le A \le 2$ (b) $\frac{3}{4} \le A \le 1$

(c) $\frac{13}{16} \le A \le 1$. (d) $\frac{3}{4} \le A \le \frac{13}{16}$

13. If $\sin x + \operatorname{cosec} x = 2$, then $\sin^n x + \operatorname{cosec}^n x$ is equal to

(a) 2 (b) 2^n (c) 2^{n-1} (d) 2^{n-2}

14. If $\sin\theta + \cos\theta = a$, then $\sin^4\theta + \cos^4\theta$ is equal to

(a) $1 - \frac{1}{2}\sqrt{a^2 - 1}$ (b) $1 - \frac{1}{2}(a^2-1)^2$

(c) $(a^2-1)^2 - \frac{1}{2}$ (d) $\sqrt{a^2 - 1} - \frac{1}{2}$

[J.N.U. M.C.A.]

15. If α and β are the solutions of the equation $a \tan\theta + b \sec\theta = c$, then $\tan(\alpha+\beta)$ is equal to

(a) $\frac{2ab}{a^2+b^2}$ (b) $\frac{2ab}{a^2-c^2}$

(c) $\frac{2ac}{a^2-b^2}$ (d) None of these

16. The equation $a \sin x + b \cos x = c$, where $|c| > \sqrt{a^2+b^2}$ has

(a) a unique solution
(b) infinite no. of solutions
(c) no solution
(d) None of these

17. If $\frac{\sin(x+y)}{\sin(x-y)} = \frac{a+b}{a-b}$, then $\frac{\tan x}{\tan y}$ is equal to

(a) $\frac{b}{a}$ (b) $\frac{a}{b}$

(c) ab (d) None of these

18. If $x\cos\alpha + y\sin\alpha = 2a$, $x\cos\beta + y\sin\beta = 2a$ and $2\sin\frac{\alpha}{2}\sin\frac{\beta}{2} = 1$, then

(a) $\cos\alpha + \cos\beta = \frac{2ax}{x^2+y^2}$

(b) $\cos\alpha\cos\beta = \frac{2a^2-y^2}{x^2+y^2}$

(c) $y^2 = 4a(\alpha - x)$

(d) $\cos\alpha + \cos\beta = 2\cos\alpha\cos\beta$

19. If an angle α is divided into two parts A and B such that $A - B = x$ and $\tan A : \tan B = k : 1$, then the value of $\sin x$ is

(a) $\frac{k-1}{k+1}\sin\alpha$ (b) $\frac{k+1}{k-1}\sin\alpha$

(c) $\frac{k}{k+1}\sin\alpha$ (d) None of these

20. If $\sin A + \cos A = m$ and $\sin^3 A + \cos^3 A = n$, then

(a) $m^3 - 3m - n = 0$ (b) $m^3 + 3m + 2n = 0$
(c) $n^3 - 3n + 2m = 0$ (d) $m^3 - 3m + 2n = 0$

21. The area of the circle and the area of a regular polygon of n sides and of perimeter equal to that of the circle are in the ratio of

(a) $\tan\left(\frac{\pi}{n}\right) : \frac{\pi}{n}$ (b) $\cos\left(\frac{\pi}{n}\right) : \frac{\pi}{n}$

(c) $\sin\left(\frac{\pi}{n}\right) : \frac{\pi}{n}$ (d) $\cot\left(\frac{\pi}{n}\right) : \frac{\pi}{n}$

22. In a triangle ABC, if $\frac{\cos A}{a} = \frac{\cos B}{b} = \frac{\cos C}{c}$ and the side $a = 2$, then area of the triangle is

(a) 1 (b) 2 (c) $\frac{\sqrt{3}}{2}$ (d) $\sqrt{3}$

23. In a triangle ABC, the line joining the circumcentre to the incentre is parallel to BC, then $\cos B + \cos C$ equals to

(a) $\frac{3}{2}$ (b) 1 (c) $\frac{3}{4}$ (d) $\frac{1}{2}$

24. In a ΔABC

$\frac{2\cos A}{a} + \frac{\cos B}{b} + \frac{2\cos C}{c} = \frac{a}{bc} + \frac{b}{ca}$, then the value of the angle A is

(a) 30° (b) 45° (c) 60° (d) 90°

25. The ex-radii of a triangle r_1, r_2, r_3 are in harmonic progression, then the sides a, b, c are in

(a) HP (b) GP
(c) AP (d) None of these

26. In an equilateral triangle the in-radius and the circumradius are connected by

(a) $r = 4R$ (b) $r = \frac{R}{2}$

(c) $r = \frac{R}{3}$ (d) None of these

27. In any ΔABC, if $\cot\frac{A}{2}$, $\cot\frac{B}{2}$, $\cot\frac{C}{2}$ are in A.P., then a, b, c are in

(a) AP (b) GP
(c) HP (d) None of these

28. In an equilateral triangle, in-radius, circum-radius and one of the ex-radii are in the ratio

(a) 1 : 2 : 3 (b) 2 : 3 : 1
(c) 1 : 3 : 7 (d) 3 : 7 : 9

29. If in a triangle ABC, $\angle B = 45°$, $a = 2(\sqrt{3}+1)$ units and its area is $6+2\sqrt{3}$ square units the value of side b is

(a) 2 (b) 5
(c) 9 (d) None of these

[J.N.U. M.C.A]

30. If the angles A, B, C of a triangle are in A.P. and sides a, b, c are in G.P., then a^2, b^2, c^2 are in

(a) AP (b) HP
(c) GP (d) None of these

31. The equation $(\cos p - 1)x^2 + (\cos p)x + \sin p = 0$, where x is a variable, has real roots. Then the interval of p may be any one of the following

(a) $(0, 2\pi)$ (b) $(-\pi, 0)$
(c) $\left(-\frac{\pi}{2}, \frac{\pi}{2}\right)$ (d) $(0, \pi)$

32. In a right angled triangle the hypotenuse is $2\sqrt{2}$ times the length of perpendicular drawn from the opposite vertex on the hypotenuses, then the other two angles are

(a) $\frac{\pi}{3}, \frac{\pi}{6}$ (b) $\frac{\pi}{4}, \frac{\pi}{4}$
(c) $\frac{\pi}{8}, \frac{3\pi}{8}$ (d) $\frac{\pi}{12}, \frac{5\pi}{12}$

33. One of the value of θ lying between $\theta = 0$ and $\theta = \frac{\pi}{2}$ and satisfying the equation

$$\begin{vmatrix} 1+\cos^2\theta & \sin^2\theta & 4\sin 4\theta \\ \cos^2\theta & 1+\sin^2\theta & 4\sin 4\theta \\ \cos^2\theta & \sin^2\theta & 1+4\sin 4\theta \end{vmatrix} = 0 \text{ is}$$

(a) $\frac{\pi}{24}$ (b) $\frac{7\pi}{24}$
(c) $\frac{5\pi}{24}$ (d) None of these

34. The number of solutions of $2\cos^2\left(\frac{x}{2}\right)\sin^2 x = x^2 + \frac{1}{x^2}$, $0 \le x \le \frac{\pi}{2}$ is

(a) 0 (b) 1
(c) infinite (d) None of these

[J.N.U. M.C.A.]

35. The number of all possible triplets (a_1, a_2, a_3) such that $a_1 + a_2 \cos 2x + a_3 \sin^2 x = 0$ for all x is

(a) zero (b) 1
(c) 2 (d) infinite

36. If $\theta_1, \theta_2, \theta_3, \theta_4$ are roots of the equation $\sin(\theta+\alpha) = k\sin 2\theta$, *no* two of which differ by a multiple of 2π, then $\theta_1+\theta_2+\theta_3+\theta_4$ is equal to

(a) $2n\pi, n \in Z$ (b) $(2n+1)\pi, n \in Z$
(c) $n\pi, n \in Z$ (d) None of these

37. The equation

$3^{\sin 2x + 2\cos^2 x} + 3^{1-\sin 2x + 2\sin^2 x} = 28$ is satisfied for the values of x given by

(a) $\sin x = 0$ (b) $\tan x = -1$
(c) $\tan x = 1$ (d) None of these

38. The smallest positive x satisfying $\log_{\cos x}\sin x + \log_{\sin x}\cos x = 2$ equal to

(a) $\frac{\pi}{2}$ (b) $\frac{\pi}{3}$ (c) $\frac{\pi}{4}$ (d) $\frac{\pi}{6}$

39. If $0 \le x \le \pi$ and $81^{\sin^2 x} + 81^{\cos^2 x} = 30$, then one of the value of x is equal to

(a) $\frac{\pi}{6}$ (b) $\frac{5\pi}{6}$
(c) $\frac{2\pi}{3}$ (d) None of these

40. $4\tan^{-1}\frac{1}{5} - \tan^{-1}\frac{1}{239}$ is equal to

(a) π (b) $\frac{\pi}{2}$ (c) $\frac{\pi}{3}$ (d) $\frac{\pi}{4}$

[J.N.U. M.C.A.]

41. $\tan^{-1}\left(\frac{x}{y}\right) - \tan^{-1}\left(\frac{x-y}{x+y}\right)$ is

(a) $\frac{\pi}{2}$ (b) $\frac{\pi}{3}$
(c) $\frac{\pi}{4}$ (d) None of these

42. The solution of

$$\sin^{-1}\left(\frac{2a}{1+a^2}\right)-\cos^{-1}\left(\frac{1-b^2}{1+b^2}\right)$$

$$=\tan^{-1}\left(\frac{2x}{1-x^2}\right) \text{ is}$$

(a) $\frac{a-b}{1-ab}$ (b) $\frac{1+ab}{a-b}$

(c) $\frac{ab-1}{a+b}$ (d) $\frac{a-b}{1+ab}$

43. A pole stands vertically on the centre of a square. When α is the elevation of the sun its shadow just reaches the side of the square and is at a distance x and y from the ends of that side. Then the height of the pole is

(a) $\sqrt{x^2+y^2}\tan\alpha$ (b) $\sqrt{x^2+y^2}\cot\alpha$

(c) $\sqrt{\frac{x^2+y^2}{2}}\tan\alpha$ (d) $\sqrt{\frac{x^2+y^2}{2}}\cot\alpha$

44. A spherical ball of diameter d subtends an angle α at a man's eye when the elevation of its centre is β. The height of the centre of the ball is

(a) $\frac{1}{2}d\sin\beta\,\text{cosec}\left(\frac{\alpha}{2}\right)$

(b) $\frac{1}{2}d\sin\alpha\,\text{cosec}\left(\frac{\beta}{2}\right)$

(c) $\frac{1}{2}d\sin\left(\frac{\beta}{2}\right)\text{cosec}\,\alpha$

(d) $\frac{1}{2}d\sin\left(\frac{a}{2}\right)\text{cosec}\,\beta$

45. A ladder rests against a wall at an angle α to the horizontal. Its foot is pulled away from the wall through a distance a, so that it slides a distance b down the wall making an angle β with the horizontal. Then a equals to

(a) $b\tan\frac{1}{2}(\alpha-\beta)$ (b) $b\tan\frac{1}{2}(\alpha+\beta)$

(c) $\frac{b}{2}\tan(\alpha-\beta)$ (d) None of these

46. The top of a hill observed from the top and bottom of a building of height h is at angles of elevation p and q respectively. The height of the hill is

(a) $\frac{h\cot q}{\cot q-\cot p}$ (b) $\frac{h\cot p}{\cot p-\cot q}$

(c) $\frac{h\tan p}{\tan p-\tan q}$ (d) None of these

47. At a distance a from the foot of a tower AB, of height b, a flagstaff BC and the tower subtends equal angles. The length of the flagstaff is

(a) $\frac{a(b^2+a^2)}{a^2-b^2}$ (b) $\frac{b(a^2+b^2)}{a^2-b^2}$

(c) $\frac{a^2(a^2+b^2)}{a^2-b^2}$ (d) None of these

[J.N.U. M.C.A.]

48. The angle of elevation of a cloud from a point h mt. above is θ° and the angle of depression of its reflection in the lake is ϕ. Then the height is

(a) $\frac{h\sin(\phi-\theta)}{\sin(\phi+\theta)}$ (b) $\frac{h\sin(\phi+\theta)}{\sin(\phi-\theta)}$

(c) $\frac{h\sin(\theta+\phi)}{\sin(\theta-\phi)}$ (d) None of these

49. AB is a vertical pole. The end A is on the level ground. C is the middle point of AB. P is a point on the level ground. The portion BC subtends an angle β at P. If AP $= n$AB, then $\tan\beta$ equals to

(a) $\frac{n}{2n^2+1}$ (b) $\frac{n}{n^2-1}$

(c) $\frac{n}{n^2+1}$ (d) None of these

50. From an aeroplane vertically over a straight horizontal road, the angles of depression of two consecutive milestones on opposite sides of the aeroplane are observed to be α and β. The height of the aeroplane above the road is

(a) $\frac{\tan\alpha+\tan\beta}{\tan\alpha\tan\beta}$ (b) $\frac{\tan\alpha\tan\beta}{\tan\alpha+\tan\beta}$

(c) $\frac{\cot\alpha\cot\beta}{\cot\alpha+\cot\beta}$ (d) None of these

ANSWERS

1	2	3	4	5	6	7	8	9	10
(b)	(a)	(a)	(d)	(d)	(b)	(a)	(d)	(c)	(a)
11	12	13	14	15	16	17	18	19	20
(a)	(b)	(a)	(b)	(c)	(c)	(b)	(c)	(a)	(d)
21	22	23	24	25	26	27	28	29	30
(a)	(d)	(b)	(d)	(c)	(b)	(a)	(a)	(d)	(a)
31	32	33	34	35	36	37	38	39	40
(d)	(c)	(b)	(a)	(d)	(b)	(b)	(c)	(a)	(d)
41	42	43	44	45	46	47	48	49	50
(c)	(d)	(c)	(a)	(b)	(b)	(b)	(b)	(a)	(b)

SOME SELECTED EXPLANATORY ANSWERS

1. In between cos 1° and cos 179° we get a term cos 90° whose value is zero.

2. Here tan 89° = tan (90° – 1°) = cot 1°
tan 88° = tan (90° – 2°) = cot 2°, so on.

$\therefore$ tan 1° tan 2° tan3°.... tan 88° tan 89°

= tan 1° tan 2° tan3°.... tan 45° cot 44° cot 43°....cot 3° cot 2° cot 1°

= tan 45° = 1.

3. log tan 1° + log tan 2° + log tan 3° +...+ log tan 89°

= log {tan 1° tan 2° tan 3°....tan 89°}

= log 1 (By Q. 2)

= 0.

4. Here $0 < x < \pi$ (given). Therefore $\sin x > 0$

We have $1 + \sin x + \sin^2 x + ... + \infty = 4 + 2\sqrt{3}$

or $\lim_{x\to\infty} \dfrac{1-(\sin x)^n}{1-\sin x} = 4 + 2\sqrt{3}$

or $\dfrac{1}{1-\sin x} = 4+2\sqrt{3}$ $(\because 0<\sin x \le 1)$

or $\sin x = 1 - \dfrac{1}{4+2\sqrt{3}}$

or $\sin x = \dfrac{\sqrt{3}}{2}$

Solving the trigonometrical equation we get

$$x = n\pi + (-1)^n \frac{\pi}{3} \text{ for } n = 0, 1$$

i.e. $x = \dfrac{\pi}{3}$ or $\dfrac{2\pi}{3}$.

5. Here $e^{\log_{10}\tan 1^\circ + \log_{10}\tan 2^\circ .... + \log_{10}\tan 89^\circ}$

$= e^0$ (By Q. 3) = 1.

6. We know that $\sin(\pi + \theta) = -\sin\theta$

$\therefore$ sin 190° = sin (180° + 10°) = – sin 10°
sin 200° = sin (180° + 20°) = – sin 20°
sin 210° = sin (180° + 30°) = – sin 30°
....
sin 360° = sin (180° + 180°) = – sin 180°

Thus, all the terms cancel each other when we add.

7. $\sin\alpha\,(\sec x_1 \sec x_2 + \sec x_2 \sec x_3 + ... + \sec x_{n-1} \sec x_n)$

$$= \frac{\sin\alpha}{\cos x_1 \cos x_2} + \frac{\sin\alpha}{\cos x_2 \cos x_3} + ... + \frac{\sin\alpha}{\cos x_{n-1}\cos x_n}$$

$$= \frac{\sin(x_2 - x_1)}{\cos x_1 \cos x_2} + \frac{\sin(x_3 - x_2)}{\cos x_2 \cos x_3} + ... + \frac{\sin(x_n - x_{n-1})}{\cos x_{n-1}\cos x_{n-1}}$$

$(\because \alpha = \text{common difference})$

$= \tan x_2 - \tan x_1 + \tan x_3 - \tan x_2 + \tan x_4 - \tan x_3 + ... + \tan x_n - \tan x_{n-1}.$

$= \tan x_n - \tan x_1$

$$= \frac{\sin(x_n - x_1)}{\cos x_n \cos x_1} = \frac{\sin(n-1)\alpha}{\cos x_n \cos x_1}$$

$[\because x_n = x_1 + (n-1)\alpha]$

8. $\sin x + \sin^2 x = 1$ (given)

or $\sin x = 1 - \sin^2 x$

or $\sin x = \cos^2 x$.

Thus, $\cos^8 x + 2\cos^6 x + \cos^4 x$

$$= \sin^4 x + 2\sin^3 x + \sin^2 x$$

$$= \left(\sin x + \sin^2 x\right)^2 = 1.$$

9. $\cos\theta.\cos 2\theta.\cos 2^2\theta....\cos 2^{n-1}\theta$

$$= \frac{1}{2\sin\theta}(2\sin\theta.\cos\theta.\cos 2\theta.\cos 2^2\theta...\cos 2^{n-1}\theta)$$

$$= \frac{1}{2\sin\theta}(\sin 2\theta.\cos 2\theta.\cos 2^2\theta....\cos 2^{n-1}\theta)$$

$$= \frac{1}{2^2\sin\theta}\times(2\sin 2\theta.\cos 2\theta.\cos 2^2\theta....\cos 2^{n-1}\theta)$$

$$= \frac{1}{2^2\sin\theta}(\sin 2^2\theta.\cos 2^2\theta....\cos 2^{n-1}\theta)$$

....

$$= \frac{1}{2^{n-1}\sin\theta}.\sin 2^{n-1}\theta.\cos 2^{n-1}\theta$$

$$= \frac{1}{2^n\sin\theta}\sin 2^n\theta$$

$$= \frac{1}{2^n\sin\theta}[\sin(\pi-\theta)] \qquad \left(\because \theta = \frac{\pi}{2^n+1}\right)$$

$$= \frac{1}{2^n}.$$

10. We have

$\sin^3 x \sin 3x$

$= \sin^3 x(3\sin x - 4\sin^3 x)$

$= 3\sin^4 x - 4\sin^6 x$

$$= 3\left(\frac{1-\cos 2x}{2}\right)^2 - 4\left(\frac{1-\cos 2x}{2}\right)^3$$

$$= \left(\frac{1-\cos 2x}{2}\right)^2[3-2(1-\cos 2x)]$$

$$= \frac{1}{4}\left(1-2\cos 2x+\frac{1+\cos 4x}{2}\right)(1+2\cos 2x)$$

$$= \frac{1}{8}[3-4\cos 2x+\cos 4x][1+2\cos 2x]$$

$$= \frac{1}{8}[3-4\cos 2x+\cos 4x+6\cos 2x-4(1+\cos 4x)+\cos 6x+\cos 2x]$$

$$= \frac{1}{8}[-1+3\cos 2x-3\cos 4x+\cos 6x] \quad ...(i)$$

It is given that

$$\sin^3 x\sin 3x = c_0 + c_1\cos x + c_2\cos 2x + ... + c_6\cos 6x \quad ...(ii)$$

Compairing *(i)* and *(ii)* we get

$$c_0 + c_2 + c_4 + c_6 = \frac{1}{8}(-1+3-3+1) = 0.$$

11. We have

$\sin^2 x + \sin^4 x + \sin^6 x + ... + \infty$

$$= \lim_{x\to\infty}\frac{\sin^2 x - \left(\sin^2 x\right)^n}{1-\sin^2 x}$$

$$= \frac{\sin^2 x}{1-\sin^2 x} \quad (\because 0\le\sin^2 x\le 0)$$

$= \tan^2 x.$

$$\therefore e^{(\sin^2 x+\sin^4 x+....+\infty)\log_e 2}$$

$$= e^{\tan^2 x\log_e 2}$$

$$= 2^{\tan^2 x} \quad ...(i)$$

Roots of $x^2 - 9x - 8 = 0$ are $\perp$ and 8. ...*(ii)*

From the given condition taking *(i)* and *(ii)* into consideration we get

$2^{\tan^2 x} = 1 = 2^{\circ}$

and $2^{\tan^2 x} = 8 = 2^3$

or $\tan^2 x = 0$ and 3

or $\tan x = 0$ and $\pm\sqrt{3}$.

But $\tan x = 0, -\sqrt{3}$ is not possible because $0 < x < \frac{\pi}{2}$.

$$\therefore \tan x = \sqrt{3} = \tan\left(\frac{\pi}{3}\right) \Rightarrow x = \frac{\pi}{3}.$$

$$\therefore \frac{\cos x}{\sin x+\cos x} = \frac{1}{1+\tan x}$$

$$= \frac{1}{1+\sqrt{3}} = \frac{\sqrt{3}-1}{3-1}$$

$$= \frac{1}{2}\left(\sqrt{3}-1\right).$$

12. We have

$$A = \sin^2\theta + \cos^2\theta$$

$$= \frac{1-\cos 2\theta}{2} + \left(\frac{1+\cos 2\theta}{2}\right)^2$$

$$= \frac{1}{2} - \frac{1}{2}\cos 2\theta + \frac{1}{4} + \frac{1}{2}\cos 2\theta + \frac{1}{4}\cos^2 2\theta$$

$$= \frac{3}{4} + \frac{1}{4}\left(\frac{1+\cos 4\theta}{2}\right)$$

$$= \frac{3}{4} + \frac{1}{8} + \frac{1}{8}\cos 4\theta$$

But $-1 \le \cos 4\theta \le 1$

or $\frac{-1}{8} \le \frac{\cos 4\theta}{8} \le \frac{1}{8}$

or $\frac{3}{4} + \frac{1}{8} - \frac{1}{8} \le \frac{3}{4} + \frac{1}{8} + \frac{1}{8}\cos 4\theta \le \frac{3}{4} + \frac{1}{8} + \frac{1}{8}$

or $\frac{3}{4} \le A \le 1.$

13. $\sin x + \operatorname{cosec} x = 2$

or $\sin^2 x - 2\sin x + 1 = 0$

or $(\sin x - 1)^2 = 0$

or $\sin x = 1.$

Thus, $\sin^n x + \operatorname{cosec}^n x = 1 + 1 = 2.$

14. $\sin\theta + \cos\theta = a$

$\therefore$ $(\sin\theta + \cos\theta)^2 = a^2$

or $1 + 2\sin\theta\cos\theta = a^2$

or $\sin\theta\cos\theta = \frac{a^2-1}{2}$

But $\sin^4\theta + \cos^4\theta = (\sin^2\theta + \cos^2\theta)^2 - 2\sin^2\theta\cos^2\theta$

$$= 1 - 2\left(\frac{a^2-1}{2}\right)^2$$

$$= 1 - \frac{1}{2}(a^2-1)^2.$$

15. We have

$a\tan\theta + b\sec\theta = c$

or $b\sec\theta = c - a\tan\theta$

or $b^2\sec^2\theta = (c - a\tan\theta)^2$

or $b^2(1+\tan^2\theta) = c^2 - 2ac\tan\theta + a^2\tan^2\theta$

or $(a^2-b^2)\tan^2\theta - 2ac\tan\theta + (c^2-b^2) = 0$

Let $\tan\alpha$ and $\tan\beta$ are the roots of this quadratic equation in $\tan\theta$.

$\therefore$ $\tan\alpha + \tan\beta = \frac{2ac}{a^2-b^2}$

and $\tan\alpha\tan\beta = \frac{c^2-b^2}{a^2-b^2}$

$\therefore$ $\tan(\alpha+\beta) = \frac{\tan\alpha + \tan\beta}{1 - \tan\alpha\tan\beta}$

$$= \frac{\frac{2ac}{a^2-b^2}}{1 - \frac{c^2-b^2}{a^2-b^2}} = \frac{2ac}{(a^2-b^2)-(c^2-b^2)}$$

$$= \frac{2ac}{(a^2-c^2)}.$$

16. $|a\sin x + b\cos x| \le \sqrt{a^2+b^2}$ for all $x \in R$.

$\therefore$ $|c| \le \sqrt{a^2+b^2}$. But $|c| > \sqrt{a^2+b^2}$ (given)

$\therefore$ $a\sin x + b\cos x = c$ does not hold for any $x \in R$.

18. From the given two equations, we can say that α and β are roots of

$x\cos\theta + y\sin\theta = 2a$

or $2a - x\cos\theta = y\sin\theta$

or $(2a - x\cos\theta)^2 = y^2\sin^2\theta$

or $(x^2+y^2)\cos^2\theta - 4ax\cos\theta + 4a^2 - y^2 = 0$

$\therefore$ $\cos\alpha + \cos\beta = \frac{4ax}{x^2+y^2}$ and

$\cos\alpha\cos\beta = \frac{4a^2-y^2}{x^2+y^2}.$

It is given that

$$2\sin\frac{\alpha}{2}\sin\frac{\beta}{2} = 1$$

or $4\sin^2\frac{\alpha}{2}\sin^2\frac{\beta}{2} = 1$

or $(1-\cos\alpha)(1-\cos\beta) = 1$

or $\cos\alpha + \cos\beta = \cos\alpha\cos\beta$

or $\dfrac{4ax}{x^2+y^2} = \dfrac{4a^2-y^2}{x^2+y^2}$

or $y^2 = 4a(a-x)$.

19. $\dfrac{\tan A}{\tan B} = \dfrac{k}{1}$

$\dfrac{\tan A + \tan B}{\tan A - \tan B} = \dfrac{k+1}{k-1}$

(By Componendo Dividendo)

or $\dfrac{\sin(A+B)}{\sin(A-B)} = \dfrac{k+1}{k-1}$

or $\dfrac{\sin\alpha}{\sin x} = \dfrac{k+1}{k-1}$

or $\sin x = \dfrac{k+1}{k-1}\sin\alpha$.

20. We have

$\sin A + \cos A = m$ and $\sin^3 A + \cos^3 A = n$

Here $\sin A + \cos A = m$

or $(\sin A + \cos A)^3 = m^3$

or $\sin^3 A + \cos^3 A + 3\sin A\cos A(\sin A + \cos A) = m^3$.

or $n + 3\sin A\cos A.m = m^3$ ...(i)

or $\sin A\cos A = \dfrac{m^2-1}{2}$ (ii)

From (i) and (ii), we have

$$n + 3m.\frac{(m^2-1)}{2} = m^3$$

or $2n + 3m^3 - 3m = 2m^3$

or $m^3 - 3m + 2n = 0$.

21. Let $A_1 = \pi r^2$, where A_1 and r are area of the circle and its radius.

As the perimeter of the circle is same as the perimeter of a regular polygon of n sides, therefore $2\pi r = na$, where 'a' is the length of one side of the regular polygon.

$\therefore a = \dfrac{2\pi r}{n}$

Let A_2 be the area of the polygon. Then

$$A_2 = \frac{1}{4}\pi a^2 \cot\left(\frac{\pi}{n}\right)$$

$$= \frac{\pi^2 r^2}{n}\cot\left(\frac{\pi}{n}\right)$$

$$\therefore A_1 : A_2 = \pi r^2 : \frac{\pi^2 r^2}{n}\cot\left(\frac{\pi}{n}\right) = \tan\left(\frac{\pi}{n}\right) : \frac{\pi}{n}.$$

22. Given

$\dfrac{\cos A}{a} = \dfrac{\cos B}{b} = \dfrac{\cos C}{c}$

$\Rightarrow \dfrac{\cos A}{k\sin A} = \dfrac{\cos B}{k\sin B} = \dfrac{\cos C}{k\sin C}$

$\left(\because \dfrac{a}{\sin A} = \dfrac{b}{\sin B} = \dfrac{c}{\sin C} = k\right)$

$\Rightarrow \cot A = \cot B = \cot C$

$\Rightarrow A = B = C = 60°$

$\Rightarrow \Delta ABC$ is equilateral.

Hence $\Delta = \dfrac{\sqrt{3}}{4}a^2 = \sqrt{3}$ $(\because a = 2)$.

24. $\dfrac{2\cos A}{a} + \dfrac{2\cos C}{c} + \dfrac{2\cos B}{b} = \dfrac{a}{bc} + \dfrac{b}{ca}$

$\Rightarrow \dfrac{2(c\cos A + a\cos C)}{ac} + \dfrac{\cos B}{b} = \dfrac{a^2+b^2}{abc}$

$\Rightarrow \dfrac{2b}{ac} + \dfrac{a^2+c^2-b^2}{2abc} = \dfrac{a^2+b^2}{abc}$

$\Rightarrow 4b^2 + c^2 + a^2 - b^2 = 2a^2 + 2b^2$

$\Rightarrow b^2 + c^2 = a^2$

$\Rightarrow \Delta ABC$ is a right angle triangle with $\angle A = 90°$.

25. r_1, r_2, r_3 are in H.P.

$\Rightarrow \dfrac{2}{r_1} = \dfrac{1}{r_1} + \dfrac{1}{r_2}$

$\Rightarrow \dfrac{2(S-b)}{\Delta} = \dfrac{S-a}{\Delta} + \dfrac{S-c}{\Delta}$

$\Rightarrow 2S - 2b = 2S - a - c$

$\Rightarrow 2b = a + c$

$\Rightarrow a, b, c$ are in A.P.

26. We have : $r = 4R \sin\frac{A}{2}\sin\frac{B}{2}\sin\frac{C}{2}$

$\Rightarrow \quad r = 4R\sin^3 30°$

$[\because A = B = C = 60°]$

$\Rightarrow \quad r = 4R\left(\frac{1}{2}\right)^3 \Rightarrow r = \frac{R}{2}.$

27. As $\cot\frac{A}{2}, \cot\frac{B}{2}, \cot\frac{C}{2}$ are in AP

$$2\cot\frac{B}{2} = \cot\frac{A}{2} + \cot\frac{C}{2}$$

$$\Rightarrow 2\sqrt{\frac{s(s-b)}{(s-a)(s-c)}} = \sqrt{\frac{s(s-a)}{(s-b)(s-c)}} + \sqrt{\frac{s(s-c)}{(s-a)(s-b)}}$$

$\Rightarrow \quad 2(s-b) = s-a+s-c$

$\Rightarrow \quad 2b = a + c$

$\therefore$ *a, b, c* are in AP.

28. We have $\Delta = \frac{\sqrt{3}}{4}a^2, s = \frac{3a}{2}$

$$\therefore r = \frac{\Delta}{S} = \frac{a}{2\sqrt{3}}, R = \frac{abc}{4\Delta} = \frac{a^3}{\sqrt{3}a^2} = \frac{a}{\sqrt{3}}$$

and $r_1 = \frac{\Delta}{s-a} = \frac{\sqrt{3}/4a^2}{a/2} = \frac{\sqrt{3}}{2}a$

$$\therefore r : R : r_1 = \frac{a}{2\sqrt{3}} : \frac{a}{\sqrt{3}} : \frac{\sqrt{3}}{2}a = 1:2:3.$$

29. We know that

Area $\quad \Delta = \frac{1}{2}ac\sin B$

$$\therefore \quad 6+2\sqrt{3} = \frac{1}{2}\left(\sqrt{3}+1\right).c.\sin 45°$$

or $\quad c = \frac{2\sqrt{2}.\sqrt{3}\left(1+\sqrt{3}\right)}{\sqrt{3}+1} = 2\sqrt{6}$

We also know that

$$\cos B = \frac{a^2+c^2-b^2}{2ac}$$

$$\text{or } \cos 45° = \frac{\left\{2\left(\sqrt{3}+1\right)\right\}^2 + \left(2\sqrt{6}\right)^2 - b^2}{2.2\left(\sqrt{3}+1\right).2\sqrt{6}}$$

or $\quad \frac{1}{\sqrt{2}} = \frac{4\left(4+2\sqrt{3}\right)+24-b^2}{8\sqrt{6}\left(\sqrt{3}+1\right)}$

or $8\sqrt{3}+24 = 16+8\sqrt{3}+24-b^2$

or $\quad b^2 = 16$

or $\quad b = 4.$

30. Here the angles are in AP

$\therefore \quad 2B = A + C$

or $\quad 3B = A + B + C$

or $\quad 3B = 180°$

or $\quad B = 60°$

Now $\quad \cos B = \frac{a^2+c^2-b^2}{2ac}$

or $\quad \cos 60° = \frac{a^2+c^2-b^2}{2ac}$

or $\quad \frac{1}{2} = \frac{a^2+c^2-b^2}{2ac}$

or $\quad a^2+c^2-b^2 = ac$

or $\quad a^2+c^2-b^2 = b^2 \quad [\because$ a, b, c are in GP]

or $\quad a^2+c^2 = 2b^2$

$\therefore a^2, b^2, c^2$ are in GP.

31. The equation

$(\cos p - 1)x^2 + (\cos p)x + \sin p = 0$

has real roots if

$\cos^2 p - 4\sin p(\cos p - 1) \geq 0$

$\Rightarrow (\cos p - 2\sin p)^2 - 4\sin^2 p + 4\sin p \geq 0$

$\Rightarrow (\cos p - 2\sin p)^2 + 4\sin p(1-\sin p) \geq 0$

Now, $0 < p < \pi$,

$\Rightarrow 4\sin p(1-\sin p) > 0$

and $(\cos p - 2\sin p)^2 \geq 0$

Thus, $(\cos p - 2\sin p)^2 + 4\sin p(1-\sin p) \geq 0$ for $0 < p < \pi$.

Hence, the equation has real roots for $0 < p < \pi$.

32. Here AD = p and BC = $2\sqrt{2}p$

Diagram shows $p = a\sin\theta = b\cos\theta$

and $a^2 + b^2 = \left(2\sqrt{2}p\right)^2$

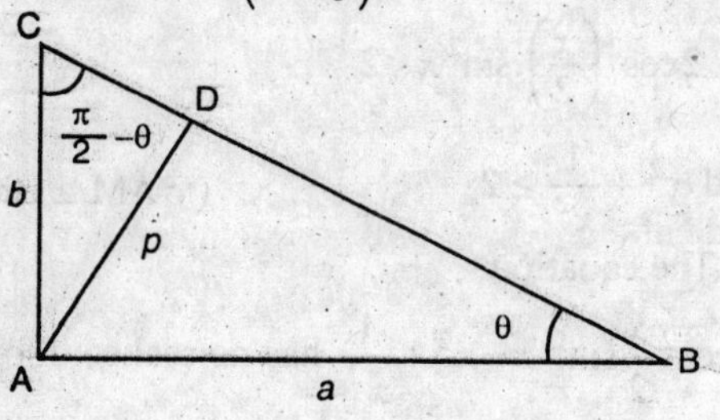

$$\Rightarrow p^2\left(\frac{1}{\sin^2\theta}+\frac{1}{\cos^2\theta}\right) = 8p^2$$

$$\Rightarrow \quad 2\sin^2 2\theta = 1$$

$$\Rightarrow \quad \sin 2\theta = \pm\frac{1}{\sqrt{2}}$$

$$\Rightarrow \quad \sin 2\theta = \frac{1}{\sqrt{2}}$$

($\because \theta$ is acute angle)

$$\Rightarrow 2\theta = \frac{\pi}{4} \Rightarrow \theta = \frac{\pi}{8}.$$

So, other angle is $\frac{\pi}{2}-\frac{\pi}{8}=\frac{3\pi}{8}$.

33. Applying $R_3 \to R_3 - R_2$ and $R_2 \to R_2 - R_1$, we get

$$\begin{vmatrix} 1+\cos^2\theta & \sin^2\theta & 4\sin 4\theta \\ -1 & 1 & 0 \\ 0 & -1 & 1 \end{vmatrix} = 0$$

$$\Rightarrow \begin{vmatrix} 2 & \sin^2\theta & 4\sin 4\theta \\ 0 & 1 & 0 \\ -1 & -1 & 1 \end{vmatrix} = 0,$$

Applying $C_1 \to C_1 + C_2$

$$\Rightarrow \quad 2 + 4\sin 4\theta = 0$$

$$\Rightarrow \quad \sin 4\theta = -\frac{1}{2}$$

$$\Rightarrow \quad 4\theta = n\pi + (-1)^n\left(-\frac{\pi}{6}\right)$$

$$\Rightarrow \quad \theta = \frac{n\pi}{4} + (-1)^n\frac{\pi}{24}.$$

Clearly $\theta = \frac{7\pi}{24}, \frac{11\pi}{24}$ are two values of θ lying between 0 and $\frac{\pi}{2}$.

34. Since, $\cos^2\left(\frac{x}{2}\right)$ and $\sin^2 x$ both can not be greater than 1,

So $2\cos^2\left(\frac{x}{2}\right).\sin^2 x < 2$ ...(i)

and $x^2 + \frac{1}{x^2} \geq 2$ ($\because$ AM $\geq$ GM)

$\therefore$ The equation

$2\cos^2\frac{x}{2}\sin^2 x = x^2 + \frac{1}{x^2}$ has no real solution.

35. We have

$$a_1 + a_2\cos 2x + a_3\sin^2 x = 0, \quad \forall x.$$

$$\Rightarrow a_1 + a_2\cos 2x + a_3\left(\frac{1-\cos 2x}{2}\right) = 0, \quad \forall x.$$

$$\Rightarrow \left(a_1 + \frac{1}{2}a_3\right) + \left(a_2 - \frac{1}{2}a_3\right)\cos 2x = 0, \quad \forall x.$$

$$\Rightarrow a_1 + \frac{1}{2}a_3 = 0 \text{ and } a_2 - \frac{1}{2}a_3 = 0$$

$$\Rightarrow a_1 = -\frac{k}{2}, a_2 = \frac{k}{2}, a_3 = k, \text{ where } k \in R.$$

Hence, the solutions are $\left(-\frac{k}{2}, \frac{k}{2}, k\right)$, where k is any real number.

Thus, the number of triplets is infinte.

36. We have

$$\sin\theta\cos\alpha + \cos\theta\sin\alpha = 2k\sin\theta\cos\theta$$

$$\Rightarrow \cos\alpha.\frac{2t}{1+t^2} + \sin\alpha.\frac{1-t^2}{1+t^2} = 2k.\frac{2t}{1+t^2}.\frac{1-t^2}{1+t^2}$$

where $t = \tan\frac{\theta}{2}$

$$\Rightarrow \sin\alpha\, t^4 - (2\cos\alpha + 4k)t^3 + (4k - 2\cos\alpha)t - \sin\alpha = 0$$

$$\Rightarrow \sum t_1 = 2\cos\alpha + 4k, \sum t_1t_2 = 0,$$

$$\sum t_1t_2t_3 = 2\cos\alpha - 4k, \text{ and } t_1t_2t_3t_4 = -\sin\alpha.$$

Now

$$\tan\left(\frac{\theta_1}{2}+\frac{\theta_2}{2}+\frac{\theta_3}{2}+\frac{\theta_4}{2}\right) = \frac{\sum t_1 - \sum t_1t_2t_3}{1+\sum t_1t_2 + t_1t_2t_3t_4} = \infty = \tan\left(\frac{\pi}{2}\right).$$

$$\Rightarrow \frac{\theta_1}{2}+\frac{\theta_2}{2}+\frac{\theta_3}{2}+\frac{\theta_4}{2} = n\pi + \frac{\pi}{2}$$

$$\Rightarrow \theta_1 + \theta_2 + \theta_3 + \theta_4 = (2n+1)\pi.$$

37. The given equation is

$$3^{\sin 2x + 2\cos^2 x} + 3^{1-\sin 2x + 2\sin^2 x} = 28$$

or $3^{\sin 2x + 2\cos^2 x} + 3^{3-(\sin 2x + 2\cos^2 x)} = 28$

Let $3^{\sin 2x + 2\cos^2 x} = y$, then the given equation takes the form

$$y + \frac{27}{y} = 28$$

or $y^2 - 28y + 27 = 0$

or $y = 27, 1$

If $y = 27$, then

$3^{\sin 2x + 2\cos^2 x} = 3^3 \Rightarrow \sin 2x + 2\cos^2 x = 3$

$\Rightarrow 2\sin x \cos x + 2\cos^2 x = 3$

$\Rightarrow 2\tan x + 2 = 3\sec^2 x$

$\Rightarrow 2\tan x + 2 = 3 + 3\tan^2 x$

$\Rightarrow 2\tan^2 x - 2\tan x + 1 = 0$

This equations does not have any solution as $\tan x \notin R$.

If $y = 1$, then

$3^{\sin 2x + 2\cos^2 x} = 3^0$

$\Rightarrow \sin 2x + 2\cos^2 x = 0$

$\Rightarrow 2\cos x(\sin x + \cos x) = 0$

$\Rightarrow \cos x = 0$ or $\tan x = -1$.

38. $\log_{\cos x} \sin x + \log_{\sin x} \cos x = 2$

$\Rightarrow y + \frac{1}{y} = 2$, where $y = \log_{\cos x} \sin x$.

$\Rightarrow y^2 - 2y + 1 = 0$

$\Rightarrow \log_{\cos x} \sin x = 1$

$\Rightarrow \sin x = \cos x \quad (\because \log_y a = x \Rightarrow a^x = y)$

$\Rightarrow x = \frac{\pi}{4}$.

39. Let $81^{\sin^2 x} = y$. Then $81^{\cos^2 x} = 81^{1-\sin^2 x} = \frac{81}{y}$

$\therefore 81^{\sin^2 x} + 81^{\cos^2 x} = 30$

$\Rightarrow y + \frac{81}{y} = 30$

$\Rightarrow y^2 - 30y + 81 = 0$

$\Rightarrow y = 3$ or 27

$\Rightarrow 4\sin^2 x = 1$ or 3

$\Rightarrow \sin^2 x = \frac{1}{4}$ or $\frac{3}{4}$

$\Rightarrow \sin x = \pm\frac{1}{2}$ or $\pm\frac{\sqrt{3}}{2}$

$\Rightarrow x = \frac{\pi}{6}$ or $\frac{\pi}{3}$.

40. $4\tan^{-1}\frac{1}{5} - \tan^{-1}\frac{1}{239}$

$= 2\tan^{-1}\frac{2/5}{1 - 1/25} - \tan^{-1}\frac{1}{239}$

$= 2\tan^{-1}\frac{5}{12} - \tan^{-1}\frac{1}{239}$

$= \tan^{-1}\left[\frac{2.5/12}{1 - (5/12)^2}\right] - \tan^{-1}\frac{1}{239}$

$= \tan^{-1}\frac{120}{119} - \tan^{-1}\frac{1}{239}$

$= \tan^{-1}\left\{\frac{120/119 - 1/239}{1 + 120/119 \times 1/239}\right\}$

$= \tan^{-1}\left(\frac{28569}{28569}\right) = \frac{\pi}{4}$.

41. $\tan^{-1}\left(\frac{x}{y}\right) - \tan^{-1}\left(\frac{x-y}{x+y}\right)$

$= \tan^{-1}\left(\frac{x}{y}\right) - \tan^{-1}\left(\frac{1 - y/x}{1 + y/x}\right)$

$= \tan^{-1}\left(\frac{x}{y}\right) - \tan^{-1}\left(\tan^{-1}1 - \tan^{-1}\frac{y}{x}\right)$

$= \tan^{-1}\left(\frac{x}{y}\right) + \cot^{-1}\left(\frac{x}{y}\right) - \tan^{-1}1$.

$\left[\because \tan^{-1} x = \cot^{-1}\frac{1}{x}\right]$

$= \frac{\pi}{2} - \frac{\pi}{4} = \frac{\pi}{4}$.

42. $\sin^{-1}\left(\frac{2a}{1+a^2}\right) - \cos^{-1}\left(\frac{1-b^2}{1+b^2}\right)$

$= \tan^{-1}\left(\frac{2x}{1-x^2}\right)$

$\Rightarrow 2\tan^{-1} a - 2\tan^{-1} b = 2\tan^{-1} x$

$\Rightarrow \tan^{-1} x = \tan^{-1}\left(\frac{a-b}{1+ab}\right) \Rightarrow x = \frac{a-b}{1+ab}$.

43. Let O be the centre of the square, OP the pole. Shadow of the pole OP is OQ. It is given that $BQ = y$ and $CQ = x$.

Then BC = $x + y$.

Let OR ⊥ BC

$$\therefore \quad OR = \frac{x+y}{2} \text{ and } BR = \frac{x+y}{2}$$

$$RQ = \frac{x+y}{2} - y = \frac{x-y}{2}$$

Let the height of the pole be h.

From right angled triangle POQ, we have

$$\tan\alpha = \frac{h}{OQ} \qquad \therefore OQ = h\cot\alpha$$

Now, from right angled triangle ORQ

$$OQ^2 = OR^2 + RQ^2$$

$$\text{or} \quad h^2\cot\alpha = \left(\frac{x+y}{2}\right)^2 + \left(\frac{x-y}{2}\right)^2$$

$$\text{or} \quad h^2\cot\alpha = \frac{2(x^2+y^2)}{4}$$

$$\therefore \quad h = \sqrt{\frac{(x^2+y^2)}{4}\,.\tan\alpha}\,.$$

44. Let O be the centre of the ball and E, the man's eye. EA and EB are the tangents covering the ball and hence

$\angle AEB = \alpha$

OO' is drawn perpendicular to EO'

and $\angle OEO' = \beta$.

Let $OO' = h$

From right angled triangle $OO'E$,

$$\sin\beta = \frac{h}{EO}$$

$$\therefore \quad h = EO\sin\beta \qquad ...(i)$$

From geometry, it is clear that

$$\angle AEO = \angle BEO = \frac{\alpha}{2} \qquad (\because \angle AEB = \alpha)$$

Now, from right angled triangle OAE,

$$\sin\frac{\alpha}{2} = \frac{d/2}{OE}$$

$$\text{or} \quad OE = \frac{1}{2}d\,\text{cosec}\,\frac{\alpha}{2} \qquad ...(ii)$$

From *(i)* and *(ii)*, we get

$$h = \frac{1}{2}d\sin\beta\,\text{cosec}\,\frac{\alpha}{2}.$$

45. Let l be the length of the ladder

$a = OA - OB = l\cos\beta - l\cos\alpha$

$b = OP - OQ = l\sin\beta - l\sin\beta$

$$\therefore \quad \frac{a}{b} = \frac{\cos\beta - \cos\alpha}{\sin\alpha - \sin\beta}$$

$$= \frac{2\sin\frac{\alpha+\beta}{2}\sin\frac{\alpha-\beta}{2}}{2\sin\frac{\alpha-\beta}{2}\cos\frac{\alpha+\beta}{2}}$$

$$\Rightarrow \quad a = b\tan\frac{\alpha+\beta}{2}.$$

46. Let AD be the building of height h and BP be the hill. Then

$$\tan q = \frac{h+x}{y} \text{ and } \tan p = \frac{x}{y}$$

$$\tan q = \frac{h+x}{x\cot p}$$

$$\text{or} \quad x\cot p = (h+x)\cot q$$

$$\text{or} \quad x = \frac{h\cot q}{\cot p - \cot q}$$

$$\text{or} \quad h + x = h + \frac{h\cot q}{\cot p - \cot q}$$

$$= \frac{h\cot q}{\cot p - \cot q}.$$

47. Let angle made by flagstaff and tower at C be α.

$$\tan\alpha = \frac{AB}{BC} = \frac{b}{a}.$$

In ΔBCD

$$\tan 2\alpha = \frac{b+h}{a} = \frac{2\tan\alpha}{1-\tan^2\alpha}.$$

$$\text{or} \quad \frac{b+h}{a} = \frac{2(b/a)}{1-(b/a)^2}$$

$$\text{or} \quad \frac{b+h}{a} = b\left(\frac{2ab}{a^2-b^2}\right)$$

$$\Rightarrow h = b\left(\frac{a^2+b^2}{a^2-b^2}\right).$$

48. Let P be the cloud and P' its reflection in the lake. Let T be a point h metres above the surface of the lake.

∴ ST = hm

Let $\angle PTM = \theta$ and $\angle P'TM = \phi$

also let $NP = NP' = x$

$\therefore PM = x - h,\ P'M = x + h$

In $\Delta P'TM$, $\dfrac{P'M}{TM} = \tan\theta$

or $\qquad x - h = TM \tan\theta \qquad ...(i)$

In $\Delta P'TM$, $\dfrac{P'M}{TM} = \tan\phi$

or $\qquad x + h = TM \tan\phi \qquad ...(ii)$

Dividing *(i)* by *(ii)*, we get

$$\frac{x-h}{x+h} = \frac{\tan\theta}{\tan\phi} \quad \text{or} \quad \frac{x}{h} = \frac{\tan\theta + \tan\phi}{\tan\phi - \tan\theta}$$

$$= \frac{\sin\theta\cos\phi + \cos\theta\sin\phi}{\sin\phi\cos\theta - \cos\phi\sin\alpha} = \frac{\sin(\theta+\phi)}{\sin(\phi-\theta)}$$

$$\therefore \quad x = h\frac{\sin(\theta+\phi)}{\sin(\phi-\theta)}.$$

49. Let $\angle APC = \alpha$. Then

$$\tan\alpha = \frac{AC}{AP} = \frac{AC}{nAB} = \frac{AB}{2nAB} = \frac{1}{2n}.$$

In ΔAPB, $\tan(\alpha+\beta) = \dfrac{AB}{AP} = \dfrac{AB}{nAB} = \dfrac{1}{n}$

Now, $\beta = \alpha + \beta - \alpha$

$$\Rightarrow \tan\alpha = \frac{\tan(\alpha+\beta) - \tan\alpha}{1 + \tan(\alpha+\beta).\tan\alpha}$$

$$= \frac{\frac{1}{n} - \frac{1}{2n}}{1 + \frac{1}{n}.\frac{1}{2n}} = \frac{n}{2n^2+1}.$$

12. DIFFERENTIAL CALCULUS

Let u be a function of two variables x and y.

Let $u = f(x, y)$

Then $\lim_{h \to 0} \frac{f(x+h, y) - f(x, y)}{h}$, if it exists, is called the partial derivative or partial differential coefficient of $f(x, y)$ with respect to x and is denoted by the symbols

$$\frac{\partial f}{\partial x} \text{ or } \frac{\partial u}{\partial x} \text{ or } f_x \text{ or } u_x$$

Similarly, if the

$$\lim_{k \to 0} \frac{f(x, y+k) - f(x, y)}{k} \text{ exists}$$

then this limit is called the partial derivative of $f(x, y)$ with respect to y and is denoted by the symbols

$$\frac{\partial f}{\partial y} \text{ or } \frac{\partial u}{\partial y} \text{ or } f_y \text{ or } u_y$$

So, by f_x, we mean that we have to differentiate the function $f(x, y)$ with respect to x, treating y as constant and by f_y. We mean that we have to differentiate the function $f(x, y)$ with respect to y, keeping x as constant.

We may further differentiate them partially with respect to x and y.

The partial derivatives of $\frac{\partial f}{\partial x}$ with respect to x and y are denoted by

$$\frac{\partial^2 f}{\partial x^2} \text{ and } \frac{\partial^2 f}{\partial y \partial x} \text{ or } f_{xx} \text{ and } f_{yx}$$

Similarly, the partial derivatives of $\frac{\partial f}{\partial y}$ with respect to x and y are denoted by

$$\frac{\partial^2 f}{\partial x \partial y} \text{ and } \frac{\partial^2 f}{\partial y^2} \text{ or } f_{xy} \text{ and } f_{yy}$$

Note : If $f(x, y)$ possesses continuous partial derivatives, then

$$\frac{\partial^2 f}{\partial x \partial y} = \frac{\partial^2 f}{\partial y \partial x} \text{ or } f_{xy} = f_{yx}$$

Illustration

1. Prove that $x\frac{\partial u}{\partial x} + y\frac{\partial u}{\partial y} = 0$ if

$$u = \sin^{-1}\left(\frac{x}{y}\right) + \tan^{-1}\left(\frac{y}{x}\right)$$

Solution : Given $u = \sin^{-1}\left(\frac{x}{y}\right) + \tan^{-1}\left(\frac{y}{x}\right)$

so, $$\frac{\partial u}{\partial x} = \frac{1}{\sqrt{\left\{1 - \left(\frac{x}{y}\right)^2\right\}}} \cdot \left(\frac{1}{y}\right) + \frac{1}{1 + \left(\frac{y}{x}\right)^2} \cdot \left(\frac{-y}{x^2}\right)$$

$$\therefore\ x\frac{\partial u}{\partial x} = \frac{x}{\sqrt{(y^2 - x^2)}} - \frac{xy}{x^2 + y^2} \qquad \text{...(i)}$$

Also

$$\frac{\partial u}{\partial y} = \frac{1}{\sqrt{\left\{1 - \left(\frac{x}{y}\right)^2\right\}}} \cdot \left(-\frac{x}{y^2}\right) + \frac{1}{1 + \left(\frac{y}{x}\right)^2} \cdot \left(\frac{1}{x}\right)$$

$$\therefore\ y\frac{\partial u}{\partial y} = -\frac{x}{\sqrt{(y^2 - x^2)}} + \frac{xy}{x^2 + y^2} \qquad \text{...(ii)}$$

Adding *(i)* and *(ii)* we have

$$x\frac{\partial u}{\partial x} + y\frac{\partial u}{\partial y} = 0.$$

2. If $u = \tan^{-1}\left(\frac{y}{x}\right)$, verify that $\frac{\partial^2 z}{\partial x^2} + \frac{\partial^2 z}{\partial y^2} = 0$

Solution : $u = \tan^{-1}\left(\frac{y}{x}\right)$

So $$\frac{\partial u}{\partial x} = \frac{1}{1 + \left(\frac{y}{x}\right)^2} \cdot \left(-\frac{y}{x^2}\right) = -\frac{y}{x^2 + y^2}$$

and $$\frac{\partial u}{\partial y} = \frac{1}{1 + \left(\frac{y}{x}\right)^2} \cdot \left(\frac{1}{x}\right) = \frac{x}{x^2 + y^2}$$

Now $$\frac{\partial^2 z}{\partial x^2} = \frac{\partial}{\partial x}\left(\frac{\partial z}{\partial x}\right) = \frac{\partial}{\partial x}\left(-\frac{y}{x^2+y^2}\right)$$

$$= -y\frac{\partial}{\partial x}\left(x^2+y^2\right)^{-1}$$

$$= (-y)(-1).\left(x^2+y^2\right)^{-2}.(2x)$$

$$= \frac{2xy}{\left(x^2+y^2\right)^2}$$

and $$\frac{\partial^2 z}{\partial y^2} = \frac{\partial}{\partial y}\left(\frac{\partial z}{\partial y}\right) = \frac{\partial}{\partial y}\left(\frac{x}{x^2+y^2}\right)$$

$$= x\frac{\partial}{\partial y}\left\{\left(x^2+y^2\right)^{-1}\right\}$$

$$= x.(-1)\left(x^2+y^2\right)^{-2}.(2y)$$

$$= -\frac{2xy}{\left(x^2+y^2\right)^2}$$

$$\therefore \frac{\partial^2 z}{\partial x^2} + \frac{\partial^2 z}{\partial y^2} = \frac{2xy}{\left(x^2+y^2\right)^2} - \frac{2xy}{\left(x^2+y^2\right)^2} = 0.$$

Euler's Theorem on Homogeneous Function

If $f(x, y)$ be a homogeneous function of x and y of degree n, then

$$x\frac{\partial f}{\partial x} + y\frac{\partial f}{\partial y} = nf.$$

Proof : Since $f(x, y)$ is a homogeneous function of degree n, it can be expressed as

$$f(x, y) = x^n\,\phi\left(\frac{y}{x}\right) \quad ...(i)$$

Differentiating partially with respect to x, have

$$\frac{\partial f}{\partial x} = \frac{\partial}{\partial x}\left\{x^n\,\phi\left(\frac{y}{x}\right)\right\}$$

$$= n\,x^{n-1}\,\phi\left(\frac{y}{x}\right) + x^n\,\phi'\left(\frac{y}{x}\right)\left(-\frac{y}{x^2}\right)$$

$$= n\,x^{n-1}\,\phi\left(\frac{y}{x}\right) - yx^{n-2}\,\phi'\left(\frac{y}{x}\right)$$

$$\therefore \quad x\frac{\partial f}{\partial x} = n\,x^n\,\phi\left(\frac{y}{x}\right) - x^{n-1}.y\,\phi'\left(\frac{y}{x}\right) \quad ...(ii)$$

Again differentiating partially with respect to y, we have

$$\frac{\partial f}{\partial x} = x^n\,\phi'\left(\frac{y}{x}\right).\left(\frac{1}{x}\right) = x^{n-1}\,\phi'\left(\frac{y}{x}\right)$$

$$\therefore \quad y\frac{\partial f}{\partial y} = x^{n-1}.y.\phi'\left(\frac{y}{x}\right) \quad ...(iii)$$

Adding *(ii)* and *(iii)*, we get

$$x\frac{\partial f}{\partial x} + y\frac{\partial f}{\partial y} = n\,x^n\,\phi\left(\frac{y}{x}\right) = nf(x, y)$$

Hence $x\frac{\partial f}{\partial x} + y\frac{\partial f}{\partial y} = nf.$

Note : If $f(x_1, x_2, \ldots, x_m)$ be a homogeneous function of m variables $x_1, x_2, \ldots, x_m$ of degree n, then

$$x_1\frac{\partial f}{\partial x_1} + x_2\frac{\partial f}{\partial x_2} + \ldots + x_m\frac{\partial f}{\partial x_m} = nf.$$

Results of Euler's Theorem : If $f(x, y)$ is a homogeneous function of degree n, then

(i) $x\frac{\partial^2 f}{\partial x^2} + y\frac{\partial^2 f}{\partial x \partial y} = (n-1)\frac{\partial f}{\partial x}$

(ii) $x\frac{\partial^2 f}{\partial x \partial y} + y\frac{\partial^2 f}{\partial y^2} = (n-1)\frac{\partial f}{\partial y}$

(iii) $x^2\frac{\partial^2 f}{\partial x^2} + 2xy\frac{\partial f}{\partial x \partial y} + y^2\frac{\partial^2 f}{\partial y^2} = n(n-1)f(x, y)$

Illustration

1. If $u = \cos^{-1}\frac{x+y}{\sqrt{x}+\sqrt{y}}$, show that

$$x\frac{\partial u}{\partial x} + y\frac{\partial u}{\partial y} + \frac{1}{2}\cot u = 0.$$

Solution : Here u is not a homogeneous function.

But $f(x, y) = \cos u = \frac{x+y}{\sqrt{x}+\sqrt{y}}$ is a homogeneous function of degree $\frac{1}{2}$, because $f(\lambda x, \lambda y) = \frac{\lambda x + \lambda y}{\sqrt{\lambda x} + \sqrt{\lambda y}}$

$$= \lambda^{1/2} \frac{x+y}{\sqrt{x}+\sqrt{y}} = \lambda^{1/2} f(x, y)$$

Hence by Euler's theorem

$$x\frac{\partial f}{\partial x} + y\frac{\partial f}{\partial y} = \frac{1}{2} f$$

or $x\frac{\partial}{\partial x}(\cos u) + y\frac{\partial}{\partial y}(\cos u) = \frac{1}{2}\cos u$

or $-x\sin u\frac{\partial u}{\partial x} - y\sin u\frac{\partial u}{\partial y} = \frac{1}{2}\cos u$

or $x\frac{\partial u}{\partial x} + y\frac{\partial u}{\partial y} = -\frac{1}{2}\cot u$

or $x\frac{\partial u}{\partial x} + y\frac{\partial u}{\partial y} + \frac{1}{2}\cot u = 0$

(proved).

2. If $u = \sin\left(\sqrt{x}+\sqrt{y}\right)$, then show that

$$x\frac{\partial u}{\partial x} + y\frac{\partial u}{\partial y} = \frac{1}{2}\left(\sqrt{x}+\sqrt{y}\right)\cos\left(\sqrt{x}+\sqrt{y}\right).$$

Solution : Here u is not a homogeneous function. But $f(x, y) = \sin^{-1} u = \sqrt{x}+\sqrt{y}$ is a homogeneous function of degree $\frac{1}{2}$, because $f(\lambda x, \lambda y) = \sqrt{\lambda x} + \sqrt{\lambda y}$

$$= \lambda^{1/2}\left(\sqrt{x}+\sqrt{y}\right) = \lambda^{1/2} f(x, y).$$

Hence by Euler's theorem

$$x\frac{\partial f}{\partial x} + y\frac{\partial f}{\partial y} = \frac{1}{2} f$$

or $x\frac{\partial}{\partial x}(\sin^{-1} u) + y\frac{\partial}{\partial y}(\sin^{-1} u) = \frac{1}{2}\sin^{-1} u$

or $x\frac{1}{\sqrt{1-u^2}}\cdot\frac{\partial u}{\partial x} + y\frac{1}{\sqrt{1-u^2}}\cdot\frac{\partial u}{\partial y} = \frac{1}{2}\sin^{-1} u$

or $x\frac{\partial u}{\partial x} + y\cdot\frac{\partial u}{\partial y} = \frac{1}{2}\sin^{-1} u\cdot\sqrt{1-u^2}$

or $x\frac{\partial u}{\partial x} + y\frac{\partial u}{\partial y} = \frac{1}{2}\left(\sqrt{x}+\sqrt{y}\right)\cdot\cos\left(\sqrt{x}+\sqrt{y}\right)$

(proved)

3. If $u = x\,\phi\left(\frac{y}{x}\right) + \psi\left(\frac{y}{x}\right)$, prove that

$$x^2\frac{\partial^2 u}{\partial x^2} + 2xy\frac{\partial^2 u}{\partial x\partial y} + y^2\frac{\partial^2 u}{\partial y^2} = 0$$

Solution : Let $\upsilon = x\,\phi\left(\frac{y}{x}\right)$ and $\omega = \psi\left(\frac{y}{x}\right)$, then $u = \upsilon + \omega$. Clearly, υ and ω are homogeneous functions of degree 1 and 0 respectively. Therefore, by Euler's theorem (for second order)

$$x^2\frac{\partial^2 \upsilon}{\partial x^2} + 2xy\frac{\partial^2 \upsilon}{\partial x\partial y} + y^2\frac{\partial^2 \upsilon}{\partial y^2} = 1.(1-1)\,\upsilon = 0 \quad ...(i)$$

and $$x^2\frac{\partial^2 \omega}{\partial x^2} + 2xy\frac{\partial^2 \omega}{\partial x\partial y} + y^2\frac{\partial^2 \omega}{\partial y^2} = 0.(0-1)\,\omega = 0 \quad ...(ii)$$

Adding *(i)* and *(ii)* we get

$$x^2\frac{\partial}{\partial x^2}(\upsilon+\omega) + 2xy\frac{\partial^2}{\partial x\partial y}(\upsilon+\omega) + y^2\frac{\partial^2}{\partial y^2}(\upsilon+\omega) = 0$$

or $x^2\frac{\partial^2 u}{\partial x^2} + 2xy\frac{\partial^2 u}{\partial x\partial y} + y^2\frac{\partial^2 u}{\partial y^2} = 0.$

Some Important Facts

1. *(a)* If u is a function of x and y, then

$$du = \frac{\partial u}{\partial x}dx + \frac{\partial u}{\partial y}dy$$

(b) If u is a function of x, y and z, then

$$du = \frac{\partial u}{\partial x}dx + \frac{\partial u}{\partial y}dy + \frac{\partial u}{\partial z}dz$$

2. *(a)* If $u = f(x, y)$, then

$$\frac{du}{dx} = \frac{\partial u}{\partial x} + \frac{\partial u}{\partial y}\cdot\frac{\partial y}{\partial x}$$

(b) If $f(x, y) = 0$, then

$$\frac{dy}{dx} = -\frac{\frac{\partial f}{\partial x}}{\frac{\partial f}{\partial y}} = \frac{f_x}{f_y}$$

(c) If $f(x, y) = 0$, then

$$\frac{d^2y}{dx^2} = \frac{d}{dx}\left(\frac{dy}{dx}\right) = \frac{d}{dx}\left(-\frac{f_x}{f_y}\right)$$

$$= -\left[\frac{f_{xx}(f_y)^2 - 2f_xf_yf_{xy} + f_{yy}(f_x)^2}{(f_y)^3}\right]$$

provided $f_y \neq 0$

or $\frac{d^2y}{dx^2} = -\frac{q^2r - 2qps + p^2t}{q^3}$

where $p = \frac{\partial f}{\partial x}, q = \frac{\partial f}{\partial y}, r = \frac{\partial^2 f}{\partial x^2}$,

$$s = \frac{\partial^2 f}{\partial x^2}, s = \frac{\partial^2 f}{\partial x \partial y}, t = \frac{\partial^2 f}{\partial y^2}$$

Illustration : If $y^3 - 3ax^2 + x^3 = 0$, then what is the value of $\frac{\partial^2 y}{\partial x^2}$

Solution : Given $f(x, y) = y^3 - 3ax^2 + x^3 = 0$

$\therefore \quad f_x = -6ax + 3x^2$

$f_y = 3y^2$

$f_{xx} = -6a + 6x, f_{yy} = 6y, f_{xy} = 0$

$$\therefore \frac{d^2y}{dx^2} = -\left[\frac{f_{xx}(f_y)^2 - 2f_xf_yf_{xy} + f_{yy}(f_x)^2}{(f_x)^3}\right]$$

$$= -\left[\frac{(6x - 6a)\left(3y^2\right)^2 - 0 + 6y\,(3x^2 - 6ax)}{\left(3y^2\right)^3}\right]$$

$$= -\frac{2}{y^5}(-ax^3 - ay^3 + 4a^2x^2)$$

$$= -\frac{2}{y^5}\left[-a\,(x^3 + y^3) + 4a^2x^2\right]$$

$$= -\frac{2}{y^5}\left[-a\,(3ax^2) + 4a^2x^2\right]$$

$[\because x^3 + y^3 - 3ax^2 = 0]$

$$= -\frac{2a^2x^2}{y^5}$$

Approximations : If u is a function of x and y, then a small change of dx and dy in x and y corresponds a small change in u and is given by

$$du = \frac{\partial u}{\partial x}dx + \frac{\partial u}{\partial y}dy$$

Illustration

1. What is the error in density of a cube when its mass is uncertain by $\pm 2\%$ and lenth of its edge is uncertain by $\pm 1\%$.

Solution : We have Density $= \frac{\text{Mass}}{\text{Volume}}$

or $\quad \rho = \frac{m}{a^3}$ where a = length of its edge

Now $\quad d\rho = \frac{\partial \rho}{\partial m}.dm + \frac{\partial \rho}{\partial a}da$

$$= \frac{1}{a^3}dm + 3.\frac{m}{a^4}da \quad ...(i)$$

(Here – sign is omitted because changes always taken +ive)

Here $\quad dm = 2\%$ of $m = \frac{2m}{100} \quad ...(ii)$

and $\quad da = 1\%$ of $a = \frac{a}{100} \quad ...(iii)$

From (i), (ii) and (iii) we get

$$d\rho = \frac{1}{a^3}\cdot\left(\frac{2m}{100}\right) + 3.\frac{m}{a^4}\cdot\left(\frac{a}{100}\right)$$

$$= \frac{2m}{100a^3} + \frac{3m}{100a^3} = \frac{5}{100}.\frac{m}{a^3} = \frac{5\rho}{100}$$

$= \pm 5\%$ of density.

EXERCISE

Mark the correct alternative(s) in each of the following :

1. If $u = x^2 \tan^{-1}\frac{y}{x} - y^2 \tan^{-1}\frac{x}{y}$, then $\frac{\partial^2 u}{\partial x \partial y}$ is equal to

(a) $\frac{x^2y}{x^2 + y^2}$ (b) $\frac{xy^2}{x^2 + y^2}$

(c) $\dfrac{x^2 - y^2}{x^2 + y^2}$ (d) $\dfrac{x^2 + y^2}{x^2 - y^2}$

2. If $f(x, y) = \log(x^2 + y^2)$, then $f_{xx} + f_{yy}$ is equal to

(a) $\dfrac{1}{x^2 + y^2}$ (b) 0

(c) $\dfrac{x^2 - y^2}{(x^2 + y^2)^2}$ (d) $\dfrac{y^2 - x^2}{(x^2 + y^2)^2}$

3. If $u = \dfrac{x^2 + y^2}{x + y}$, then $\left(\dfrac{\partial u}{\partial x} - \dfrac{\partial u}{\partial y}\right)^2$ is equal to

(a) $\left\{1 - \dfrac{\partial u}{\partial x} - \dfrac{\partial u}{\partial y}\right\}$ (b) $4\left\{1 - \dfrac{\partial u}{\partial x} - \dfrac{\partial u}{\partial y}\right\}$

(c) $\left\{1 + \dfrac{\partial u}{\partial x} - \dfrac{\partial u}{\partial y}\right\}$ (d) $4\left\{1 + \dfrac{\partial u}{\partial x} - \dfrac{\partial u}{\partial y}\right\}$

4. If $u = a \sin\left(\dfrac{x}{y}\right) + b \cos\left(\dfrac{y}{x}\right)$, then $x\dfrac{\partial u}{\partial x} + y\dfrac{\partial u}{\partial y}$ is equal to

(a) $2a\left(\dfrac{x}{y}\right)\cos\left(\dfrac{x}{y}\right)$ (b) $2b\left(\dfrac{y}{x}\right)\cos\left(\dfrac{y}{x}\right)$

(c) 0 (d) None of these

5. If $u = f(y + ax) + \phi(y - ax)$, then $\dfrac{\partial^2 u}{\partial x^2}$ is equal to

(a) $\dfrac{\partial^2 u}{\partial y^2}$ (b) $a^2\dfrac{\partial^2 u}{\partial y^2}$

(c) $-a^2\dfrac{\partial^2 u}{\partial y^2}$ (d) $a\dfrac{\partial^2 u}{\partial y^2}$

6. If $u = \dfrac{x^2(x^2 - y^2)^3}{(x^2 + y^2)^2}$, then $x\dfrac{\partial u}{\partial x} + y\dfrac{\partial u}{\partial y}$ equal to

(a) u (b) $2u$

(c) $3u$ (d) $4u$

7. If $u = \begin{vmatrix} x^2 & y^2 & z^2 \\ x & y & z \\ 1 & 1 & 1 \end{vmatrix}$, then $\dfrac{\partial u}{\partial x} + \dfrac{\partial u}{\partial y} + \dfrac{\partial u}{\partial z}$ is equal to

(a) 0 (b) 1

(c) $x + y + z$ (d) $2(x + y + z)$

8. If $u = \log(x^3 + y^3 + z^3 - 3xyz)$, then $x\dfrac{\partial u}{\partial x} + y\dfrac{\partial u}{\partial y} + z\dfrac{\partial u}{\partial z}$ is equal to

(a) $3u$ (b) $2u$

(c) 3 (d) 0

9. If $u = \dfrac{y}{z} + \dfrac{z}{x} + \dfrac{x}{y}$, then $x\dfrac{\partial u}{\partial x} + y\dfrac{\partial u}{\partial y} + z\dfrac{\partial u}{\partial z}$ is equal to

(a) u (b) 1

(c) 0 (d) None of these

10. If $u = \log r$, where $r^2 = (x-a)^2 + (y-b)^2 + (z-c)^2$, then $u_{xx} + u_{yy} + u_{zz}$ is equal to

(a) 0 (b) $\dfrac{1}{r}$

(c) $\dfrac{1}{r^2}$ (d) None of these

11. If $u = e^{ax + by} f(ax - by)$, then $\dfrac{1}{u}(bu_x + au_y)$ is equal to

(a) ab (b) $2ab$

(c) $\dfrac{ab}{2}$ (d) None of these

12. If $u = 3x^2yz + 5xy^2z + 4z^4$, then $x\dfrac{\partial u}{\partial x} + y\dfrac{\partial u}{\partial y} + z\dfrac{\partial u}{\partial z}$ is equal to

(a) $2u$ (b) $3u$

(c) $4u$ (d) None of these

13. If $u = \sin^{-1}\dfrac{x^2 + y^2}{x + y}$, then $x\dfrac{\partial u}{\partial x} + y\dfrac{\partial u}{\partial y}$ is equal to

(a) $\sin u$ (b) $\tan u$

(c) $\cot u$ (d) None of these

14. If $u = \tan^{-1}\dfrac{x^2 + y^2}{x - y}$, then $x\dfrac{\partial u}{\partial x} + y\dfrac{\partial u}{\partial y}$ is equal to

(a) $\sin u$ (b) $\tan 2u$

(c) $\frac{1}{2}\sin^2 u$ (d) $\frac{1}{2}\tan u$

15. If $u = \log \frac{x^2 + y^2}{x + y}$, then $x\frac{\partial u}{\partial x} + y\frac{\partial u}{\partial y}$ is equal to

(a) 0 (b) 1

(c) u (d) eu

[J.N.U. M.C.A.]

16. If $u = \tan^{-1}\left(\frac{x^3 + y^3}{x - y}\right)$, the value of

$x^2\frac{\partial^2 u}{\partial x^2} + 2xy\frac{\partial^2 u}{\partial x \partial y} + y^2\frac{\partial^2 u}{\partial y^2}$ is

(a) $\sin 3u \sin 2u \sin u$

(b) $\cos 2u\,(2 - \cos^2 u)$

(c) $\tan 2u\,(\cos 2u - \sin 2u)$

(d) $\sin 2u\,(1 - 4\sin^2 u)$

[J.N.U. M.C.A.]

17. If $u = \log(\tan x + \tan y + \tan z)$, then

$(\sin 2x)\frac{\partial u}{\partial x} + (\sin 2y)\frac{\partial u}{\partial y} + (\sin 2z)\frac{\partial u}{\partial z}$ is equal to

(a) 1 (b) 2 (c) u (d) $2u$

18. If $x^x y^y z^z = c$, then $\frac{\partial z}{\partial x}$ is equal to

(a) $\frac{1 + \log x}{1 + \log z}$ (b) $-\left(\frac{1 + \log x}{1 + \log z}\right)$

(c) $-\left(\frac{1 + \log y}{1 + \log z}\right)$ (d) None of these

19. If $u = \sec^{-1}\frac{x^2 + y^2}{x - y}$, then $x\frac{\partial u}{\partial x} + y\frac{\partial u}{\partial y}$ is equal to

(a) $\tan u$ (b) $\cot u$

(c) $\cos u$ (d) None of these

20. If $u = \log(x^3 + y^3 + z^3 - 3xyz)$, then $\frac{\partial^2 u}{\partial x^2} + \frac{\partial^2 u}{\partial y^2} + \frac{\partial^2 u}{\partial z^2}$ is equal to

(a) $\frac{3}{(x + y + z)^2}$ (b) $-\frac{3}{(x + y + z)^2}$

(c) $\frac{3}{(x + y + z)^3}$ (d) $-\frac{3}{(x + y + z)^3}$

21. If $u = x^2\tan^{-1}\frac{y}{x} - y^2\tan^{-1}\frac{x}{y}$, then $\frac{\partial^2 u}{\partial x \partial y}$ is equal to

(a) $\frac{x - y}{x + y}$ (b) $\frac{x + y}{x - y}$

(c) $\frac{x^2 - y^2}{x^2 + y^2}$ (d) $\frac{x^2 + y^2}{x^2 - y^2}$

22. If $u = (ax + by)^2 - (x^2 + y^2)$ and $a^2 + b^2 = 1$, $\frac{\partial^2 u}{\partial x^2} + \frac{\partial^2 u}{\partial y^2}$ is equal to

(a) $(x^2 + y^2)$ (b) $x^2 - y^2$

(c) 0 (d) $2abxy$

23. If $u = \frac{1}{(x^2 + y^2 + z^2)^{1/2}}$, then $\frac{\partial^2 u}{\partial x^2} + \frac{\partial^2 u}{\partial y^2} + \frac{\partial^2 u}{\partial z^2}$ is equal to

(a) -2 (b) $\frac{1}{2}$

(c) 0 (d) None of these

24. If $u = \cos(x + y) + \cos(x - y)$, then which of the following are true?

I. $\frac{\partial^2 u}{\partial x^2} = \frac{\partial^2 u}{\partial y^2}$

II. $\frac{\partial^2 u}{\partial x^2} = \frac{\partial^2 u}{\partial x \partial y}$

III. $\frac{\partial^2 u}{\partial y^2} = \frac{\partial^2 u}{\partial y \partial x}$

(a) I only (b) I and II only

(c) II only (d) I, II and III only

[J.N.U. M.C.A.]

25. A physical quantity x is calculated from the relation $x = \frac{a^2 b^3}{c\sqrt{d}}$

If percentage error in a, b, c, d are 2%, 3% and 4% respectively, then the percentage error in x is

(a) 6% (b) 8%

(c) 10% (d) 12%

26. What is the % error in measurement of 'T' of a pendulum if maximum errors in the measurement of 'l' and 'g' are 2% and 4% respectively

(a) 6% (b) 4%

(c) 3% (d) 5%

27. If an error of 1% is made in measuring the major and minor axes of an ellipse, then the percentage error in the area is approximately

(a) 1% (b) 2%

(c) 1.5% (d) 2.5% *[J.N.U. M.C.A]*

28. The torsional rigidity of the length of a wire is obtained by $N = \frac{8\pi IL}{T^2R^3}$, I is constant. If L is decreased by 2%, R is increased by 2% and T is increased by 1.5%, then the value of N is

(a) increased by 7%

(b) diminishes by 13%

(c) increased by 11%

(d) diminishes by 9% *[J.N.U. M.C.A.]*

29. In the formula $D = \frac{d^2}{2h} + \frac{h}{2}$. If the percentage of error in D is not to exceed 0.3% then the allowable percentage error in d and h will be

(a) 0.177 and 0.98 (b) 0.98 and 0.177

(c) 0.47 and 0.98 (d) 0.98 and 0.47

[J.N.U. M.C.A.]

30. The side a and the opposite angle A of a ΔABC remain constant when other sides and angles are slightly varied, then

(a) $\frac{\delta b}{\cos C} + \frac{\delta c}{\cos B} = 0$ (b) $\frac{\delta b}{\cos C} = \frac{\delta c}{\cos C}$

(c) $\frac{\delta b}{\cos B} + \frac{\delta c}{\cos C} = 0$ (d) $\frac{\delta b}{\cos B} = \frac{\delta c}{\cos C}$

31. If $u = f(n)$, where $r = \sqrt{x^2 + y^2}$, then $u_{xx} + u_{yy}$ is equal to

(a) $f''(r)$ (b) $f''(r) + f(r)$

(c) $f''(r) + \frac{1}{r}f'(r)$ (d) None of these

ANSWERS

1	2	3	4	5	6	7	8	9	10
(c)	(b)	(b)	(c)	(b)	(d)	(a)	(c)	(c)	(c)
11	**12**	**13**	**14**	**15**	**16**	**17**	**18**	**19**	**20**
(b)	(c)	(b)	(c)	(b)	(d)	(b)	(b)	(b)	(b)
21	**22**	**23**	**24**	**25**	**26**	**27**	**28**	**29**	**30**
(c)	(c)	(c)	(a)	(d)	(c)	(b)	(b)	(c)	(c)
31									
(c)									

SOME SELECTED EXPLANATORY ANSWERS

1. Given $u = x^2 \tan^{-1}\frac{y}{x} - y^2 \tan^{-1}\frac{x}{y}$

Then

$$\frac{\partial u}{\partial x} = 2x\tan^{-1}\frac{y}{x} + x^2 \cdot \frac{1}{1+\left(\frac{y}{x}\right)^2}\cdot\left(-\frac{y}{x^2}\right) - y^2 \cdot \frac{1}{1+\left(\frac{x}{y}\right)^2}\cdot\left(\frac{1}{y}\right)$$

$$= 2x\tan^{-1}\frac{y}{x} - \frac{x^2y}{x^2+y^2} - \frac{y^3}{x^2+y^2}$$

$$= 2x\tan^{-1}\frac{y}{x} - y$$

$$\therefore \quad \frac{\partial u}{\partial x} = 2x\tan^{-1}\frac{y}{x} - y$$

Partially differentiating w.r.t. y, we get

$$\frac{\partial^2 z}{\partial y\,\partial x} = 2x \cdot \frac{1}{1+\left(\frac{y}{x}\right)^2}\cdot\left(\frac{1}{x}\right) - 1$$

$$= \frac{2x^2}{x^2+y^2} - 1 = \frac{x^2-y^2}{x^2+y^2}$$

or $$\frac{\partial^2 z}{\partial y\,\partial x} = \frac{x^2-y^2}{x^2+y^2}.$$

2. Given $f(x, y) = \log(x^2 + y^2)$

$$\therefore \quad f_x = \frac{\partial f}{\partial x} = \frac{2x}{x^2+y^2}$$

$$f_{xx} = \frac{\partial^2 f}{\partial x^2} = \frac{\partial}{\partial f}\left(\frac{2x}{x^2+y^2}\right)$$

$$= \frac{2(x^2+y^2) - 2x(2x)}{(x^2+y^2)^2} = \frac{2(y^2-x^2)}{(x^2+y^2)^2}$$

Since f is symmetric in x, y, therefore

$$f_{yy} = \frac{2(x^2-y^2)}{(x^2+y^2)^2}.$$

$$\therefore f_{xx} + f_{yy} = \frac{2(y^2-x^2)}{(x^2+y^2)^2} + \frac{2(x^2-y^2)}{(x^2+y^2)^2} = 0.$$

3. Given $u = \dfrac{x^2+y^2}{x+y}$

$$\therefore \quad \frac{\partial u}{\partial x} = \frac{2x(x+y) - 1.(x^2+y^2)}{(x+y)^2}$$

$$= \frac{x^2+2xy-y^2}{(x+y)^2}$$

$$\frac{\partial u}{\partial y} = \frac{2y(x+y) - 1.(x^2+y^2)}{(x+y)^2}$$

$$= \frac{y^2+2xy-x^2}{(x+y)^2}$$

Subtracting we get

$$\frac{\partial u}{\partial x} - \frac{\partial u}{\partial y} = \frac{2(x^2-y^2)}{(x+y)^2} = \frac{2(x-y)}{x+y}$$

Adding we get

$$\frac{\partial u}{\partial x} + \frac{\partial u}{\partial y} = \frac{4xy}{(x+y)^2}$$

Now $$\left(\frac{\partial u}{\partial x} - \frac{\partial u}{\partial y}\right)^2 = \frac{4(x-y)^2}{(x+y)^2} \qquad ...(i)$$

Also $$4\left\{1 - \frac{\partial u}{\partial x} - \frac{\partial u}{\partial y}\right\} = 4\left\{1 - \frac{4xy}{(x+y)^2}\right\}$$

$$= 4.\frac{(x-y)^2}{(x+y)^2} \qquad ...(ii)$$

From *(i)* and *(ii)* we get

$$\left(\frac{\partial u}{\partial x} - \frac{\partial u}{\partial y}\right)^2 = 4\left\{1 - \frac{\partial u}{\partial x} - \frac{\partial u}{\partial y}\right\}.$$

4. Given $u = a\sin\left(\dfrac{x}{y}\right) + b\cos\left(\dfrac{y}{x}\right)$

$$\therefore \quad \frac{\partial u}{\partial x} = a\cos\left(\frac{x}{y}\right).\left(\frac{1}{y}\right) - b\sin\left(\frac{y}{x}\right).\left(-\frac{y}{x^2}\right)$$

and $$\frac{\partial u}{\partial y} = a\cos\left(\frac{x}{y}\right).\left(\frac{-x}{y^2}\right) - b\sin\left(\frac{y}{x}\right).\left(\frac{1}{x}\right)$$

$$\therefore \quad x\frac{\partial u}{\partial x} + y\frac{\partial u}{\partial y}$$

$$= a\left(\frac{x}{y}\right)\cos\left(\frac{x}{y}\right) + b\left(\frac{y}{x}\right)\sin\left(\frac{y}{x}\right)$$

$$- a\left(\frac{x}{y}\right)\cos\left(\frac{x}{y}\right) - b\left(\frac{y}{x}\right)\sin\left(\frac{y}{x}\right) = 0.$$

5. Given $u = f(y+ax) + \phi(y-ax)$

$$\therefore \quad \frac{\partial u}{\partial x} = af'(y+ax) - a\phi'(y-ax)$$

$$\frac{\partial^2 u}{\partial x^2} = a^2 f''(y+ax) - a^2\phi''(y-ax)$$

$$= a^2\left[f''(y+ax) + \phi''(y-ax)\right] \qquad ...(i)$$

Also $$\frac{\partial u}{\partial y} = f'(y+ax) + \phi'(y-ax)$$

$$\frac{\partial^2 u}{\partial y^2} = f''(y+ax) + \phi'(y-ax) \qquad ...(ii)$$

From *(i)* and *(ii)* we get

$$\frac{\partial^2 u}{\partial x^2} = a^2\frac{\partial^2 u}{\partial y^2}.$$

6. Given $u = \dfrac{x^2(x^2-y^2)^3}{(x^2+y^2)^2}$

Here u is a homogeneous function of degree 4.

∴ By Euler's theorem, we have

$$x\frac{\partial u}{\partial x}+y\frac{\partial u}{\partial y}=4u.$$

7. Given $u=\begin{vmatrix}x^2 & y^2 & z^2\\ x & y & z\\ 1 & 1 & 1\end{vmatrix}$

$$\therefore\quad \frac{\partial u}{\partial x}=\begin{vmatrix}2x & 0 & 0\\ 1 & 0 & 0\\ 0 & 0 & 0\end{vmatrix}$$

$$\frac{\partial u}{\partial y}=\begin{vmatrix}0 & 2y & 0\\ 0 & 1 & 0\\ 0 & 0 & 0\end{vmatrix}$$

$$\frac{\partial u}{\partial z}=\begin{vmatrix}0 & 0 & 2z\\ 0 & 0 & 1\\ 0 & 0 & 0\end{vmatrix}$$

$$\therefore\quad \frac{\partial u}{\partial x}+\frac{\partial u}{\partial y}+\frac{\partial u}{\partial z}=\begin{vmatrix}2x & 2y & 2z\\ 1 & 1 & 1\\ 0 & 0 & 0\end{vmatrix}=0.$$

8. Given $u=\log(x^3+y^3+z^3-3xyz)$

$$\therefore\quad \frac{\partial u}{\partial x}=\frac{3x^2-3yz}{x^3+y^3+z^3-3xyz}$$

Similarly $\dfrac{\partial u}{\partial y}=\dfrac{3y^2-3xz}{x^3+y^3+z^3-3xyz}$

$$\frac{\partial u}{\partial z}=\frac{3z^2-3xy}{x^3+y^3+z^3-3xyz}$$

$$\therefore\quad x\frac{\partial u}{\partial x}+y\frac{\partial u}{\partial y}+z\frac{\partial u}{\partial z}=\frac{3(x^3-xyz)}{x^3+y^3+z^3-3xyz}$$

$$+\frac{3(y^3-xyz)}{x^3+y^3+z^3-3xyz}+\frac{3(z^3-xyz)}{x^3+y^3+z^3-3xyz}$$

$$=\frac{3(x^3+y^3+z^3-xyz)}{x^3+y^3+z^3-3xyz}=3.$$

9. Given $u=\dfrac{y}{z}+\dfrac{z}{x}+\dfrac{x}{y}$

$$\therefore\quad \frac{\partial u}{\partial x}=-\frac{z}{x^2}+\frac{1}{y}\Rightarrow x\frac{\partial u}{\partial x}=-\frac{z}{x}+\frac{x}{y}$$

$$\frac{\partial u}{\partial y}=\frac{1}{z}+\frac{x}{y^2}\Rightarrow y\frac{\partial u}{\partial y}=\frac{y}{z}-\frac{x}{y}$$

$$\frac{\partial u}{\partial z}=-\frac{y}{z^2}+\frac{1}{x}\Rightarrow z\frac{\partial u}{\partial z}=-\frac{y}{z}+\frac{z}{x}$$

$$\therefore\quad x\frac{\partial u}{\partial x}+y\frac{\partial u}{\partial y}+z\frac{\partial u}{\partial z}$$

$$=\left(-\frac{z}{x}+\frac{x}{y}\right)+\left(\frac{y}{z}-\frac{x}{y}\right)+\left(-\frac{y}{z}+\frac{z}{x}\right)$$

$= 0.$

Alternate Methode

Given $u=\dfrac{y}{z}+\dfrac{z}{x}+\dfrac{x}{y}$

Here u is a homogeneous function of degree zero.

$$\therefore\quad x\frac{\partial u}{\partial x}+y\frac{\partial u}{\partial y}+z\frac{\partial u}{\partial z}=nu=0.u=0$$

where n is the degree of the function.

10. Given $u=\log r$, where $r^2=(x-a)^2+(y-b)^2+(z-c)^2$.

$$\therefore\quad u_x=\frac{\partial u}{\partial x}=\frac{1}{r}.\frac{\partial r}{\partial x}\text{ and } 2r.\frac{\partial r}{\partial x}=2(x-a)$$

$$\therefore\quad u_x=\frac{1}{r^2}(x-a)$$

$$\Rightarrow\quad u_{xx}=-\frac{2}{r^3}\frac{\partial r}{\partial x}(a-a)+\frac{1}{r^2}$$

$$=-\frac{2}{r^3}.\frac{(x-a)}{r}.(x-a)+\frac{1}{r^2}$$

$$=-\frac{2}{r^4}(x-a)^2+\frac{1}{r^2}$$

Similarly $u_{yy}=-\dfrac{2}{r^4}(y-a)^2+\dfrac{1}{r^2}$

$$u_{zz}=-\frac{2}{r^4}(z-a)^2+\frac{1}{r^2}$$

$\therefore\ u_{xx}+u_{yy}+u_{zz}$

$$=-\frac{2}{r^4}\left\{(x-a)^2+(y-b^2)+(x-c)^2\right\}+\frac{3}{r^2}$$

$$=-\frac{2}{r^4}r^2+\frac{3}{r^2}=\frac{1}{r^2}.$$

11. Given $u=e^{ax+by}.f(ax-by)$

$$u_x=\frac{\partial u}{\partial x}=a.e^{ax+by}.f(ax-by)$$

$$+a.e^{ax+by}.f'(ax-by)$$

$$= a.e^{ax+by}.[f(ax-by)+f'(ax-by)]$$

Also $u_y = \dfrac{\partial u}{\partial y} = b.e^{ax+by}.f(ax-by)$

$$-b.e^{ax+by}.f'(ax-by)$$

$$\therefore \frac{1}{u}(bu_x + au_y) = \frac{ab}{u}[2f(ax-by)].e^{ax+by}$$

$$= \frac{2ab}{u}.e^{ax+by}.f(ax-by) = \frac{2ab}{u}.u = 2ab.$$

12. Given $u = 3x^2yz + 5xy^2z + 4z^4$.

$$\therefore \quad \frac{\partial u}{\partial x} = 6xyz + 5y^2z$$

or $\quad x\dfrac{\partial u}{\partial x} = 6x^2yz + 5xy^2z$

Similarly $y\dfrac{\partial u}{\partial y} = 3x^2yz + 10xy^2z$

and $\quad z\dfrac{\partial u}{\partial z} = 3x^2yz + 5xy^2z + 16z^4$

$$\therefore \quad x\frac{\partial u}{\partial x} + y\frac{\partial u}{\partial y} + z\frac{\partial u}{\partial z} = 4(3x^2yz + 5xy^2z + 4z^4) =$$

$4u$.

Alternate Methode

Given $u = 3x^2yz + 5xy^2z + 4z^4$

Here u is homogeneous function of degree 4.

$$\therefore \quad x\frac{\partial u}{\partial x} + y\frac{\partial u}{\partial y} + z\frac{\partial u}{\partial z} = 4u.$$

13. Given $u = \sin^{-1}\dfrac{x^2+y^2}{x+y}$

$\Rightarrow \sin u = \dfrac{x^2+y^2}{x+y}$, a homogeneous function of degree one.

$\therefore$ By Euler's theorem for $\sin u$, we have

$$x\frac{\partial}{\partial x}(\sin u) + y\frac{\partial}{\partial y}(\sin u) = 1.\sin u$$

i.e. $x\cos u\dfrac{\partial u}{\partial x} + y\cos u\dfrac{\partial u}{\partial y} = \sin u$

$$\therefore \quad x\frac{\partial u}{\partial x} + y\frac{\partial u}{\partial y} = \tan u.$$

14. Given $u = \tan^{-1}\dfrac{x^2+y^2}{x-y}$

or $\tan u = \dfrac{x^2+y^2}{x-y}$, a homogeneous function of degree one.

$\therefore$ By Euler's theorem for $\tan u$, we have

$$x\frac{\partial}{\partial x}(\tan u) + y\frac{\partial}{\partial y}(\tan u) = 1.\tan u$$

i.e. $x\sec^2 u\dfrac{\partial u}{\partial x} + y\sec^2 u\dfrac{\partial u}{\partial y} = \tan u$

i.e. $x\dfrac{\partial u}{\partial x} + y\dfrac{\partial u}{\partial y} = \tan u.\cos^2 u = \dfrac{1}{2}\sin 2u.$

15. Given $u = \log\dfrac{x^2+y^2}{x+y}$

$$\Rightarrow e^u = \frac{x^2+y^2}{x+y} = f(x, y).$$

Here f is a homogeneous function of degree one.

$$\therefore \quad x\frac{\partial f}{\partial x} + y\frac{\partial f}{\partial y} = f$$

$$\therefore \quad x\frac{\partial e^u}{\partial x} + y\frac{\partial e^u}{\partial y} = f$$

or $\quad xe^u\dfrac{\partial u}{\partial x} + ye^u\dfrac{\partial u}{\partial y} = e^u$

or $\quad x\dfrac{\partial u}{\partial x} + y\dfrac{\partial u}{\partial y} = 1.$

16. Given $u = \tan^{-1}\left(\dfrac{x^3+y^3}{x-y}\right)$

or $\tan u = \dfrac{x^3+y^3}{x-y} = f(\text{say})$

is a homogeneous function of degree two.

$\therefore$ By Euler's theorem we have

$$x\frac{\partial f}{\partial x} + y\frac{\partial f}{\partial y} = 2f$$

or $x\dfrac{\partial(\tan u)}{\partial x} + y\dfrac{\partial(\tan u)}{\partial y} = 2\tan u$

or $x\sec^2 u\dfrac{\partial u}{\partial x} + y\sec^2 u\dfrac{\partial u}{\partial y} = 2\tan u$

or $x\frac{\partial u}{\partial x}+y\frac{\partial u}{\partial y}=\sin 2u.$

Differentiating partially w.r.t. x we get

$$x\frac{\partial^2 u}{\partial x^2}+\frac{\partial u}{\partial x}+y\frac{\partial^2 u}{\partial x\partial y}=2\cos 2u\frac{\partial u}{\partial x} \quad ...(i)$$

Differentiating partially w.r.t. y we get

$$x\frac{\partial^2 u}{\partial x\partial y}+y\frac{\partial^2 u}{\partial y^2}+\frac{\partial u}{\partial y}=2\cos 2u\frac{\partial u}{\partial y} \quad ...(ii)$$

Multiplying *(i)* by x and *(ii)* by y and then adding we get

$$x^2\frac{\partial^2 u}{\partial x^2}+2xy\frac{\partial^2 u}{\partial x\partial y}+y^2\frac{\partial^2 u}{\partial y^2}$$

$$=(2\cos 2u-1)\left(x\frac{\partial u}{\partial x}+y\frac{\partial u}{\partial y}\right)$$

$= (2\cos 2u - 1)(\sin 2u)$

$= \sin 2u\,(1 - 4\sin^2 u).$

17. Given $u = \log(\tan x + \tan y + \tan z)$

or $e^u = \tan x + \tan y + \tan z$

$$\therefore\ \frac{\partial}{\partial x}(e^u)=\sec^2 x \Rightarrow e^u.\frac{\partial u}{\partial x}=\sec^2 x$$

$$\Rightarrow\ \frac{\partial u}{\partial x}=\frac{\sec^2 x}{e^u}$$

$$\Rightarrow\ (\sin 2x)\frac{\partial u}{\partial x}=\frac{\sin 2x.\sec^2 x}{e^u}=2\frac{\tan x}{e^u}$$

Similarly $u_y \sin 2y = 2\frac{\tan y}{e^u}$ and

$u_z \sin 2z = 2\frac{\tan z}{e^u}$

$$\therefore\ (\sin 2x)\frac{\partial u}{\partial x}+(\sin 2y)\frac{\partial u}{\partial y}+(\sin 2z)\frac{\partial u}{\partial z}$$

$$=2.\frac{(\tan x+\tan y+\tan z)}{e^u}=2.$$

18. Given $x^x y^y z^z = c.$

Taking log on both sides, we get

$x\log x + y\log y + z\log z = \log c \quad ...(i)$

Differentiating *(i)* partially w.r.t. x, regarding z as a function of x and y, we have

$$\left(x.\frac{1}{x}+\log x\right)+0+\left(z\frac{1}{z}+\log z\right)\frac{dz}{dx}=0$$

or $$\frac{\partial z}{\partial x}=-\left(\frac{1+\log x}{1+\log z}\right)$$

19. Given $u=\sec^{-1}\left(\frac{x^2+y^2}{x-y}\right)$

or $\sec u=\frac{x^2+y^2}{x-y}$, a homogeneous function of degree one.

$\therefore$ By Euler's theorem for $\sec u$, we have

$$x\frac{\partial}{\partial x}(\sec u)+y\frac{\partial}{\partial y}(\sec u)=1.\sec u$$

or $x\sec u.\tan u.\frac{\partial u}{\partial x}+y\sec u.\tan u.\frac{\partial u}{\partial y}=\sec u$

or $x\frac{\partial u}{\partial x}+y\frac{\partial u}{\partial y}=\cot u.$

20. Given $u = \log(x^3 + y^3 + z^3 - 3xyz)$

or $u = \log\left[(x+y+z)(x^2+y^2+z^2-xy-yz-zx)\right]$

$= \log(x+y+z) + \log(x^2+y^2+z^2-xy-yz-zx)$

Differentiating partially w.r.t. x (keeping y and z as constans), we get

$$\frac{\partial u}{\partial x}=\frac{1}{x+y+z}+\frac{2x-y-z}{x^2+y^2+z^2-xy-yz-zx}$$

Differentiating this partially w.r.t. x (keeping y and z as constanst), we get

$$\frac{\partial^2 u}{\partial x^2}=-\frac{1}{(x+y+z)^2}+\frac{2}{\left(x^2+y^2+z^2-xy-yz-zx\right)}-\frac{(2x-y-z)(2x-y-z)}{\left(x^2+y^2+z^2-xy-yz-zx\right)^2}$$

$$=-\frac{1}{(x+y+z)^2}+\frac{2\left(x^2+y^2+z^2-xy-yz-zx\right)-\left(4x^2+y^2+z^2-4xy+2yz-4xz\right)}{\left(x^2+y^2+z^2-xy-yz-zx\right)^2}$$

$$=-\frac{1}{(x+y+z)^2}+\frac{y^2+z^2+2xy+2xz-2x^2-4yz}{\left(x^2+y^2+z^2-xy-yz-zx\right)^2}$$

Similarly $\frac{\partial^2 u}{\partial y^2} = -\frac{1}{(x+y+z)^2}$

$$+\frac{z^2+x^2+2yz+2yx-2y^2-4zx}{\left(x^2+y^2+z^2-xy-yz-zx\right)^2}$$

$$\frac{\partial^2 u}{\partial z^2} = -\frac{1}{(x+y+z)^2}$$

$$+\frac{x^2+y^2+2zx+2zy-2z^2-4xy}{\left(x^2+y^2+z^2-xy-yz-zx\right)^2}$$

Hence $\frac{\partial^2 u}{\partial x^2}+\frac{\partial^2 u}{\partial y^2}+\frac{\partial^2 u}{\partial z^2} = -\frac{3}{(x+y+z)^2}$.

21. Given $u = x^2 \tan^{-1}\frac{y}{x} - y^2 \tan^{-1}\frac{x}{y}$.

$$\therefore \frac{\partial u}{\partial y} = x^2 . \frac{1}{1+\frac{y^2}{x^2}} . \frac{1}{x} - 2y\tan^{-1}\frac{x}{y}$$

$$+ y^2 . \frac{1}{1+\frac{x^2}{y^2}} . \frac{x}{y^2}$$

or $\frac{\partial u}{\partial y} = \frac{x^3}{x^2+y^2} - 2y\tan^{-1}\frac{x}{y} + \frac{xy^2}{x^2+y^2}$

$$= x - 2y\tan^{-1}\frac{x}{y}.$$

Differentiating partially w.r.t. x, we get

$$\frac{\partial^2 u}{\partial x \partial y} = 1 - 2y . \frac{1}{1+\frac{x^2}{y^2}} . \frac{1}{y}$$

$$= 1 - \frac{2y^2}{x^2+y^2} = \frac{x^2-y^2}{x^2+y^2}$$

22. Here $u = 2(ax+by)^2 - (x^2+y^2)$

$$\therefore \frac{\partial u}{\partial x} = 4a\,(ax+by) - 2x \text{ and}$$

$$\frac{\partial^2 u}{\partial x^2} = 4a^2 - 2$$

Also $\frac{\partial u}{\partial y} = 4b\,(ax+by) - 2y$

and $\frac{\partial^2 u}{\partial y^2} = 4b^2 - 2$

$$\therefore \frac{\partial^2 u}{\partial x^2} + \frac{\partial^2 u}{\partial y^2} = (4a^2-2) + (4b^2-2)$$

$= 4\,(a^2+b^2) - 4$

$= 4 - 4 = 0$ ($\because a^2 + b^2 = 1$).

23. Given $u = \frac{1}{\left(x^2+y^2+z^2\right)^{1/2}}$

$$\therefore \frac{\partial u}{\partial x} = -\frac{1}{2} . \left(x^2+y^2+z^2\right)^{-3/2} . (2x)$$

$$= \frac{-x}{\left(x^2+y^2+z^2\right)^{3/2}}$$

$$\therefore \frac{\partial^2 u}{\partial x^2} =$$

$$\frac{-\left(x^2+y^2+z^2\right)^{3/2} + x . \frac{3}{2} . \left(x^2+y^2+z^2\right)^{1/2} . 2x}{\left(x^2+y^2+z^2\right)^3}$$

$$= -\frac{1}{\left(x^2+y^2+z^2\right)^{3/2}} + \frac{3x^2}{\left(x^2+y^2+z^2\right)^{5/2}}$$

Similarly

$$\frac{\partial^2 u}{\partial y^2} = -\frac{1}{\left(x^2+y^2+z^2\right)^{3/2}} + \frac{3y^2}{\left(x^2+y^2+z^2\right)^{5/2}}$$

$$\frac{\partial^2 u}{\partial z^2} = -\frac{1}{\left(x^2+y^2+z^2\right)^{3/2}} + \frac{3z^2}{\left(x^2+y^2+z^2\right)^{5/2}}$$

$$\therefore \frac{\partial^2 u}{\partial x^2} + \frac{\partial^2 u}{\partial y^2} + \frac{\partial^2 u}{\partial z^2} =$$

$$-\frac{3}{\left(x^2+y^2+z^2\right)^{3/2}} + \frac{3\left(x^2+y^2+z^2\right)}{\left(x^2+y^2+z^2\right)^{5/2}}$$

$$= -\frac{3}{\left(x^2+y^2+z^2\right)^{3/2}} + \frac{3}{\left(x^2+y^2+z^2\right)^{3/2}} = 0.$$

24. Given $u = \cos(x+y) + \cos(x-y)$

$$\therefore \frac{\partial u}{\partial x} = -\sin(x+y) - \sin(x-y)$$

$$\frac{\partial^2 u}{\partial x^2} = -\cos(x+y) - \cos(x-y) = -u$$

Also $\frac{\partial u}{\partial y} = -\sin(x+y) + \sin(x-y)$

$$\frac{\partial^2 u}{\partial y^2} = -\cos(x+y) + \cos(x-y) = -u$$

Also $\frac{\partial^2 u}{\partial x \partial y} = -\cos(x+4) + \cos(x-y)$

$\therefore \frac{\partial^2 u}{\partial x^2} = \frac{\partial^2 u}{\partial y^2}$; is the only possibility.

25. Given $x = \frac{a^2 b^3}{c\sqrt{d}}$

$$\therefore \frac{\Delta x}{x} = \pm\left[2\frac{\Delta a}{a} + 3\frac{\Delta b}{b} + \frac{\Delta c}{c} + \frac{1}{2}\frac{\Delta d}{d}\right]$$

$$\therefore \frac{\Delta x}{x} \times 100 =$$

$$= \pm\left[2 \times 2\% + 3 \times 1\% + 3\% + \frac{1}{2} \times 4\%\right] = \pm 12\%.$$

26. Time period of a pendulum is given by the formula

$$T = 2\pi\sqrt{\frac{l}{g}} = 2\pi\frac{l^{1/2}}{g^{1/2}} = 2\pi\, l^{1/2}.g^{-1/2}$$

$$\therefore \frac{\Delta T}{T} = \pm\left[\frac{1}{2}\frac{\Delta l}{l} + \frac{1}{2}\frac{\Delta g}{g}\right]$$

$$\therefore \frac{\Delta T}{T} \times 100 = \pm\left[\frac{1}{2} \times 2\% + \frac{1}{2} \times 4\%\right] = \pm 3\%.$$

$\therefore$ Percentage error $= \pm 3\%$.

27. Area of an ellipse is

$A = \pi ab$, where $2a$ and $2b$ are major and minor axis.

$$\therefore \quad \Delta A = \pm(\pi a\Delta b + \pi b\Delta a)$$

$$\therefore \frac{\Delta A}{A} = \frac{\pm(\pi a\Delta b + \pi b\Delta a)}{\pi ab} = \pm\left[\frac{\Delta b}{b} + \frac{\Delta a}{a}\right]$$

$$\therefore \frac{\Delta A}{A} \times 100 = \pm[1\% + 1\%] = \pm 2\%.$$

$\therefore$ Percentage error $= 2\%$.

28. Given $N = \frac{8\pi IL}{T^2 R^4}$ where I is constant.

Taking log both the sides we get

$\log N = \log 8\pi I + \log L - 2\log T - 4\log R$

Differentiating both the sides we get

$$\frac{dN}{N} = \frac{dL}{L} - 2\frac{dT}{T} - 4\frac{dR}{R}$$

$$\therefore \frac{dN}{N} \times 100 = \frac{dL}{L} \times 100 - 2 \times \frac{dT}{T} \times 100 - 4 \times \frac{dR}{R} \times 100$$

Given $\frac{dL}{L} \times 100 = -2$; $\frac{dR}{R} \times 100 = 2$

and $\frac{dT}{T} \times 100 = 1.5$

$$\therefore \frac{dN}{N} \times 100 = -2\% - 2 \times 1.5\% - 4 \times 2\%$$

$= -13\%$

$\therefore$ N diminishes by 13%.

30. In any triangle

$a = b\cos C + c\cos B$.

$$\therefore 0 = \delta b\cos C + \delta c\cos B - b\sin C\,\delta C - c\sin B\,\delta B$$

($\because$ a is constant)

$$\therefore \delta b\cos C + \delta c\cos B = b\sin C\,(\delta B + \delta C)$$

($\because$ $c\sin B = b\sin C$)

$$= b\sin C.\delta(B + C)$$
$$= b\sin C.\delta(\pi - A)$$
$$= 0 \;(\because \text{A is constant})$$

Dividing both the sides by cos C cos B we get

$$\frac{\delta b}{\cos B} + \frac{\delta c}{\cos C} = 0.$$

31. Given $u = f(r)$, where $r^2 = x^2 + y^2$

$$\therefore \frac{\partial u}{\partial x} = u_x = f'(r).\frac{\partial r}{\partial x} = f'(r).\frac{x}{r}$$

$$\frac{\partial^2 u}{\partial x^2} = u_{xx} = \frac{\partial}{\partial x}\left[f'(r).\frac{x}{r}\right]$$

$$= \frac{r\left\{f'(r) + xf''(r).\frac{\partial r}{\partial x}\right\} - xf'(r).\frac{\partial r}{\partial x}}{r^2}$$

$$= \frac{1}{r^2}\left\{r\,f'(r) + x^2 f''(r) - \frac{x^2}{r}f'(r)\right\} \quad ...(i)$$

Similarly

$$\frac{\partial^2 u}{\partial y^2} = \frac{1}{r^2}\left\{r\,f'(r) + y^2 f''(r) - \frac{y^2}{r}f'(r)\right\} \quad ...(ii)$$

Adding *(i)* and *(ii)* we have

$$\frac{\partial^2 u}{\partial x^2} + \frac{\partial^2 u}{\partial y^2}$$

$$= \frac{1}{r^2}\left\{2r\,f'(r) + (x^2 + y^2)f''(r) - \frac{1}{r}(x^2 + y^2)f'(r)\right\}$$

$$= \frac{1}{r^2}\left\{2r\,f'(r) + r^2 f''(r) - r\,f'(r)\right\}$$

$$= f''(r) + \frac{1}{r}f'(r).$$

13. APPLICATION OF DERIVATIVES

Let P be a point (x, y) on the curve and Q be another point $(x+\delta x, y+\delta y)$ very near to P.

The straight line PQ, when Q approaches P along the curve is called the tangent to the curve at the point P.

Normal at P is a line through P at right angle to the tangent at P.

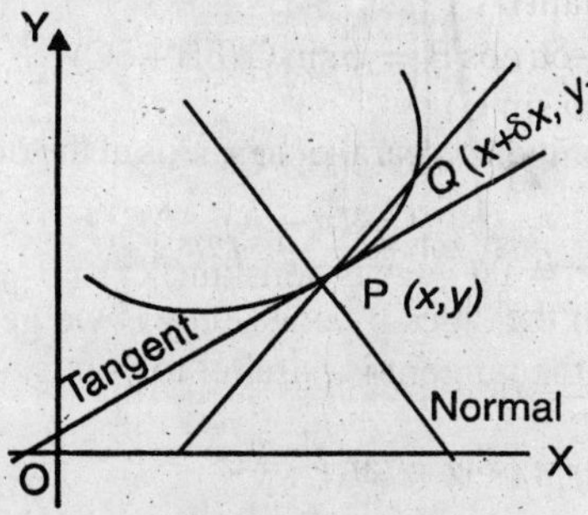

Equation of the Tangent at (x, y)

Let the equation to the curve be $y = f(x)$.

Then $y+\delta y = f(x+\delta x)$, as Q $(x+\delta x, y+\delta y)$ is on the curve.

$$\therefore \frac{\delta y}{\delta x} = \frac{f(x+\delta x) - f(x)}{\delta x}$$

Let (X, Y) be the current co-ordinates.

Then the equation to the straight line PQ joining the points P (x, y) and Q $(x+\delta x, y+\delta y)$ is

$$\frac{Y-y}{X-x} = \frac{(y+\delta y)-y}{(x+\delta x)-x}$$

$$i.e., \quad \frac{Y-y}{X-x} = \frac{\delta y}{\delta x} = \frac{f(x+\delta x)-f(x)}{\delta x}$$

Now let Q tends to P. Then $\delta x \to 0$ and the straight line PQ will become the tangent to the curve at P (x, y).

$$\therefore \quad \frac{Y-y}{X-x} = \lim_{\delta x \to 0} \frac{f(x+\delta x)-f(x)}{\delta x}$$

$$= f'(x) = \frac{dy}{dx}.$$

Hence the equation to the tangent to the curve $y = f(x)$ at P (x, y) is

$$Y - y = \frac{dy}{dx}(X - x) \quad ...(i)$$

Now if the equation of the curve be given in the form $f(x, y) = 0$, then

$$\frac{dy}{dx} = -\frac{\frac{\partial f}{\partial x}}{\frac{\partial f}{\partial y}}$$

Substituting the value of $\frac{dy}{dx}$ in *(i)*, we get

$$Y - y = \frac{\frac{\partial f}{\partial x}}{\frac{\partial f}{\partial y}}(X - x)$$

or $(X - x)\frac{\partial f}{\partial x} + (Y - y)\frac{\partial f}{\partial y} = 0$

or $(X - x) f_x + (Y - y) f_y = 0$

which is the equation of the tangent to the curve $f(x, y) = 0$ at P (x, y).

Equation of the Normal at (x, y) : The equation of the tangent to the curve $y = f(x)$ at a point (x, y) is

$Y - y = \frac{dy}{dx}(X - x)$, whose slope is $\frac{dy}{dx}$.

As ***normal*** at P is a line through P at right angle to the tangent at P, so the slope of the normal $= -\frac{1}{\frac{dy}{dx}}$.

Hence the equation to the normal at the point (x, y) is

$$Y - y = -\frac{1}{\frac{dy}{dx}}(X - x)$$

i.e., $(X - x) + (Y - y)\dfrac{dy}{dx} = 0$

If the equation of the curve be $f(x, y) = 0$, then equation of the tangent is

$(X - x)f_x + (Y - y)f_y = 0$

Whose slope is $-\dfrac{f_x}{f_y}$.

Therefore the slope of the normal is $\dfrac{f_y}{f_x}$.

Hence the equation of the normal is

$$Y - y = \frac{f_y}{f_x}(X - x)$$

i.e., $$\frac{X - x}{f_x} = \frac{Y - y}{f_y}.$$

Illustration

1. Find at what points on the curve $\dfrac{x^3}{a} + \dfrac{y^3}{b} = xy$, the tangent is parallel to one of the co-ordinate axes.

Solution : (*a*) Let the tangent at (x, y) be parallel to the x-axis

At that point $\dfrac{dy}{dx} = \tan\psi = \tan 0° = 0$

Now, differentiating $\dfrac{x^3}{a} + \dfrac{y^3}{b} - xy = 0$, with respect to x, we get

$$\frac{3x^2}{a} + \frac{3y^2}{b}.\frac{dy}{dx} - y - x\frac{dy}{dx} = 0$$

or $$\frac{dy}{dx} = \frac{y - \dfrac{3x^2}{a}}{\dfrac{3y^2}{b} - x} \quad ...(i)$$

But $\dfrac{dy}{dx} = 0$; $\therefore$ $y - \dfrac{3x^2}{a} = 0$ or $y = \dfrac{3x^2}{a}$ ...(*ii*)

Again (x, y) is on the curve,

so $\dfrac{x^3}{a} + \dfrac{y^3}{b} = xy$ ...(*iii*)

Eliminating y between (*ii*) and (*iii*), we get

$$\frac{x^3}{a} + \frac{1}{b}.\left(\frac{3x^2}{a}\right)^3 = x.\left(\frac{3x^2}{a}\right)$$

or $$\frac{x^3}{a} + \frac{1}{b}.\frac{27x^6}{a^3} = x.\frac{3x^2}{a}$$

or $$\frac{2}{a}x^3 = \frac{27}{ba^3}x^6;$$

$\therefore$ $$x = 0 \text{ or } \left(\frac{2ba^2}{27}\right)^{1/3}$$

from (*ii*), $y = 0$ or $\dfrac{3}{a}.\left(\dfrac{2ba^2}{27}\right)^{1/3}$.

Hence the tangent is parallel to x-axis at the origin and also at $\left(\dfrac{2^{1/3}}{3}b^{1/3}a^{2/3}, \dfrac{2^{2/3}}{3}a^{1/3}b^{2/3}\right)$.

(*b*) Now if the tangent is parallel to y-axis.

$$\frac{dy}{dx} = \tan\psi = \tan\frac{\pi}{2} = \infty$$

From (*i*), we have $x = \dfrac{3y^2}{b}$.

By similar procedure (x, y) we have

$$y = 0 \text{ or } \left(\frac{2ab^2}{27}\right)^{1/2}$$

and $$x = 0 \text{ or } \frac{3}{b}\left(\frac{2ab^2}{27}\right)^{2/3}$$

Hence the tangent is parallel to y-axis at the origin and also at $\left(\dfrac{2^{2/3}}{3}a^{2/3}b^{1/3}, \dfrac{2^{1/3}}{3}a^{1/3}b^{2/3}\right)$

2. Find the condition that $x\cos\theta + y\sin\theta = p$ is normal to the curve

$$\frac{x^2}{a^2} + \frac{y^2}{b^2} = 1$$

Solution : The curve is $\dfrac{x^2}{a^2} + \dfrac{y^2}{b^2} = 1$

Differentiating both the sides with respect to x we have

$$\frac{2x}{a^2}+\frac{2y}{b^2}\cdot\frac{dy}{dx}=0$$

i.e.,
$$\frac{dy}{dx}=-\frac{x}{y}\cdot\frac{b^2}{a^2}$$

The equation of the normal at (x, y) is

$$Y-y=-\frac{dx}{dy}(X-x)$$

$$=\frac{y}{x}\cdot\frac{a^2}{b^2}(X-x)$$

or
$$\frac{Yb^2}{y}-b^2=\frac{Xa^2}{x}-a^2$$

or
$$\frac{Xa^2}{x}-\frac{Yb^2}{y}=a^2-b^2$$

By question, $X\cos\theta+Y\sin\theta=p$ is normal to the curve. Comparing these two equation we get

$$\frac{\cos\theta}{a^2/x}=\frac{\sin\theta}{-b^2/y}=\frac{p}{a^2-b^2}$$

or
$$\frac{x/a}{a\sec\theta}=\frac{y/b}{-b\operatorname{cosec}\theta}=\frac{p}{a^2-b^2}$$

or
$$\frac{\sqrt{\left\{\left(\frac{x}{a}\right)^2+\left(\frac{y}{b}\right)^2\right\}}}{\sqrt{a^2\sec^2\theta+b^2\operatorname{cosec}^2\theta}}=\frac{p}{a^2-b^2}$$

or
$$\frac{1}{\sqrt{a^2\sec^2\theta+b^2\operatorname{cosec}^2\theta}}=\frac{p}{a^2-b^2}$$

or $p=\dfrac{a^2-b^2}{\sqrt{a^2\sec^2\theta+b^2\operatorname{cosec}^2\theta}}$ is the required condition.

Some Geometrical Results

(i) Sub-tangent = TM = $y\cot\psi=\dfrac{y}{\tan\psi}=\dfrac{y}{\frac{dy}{dx}}=\dfrac{y}{y_1}$.

(ii) Sub-normal = MN = $y\tan\psi=y\dfrac{dy}{dx}=yy_1$.

(iii) Tangent = PT $=y\operatorname{cosec}\psi$

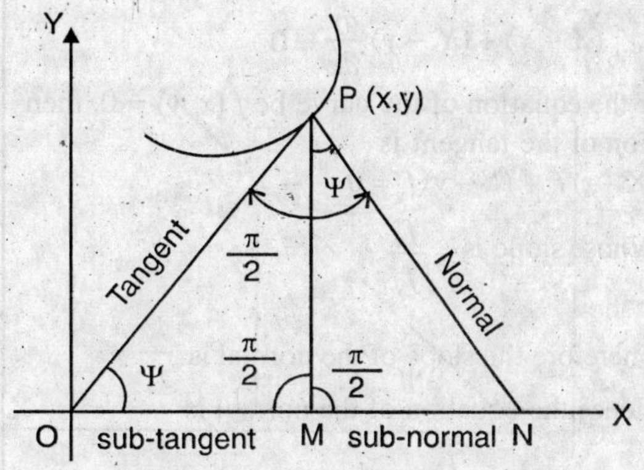

$$=y\sqrt{1+\cot^2\psi}=y\frac{\sqrt{1+\tan^2\psi}}{\tan\psi}$$

$$=y\frac{\sqrt{1+\left(\frac{dy}{dx}\right)^2}}{\frac{dy}{dx}}=\frac{y}{y_1}\sqrt{1+y_1^2}$$

(iv) Normal = PN = $y\sec\psi=y\sqrt{1+\tan^2\psi}$

$$=y\sqrt{1+\left(\frac{dy}{dx}\right)^2}=y\sqrt{1+y_1^2}$$

(v) Sub-tangent × Sub-normal $=y^2$ = Square of the ordinate

(vi) Sub-normal/Sub-tangent $=y_1^2$

Illustration

1. Show that in the curve $y=a\log(x^2-a^2)$, the sum of the tangent and subtangent varies as the product of the co-ordinates of the point.

Solution : We know that the length of the tangent $=y\operatorname{cosec}\psi$.

Also length of its subtangent $=\dfrac{y}{y_1}$

Given equation of the curve is $y=a\log(x^2-a^2)$. Differentiating both the sides we get

$$y_1=\frac{a}{x^2-a^2}\cdot 2x=\frac{2ax}{x^2-a^2}$$

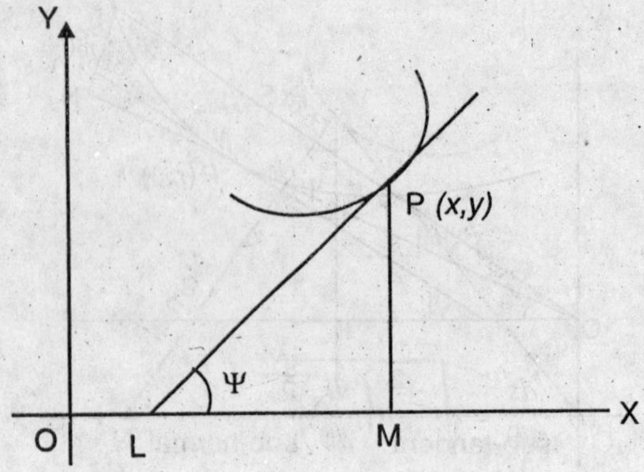

Now $\operatorname{cosec}\psi = \sqrt{1+\cot^2\psi}$

$$= \sqrt{1+\frac{1}{\tan^2\psi_1}} = \sqrt{1+\frac{1}{y_1^2}}$$

$$= \sqrt{1+\frac{\left(x^2-a^2\right)^2}{4a^2x^2}} = \frac{x^2+a^2}{2ax}.$$

$\therefore$ Sum of the tangent and subtangent

$$= y\cos\psi + \frac{y}{y_1} = y\left[\operatorname{cosec}\psi + \frac{1}{y_1}\right]$$

$$= y\left[\frac{x^2+a^2}{2ax} + \frac{x^2-a^2}{2ax}\right] = y.\frac{2x^2}{2ax} = \frac{xy}{a}.$$

Thus the result follows.

2. Show that in the curve $by^2 = (a+x)^3$ the square of the subtangent varies as the subnormal.

Solution : The curve is $by^2 = (a+x)^3$ ...*(i)*

Differentiating it with respect to x, we have

$$2byy_1 = 3(a+x)^2$$

or $$yy_1 = \frac{3(a+x)^2}{2b} \quad ...(ii)$$

Hence sub-normal $= \dfrac{3(a+x)^2}{2b}$ ...*(iii)*

Also dividing *(i)* by *(ii)*, we have

$$b.\left(\frac{y}{y_1}\right) = \frac{2b.(a+x)}{3}$$

or $$\frac{y}{y_1} = \frac{2(a+x)}{3}$$

$$\therefore \text{ Subtangent} = \frac{y}{y_1} = \frac{2(a+x)}{3}$$

$$\therefore (\text{Subtangent})^2 = \frac{4(a+x)^2}{9}$$

$$= \frac{8b}{27}.\frac{3(a+x)^2}{2b} = \frac{8b}{27}.(\text{Sub-normal}) \text{ from } (ii)$$

i.e., $(\text{Subtangent})^2 \propto$ Sub-normal.

Derivative of arc (Cartesian Co-ordinate) : Let P (x, y) be a point on the curve and Q $(x+\delta x, y+\delta y)$ another point very near to P. Also let that the length of the arc AP and AQ are respectively s and $s+\delta s$.

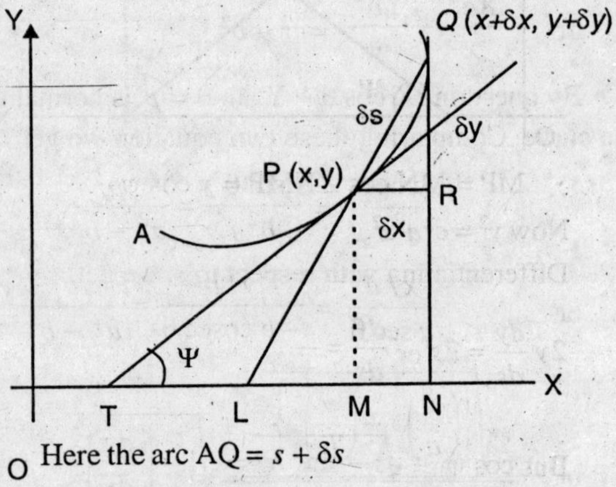

Here the arc AQ $= s + \delta s$

$\therefore$ Arc PQ $= \delta s$.

Then

(i) $$\frac{ds}{dx} = \sqrt{1+\left(\frac{dy}{dx}\right)^2}$$

(ii) $$\frac{ds}{dy} = \sqrt{1+\left(\frac{dx}{dy}\right)^2}$$

(iii) $$\cos\psi = \frac{dx}{ds}$$

(iv) $$\sin\psi = \frac{dy}{ds}$$

(v) $$\left(\frac{dx}{ds}\right)^2 + \left(\frac{dy}{ds}\right)^2 = 1$$

(vi) $\left(\frac{ds}{dt}\right)^2 = \left(\frac{dx}{dt}\right)^2 + \left(\frac{dy}{dt}\right)^2$, when the curve is inparametric form.

Illustration : Show that in the curve for which $y^2 = c^2 + s^2$, the perpendicular for the foot of the ordinate upon the tangent is of constant length.

Solution : Here MP is the perpendicular from M, the foot of the ordinate, upon the tangent at N.

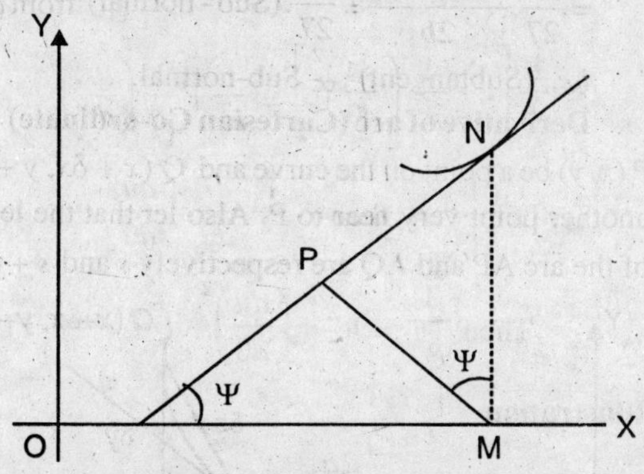

$\therefore$ MP = MN cos ∠NMP = $y \cos \psi$

Now $y^2 = c^2 + s^2$.

Differentiating with respect to s, we get

$$2y\frac{dy}{ds} = 2s \text{ or } \frac{dy}{ds} = \frac{s}{y}.$$

$$\text{But } \cos\psi = \sqrt{1-\sin^2\psi} = \sqrt{1-\left(\frac{dy}{dx}\right)^2}$$

$$= \sqrt{1-\left(\frac{s}{y}\right)^2} = \sqrt{\frac{y^2-s^2}{y^2}} = \frac{c}{y}.$$

$$\therefore \quad \text{MP} = y.\frac{c}{y} = c \text{ (constant)}.$$

Derivative of arc (Polar Co-ordinate) : P (r, θ) be a point on the curve and Q $(r + \delta r, \theta + \delta\theta)$ be another point very near to P.

Here equation of the curve is $r = f(\theta)$

Arc AP $= s$

and arc AQ $= s + \delta s$

$\therefore$ arc PQ $= \delta s$.

From the ΔPQN, we get

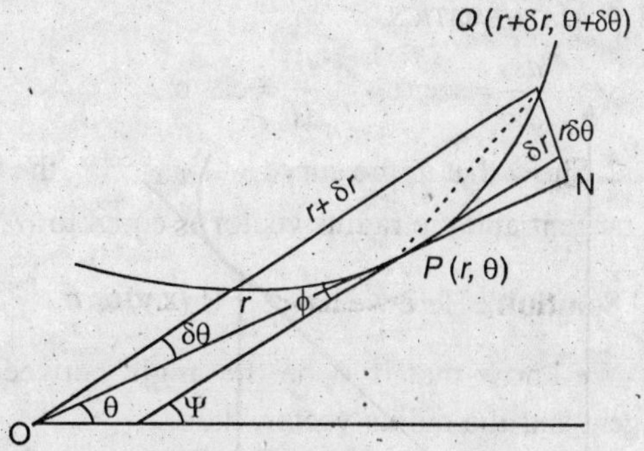

(i) $\frac{ds}{d\theta} = \sqrt{r^2 + \left(\frac{dr}{d\theta}\right)^2}$

(ii) $\frac{ds}{dr} = \sqrt{1 + r^2\left(\frac{d\theta}{dr}\right)^2}$

(iii) $\cos\phi = \frac{dr}{ds}$, where ϕ is the angle between radius vector and tangent

(iv) $\sin\phi = r\frac{d\theta}{ds}$

(v) $\psi = \theta + \phi$

(vi) $\left(\frac{dr}{ds}\right)^2 + r^2\left(\frac{d\theta}{ds}\right)^2 = 1$

(vii) $ds^2 = dr^2 + r^2 d\theta^2$.

Illustration

1. In the equiangular spiral $r = a\,e^{\theta \cot \alpha}$, prove that $\frac{dr}{ds} = \cos\alpha$.

Solution : Given $r = a\,e^{\theta \cot \alpha}$.

Differentiating with respect to θ, both the sides we get

$$\frac{dr}{d\theta} = a\,e^{\theta\cot\alpha}.\cot\alpha = r.\cot\alpha$$

$$\therefore \quad r\frac{d\theta}{dr} = \tan\alpha.$$

$$\text{Now} \quad ds^2 = dr^2 + r^2(d\theta)^2$$

$$\therefore \quad \left(\frac{ds}{dr}\right)^2 = 1 + r^2\left(\frac{d\theta}{dr}\right)^2 = 1 + \left(r\frac{d\theta}{dr}\right)^2$$

$$= 1 + \tan^2\alpha = \sec^2\alpha.$$

$$\therefore \quad \frac{ds}{dr} = \sec\alpha, \therefore \frac{dr}{ds} = \cos\alpha.$$

2. Show that in the curve $r = a\,e^{\theta \cot \alpha}$, the angle the tangent and the radius vector is equal to α.

Solution : Here we have $\dfrac{dr}{d\theta} = \cot\alpha \,.\, a\,e^{\theta\cot\alpha}$

We know that if ϕ be the angle between the tangent and the radius vector, then

$$\tan\phi = r\frac{d\theta}{dr} = \frac{r}{\dfrac{dr}{d\theta}} = \frac{a\,e^{\theta\cot\alpha}}{\cot\alpha\,.\,a\,e^{\theta\cot\alpha}} = \frac{1}{\cot\alpha}$$

$\therefore \tan\phi = \tan\alpha$

i.e., $\quad \phi = \alpha$, which is constant.

Some Geometrical Result (Polar Co-ordinates)

Let (r, θ) be any point P on the curve $r = f(\theta)$.

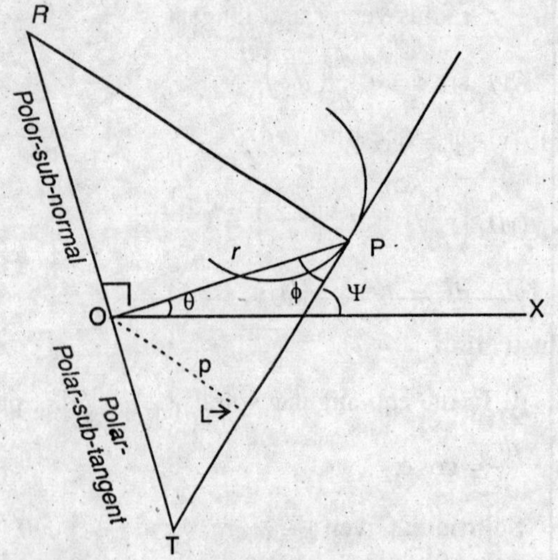

Then,

(*i*) Polar Sub-tangent = OT = OP . tan ϕ

$$= r.\left(r\frac{d\theta}{dr}\right) = r^2\frac{d\theta}{dr} = -\frac{d\theta}{du},$$

where $r = \dfrac{1}{u}$

(*ii*) Polar Sub-normal= OR = OP . cot ϕ

$$= \frac{r}{\left(r\dfrac{d\theta}{dr}\right)} = \frac{dr}{d\theta}$$

(*iii*) Let OL be perpendicular to the tangent PT. Let OL = p. Then $p = r\sin\phi$.

$\therefore \dfrac{dp}{d\phi} = r\cos\phi$ = projection of radius vector on tangent.

(*iv*) Now. $\dfrac{1}{p^2} = \dfrac{1}{r^2}\operatorname{cosec}^2\phi = \dfrac{1}{r^2}(1+\cot^2\phi)$

$$= \frac{1}{r^2}\left[1 + \frac{1}{r^2}\left(\frac{dr}{d\theta}\right)^2\right] = \frac{1}{r^2} + \frac{1}{r^4}\left(\frac{dr}{d\theta}\right)^2$$

(*v*) Let $\dfrac{1}{r} = u$; then $-\dfrac{1}{r^2}.\dfrac{dr}{d\theta} = \dfrac{du}{d\theta}$

$$\text{Then } \frac{1}{p^2} = u^2 + \left(\frac{du}{d\theta}\right)^2$$

Illustration

1. For the curve $\dfrac{2a}{r} = 1 - \cos\theta$, prove that

(*i*) $\phi = \pi - \dfrac{1}{2}\theta$

(*ii*) $p = a\operatorname{cosec}\dfrac{1}{2}\theta$

(*iii*) polar subtangent = $2a\operatorname{cosec}\theta$

(*iv*) $p^2 = ar$

Solution : (*i*) The curve is $\dfrac{2a}{r} = 1 - \cos\theta$

$$= 2\sin^2\frac{\theta}{2}.$$

i.e., $\quad r = a\operatorname{cosec}^2\dfrac{\theta}{2}$ ...(*i*)

$\therefore \log r = \log a + 2\log\operatorname{cosec}\dfrac{1}{2}\theta$

Differentiating w.r.t. θ we get

$$\frac{1}{r}.\frac{dr}{d\theta} = 2.\frac{-\operatorname{cosec}\dfrac{\theta}{2}.\cot\dfrac{\theta}{2}\left(\dfrac{1}{2}\right)}{\operatorname{cosec}\dfrac{\theta}{2}}$$

$$= -\cot\frac{\theta}{2}.$$

$$\therefore \cot\phi = -\cot\frac{\theta}{2} = \cot\left(\pi - \frac{1}{2}\theta\right)$$

or $\phi = \pi - \frac{1}{2}\theta.$

(ii) Also $p = r\sin\phi = r\sin\left(\pi - \frac{1}{2}\theta\right)$

$$= r\sin\frac{1}{2}\theta$$

$$= a\,\text{cosec}^2\frac{1}{2}\theta.\sin\frac{1}{2}\theta \text{ using } (i)$$

$$\therefore \quad p = a\,\text{cosec}\frac{1}{2}\theta.$$

(iii) Polar-subtangent $= r^2\frac{d\theta}{dr} = r\left(r\frac{d\theta}{dr}\right)$

$= a\,\text{cosec}^2\frac{1}{2}\theta.\left(-\tan\frac{1}{2}\theta\right)$ using *(i)* and *(ii)*

$= \frac{-2a}{\sin\theta} = -2a\,\text{cosec}\,\theta = 2a\,\text{cosec}\,\theta$ (in length).

(iv) Now $p = a\,\text{cosec}\frac{1}{2}\theta$

$$= a\left(\frac{r}{a}\right)^{1/2} \text{ using } (i)$$

or $p^2 = a^2\left(\frac{r}{a}\right)$

$$p^2 = ar.$$

2. Find the polar normal and polar subnormal for the cardioid $r = a(1+\cos\theta)$.

Solution : The curve is $r = a(1+\cos\theta)$

$$\therefore \quad \frac{dr}{d\theta} = -a\sin\theta$$

$$\therefore \text{ Polar normal} = \sqrt{r^2 + \left(\frac{dr}{d\theta}\right)^2}$$

$$= \sqrt{a^2(1+\cos\theta)^2 + a^2\sin^2\theta}$$

$$= a\sqrt{2(1+\cos\theta)} = 2a\cos\frac{\theta}{2}$$

Polar sub-normal $= \frac{dr}{d\theta} = -\sin\theta$

Angle of Intersection of Two Curves

If two curves intersect each other at a point then the angle of intersection of the curves is defined as the angle between the tangents to the curves at the points, such that $0 \le \theta \le \frac{\pi}{2}$.

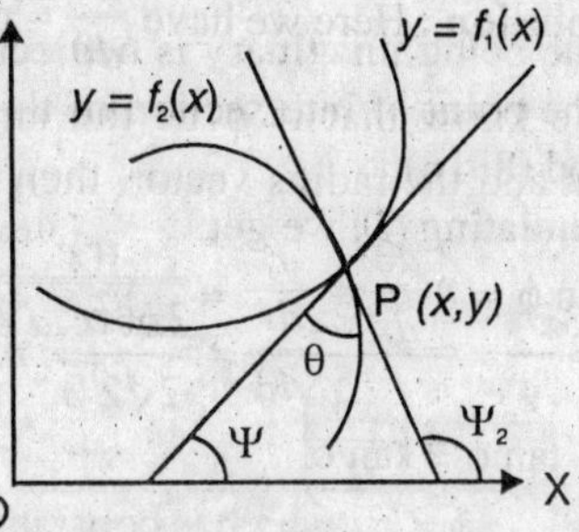

Let ψ_1 and ψ_2 be the angles which the tangents to the curve at a point of intersection makes with x-axis.

Let $\tan\psi_1 = \left(\frac{dy}{dx}\right)_1$ and $\tan\psi_2 = \left(\frac{dy}{dx}\right)_2$

Let P be the point of intersection, where $\psi_2 = \psi_1 + \theta$.

i.e., $\theta = \psi_2 - \psi_1$

or $\tan\theta = \tan(\psi_2 - \psi_1)$

$$= \frac{\tan\psi_2 - \tan\psi_1}{1+\tan\psi_1.\tan\psi_2}$$

or $\theta = \tan^{-1}\left(\frac{\tan\psi_2 - \tan\psi_1}{1+\tan\psi_1.\tan\psi_2}\right)$

Since θ lies between 0 and $\frac{\pi}{2}$, $\tan\theta$ is non-negative.

Hence $\tan\theta = \left|\frac{\tan\psi_2 - \tan\psi_1}{1+\tan\psi_1.\tan\psi_2}\right|$

Note : 1. If the curves cut each other orthogonally *i.e.,* $\theta = 90°$ then $\tan\Psi_2.\tan\Psi_1 = -1$.

2. If two curves touch each other *i.e.,* having common tangents, iff $\theta = 0$ then $\tan\psi_2 = \tan\psi_1$.

Illustration : Find the angle of intersection of the curves

$2y^2 = x^3$ and $y^2 = 32x$.

Solution : The given curves are

$2y^2 = x^3$ ...(i)

$y^2 = 32x$ ...(ii)

Solving equations *(i)* and *(ii)* we get $x = 0, 8, -8$.

Equations *(ii)* gives the corresponding values of y as 0, 16 and $\sqrt{-256}$.

Last one being imaginary is neglected.

Thus the point of intersection of the two curves are (0, 0) and (8, 16).

Differentiating *(i)*, we get

$$\frac{dy}{dx} = \frac{3x^2}{4y} = \frac{3x^2}{4\left(\frac{x^3}{2}\right)^{1/2}} = \frac{3x^{1/2}}{2\sqrt{2}} = m_1$$

Differentiating *(ii)*, we get

$$\frac{dy}{dx} = \frac{16}{y} = m_2.$$

At the point (0, 0), $m_1 = 0 = \tan\psi_1 \Rightarrow \psi_1 = 0$

$$m_2 = \frac{16}{0} = \infty = \tan\psi_2 \Rightarrow \psi_2 = \frac{\pi}{2}$$

At the point (8, 16)

$$m_1 = \frac{3(8)^{1/2}}{2\sqrt{2}} = 3 \text{ and } m_2 = \frac{16}{16} = 1$$

∴ The angle of intersection of the curves at (0, 0) is $\psi_1 \sim \psi_2 = \frac{\pi}{2} - 0 = \frac{\pi}{2}$

Also angle of intersection of the curves at (8, 16)

$$= \tan^{-1}\frac{m_1 \sim m_2}{1 + m_1 m_2} = \tan^{-1}\frac{3-1}{1+3.1} = \tan^{-1}\left(\frac{1}{2}\right).$$

Maxima and minima of function of one variable: A function $f(x)$ of one variable x is said to have a **maximum** at $x = a$ if there exists a positive number δ such that

$$f(a+h) \leq f(a)$$

for all h in the interval $(a - \delta, a + \delta)$.

A function $f(x)$ is said to have a **minimum** at $x = a$ if there exists a positive number δ, such that

$$f(a+h) \geq f(a)$$

for all h in the interval $(a - \delta, a + \delta)$.

The maximum and minimum values of a function are called its **extreme values** and the points at which they are attained are called points of **Maxima** and **Minima**.

Maxima and minima of functions of one variable : A function $f(x, y)$ of two independent variables x, y is said to have a **maximum** or a **minimum** at (a, b) if for every (x, y) $\{\neq (a, b)\}$ in some neighbourhood of (a, b) we have

$f(x, y) - f(a, b) < 0$ or > 0

respectively and $f(a, b)$ is called a maximum or minimum value.

Conditions for maxima or minima of functions of one variable

1. The necessary condition for a function $y = f(x)$ of one variable to have maximum or a minimum at $x = \alpha$ is that $f'(\alpha) = 0$ *i.e.*, if the derivative exists.

2. If for a function $y = f(x)$ we have $f'(\alpha) = f''(\alpha) = \ldots = f^{n-1}(\alpha) = 0$ and $f^n(\alpha) \neq 0$ then $f(x)$ has

(i) a maximum if n is even and $f^n(\alpha) < 0$

(ii) a minimum if n is even and $f^n(\alpha) > 0$

(iii) neither a maximum nor a minimum if n is odd

Working rule for the determination of maxima or minima for a function of one variable

Rule I : Let the function be $f(x)$. Find $f'(x)$ and equate it to zero. Solve this equation for x. Let the roots be $\alpha, \beta, \gamma, \ldots$.

Find $f''(x)$ and then $f''(\alpha), f''(\beta), \ldots$.

If $f''(\alpha)$ is not zero and is negative we have a maximum at $x = \alpha$ and if $f''(\alpha)$ is positive we have minimum at $x = \alpha$.

If $f''(\alpha) = 0$, find $f'''(x)$ and then $f'''(\alpha)$, $f'''(\beta), \ldots$

Let us test for $x = \alpha$. If $f'''(\alpha)$ is not equal to zero, there is neither a maximum nor a minimum at $x = a$ *i.e.*, for a maximum or a minimum at $x = \alpha$, $f'''(\alpha)$ must be zero.

If it is so then find $f^{iv}(\alpha)$. If $f^{iv}(\alpha)$ is negative, there is a maximum at $x = \alpha$ and if $f^{iv}(\alpha)$ is positive, then there is minimum at $x = \alpha$. If $f^{iv}(\alpha) = 0$, we proceed to test with other derivatives. This gives the criteria for determination of Maxima and Minima values.

Rule II : Let $f(x)$ be the function. Find $f'(x)$ and equate it to zero. Solve this equation for x.

Let the values be $\alpha, \beta, \ldots$.

If $f'(\alpha - \epsilon) > 0$ and $f'(\alpha + \epsilon) < 0$ then $f(x)$ has a maximum at $x = \alpha$.

If $f'(\alpha - \epsilon) < 0$ and $f'(\alpha + \epsilon) > 0$ then $f(x)$ has a minimum at $x = \alpha$.

(Here ϵ is a small +ive quantity).

Illustration

1. Show that x^x is a minnimum for $x = \frac{1}{e}$.

Solution : Let $y = x^x$

Taking log both the sides we get

$$\log y = x \log x.$$

Now a function is minimum when its logarithm is minimum.

$\therefore$ Let $u = x \log x$

$$\frac{du}{dx} = x.\left(\frac{1}{x}\right) + \log x = 1 + \log x$$

Now $\frac{du}{dx} = 0$ gives $\log x = -1$

or $x = e^{-1}$

Now $\frac{d^2u}{dx^2} = \frac{1}{x}$, is positive when $x = e^{-1}$

Hence u and therefore y is minimum when $x = \frac{1}{e}$

2. Show that $x^{1/x}$ is a maximum for $x = e$

Solution : Let $y = x^{1/x}$

Taking log both the sides we get

$$\log y = \frac{\log x}{x}$$

Now a function is maximum when its logarithm is maximum.

Let $u = \frac{\log x}{x}$

$$\therefore \quad \frac{du}{dx} = \frac{1 - \log x}{x^2}$$

Now $\frac{du}{dx} = 0$ gives $\log x = 1$ or $x = e$

Also
$$\frac{d^2u}{dx^2} = \frac{x^2\left(-\frac{1}{x}\right) - (1 - \log x).2x}{x^4}$$

$$= \frac{-1 - 2(1 - \log x)}{x^3}$$

which is negative when $x = e$

Hence u and therefore y is maximum when $x = e$

Conditions for maxima or minima of functions of two independent variables

1. The necessary conditions for a function $z = f(x, y)$ of two independent variables x, y to have a maximum at (a, b) *i.e.*, $x = a, y = b$ are

$$\left(\frac{\partial f}{\partial x}\right)_{a,b} = 0 \text{ and } \left(\frac{\partial f}{\partial y}\right)_{a,b} = 0$$

if the partial derivatives exist.

2. If for a function $z = f(x, y)$ we have $\frac{\partial f}{\partial x} = 0$ and $\frac{\partial f}{\partial y} = 0$ at $x = a, y = b$ and we denote

$$\left(\frac{\partial^2 f}{\partial x^2}\right)_{a,b} = r, \left(\frac{\partial^2 f}{\partial x \partial y}\right)_{a,b} = s, \left(\frac{\partial^2 f}{\partial y^2}\right)_{a,b} = t.$$

Then $f(x, y)$ will have

(i) a maximum at $x = a, y = b$ if $r < 0$ and $rt - s^2 > 0$

(ii) a minimum at $x = a, y = b$ if $r > 0$ and $rt - s^2 > 0$

(iii) neither a maximum nor a minimum at $x = a, y = b$ if $rt - s^2 < 0$ and $r \neq 0$

Working Rule for determination of maxima or minima of a function of two independent variables Let $z = f(x, y)$ be the function. Find $\frac{\partial f}{\partial x}$ and $\frac{\partial f}{\partial y}$

Then solve the equations $\frac{\partial f}{\partial x} = 0$ and $\frac{\partial f}{\partial y} = 0$

Let the solutions be $x = \alpha_1, \alpha_2, \ldots$ and $y = \beta_1, \beta_2, \ldots$

Next find $\frac{\partial^2 f}{\partial x^2}, \frac{\partial^2 f}{\partial x \partial y}$ and $\frac{\partial^2 f}{\partial y^2}$

Now find $\frac{\partial^2 f}{\partial x^2}\cdot\frac{\partial^2 f}{\partial y^2}-\left(\frac{\partial^2 f}{\partial x\partial y}\right)^2$ at $x=\alpha_1$, $y=\beta_1$.

If it is greater then 0, observe the sign of $\left(\frac{\partial^2 f}{\partial x^2}\right)_{\alpha_1,\beta_1}$

If this sign is negative, $f(x, y)$ has a maximum at (α_1, β_1) which if it is positive, $f(x, y)$ has a minimum at (α_1, β_1)

Illustration

1. Examine the maxima or minima of the function

$$x^3 + y^3 - 12x - 3y + 20$$

Solution : Here $f(x, y) = x^3 + y^3 - 12x - 3y + 20$

$$\therefore \quad \frac{\partial f}{\partial x} = 3x^2 - 12; \frac{\partial f}{\partial y} = 3y^2 - 3$$

For maxima or minima, $\frac{\partial f}{\partial x} = 0$ and $\frac{\partial f}{\partial y} = 0$

i.e., $3x^2 - 12 = 0; 3y^2 - 3 = 0$

i.e., $x^2 = 4; y^2 = 1$

$\therefore x = \pm 2; x = \pm 1$

$\therefore$ The stationary points are (2, – 1), (2, 1), (– 2, – 1), (– 2, 1)

Now $\frac{\partial^2 f}{\partial x^2} = 6x; \frac{\partial^2 f}{\partial x\partial y} = 0; \frac{\partial^2 f}{\partial y^2} = 6y$

$\therefore$ At (2, – 1), $r = \frac{\partial^2 f}{\partial x^2} = 6 \times 2 = 12;$

$$s = \frac{\partial^2 f}{\partial x\partial y} = 0$$

$$t = \frac{\partial^2 f}{\partial y^2} = 6(-1) = -6$$

$\therefore rt - s^2 = 12.(-6) - 0^2 = -72 < 0$ and $r = 12 \neq 0$

$\therefore$ The function has neither a maximum nor a minimum at (2, – 1)

At (2, 1), $r = 6 \times 2 = 12; s = 0; t = 6$

$\therefore rt - s^2 = 12 \times 6 - 0^2 = 72 > 0$ and $r = 12 > 0$

$\therefore$ The function has a minimum at (2, 1)

At (– 2, – 1), $r = \frac{\partial^2 f}{dx^2} = 6 \times (-2) = -12;$

$$s = \frac{\partial^2 f}{\partial x\partial y} = 0$$

$$t = \frac{\partial^2 f}{\partial y^2} = 6 \times (-1) = -6$$

$\therefore rt - s^2 = -12(-6) - 0^2 = 72 > 0$ and $r = -12 < 0$

$\therefore$ The function has a maximum at (– 2, – 1)

At (– 2, – 1), $r = \frac{\partial^2 f}{\partial x^2} = 6(-2) = -12;$

$$s = \frac{\partial^2 f}{\partial x\partial y} = 0$$

$$t = \frac{\partial^2 f}{\partial y^2} = 6 \times 1 = 6$$

$\therefore rt - s^2 = (-12)\,6 - 0^2 = -72 < 0$ and $r = -12 \neq 0.$

$\therefore$ The function has neither a maximum nor a minimum at (– 2, – 1)

EXERCISE

Mark the correct alternative(s) of the following:

1. Let P be any point on the curve $x^{2/3} + y^{2/3} = a^{2/3}$. Then the length of the segment of the tangent between the co-ordinate axes is of length

(a) 2*a* *(b)* *a* *(c)* 3*a* *(d)* 4*a*

2. The equation of the tangent to the curve $y = (2x - 1)\, e^{2(1-x)}$ at the point of its maximum is

(a) $x - 1 = 0$ *(b)* $x + y - 1 = 0$

(c) $y - 1 = 0$ *(d)* $x - y + 1 = 0$

3. If the sum of the squares of the intercepts on the axes cut off by the tangent to the curve $x^{1/3} + y^{1/3} = a^{1/3}$ (with $a > 0$) at $(a/8, , a/8)$ is 2, then a has the value

(a) 1 *(b)* 2

(c) 3 *(d)* 4

4. The equation of the tangent to the curve $x = t^3 - 4$, $y = 2t^2 + 1$ at the point, where $t = 2$ is
(a) $2x - 3y - 19 = 0$
(b) $2x - 3y + 19 = 0$
(c) $2x + 3y - 19 = 0$
(d) $3x + 2y + 6 = 0$

[J.N.U. M.C.A.]

5. The point at which $y = x$ is the normal to the curve $x^{2/3} + y^{2/3} = a^{2/3}$ is
(a) $\left(\frac{1}{2\sqrt{2}}, \frac{1}{2\sqrt{2}}\right)$ (b) $\left(\frac{a}{\sqrt{2}}, \frac{a}{\sqrt{2}}\right)$
(c) $\left(\frac{a}{\sqrt{2}}, \frac{a}{2}\right)$ (d) $\left(\frac{a}{2\sqrt{2}}, \frac{a}{2\sqrt{2}}\right)$

6. The sum of the intercepts on the axes cut by the tangent to the curve $x^{1/2} + y^{1/2} = a^{1/2}$ is
(a) $2a$ (b) a (c) $2a^{1/2}$ (d) $2a^2$

[D.U. M.C.A.]

7. The line $\frac{x}{a} + \frac{y}{b} = 1$ touches the curve $y = be^{-x/a}$ at the point
(a) (a, b) (b) $\left(a, \frac{b}{a}\right)$
(c) $\left(-a, \frac{b}{a}\right)$ (d) None of these

8. The tangent to the curve $x = e^t \cos t$; $y = e^t \sin t$; at the point $t = \frac{\pi}{4}$ makes with axis of x, the angle
(a) 0 (b) $\frac{\pi}{4}$ (c) $\frac{\pi}{3}$ (d) $\frac{\pi}{2}$

9. The curve $\left(\frac{x}{a}\right)^n + \left(\frac{y}{b}\right)^n = 2$ touches the line $\frac{x}{a} + \frac{y}{b} = 2$ at the point (a, b) for n equal to
(a) 1 (b) 2
(c) 3 (d) every non-zero value

10. Equations of the normal to the curve $y(x^2 + a^2) = ax^2$ at points where $y = \frac{1}{4}a$ is
(a) $y = \mp \frac{8}{3\sqrt{3}}x + \frac{36}{41}a$
(b) $\mp \frac{3\sqrt{3}}{8}x + \frac{36}{41}a$
(c) $y = \mp \frac{8}{3\sqrt{3}}x + \frac{41}{36}a$
(d) $y = \mp \frac{3\sqrt{3}}{8}x + \frac{41}{36}a$

11. Condition that the line $x\cos\theta + y\sin\theta = p$ may touch the curve $x^m y^n = a^{m+n}$ is
(a) $p^{m+n}.m^m n^n = (m+n)^{m+n}.a^{m+n} \cos^m\theta \sin^n\theta$
(b) $p^{m+n}.m^n n^m = (m+n)^{m+n}.a^{m+n} \cos^m\theta \sin^n\theta$
(c) $p^{m+n}.m^m n^n = (m+n)^{m+n}.a^{m+n} \cos^n\theta \sin^m\theta$
(d) None of these

12. The condition that the line $x\cos\alpha + y\sin\alpha = p$ touches the curve $\left(\frac{x}{a}\right)^m + \left(\frac{y}{b}\right)^m = 1$ is
(a) $(a\cos\alpha)^{\frac{m-1}{m}} + (b\sin\alpha)^{\frac{m-1}{m}} = p^{\frac{m-1}{m}}$
(b) $\left(\frac{\cos\alpha}{a}\right)^{\frac{m-1}{m}} + \left(\frac{\cos\alpha}{b}\right)^{\frac{m-1}{m}} = p^{\frac{m-1}{m}}$
(c) $(a\cos\alpha)^{\frac{m}{m-1}} + (b\sin\alpha)^{\frac{m}{m-1}} = p^{\frac{m}{m-1}}$
(d) None of these

13. The length of the sub-tangent at the point θ of the curve $x = a(\theta + \sin\theta)$ $y = a(1 - \cos\theta)$ is given by
(a) $a\cos\frac{\theta}{2}$ (b) $a\cos\theta$
(c) $a\sin\frac{\theta}{2}$ (d) $a\sin\theta$

14. In the curve $y = b\,e^{x/a}$, the sub-tangent
(a) varies as the abscissa
(b) varies as the ordinate
(c) is of constant length
(d) varies as the square of the length

15. For a curve $\frac{(\text{length of normal})^2}{(\text{length of tangent})^2}$ is equal to
(a) (sub - normal)/(sub - tangent)
(b) (sub - tangent)/(sub - normal)
(c) (tangent)/(normal)
(d) constant

16. The value of n for which the sub-normal of the curve $y = a^{(1-n)}.x^n$ may be of constant length is

(a) $\frac{1}{2}$ (b) 2

(c) 1 (d) None of these

17. In the cantenary $y = c\cosh\left(\frac{x}{c}\right)$, the length of the normal intercepted between the curve and the axis of x is

(a) $c\,y^2$ (b) $\frac{1}{c}y^2$

(c) $\frac{x^2}{c}$ (d) None of these

18. If at any point on a curve the sub-tangent and sub-normal are equal, then the length of the tangent is equal to

(a) ordinate (b) $\sqrt{2}$ ordinate

(c) $\sqrt{2\text{ (ordinate)}}$ (d) None of these

19. If the area of the triangle, included between the axes and any tangent to the curve $x\,y^n = a^{n+1}$ is constant then the value of n is

(a) – 1 (b) – 2 (c) 1 (d) 2

20. In the curve $y = a\log(x^2 - a^2)$, the sum of the tangent and sub-tangent

(a) varies as abscissa

(b) varies ordinate

(c) varies as product of abscissa and ordinate

(d) None of these

21. If $f(x) = a\log|x| + bx^2 + x$ has its extremum values at $x = -1$ and $x = 2$, then

(a) $a = 2, b = -1$ (b) $a = 2, b = -\frac{1}{2}$

(c) $a = -2, b = \frac{1}{2}$ (d) None of these

22. The difference between the greatest and least values of the function

$f(x) = \sin 2x - x$ on $\left[-\frac{\pi}{2}, \frac{\pi}{2}\right]$ is

(a) $\frac{\sqrt{3}+\sqrt{2}}{2}$ (b) $\frac{\sqrt{3}+\sqrt{2}}{2} + \frac{\pi}{6}$

(c) $\frac{\sqrt{3}}{2} + \frac{\pi}{3}$ (d) π

23. The function

$$f(x) = \int_1^x \left\{2(t-1)(t-2)^3 + 3(t-1)^2(t-2)^2\right\}dt$$

attains its maximum at $x =$

(a) 1 (b) 2 (c) 3 (d) 4

24. The shortest distance of the point $(0, c)$ where $0 \le c \le 5$, from the parabola $y = x^2$ is

(a) $\sqrt{4c+1}$ (b) $\frac{\sqrt{4c+1}}{2}$

(c) $\frac{\sqrt{4c-1}}{2}$ (d) $\sqrt{4c-1}$

25. $f(x) = \sin^p\theta\cos^q\theta, \left(p, q > 0, 0 < \theta < \frac{\pi}{2}\right)$ has a point of maxima at

(a) $\theta = \tan^{-1}\sqrt{\frac{p}{q}}$ (b) $\theta = \tan^{-1}\sqrt{\frac{q}{p}}$

(c) $\theta = \tan^{-1}\left(\frac{q}{p}\right)$ (d) None of these

26. The minimum value of $|x^2 - 5x + 2|$ is

(a) 2 (b) 0 (c) – 1 (d) – 2

27. The minimum value of $px + qy$ when $xy = r^2$ is

(a) $2r\sqrt{pq}$ (b) $2pq\sqrt{r}$

(c) $-2r\sqrt{pq}$ (d) None of these

28. The least value of $f(x) = 2x + \frac{8}{x^2}, x > 0$ is

(a) 4 (b) 6

(c) 8 (d) None of these

[J.N.U. M.C.A.]

29. When x is positive, the minimum value of x^x is

(a) e^{-1} (b) $e^{-1/e}$

(c) $e^{1/e}$ (d) None of these

30. The maximum value of $\left(\frac{1}{x}\right)^x$ is

(a) a (b) e^{-e}

(c) $e^{-1/e}$ (d) $e^{1/e}$

[J.N.U. M.C.A.]

31. The function $f(x) = x^{1/x}$ has a miximum value at

(a) $x = e$ (b) $x = \frac{1}{e}$

(c) $x = e^2$ (d) $x = 0$

[J.N.U. M.C.A.]

32. The function $f(x) = \frac{x}{\log x}$ has a minimum value at

(a) 1 (b) e^{-1}

(c) e (d) None of these

33. The function $f(x) = \frac{\log x}{x}$ has a maximum value at

(a) 1 (b) e^{-1}

(c) e (d) None of these

34. The function $f(x) = x^2$ has a minimum value at

(a) $x = 0$ (b) $x = 1$

(c) $x = -1$ (d) None of these

35. Let $f(x) = |x|$, then

(a) $f'(0) = 0$

(b) $f(x)$ is maximum at $x = 0$

(c) $f(x)$ is minimum at $x = 0$

(d) None of these

36. Maximum value of $x^p y^q$ when $x + y = a$ is

(a) $\frac{a^{pq} p^p q^q}{(p+q)^{p+q}}$ (b) $\frac{a^{p+q} p^q q^p}{(p+q)^{p+q}}$

(c) $\frac{a^{p+q} p^p q^q}{(p+q)^{p+q}}$ (d) None of these

37. What fraction exceeds its pth power by the greatest number possible

(a) p^{p-1} (b) $\frac{1}{p^{p-1}}$

(c) $\left(\frac{1}{p}\right)^{p-1}$ (d) $\left(\frac{1}{p}\right)^{\frac{1}{p-1}}$

38. Assume that the petrol burnt (per hour) in driving a motorboat varies as the cube of its velocity. Then the most economical speed when going against a current of c miles per hour is

(a) $\frac{1}{2}c$ miles per hour

(b) c miles per hour

(c) $\frac{3}{2}c$ miles per hour

(d) None of these

39. The points of extremum of the function

$$\phi(x) = \int_1^x e^{-t^2/2}.(1-t^2)\,dt \text{ are}$$

(a) $x = 0$ (b) $x = 1$

(c) $x = \frac{1}{2}$ (d) None of these

40. On the interval [0, 1] the function $x^{25}(1-x)^{75}$ takes its maximum value at the point

(a) 0 (b) $\frac{1}{2}$

(c) $\frac{1}{3}$ (d) $\frac{1}{4}$

ANSWERS

1	2	3	4	5	6	7	8	9	10
(b)	(c)	(d)	(b)	(d)	(b)	(d)	(d)	(d)	(c)
11	12	13	14	15	16	17	18	19	20
(a)	(c)	(d)	(c)	(c)	(a)	(b)	(b)	(c)	(c)
21	22	23	24	25	26	27	28	29	30
(b)	(d)	(a)	(c)	(a)	(b)	(a)	(b)	(b)	(d)
31	32	33	34	35	36	37	38	39	40
(a)	(c)	(b)	(a)	(c)	(c)	(d)	(c)	(b)	(d)

SOME SELECTED EXPLANATORY ANSWERS

1. Let the co-ordinate of R be (x_1, y_1).

Given, $x^{2/3} + y^{2/3} = a^{2/3}$.

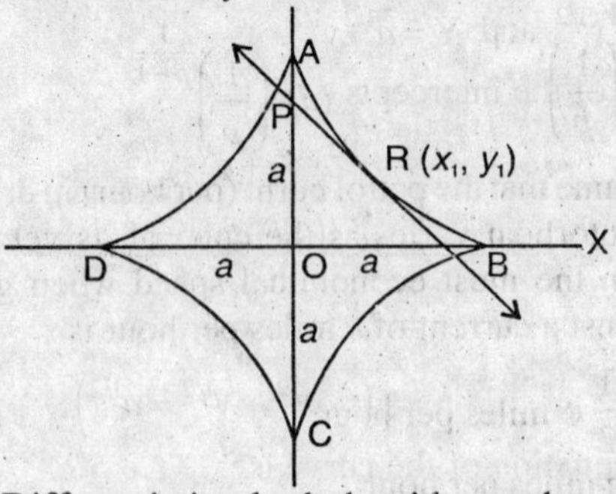

Differentiating both the sides we have

$$\frac{2}{3}x^{-1/3} + \frac{2}{3}y^{-1/3}.\frac{dy}{dx} = 0$$

$$\Rightarrow \quad \frac{dy}{dx} = -\frac{y^{1/3}}{x^{1/3}}$$

$$\Rightarrow \quad \left(\frac{dy}{dx}\right)_{(x_1, y_1)} = -\frac{y_1^{1/3}}{x_1^{1/3}}.$$

The equation of the tangent at (x_1, y_1) to the given curve is

$$y - y_1 = \frac{-y_1^{1/3}}{x_1^{1/3}}(x - x_1)$$

$$\Rightarrow \quad \frac{y - y_1}{y_1^{1/3}} = \frac{x - x_1}{x_1^{1/3}}$$

$$\Rightarrow \quad xx_1^{-1/3} + yy_1^{-1/3} = x_1^{2/3} + y_1^{2/3}$$

$$\Rightarrow \quad xx_1^{-1/3} + yy_1^{-1/3} = a^{2/3}$$

$\left(\because x_1^{2/3} + y_1^{2/3} = a^{2/3} \text{ as } (x_1, y_1) \text{ lies in it}\right)$

This meets the co-ordinates axes at $P\left(a^{2/3}x_1^{1/3}, 0\right)$ and $Q\left(0, a^{2/3}y_1^{1/3}\right)$

$$\therefore \quad PQ = \sqrt{a^{4/3}x_1^{2/3} + a^{4/3}y_1^{2/3}}$$

$$= \sqrt{a^{4/3}\left(x_1^{2/3} + y_1^{2/3}\right)} = \sqrt{a^{4/3}a^{2/3}}$$

$$= a.$$

2. Given $y = (2x - 1)\,e^{2(1-x)}$

$$\Rightarrow \quad \frac{dy}{dx} = 2.e^{2(1-x)} - 2(2x-1)\,e^{2(1-x)}$$

$$= 2e^{2(1-x)}.(2 - 2x)$$

$$= 4.e^{2(1-x)}.(1 - x)$$

$$\Rightarrow \quad \frac{d^2y}{dx^2} = -8.e^{2(1-x)}.(1 - x) - 4.e^{2(1-x)}$$

Now for maxima or minima

$$\frac{dy}{dx} = 0 \Rightarrow e^{2(1-x)}.(1 - x) = 0$$

$$\Rightarrow x = 1 \qquad \left(\because e^{2(1-x)} \neq 0\right)$$

$$\text{Now} \left(\frac{d^2y}{dx^2}\right)_{x=1} = -4 < 0.$$

$\therefore$ y is maximum at $x = 1$. When $x = 1$, we get $y = 1$.

$\therefore$ Point of maximum is $(1, 1)$.

Now the equation of the tangent at $(1, 1)$ is

$$y - 1 = 0\,(x - 1) \left(\because \frac{dy}{dx} = 0\right)$$

or $y = 1$.

3. Given equation is $x^{1/3} + y^{1/3} = a^{1/3}, \ \forall \ a > 0$.

Differentiating both the sides of the given equation we get

$$\frac{1}{3}x^{-2/3} + \frac{1}{3}y^{-2/3}.\frac{dy}{dx} = 0$$

$$\text{or} \quad \frac{dy}{dx} = -\frac{x^{-2/3}}{y^{-2/3}} = -\frac{y^{2/3}}{x^{2/3}}$$

$$\text{or} \quad \left(\frac{dy}{dx}\right)_{(a/8, a/8)} = -\frac{a^{2/3}/4}{a^{2/3}/4} = -1.$$

The given equation of the tangent at $\left(\frac{a}{8}, \frac{a}{8}\right)$ is given by

$$y - \frac{a}{8} = -1\left(x - \frac{a}{8}\right)$$

$$\text{or} \quad x + y = \frac{a}{4}$$

$\therefore$ x and y intercepts of this line on the co-ordinates axes are equal to $\frac{a}{4}$.

$\therefore$ By given condition we get

$$\left(\frac{a}{4}\right)^2+\left(\frac{a}{4}\right)^2=2 \Rightarrow \frac{a^2}{8}=2 \Rightarrow a=4.$$

4. Given equation of the tangent is

$x=t^3-4, y=2t^2+1.$

Differentiating x and y w.r.t. t we get

$$\frac{dx}{dt}=3t^2 \text{ and } \frac{dy}{dt}=4t$$

Now $\frac{dy}{dx}=\frac{dy/dt}{dx/dt}=\frac{4t}{3t^2}=\frac{4}{3t}.$

$$\therefore \left(\frac{dy}{dx}\right)_{t=2}=\frac{2}{3}$$

At this point equation where $t=2$, we have $x=4, y=9$.

The equation of the tangent is

$$(y-9)=\frac{2}{3}(x-4) \text{ or } 2x-3y+19=0.$$

5. Given equation is $x^{2/3}+y^{2/3}=a^{2/3}$.

Also the given normal is $y=x$ to the curve.

So, the normal intersect the curve at the point (x, y) where

$$x=\frac{a}{2\sqrt{2}}=y.$$

$\therefore$ Required point $(x, y)=\left(\frac{a}{2\sqrt{2}},\frac{a}{2\sqrt{2}}\right)$

6. Given equation of the curve is

$x^{1/2}+y^{1/2}=a^{1/2}.$

Now differentiating both the sides, we get

$$\frac{1}{2}x^{-1/2}+\frac{1}{2}y^{-1/2}.\frac{dy}{dx}=0$$

$$\Rightarrow \frac{dy}{dx}=-\left(\frac{y}{x}\right)^{1/2}.$$

$\therefore$ Equation of the tangent at the point (x, y) is

$$(Y-y)=\left(\frac{y}{x}\right)^{1/2}(X-x)$$

or $$\frac{X}{x^{1/2}}+\frac{Y}{y^{1/2}}=x^{1/2}+y^{1/2}$$

or $$\frac{X}{x^{1/2}}+\frac{Y}{y^{1/2}}=a^{1/2}.$$

Thus X and Y intercepts of this line on the co-ordinate axes are

$X=a^{1/2}x^{1/2}$ and $Y=a^{1/2}y^{1/2}$.

$\therefore$ Sum of the intercepts

$$=a^{1/2}x^{1/2}+a^{1/2}y^{1/2}$$

$$=a^{1/2}\left(x^{1/2}+y^{1/2}\right)$$

$$=a^{1/2}.a^{1/2}=a$$

$$\left(\because x^{1/2}+y^{1/2}=a^{1/2}\right)$$

7. Given equation of the curve is

$$y=b\,e^{-x/a}.$$

Differentiating both the sides w.r.t. x we get

$$\frac{dy}{dx}=-\frac{b}{a}e^{-x/a}=-\frac{y}{a} \quad ...(i)$$

Let the point of contact be (α,β).

$\therefore$ From *(i)* we get $\left(\frac{dy}{dx}\right)_{(\alpha,\beta)}=-\frac{\beta}{a}$ ...*(ii)*

Now equation of the tangent is

$$\frac{y-\beta}{x-\alpha}=-\frac{\beta}{a}$$

or $$\frac{x}{a}+\frac{y}{\beta}=1+\frac{\alpha}{a} \quad ...(i)$$

Compairing *(i)* with $\frac{x}{a}+\frac{y}{b}=1$, we get

$\beta=b$ and $1+\frac{\alpha}{a}=1$ ro $\alpha=0$.

$\therefore$ The required point i.e. $(\alpha, \beta)=(0, b)$.

8. Given $x=e^t\cos t$; $y=e^t\sin t$

$$\therefore \frac{dx}{dt}=-e^t\sin t+e^t\cos t.$$

$$\frac{dy}{dt}=e^t\cos t+e^t\sin t.$$

$$\therefore \frac{dy}{dx}=\frac{dy/dt}{dx/dt}=\frac{e^t(\cos t+\sin t)}{e^t(\cos t-\sin t)}$$

$$=\frac{\cos t+\sin t}{\cos t-\sin t} \quad (\because e^t\neq 0)$$

$$\therefore \left(\frac{dy}{dx}\right)_{t=\pi/4} = \frac{\cos\pi/4+\sin\pi/4}{\cos\pi/4-\sin\pi/4} = \infty$$

$$\Rightarrow \left(\frac{dx}{dy}\right)_{t=\pi/4} = 0.$$

$\therefore$ The tangent is parallel to y-axis and therefore perpendicular to x-axis.

9. Given equation is $\left(\frac{x}{a}\right)^n + \left(\frac{y}{b}\right)^n = 2$

Differentiating w.r.t. x we get

$$n.\left(\frac{x}{a}\right)^{n-1}.\frac{1}{a} + n.\left(\frac{y}{b}\right)^{n-1}.\frac{1}{b}\frac{dy}{dx} = 0$$

or $$\frac{dy}{dx} = -\frac{b^n}{a^n}.\left(\frac{y}{x}\right)^{n-1}$$

$$\therefore \left(\frac{dy}{dx}\right)_{(a,b)} = -\frac{b}{a}.$$

Now equation of the tangent at (a, b) is

$$(y-b) = -\frac{b}{a}(x-a)$$

$$\left[\because \left(\frac{dy}{dx}\right)_{(a,b)} = -\frac{b}{a}\right]$$

or $$ay + bx = 2ab$$

or $$\frac{x}{a}+\frac{y}{b} = 2.$$

$\therefore$ It is true for every non-zero value of n.

10. The given curve is $y(x^2 + a^2) = ax^2$ ...(*i*)

Putting $y = \frac{1}{4}a$ in (*i*) we get $3x^2 = a^2$ i.e. $x = \pm\frac{a}{\sqrt{3}}$.

Therefore we are to determine normals at the points $\left(\pm\frac{a}{\sqrt{3}}, \frac{a}{4}\right)$.

Now differentiating (*i*) w.r.t. x, we have

$$\frac{dy}{dx}(x^2+a^2) + y.2x = 2ax$$

or $$\frac{dy}{dx} = \frac{2ax-2xy}{(x^2+a^2)}$$

$$\therefore \left(\frac{dy}{dx}\right)_{\left(\pm\frac{a}{\sqrt{3}},\frac{a}{4}\right)} = \frac{2a.\left(\pm\frac{a}{\sqrt{3}}\right) - 2.\left(\pm\frac{a}{\sqrt{3}}\right)\left(\frac{a}{4}\right)}{\left(\pm\frac{a}{\sqrt{3}}\right)^2 + \left(\frac{a}{4}\right)^2}$$

$$= \pm\frac{3\sqrt{3}}{8}.$$

$\therefore$ Equation of the normal is

$$y - \frac{a}{4} = \mp\frac{8}{3\sqrt{3}}\left(x \mp \frac{a}{\sqrt{3}}\right)$$

i.e. $$y = \mp\frac{8}{3\sqrt{3}} + \frac{8a}{9} + \frac{1}{4}a$$

i.e. $$y = \mp\frac{8}{3\sqrt{3}}x + \frac{41}{36}a.$$

11. The given is $x^m y^n = a^{m+n}$.
Taking log both sides we get
$m\log x + n\log y = (m+n)\log a.$
Differentiating both the sides w.r.t. x we get

$$\frac{m}{x} + \frac{n}{y}.\frac{dy}{dx} = 0 \text{ or } \frac{dy}{dx} = -\frac{my}{nx}$$

At the point (α,β), $\frac{dy}{dx} = -\frac{m\beta}{n\alpha}$.

$\therefore$ Tangent at the point (α,β) is

$$y - \beta = -\frac{m\beta}{n\alpha}(x-\alpha)$$

or $$\frac{mx}{\alpha} + \frac{ny}{\beta} = m + n \quad ...(i)$$

Also the line $x\cos\theta + y\sin\theta = p$ is the tangent. ...(*ii*)

Compairing (*i*) and (*ii*), we have

$$\frac{\cos\theta}{m/\alpha} = \frac{\sin\theta}{n/\beta} = \frac{p}{m+n}$$

i.e. $\alpha = \frac{mp}{(m+n)\cos\theta}$, $\beta = \frac{np}{(m+n)\sin\theta}$

But (α,β) lies on the curve,

$\therefore \alpha^m.\beta^n = a^{m+n}$

Substituting for α and β from (*iii*), we get

$$\frac{m^m p^m}{(m+n)^m.\cos^m\theta}.\frac{n^n p^n}{(m+n)^n.\sin^n\theta} = a^{m+n}.$$

$\therefore p^{m+n}.m^m.n^n = (m+n)^{m+n}.a^{m+n}\cos^m\theta.\sin^n\theta$

Which is the required solution.

12. Given equation of the curve is

$$\left(\frac{x}{a}\right)^m + \left(\frac{y}{b}\right)^m = 1$$

Differentiating w.r.t. x we get

$$\frac{m\,x^{m-1}}{a^m} + \frac{n\,y^{m-1}}{b^m}.\frac{dy}{dx} = 0$$

or $$\frac{dy}{dx} = -\frac{x^{m-1}}{a^m}.\frac{b^m}{y^{m-1}}$$

$$\therefore \left(\frac{dy}{dx}\right)_{(x_1, y_1)} = -\frac{x_1^{m-1}}{a^m}.\frac{b^m}{y_1^{m-1}}$$

$\therefore$ Tangent at the point (x_1, y_1) is

$$y - y_1 = -\frac{x_1^{m-1}}{a^m}.\frac{b^m}{y_1^{m-1}}(x - x_1)$$

or $$\frac{y_1^{m-1}}{b^m}(y - y_1) + \frac{x_1^{m-1}}{a^m}(x - x_1) = 0$$

or $$\frac{x_1^{m-1}}{a^m}x + \frac{y_1^{m-1}}{b^m}y = \frac{x^m}{a^m} + \frac{y^m}{b^m} \quad ...(i)$$

But (x_1, y_1) lies on the curve

$$\therefore \frac{x_1^m}{a^m} + \frac{y_1^m}{b^m} = 1$$

$\therefore$ From (i) we get

$$\frac{x_1^m}{a^m}x + \frac{y_1^m}{b^m}y = 1 \quad ...(ii)$$

Also $x\cos\alpha + y\sin\alpha = p$ ...*(iii)*
is the equation of the tangent.
Comparing *(ii)* and *(iii)* we have

$$\frac{\cos\alpha}{x_1^{m-1}/a^m} = \frac{\sin\alpha}{y_1^{m-1}/b^m} = \frac{p}{1}$$

$$\therefore a\cos\alpha = p\left(\frac{x_1}{a}\right)^{m-1} \text{ and } b\sin\alpha = p\left(\frac{y_1}{a}\right)^{m-1}$$

Raising to power $\frac{m}{m-1}$ and adding we have

$$(a\cos\alpha)^{m/m-1} + (b\sin\alpha)^{m/m-1}$$

$$= p^{m/m-1}.\left\{\left(\frac{x_1}{a}\right)^m + \left(\frac{y_1}{b}\right)^m\right\}$$

$$\therefore (a\cos\alpha)^{m/m-1} + (b\sin\alpha)^{m/m-1} = p^{m/m-1}$$

which is the required condition.

13. Equation of the given curve are
$x = a(\theta + \sin\theta)$; $y = a(1 - \cos\theta)$.

$$\therefore \frac{dx}{d\theta} = a(1 + \cos\theta); \quad \frac{dy}{d\theta} = a\sin\theta$$

$$\therefore \frac{dy}{dx} = \frac{dy/d\theta}{dx/d\theta} = \frac{a\sin\theta}{a(1+\cos\theta)}$$

$$= \frac{2\sin\theta/2\,\cos\theta/2}{2\cos^2\theta/2} = \tan\frac{\theta}{2}.$$

Length of the sub-tangent

$$= \frac{y}{dy/dx} = \frac{a(1-\cos\theta)}{\tan\theta/2}$$

$$= \frac{a.2\sin^2\theta/2}{\tan\theta/2} = a\sin\theta.$$

14. Given $y = b\,e^{x/a}$

$$\Rightarrow \frac{dy}{dx} = \frac{b}{a}e^{x/a}$$

Length of sub-tangent

$$= \frac{y}{dy/dx} = \frac{b.e^{x/a}}{b/a.e^{x/a}} = a.$$

16. Given curve is $y = a^{(1-n)}.x^n$.

$$\therefore \frac{dy}{dx} = n.a^{(1-n)}.x^{n-1}.$$

Now sub-normal $= y\frac{dy}{dx} = n.a^{2(1-n)}.x^{2n-1}$.

It will be of constant length if power of x i.e. $2n - 1 = 0$ or $n = \frac{1}{2}$.

17. Given equation of catenary is

$$y = c\cosh\left(\frac{x}{c}\right).$$

$$\Rightarrow \frac{dy}{dx} = c\sinh\left(\frac{x}{c}\right).\frac{1}{c} = \sinh\left(\frac{x}{c}\right).$$

Now Normal $= y.\sqrt{1 + \left(\frac{dy}{dx}\right)^2}$

$$= c\cosh\left(\frac{x}{c}\right).\sqrt{1 + \sinh^2\left(\frac{x}{c}\right)}$$

$$= c\cosh^2\left(\frac{x}{c}\right) = \left(\frac{y^2}{c}\right)$$

18. Given Subtangent = Subnormal

$$\Rightarrow \frac{y}{dy/dx} = y\frac{dy}{dx}$$

$$\Rightarrow \left(\frac{dy}{dx}\right)^2 = 1 \Rightarrow \frac{dy}{dx} = \pm 1.$$

∴ Length of the tangent

$$= \frac{y\sqrt{1+\left(\frac{dy}{dx}\right)^2}}{dy/dx} = y\sqrt{2} = \sqrt{2} \text{ ordinate.}$$

19. Given curve is $xy^n = a^{n+1}$

Differentiating both the sides w.r.t. x we get

$$y^n + x.ny^{n-1}.\frac{dy}{dx} = 0 \Rightarrow \frac{dy}{dx} = -\frac{y}{nx}.$$

Let (α, β) be a point on $xy^n = a^{n+1}$. Then the equation of the tangent at (α, β) is

$$y - \beta = -\frac{\beta}{n\alpha}(x - \alpha)$$

It meets the co-ordinates axes at $A[(n+1)\alpha, 0]$ and $B\left[0, \frac{(n+1)\beta}{n}\right]$.

Now the area of the $\Delta AOB = \frac{1}{2} OA \times OB$

$$= \frac{1}{2}(n+1)\alpha.\frac{(n+1)}{n}\beta$$

$$= \frac{1}{2}\frac{(n+1)^2}{n}.\alpha\beta \quad ...(i)$$

(α, β) lies on $xy^n = a^{n+1}$, so $\alpha\beta^n = a^{n+1}$

or $\alpha = \frac{a^{n+1}}{\beta^n}$.

Putting the value of α in *(i)*, we get

$$\Delta = \frac{1}{2}\frac{(n+1)^2}{n}.a^{n+1}.\beta^{-n+1}$$

For area of the triangle to be constant, power of β should be zero.

i.e. $-n + 1 = 0$ or $n = 1$.

20. Given curve is $y = a \log (x^2 - a^2)$

Differentiating both the sides we get

$$\frac{dy}{dx} = \frac{2ax}{x^2 - a^2}$$

$$\Rightarrow \quad \tan\psi = \frac{2ax}{x^2 - a^2}$$

Now Subtangent $= y\frac{dx}{dy} = y.\frac{x^2 - a^2}{2ax}$

∴ Length of the tangent $= y \operatorname{cosec}\psi$

$$= y\sqrt{1+\cot^2\psi} = y\sqrt{\left\{1+\frac{(x^2-a^2)^2}{4a^2x^2}\right\}}$$

$$= y\sqrt{\frac{(x^2+a^2)^2}{4a^2x^2}} = y.\frac{x^2+a^2}{2ax}$$

Hence the sum of the sub-tangent and the length of the tangent

$$= \frac{y(x^2-a^2)}{2ax} + \frac{y(x^2+a^2)}{2ax} = \frac{xy}{a}$$

i.e., varies as product of the co-ordinate of the point.

21. Given $f(x) = a \log|x| + bx^2 + x$

$$\therefore \quad f'(x) = \frac{a}{x} + 2bx + 1$$

Now $f(x)$ attains extremum values at $x = -1$ and $x = 2$.

So $f'(-1) = 0$ and $f'(2) = 0$

$$\Rightarrow -a - 2b + 1 = 0 \text{ and } \frac{a}{2} + 4b + 1 = 0$$

Solving these two equation we get $a = 2$ and $b = -\frac{1}{2}$.

22. Given $f(x) = \sin 2x - x$, for $x \in \left[-\frac{\pi}{2}, \frac{\pi}{2}\right]$

$$\therefore \quad f'(x) = 2\cos 2x - 1$$

Now for $f(x)$ to attains extremum values we must have

$$f'(x) = 2\cos 2x - 1 = 0$$

$$\Rightarrow \cos 2x = \frac{1}{2} \Rightarrow 2x = -\frac{\pi}{3}, \frac{\pi}{3}$$

$$\Rightarrow \quad x = -\frac{\pi}{6}, \frac{\pi}{6}$$

Now $f\left(-\frac{\pi}{2}\right) = \frac{\pi}{2}$, $f\left(\frac{\pi}{2}\right) = -\frac{\pi}{2}$.

$$f\left(-\frac{\pi}{6}\right) = -\frac{\sqrt{3}}{2} + \frac{\pi}{6} \text{ and } f\left(\frac{\pi}{6}\right) = \frac{\sqrt{3}}{2} - \frac{\pi}{6}.$$

These values shows that $\frac{\pi}{2}$ is the greatest value of $f(x)$ and its least value is $-\frac{\pi}{2}$.

Hence the required difference is $\frac{\pi}{2}-\left(-\frac{\pi}{2}\right)=\pi$.

23. Given $f(x) =$

$$\int_1^x \left\{2(t-1)(t-2)^3+3(t-1)^2(t-2)^2\right\} dt$$

$$= \int_1^x (t-1)(t-2)^2(5t-7)\,dt$$

$\Rightarrow f'(x) = (x-1)(x-2)^2(5x-7)$.

For maximum or minimum value

$f'(x)=0 \Rightarrow x=1, 2, \frac{7}{5}$.

Now $f''(x) = (x-2)^2(5x-7) + 2(x-1)(x-2)(5x-7) + 5(x-1)(x-2)^2$.

$\Rightarrow f''(1)<0,\ f''\left(\frac{7}{5}\right)>0$ and $f''(2)=0$

Hence, $f(x)$ attains its maximum at $x = 1$.

24. Any point on the parabola $y = x^2$ is (t, t^2)

$\therefore$ Distance between them is

$$D = \sqrt{(t-0)^2+(t^2-c)^2}$$

or $\quad D^2 = t^2 + (t^2-c)^2$

Let us denote D^2 by F. Now F will be maximum or minimum if D is so.

$\therefore \quad F = t^2 + (t^2-c)^2$.

$$\Rightarrow \frac{dF}{dt} = 2t + 2(t^2-c).2t$$

$$= 2t\left\{1+2(t^2-c)\right\}$$

Now $\frac{dF}{dt}=0 \Rightarrow 2t\left\{1+2(t^2-c)\right\}=0$

$$\Rightarrow \quad t = 0 \text{ or } \sqrt{\left(c-\frac{1}{2}\right)}$$

Also $\quad \frac{d^2F}{dt^2} = 2 + 4(t^2-c) + 4t.2t$

$$= 2 + 4t^2 + 8t^2 - 4c$$

$$= 12t^2 - 4c + 2$$

$$= 12.\frac{(2c-1)}{2} - 4c + 2$$

$$= 8c - 4 > 0 \ (\because 0 \le c \le 5)$$

$\therefore$ F is minimum when $t = \sqrt{\left(c-\frac{1}{2}\right)}$

$\therefore$ Minimum distance i.e.

$$D = \sqrt{t^2+(t^2-c)^2}$$

$$= \sqrt{\left(c-\frac{1}{2}\right)+\left(c-\frac{1}{2}-c\right)^2}$$

$$= \sqrt{\left(c-\frac{1}{4}\right)} = \frac{\sqrt{4c-1}}{2}$$

25. Given $f(x) = \sin^p\theta\cos^q\theta$, where $p, q > 0$, $0<\theta<\frac{\pi}{2}$

$\Rightarrow y = \sin^p\theta\cos^q\theta$ where $y = f(x)$.

Taking log both the sides we get

$\log y = p\log\sin\theta + q\log\cos\theta$

Differentiating both the sides we get

$$\frac{1}{y}.\frac{dy}{d\theta} = p\cot\theta - q\tan\theta$$

or $$\frac{dy}{d\theta} = y(p\cot\theta - q\tan\theta)$$

Now $\frac{dy}{d\theta}=0 \Rightarrow y(p\cot\theta-q\tan\theta)=0$

$$\Rightarrow \quad \tan^2\theta = \frac{p}{q} \quad (\because y\ne 0)$$

$$\Rightarrow \quad \theta = \tan^{-1}\left(\sqrt{\frac{p}{q}}\right).$$

Also $$\frac{d^2y}{d\theta^2} = -y(p\,\text{cosec}^2\theta + q\sec^2\theta) + (p\cot\theta - q\tan\theta).\frac{dy}{d\theta}$$

$$< 0, \text{ as } \frac{dy}{d\theta}=0 \text{ and } \tan^2\theta = \left(\frac{p}{q}\right).$$

$\therefore$ y is maximum when $\theta = \tan^{-1}\sqrt{\frac{p}{q}}$.

26. Mod of any function can not be less than zero.

$\therefore$ Minimum value of $f(x) = |x^2-5x+2|$ is zero.

27. Let $F = px + qy$

Then $F = px + \frac{qr^2}{x}$ $(\because xy = r^2)$

$\Rightarrow \frac{dF}{dx} = p - \frac{qr^2}{x^2}$

Now $\frac{dF}{dx} = 0 \Rightarrow p - \frac{qr^2}{x^2} = 0 \Rightarrow x = \pm\sqrt{\frac{qr^2}{p}}$

Also $\frac{d^2F}{dx^2} = \frac{2qr^2}{x^3} > 0$ for $x = \sqrt{\frac{qr^2}{p}}$.

$\therefore$ F is minimum when $x = \sqrt{\frac{qr^2}{p}}$.

$\therefore F = p.\sqrt{\frac{qr^2}{p}} + \frac{qr^2}{\sqrt{qr^2/p}} = 2r\sqrt{pq}$.

28. Given $f(x) = 2x + \frac{8}{x^2}, x > 0$

$\therefore f'(x) = 2 - \frac{16}{x^3}$

$f''(x) = \frac{48}{x^4}$

Now for maxima or minima

$f'(x) = 0$

$\Rightarrow 2 - \frac{16}{x^3} = 0 \Rightarrow x = 2.$

$\therefore f''(x) = \frac{48}{x^4} = \frac{48}{2^4} = 3 > 0$

$\therefore$ Minimum value of $f(x)$ is obtained at $x = 2$.

$\therefore f(2) = 2 \times 2 + \frac{8}{2^2} = 6.$

29. Let $y = x^x$

Taking log both the sides, we have

$\log y = x \log x$

$\Rightarrow \frac{1}{y}.\frac{dy}{dx} = x.\frac{1}{x} + \log x$

$\Rightarrow \frac{dy}{dx} = y(1 + \log x)$

$\Rightarrow \frac{d^2y}{dx^2} = \frac{dy}{dx}(1 + \log x) + y.\frac{1}{x}$

Now for maxima or minima

$\frac{dy}{dx} = 0$

$\Rightarrow y(1 + \log x) = 0$

$\Rightarrow \log x = -1$ $(\because y \neq 0)$

$\Rightarrow x = e^{-1}$

$\therefore \frac{d^2y}{dx^2} = x^{x-1} > 0$ for $x = e^{-1}$

$\therefore$ Minimum value of $f(x)$ is obtained at $x = e^{-1}$.

$\therefore f(e^{-1}) = \left(e^{-1}\right)^{e^{-1}} = e^{-1/e}$.

30. Let $y = \left(\frac{1}{x}\right)^x$ or $y = x^{-x}$

Taking log both the sides we get

$\log y = -x \log x$

$\Rightarrow \frac{1}{y}.\frac{dy}{dx} = -x\frac{1}{x} - \log x$

$\Rightarrow \frac{dy}{dx} = -y(1 + \log x)$

$\Rightarrow \frac{d^2y}{dx^2} = -\frac{dy}{dx}(1 + \log x) - \frac{y}{x}$

Now for maxima or minima

$\frac{dy}{dx} = 0$

$\Rightarrow -y(1 + \log x) = 0$

$\Rightarrow \log x = -1$ $(\because y \neq 0)$

$\Rightarrow x = e^{-1}$

$\therefore \frac{d^2y}{dx^2} = -x^{1-x} < 0$ $\left(\because \frac{dy}{dx} = 0\right)$

for $x = e^{-1}$.

$\therefore$ Maximum value of y is obtained at $x = e^{-1}$.

$\therefore y_{\max} = e^{1/e}$.

31. Given $f(x) = x^{1/x}$

$\Rightarrow \log f(x) = \frac{\log x}{x}$

$\Rightarrow \frac{1}{f(x)}\frac{df(x)}{dx} = \frac{x.\frac{1}{x} - \log x}{x^2}$

$\Rightarrow \frac{df(x)}{dx} = f(x).\left[\frac{1 - \log x}{x^2}\right]$

$$\Rightarrow \quad \frac{d^2f(x)}{dx^2} = \frac{df(x)}{dx}\cdot\left[\frac{1-\log x}{x^2}\right]$$

$$+ f(x)\left[\frac{(2\log x - 3)x + (1-\log x)^2}{x^4}\right]$$

For maxima or minima

$$\frac{df(x)}{dx} = 0$$

$$\Rightarrow \quad \frac{1-\log x}{x^2} = 0$$

$$\Rightarrow \quad x = e$$

$$\therefore \quad \frac{d^2f(x)}{dx^2} = f(x)\left[\frac{(2\log x - 3)x + (1-\log x)^2}{x^4}\right]$$

$$\left(\because \frac{df(x)}{dx} = 0\right)$$

$$\Rightarrow \quad \frac{d^2f(e)}{dx^2} = f(e)\left[\frac{(2-3)e}{e^4}\right] < 0$$

$\therefore$ Maximum value of $f(x)$ is obtained at $x = e$.

$$\therefore \quad f(e) = e^{1/e}.$$

32. Given $\quad f(x) = \dfrac{x}{\log x}$

$$\Rightarrow \quad \frac{df(x)}{dx} = \frac{\log x - x.\frac{1}{x}}{(\log x)^2} = \frac{\log x - 1}{(\log x)^2}$$

$$\Rightarrow \quad \frac{d^2f(x)}{dx^2} = \frac{(\log x)^2(1/x) - 2\log x(1/x)(\log x - 1)}{(\log x)^4}$$

Now for maxima or minima

$$\frac{df(x)}{dx} = 0 \Rightarrow \frac{\log x - 1}{(\log x)^2} = 0$$

$$\Rightarrow \log x = 1 \Rightarrow x = e.$$

Also $\dfrac{d^2f(x)}{dx^2} = \dfrac{2-\log x}{x(\log x)^3} > 0$ for $x = e$.

$\therefore$ Minimum value of $f(x)$ is obtained at $x = e$.

33. Given $\quad f(x) = \dfrac{\log x}{x}$

$$\Rightarrow \quad \frac{df(x)}{dx} = \frac{x.\frac{1}{x} - \log x}{x^2} = \frac{1-\log x}{x^2}$$

$$\Rightarrow \quad \frac{d^2f(x)}{dx^2} = \frac{\left(-\frac{1}{x}\right)x^2 - (1-\log x)\,2x}{x^4}$$

$$= \frac{-3 + 2\log x}{x^2}$$

Now for maxima or minima

$$\frac{df(x)}{dx} = 0 \Rightarrow 1 - \log x = 0 \Rightarrow x = e.$$

Also $\dfrac{d^2f(x)}{dx^2} = -\dfrac{1}{e^3} < 0$ for $x = e$.

$\therefore$ Maximum value of $f(x)$ is obtained at $x = e$.

34. Given $\quad f(x) = x^2$

$$\Rightarrow \quad \frac{df(x)}{dx} = 2x \Rightarrow \frac{d^2f(x)}{dx^2} = 2 > 0$$

Now $\dfrac{df(x)}{dx} = 0 \Rightarrow 2x = 0 \Rightarrow x = 0$

$\dfrac{d^2f(x)}{dx^2} > 0 \Rightarrow f(x)$ is minimum at $x = 0$.

36. Let $z = x^py^q = x^p(a-x)^q$ $(\because y = a - x)$

Taking log both the sides we get

$$\log z = p\log x + q\log(a-x)$$

Now *a* function is maximum when its logarithm is maximum

$\therefore$ Let $\quad u = p\log x + q\log(a-x)$

$$\Rightarrow \quad \frac{du}{dx} = \frac{p}{x} - \frac{q}{a-x} = \frac{ap - x(p+q)}{x(a-x)}$$

$$\Rightarrow \quad \frac{d^2u}{dx^2} = \frac{-(p+q)x(a-x) - (a-2x)\{ap - x(p+q)\}}{x^2(a-x)^2}$$

Now $\dfrac{du}{dx} = 0 \Rightarrow x = \dfrac{ap}{(p+q)}$

Clearly $\dfrac{d^2u}{dx^2} = -$ive at $x = \dfrac{ap}{(p+q)}$

Hence z is maximum at $x=\dfrac{ap}{(p+q)}$

$\therefore$ Maximum value of z (or $x^p y^q$)

$$=\left\{\frac{ap}{(p+q)}\right\}^p\left\{a-\frac{ap}{(p+q)}\right\}^q$$

$$=\left\{\frac{ap}{(p+q)}\right\}^p\left\{\frac{aq}{(p+q)}\right\}^q=\frac{a^{p+q}.p^p.q^q}{(p+q)^{p+q}}.$$

37. Let x be the required fraction, then

$$y = x - x^p$$

$$\Rightarrow \quad \frac{dy}{dx} = 1 - p.x^{p-1}$$

$$\Rightarrow \quad \frac{d^2y}{dx^2} = p(p-1).x^{p-2}$$

Now $\dfrac{dy}{dx}=0 \Rightarrow x^{p-1}=\dfrac{1}{p} \Rightarrow x=\left(\dfrac{1}{p}\right)^{1/p-1}$

Clearly $\dfrac{d^2y}{dx^2}=-\text{ive}$ at $x=\left(\dfrac{1}{p}\right)^{1/p-1}$

Hence y is the greatest when $x=\left(\dfrac{1}{p}\right)^{1/p-1}$

38. Let y miles/hour be the velocity of the motorboat. Then velocity of the boat relative to current = $(v-c)$ miles/hour.

Let a miles be the distance to be covered up, where a is constant.

$\therefore$ The time of run $=\dfrac{a}{v-c}$ hours.

The petrol burnt, per hour = kv^3, where k is a constant. Let y be the total amount of petrol burnt, then

$$y = kv^3.\frac{a}{v-c}=ak.\frac{v^3}{v-c}$$

For maxima or minima

$$\frac{dy}{dv} = ka.\frac{(v-c).3v^2-v^3}{(v-c)^2}$$

$$= ka.\frac{v^2(2v-3c)}{(v-c)^2}=0$$

$$\Rightarrow \quad v = \frac{3c}{2}.$$

Also $\dfrac{dy}{dv}$ changes sign from –ive to +ive as x passes through $\dfrac{3c}{2}$.

Hence y is minimum when $v=\dfrac{3c}{2}$.

39. Given $\phi(x) = \displaystyle\int_1^x e^{-t^2/2}(1-t^2)\,dt$

$$\Rightarrow \quad \phi'(x) = e^{-x^2/2}(1-x^2)$$

For maxima or minima i.e. extremum value we must have

$\phi'(x)=0$

$\Rightarrow e^{-x^2/2}(1-x^2)=0$

$\Rightarrow x=\pm 1 \left(\because e^{-x^2/2}\neq 0\right)$

40. Given $f(x) = x^{25}(1-x)^{75}$

$$\Rightarrow \quad f'(x) = 25x^{24}(1-x)^{75} - 75x^{25}(1-x)^{74}$$

$$= 25x^{24}(1-x)^{74}(1-4x)$$

Now $f'(x)=0 \Rightarrow x=0,1,\dfrac{1}{4}.$

For $x<\dfrac{1}{4}$,

$$f'(x) = 25x^{24}(1-x)^{74}(1-4x)>0$$

and for $x>\dfrac{1}{4}$,

$$f'(x) = 25x^{24}(1-x)^{74}(1-4x)<0$$

$\therefore$ $f'(x)$ changes its sign from +ive and –ive as x passes through $\dfrac{1}{4}$ from left to right.

So, $f(x)$ attains its maximum at $x=\dfrac{1}{4}$.

14. INTEGRAL CALCULUS

1. Integration: Integration is the reverse process of differentiation. The process of finding the function $f(x)$ whose differential coefficient w.r.t. 'x', say $F(x)$, is given, is called the **integration** of $f(x)$ w.r.t. x and is written as $\int F(x)\,dx = f(x)$ where $\frac{d}{dx} f(x) = F(x)$.

We know that the differential coefficient of a constant is zero. Thus if c is an arbitrary constant independent of x, then $\frac{d}{dx}[f(x)+c] = F(x)$, where $\frac{d}{dx} f(x) = F(x)$. Thus $\int F(x)\,dx = f(x) + c$ ... (1)

This arbitrary constant c is called the constant of integration. The integration given in (1) is called the indefinite integral or simply an integral of $f(x)$ w.r.t. x.

2. Methods of Integration: The various methods of integration can be classified as follow:

Integration by using standard formulae:

(i) $\int k\,dx = kx + c$, k is a constant

(ii) $\int kf(x)\,dx = k\int f(x)\,dx + c$

(iii) $\int [f_1(x) \pm f_2(x)]\,dx = \int f_1(x)\,dx \pm \int f_2(x)\,dx + c$

(iv) $\int x^n\,dx = x^{n+1}/(n+1) + c, (n \neq -1)$.

(v) $\int (1/x)\,dx = \log_e |x| + c$

(vi) $\int a^x\,dx = a^x/\log_e a + c, a > 0$

(vii) $\int e^x\,dx = e^x + c$

(viii) $\int \sin x\,dx = -\cos x + c$

(ix) $\int \cos x\,dx = \sin x + c$

(x) $\int \sec^2 x\,dx = \tan x + c$

(xi) $\int \operatorname{cosec}^2 x\,dx = -\cot x + c$

(xii) $\int \sec x \tan x\,dx = \sec x + c$

(xiii) $\int \operatorname{cosec} x \cot x\,dx = -\operatorname{cosec} x + c$

(xiv) $\int \tan x\,dx = \log|\sec x| + c = -\log|\cos x| + c$

(xv) $\int \cot x\,dx = \log|\sin x| + c$

(xvi) $\int \sec x\,dx = \log|\tan(1/4\,\pi + 1/2\,\pi) + c = \log|(\sec x + \tan x| + c$

(xvii) $\int \operatorname{cosec} x = \log|\tan 1/2\,x| + c = \log|(\operatorname{cosec} x - \cot x| + c$

(xviii) $\int \sinh x\,dx = \cosh x + c$

(xix) $\int \cosh x\,dx = \sinh x + c$

(xx) $\int \operatorname{sech}^2 x\,dx = \tanh x + c$

(xxi) $\int \operatorname{cosech}^2 x\,dx = -\coth x + c$

(xxii) $\int \operatorname{sech} x \tanh x\,dx = -\operatorname{sech} x + c$

(xxiii) $\int \operatorname{cosech} x \coth x\,dx = -\operatorname{cosech} x + c$

(xxiv) $\int \tanh x\,dx = \log\cosh x + c$

(xxv) $\int \coth x\,dx = \log|\sinh x| + c$

(xxvi) $\int \frac{1}{\sqrt{(1-x^2)}}\,dx = \sin^{-1} x + c \text{ or } -\cos^{-1} x + c$

(xxvii) $-\int \frac{1}{\sqrt{(1-x^2)}}\,dx = \cos^{-1} x + c \text{ or } -\sin^{-1} x + c$

(xxviii) $\int \frac{1}{1+x^2}\,dx = \tan^{-1} x + c \text{ or } -\cot^{-1} x + c$

(xxix) $\int \frac{1}{1+x^2} - dx = \cot^{-1} x + c \text{ or } -\tan^{-1} x + c$

(xxx) $\int \frac{1}{x\sqrt{(x^2-1)}}\,dx = \sec^{-1} x + c \text{ or } -\operatorname{cosec}^{-1} x + c$

(xxxi) $-\int \frac{1}{x\sqrt{(x^2-1)}}\,dx = \operatorname{cosec}^{-1} x + c \text{ or } -\sec^{-1} x + c$

(xxxii) $\int \frac{dx}{a^2+x^2} = \frac{1}{a} \tan^{-1}\left(\frac{x}{a}\right) + c$

(xxxiii) $\int \frac{dx}{x^2-a^2} = \frac{1}{2a} \log\left|\frac{x-a}{x+a}\right| + c, x > a$

(xxxiv) $\int \frac{dx}{a^2 - x^2} = \frac{1}{2a} \log \left|\frac{a+x}{a-x}\right| + c, x < a$

(xxxv) $\int \frac{dx}{\sqrt{(a^2 - x^2)}} = \sin^{-1}\left(\frac{x}{a}\right) + c$

(xxxvi) $\int \frac{dx}{\sqrt{(x^2 + a^2)}} = \sinh^{-1}\left(\frac{x}{a}\right) + c$ or

$\log |[x + \sqrt{(a^2 + x^2)}]| + c$

(xxxvii) $\int \frac{dx}{\sqrt{(x^2 - a^2)}} = \cosh^{-1}\left(\frac{x}{a}\right) + c$ or

$\log |[x + \sqrt{(x^2 - a^2)}]| + c$

(xxxviii) $\int \frac{dx}{x\sqrt{(x^2 - a^2)}} = \frac{1}{a} \sec^{-1}\left(\frac{x}{a}\right) + c$

(xxxix) $\int \sqrt{(a^2 - x^2)}\, dx = \frac{1}{2} x \sqrt{(a^2 - x^2)} + \frac{1}{2} a^2$

$\sin^{-1} (x/a) + c$

(xxxx) $\int \sqrt{(a^2 + x^2)}\, dx = \frac{1}{2} x \sqrt{(a^2 + x^2)} + \frac{1}{2} a^2 \sinh^-$

$^1 (x/a) + c$

or $= \frac{1}{2} x \sqrt{(a^2 + x^2)} + \frac{1}{2} a^2 \log |[x + \sqrt{(a^2 +}$

$x^2)]| + c$

(xxxxi) $\int \sqrt{(x^2 - a^2)}\, dx = \frac{1}{2} x \sqrt{(x^2 + a^2)} - \frac{1}{2} a^2 \cosh^-$

$^1 (x/a) + c$

or $= \frac{1}{2} x \sqrt{(x^2 - a^2)} - \frac{1}{2} a^2 \log |[x + \sqrt{(x^2 +}$

$a^2)]| + c$

(xxxxii) $\int e^{ax} \sin bx\, dx = \frac{e^{ax}}{a^2 + b^2} (a \sin bx - b \cos bx)$

$+ c = \frac{e^{ax}}{\sqrt{(a^2 + b^2)}} \sin\left(bx - \tan^{-1}\frac{b}{a}\right) + c.$

(xxxxiii) $\int e^{ax} \cos bx\, dx = \frac{e^{ax}}{a^2 + b^2} (a \cos bx + b \sin$

$bx) = \frac{e^{ax}}{\sqrt{(a^2 + b^2)}} \cos\left(bx - \tan^{-1}\frac{b}{a}\right).$

3. Integration by parts: $\int u.v\, dx = u. \int v\, dx - \int\left[\frac{du}{dx}.\int v\, dx\right]dx$

i.e., the integral of the product of two funcrtions = (first function) × (integral of the second function) – integral of {(differential of first function) × (Integral of second function)}.

4. Chain rule: (For successive integration by parts) $\int u.v\, dx = uv_1 - u'v_2 + u''v_3 - u'''v_4 + ... + (-1)^{n-1} u^{n-1} v_n + (-1)^n \int u^n v_n\, dx$, where u^n stands for nth differential coefficient of u and v_n stands for nth integral of v.

5. Integration by Substitution

(a) To evaluate the integral $\int f(ax + b)\, dx$

Putting $ax + b = t$, so that $a\, dx = dt$., *i.e.*, $dx = (1/a)\, dt$,

$\int f(ax + b)\, dx = \int f(t).(1/a)\, dt = (1/a)\, F(t)$,

where $\int f(t)\, dt = F(t) = (1/a)\, F(ax + b)$.

Thus to evaluate the integral $\int f(ax + b)\, dx$, integrate $f(ax + b)$ supposing $(ax + b)$ as a variable like x and divide it by a (the coefficient of x in $ax + b$).

(i) $\int (ax + b)^n\, dx = \frac{(ax + b)^{n+1}}{a(n+1)} + c,\ n \neq -1$

(ii) $\int \frac{1}{ax + b}\, dx = \log |(ax + b)| + c$

(iii) $\int e^{ax}\, dx = (1/a)\, e^{ax}$

(iv) $\int \sin (ax + b)\, dx = -(1/a) = -(1/a) \cos (ax + b) + c$

(v) $\int \cos(ax + b)\, dx = (1/a) \sin (ax+b) + c$

(vi) $\int \sec^2 (ax+b)\, dx = (1/a) \tan (ax+b) + c$

(vii) $\int \operatorname{cosec}^2 (ax+b)\, dx = -(1/a) \cot (ax+b) + c$

(viii) $\int \sec (ax+b) \tan (ax+b)\, dx = (1/a) \sec (ax+b) + c$

(ix) $\int \operatorname{cosec} (ax + b) \cot (ax + b)\, dx = -(1/a) \operatorname{cosec} (ax+b) + c$

(b) $\displaystyle\int \frac{f'(x)}{f(x)}\, dx = \log f(x) + c$

(c) $\int [f(x)]^n f'(x)\, dx = [f(x)^{n+1}/(n+1) + c$

(d) Some important substitutions

Function	Substitutions
$\sqrt{(a^2 - x^2)}$	$x = a \sin\theta$ or $x = a \cos\theta$
$\sqrt{(a^2 + x^2)}$	$x = a \tan\theta$ or $x = a \sinh\theta$
$\sqrt{(x^2 + a^2)}$	$x = a \sec\theta$ or $x = a \cosh\theta$

Method III: Integration by Decomposition into Sum:

(a) Trigonometrical transformations: For the integration of the trigonometrical products such as $\sin^2 x$, $\cos^2 x$, $\sin^3 x$, $\cos^3 x$, $\sin ax$, $\cos bx$, etc., they are expressed as the sum or difference of the sines and cosines of multiples of angles.

(b) Partial fractions: If the given function is in the form of fractions of two polynomials, then for its integration decompose it into fractions. (If possible).

6. Integration of Some Special Integrals:

(a) Integration of $\displaystyle\int \frac{dx}{ax^2 + bx + c}$ **:** This may be reproduced to one of the forms *(xxxii)*, *(xxxiii)*, *(xxxiv)*.

(b) Integration of $\displaystyle\int \frac{dx}{\sqrt{(ax^2 + bx + c)}}$ **:** This can be reduced to one of the forms *(xxxv)*, *(xxxvi)* or *(xxxvii)*.

(c) Integration of $\sqrt{(ax^2 + bx + c)}\, dx$**:** This can be reduced to one of the forms *(xxxix)*, *(xxxx)* or *(xxxxi)*.

(d) Integration of $\displaystyle\int \frac{(px+q)\, dx}{ax^2 + bx + c}$, $\displaystyle\int (px+q)\sqrt{(ax^2 + bx + c)}\, dx$, **:** For the evaluation of any of these integrals, put $px + q = A$ {differential of $(ax^2 + bx + c)$} + B.

Find A and B by comparing the coefficients of like powers of x on the two sides.

(e) Integration of $\displaystyle\int \frac{dx}{(x+k)\sqrt{(ax^2 + bx + c)}}$: Put $x + k = 1\, t$.

(f) Integration of $\displaystyle\int \frac{dx}{(Ax^2 + B)\sqrt{(Cx^2 + D)}}$: Put $x = 1/t$.

(g) Integration of $\displaystyle\int \frac{dx}{\sqrt{[(x-\alpha)(x-\beta)]}}$, $\displaystyle\int \sqrt{\left(\frac{x-\alpha}{\beta - x}\right)}\, dx$, $\int \sqrt{[(x-\alpha)(\beta - x)]}\, dx$, put $x = \alpha \cos^2\theta + \beta \sin^2\theta$.

(h) Integration of $\displaystyle\int \frac{dx}{a + b \cos x}$, $\displaystyle\int \frac{dx}{a + b \sin x}$, $\displaystyle\int \frac{dx}{a + b \cos x + c \sin x}$

Replace, $\sin x = (2 \tan 1/2\, x)/(1 + \tan^2 1/2\, x)$ and $\cos x = (1 - \tan^2 1/2\, x)/(1 + \tan^2 1/2 x)$

Then put $\tan 1/2x = t$.

(i) Integration of $\displaystyle\int \frac{p \cos x + q \sin x}{a + b \cos x + b \sin x}\, dx$: Put $p \cos x + q \sin x = A (a + b \cos x + b \sin x) + B$. Differential of $(a + b \cos x + b \sin x) + C$.

A, B and C can be calculated by equating the coefficients of $\cos x$, $\sin x$ and the constant terms.

DEFINITE INTEGRATION

7. Definite Integral: The definite integral of $f(x)$ between the limits a to b, *i.e.*, in the interval $[a, b]$ is denoted by $\int_a^b f(x)\, dx$ and is defined as follows:

$$\int_a^b f(x)\, dx = [F(x)]_a^b = F(b) - F(a) \text{ where } \int f(x)\, dx = F(x).$$

8. General Properties of Definite Integrals:

I. $\int_a^b f(x)\, dx = \int_a^b f(t)\, dt.$

II. $\int_a^b f(x)\, dx = -\int_b^a f(x)\, dx.$

III. $\int_a^b f(x)\, dx = \int_a^c f(x)\, dx + \int_c^b f(x)\, dx$, where $a < c < b$.

IV. $\int_a^b f(x)\, dx = \int_a^b f(a+b-x)\, dx$ In particular, $\int_0^a f(x)\, dx = \int_0^a f(a-x)\, dx$.

V. $\int_{-a}^a f(x)\, dx = 2\int_0^a f(x)\, dx$, if $f(x)$ is even function.

VI. $\int_{-a}^a f(x)\, dx = 0$, if $f(x)$ is odd function.

VII. $\int_{-a}^{2a} f(x)\, dx = 2\int_0^a f(x)\, dx$, if $f(2a-x) = f(x)$

VIII. $\int_0^{2a} f(x)\, dx = 0$, if $f(2a-x) = -f(x)$.

9. Summation of Series by Integration:

$$\lim_{n\to\infty} \sum_{r=1}^{n-1} \left(\frac{r}{n}\right) \cdot \frac{1}{n} = \int_0^1 f(x)\, dx.$$

Working Rule: Here proceed as follows:

(i) Find the $(r-1)$ th or rth or $(r+1)$th term of the series and express it as $(1/n) f(r/n)$. Thus the given series is put in the form

$$\lim_{n\to\infty} \sum_{r=0}^{n-1} f\left(\frac{r}{n}\right) \cdot \left(\frac{1}{n}\right)$$

(ii) Now write the above series equal to a definite integral by replacing $\left(\lim_{n\to\infty} \sum\right)$ by $\int$, (r/n) by x and $1/n$ by dx.

(iii) The limits of integration are calculated as follows:

Lower limit $= \lim_{n\to\infty} \left[\frac{r}{n}\right]_{r=0}$, $r = 0$ correspond to the first term.

Upper limit $= \lim_{n\to\infty} \left[\frac{r}{n}\right]_{r=n-1}$, $r = (n-1)$ correspond to the term.

10. Some Important Results:

(i) $\sum_{r=1}^{n} r = \frac{1}{2} n(n+1)$

(ii) $\sum_{r=1}^{n} r^2 = \frac{1}{6} n(n+1)(2n+1)$

(iii) $\sum_{r=1}^{n} r^3 = \frac{1}{4} n^2 (n+1)^2$

(iv) $\sum_{r=0}^{n-1} \sin(\alpha + r\beta) = \sin(\alpha + 1/2\,(n-1)\beta\}\sin(1/2 n\beta)/\sin(1/2\beta)$

(v) $\sum_{r=0}^{n-1} \cos(\alpha + r\beta) = \cos\{\alpha + 1/2\,(n-1)\beta\}\sin(1/2\, n\beta)/\sin(1/2\beta)$

(vi) $1/1^2 - 1/2^2 + 1/3^2 - \ldots = \pi^2/12$

(vii) $1/1^2 + 1/2^2 + 1/3^2 + \ldots = \pi^2/6.$

EXERCISE

1. $\int$(tan x + cot x) dx equals
   (a) $\sec^2 x + \text{cosec}^2 x + c$
   (b) $\log|\sin 2x| + c$
   (c) $\log|\cot x| + c$
   (d) $\log|\tan x| + c$

2. $\int_0^{\pi/2} \frac{dx}{1+\sin x}$ equals
   (a) 0 (b) 1/2
   (c) 1 (d) 3/2

3. The value of $\int_0^{2\pi} \sqrt{1 + \sin 1/2\, x)}\, dx$ is
   (a) 0 (b) 2
   (c) 4 (d) 8

4. The value of $\int_a^b \frac{|x|}{x}\, dx$, $a < b$ is
   (a) $b - a$ (b) $a - b$
   (c) $b + a$ (d) $|b| - |a|$

5. $\int_{-1}^{2} \frac{|x|}{x}\, dx =$
   (a) 1 (b) 3
   (c) Not exists (d) None of these

6. $\int_{-1}^{1} |(1-x)|\, dx$ equals
   (a) – 2 (b) 0
   (c) 2 (d) 4

7. The value of $\int_0^4 (\sqrt{x})\, dx$, where () denotes the fractional part of x is
   (a) 16/3 (b) 25/3
   (c) 7/3 (d) None of these

8. $\int \frac{xe^x}{(x+1)^2}\, dx =$
   (a) $e^x/(x+1)$ (b) $e^x/(x+1)^2$
   (c) $-e^x/(x+1)^3$ (d) None of these

9. Let $I_1 = \int_1^2 \frac{dx}{\sqrt{(1+x^2)}}$ and $I_2 = \int_1^2 \frac{dx}{x}$. Then
   (a) $I_1 > I_2$ (b) $I_2 > I_1$
   (c) $I_1 = I_2$ (d) $I_2 > 2I_2$

10. The smallest interval $[a, b]$ such that
    $\int_0^1 \frac{dx}{\sqrt{(1+x^4)}} \in [a, b]$ is given by
    (a) $[1/\sqrt{2}, 1]$ (b) $[0, 1]$
    (c) $[1/2, 1]$ (d) $[3/4, 1]$

11. $\int \frac{(\sin x + \cos x)\, dx}{\sqrt{(1+\sin 2x)}}$ equals
    (a) log (sin x + cos x) (b) x
    (c) log x (d) log sin (cos x)

12. dx, $3\pi/4 < x < 7\pi/4$ is equal to
    (a) log (sin x + cos x) (b) x
    (c) log x (d) None of these

13. $\int \frac{\sin x + \cos x}{\sqrt{(1+\sin 2x)}}$ $\int \sqrt{x}\, e^{\sqrt{x}}\, dx =$
    (a) $2\sqrt{x} - e^{\sqrt{x}} - 4\sqrt{x}\, e^{\sqrt{x}}$(b) $(2x - 4\sqrt{x} + 4)\, e^{\sqrt{x}}$
    (c) $(1 - 4\sqrt{x})\, e^{\sqrt{x}}$ (d) None of these

14. $\int [\sqrt{\tan x} + \sqrt{\cot x}]\, dx =$
    (a) $\sqrt{2} \tan^{-1} [(\sqrt{\tan x} - \sqrt{\cot x})/\sqrt{2}] + c$
    (b) $\sqrt{2} \tan^{-1} [(\sqrt{\tan x} + \sqrt{\cot x})/\sqrt{2}] + c$
    (c) $(1/\sqrt{2}) \tan^{-1} [\sqrt{2}\, (\sqrt{\tan x} - \sqrt{\cot x})] + c$
    (d) None of these

15. $\int_0^4 \frac{\sqrt{(x^2-4)}}{x}\, dx =$
    (a) $2\,(3\sqrt{3} - \pi)/3$ (b) π

(c) $2(3\sqrt{3}-\pi)$ (d) None of these

16. The value of $\int \frac{\log x^2}{x}\,dx$ is

(a) $(\log x)^2 + c$ (b) $1/2\,(\log x)^2 + c$
(c) $\log x^2 + c$ (d) None of these

17. $\int x^3 (\log x)^2\,dx$

(a) $\frac{1}{32}x^4\,[8(\log x)^2 + 4\log x - 1]$

(b) $\frac{1}{32}x^4\,[8(\log x)^2 + 4\log x + 1]$

(c) $\frac{1}{32}x^4[8(\log x)^2 - 4\log x - 1]$

(d) None of these

18. $\int_{-\pi/2}^{\pi/2} \sqrt{(\cos x - \cos^3 x)}\,dx =$

(a) 3/4 (b) – 3/4
(c) 4/3 (d) 0

19. $\int_{-\pi/2}^{0} \sqrt{[(\cos x - \cos^3 x)]}\,dx =$

(a) 2/3 (b) – 2/3
(c) 3/2 (d) –3/2

20. The value of $\int \frac{dx}{e^x+1}$ is

(a) $\log(e^x - 1) + c$ (b) $\log(e^x + 1) + c$
(c) $x - \log(e^x + 1)$ (d) None of these

21. $\int_3^8 \frac{2-3x}{x\sqrt{(1+x)}}\,dx =$

(a) $2\log 3/(2e^3)$ (b) $\log(3/e^3)$
(c) $4\log(3/e^3)$ (d) None of these

22. If $(n - m)$ is odd, and $|m| \neq |n|$, then

$\int_0^{\pi} \cos mx\,\sin nx\,dx$ is

(a) $2n/(n^2 - m^2)$ (b) 0
(c) $2n/(m^2 - n^2)$ (d) $2m/(n^2 - m^2)$

23. Given that $\int_0^{\infty} \frac{x^2\,dx}{(x^2+a^2)(x^2+b^2)(x^2+c^2)}$

$\frac{\pi}{2(a+b)(b+c)(c+a)}$ = then the value of

$\int_0^{\infty} \frac{dx}{(x^2+4)(x^2+9)}$

is

(a) $\pi/60$ (b) $\pi/20$
(c) $\pi/40$ (d) $\pi/80$

24. The value of the integral $\int_0^{\pi/4} \frac{\sin x + \cos x}{9 + 16\sin 2x}\,dx$ is

(a) log 3 (b) log 2
(c) log 3 (d) log 2

25. The value of $\int \frac{x\sin^{-1} x}{\sqrt{(1-x^2)}}\,dx$ is

(a) $\sqrt{(1-x^2)}\sin^{-1} x + c$
(b) $x\sin^{-1} x + c$
(c) $x - \sqrt{(1-x^2)}\sin^{-1} x + c$
(d) $(\sin^{-1} x)^2 + c$

26. $\int \cos\sqrt{x}\,dx =$

(a) $2[\sqrt{x}\sin\sqrt{x} + \cos\sqrt{x}] + c$
(b) $[\sqrt{x}\sin\sqrt{x} - \cos\sqrt{x}] + c$
(c) $2[\sqrt{x}\sin\sqrt{x} - \cos\sqrt{x}] + c$
(d) None of these

27. $\int \frac{1}{x\log_a x} = \log_e a\,\log_e(\log_e x)$ is true for

(a) all $x \in R$ (b) $x > e$
(c) $x > 1$ (d) for no real x

28. $\int \sec^3\theta\,d\theta =$

(a) $1/2[\tan\theta\sec\theta + \log(\tan\theta + \sec\theta)] + c$
(b) $1/2[\tan\theta\sec\theta - \log(\tan\theta + \sec\theta)] + c$
(c) $1/2[\tan\theta\sec\theta - \log(\sec\theta - \tan\theta)] + c$
(d) None of these

29. $\int_0^{\pi/2} e^x (\sin x + \cos x)\, dx$ is equal to

(a) 1 (b) $e^{\pi/4}$
(c) e^{π} (d) $e^{\pi/2}$

30. $\int \frac{1+x+x^2}{1+x^2} e \tan^{-1} x\, dx =$

(a) $x^2 e \tan^{-1} x + c$ (b) $e \tan^{-1} x + c$
(c) $x e \tan^{-1} x + c$ (d) None of these

31. $\int [\log \log x + (\log x)^{-2}]\, dx$ is

(a) $x \log (\log x)$
(b) $x \log (\log x) + x/(\log x)$
(c) $x \log (\log x) - x/(\log x)$
(d) None of these

32. $\int e^x (\sinh x + \cosh x)\, dx =$

(a) e^x sech x (b) $e^x \cosh x$
(c) $\sinh 2x$ (d) $\cosh 2x$

33. Area lying between the parabola $y^2 = 4ax$ and its latus rectum is

(a) $(8/3)a^2$ (b) $(8/3)a$
(c) $4a/3$ (d) $4a^2/3$

34. Area between the curve $y = 4 + 3x - x^2$ and x-axis is

(a) (125/3) sq units (b) (125/4) sq units
(c) (125/6) sq units (d) None of these

35. The area covered by a curve $y^2 = x$, straight line $y = 4$ and y-axis is .

(a) 16/3 (b) 64/3
(c) $7\sqrt{2}$ (d) None of these

36. Area lying in the first quadrant and bounded by the circle $x^2 + y^2 = 4$ and the line $x = y\sqrt{3}$ is

(a) π (b) $\pi/2$
(c) $\pi/3$ (d) None of these

37. In the interval $(0, \pi/2]$, area lying between the curves $y = \tan x$, $y = \cot x$ and x-axis is

(a) log 2 (b) 1/2 log 2
(c) 2 log $(1/\sqrt{2})$ (d) None of these

38. Area bounded by the curves $y = x \sin x$ and x-axis between $x = 0$ and $x = 2\pi$ is

(a) 2π (b) 3π
(c) 4π (d) None of these

39. Area included between the parabolas $y^2 = 4ax$ and $x^2 = 4ay$ is equal to

(a) $8a^2/3$ (b) $16a^2/3$
(c) $4a^2/3$ (d) None of these

40. Area bounded by the curve $y = (x - 1)(x - 2)(x - 3)$ and x-axis, lying between the ordinates $x = 0$ and $x = 3$ is equal to

(a) 9/4 sq units (b) 11/4 sq units
(c) 11/2 sq units (d) None of these

ANSWERS

1	2	3	4	5	6	7	8	9	10
(d)	(c)	(d)	(d)	(a)	(c)	(c)	(a)	(b)	(a)
11	12	13	14	15	16	17	18	19	20
(b)	(d)	(b)	(a)	(a)	(a)	(d)	(c)	(a)	(c)
21	22	23	24	25	26	27	28	29	30
(a)	(a)	(a)	(c)	(c)	(a)	(c)	(a)	(d)	(c)
31	32	33	34	35	36	37	38	39	40
(c)	(b)	(a)	(c)	(b)	(c)	(a)	(c)	(b)	(b)

SOME SELECTED EXPLANATORY ANSWERS

1. $\int (\tan x + \cot x)\, dx$

$= \log |\sec x| + \log |\sin x| + c$

$= \log |\sec x \sin x| + c$

$= \log |\tan x| + c.$

2. Given integral

$$= \int_0^{\pi/2} \frac{dx}{1+\cos\left(\frac{1}{2}\pi - x\right)}$$

$$= \frac{1}{2}\int_0^{\pi/2} \sec^2\left(\frac{1}{4}\pi - \frac{1}{2}x\right)dx$$

$$= \left[-\tan\left(\frac{1}{4}\pi - \frac{1}{2}x\right)\right]_0^{\pi/2} = 1.$$

3. Given integral

$$= \int_0^{2\pi}\left(\sin\frac{1}{4}x + \cos\frac{1}{4}x\right)dx$$

$$= \left[4\left(-\cos\frac{1}{4}x + \sin\frac{1}{4}x\right)\right]_0^{2\pi} = 8$$

4. Let $\mathrm{I} = \int_a^b \frac{|x|}{x}\,dx, a < b.$

(i) If $0 \le a < b$, then $|x| = x$,

$$\therefore\ \mathrm{I} = \int_a^b \frac{x}{x}dx = \int_a^b 1.dx = b - a.$$

(ii) If $a < b \le 0$, then $|x| = -x$

$$\therefore\ \mathrm{I} = \int_a^b \frac{-x}{x}\,dx = a - b = -b - (-a)$$

$$= |b| - |a|.$$

(iii) If $a < 0 < b$, then

$$\mathrm{I} = \int_a^0 \frac{|x|}{x}\,dx + \int_0^b \frac{|x|}{x}\,dx$$

$$= \int_a^0 \frac{-x}{x}dx + \int_0^b \frac{x}{x}\,dx$$

$$= -\int_a^0 dx + \int_0^b dx = a + b = b - (-a)$$

$$= |b| - |a|.$$

5. $\int_{-1}^{2} \frac{|x|}{x}\,dx = \int_{-1}^{0} \frac{|x|}{x}dx + \int_0^2 \frac{|x|}{x}\,dx$

$$= \int_{-1}^{0} \frac{-x}{x}\,dx + \int_0^2 \frac{x}{x}\,dx = [-x]_{-1}^0 + [x]_0^2 = 1.$$

6. $\int_{-1}^{1} |(1-x)|dx = \int_{-1}^{1}(1-x)\ dx$

$1 - x \ge$ when $-1 \le x \le 1$

$$= \left[x - \frac{1}{2}x^2\right]_{-1}^1 = 2$$

7. $\int_0^4 (\sqrt{x})\,dx = \int_0^1 (\sqrt{x})\,dx + \int_1^4 (\sqrt{x})\,dx$

$$= \int_0^1 \sqrt{x}\,dx + \int_1^4 \{\sqrt{x} - 1\}\,dx$$

$$= \int_0^4 \sqrt{x}\,dx - \int_1^4 dx = .\ 8 - 3 = 7/3.$$

8. $\mathrm{I} = \int \frac{[(x+1)-1]e^x}{(x+1)^2}dx$

$$= \int \underset{\text{II}}{e^x}\ \underset{\text{I}}{\frac{1}{x+1}}dx - \int e^x \cdot \frac{1}{(x+1)^2}.dx$$

$$= \frac{1}{x+1}.e^x - \int\left(-\frac{1}{(x+1)^2}\right)e^x\ dx$$

$$- \int \frac{1}{(x+1)^2}e^x dx$$

$= e^x/(x+1).$

9. We have $1 + x^2 > x^2$, □x

$\Rightarrow \sqrt{(1+x^2)} < x$, □$x$, $\in [1, 2]$

$$\Rightarrow \square\frac{1}{\sqrt{(1+x^2)}} < \frac{1}{x}\ \ x \in [1,2]$$

$$\Rightarrow \int_1^2 \frac{dx}{\sqrt{(1+x^2)}} < \int_1^2 \frac{dx}{x} \Rightarrow \mathrm{I}_1 < \mathrm{I}_2$$

$$\left[\begin{array}{l} \because f(x) < g(x) \text{ in } [a,b] \\ \Rightarrow \int_a^b f(x)dx < \int_a^b g(x)dx \end{array}\right]$$

10. Let $I = \int_0^1 \frac{dx}{\sqrt{(1+x^4)}}$

Here $0 \le x \le 1 \quad \Rightarrow 1 \le 1 + x^4 \le 2$

$\Rightarrow 1 \le \sqrt{(1 + x^4)} \le \sqrt{2}$

$$\Rightarrow \frac{1}{\sqrt{2}} \le \frac{1}{\sqrt{(1+x^4)}} \le 1$$

$$\Rightarrow \frac{1}{\sqrt{2}} \le \int_0^1 \frac{dx}{\sqrt{(1+x^4)}} \le 1$$

Hence $[1/\sqrt{2}, 1]$ is the smallest interval such that $I \in [1/\sqrt{2}, 1]$.

11. We have $\sqrt{(1 + \sin 2x)} = \sin x + \cos x$, taking $\sin x + \cos x > 0$

$\therefore$ Given integral $= \int 1.dx = x$.

12. We have $\sqrt{(1 + \sin 2x)} = \sqrt{[\sin x + \cos x)^2]}$

$= -(\sin x + \cos x)$

$\sin x + \cos x < 0$ in $3\pi/4 < x < 7\pi/4$.

$\therefore$ Given integral $= \int -1.\,dx = -x$.

13. Putting $x = t^2$, $dx = 2t\,dt$

$I = \int t\,e^t.\,2t\,dt = 2\int t^2\,e^t\,dt$

$= 2t^2.\,e^t - 4\int t\,e^t\,dt$

$= 2t^2\,e^t - 4\,(t\,e^t - e^t)$

$= (2x - 4\sqrt{x} + 4)\,e^{\sqrt{x}}$.

14. Putting $\tan x = t^2$, we have

$dx = 2t\,dt/\sec^2 x = 2t\,dt/(1 + t^4)$

$$\therefore I = \int \frac{(t+1/t)2t\,dt}{(t^4+1)}$$

$$= 2\int \frac{t^2+1}{t^4+1}dt = 2\int \frac{(1+l/t^2)dt}{t^2+1/t^2}$$

$$= 2\int \frac{(1+1/t^2)dt}{(t-1/t)^2+2}$$ Putting $t - (1/t) = u$,

$$= 2\int \frac{du}{u^2+2} = \frac{2}{\sqrt{2}}\tan^{-1}\left(\frac{u}{\sqrt{2}}\right) + c$$

$= \sqrt{2}\tan^{-1}[\sqrt{\{(\tan x)} - \sqrt{(\cot x)\}}/\sqrt{2}] + c$.

15. Putting $x = 2\sec\theta$

$$I = \int_0^{\pi/3} \frac{2\tan\theta}{2\sec\theta}\,2\sec\theta\tan\theta\,d\theta$$

$$= 2\int_0^{\pi/3} (\sec^2\theta - 1)d\theta$$

$= 2[\tan\theta - \theta]_0^{\pi/3} = 2\,(3\sqrt{3} - \pi)/3$.

16. $I = \int \frac{\log(x^2)}{x}dx$

$= 2\int \frac{\log x}{x}\,dx = 2\,\frac{1}{2}\,(\log x)^2 + c$

$= (\log x)^2 + c$.

17. $I = \int x^3.\,(\log x)^2\,dx$

(II) (I)

$= 1/4\,x^4.\,(\log x)^2 - \int 1/4\,x^4.\,2\log x\,(1/x)\,dx$

$= 1/4.\,x^4\,(\log x)^2 - 1/2\int x^3\log x\,dx$

(II) (I)

$= 1/4x^4\,(\log x)^2 - 1/2\,[1/4\,x^4\log x - \int 1/4\,x^4\cdot(1/x)\,dx]$

$= 1/4\,x^4\,(\log x)^2 - 1/8\,x^4\log x + 1/8\int x^3\,dx$

$= 1/4\,x^4\,(\log x^2) - 1/8.\,x^4\log x + 1/32\,x^4 + c$

$= 1/32\,x^4\,[8\,(\log x)^2 - 4\log x + 1] + c$.

18. $I = \int_{-\pi/2}^{\pi/2} \sqrt{(\cos x - \cos^3 x)}\,dx$

Since $f(-x) = \cos(-x) - \cos^3(-x)$

$= \cos x - \cos^3 x = f(x)$

$$\therefore I = 2\int_0^{\pi/2} \sqrt{(\cos x - \cos^3 x)}\,dx$$

$$= 2\int_0^{\pi/2} \sqrt{(\cos x)}.\,\sin x\,dx$$

$$= -2\left[\frac{2}{3}(\cos x)^{3/2}\right]_0^{\pi/2} = \frac{4}{3}.$$

19. Given integral

$$= \int_{-\pi/2}^{0} \sqrt{(\cos x.\ \sin^2 x)}\, dx$$

$$= -\int_{-\pi/2}^{0} \sqrt{(\cos x)}.\sin x\, dx$$

$\sqrt{(\sin^2 x)} = -\sin x$, as
$\sin x$ is –ve, when $-\pi/2 < x < 0$,

$$= \left[\frac{2}{3}(\cos x)^{3/2}\right]_{-\pi/2}^{0} = \frac{2}{3}.$$

20. Given integral

$$= \int\left(1 - \frac{e^x}{e^x + 1}\right)dx = x - \log(e^x + 1) + c.$$

21. Putting $1 + x = t^2$, $dx = 2t\, dt$, the given integral

$$= 2\int_2^3 \frac{5 - 3t^2}{t^2 - 1}\, dt = 2\int_2^3 \left(\frac{2}{t^2 - 1} - 3\right) dt$$

$$= 2\left[\frac{2}{2.1}\log\frac{t-1}{t+1} - 3t\right]_2^3 = 2\log\left(\frac{3}{2e^3}\right).$$

22. Given integral

$$I = \frac{1}{2}\int_0^{\pi} [\sin(m+n)x - \sin(m-n)x]\, dx$$

$$= -\frac{1}{2}\left[\frac{\cos(m+n)x}{m+n} - \frac{\cos(m-n)x}{m-n}\right]_0^{\pi}$$

$$= -\frac{1}{2}\left[\left\{\frac{(-1)^{m+n}}{m+n} - \frac{(-1)^{m-n}}{m-n}\right\} - \left\{\frac{1}{m+n} - \frac{1}{m-n}\right\}\right]$$

Since $n - m$ is odd, $\therefore$ $n + m$ must be odd,
so $(-1)^{m+n} = (-1)^{m-n} = -1$.
Also since
$|m| \neq |n|$, $m + n \neq 0$, $m - n \neq 0$

$$\therefore I = \frac{1}{m+n} - \frac{1}{m-n}$$

$$= \frac{m - n - m - n}{m^2 - n^2} = \frac{2n}{n^2 - m^2}.$$

23. Hint: Put $a = 2$, $b = 3$ and $c = 0$ in the given integral.

24. Let $\sin x - \cos x = t$,
$(\cos x + \sin x)\, dx = dt$,
($\sin x + \cos x$ in numerator is differential of $\sin x - \cos x$)
$t^2 = (\sin x - \cos x)^2 = 1 - \sin 2x$
or $\sin 2x = 1 - t^2$,
given integral

$$= \int_{t=-1}^{0} \frac{dt}{9 + 16(1 - t^2)} = \frac{1}{16}\int_{-1}^{0} \frac{dt}{(5/4)^2 - t^2}$$

$$= \frac{1}{16}.\frac{1}{2.(5/4)}\left[\log\frac{5/4 + t}{5/4 - t}\right]_{-1}^{0}$$

$$= \frac{1}{40}[\log 1 - \log(1/9)]$$

$= (1/40)\log 3^2 = (1/20)\log 3.$

25. Putting $\sin^{-1} x = t$, $x = \sin t$,
$dx = \cos t\, dt$, the given integral
$= \int t \sin t\, dt = -t\cos t + \sin t + c$
$= -t\sqrt{(1 - \sin^2 t)} + \sin t + c$,
$= x - \sqrt{(1 - x^2)}\sin^{-1} x + c$

26. Put $x = t^2$, $dx = 2t\, dt$.
$\therefore$ $I = 2\int t \cos t\, dt$
I II
$= 2(t\sin t + \cos t) + c$
$= 2[\sqrt{x}\sqrt{x} + \cos\sqrt{x}] + c.$

27. Since $\log_e(\log_e x)$ is real if
$\log_e x > 0$, *i.e.*, $x > 1$.

28. $I = \int \sec\theta \sec^2\theta\, d\theta$
I II
$= \sec\theta\tan\theta - \int \sec\theta\tan^2\theta\, d\theta$
$= \sec\theta\tan\theta - \int \sec^3\theta\, d\theta + \int \sec\theta\, d\theta$
$\therefore 2I = \sec\theta\tan\theta + \log(\sec\theta + \tan\theta) + c$
$\Rightarrow I = [\tan\theta\sec\theta + \log(\tan\theta + \sec\theta)] + c.$

29. Given integral

$$= \int_0^{\pi/2} e^x \sin x\, dx + \int_0^{\pi/2} e^x \cos x\, dx$$

$$= \int_0^{\pi/2} e^x \sin x\, dx + \left[e^x \sin x\right]_0^{\pi/2}$$

$$- \int_0^{\pi/2} e^x \sin x\, dx = e^{\pi/2}.$$

30. Given integral

$$= \int e^{\tan^{-1} x} . 1\, dx + \int \frac{x}{1+x^2} e^{\tan^{-1}} x\, dx$$

$$= e^{\tan^{-1} x} . x - \int e^{\tan^{-1} x} \cdot \frac{\cdot 1}{1+x^2} . x\, dx$$

$$+ \int \frac{x}{1+x^2} e^{\tan^{-1} x}\, dx + c = + c.$$

31. Given integral

$= \int \log \log x .\ 1\, dx + \int (\log x)^{-2}\, dx.$

$$= (\log \log x)x - \int \frac{1}{x \log x} x\, dx$$

$+ \int (\log x)^{-2}\, dx$

$= x \log \log x - \int (\log x)^{-1} .\ 1\, dx$

$+ \int (\log x)^{-2}\, dx$

$= x \log \log x - (\log x)^{-1} x$

$- \int (\log x)^{-2} . (1/x)\, x\, dx + \int (\log x)^{-2}\, dx$

$= x \log \log x - x/(\log x).$

32. Given integral

$= \int e^x \sinh x\, dx + \int e^x \cosh x\, dx$

I II

$= e^x \cosh x - \int e^x \cosh x\, dx + \int e^x \cosh x\, dx$

$= e^x \cosh x.$

33. Parabola $y^2 = 4ax$ is symmetrical about x-axis and latus rectum is $x = a$, so required area

$$= 2\int_0^a \sqrt{(4ax)}\, dx = 8a^2/3 \text{ sq units.}$$

34. Solving $y = 0$ and $y = 4 + 3x - x^2$, we get $x = -1, 4$. Curve does not intersect x-axis between $x = -1$ and $x = 4$.

$$\therefore \text{Area} = \int_{-1}^{4} (4 + 3x - x^2)\, dx = 125/6 \text{ sq units.}$$

35. Curve does not intersect x-axis between $x = 1$ and $x = 3$, so required area

$$= \int_1^3 y\, dx \int_1^3 (1/x) = dx$$

$= \log 3 - \log 1 = \log 3.$

36. Required area

= Area of Δ OAC + Area of Δ ABC

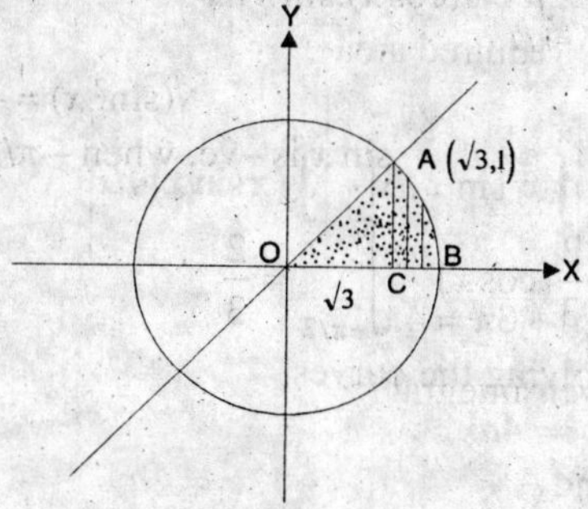

$$= \frac{1}{2} \sqrt{3} \times 1 + \int_{\sqrt{3}}^{2} \sqrt{\left(4 - x^2\right)}\, dx = \frac{\pi}{3}.$$

37. In $[0, \pi/2]$, $\tan x$ and $\cot x$ intersect at $x = \pi/4$.

$\therefore$ Required area

= Area OPBO + Area BPAB

$$= \int_0^{\pi/4} \tan x\, dx + \int_{\pi/4}^{\pi/2} \cot x\, dx$$

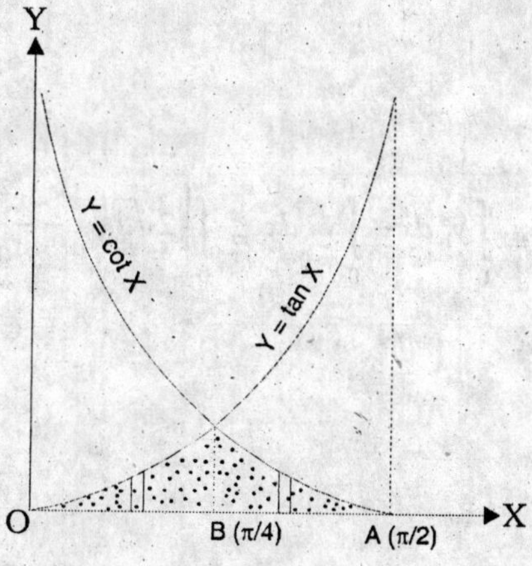

$$= \left[\log |\sec x|\right]_0^{\pi/4} + \left[\log |\sin x|\right]_{\pi/4}^{\pi/2}$$

$= \log \sqrt{2} + \log \sqrt{2} = \log 2.$

38. In $[0, 2\pi]$, $y = x \sin x = 0$ at

$x = \pi$,

y is +ve when $0 < x < \pi$,

and y is – ve when $\pi < x < 2\pi$.

Thus the curve is above the axis of x from $x = 0$ to $x = \pi$ and below the axis of x from $x = \pi$ to $x = 2\pi$.

$\therefore$ Required area

$$= \left|\int_0^\pi x \sin x \, dx\right| + \left|\int_\pi^{2\pi} (x \sin x) \, dx\right|$$

$= \pi + 3\pi = 4\pi$.

39. Solving the curves,

$y^2 = 4ax$ ... (1)

and $x^2 = 4ay$ ... (2)

we get $x = 0$ and $4a$.

$\therefore$ Required area

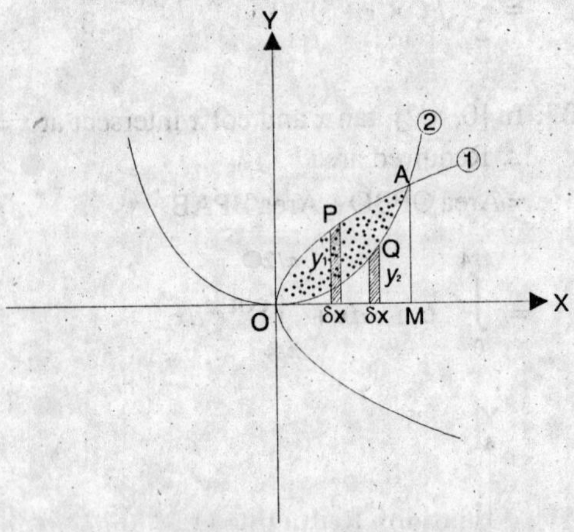

$$= \int_0^{4a} y_1 \, dx - \int_0^{4a} y_2 \, dx = \int_0^{4a}\left[2\sqrt{a}\sqrt{x} - \frac{x^2}{4a}\right] dx$$

$$= \left[2\sqrt{a}.\frac{2}{3}.x^{3/2} - \frac{x^3}{12a}\right]_0^{4a}$$

$$= \frac{32}{3}a^2 - \frac{64a^3}{12a} = \frac{16}{3}a^2 \text{ sq units.}$$

40. Clearly $y < 0$ in $]0, 1[$ and$]2, 3[$ and $y > 0$ in $]1, 2[$.

$\therefore$ Required area

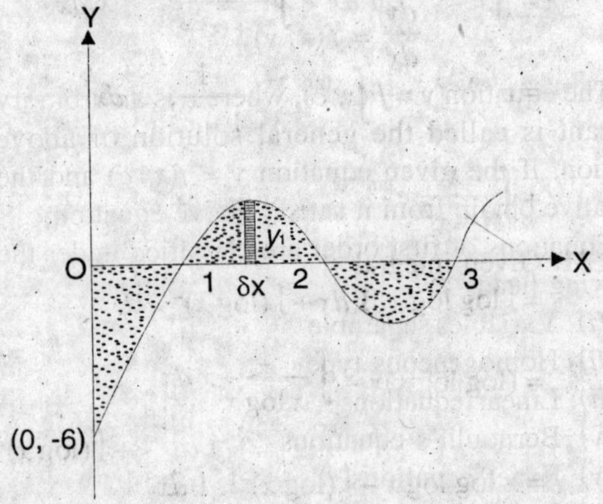

$$= \left|\int_0^1 (x-1)(x-2)(x-3) \, dx\right|$$

$$+ \left|\int_1^2 (x-1)(x-2)(x-3) \, dx\right|$$

$$+ \left|\int_2^3 (x-1)(x-2)(x-3) \, dx\right|$$

$= 11/4$ sq. units.

15. DIFFERENTIAL EQUATION

Differential Equations of First Order and First Degree

Ordinary differential equation of first order and of first degree may be written as

$$\frac{dy}{dx} = f(x, y).$$

The equation $y = f(x, c)$, where c is an arbitrary constant is called the general solution of above equation, if the given equation $y = f(x, c)$ and the derivative obtain from it satisfy above equation.

Equations of first order are classified under the following heads

(i) Variables separable
(ii) Homogeneous type
(iii) Linear equations
(iv) Bernoulli's equations
(v) Exact equations
(vi) Integrating factors

Type I : Variable Separables

If an equation can be written as $\frac{dy}{dx} = \frac{f(x)}{g(y)}$, then such an equation "variables separable type" and can be solved by seperating the variables and integrating separately functions of x and functions of y *i.e.*,

$$\int g(y)\,dy = \int f(x)\,dx$$

Type II : Homegeneous Equations

It is a differential equation of the form

$\frac{dy}{dx} = \frac{\phi(x, y)}{\psi(x, y)}$, where $\phi(x, y)$ and $\psi(x, y)$ are homogeneous functions of x and y of the same degree, n (say).

Such equations can be solved by putting $y = vx$.

Hence $$\frac{dy}{dx} = v + x\frac{dy}{dx}.$$

Now the given differential equation is

$$\frac{dy}{dx} = \frac{\phi(x, y)}{\psi(x, y)} = \frac{x^n\phi\left(\frac{y}{x}\right)}{x^n\psi\left(\frac{y}{x}\right)},$$ taking x^n common from both the numerator and denominator.

$$\therefore \quad \frac{dy}{dx} = \frac{\phi\left(\frac{y}{x}\right)}{\psi\left(\frac{y}{x}\right)} = f\left(\frac{y}{x}\right) \text{ say.}$$

Substituting the values of y and $\frac{dy}{dx}$ in the above equation we have

$$v + x\frac{dv}{dx} = f(v)$$

or $$x\frac{dv}{dx} = f(v) - v$$

or $$\frac{dv}{f(v) - v} = \frac{dx}{x}$$

The variables has now been separated and its solution is

$$\int \frac{dv}{f(v) - v} = \log x + c$$

After integrating v should be replaced by $\left(\frac{y}{x}\right)$ to get the required solution.

Type III : Equations Reducible to Homogeneous Form:

An equation of the form

$$\frac{dy}{dx} = \mathrm{F}\left(\frac{ax + by + c}{\mathrm{A}x + \mathrm{B}y + \mathrm{C}}\right) \qquad ...(i)$$

in which $a, b, c, \mathrm{A, B, C}$ are fixed constants such that $a\mathrm{B} - b\mathrm{A} \neq 0$ can be made homogeneous and hence can be solved as follows :

We note that under the given restriction (*i.e.*, $a\mathrm{B} - b\mathrm{A} \neq 0$) the equations

$$ax + by + c = 0$$
$$\mathrm{A}x + \mathrm{B}y + \mathrm{C} = 0$$

will represent two intersecting straight lines. The point of intersection (h, k) is given by

$$h = \frac{bC - cB}{aB - bA} \text{ and } k = \frac{cA - aC}{aB - bA} \quad ...(ii)$$

We now transfer the origin there [*i.e.*, (h, k)] by putting

$x = h + X, y = k + Y$

This leaves $dx = dX$ and $dy = dY$.

The equation *(i)* now becomes

$$\frac{dY}{dX} = F\left(\frac{aX + bY}{AX + BY}\right).$$

So that F is a homogeneous function of X and Y of degree zero.

Proceeding similar as in homogeneous function, we put $Y = v$ we obtain

$$v + X\frac{dv}{dX} = F\left(\frac{a + bv}{A + Bv}\right) = \phi(v), \text{ say}$$

Separating the variables we get

$$\frac{dv}{\phi(v) - v} = \frac{dX}{X}$$

The primitive will be then

$$\int \frac{dv}{\phi(v) - v} = \log C_1 X,$$

where after integration is performed, the value of

$v = \dfrac{Y}{X} = \dfrac{y - k}{x - h}$ is to be substituted.

Particular Case : When $aB - bA = 0$, let X be a new dependent variable defined by

$$X = x + \frac{by}{a} = x + \frac{By}{A} \left[\because \frac{b}{a} = \frac{B}{A}\right]$$

So that $\dfrac{dX}{dx} = 1 + \dfrac{b}{a}\dfrac{dy}{dx}$.

The equation *(i)* then becomes

$$\frac{a}{b}\left(\frac{dX}{dx} - 1\right) = F\left(\frac{aX + c}{AX + C}\right)$$

or $$\frac{dX}{dx} = 1 + \frac{b}{a}F\left(\frac{aX + c}{AX + C}\right)$$

The variables X and x are now separable.

In practice, the following process is adopted.

Since $\dfrac{a}{A} = \dfrac{b}{B} = $ (say), we observe that $ax + by = k$ $(Ax + By)$.

Putting $ax + by = v$, so that $\dfrac{dv}{dx} = a + b\dfrac{dy}{dx}$, in equation *(i)* we get

$$\frac{1}{b}\left(\frac{dv}{dx} - a\right) = F\left(\frac{v + c}{kv + C}\right) = \phi(v), \text{ say}$$

The variables v and x can now be easily separated.

Type IV : Linear Equations

A differential equation of the form $\dfrac{dy}{dx} + Py = Q$, where P and Q are functions of x or constants, is called a linear differential equation of the first order.

To solve the equation $\dfrac{dy}{dx} + Py = Q$, we multiply both sides by $e^{\int P\,dx}$

The equation becomes

$$e^{\int P\,dx}\left[\frac{dy}{dx} + Py\right] = Q\,e^{\int P\,dx}$$

Integrating both sides w.r.t. x, we get

$$y\,e^{\int P\,dx} = \int Q\,e^{\int P\,dx}\,dx + C$$

which is the required solution. Here $e^{\int P\,dx}$ is called the integrating factor.

Type V : Equations Reducible to Linears Form : (Bernoulli's Equations)

The equation $\dfrac{dy}{dx} + Py = Q\,y^n$ ...*(i)*

in which P and Q are function of x alone or constants, is known as *Bernoulli's Equation*. It may be brought into the linear form by a change of dependent variable.

We divide both the sides of equation *(i)* by y^n and we get

$$y^{-n}\frac{dy}{dx} + P\,y^{1-n} = Q$$

Now let $v = y^{1-n}$, then $\dfrac{dv}{dx} = (1 - n)y^{-n}\dfrac{dy}{dx}$

∴ The equation becomes

$$\frac{1}{1-n}\frac{dv}{dx} + Pv = Q$$

or $$\frac{dv}{dx} + P(1-n)v = (1-n)Q \quad ...(ii)$$

which is a linear equatiotn in v. It's integrating factor is $e^{(1-n)\int P\,dx}$

Multiplying both the sides by integrating factor, we obtain

$$\frac{d}{dx}\left\{v.e^{(1-n)\int P\,dx}\right\} = (1-n)Qe^{(1-n)\int P\,dx}$$

Integrating we get

$$v = e^{-(1-n)\int P dx}\left[C + \int\left\{(1-n)Qe^{(1-n)\int P dx}\right\}dx\right]$$

∴ The general solution is

$$y^{1-n} = e^{-(1-n)\int P dx}\left[C + \int\left\{(1-n)Q\,e^{(1-n)\int P dx}\right\}dx\right]$$

Type VI : Exact Differential Equations

If M and N are functions of x and y, the equation

$$Mdx + Ndy = 0$$

is called an exact differential equation, when there exists a function $f(x, y)$ such that

$$d[f(x, y)] = Mdx + Ndy$$

i.e., $$\frac{\partial f}{\partial x}dx + \frac{\partial f}{\partial y}dy = Mdx + Ndy$$

Theorem : The necessary and sufficient condition for the differential equation

$Mdx + Ndy = 0$ to be exact is ...(i)

$$\frac{\partial M}{\partial y} = \frac{\partial N}{\partial x}$$

Working rule for solving an exact differential equation

Let the equation $Mdx + Ndy = 0$ satisfy the condition

$$\frac{\partial M}{\partial y} = \frac{\partial N}{\partial x}$$

Then it is exact. To integrate it

1. Integrate M w.r.t. x, treating y as a constant.

2. Integrate N w.r.t. y, treating x as a constant and omit those terms which have already been obtained by integrating M.

3. Add the two expression so obtained and equate the sum of to an arbitrary constant.

Integrating Factors : If an equation of the form $Mdx + Ndx = 0$ is not exact, it can always be made exact, multiplying by some function of x and y. Such a multiplier is called an integrating factor. The equation $\tan y\,dx + \tan x\,dy = 0$

is not exact as can be easily verified. But if we multiply by $\cos x \cos y$, the equation becomes

$$\sin y \cos x\,dx + \sin x \cos y\,dy = 0$$

or $$d(\sin x \sin y) = 0$$

Consequently the primitive is $\sin x \sin y = C$.

The function $\cos x \cdot \cos y$ is called as Integrating Factor of the equation.

In general, a function $\mu(x, y)$ is said to be an Integral Factor (I.F.) of the equation

$$Mdx + Ndy = 0$$

if it is possible to obtain a function $u(x, y)$ such that

$$\mu(Mdx + Ndx) = du.$$

In other words, an I.F. is a multiplying factor by which the equation can be made exact.

Group of terms	*Integrating factor*	*Exact differential*
1. $xdy - ydx$	$\frac{1}{x^2}$	$\frac{xdy - ydx}{x^2} = d\left(\frac{y}{x}\right)$
2. $xdy - ydx$	$\frac{1}{y^2}$	$\frac{xdy - ydx}{y^2} = d\left(\frac{-x}{y}\right)$
3. $xdy - ydx$	$\frac{1}{xy}$	$\frac{dy}{y} - \frac{dx}{x} = d\log\left(\frac{y}{x}\right)$
4. $xdy - ydx$	$\frac{1}{x^2+y^2}$	$\frac{xdy - ydx}{x^2+y^2} = d\left\{\tan^{-1}\frac{y}{x}\right\}$
5. $xdy + ydx$	$\frac{1}{xy}$	$\frac{xdy + ydx}{xy} = d(\log xy)$
6. $xdx + ydy$	$\frac{1}{x^2+y^2}$	$\frac{xdx + ydy}{x^2+y^2} = d\left[\frac{1}{2}\log(x^2+y^2)\right]$

Illustration : Solve : $xdy - ydx = xy^2dx$.

Solution : The given equation can be written as

$xdy - y(1 + xy)\,dx = 0$

$$M = -(y + xy^2) \text{ and } N = x$$

$$\frac{\partial M}{\partial y} = -(y + 2xy),\ \frac{\partial N}{\partial x} = 1$$

Since $\frac{\partial M}{\partial y} \neq \frac{\partial N}{\partial x}$, the equation is not exact.

The equation can be re-written as

$ydx - xdy + xy^2dx = 0$

or $\frac{ydx - xdy}{y^2} + xdx = 0$

or $d\left(\frac{x}{y}\right) + xdx = 0$

Integrating, $\frac{x}{y} + \frac{x^2}{2} = C$.

Rules for Finding the Integration Factors

1. If $\dfrac{\frac{\partial M}{\partial y} - \frac{\partial N}{\partial x}}{N} = f(x)$, a function of x only, then $e^{\int f(x)\,dx}$ is an integrating factor.

2. If $\dfrac{\frac{\partial M}{\partial y} - \frac{\partial N}{\partial x}}{M} = -g(y)$, a function of y only, then $e^{\int g(y)\,dy}$ is an integrating factor.

3. If $Mdx + Ndy = 0$ is homogeneous and $Mx + Ny \neq 0$, then $\frac{1}{Mx + Ny}$ is an integrating factor.

4. If the given equation $Mdx + Ndy = 0$ is such that $M = yf(x, y)$ and $N = xg(x, y)$ and if $Mx + Ny \neq 0$, then $\frac{1}{Mx - Ny}$ is an integrating factor.

5. The equation of the form $x^a y^b (mydx + nxdy) + x^c y^d (\mu ydx + \nu xdy)$ where $a, b, c, d, m, n, \mu, \nu$ are all constants have an integrating factor $x^\alpha y^\beta$ where α, β are so chosen that after multiplying by $x^\alpha y^\beta$ the equation becomes exact.

EXERCISE

Mark the correct alternative(s) in each of the following :

1. The degree of the differential equation

$$\sqrt[3]{y + x\left(\frac{dy}{dx}\right)^2} = \frac{d^2y}{dx^2} \text{ is}$$

(a) not defined (b) 1
(c) 2 (d) 3

[J.N.U. M.C.A.]

2. The degree of the differential equation satisfying the relation

$$\sqrt{1 + x^2} + \sqrt{1 + y^2} = \lambda\left(x\sqrt{1 + y^2} - y\sqrt{1 + x^2}\right)$$

is

(a) 1 (b) 2
(c) 3 (d) None of these

3. The differential equation representing the family of curves $y^2 = 2c\left(x + \sqrt{c}\right)$, where c is a positive parameter is of

(a) degree 1 (b) degree 2
(c) degree 3 (d) degree 4

4. The solution to the differential equation

$$\frac{dy}{dx} = e^{x+y} + x^2e^y \text{ is}$$

(a) $e^{-x} + e^y + \frac{1}{3}x^3 = c$

(b) $e^x + e^{-y} + \frac{1}{3}y^3 = c$

(c) $e^x + e^{-y} + \frac{1}{3}x^3 = c$

(d) None of these

5. The solution to the differential equation

$$(x - y)^2 \frac{dy}{dx} = a^2 \text{ is}$$

(a) $\frac{a}{2}\log\left(\frac{x-y-a}{x-y+a}\right)-y=c$

(b) $\frac{1}{2}\log\left(\frac{x-y+a}{x-y-a}\right)-y=c$.

(c) $\frac{1}{2}\log\left(\frac{x-y+a}{x-y-a}\right)+y=c$

(d) None of these

6. The solution to the differential equation $\frac{dy}{dx}=\sin(x+y)+\cos(x+y)$ is

(a) $x+c=\log\left[1-\tan\frac{(x+y)}{2}\right]$

(b) $x+c=\log\left[1+\tan\frac{(x+y)}{2}\right]$

(c) $x+\log\left[1-\tan\frac{(x+y)}{2}\right]=c$

(d) $x+\log\left[1+\tan\frac{(x+y)}{2}\right]=c$

7. The solution to the differential equation $\left(x\sin\frac{y}{x}\right)\frac{dy}{dx}=\left(y\sin\frac{y}{x}-x\right)$ is

(a) $\cos\left(\frac{x}{y}\right)=\log cx$

(b) $\cos\left(\frac{x}{y}\right)+\frac{y}{x}=\log cx$

(c) $\cos\left(\frac{y}{x}\right)+\frac{x}{y}=\log cx$

(d) $\cos\left(\frac{y}{x}\right)=\log cx$

8. The solution to the differential equation $\sin^{-1}\frac{dy}{dx}=x+y$ is

(a) $\tan(x+y)-\sec(x+y)=x+c$

(b) $\tan(x+y)+\sec(x+y)=x+c$

(c) $\cot(x+y)-\operatorname{cosec}(x+y)=\frac{1}{x}+c$

(d) $\cot(x+y)+\operatorname{cosec}(x+y)=\frac{1}{x}+c$

9. The solution to the differential equation $x\cos\frac{y}{x}(ydx+xdy)=y\sin\frac{y}{x}(xdy-ydx)$ is

(a) $xy\cos\frac{x}{y}=c$ (b) $xy\cos\frac{y}{x}=c$

(c) $xy+\cos\frac{x}{y}=c$ (d) None of these

10. The solution to the differential equation $(x^2-y^2)\frac{dy}{dx}=2xy$ for $y=1$, when $x=1$ is

(a) $x^2-y^2=2x$ (b) $x^2-y^2=2y$

(c) $x^2+y^2=2x$ (d) $x^2+y^2=2y$

11. The solution to the differential equation $\left(1+e^{x/y}\right)dx+e^{x/y}\left(1-\frac{x}{y}\right)dy=0$ is

(a) $y+x\,e^{x/y}=c$ (b) $x+y\,e^{y/x}=c$

(c) $x+y\,e^{x/y}=c$ (d) None of these

12. The solution to the differential equation $\left[x\sqrt{(x^2+y^2)}-y^2\right]dx+xy\,dy=0$ is

(a) $\sqrt{(x^2+y^2)}=y\log\left(\frac{c}{x}\right)$

(b) $\sqrt{(x^2+y^2)}=x\log\left(\frac{c}{y}\right)$

(c) $\sqrt{(x^2+y^2)}=x\log\left(\frac{c}{x}\right)$

(d) None of these

13. If $\frac{dy}{dx}=\frac{x+2y+3}{2x+y+3}$, then

(a) $c(x+y+3)=(x-y)^3$

(b) $c(x+y+2)=(x+y)^3$

(c) $c(x+y+3)=(x+y)^3$

(d) $c(x+y+2)=(x-y)^3$

14. The solution to the differential equation $\frac{dy}{dx}+\frac{10x+8y-12}{7x+5y-9}$ is

(a) $c=(x+y-1)(2x+y-3)^3$

(b) $c=(x+y-1)^2(2x+y-3)^3$

(c) $c=(x+y-1)(2x+y-3)^2$

(d) $c=(x+y-1)^2(2x+y-3)^2$

15. If $\frac{dy}{dx}=\frac{x+y+1}{2x+2y+3}$, then

(a) $3x + 6y = \log (3x + 3y + 4) + c$
(b) $3x - 6y = \log (3x + 3y + 4) + c$
(c) $3x + 6y = \log (3x - 3y + 4) + c$
(d) None of these

16. The solution to the differential equation

$$\frac{dy}{dx}=\frac{3x-4y-2}{6x-8y-5} \text{ is}$$

(a) $\log (6x - 8y - 7) = c - 2x + 4y$
(b) $6x - 8y - 7 = \log (c - 2x + 4y)$
(c) $6x - 8y - 7 = c - \log (2x - 4y)$
(d) None of these

17. The integrating factor of the differential equation

$$\sin x \frac{dy}{dx} + 3y = \cos x \text{ is}$$

(a) $e^{\tan^3 \frac{x}{2}}$ (b) $\log \tan \frac{x}{2}$
(c) $\tan^3 \frac{x}{2}$ (d) $\tan \frac{x}{2}$

[J.N.U. M.C.A.]

18. A differential equation $\frac{dy}{dx} = y \tan x - 2 \sin x$ has an integrating factor

(a) $\cos x$ (b) $e^{\int \tan x\, dx}$
(c) $e^{-\int \sin x\, dx}$ (d) $e^{\int \cos x\, dx}$

[J.N.U. M.C.A.]

19. The integrating factor for the differential equation

$$(x^3 - x)\frac{dy}{dx} - (3x^2 - 1)y = x^5 - 2x^3 + x \text{ is}$$

(a) $\frac{1}{x^3 - x}$ (b) $x^3 - x$
(c) $\frac{1}{3x^2 - 1}$ (d) $3x^2 - 1$

20. The solution to the differential equation

$$\frac{dy}{dx} - 2y\cos x = -2\sin 2x \text{ is}$$

(a) $y = c\, e^{\sin^2 x} + 2 \sin x + 1$
(b) $y = c\, e^{2 \sin x} + 2 \sin x + 1$
(c) $y = c\, e^{\sin x} + 2 \sin x + 1$
(d) None of these

21. The solution to the differential equation

$$x\frac{dy}{dx} - 2y = x^2 + \sin\left(\frac{1}{x^2}\right) \text{ is}$$

(a) $\frac{x}{y^2} = \log x + \frac{1}{2}\cos\left(\frac{1}{y^2}\right) + c$

(b) $\frac{y}{x^2} = \log x + \frac{1}{2}\cos\left(\frac{1}{x^2}\right) + c$

(c) $xy^2 = \log x + \frac{1}{2}\cos\left(\frac{1}{y^2}\right) + c$

(d) $yx^2 = \log x + \frac{1}{2}\cos\left(\frac{1}{x^2}\right) + c$

22. The solution to the differential equation $y \log y\, dx + (x - \log y)\, dy = 0$ is

(a) $y \log x = \frac{(\log x)^2}{2} + c$

(b) $y \log x = \frac{(\log y)^2}{2} + c$

(c) $x \log y = \frac{(\log y)^2}{2} + c$

(d) None of these

23. The solution to the differential equation

$$x \log x \frac{dy}{dx} + y = 2 \log x \text{ is}$$

(a) $y \log x = (\log y)^2 + c$
(b) $y \log x = (\log x)^2 + c$
(c) $x \log y = (\log x)^2 + c$
(d) $x \log y = (\log y)^2 + c$

24. The solution to the differential equation

$$(x + 1)\frac{dy}{dx} - ny = e^x (x + 1)^{n+1} \text{ is}$$

(a) $y = (e^x + c)(x + 1)^n$
(b) $y = (e^{nx} + c)(x + 1)$
(c) $y = e^x + (x + 1)^n + c$
(d) None of these

25. The differential equation of the form

$\frac{dy}{dx} + P(x)\, y = Q(x)\, y^n$ is called

(a) Auxiliary equation
(b) Clairaut's equation
(c) Bessel's equation
(d) Bernoulli's equation

26. The solution to the differential equation

$xy - \frac{dy}{dx} = y^3 e^{-x^2}$ is

(a) $\frac{e^{y^2}}{x^2} = 2y + c$ (b) $x^2 e^{y^2} = 2y + c$

(c) $\frac{e^{x^2}}{y^2} = 2x + c$ (d) $y^2 e^{x^2} = 2x + c$

27. The solution to the differential equation

$\frac{dy}{dx} = e^{x-y}(e^x - e^y)$ is

(a) $e^y = e^x + 1 + c\, e^{-e^x}$

(b) $e^x = e^y + 1 + c.e^{e^x}$

(c) $e^y = e^x - 1 + c.e^{-e^x}$

(d) $e^y = e^x + 1 + c.e^{-e^x}$

28. The solution to the differential equation $(y \log x - 1)\, ydx = xdy$ is

(a) $\frac{1}{y} = x \log x + 1 + cx$

(b) $\frac{1}{y} = \log x + 1 + cx$

(c) $\frac{1}{x} = \log y + 1 + cy$

(d) $\frac{1}{x} = \log y + 1 + cx$

29. The solution to the differential equation $(1 + y^2)\, dx = (\tan^{-1} y - x)\, dy$ is

(a) $y = (\tan^{-1} x - 1) + c.e^{-\tan^{-1} y}$

(b) $y = c(\tan^{-1} x - 1) + e^{-\tan^{-1} y}$

(c) $x = (\tan^{-1} y - 1) + c.e^{-\tan^{-1} y}$

(d) $x = c(\tan^{-1} x - 1) + e^{-\tan^{-1} x}$

30. The solution to the differential equation $(x^3y^2 + xy)\, dx = dy$ is

(a) $1 = (2 - x^2 + c\, e^{-x^2/2})\, y$

(b) $y = 2 - x^2 + c\, e^{-x^2/2}$

(c) $\frac{1}{y} = 2 + x^2 + c\, e^{-x^2/2}$

(d) None of these

31. Which of the following equation is not exact?

(a) $y \sin 2x\, dx - (y^2 + \cos^2 x)\, dy$

(b) $\left(1 + e^{x/y}\right) dx + e^{x/y}\left(1 - \frac{x}{y}\right) dy = 0$

(c) $xdy - ydx = xy^2\, dx$

(d) None of these

32. The solution of the differential equation

$\left(1 + e^{x/y}\right) dx + e^{x/y}\left(1 - \frac{x}{y}\right) dy = 0$ is

(a) $x + y\, e^{-x/y} = c$ (b) $x + y\, e^{x/y} = c$
(c) $x - y\, e^{-x/y} = c$ (d) $x - y\, e^{x/y} = c$

33. The solution of the differential equation

$\left[y\left(1 + \frac{1}{x}\right) + \cos y\right] dx + (x + \log x - x \sin y)\, dy = 0$ is

(a) $xy + y \log x + x \cos y = c$
(b) $xy - x \log y + x \cos y = c$
(c) $xy + x \log y + y \cos x = c$
(d) None of these

34. The solution of the differential equation

$xdx + ydy = \frac{a^2(xdy - ydx)}{x^2 + y^2}$ is

(a) $x^2 - y^2 + 2a^2 \tan^{-1}\frac{x}{y} = c$

(b) $x^2 + y^2 + 2a^2 \tan^{-1}\frac{x}{y} = c$

(c) $x^2 - y^2 + a^2 \tan^{-1}\frac{x}{y} = c$

(d) None of these

35. The solution of the differential equation $(2ax + by + g)\, dx + (2cy + bx + e)\, dy = 0$ is

(a) $ax^2 + cxy + by^2 + gx + ey = k$

(b) $ax^2 + bxy + cy^2 + gx + ey = k$

(c) $ax^2 + cxy + by^2 + ex + gy = k$

(d) None of these

36. If $Mdx + Ndy = 0$ is homogeneous, then the integrating factor is

(a) $\frac{1}{Mx + Ny}$ (b) $\frac{1}{Mx - Ny}$

(c) $\frac{1}{My + Nx}$ (d) $\frac{1}{My - Nx}$

37. The integrating factor of the differential equation $(1 + xy)\, y\, dx + (1 - xy)\, x\, dy = 0$ is

(a) $\frac{1}{xy}$ (b) $\frac{1}{x^2 + y^2}$

(c) $\frac{1}{x^2 y^2}$ (d) $\frac{1}{x^2 - y^2}$

38. The solution of the differential equation $(1 + xy)\, ydx + (1 - xy)\, x\, dy = 0$ is

(a) $\frac{1}{xy} + \log x - \log y = c$

(b) $-\frac{1}{xy} + \log \frac{x}{y} = c$

(c) $\frac{1}{xy} + \log \frac{x}{y} = c$

(d) None of these

39. The integration factor of the differential equation $(x^2 + y^2 + x)\, dx + xy\, dy = 0$ is

(a) e^{x^2} (b) e^x

(c) x (d) $\frac{1}{x}$

40. The integrating factor of the differential equation $(y^4 + 2y)\, dx + (xy^3 + 2y^4 - 4x)\, dy = 0$ is

(a) y^3 (b) $\frac{1}{y^3}$ (c) x^3 (d) $\frac{1}{x^3}$

ANSWERS

1	2	3	4	5	6	7	8	9	10
(d)	(a)	(c)	(a)	(a)	(b)	(d)	(a)	(b)	(d)
11	**12**	**13**	**14**	**15**	**16**	**17**	**18**	**19**	**20**
(c)	(c)	(d)	(b)	(b)	(a)	(c)	(a)	(a)	(b)
21	**22**	**23**	**24**	**25**	**26**	**27**	**28**	**29**	**30**
(b)	(c)	(b)	(a)	(d)	(c)	(c)	(b)	(c)	(a)
31	**32**	**33**	**34**	**35**	**36**	**37**	**38**	**39**	**40**
(c)	(b)	(a)	(b)	(b)	(a)	(c)	(b)	(c)	(b)

SOME SELECTED EXPLANATORY ANSWERS

1. Given differential equation is

$$\sqrt[3]{y + x\left(\frac{dy}{dx}\right)^2} = \frac{d^2y}{dx^2}$$

Cubing both the sides we get

$$\left(\frac{d^2y}{dx^2}\right)^3 = y + x\left(\frac{dy}{dx}\right)^2.$$

∴ Degree of the equation is 3.

2. Let $x = \tan\alpha$ and $y = \tan\beta$ and put it in the given equation,

$$\sqrt{1+x^2} + \sqrt{1+y^2}$$
$$= \lambda\left(x\sqrt{1+y^2} - y\sqrt{1+x^2}\right)$$

Putting we get

$$\cos\alpha + \cos\beta = \lambda(\sin\alpha - \sin\beta)$$

$$\Rightarrow \frac{\sin\alpha - \sin\beta}{\cos\alpha + \cos\beta} = \frac{1}{\lambda}$$

$$\Rightarrow \tan\left(\frac{\alpha - \beta}{2}\right) = \frac{1}{\lambda}$$

$\Rightarrow \alpha - \beta = 2\tan^{-1}\left(\frac{1}{\lambda}\right)$

$\Rightarrow \tan^{-1}x - \tan^{-1}y = 2\tan^{-1}\left(\frac{1}{\lambda}\right)$

Differentiating the above w.r.t. x we get

$$\frac{1}{1+x^2} - \frac{1}{1+y^2}.\frac{dy}{dx} = 0$$

$$\Rightarrow \frac{dy}{dx} = \frac{1+y^2}{1+x^2}.$$

∴ It is a differential equation of degree 1.

3. Given $y^2 = 2c\left(x+\sqrt{c}\right)$ ...(*i*)

Differentiating both the sides w.r.t. x we get

$$2y.\frac{dy}{dx} = 2c$$

$$\Rightarrow y.\frac{dy}{dx} = c \quad ...(ii)$$

Eliminating c from (*i*) and (*ii*) we get

$$y^2 = 2y\frac{dy}{dx}\left[x+\sqrt{y\frac{dy}{dx}}\right]$$

$$\Rightarrow y^2 = 2xy\frac{dy}{dx} + 2y^{3/2}\left(\frac{dy}{dx}\right)^{3/2}$$

$$\Rightarrow y^2 - 2xy\frac{dy}{dx} = 2y^{3/2}\left(\frac{dy}{dx}\right)^{3/2}$$

$$\Rightarrow y - 2x\frac{dy}{dx} = 2y^{1/2}\left(\frac{dy}{dx}\right)^{3/2}$$

Squaring both the sides we get

$$\left(y-2x\frac{dy}{dx}\right)^2 = 4y\left(\frac{dy}{dx}\right)^3.$$

∴ Degree of the differential equation is 3.

4. Given differential equation is

$$\frac{dy}{dx} = e^{x+y} + x^2e^y$$

$$\Rightarrow \frac{dy}{dx} = e^y(e^x + x^2)$$

$$\Rightarrow (e^x + x^2)\,dx = e^{-y}.dy$$

Integrating both the sides we get

$\left(e^x + \frac{x^3}{3}\right) = -e^{-y} + c$, where c is a constant.

or $e^x + e^{-y} + \frac{x^3}{3} = c$, is the required solution.

5. Given differential equation is

$$(x-y)^2\frac{dy}{dx} = a^2$$

Let $x - y = z$ so that $1 - \frac{dy}{dx} = \frac{dz}{dx}$

or $\frac{dy}{dx} = 1 - \frac{dz}{dx}$.

∴ The given equation reduces to

$$z^2\left(1-\frac{dz}{dx}\right) = a^2$$

or $\frac{dz}{dx} = \frac{z^2-a^2}{z^2}$

or $\frac{z^2}{z^2-a^2}dz = dx.$

Integrating we get

$$\int\frac{z^2}{z^2-a^2}dz = \int dx$$

or $\int\left\{1+\frac{a^2}{z^2-a^2}\right\}dz = \int dx$

or $z + a^2.\frac{1}{2a}\log\frac{z-a}{z+a} = x + c$

or $x - y + \frac{a}{2}\log\frac{x-y-a}{x+y+a} = x + c$

or $\frac{a}{2}\log\frac{x-y-a}{x+y+a} - y = c,$

is the required solution.

6. Given equation is

$$\frac{dy}{dx} = \sin(x+y) + \cos(x+y)$$

Let us put $x + y = z$ so that $1 + \frac{dy}{dx} = \frac{dz}{dx}$

Replacing $\frac{dy}{dx}$ with $\frac{dz}{dx}$ we get

$$\frac{dz}{dx} = 1 + \sin z + \cos z$$

or $\frac{dz}{1+\sin z+\cos z} = dx$

or $\dfrac{dz}{2\cos^2\frac{z}{2}+2\sin\frac{z}{2}\cos\frac{z}{2}} = dx$

or $\dfrac{dz}{2\cos^2\frac{z}{2}\left(1+\tan\frac{z}{2}\right)} = dx$

or $\dfrac{\sec^2\frac{z}{2}dz}{2\left(1+\tan\frac{z}{2}\right)} = dx$

Integrating both the sides we get

$$\int\frac{\sec^2\frac{z}{2}dz}{2\left(1+\tan\frac{z}{2}\right)} = \int dx$$

or $\log\left(1+\frac{z}{2}\right) = x + c$

or $\log\left[1+\tan\frac{(x+y)}{2}\right] = x + c$, is the required solution.

7. Given eqation is

$$\left(x\sin\frac{y}{x}\right)\frac{dy}{dx}=\left(y\sin\frac{y}{x}-x\right)$$

Let $\frac{y}{x}=z$ i.e. $y = zx$.

Differentiating w.r.t. x we get $\frac{dy}{dx}=z+x\frac{dz}{dx}$

∴ The new equation becomes

$$x\sin z.\left(z+x\frac{dz}{dx}\right) = y\sin z - x$$

or $zx\sin z + x^2\sin z.\frac{dz}{dx} = y\sin z - x$

$y\sin z + x^2\sin z.\frac{dx}{dx} = y\sin z - x$

or $\sin z\,dz = -\frac{dx}{x}$

Integrating both the sides we get

$-\cos z = -\log x - \log c.$

or $-\cos z = -\log cx$

or $\cos\left(\frac{y}{x}\right)= \log cx$ is the required solution.

8. Given differentiation equation is

$$\sin^{-1}\left(\frac{dy}{dx}\right)=x+y$$

Putting $z = x + y$, the equation becomes

$$\frac{dz}{dx}-1 = \sin z$$

or $\dfrac{dz}{1+\sin z} = dx$

or $\dfrac{(1-\sin z)}{\cos^2 z}dz = dx$

or $(\sec^2 z - \tan z\sec z)\,dz = dx$

Integrating both the sides we get

$\tan z - \sec z = x + c$

or $\tan(x+y) - \sec(x+y) = x + c$, is the required solution.

9. Given equation is

$$x\cos\frac{y}{x}(ydx+xdy) = y\sin\frac{y}{x}(xdy-ydx)$$

Rewriting the given equation we get

$$y\left[x\cos\frac{y}{x}+y\sin\frac{y}{x}\right] = \frac{dy}{dx}\left[xy\sin\frac{y}{x}-x^2\cos\frac{y}{x}\right]$$

or $\dfrac{dy}{dx} = \dfrac{y\left[x\cos\frac{y}{x}+y\sin\frac{y}{x}\right]}{x\left[y\sin\frac{y}{x}-x\cos\frac{y}{x}\right]}$

Puttin $y = zx$, so that $\frac{dy}{dx}=z+x\frac{dz}{dx}$, we get

$$z+x\frac{dy}{dx} = \frac{z[x\cos z+zx\sin z]}{[zx\sin z - x\cos z]}$$

or $z+x\dfrac{dz}{dx} = \dfrac{z[\cos z+z\sin z]}{z\sin z-\cos z}$

or $x\dfrac{dy}{dx} = \dfrac{z[\cos z+z\sin z]}{z\sin z-\cos z}-z$

$$= \frac{z\cos z+z^2\sin z-z^2\sin z+z\cos z}{z\sin z-\cos z}$$

or $x\dfrac{dz}{dx} = \dfrac{2z\cos z}{z\sin z-\cos z}$

or $\dfrac{(z\sin z-\cos z)\,dz}{z\cos z} = \dfrac{2dx}{x}$

or $\left(\dfrac{\sin z}{\cos z}-\dfrac{1}{z}\right)dz = \dfrac{2dx}{x}$

Integrating we get

$$-\log\cos z-\log z = 2\log x-\log c$$

or $2\log x = \log\left(\dfrac{c}{z\cos z}\right)$

or $x^2 = \dfrac{c}{z\cos z}$ or $xy\cos\dfrac{y}{x} = c.$

10. The given equation is

$$\frac{dy}{dx}=\frac{2xy}{x^2-y^2} \quad ...(i)$$

Put $y = zx$, so $\dfrac{dy}{dx}=z+x\dfrac{dz}{dx}$

Substituting in *(i)* we get

$$z+x\frac{dz}{dx} = \frac{2zx^2}{x^2(1-z^2)}=\frac{2z}{1-z^2}$$

or $x\dfrac{dz}{dx} = \dfrac{2z}{1-z^2}-z=\dfrac{z+z^3}{1-z^2}$

or $\dfrac{(1-z^2)}{z(1+z^2)}dz = \dfrac{dx}{x}$

Integrating we get

$$\log x = \int\frac{(1-z^2)}{z(1+z^2)}dz$$

$$= \int\left(\frac{1}{z}-\frac{2z}{1+z^2}\right)dz$$

$$= \log z-\log(1+z^2)+\log c$$

$\therefore$ $\log x = \log\dfrac{zc}{1+z^2}$

or $x(1+z^2) = zc$

or $x\left(1+\dfrac{y^2}{x^2}\right) = \dfrac{y}{x}.c$

or $x^2+y^2 = cy.$

Given that $y = 1$, when $x = 1$. Then $c = 2$.

$\therefore$ Required Solution is $x^2 + y^2 = 2y$.

11. Given $\left(1+e^{x/y}\right)dx+e^{x/y}\left(1-\dfrac{x}{y}\right)dy=0$

Put $x = zy$, so that $\dfrac{dx}{dy}=z+y\dfrac{dz}{dy}$.

The equation becomes

$$\left(1+e^z\right)\left[z+y\frac{dz}{dy}\right]+e^z(1-z)=0$$

or $z+y\dfrac{dz}{dy} = \dfrac{e^z(z-1)}{e^z+1}$

or $y\dfrac{dz}{dy} = \dfrac{e^z(z-1)}{e^z+1}-z=\dfrac{-(e^z+z)}{e^z+1}$

or $\dfrac{dy}{y} = -\dfrac{(e^z+1)}{e^z+z}dz$

Integrating, both the sides we get

$$\log y = -\log\left|e^z+z\right|+\log c$$

or $y(e^z+z) = c$

or $y\left[e^{x/y}+\dfrac{x}{y}\right] = c$

or $x + y\,e^{x/y} = c$, is the required solution of the given equation.

12. The given equation is

$$\left[x\sqrt{(x^2+y^2)}-y^2\right]dx+xy\,dy=0$$

Equation can be rewritten as

$$xy\frac{dy}{dx}+\left[x\sqrt{x^2+y^2}-y^2\right]=0$$

Putting $y = zx$, the above equation reduces to

$$x.zx\left(z+x\frac{dz}{dx}\right)+\left[x\sqrt{(x^2+z^2x^2)}-z^2x^2\right]=0$$

or $z\left(z+x\dfrac{dy}{dx}\right)+\sqrt{(1+z^2)}-z^2=0$

or $zx\dfrac{dz}{dx}+\sqrt{(1+z^2)}=0$

or $\dfrac{z\,dz}{\sqrt{(1+z^2)}}+\dfrac{dx}{x}=0$

or $\dfrac{v\,dv}{v}+\dfrac{dx}{x}=0$, putting $1+z^2=v^2$

or $\qquad dv+\left(\frac{1}{x}\right)dx = 0$

Integrating we get $v + \log x = \log c$, where c is an arbitrary constant.

or $v = \log\left(\frac{c}{x}\right)$ or $\sqrt{(1+z^2)} = \log\left(\frac{c}{x}\right)$

$$\because v^2 = 1 + z^2$$

or $\sqrt{\left[1+\left(\frac{y}{x}\right)^2\right]} = \log\left(\frac{c}{x}\right)$ or $\sqrt{(x^2+y^2)}$

$= x\log\left(\frac{c}{x}\right)$.

13. Given $\frac{dy}{dx}=\frac{x+2y+3}{2x+y+3}$

Putting, $x = X + h,\ y = Y + k$, the equation becomes

$$\frac{dY}{dX}=\frac{X+2Y+h+2k+3}{2X+Y+2h+k+3}$$

Choose h and k so that $h + 2k + 3 = 0$ and

$$2h + k + 3 = 0$$

On solving these equations, we get $h = -1,\ k = -1$.

The equation becomes, $\frac{dY}{dX}=\frac{X+2Y}{2X+Y}$

Put $Y = zX$, so $\frac{dY}{dX}=z+X\frac{dz}{dX}$

$$\therefore \quad z+X\frac{dz}{dX} = \frac{1+2z}{2+z}$$

or $\quad X\frac{dz}{dX} = \frac{1+2z}{2+z}-z=\frac{1-z^2}{2+z}$

or $\quad \frac{(2+z)\,dz}{1-z^2} = \frac{dX}{X}$

Integrating we get

$$\frac{2}{2}\log\frac{1-z}{1+z}-\frac{1}{2}\log(1-z^2)=\log X-\frac{1}{2}\log C$$

$$\frac{1}{2}\log C+\frac{1}{2}\left[\log\frac{(1+z)^2}{(1-z)^2\,(1-z^2)}\right] = \log X$$

$$\therefore \log\frac{(1+z)}{(1-z^3)} = 2\log X = \log X^2$$

$$\therefore X^2=\frac{C[X+Y]X^3}{X[X-Y]^3}=C\frac{X^2\,(X+Y)}{(X-Y)^3}.$$

$$\therefore C[X+Y]=(X-Y)^3$$

or $C\,(x + y + 2) = (x - y)^3$ is the required solution.

14. Given $\frac{dy}{dx}+\frac{10x+8y-12}{7x+5y-9}=0$

$$\therefore \quad \frac{dy}{dx} = -\frac{(10x+8y-12)}{7x+5y-9}$$

Putting $x = X + h,\ y = Y + k$, the equation becomes

$$\frac{dY}{dX}=-\frac{[10X+8Y+10h+8k-12]}{7X+5Y+7h+5k-9}$$

Choose h and k so that $10h + 8k - 12 = 0,\ 7h + 5k - 9 = 0$

Solving the equation we get $h = 2,\ k = -1$.

Then the equation becomes

$$\frac{dY}{dX}=\frac{-(10X+8Y)}{7X+5Y}$$

Putting $Y = zX$, we get $\frac{dY}{dX}=z+X\frac{dz}{dX}$.

Equation now becomes

$$z+X\frac{dz}{dX} = \frac{-X\,(10+8z)}{X\,(7+5z)}$$

or $\quad X\frac{dz}{dX} = -\frac{(10+8z)}{(7+5z)}-z$

$$= \frac{-10-15z-5z^2}{7+5z}$$

or $\quad \frac{(7+5z)}{z^2+3z+2}dz = -\frac{5\,dX}{X}$

or $\quad \left\{\frac{2}{z+1}+\frac{3}{2+z}\right\}dz = -\frac{5\,dX}{X}$

Integrating we get

$2\log(z+1)+3\log(z+2) = -5\log X + \log c$

or $\log(z+1)^2(z+2)^3X^5 = \log c$

$\therefore c = (z+1)^2(z+2)^3X^5$

$$=\frac{(X+Y)^2}{X^2}.\frac{(Y+2X)^2}{X^3}X^5$$

$$=(Y+X)^2(Y+2X)^3$$

$$=(y+1+x-2)^2(y+1+2x-4)^3$$

or $c = (x + y - 1)^2\,(2x + y - 3)^3$ is the required solution.

15. Given $\frac{dy}{dx}=\frac{x+y+1}{2x+2y+3}$

Here two lines $x + y + 1 = 0$ and $2x + 2y + 3 = 0$ are parallel. We observe here that the equation may be written as

$$\frac{dy}{dx}=\frac{x+y+1}{2(x+y)+3}.$$

Put $x + y = z$, so that $\frac{dz}{dx}=1+\frac{dy}{dx}$

Equation now becomes

$$\frac{dz}{dx}-1 = \frac{z+1}{2z+3}$$

or $$\frac{dz}{dx} = 1+\frac{z+1}{2z+3}=\frac{3z+3}{2z+3}$$

or $$\left(\frac{2z+3}{2z+4}\right)dz = dx$$

or $$\left[\frac{2}{3}\left(\frac{3z+4}{3z+4}\right)+\frac{1}{3}\left(\frac{1}{3z+4}\right)\right]dz = dx.$$

Integrating both the sides we get

$$\frac{2}{3}z+\frac{1}{9}\log(3z+4) = x+c$$

or $6z + \log(3z + 4) = 9x + c$

or $6(x + y) + \log(3x + 3y + 4) = 9x + c$

or $3x - 6y = \log(3x + 3y + 4) + c$.

16. Given equation is

$$\frac{dy}{dx}=\frac{3x-4y-2}{6x-8y-5}$$

Here the two lines $3x - 4y - 2 = 0$ and $6x - 8y - 5 = 0$ are parallel. We observe that here that the equation may be written as

$$\frac{dy}{dx}=\frac{(3x-4y)-2}{2(3x-4y)-5}$$

Put $3x - 4y = z$, so that $\frac{dz}{dx}=3-4\frac{dy}{dx}$

Hence we obtain $\frac{3}{4}-\frac{1}{4}\frac{dz}{dx}=\frac{z-2}{2z-5}$

This reduces to $\frac{2z-7}{2z-5}=\frac{dz}{dx}$

Separating the variables we get

$$\frac{(2z-5)}{2z-7}dz=dx$$

Integrating we get

$z + \log(2z - 7) = x + c$

or $\log(6x - 5y - 7) = c - 2x + 4y$

$(\because z = 3x - 4y)$

Which is the required solution.

17. Given equation is

$$\sin x\frac{dy}{dx}+3y=\cos x.$$

It can be re-written as

$$\frac{dy}{dx}+3y\,\text{cosec}\,x=\cot x.$$

Which is the linear equation.

Here $P=\text{cosec}\,x$.

$$\therefore \int P\,dx=\int \text{cosec}\,x\,dx = \log\left(\tan\frac{x}{2}\right)$$

$$\text{I.F.}=e^{3\int P\,dx}=e^{3\log\left(\tan\frac{x}{2}\right)}=\tan^3\frac{x}{2}.$$

18. Given equation is

$$\frac{dy}{dx}=y\tan x-2\sin x$$

It can be rewritten as

$$\frac{dy}{dx}-y\tan x=-2\sin x$$

Here $P=-\tan x$

$$\therefore \int P\,dx=-\int \tan x\,dx$$

$$\therefore \text{I.F.}=e^{\int P\,dx}=e^{-\int \tan x\,dx}=e^{-\log\sec x}=\cos x.$$

19. Given equation is

$$\left(x^3-x\right)\frac{dy}{dx}-(3x^2-1)\,y = x^5-2x^3+x$$

or $$\frac{dy}{dx}-\frac{(3x^2-1)}{(x^3-x)}y=\frac{x^5-2x^3+x}{x^3-x}$$

or $$\frac{dy}{dx}-\frac{(3x^2-1)}{(x^3-x)}y=x^2-1$$

Here $\int P\,dx=-\int\frac{(3x^2-1)}{x^3-x}dx=-\log(x^3-x)$.

$$\therefore \text{I.F.}=e^{-\int\frac{(3x^2-1)}{(x^3-x)}dx}=e^{\log(x^3-x)^{-1}}=\frac{1}{x^3-x}.$$

20. Given differential equation is

$$\frac{dy}{dx} - 2y\cos x = -2\sin 2x$$

$$\int P\,dx = -\int 2\cos x\,dx = -2\sin x$$

$$e^{\int P\,dx} = e^{-2\sin x}$$

Solution is

$$y\,e^{-2\sin x} = \int e^{-2\sin x}.(-2\sin 2x)\,dx + c$$

$$= -2\int e^{-2\sin x} \times 2\sin x\cos x\,dx + c$$

Putting $t = -2\sin x$ to that $dt = -2\cos x\,dx$ we get

$$y\,e^{-2\sin x} = -\int t\,e^t\,dt + c$$
$$= c - (t\,e^t - e^t)$$
$$= c - e^t\,(t-1)$$
$$= c + e^{-2\sin x}\,(2\sin x + 1).$$

$\therefore$ $y = c.e^2 \sin x + 2\sin x + 1$ is the required solution.

21. Given equation is

$$x\frac{dy}{dx} - 2y = x^2 + \sin\left(\frac{1}{x^2}\right)$$

Dividing throughout by x we get

$$\frac{dy}{dx} = -\frac{2}{x}y = x + \frac{1}{x}\sin\left(\frac{1}{x^2}\right)$$

$$\therefore \text{ I.F.} = e^{\int P\,dx} = e^{\int -\frac{2}{x}dx} = e^{-2\log x} = \frac{1}{x^2}$$

$\therefore$ Solution is

$$\frac{y}{x^2} = \int\left\{\left(\frac{1}{x} + \frac{1}{x^3}\sin\left(\frac{1}{x^2}\right)\right)\right\}dx + c$$

$$= \log x + \int\frac{1}{x^3}\sin\left(\frac{1}{x^2}\right)dx + c$$

Putting $\frac{1}{x^2} = t$ in R.H.S. we get

$$\frac{y}{x^2} = \log x - \frac{1}{2}\int \sin t\,dt + c$$

or
$$\frac{y}{x^2} = \log x + \frac{1}{2}\cos\left(\frac{1}{x^2}\right) + c.$$

22. Given equation is
$y\log y\,dx + (x - \log y)\,dy = 0$
The equation takes the form

$$\frac{dx}{dy} + \frac{x - \log y}{y\log y} = 0$$

or
$$\frac{dx}{dy} + \frac{x}{y\log y} = \frac{1}{y}$$

This is a linear equation in x.

$$\int P\,dx = \int\frac{dy}{y\log y} = \log(\log y)$$

$$\therefore\ e^{\int P\,dy} = e^{\log(\log y)} = \log y.$$

$\therefore$ The solution of this equation is

$$x\log y = \int\frac{\log y}{y}dy + c$$
$$= \frac{(\log y)^2}{2} + c.$$

23. Given equation is

$$x\log x\frac{dy}{dx} + y = 2\log x$$

Dividing throughout by $x\log x$, we obtain

$$\frac{dy}{dx} + \frac{1}{x\log x}y = \frac{2}{x}.$$

Here $P = \frac{1}{x\log x}$

$$\therefore\ e^{\int P\,dx} = e^{\int\frac{dx}{x\log x}} = \log(\log x)$$

$$\therefore \text{ I.F.} = e^{\int P\,dx} = e^{\log(\log x)} = \log x.$$

Hence the required solution is

$$y\log x = \int\frac{2}{x}\log x\,dx + c$$
$$= (\log x)^2 + c.$$

24. Given equation is

$$(x+1)\frac{dy}{dx} - ny = e^x(x+1)^{n+1}$$

The given equation can be written as

$$\frac{dy}{dx} - \frac{n}{x+1}y = e^x(x+1)^n$$

Now $\int P\,dx = -n\int\frac{dx}{x+1}$

$$= -n\log(x+1) = \log(x+1)^{-n}$$

$\therefore$ I.F. $= e^{\int P\,dx} = (x+1)^{-n}$.

The solution is given by

$$y\,(x+1)^{-n} = \int e^{x}(x+1)^{n}\,(x+1)^{-n}\,dx + c$$

$$= e^{x} + c.$$

26. Given equation is

$$xy - \frac{dy}{dx} = y^{3}\,e^{-x^{2}}$$

or $$-\frac{dy}{dx} + xy = y^{3}\,e^{-x^{2}}$$

Dividing throughout by y^3, we get

$$-y^{-3}\frac{dy}{dx} + xy^{-2} = e^{-x^{2}}.$$

Putting $z = y^{-2}$, we get $\dfrac{dz}{dx} = -2y^{-3}\dfrac{dy}{dx}$.

$\therefore$ The given equation takes the form

$$\frac{1}{2}\frac{dz}{dx} + xz = e^{-x^{2}}$$

or $$\frac{dz}{dx} + 2xz = 2e^{-x^{2}}$$

$$\text{I.F.} = e^{\int P\,dx} = e^{\int 2x\,dx} = e^{x^{2}}.$$

$\therefore$ Solution is $z\,e^{x^{2}} = \int 2\,dx + c$

or $$\frac{e^{x^{2}}}{y^{2}} = 2x + c.$$

27. Given equation is

$$\frac{dy}{dx} = e^{x-y}\,(e^{x} - e^{y})$$

Simplifying we get

$$\frac{dy}{dx} = e^{2x-y} - e^{x}$$

or $$\frac{dy}{dx} + e^{x} = e^{2x}\,.\,e^{-y}$$

Dividing throughout by e^{-y} we get

$$e^{y}\frac{dy}{dx} + e^{x}\,e^{y} = e^{2x}$$

Putting $e^{y} = z$ so that $\dfrac{dz}{dx} = e^{y}\dfrac{dy}{dx}$, we get

$$\frac{dz}{dx} + e^{x}z = e^{2x}.$$

$\therefore$ I.F. $= e^{\int e^{x}\,dx} = e^{(e^{x})}$ and the solution of the equation is

$$z\,e^{(e^{x})} = \int e^{e^{x}}.e^{2x}\,dx + c.$$

Put $e^{x} = t$ $\therefore$ $e^{x}\,dx = dt$.

Thus $$z\,e^{(e^{x})} = \int e^{t}.t\,dt + c$$

$$= t\,e^{t} - e^{t} + c$$

or $$e^{y}.e^{e^{x}} = e^{e^{x}}\,(e^{x} - 1) + c$$

$\therefore$ $e^{y} = e^{x} - 1 + c\,e^{-e^{x}}$ is the required solution.

28. Given equation is

$(y \log x - 1)\,y\,dx = x\,dy$

The given equation can be rewritten as

$$x\frac{dy}{dx} = y^{2}\log x - y$$

or $$\frac{dy}{dx} + \frac{y}{x} = \frac{y^{2}\log x}{x}$$

Dividing throughout by y^2, we get

$$y^{-2}\frac{dy}{dx} + \frac{y^{-1}}{x} = \frac{\log x}{x}$$

Putting $z = y^{-1}$ so that $\dfrac{dz}{dx} = -y^{-2}\dfrac{dy}{dx}$, we get

$$-\frac{dz}{dx} + \frac{z}{x} = \frac{\log x}{x}$$

or $\dfrac{dz}{dx} - \dfrac{z}{x} = -\dfrac{\log x}{x}$, which is linear.

It's I.F. $= e^{-\int \frac{1}{x}dx} = e^{-\log x} = \dfrac{1}{x}$

$\therefore$ Solution is given by

$$\frac{z}{x} =$$

$$\int \frac{-\log x}{x^{2}}\,dx = \int \log x.d\left(\frac{1}{x}\right)$$

or $$\frac{z}{x} = \frac{1}{x}\log x + \frac{1}{x} + c$$

or $$\frac{1}{xy} = \frac{1}{x}\log x + \frac{1}{x} + c$$

or $\dfrac{1}{y} = \log x + 1 + cx$ is the required solution.

29. Given equation is

$$(1+y^2)\,dx = (\tan^{-1} y - x)\,dy$$

or $\dfrac{dx}{dy} = \dfrac{\tan^{-1} y - x}{1+y^2}$.

or $\dfrac{dx}{dy} + \dfrac{x}{1+y^2} = \dfrac{\tan^{-1} y}{1+y^2}$

$$\text{I.F.} = e^{\int \frac{dy}{1+y^2}} = e^{\tan^{-1} y}$$

∴ Solution is

$$x.e^{\tan^{-1} y} = \int e^{\tan^{-1} y}.\frac{\tan^{-1} y}{1+y^2}dy + c$$

$$= \int t\,e^t\,dt + c \text{ where } t = \tan^{-1} y$$

$$= (t\,e^t - e^t) + c$$

(∴ Integrating by parts)

$$= (\tan^{-1} y - 1)\,e^{\tan^{-1} y} + c.$$

Hence $x = (\tan^{-1} y - 1) + c\,e^{-\tan^{-1} y}$ is the required solution.

30. Given equation is

$$(x^3y^2 + xy)\,dx = dy$$

or $\dfrac{dy}{dx} - xy = x^3y^2$

or $\dfrac{1}{y^2}\dfrac{dy}{dx} - \dfrac{1}{y}.x = x^3$.

Put $\dfrac{1}{y} = z$, so that $-\dfrac{1}{y^2}\dfrac{dy}{dx} = \dfrac{dz}{dx}$

Now the equation becomes

$$\frac{dz}{dx} + x.z = -x^3$$

$$\therefore \text{I.F.} = e^{\int x\,dx} = e^{x^2/2}.$$

∴ Solution is

$$z\,e^{x^2/2} = -\int x^3\,e^{x^2/2}\,dx + c$$

$$= -2\int t\,e^t\,dt + c, \text{ where } t = \frac{x^2}{2}.$$

$$= -2\,(t-1)\,e^t + c$$

(∵ Integrating by parts)

$$= (2 - x^2)\,e^{x^2/2} + c, \text{ where } z = \frac{1}{y}.$$

Hence $1 = (2 - x^2 + c\,e^{-x^2/2})\,y$ is the required solution.

31. Given equation is

$$x\,dy - y\,dx = xy^2\,dx$$

It can be rewritten as

$$x\,dy - y\,(1+xy)\,dx = 0$$

Here $M = -(y + xy^2)$ and $N = x$

$$\therefore \frac{\partial M}{\partial y} = -(1+2xy); \quad \frac{\partial N}{\partial x} = 1$$

Since $\dfrac{\partial M}{\partial y} \neq \dfrac{\partial N}{\partial x}$, the equation is not exact.

32. Given equation is

$$\left(1+e^{x/y}\right)dx + e^{x/y}\left(1-\frac{x}{y}\right)dy = 0$$

Here $M = 1 + e^{x/y}$ and $N = e^{x/y}\left(1-\dfrac{x}{y}\right)$

$$\therefore \frac{\partial M}{\partial y} = e^{x/y}\left[\frac{-x}{y^2}\right];$$

$$\frac{\partial N}{\partial x} = e^{x/y}\left(\frac{1}{y}\right) - \left(\frac{x}{y}\right)e^{x/y}\left(\frac{1}{y}\right) - e^{x/y}\left(\frac{1}{y}\right)$$

$$= -\frac{x}{y^2}e^{x/y}$$

∴ $\dfrac{\partial M}{\partial y} = \dfrac{\partial N}{\partial x}$, so the given equation is exact.

Now $\int M\,dx = \int\left(1+e^{x/y}\right)dx = x + y\,e^{x/y}$

treating y as a constant.

$$\int N\,dy = \int e^{x/y}\left(1-\frac{x}{y}\right)dy = y\,e^{x/y}$$

treating x as a constant

= 0 omitting the term $y\,e^{x/y}$

as already present in $\int M\,dx$.

∴ Solution is $x + y\,e^{x/y} = c$.

33. Given equation is

$$\left[y\left(1+\frac{1}{x}\right) + \cos y\right]dx + (x + \log x - x\sin y)\,dy = 0$$

Here $M = y\left(1+\dfrac{1}{x}\right) + \cos y$ and N

$$= x + \log x - x\sin y$$

$\therefore \quad \dfrac{\partial M}{\partial y} = 1 + \dfrac{1}{x} - \sin y$ and $\dfrac{\partial N}{\partial x} = 1 + \dfrac{1}{x} - \sin y$

$\therefore \quad \dfrac{\partial M}{\partial y} = \dfrac{\partial N}{\partial x}$ and hence the equation is exact.

$$\int M\,dx = \int \left[y\left(1 + \frac{1}{x}\right) + \cos y \right] dx$$

$= y(x + \log x) + x\cos y$, keeping y as a constant.

$$\int N\,dy = \int (x + \log x - x\sin y)\,dx$$

$= xy + y\log x + x\cos y$, keeping x as a constant.
$= 0$ omitting all the terms as they appear in $\int M\,dx$.

$\therefore$ Solution is $xy + y\log x + x\cos y = c$.

34. Given equation is

$$x\,dx + y\,dy = \frac{a^2(x\,dy - y\,dy)}{x^2 + y^2}$$

The equation can be rewritten as

$$\left(x + \frac{a^2 y}{x^2 + y^2}\right)dx + \left(y - \frac{a^2 x}{x^2 + y^2}\right)dy = 0$$

Here $M = x + \dfrac{a^2 y}{x^2 + y^2}$ and $N = y - \dfrac{a^2 x}{x^2 + y^2}\,dy$

$$\therefore \quad \frac{\partial M}{\partial y} = \left[\frac{(x^2 + y^2)\,a^2 - a^2 y\,(2y)}{(x^2 + y^2)^2}\right]$$

$$= \frac{a^2\,(x^2 - y^2)}{(x^2 + y^2)^2}$$

$$\frac{\partial N}{\partial x} = -\left[\frac{(x^2 + y^2)\,a^2 - a^2 x\,(2x)}{(x^2 + y^2)^2}\right]$$

$$= \frac{a^2\,(x^2 - y^2)}{(x^2 + y^2)^2}$$

$\therefore \quad \dfrac{\partial M}{\partial y} = \dfrac{\partial N}{\partial x}$ and hence the equation is exact.

Now $\displaystyle\int M\,dx = \int \left(x + \frac{a^2 y}{x^2 + y^2}\right)dx$

$= \dfrac{x^2}{2} + a^2 \tan^{-1}\dfrac{x}{y}$ keeping y fixed.

and $\displaystyle\int N\,dy = \int \left(y - \frac{a^2 x}{x^2 + y^2}\right)dy$

$= \dfrac{y^2}{2} - a^2 \tan^{-1}\dfrac{y}{x}$ keeping x fixed.

$$= \frac{y^2}{2} - a^2 \cot^{-1}\frac{x}{y}$$

$$= \frac{y^2}{2} - a^2\left[\frac{\pi}{2} - \tan^{-1}\frac{x}{y}\right]$$

$$= \frac{y^2}{2} - \frac{\pi a^2}{2} + a^2 \tan^{-1}\frac{x}{y}$$

$= \dfrac{y^2}{2} - \dfrac{\pi a^2}{2}$ omitting the other term.

$\therefore$ Solution is $\dfrac{x^2}{2} + \dfrac{y^2}{2} + a^2 \tan^{-1}\dfrac{x}{y} - \dfrac{\pi a^2}{2} = c_1$

i.e. $x^2 + y^2 + 2a^2 \tan^{-1}\dfrac{x}{y} = c$

35. Given differential equation is
$(2ax + by + g)\,dx + (2cy + bx + e)\,dy = 0$
Here $M = 2ax + by + g$ and $N = 2cy + bx + e$.

$\therefore \quad \dfrac{\partial M}{\partial y} = b$ and $\dfrac{\partial N}{\partial x} = b$

$\therefore \quad \dfrac{\partial M}{\partial y} = \dfrac{\partial N}{\partial x}$ and hence the equation is exact.

Now $\displaystyle\int M\,dx = \int (2ax + by + g)\,dx$

$= ax^2 + bxy + gx$

$\displaystyle\int N\,dy = \int (2cy + bx + e)\,dy$

$= cy^2 + bxy + ey.$

$\therefore$ Solution is $ax^2 + cy^2 + bxy + gx + ey = k$.

37. Given differential equation is
$(1 + xy)\,y\,dx + (1 - xy)\,x\,dy = 0$
Equation can be rewritten as
$y\,dx + x\,dy + xy\,(y\,dx - x\,dy) = 0$

Multiplying above equations by $\dfrac{1}{(xy)^2}$ we get

$$\frac{y\,dx + x\,dy}{(xy)^2} + \frac{y\,dx - x\,dy}{xy} = 0$$

i.e. $$\frac{d\,(xy)}{(xy)^2} + \frac{dx}{x} - \frac{dy}{y} = 0$$

Thus the above equation can be integrable, so the

$$\text{I.F.} = \frac{1}{(xy)^2}.$$

38. Proceeding next, from where we left solution of Q. 37 we get

$$\frac{d(xy)}{(xy)^2} + \frac{dx}{x} - \frac{dy}{y} = 0$$

Integrating we get

$$-\frac{1}{xy} + \log\frac{x}{y} = c.$$

39. Given equation is

$(x^2 + y^2 + x)\,dx + xy\,dy = 0$

Here $M = x^2 + y^2 + x$ and $N = xy$

$$\therefore \quad \frac{\partial M}{\partial y} = 2y;\ \frac{\partial N}{\partial x} = y$$

$$\therefore \quad \frac{1}{N}\left(\frac{\partial M}{\partial y} - \frac{\partial N}{\partial x}\right) = \frac{y}{xy} = \frac{1}{x},\ \text{a function of } x.$$

$$\therefore \text{ I.F.} = e^{\int \frac{dx}{x}} = e^{\log x} = x.$$

40. Given equation is

$(x^4 + 2y)\,dx + (xy^3 + 2y^4 - 4x)\,dy = 0$

Here $M = y^4 + 2y$ and $N = xy^3 + 2y^4 - 4x$

$$\therefore \quad \frac{\partial M}{\partial y} = 4y^3 + 2 \text{ and } \frac{\partial N}{\partial x} = y^3 - 4$$

$\dfrac{\partial M}{\partial y} \neq \dfrac{\partial N}{\partial x}$ and hence the equation is not exact.

Now $$\frac{1}{N}\left(\frac{\partial M}{\partial y} - \frac{\partial N}{\partial x}\right) = \frac{3y^3 + 6}{y^4 + 2y} = \frac{3}{y},$$

a function of y.

$\therefore$ Integrating factor

$$= e^{-\int \frac{3}{y} dy} = e^{-3\log y} = y^{-3}.$$

16. VECTORS

Scalars : A scalar is a quantity which has only magnitude but does not have a direction. For example time, mass, temperature, distance and specific gravity etc.

Vectors : A vector is a quantity which has magnitude, direction and follow the law of parallelogram (addition of two vectors). For example displacement, force, acceleration.

Types of Vectors :

***(i)* Equal vector :** Two vectors are said to be equal if and only if they have equal magnitudes and same direction. Their lines of action may be different.

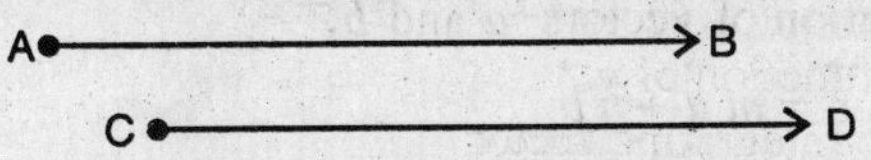

Here $|\vec{AB}| = |\vec{CD}|$ as well as direction is same.

***(ii)* Zero vector (null vector) :** A vector whose initial and terminal point are same is called null vector. For example $\vec{AA}$.

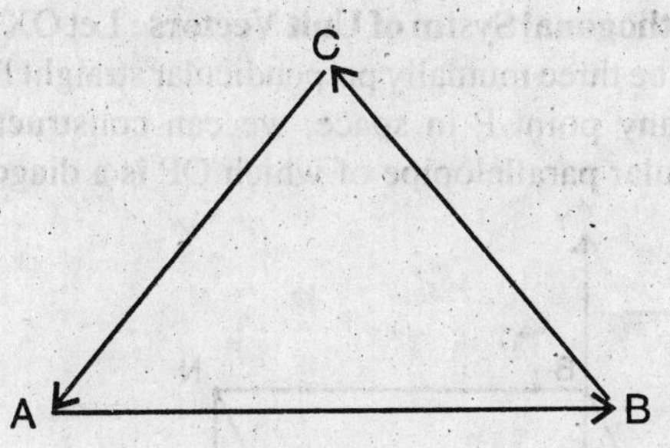

This type of vector has zero magnitude and no direction, and is denoted by $\vec{0}$

i.e. $\vec{AB} + \vec{BC} + \vec{CA} = \vec{AA}$

or $\vec{AB} + \vec{BC} + \vec{CA} = \vec{0}$

***(iii)* Like and unlike vectors :** Two vectors are said to be like when they have same direction. Unlike when they are in opposite directions.

$\vec{AB}$ and $\vec{BA}$ are two unlike vectors as their directions are opposite.

***(iv)* Unit vector :** A unit vector is a vector whose magnitude is unity. We write a unit vector as $\hat{AB}$ i.e.

$$\hat{AB} = \frac{\vec{AB}}{|\vec{AB}|}.$$

The unit vector always represents direction of any vector.

For example $\vec{AB} = |\vec{AB}|\,\hat{AB}$ where $\hat{AB}$ is the unit vector in the direction of vector $\vec{AB}$.

***(v)* Position vector :** If P is any point in the space $\vec{OP}$ is called the position vector of point P where O is the origin of reference.

Addition of two vectors : Let $\vec{OA} = \vec{a}$, $\vec{AB} = \vec{b}$ and $\vec{OB} = \vec{c}$. Here $\vec{c}$ is sum (or resultant) of vector $\vec{a}$ and $\vec{b}$. It is to be noted that the initial point of $\vec{b}$ coincides, with the terminal point of $\vec{a}$ and the line joining the initial point of $\vec{a}$ to the terminal point $\vec{b}$ represent vector $\vec{a} + \vec{b}$ in magnitude direction. The law of addition of vectors is also known as triangle law of addition.

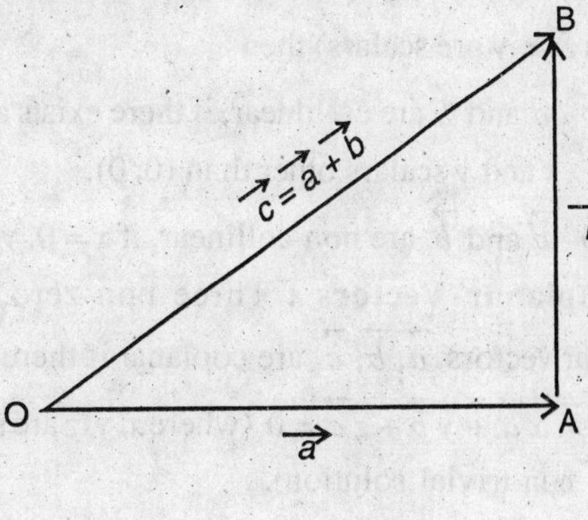

Some Properties of Vectors :

(i) $\vec{a} + \vec{b} = \vec{b} + \vec{a}$ (vector addition is commutative)

(ii) $\vec{a} + \left(\vec{b} + \vec{c}\right) = \left(\vec{a} + \vec{b}\right) + \vec{c}$ (vector addition is associative)

(iii) $\vec{a} + \vec{O} = \vec{O} + \vec{a}$ (Additive identity exist where $\vec{O}$ is null vector)

(iv) If $\vec{a} + \vec{b} = \vec{O}$, then $\vec{b} = -\vec{a}$ is called the additive inverse of $\vec{a}$.

(v) $\left|\vec{a} + \vec{b}\right| \le \left|\vec{a}\right| + \left|\vec{b}\right|$

(vi) $\left|\vec{a} + \vec{b}\right| \ge \left|\vec{a}\right| - \left|\vec{b}\right|$

(vii) $m\left(n\vec{a}\right) = mn\vec{a} = \left(m\vec{a}\right)$ where *m, n* are scalars.

(viii) $(m+n)\vec{a} = m\vec{a} + n\vec{a}$, where, *m, n* are scalars.

(ix) $m\left(\vec{a} + \vec{b}\right) = m\vec{a} + m\vec{b}$ where *m* is scalar.

Collinear Vectors : The vectors are said to be collinear if there exists a relation $\vec{a} = m\vec{b}$, where m is a scalar. Here converse is also true.

If $x\vec{a} + y\vec{b} = 0$ ($\vec{a}$ and $\vec{b}$ are two non-zero vectors & *x, y* are scalars) then

(i) $\vec{a}$ and $\vec{b}$ are collilnear, if there exists a set of *x* and *y* scalars other than (0, 0).

(ii) $\vec{a}$ and $\vec{b}$ are non-collinear, if $x = 0, y = 0$.

Coplanar Vectors : Three non-zero, non-collinear vectors $\vec{a}, \vec{b}, \vec{c}$ are coplanar if there exists a relation $x\vec{a} + y\vec{b} + z\vec{c} = 0$ (where *x, y, z* are scalars having non-trivial solution).

But if $x\vec{a} + y\vec{b} + z\vec{c} = \vec{0}$, then $x = 0, y = 0, z = 0$ if $\vec{a}, \vec{b}, \vec{c}$ are non-coplanar vectors.

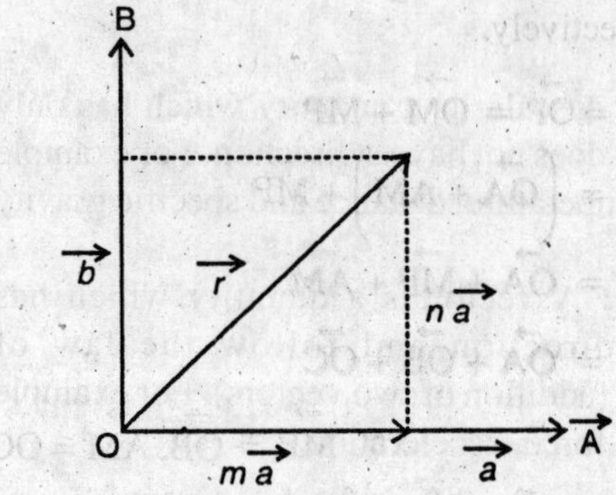

Any vector $\vec{r}$, coplanar with non-collinear vectors $\vec{a}$ and $\vec{b}$, can be expressed as a linear combination of vectors $\vec{a}$ and $\vec{b}$.

i.e. $\vec{r} = m\vec{a} + n\vec{b}$

Any vector $\vec{r}$ in space can be written as a linear combination of three non-zero, non-coplanar vector $\vec{a}, \vec{b}, \vec{c}$

i.e. $\vec{r} = l\vec{a} + m\vec{b} + n\vec{c}$, where *l, m, n* is a set of scalars.

Orthogonal Systm of Unit Vectors : Let OX, OY and OZ be three mutually perpendicular straight lines. Given any point P in space, we can construct the rectangular parallelopipe of which OP is a diagonal.

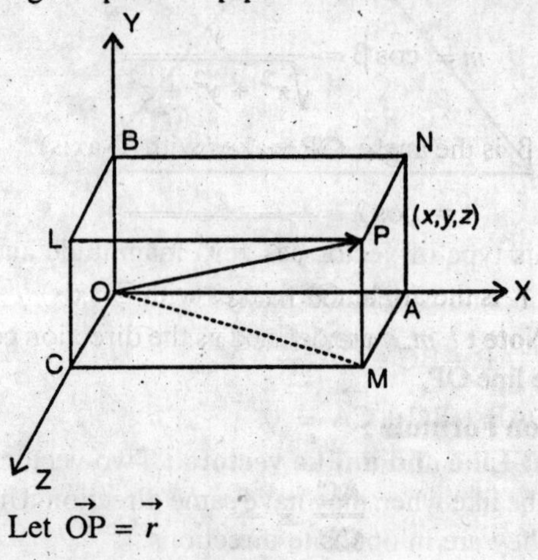

Let $\vec{OP} = \vec{r}$

and $OA = x$, $OB = y$, $OC = z$.

Then A, B, C are $(x, 0, 0)$, $(0, y, 0)$ and $(0, 0, z)$ respectively and L, M, N are $(0, y, z)$, $(x, 0, z)$ and $(x, y, 0)$ respectively.

Let $\hat{i}, \hat{j}, \hat{k}$ denote unit vectors along OX, OY and OZ respectively.

Then $\vec{r} = \vec{OP} = \vec{OM} + \vec{MP}$

$$= \left(\vec{OA} + \vec{AM}\right) + \vec{MP}$$

$$= \vec{OA} + \vec{MP} + \vec{AM}$$

$$= \vec{OA} + \vec{OB} + \vec{OC}$$

$$(\because \vec{MP} = \vec{OB}, \vec{AM} = \vec{OC})$$

$$= x\hat{i} + y\hat{j} + z\hat{k}$$

$$\left(\because \left|\vec{OA}\right| = x, \left|\vec{OB}\right| = y, \left|\vec{OC}\right| = z\right)$$

$$\therefore \quad r = \left|\vec{r}\right| = \left|\vec{OP}\right| = \sqrt{x^2 + y^2 + z^2}$$

$$\therefore \hat{r} = \frac{\vec{r}}{\left|\vec{r}\right|} = \frac{x\hat{i} + y\hat{j} + z\hat{k}}{\sqrt{x^2 + y^2 + z^2}} = l\hat{i} + m\hat{j} + n\hat{k}$$

or $\vec{r} = lr\hat{i} + mr\hat{j} + nr\hat{k}$.

Where $l = \cos\alpha = \dfrac{x}{\sqrt{x^2 + y^2 + z^2}}$

(α is the angle, OP makes with X-axis.)

$$m = \cos\beta = \frac{y}{\sqrt{x^2 + y^2 + z^2}}$$

(β is the angle, OP makes with Y-axis)

$$n = \cos\lambda = \frac{z}{\sqrt{x^2 + y^2 + z^2}}$$

(γ is the angle, OP makes with Z-axis)

Note : l, m, n are defined as the direction cosines of the line OP.

Section Formula :

$$\frac{AC}{CB} = \frac{n}{m}$$

or $\qquad mAC = nCB$

or $\qquad m\vec{AC} = n\vec{CB}$ ...*(i)*

(As vectors are in same direction)

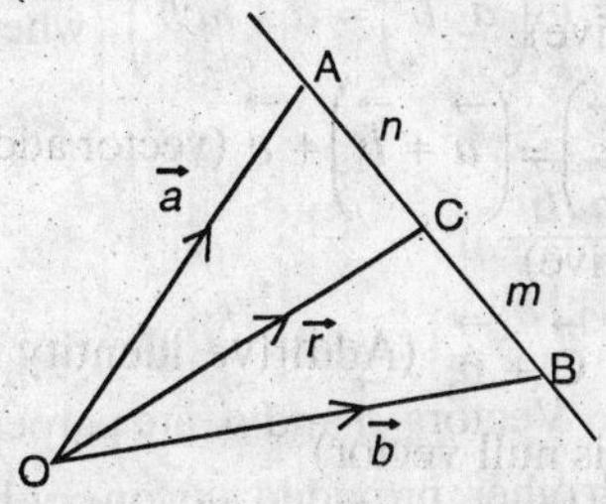

Now, $\quad \vec{OA} + \vec{AC} = \vec{OC}$

$\Rightarrow \quad \vec{AC} = \vec{OC} - \vec{OA}$

$\Rightarrow \quad \vec{AC} = \vec{r} - \vec{a}$ ...*(ii)*

Also $\quad \vec{OC} + \vec{OB} = \vec{OB}$

$\Rightarrow \quad \vec{CB} = \vec{OB} - \vec{OC}$

$\Rightarrow \quad \vec{CB} = \vec{b} - \vec{r}$ ...*(iii)*

From *(i)*, *(ii)* and *(iii)* we get

$$m\left(\vec{r} - \vec{a}\right) = n\left(\vec{b} - \vec{r}\right)$$

or $\qquad \vec{r} = \dfrac{m\vec{a} + n\vec{b}}{m+n}$.

Collinearity of three points : The necessary and sufficient condition for three points with position vectors $\vec{a}, \vec{b}, \vec{c}$ to be collinear is that there exist three scalars x, y, z not all zero, such that $x\vec{a} + y\vec{b} + z\vec{c} = 0$ where $x + y + z = 0$.

Dot Product : A scalar product of two vectors $\vec{a}$ and $\vec{b}$ is defined as $|\vec{a}||\vec{b}|\cos\theta$, where θ is the angle between the two vectors when drawn from a same initial point.

In this the angle θ is restricted to the interval $0 \le \theta \le \pi$.

It is denoted by $\vec{a}.\vec{b}$.

Properties of dot product :

(i) $\vec{a}.\vec{b} = \vec{b}.\vec{a}$ (Product is commutative)

(ii) $\vec{a}^2 = \vec{a}.\vec{a} = |\vec{a}|^2$

(iii) $\left(m\vec{a}\right).\vec{b} = m\left(\vec{a}.\vec{b}\right) = \vec{a}.\left(m\vec{b}\right)$ (where m is scalar)

(iv) $\cos\theta = \dfrac{\vec{a}.\vec{b}}{|\vec{a}|.|\vec{b}|}$

(v) $\vec{a}.\vec{b} = 0 \Rightarrow$ Vectors $\vec{a}$ and $\vec{b}$ are perpendicular to each other, provided any one or both of vector $\vec{a}, \vec{b} \neq 0$.

(vi) $\hat{i}.\hat{j} = \hat{j}.\hat{k} = \hat{k}.\hat{i} = 0$

(vii) $\vec{a}.\left(\vec{b}+\vec{c}\right) = \vec{a}.\vec{b} + \vec{a}.\vec{c}$

(viii) $\left(\vec{a}+\vec{b}\right)\left(\vec{a}-\vec{b}\right) = \left|\vec{a}\right|^2 - \left|\vec{b}\right|^2 = \vec{a}^2 - \vec{b}^2$

(ix) Let $\vec{a} = a_1\hat{i} + a_2\hat{j} + a_3\hat{k}$,

$\vec{b} = b_1\hat{i} + b_2\hat{j} + b_3\hat{k}$.

$\vec{a}.\vec{b} = \left(a_1\hat{i} + a_2\hat{j} + a_3\hat{k}\right).\left(b_1\hat{i} + b_2\hat{j} + b_3\hat{k}\right)$

$= a_1b_1 + a_2b_2 + a_3b_3$.

Projection of a vector along some other vector :

Here $ON = OB\cos\theta = \left|\vec{b}\right|.\dfrac{\vec{a}.\vec{b}}{\left|\vec{a}\right|\left|\vec{b}\right|}$

$\therefore ON = |OB\cos\theta| = \left|\hat{a}.\vec{b}\right|$

= Projection of OB along OA.

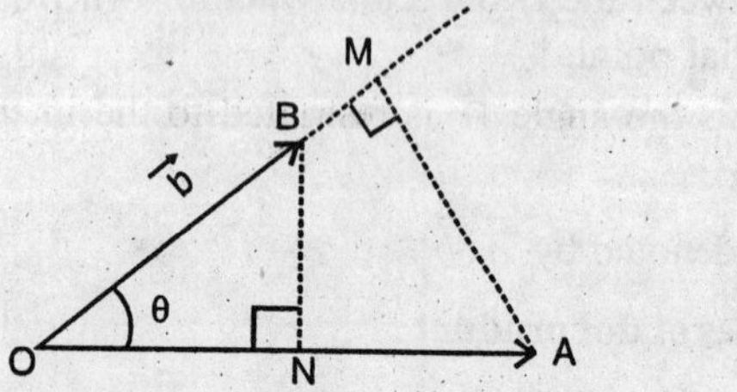

Similarly projection of OA along $OB = \left|\vec{a}.\vec{b}\right|$

Vector (cross) Product : The vector product of two vectors $\vec{a}$ and $\vec{b}$, whose modulus are $|\vec{a}|$ and $|\vec{b}|$ respectively, is the vector whose modulus is $ab\sin\theta$ where $\theta\ (0 < \theta < \pi)$ is the angle between vectors $\vec{a}$ and $\vec{b}$, whose direction is that of a unit vector $\hat{n}$ perpendicular to both $\vec{a}$ and $\vec{b}$ such that $\vec{a}, \vec{b}, \hat{n}$ are in right handed orientation.

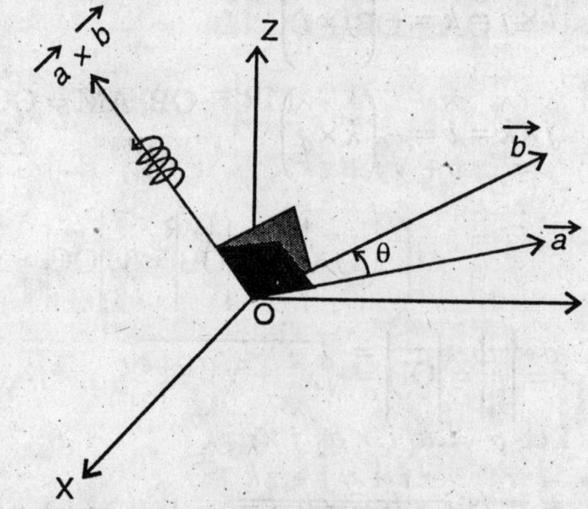

By the right handed orientation we mean that if we turn the vector $\vec{a}$ into the vector $\vec{b}$ through the angle θ, then $\hat{n}$ points in the direction in which a right handed screw would move if turned in the same manner.

$\vec{a}\times\vec{b} = \left|\vec{a}\right|\left|\vec{b}\right|\sin\theta\,\hat{n}$

$\Rightarrow \left|\vec{a}\times\vec{b}\right| = \left|\vec{a}\right|\left|\vec{b}\right|\sin\theta$

$\therefore \vec{a}\times\vec{b} = \vec{0}$ if either $\vec{a} = \vec{0}, \vec{b} = \vec{0}$ or $\vec{a} \parallel \vec{b}$.

Properties of vector (cross) product :

(i) $\vec{a}\times\vec{b} = -\left(\vec{b}\times\vec{a}\right)$

(ii) $\left(m\vec{a}\right)\times\vec{b} = m\left(\vec{a}\times\vec{b}\right) = \vec{a}\times\left(m\vec{b}\right)$

where m is a scalar.

(iii) If two vectors are parallel, we have $\vec{a}\times\vec{b} = 0$.

(iv) $\vec{a} \times \vec{a} = \vec{O}$

(v) $\vec{a} \times \vec{b} = \vec{O} \Rightarrow \vec{a}$ and $\vec{b}$ are parallel vectors (provided $\vec{a}$ and $\vec{b}$ are non-zero vectors)

(vi) $\vec{a} \times \vec{b} = |\vec{a}||\vec{b}|\hat{n}$

(vii) $\hat{i} \times \hat{i} = \hat{j} \times \hat{j} = \hat{k} \times \hat{k} = \vec{O}$

(viii) $\hat{i} \times \hat{j} = \hat{k} = -\left(\hat{j} \times \hat{i}\right)$

(ix) $\hat{j} \times \hat{k} = \hat{i} = -\left(\hat{k} \times \hat{j}\right)$

(x) $\hat{k} \times \hat{i} = \hat{i} = -\left(\hat{i} \times \hat{k}\right)$

(xi) $\vec{a} \times \left(\vec{b} + \vec{c}\right) = \vec{a} \times \vec{b} + \vec{a} \times \vec{c}$

(xii) Let $\vec{a} = a_1 \hat{i} \times a_2 \hat{j} \times a_3 \hat{k}$

$\vec{b} = b_1 \hat{i} \times b_2 \hat{j} \times b_3 \hat{k}$

Then $\vec{a} \times \vec{b} = \begin{vmatrix} \hat{i} & \hat{j} & \hat{k} \\ a_1 & a_2 & a_3 \\ b_1 & b_2 & b_3 \end{vmatrix}$

$= \hat{i}(a_2 b_3 - a_3 b_2) + \hat{j}(a_3 b_1 - a_1 b_3)$

$+ \hat{k}(a_1 b_2 - a_2 b_1)$

(xiii) $\sin\theta = \dfrac{\left|\vec{a} \times \vec{b}\right|}{|\vec{a}||\vec{b}|}$

Note : We can find the value of θ by using cross product.

(xiv) Area of triangle $= \dfrac{1}{2}\left|\vec{a} \times \vec{b}\right|$

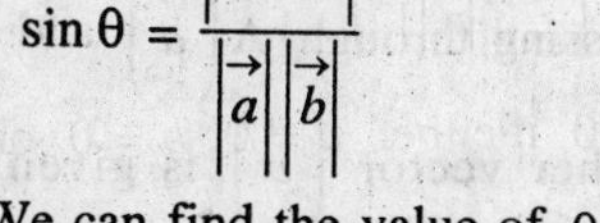

(xv) Area of parallelogram $= \left|\vec{a} \times \vec{b}\right|$

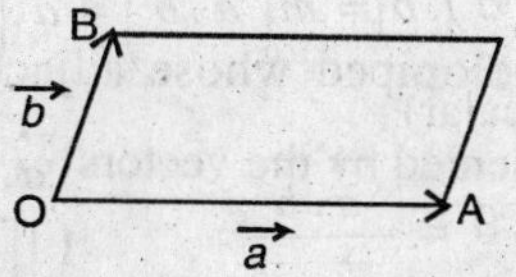

Multiple Product :

I. Scalar triple Product : The scalar product of three vectors $\vec{a}, \vec{b}$ and $\vec{c}$ is defined as $\left(\vec{a} \times \vec{b}\right).\vec{c}$.

We denote it by $\left[\vec{a}\,\vec{b}\,\vec{c}\right]$.

Here we have both cross and dot sign. First we take vector product and get a vector quantity and than its dot is taken with the third vector and get a scalar quantity.

Now $\left(\vec{a} \times \vec{b}\right).\vec{c} = \vec{a}.\left(\vec{b} \times \vec{c}\right) = \vec{c}.\left(\vec{a} \times \vec{b}\right)$

i.e. $\left[\vec{a}\,\vec{b}\,\vec{c}\right] = \left[\vec{b}\,\vec{c}\,\vec{a}\right] = \left[\vec{c}\,\vec{a}\,\vec{b}\right]$

Let $\vec{a} = a_1 \hat{i} + a_2 \hat{j} + a_3 \hat{k}$

$\vec{b} = b_1 \hat{i} + b_2 \hat{j} + b_3 \hat{k}$

$\vec{c} = c_1 \hat{i} + c_2 \hat{j} + c_3 \hat{k}$.

Here $\vec{a} \times \vec{b} = \begin{vmatrix} \hat{i} & \hat{j} & \hat{k} \\ a_1 & a_2 & a_3 \\ b_1 & b_2 & b_3 \end{vmatrix}$

$= \hat{i}\begin{vmatrix} a_2 & a_3 \\ b_2 & b_3 \end{vmatrix} - \hat{j}\begin{vmatrix} a_1 & a_3 \\ b_1 & b_3 \end{vmatrix} + \hat{k}\begin{vmatrix} a_1 & a_2 \\ b_1 & b_2 \end{vmatrix}$

$\therefore \left(\vec{a} \times \vec{b}\right).\vec{c}$

$= c_1\begin{vmatrix} a_2 & a_3 \\ b_2 & b_3 \end{vmatrix} - c_2\begin{vmatrix} a_1 & a_3 \\ b_1 & b_3 \end{vmatrix} + c_3\begin{vmatrix} a_1 & a_2 \\ b_1 & b_2 \end{vmatrix}$

$= \begin{vmatrix} c_1 & c_2 & c_3 \\ a_1 & a_2 & a_3 \\ b_1 & b_2 & b_3 \end{vmatrix}$

Properties :

(i) $\left|\left(\vec{a}\times\vec{b}\right).\vec{c}\right|$ represents the volume of the parallelopiped whose adjacent sides are represented by the vectors $\vec{a}, \vec{b}$ and $\vec{c}$.

(ii) Volume of tetrahedron $= \frac{1}{6}\left|\left[\vec{a}\ \vec{b}\ \vec{c}\right]\right|$

(iii) $\left[\vec{a}+\vec{b}\ \vec{c}\ \vec{d}\right] = \left[\vec{a}\ \vec{c}\ \vec{d}\right] + \left[\vec{b}\ \vec{c}\ \vec{d}\right]$

(iv) $\left[\vec{a}\ \vec{a}\ \vec{d}\right] = 0$

(v) $\left[\vec{a}\ \vec{b}\ \vec{c}\right] = 0 \Rightarrow \vec{a}, \vec{b}, \vec{c}$ are coplanar.

($\vec{a}, \vec{b}, \vec{c}$ are non-zero vectors)

II. Vector triple product :

$$\vec{a}\times\left(\vec{b}\times\vec{c}\right) = \left(\vec{a}.\vec{c}\right)\vec{b} - \left(\vec{a}.\vec{b}\right).\vec{c}$$

$$= \begin{vmatrix} \vec{b} & \vec{c} \\ \vec{a}.\vec{b} & \vec{a}.\vec{c} \end{vmatrix}$$

$$\left(\vec{a}\times\vec{b}\right)\times\vec{c} = \left(\vec{a}.\vec{c}\right)\vec{b} - \left(\vec{b}.\vec{c}\right).\vec{a}$$

$$= \begin{vmatrix} \vec{b} & \vec{a} \\ \vec{c}.\vec{b} & \vec{c}.\vec{a} \end{vmatrix}$$

III. Double scalar product :

$$\left(\vec{a}\times\vec{b}\right).\left(\vec{c}\times\vec{d}\right) = \begin{vmatrix} \vec{a}.\vec{c} & \vec{b}.\vec{c} \\ \vec{a}.\vec{d} & \vec{b}.\vec{d} \end{vmatrix}$$

$$\left(\vec{a}\times\vec{b}\right)^2 = \begin{vmatrix} a^2 & \vec{a}.\vec{b} \\ \vec{a}.\vec{b} & b^2 \end{vmatrix}$$

IV. Double vector product :

$$\left(\vec{a}\times\vec{b}\right)\times\left(\vec{c}\times\vec{d}\right) = -\vec{a}\left[\vec{b}\ \vec{c}\ \vec{d}\right] + \vec{b}\left[\vec{c}\ \vec{d}\ \vec{a}\right]$$

$$= \vec{c}\left[\vec{d}\ \vec{a}\ \vec{b}\right] - \vec{d}\left[\vec{a}\ \vec{b}\ \vec{c}\right]$$

V. Products of orthogonal vectors :

If $\vec{a}\times\left(\vec{b}\times\vec{c}\right) = \vec{b}\times\left(\vec{c}\times\vec{a}\right) = \vec{c}\times\left(\vec{a}\times\vec{b}\right)$

then $\vec{a}, \vec{b}, \vec{c}$ are orthogonal.

Geometrical Applications :

(i) Bisectors of two vectors :

$$\vec{r} = \lambda\left[\frac{\vec{a}}{|\vec{a}|} + \frac{\vec{b}}{|\vec{b}|}\right]$$

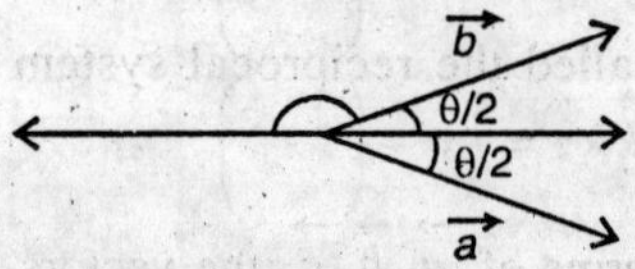

(ii) Equation of a line :

(a) $\vec{a}$ and $\vec{b}$ are position vectors of A and B. Then equation of line passing through A and B is $\vec{r} = \vec{a} + \lambda\left(\vec{b} - \vec{a}\right)$, where λ is a parameter.

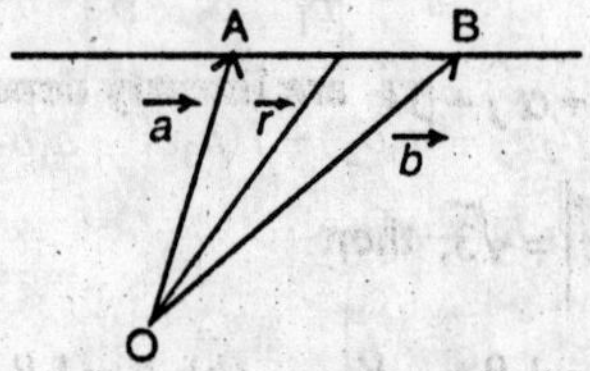

(b) Line passing through A $\left(\vec{a}\right)$ and parallel to another vector $\left(\vec{b}\right)$ is given by the equation

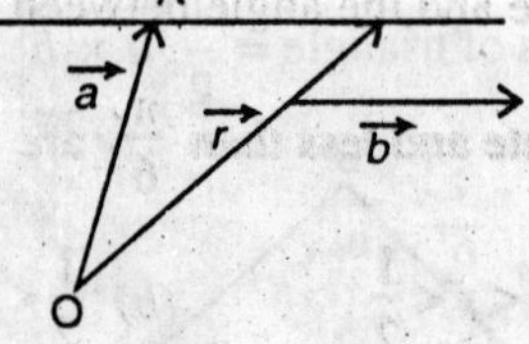

$\vec{r} = \vec{b} + \lambda\left(\vec{b}\right)$, where λ is a parameter.

(iii) *Equation of a plane :* The equation of a plane through the point $\vec{a}, \vec{b}$ and $\vec{c}$ is

$\vec{r} = (1-n-m)\vec{a} + n\vec{b} + m\vec{c}$, where n and m are two parameters.

Reciprocal Vectors : Let $\vec{a}, \vec{b}$ and $\vec{c}$ be a system of three non-coplanar vectors. Then the system of vectors $\vec{a}', \vec{b}'$ and $\vec{c}'$ which satisfies

$$\vec{a}.\vec{a}' + \vec{b}.\vec{b}' + \vec{c}.\vec{c}' = 1$$

and $\vec{a}.\vec{b}' = \vec{a}.\vec{c}' = \vec{b}.\vec{a}' = \vec{b}.\vec{c}' = \vec{c}.\vec{b}' = 0$,

is called the reciprocal system to the vectors $\vec{a}, \vec{b}, \vec{c}$.

If terms of $\vec{a}, \vec{b}, \vec{c}$ the vectors $\vec{a}', \vec{b}', \vec{c}'$ are given by

$$\vec{a}' = \frac{\vec{b} \times \vec{c}}{[\vec{a}\,\vec{b}\,\vec{c}]}, \quad \vec{b}' = \frac{\vec{c} \times \vec{a}}{[\vec{a}\,\vec{b}\,\vec{c}]}, \quad \vec{c}' = \frac{\vec{a} \times \vec{b}}{[\vec{a}\,\vec{b}\,\vec{c}]}.$$

Linear independence and dependence of vectors :

I. Linearly Independent Vector : A set of non-zero vectors $\vec{a}_1, \vec{a}_2, \ldots, \vec{a}_n$ is said to be linearly independent, if

$$x_1\vec{a}_1 + x_2\vec{a}_2 + \ldots + x_n\vec{a}_n = 0$$
$$\Rightarrow x_1 = x_2 = \ldots = x_n = 0$$

II. Linearly Dependent Vector : A set of vectors $\vec{a}_1, \vec{a}_2, \ldots, \vec{a}_n$ is said to be linearly dependent if there exist scalars $x_1, x_2, \ldots, x_n$ not all zero such that

$$x_1\vec{a}_1 + x_2\vec{a}_2 + \ldots + x_n\vec{a}_n = 0$$

It thus says that a set of vectors is linearly dependent iff one of them is expressible as a linear combination of others.

EXERCISE

Mark the correct alternatives of each of the following:

1. If $\vec{a} = \hat{i} + \hat{j} + \hat{k}$, $\vec{b} = 4\hat{i} + 3\hat{j} + 4\hat{k}$ and $\vec{c} = \hat{i} + \alpha\hat{j} + \beta\hat{k}$ are linearly dependent vectors and $|\vec{c}| = \sqrt{3}$, then

(a) $\alpha = 1, \beta = -1$ (b) $\alpha = 1, \beta = \pm 1$
(c) $\alpha = -1, \beta = \pm 1$ (d) $\alpha = \pm 1, \beta = 1$

2. The value of x for which the angle between $\vec{a} = 2x^2\hat{i} + 4x\hat{j} + \hat{k}$ and $\vec{b} = 7\hat{i} - 2\hat{j} + x\hat{k}$ is obtuse and the angle between $\vec{b}$ and the z-axis is acute and less than $\frac{\pi}{6}$, are

(a) $a < x < \frac{1}{2}$ (b) $\frac{1}{2} < x < 51$
(c) $x > \frac{1}{2}$ or $x < 0$ (d) None of these

3. The vectors $\vec{a}, \vec{b}$ and $\vec{c}$ are of same length and taken pairwise, they form equal angles. If $\vec{a} = \hat{i} + \hat{j}$ and $\vec{b} = \hat{j} + \hat{k}$ then $\vec{c}$ is equal to

(a) $\hat{i} + \hat{k}$ (b) $\hat{i} + 2\hat{j} + 3\hat{k}$
(c) $-\hat{i} + \hat{j} + 2\hat{k}$ (d) $\frac{1}{3}\left(-\hat{i} + 4\hat{j} - \hat{k}\right)$

4. A vector of magnitude 3 and perpendicular to $\left(\hat{i} - 2\hat{j} + \hat{k}\right)$ and $\left(2\hat{i} + \hat{j} - 3\hat{k}\right)$ is

(a) $\frac{2\sqrt{3}}{3}\left(\hat{i} + \hat{j} - \hat{k}\right)$ (b) $\sqrt{3}\left(\hat{i} + \hat{j} + \hat{k}\right)$
(c) $\frac{2\sqrt{3}}{3}\left(\hat{i} - \hat{j} + \hat{k}\right)$ (d) $\sqrt{3}\left(-\hat{i} + \hat{j} + \hat{k}\right)$

5. If $\vec{a}, \vec{b}$, are three coplanar vectors such that $\vec{a} = p\hat{i} + \sin\theta\,\hat{j} + \hat{k}$, $\vec{b} = 2\hat{i} + p\hat{j} + \hat{k}$, $\vec{c} = \hat{i} + \hat{j} + \hat{k}$, then all possible values of scalars p and θ are

(a) $\theta = 2n\pi + \frac{\pi}{2}, p = \frac{1}{2}$

(b) $\theta = 2n\pi, p = 1$

(c) $\theta = 2n\pi + \frac{\pi}{2}, p = 0$

(d) None of these

6. The unit vector parallel to $\vec{a} = 3\hat{i} + 4\hat{j} - 2\hat{k}$ is

(a) $\sqrt{29}\left(3\hat{i} + 4\hat{j} - 2\hat{k}\right)$

(b) $\frac{1}{\sqrt{29}}\left(3\hat{i} + 4\hat{j} - 2\hat{k}\right)$

(c) $29\left(3\hat{i} + 4\hat{j} - 2\hat{k}\right)$

(d) $\frac{1}{29}\left(3\hat{i} + 4\hat{j} - 2\hat{k}\right)$

[J.N.U. M.C.A.]

7. If $\left|\vec{a} + \vec{b}\right| = \left|\vec{a} - \vec{b}\right|$ and $\vec{a} \neq 0, \vec{b} \neq 0$, then

(a) $\vec{a} \parallel \vec{b}$ (b) $\vec{a} \perp \vec{b}$

(c) $\left|\vec{a}\right| = \left|\vec{b}\right|$ (d) None of these

8. The number of vectors of unit length perpendicular of vectors $\vec{a} = (1, 1, 0)$ and $\vec{b} = (0, 1, 1)$ is

(a) None (b) One

(c) Two (d) Infinite

9. The vector $\vec{c}$, directed along the internal bisector of the angle between the vectors $\vec{a} = 7\hat{i} - 4\hat{j} - 4\hat{k}$ and $\vec{b} = -2\hat{i} - \hat{j} + 2\hat{k}$ with $\left|\vec{c}\right| = 5\sqrt{6}$ is,

(a) $\frac{5}{3}\left(\hat{i} - 7\hat{j} + 2\hat{k}\right)$ (b) $\frac{5}{3}\left(5\hat{i} + 5\hat{j} + 2\hat{k}\right)$

(c) $\frac{5}{3}\left(\hat{i} + 7\hat{j} + 2\hat{k}\right)$ (d) $\frac{5}{3}\left(-5\hat{i} + 5\hat{j} + 2\hat{k}\right)$

10. The point with position vectors $60\hat{i} + 3\hat{j}$, $40\hat{i} - 8\hat{j}$ and $a\hat{i} - 52\hat{j}$ are collinear, if

(a) $a = -40$ (b) $a = 40$

(c) $a = 20$ (d) None of these

[D.U. M.C.A.]

11. Given two vectors $\hat{i} - \hat{j}$ and $+\hat{i} + 2\hat{j}$, the unit vector coplanar with the two vectors and perpendicular to first is

(a) $\frac{1}{\sqrt{2}}\left(\hat{i} + \hat{j}\right)$ (b) $\frac{1}{\sqrt{5}}\left(2\hat{i} + \hat{j}\right)$

(c) $\frac{1}{\sqrt{2}}\left(\hat{i} + \hat{k}\right)$ (d) None of these

12. If $\vec{a}, \vec{b}, \vec{c}$ are non-coplanar unit vectors such that

$$\vec{a} \times \left(\vec{b} \times \vec{c}\right) = \frac{\left(\vec{b} + \vec{c}\right)}{\sqrt{2}}$$

where b and c are non-parallel, then the angle between $\vec{a}$ and $\vec{b}$ is

(a) $\frac{\pi}{4}$ (b) $\frac{3\pi}{4}$

(c) $\frac{\pi}{2}$ (d) None of these

[D.U. M.C.A.]

13. The unit vectors $\vec{a}$ and $\vec{b}$ are pendicular and the unit vector $\vec{c}$ is inclind at an angle θ to both $\vec{a}$ and $\vec{b}$. If $\vec{c} = \alpha\vec{a} + \beta\vec{b} + \gamma\left(\vec{a} \times \vec{b}\right)$, then

(a) $\alpha = \beta$ (b) $\gamma^2 = 1 - 2\alpha^2$

(c) $\gamma^2 = -\cos 2\theta$ (d) All of them

14. If $\vec{e_1}, \vec{e_2}$ are two unit vectors and θ is the angle between them, then $\cos\frac{\theta}{2}$ is

(a) $\frac{1}{2}\left|\vec{e_1} + \vec{e_2}\right|$ (b) $\frac{1}{2}\left|\vec{e_1} - \vec{e_2}\right|$

(c) $\frac{\left|\vec{e_1}\vec{e_2}\right|}{2}$ (d) $\frac{1}{2}\frac{\left|\vec{e_1}+\vec{e_2}\right|}{2\left|\vec{e_1}\right|\left|\vec{e_2}\right|}$

15. If $\vec{e_1}, \vec{e_2}$ are two unit vectors and θ is the angle between them, then $\left|\frac{\vec{e_1}-\vec{e_2}}{2}\right|$ is

(a) $\sin\frac{\theta}{2}$ (b) $\sin\theta$
(c) $2\sin\theta$ (d) $\sin 2\theta$

16. If the vectors $\vec{r_1} = a\hat{i}+\hat{j}+\hat{k}$, $\vec{r_2} = \hat{i}+b\hat{j}+\hat{k}$, $\vec{r_3} = \hat{i}+\hat{j}+c\hat{k}$ $(a\neq 1, b\neq 1, c\neq 1)$ are coplanar, then the value of $\frac{1}{1-a}+\frac{1}{1-b}+\frac{1}{1-c}$ is

(a) -1 (b) 0
(c) 1 (d) None of these

17. If the vectors $\vec{a} = \hat{i}+a\hat{j}+a^2\hat{k}$, $\vec{b} = \hat{i}+b\hat{j}+b^2\hat{k}$, $\vec{c} = \hat{i}+c\hat{j}+c^2\hat{k}$ are three non-coplanar vectors and

$\begin{vmatrix} a & a^2 & 1+a^3 \\ b & b^2 & 1+b^3 \\ c & c^2 & 1+c^3 \end{vmatrix} = 0$, then the value of abc is

(a) 0 (b) 1 (c) 2 (d) -1

18. The triangle ABC whose vertices A, B and C are $7\hat{j}+10\hat{k}$, $-\hat{i}+6\hat{j}+\hat{k}$, $-4\hat{i}+9\hat{j}+6\hat{k}$ is

(a) Isosceles triangle
(b) Right angled triangle
(c) Isoceles right angle triangle
(d) None of these

[D.U. M.C.A]

19. A unit vector coplanar with $\hat{i}+\hat{j}+2\hat{k}$ and $\hat{i}+2\hat{j}+\hat{k}$ and perpendicular to $\hat{i}+\hat{j}+\hat{k}$ is

(a) $\pm\frac{1}{2}\left(\hat{j}+\hat{k}\right)$ (b) $\pm\frac{1}{\sqrt{2}}\left(\hat{j}+\hat{k}\right)$

(c) $\pm\frac{1}{\sqrt{2}}\left(\hat{j}-\hat{k}\right)$ (d) None of these

20. The position vectors of the points P and Q are $5\hat{i}+7\hat{j}-2\hat{k}$ and $-3\hat{i}+3\hat{j}+6\hat{k}$ respectively. The vector $\vec{A} = 3\hat{i}-\hat{j}+\hat{k}$ passes through the point P and the vector $\vec{B} = -3\hat{i}+3\hat{j}+4\hat{k}$, passes through the point Q. A third vector $2\hat{i}+7\hat{j}-4\hat{k}$ intersects vectors $\vec{A}$ and $\vec{B}$. Then the position vector of the points of intersection are

(a) $\hat{i}+\hat{j}+2\hat{k}, 2\hat{i}+8\hat{j}-3\hat{k}$
(b) $\hat{j}+2\hat{k}, 2\hat{i}+8\hat{j}-3\hat{k}$
(c) $\hat{i}+2\hat{k}, 2\hat{i}-3\hat{k}$
(d) $\hat{i}+\hat{j}, 2\hat{i}-3\hat{k}$

21. The volume of the paralleopiped whose edges are represented by $\vec{a} = 2\hat{i}-3\hat{j}+4\hat{k}$, $\vec{b} = \hat{i}+2\hat{j}-\hat{k}$, $\vec{c} = 3\hat{i}-\hat{j}+2\hat{k}$ is

(a) 6 (b) 7 (c) 8 (d) 9

22. If $\left|\vec{a}\right| = 2, \left|\vec{b}\right| = 5$ and $\left|\vec{a}\times\vec{b}\right| = 8$, then $\vec{a}.\vec{b}$ is equal to

(a) 2 (b) 4 (c) 6 (d) 8

23. If $\vec{a}, \vec{b}$ and $\vec{c}$ be three vectors such that $\vec{a}+\vec{b}+\vec{c} = 0$, $\left|\vec{a}\right| = 3$, $\left|\vec{b}\right| = 5$ and $\left|\vec{c}\right| = 7$. Then the angle between $\vec{a}$ and $\vec{b}$ is

(a) 15° (b) $\cos^{-1}\left(\frac{2}{3}\right)$
(c) 30° (d) 60°

24. If $\vec{r}$ satisfies the equation $\vec{r}\times\left(\hat{i}+2\hat{j}+\hat{k}\right) = \hat{i}+\hat{k}$, then for any scalar t, r is equal to

(a) $\hat{i}+t\left(\hat{i}+2\hat{j}+\hat{k}\right)$ (b) $\hat{j}+t\left(\hat{i}+2\hat{j}+\hat{k}\right)$

(c) $\hat{k}+t\left(\hat{i}+2\hat{j}+\hat{k}\right)$ (d) $\hat{i}-\hat{k}+t\left(\hat{i}+2\hat{j}+\hat{k}\right)$

25. The vectors $\vec{AB}=3\hat{i}-2\hat{j}+2\hat{k}$ and $\vec{BC}=-\hat{i}-2\hat{k}$ are the adjacent sides of a parallelogram. The angle between its diagonals is

(a) $\frac{\pi}{4}$ (b) $\frac{\pi}{3}$ (c) $\frac{3\pi}{4}$ (d) $\frac{2\pi}{3}$

26. The vectors $(x, x+1, x+2)$, $(x+3, x+4, x+5)$ and $(x+6, x+7, x+8)$ are coplanar for

(a) all values of x (b) $x<0$
(c) $x>0$ (d) None of these

27. If $\vec{a}$ and $\vec{b}$ are non-collinear vectors and if

$$\begin{vmatrix} l_1 & l_2 & l_3 \\ m_1 & m_2 & m_3 \\ 1 & 1 & 1 \end{vmatrix} = 0$$

Then the points $l_1\vec{a}+m_1\vec{b}$, $l_2\vec{a}+m_2\vec{b}$ and $l_3\vec{a}+m_3\vec{b}$ are

(a) Congruent (b) Coplanar
(c) Collinear (d) None of these

[J.N.U. M.C.A.]

28. $A_1, A_2, ..., A_n$ are the vertices of regular polygon of n sides and O is its centre. Then

$$\sum_{i=1}^{n-1}\left(\vec{OA_i}\times\vec{OA}_{i-1}\right) = K\left(\vec{OA_2}\times\vec{OA_1}\right)$$

where K is equal to

(a) n (b) $-n$ (c) $n-1$ (d) $1-n$

29. The vector $\hat{i}+\hat{j}-\hat{k}$ bisects the angle between the vectors $\vec{e}$ and $3\hat{i}+4\hat{j}$, the unit vector along $\vec{e}$ is

(a) $\frac{1}{15}\left(11\hat{i}+10\hat{j}+2\hat{k}\right)$

(b) $\frac{15}{2}\left(-11\hat{i}+10\hat{j}-2\hat{k}\right)$

(c) $\frac{1}{15}\left(-11\hat{i}+10\hat{j}-2\hat{k}\right)$

(d) None of these

[J.N.U. M.C.A.]

30. Let $\vec{a}=2\hat{i}-3\hat{j}-6\hat{k}$ and $\vec{b}=-2\hat{i}-2\hat{j}-\hat{k}$. Then the value of

$$\left[\frac{\text{The projection of } \vec{a} \text{ on } \vec{b}}{\text{The projection of } \vec{b} \text{ on } \vec{a}}\right] \text{ is equal to}$$

(a) $\frac{3}{7}$ (b) $\frac{7}{3}$ (c) 7 (d) 3

[J.N.U. M.C.A.]

31. The unit vector in ZOX plane and making angles 45° and 60° respectively with $\vec{a}=2\hat{i}+2\hat{j}-\hat{k}$ and $\vec{b}=0\hat{i}+\hat{j}-\hat{k}$ is

(a) $-\frac{1}{\sqrt{2}}\hat{i}+\frac{1}{\sqrt{2}}\hat{k}$

(b) $\frac{1}{\sqrt{2}}\hat{i}-\frac{1}{\sqrt{2}}\hat{k}$

(c) $\frac{1}{3\sqrt{2}}\hat{i}+\frac{4}{3\sqrt{2}}\hat{j}+\frac{1}{3\sqrt{2}}\hat{k}$

(d) None of these

32. Let $\vec{a}=2\hat{i}+\hat{j}+\hat{k}$, $\vec{b}=\hat{i}+2\hat{j}+\hat{k}$ and $\vec{c}=2\hat{i}-3\hat{j}+4\hat{k}$. A vector $\vec{r}$ satisfying $\vec{r}\times\vec{b}=\vec{c}\times\vec{b}$ and $\vec{r}.\vec{a}=0$ is

(a) $-2\hat{i}+2\hat{j}+2\hat{k}$ (b) $-2\hat{i}+\hat{j}+3\hat{k}$
(c) $-3\hat{i}+2\hat{j}+4\hat{k}$ (d) $\hat{i}-5\hat{j}+3\hat{k}$

33. Let the unit vectors $\vec{a}$ and $\vec{b}$ be perpendicular to each other and the unit vector $\vec{c}$ be inclined at an angle θ to both $\vec{a}$ and $\vec{b}$. If $\vec{c}=x\vec{a}+y\vec{b}+z\left(\vec{a}\times\vec{b}\right)$, then

(a) $x=\cos\theta, y=\sin\theta, z=\cos 2\theta$
(b) $x=\sin\theta, y=\cos\theta, z=-\cos 2\theta$
(c) $x=y=\cos\theta, z^2=\cos 2\theta$
(d) $x=y=\cos\theta, z^2=-\cos 2\theta$

34. If $\vec{a}, \vec{b}, \vec{c}$ are linearly independent vectors and

$$\Delta = \begin{vmatrix} \vec{a} & \vec{b} & \vec{c} \\ \vec{a}.\vec{a} & \vec{a}.\vec{b} & \vec{a}.\vec{c} \\ \vec{a}.\vec{c} & \vec{b}.\vec{c} & \vec{c}.\vec{c} \end{vmatrix}, \text{ then}$$

(a) $\Delta = 0$
(b) $\Delta = 1$
(c) $\Delta =$ any non-zero value
(d) None of these

35. The value of $\left[\vec{a}-\vec{b}, \vec{b}-\vec{c}, \vec{c}-\vec{a}\right]$ where $\left|\vec{a}\right| = 1, \left|\vec{b}\right| = 2, \left|\vec{c}\right| = 3$ is

(a) 0 (b) 1
(c) 6 (d) None of these

36. If $\left|\vec{a}\right| = 1, \left|\vec{b}\right| = 2$ and $\left|\vec{c}\right| = 3$ such that each is perpendicular to the sum of the other two, then $\left|\vec{a}+\vec{b}+\vec{c}\right| = ?$

(a) $\sqrt{6}$ (b) $\sqrt{14}$ (c) $\frac{\sqrt{7}}{2}$ (d) $2\sqrt{7}$

37. If the position vectors of three consecutive vertices of a parallelogram are $\hat{i}+\hat{j}+\hat{k}$, $\hat{i}+3\hat{j}+5\hat{k}$ and $7\hat{i}+9\hat{j}+11\hat{k}$, then the position vector of the fourth vertex is

(a) $\left(2\hat{i}-5\hat{k}\right)$ (b) $4\hat{i}+5\hat{j}+6\hat{k}$
(c) $7\left(\hat{i}+\hat{j}+\hat{k}\right)$ (d) $3\hat{i}-4\hat{j}$

38. If $\vec{a}, \vec{b}, \vec{c}$ are three non-coplanar vectors, then $\left[\vec{a}\times\vec{b}, \vec{b}\times\vec{c}, \vec{c}\times\vec{a}\right]$ is equal to

(a) 0 (b) $\left[\vec{a}\,\vec{b}\,\vec{c}\right]$
(c) $\left[\vec{a}\;\vec{b}\;\vec{c}\right]^2$ (d) $2\left[\vec{a}\;\vec{b}\;\vec{c}\right]$

39. The three vector $\hat{i}+\hat{j}$, $\hat{j}+\hat{k}$, $\hat{k}+\hat{i}$ taken two at a time form three planes. The three unit vectors drawn perpendicular to three planes form a paralleopiped of volume.

(a) $\frac{1}{3\sqrt{3}}$ cubic units (b) 3 cubic units
(c) $4\sqrt{3}$ cubic units (d) $\frac{4}{3\sqrt{3}}$ cubic units

40. Let $\vec{a} = 2\hat{i}+\hat{j}-2\hat{k}$ and $\vec{b} = \hat{i}+\hat{j}$. If $\vec{c}$ is a vector such that $\vec{a}.\vec{c} = \left|\vec{c}\right|$, $\left|\vec{c}-\vec{a}\right| = 2\sqrt{2}$ and the angle between $\vec{a}\times\vec{b}$ and $\vec{c}$ is 30°, such that $\left|\left(\vec{a}\times\vec{b}\right)\times\vec{c}\right| =$.

(a) $\frac{2}{3}$ (b) $\frac{3}{2}$ (c) 2 (d) 3

ANSWERS

1	2	3	4	5	6	7	8	9	10
(d)	(d)	(a), (d)	(b)	(d)	(b)	(b)	(c)	(a)	(a)
11	**12**	**13**	**14**	**15**	**16**	**17**	**18**	**19**	**20**
(b)	(b)	(d)	(a)	(a)	(c)	(d)	(d)	(c)	(b)
21	**22**	**23**	**24**	**25**	**26**	**27**	**28**	**29**	**30**
(b)	(c)	(d)	(b)	(a),(c)	(a), (b),(c)	(b)	(c)	(c)	(b)
31	**32**	**33**	**34**	**35**	**36**	**37**	**38**	**39**	**40**
(b)	(d)	(d)	(c)	(a)	(b)	(c)	(c)	(d)	(b)

SOME SELECTED EXPLANATORY ANSWERS

1. As $\vec{a}, \vec{b}, \vec{c}$ are linearly dependent vectors, then

$$\left[\vec{a}\,\vec{b}\,\vec{c}\right] = 0$$

$$\Rightarrow \begin{vmatrix} 1 & 1 & 1 \\ 4 & 3 & 4 \\ 1 & \alpha & \beta \end{vmatrix} = 0 \Rightarrow -\beta+1=0 \Rightarrow \beta=1.$$

Now $\left|\vec{c}\right| = \sqrt{3} \Rightarrow \sqrt{1+\alpha^2+\beta^2} = \sqrt{3}$

$\Rightarrow \quad 1+1+\alpha^2 = \sqrt{3}$

$\Rightarrow \quad \alpha^2 = 1$

$\Rightarrow \quad \alpha = \pm 1.$

2. Given that the angle between $\vec{a}$ and $\vec{b}$ is obtuse

$\therefore \quad \vec{a}.\vec{b} < 0$

$\Rightarrow 14x^2 - 8x + x < 0$

$\Rightarrow \quad 7x(2x-1) < 0$

$\Rightarrow \quad 0 < x < \frac{1}{2}$ ...(i)

The angle between $\vec{b}$ and z-axis is acute and less than $\frac{\pi}{6}$.

$$\therefore \quad \frac{\vec{b}.\hat{k}}{\left|\vec{b}\right|\left|\hat{k}\right|} > \cos\frac{\pi}{6}$$

$$\left\{ \begin{array}{l} \because \theta < \frac{\pi}{6} \Rightarrow \cos\theta > \cos\frac{\pi}{6} \\ \Rightarrow \frac{\vec{b}.\hat{k}}{\left|\vec{b}\right|\left|\hat{k}\right|} > \cos\frac{\pi}{6} \end{array} \right.$$

$\Rightarrow \quad \frac{x}{\sqrt{x^2+53}} > \frac{\sqrt{3}}{2}$

$\Rightarrow \quad 4x^2 > 3x^2 + 159$

$\Rightarrow \quad x^2 > 159$

$\Rightarrow x > \sqrt{159}$ or $x < -\sqrt{159}$ ...(ii)

(i) and *(ii)* do not satisfy together.

3. Let $\vec{c} = x\hat{i} + y\hat{j} + z\hat{k}$.

Given $\left|\vec{a}\right| = \left|\vec{b}\right| = \sqrt{2}$

$\therefore \quad \left|\vec{c}\right| = \sqrt{x^2+y^2+z^2} = \sqrt{2}$

$\Rightarrow \quad x^2+y^2+z^2 = 2$ ...(i)

Given that the angles between the vectors taken in pairs are equal, say θ.

$$\therefore \quad \cos\theta = \frac{\vec{a}.\vec{b}}{\left|\vec{a}\right|\left|\vec{b}\right|} = \frac{0+1+0}{\sqrt{2}\sqrt{2}} = \frac{1}{2}$$

$$\Rightarrow \quad \frac{\vec{a}.\vec{c}}{\left|\vec{a}\right|\left|\vec{c}\right|} = \frac{1}{2} \text{ and } \frac{\vec{b}.\vec{c}}{\left|\vec{b}\right|\left|\vec{c}\right|} = \frac{1}{2}$$

$$\Rightarrow \quad \frac{x+y}{\sqrt{2}.\sqrt{2}} = \frac{1}{2} \text{ and } \frac{y+z}{\sqrt{2}.\sqrt{2}} = \frac{1}{2}$$

$\Rightarrow \quad x+y=1$ and $y+z=1$

$\Rightarrow y = 1-x$ and $z = 1-y = 1-(1-x) = x$

$\therefore \quad x^2+y^2+z^2 = 2$

$\Rightarrow \quad x^2+(1-x)^2+x^2 = 2$

$\Rightarrow \quad (3x+1)(x-1) = 0$

$\Rightarrow x = 1, -\frac{1}{3}.$

For $x = 1$ — For $x = -\frac{1}{3}$

$y = 1-x = 0$ — $y = 1-x = -\frac{4}{3}$

Hence

$\vec{c} = \hat{i} + 0\hat{j} + \hat{k}$ and $\vec{c} = -\frac{1}{3}\hat{i} + \frac{4}{3}\hat{j} - \frac{1}{3}\hat{k}.$

4. Let $\vec{a} = \left(\hat{i} - 2\hat{j} + \hat{k}\right)$ and $\vec{b} = 2\hat{i} + \hat{j} - 3\hat{k}$.

$$\text{Then} \quad \vec{a}\times\vec{b} = \begin{vmatrix} \hat{i} & \hat{j} & \hat{k} \\ 1 & -2 & 1 \\ 2 & 1 & -3 \end{vmatrix} = 5\left(\hat{i}+\hat{j}+\hat{k}\right)$$

$$\therefore \quad \left|\vec{a} \times \vec{b}\right| = \sqrt{5^2+5^2+5^2} = 5\sqrt{3}$$

Unit vector along $\left(\vec{a} \times \vec{b}\right) = \dfrac{5\left(\hat{i}+\hat{j}+\hat{k}\right)}{5\sqrt{3}}$

$$= \frac{\sqrt{3}}{3}\left(\hat{i}+\hat{j}+\hat{k}\right)$$

$\therefore$ Required vector $= \dfrac{3\sqrt{3}}{3}\left(\hat{i}+\hat{j}+\hat{k}\right)$

$$= \sqrt{3}\left(\hat{i}+\hat{j}+\hat{k}\right).$$

5. As $\vec{a}, \vec{b}, \vec{c}$ are coplanar so

$$\begin{vmatrix} p & \sin\theta & 1 \\ 2 & p & 1 \\ 1 & 1 & 1 \end{vmatrix} = 0$$

or $\quad p(p-1)-\sin\theta+(2-p) = 0$

or $\quad p^2-2p+1 = \sin\theta-1$

or $\quad (p-1)^2 = (\sin\theta-1)$

$\Rightarrow \sin\theta-1 \geq 0$ as $(p-1)^2 \geq 0$

$\Rightarrow \sin\theta=1$ and $p = 1$

$\Rightarrow \theta = 2n\pi + \dfrac{\pi}{2}$ amd $p = 1$.

7. $\quad \left|\vec{a}+\vec{b}\right| = \left|\vec{a}-\vec{b}\right|$

$\Rightarrow \quad \left|\vec{a}+\vec{b}\right|^2 = \left|\vec{a}-\vec{b}\right|^2$

$\Rightarrow \quad a^2+b^2+2\vec{a}.\vec{b} = a^2+b^2-2\vec{a}.\vec{b}$

$\Rightarrow \quad 4\vec{a}.\vec{b} = 0$

$\Rightarrow \quad \vec{a}.\vec{b} = 0$

$\Rightarrow \quad \vec{a} \perp \vec{b}$.

8. Given $\vec{a} = \hat{i}+\hat{j}+0\hat{k}$ and $\vec{b} = 0\hat{i}+\hat{j}+\hat{k}$.

$$\therefore \vec{a} \times \vec{b} = \begin{vmatrix} \hat{i} & \hat{j} & \hat{k} \\ 1 & 1 & 0 \\ 0 & 1 & 1 \end{vmatrix} = \hat{i}-\hat{j}+\hat{k}.$$

Thus, $\vec{a} \times \vec{b} = \hat{i}-\hat{j}+\hat{k}$ is perpendicular to both $\vec{a}$ and $\vec{b}$.

Hence, unit vector $= \pm\dfrac{\hat{i}-\hat{j}+\hat{k}}{\sqrt{3}}$.

9. The required vector $\vec{c}$ is given by

$$\vec{c} = \lambda\left(\hat{a}+\hat{b}\right)$$

$$= \lambda\left(\frac{\vec{a}}{\left|\vec{a}\right|}+\frac{\vec{b}}{\left|\vec{b}\right|}\right)$$

$$= \lambda\left\{\frac{1}{9}\left(7\hat{i}-4\hat{j}-4\hat{k}\right)+\frac{1}{3}\left(-2\hat{i}-\hat{j}+2\hat{k}\right)\right\}$$

or $\quad \vec{c} = \dfrac{\lambda}{9}\left(\hat{i}-7\hat{j}+2\hat{k}\right)$

or $\quad \left|\vec{c}\right| = \pm\dfrac{\lambda}{9}\sqrt{1+49+4} = \pm\dfrac{\lambda}{9}\sqrt{54}$

But $\quad \left|\vec{c}\right| = 5\sqrt{6}$ (given)

$\therefore \quad \pm\dfrac{\lambda}{9}\sqrt{54} = 5\sqrt{6}$ or $\lambda = \pm 15$

Hence $\quad \vec{c} = \pm\dfrac{15}{9}\left(\hat{i}-7\hat{j}+2\hat{k}\right)$

$$= \pm\frac{5}{3}\left(\hat{i}-7\hat{j}+2\hat{k}\right).$$

10. Points with position vectors $60\hat{i}+3\hat{j}$, $40\hat{i}-8\hat{j}$ and $a\hat{i}-52\hat{j}$ are colilnear if

$$\frac{1}{2}\begin{vmatrix} 60 & 3 & 1 \\ 40 & -8 & 1 \\ a & -52 & 1 \end{vmatrix} = 0$$

($\because$ Area of the triangle is zero if colilnear)

$\Rightarrow a = 40$.

11. Let $\vec{a} = \hat{i}-\hat{j}$ and $\vec{b} = \hat{i}+2\hat{j}$.

Since $\vec{a} \times \left(\vec{b} \times \vec{c}\right)$ is a vector coplanar with $\vec{b}$ and $\vec{c}$ and perpendicular to $\vec{a}$.

So, the required vector is along the vector

$$\vec{a}\times\left(\vec{a}\times\vec{b}\right) = \left(\vec{a}.\vec{b}\right)\vec{a}-\left(\vec{a}.\vec{a}\right)\vec{b}$$

$$= -\left(\hat{i}-\hat{j}\right)-2\left(\hat{i}+2\hat{j}\right)$$

$$= -3\hat{i}-3\hat{j}$$

Hence, the required vectors are given by

$$\pm\frac{\left(-3\hat{i}-3\hat{j}\right)}{\sqrt{(-3)^2+(-3)^2}} = \pm\frac{1}{\sqrt{2}}\left(\hat{i}+\hat{j}\right).$$

12. $$\vec{a}\times\left(\vec{b}\times\vec{c}\right) = \left(\vec{a}.\vec{c}\right)\vec{b}-\left(\vec{a}.\vec{b}\right)\vec{c}$$

$$\therefore\quad \vec{a}\times\left(\vec{b}\times\vec{c}\right) = \frac{\left(\vec{b}+\vec{c}\right)}{\sqrt{2}}$$

$$\Rightarrow \left(\vec{a}.\vec{c}\right)\vec{b}-\left(\vec{a}.\vec{b}\right)\vec{c} = \frac{\left(\vec{b}+\vec{c}\right)}{\sqrt{2}}$$

$$\Rightarrow \left(\vec{a}.\vec{c}-\frac{1}{\sqrt{2}}\right)\vec{b}-\left(\vec{a}.\vec{b}+\frac{1}{\sqrt{2}}\right)\vec{c} = 0$$

$$\Rightarrow \quad x\vec{b}-y\vec{c} = 0$$

As $\vec{b}$ and $\vec{c}$ are non-parallel vectors, so $x = 0$ and $y = 0$

$$\therefore\quad \vec{a}.\vec{b} = -\frac{1}{\sqrt{2}}$$

or $\quad 1.1.\cos\theta = -\frac{1}{\sqrt{2}}$

or $\quad \cos\theta = \cos\left(\pi-\frac{\pi}{4}\right)=\cos\frac{3\pi}{4}$

or $\quad \theta = \frac{3\pi}{4}.$

13. Since $\vec{a}, \vec{b}$ and $\vec{c}$ are unit vectors inclined at an angle θ,

so $\left|\vec{a}\right|=\left|\vec{b}\right|=\left|\vec{c}\right|=1$ and $\cos\theta=\vec{a}.\vec{c}=\vec{b}.\vec{c}$.

Now, $\vec{c} = \alpha\vec{a}+\beta\vec{b}+\gamma\left(\vec{a}\times\vec{b}\right)$ ...(i)

$$\therefore\quad \vec{a}.\vec{c} = \alpha\left(\vec{a}.\vec{a}\right)+\beta\left(\vec{a}.\vec{b}\right)+\gamma\left\{\vec{a}.\left(\vec{a}\times\vec{b}\right)\right\}$$

$$\Rightarrow \cos\theta = \alpha\left|\vec{a}\right|^2$$

$$\left[\because \vec{a}.\vec{b}=0,\ \ \vec{a}.\left(\vec{a}\times\vec{b}\right)=0\right]$$

$$\Rightarrow \cos\theta = \alpha$$

Similarly, by taking dot product on both sides of *(i)* by $\vec{b}$, we get

$$\cos\theta = \beta$$

$$\therefore\quad \alpha = \beta$$

Again $\vec{c} = \alpha\vec{a}+\beta\vec{b}+\gamma\left(\vec{a}\times\vec{b}\right)$

$$\Rightarrow \left|\vec{c}\right|^2 = \left|\alpha\vec{a}+\beta\vec{b}+\gamma\left(\vec{a}\times\vec{b}\right)\right|^2$$

$$= \alpha^2\left|\vec{a}\right|^2+\beta^2\left|\vec{b}\right|^2+\gamma^2\left|\vec{a}\times\vec{b}\right|^2$$

$$+2\alpha\beta\left(\vec{a}.\vec{b}\right)+2\alpha\gamma\left\{\vec{a}.\left(\vec{a}\times\vec{b}\right)\right\}$$

$$+2\beta\gamma.\left\{\vec{b}.\left(\vec{a}\times\vec{b}\right)\right\}$$

$$\Rightarrow \quad 1 = \alpha^2+\beta^2+\gamma^2\left|\vec{a}\times\vec{b}\right|^2$$

$$\Rightarrow \quad 1 = 2\alpha^2+\gamma^2\ \left(\because\left|\vec{a}\right|^2=\left|\vec{b}\right|^2=\sin^2\frac{\pi}{2}=1\right)$$

$$\Rightarrow \quad \alpha^2 = \frac{1-\gamma^2}{2}$$

But $\alpha=\beta=\cos\theta$.

Therefore $1=2\alpha^2+\gamma^2 \Rightarrow \gamma^2=1-2\cos^2\theta$

$$= -\cos 2\theta.$$

14. $$\left(\vec{e_1}+\vec{e_2}\right)^2 = \vec{e_1}.\vec{e_1}+2\vec{e_1}.\vec{e_2}+\vec{e_2}.\vec{e_2}$$

$$\Rightarrow \left|\vec{e_1}+\vec{e_2}\right|^2 = \left|\vec{e_1}\right|^2+2\left|\vec{e_1}\right|\left|\vec{e_2}\right|\cos\theta+\left|\vec{e_2}\right|^2$$

$$\Rightarrow \left|\vec{e_1}+\vec{e_2}\right|^2 = 1+2.1.1\cos\theta+1\ \left(\because\left|\vec{e_1}\right|=\left|\vec{e_2}\right|=1\right)$$

$$\Rightarrow \left|\vec{e_1}+\vec{e_2}\right|^2 = 2(1+\cos\theta)$$

$$\Rightarrow 4\cos^2\frac{\theta}{2} = \left|\vec{e_1}+\vec{e_2}\right|^2 \Rightarrow \cos\frac{\theta}{2} = \frac{\left|\vec{e_1}+\vec{e_2}\right|}{2}.$$

15. We have

$$\left|\vec{e_1}-\vec{e_2}\right|^2 = \left|\vec{e_1}\right|^2+\left|\vec{e_2}\right|^2 - 2\vec{e_1}.\vec{e_2}$$

$$\Rightarrow \left|\vec{e_1}-\vec{e_2}\right|^2 = 1+1-2\left|\vec{e_1}\right|\left|\vec{e_2}\right|\cos\theta$$

$$\Rightarrow \left|\vec{e_1}-\vec{e_2}\right|^2 = 2-2\cos\theta$$

$$\Rightarrow \left|\vec{e_1}-\vec{e_2}\right|^2 = 4\sin^2\frac{\theta}{2}$$

$$\Rightarrow \sin\frac{\theta}{2} = \frac{\left|\vec{e_1}-\vec{e_2}\right|}{2}.$$

16. $\vec{r_1}, \vec{r_2}, \vec{r_3}$ are coplanar, therefore

$$\left[\vec{r_1}\,\vec{r_2}\,\vec{r_3}\right] = 0$$

$$\Rightarrow \begin{vmatrix} a & 1 & 1 \\ 1 & b & 1 \\ 1 & 1 & c \end{vmatrix} = 0$$

$$\Rightarrow abc = a+b+c-2 \quad ...(i)$$

Now $\dfrac{1}{1-a}+\dfrac{1}{1-b}+\dfrac{1}{1-c}$

$$= \frac{3-2(a+b+c)+ab+bc+ca}{1-(a+b+c)+ab+bc+ca-abc}$$

$$= \frac{3-2(a+b+c)+ab+bc+ca}{1-(a+b+c)+ab+bc+ca-abc}$$

$$= \frac{3-2(a+b+c)+ab+bc+ca}{3-2(a+b+c)+ab+bc+ca} \text{ (using (i))}$$

$= 1.$

18.

$$\vec{AB} = \vec{OB}-\vec{OA}$$

$$= \left(-\hat{i}+6\hat{j}+\hat{k}\right)-\left(7\hat{i}+10\hat{k}\right)$$

$$= -\hat{i}-\hat{j}-9\hat{k}.$$

Similarly $\vec{BC} = -3\hat{i}+3\hat{j}+5\hat{k}$

$$\vec{CA} = 4\hat{i}-2\hat{j}+4\hat{k}.$$

Here $\vec{AB}+\vec{BC}+\vec{CA}=0$, so ABC is a triangle.

But $\left|\vec{AB}\right| = \sqrt{1+1+81} = \sqrt{83}$

$$\left|\vec{BC}\right| = \sqrt{9+9+25} = \sqrt{43}$$

$$\left|\vec{CA}\right| = \sqrt{16+4+16} = 6.$$

$\therefore$ ABC is a triangle neither right angled nor isosceles.

19. Let the required vector be $x\hat{i}+y\hat{j}+z\hat{k}$.

Then $\begin{vmatrix} x & y & z \\ 1 & 1 & 2 \\ 1 & 2 & 1 \end{vmatrix} = 0$ (Condition for coplanarity of three vectors)

$$\Rightarrow 3x-y-z=0 \quad ...(i)$$

Now $\left(x\hat{i}+y\hat{j}+z\hat{k}\right)\perp\left(\hat{i}+\hat{j}+\hat{k}\right)$ (given)

$$\Rightarrow x+y+z=0 \quad ...(ii)$$

Solving *(i)* and *(ii)* we get

$$x=0, y=-z.$$

$\therefore$ The required vector is

$$x\hat{i}+y\hat{j}+z\hat{k} = y\hat{j}-y\hat{k}.$$

$\therefore$ Required unit vector $= \dfrac{y\hat{j}-y\hat{k}}{\left|y\hat{j}-y\hat{k}\right|}$

$$= \pm\frac{1}{\sqrt{2}}\left(\hat{j}-\hat{k}\right).$$

20. Let L and M are the point of intersection.

Since $\vec{PL}$, A are collinear

$$\vec{PL} = \lambda_1\vec{A}$$

$$\Rightarrow (x_1-5)\hat{i}+(y_1-7)\hat{j}+(z_1+2)\hat{k} = \lambda_1\left(3\hat{i}-\hat{j}+\hat{k}\right)$$

$$\Rightarrow \frac{x_1-5}{3} = \frac{y_1-7}{-1} = \frac{z_1+2}{1} = \lambda_1$$

$\Rightarrow \quad L \equiv (3\lambda_1+5, 7-\lambda_1, \lambda_1-2)$

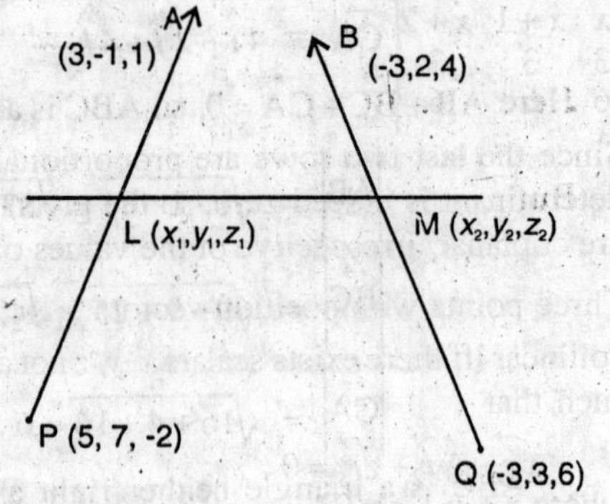

Since $\vec{Q}, \vec{M}, \vec{B}$ are collinear

$$\vec{QM} = \lambda_2 \vec{B}$$

$$\Rightarrow (x_2+3)\hat{i}+(y_2-3)\hat{j}+(z_2-6)\hat{k} = \lambda_2\left(-3\hat{i}+2\hat{j}+4\hat{k}\right)$$

$$\Rightarrow \frac{x_2+3}{-3} = \frac{y_2-3}{2} = \frac{z_2-6}{4} = \lambda_2.$$

$$M \equiv (-3\lambda_2-3, 2\lambda_2+3, 4\lambda_2+6).$$

Again L and M are collinear with (2, 7, – 5).

$$\Rightarrow \frac{x_2-x_1}{2} = \frac{y_2-y_1}{7} = \frac{z_2-z_1}{-5} = \lambda_3$$

$$\Rightarrow \frac{-3\lambda_2-3\lambda_1-8}{2} = \frac{2\lambda_2+\lambda_1-4}{7} = \frac{4\lambda_2-\lambda_1+8}{-5} = \lambda_3$$

$$\Rightarrow 3\lambda_1+3\lambda_2+2\lambda_3 = -8 \quad ...(i)$$

$$\lambda_1+2\lambda_2-7\lambda_3 = 4 \quad ...(ii)$$

$$\Rightarrow -\lambda_1+4\lambda_2+5\lambda_3 = 8 \quad ...(iii)$$

Solving *(i)*, *(ii)* and *(iii)* we get $\lambda_1 = \lambda_2 = \lambda_3 = -1$

Hence $L \equiv (2, 8, -3)$ or $2\hat{i}+8\hat{j}-3\hat{k}$ and $M \equiv (0,1,2)$ or $\hat{j}+2\hat{k}$.

21. The required volume of the paralleopiped is equal to the absolute value of $\left[\vec{a}, \vec{b}, \vec{c}\right]$ i.e. $\vec{a}.\left(\vec{b}\times\vec{c}\right)$

Now $\vec{b}\times\vec{c} = \left(\hat{i}+2\hat{j}-\hat{k}\right)\times\left(3\hat{i}-\hat{j}+2\hat{k}\right)$

$$= \begin{vmatrix} \hat{i} & \hat{j} & \hat{k} \\ 1 & 2 & -1 \\ 3 & -1 & 2 \end{vmatrix} = 3\hat{i}-5\hat{j}-7\hat{k}$$

Here

$$\vec{a}.\left(\vec{b}\times\vec{c}\right) = \left(2\hat{i}-3\hat{j}+4\hat{k}\right).\left(3\hat{i}-5\hat{j}-7\hat{k}\right)$$

$$= 6+15-28 = -7.$$

Neglecting the negative sign, we get the volume of the paralleopiped = 7.

22. Given $\left|\vec{a}\right| = 2, \left|\vec{b}\right| = 5$ and $\left|\vec{a}\times\vec{b}\right| = 8$

So $\left|\vec{a}\times\vec{b}\right| = 8 \Rightarrow \left|\vec{a}\times\vec{b}\right|^2 = 64$

$$\Rightarrow a^2b^2\sin^2\theta = 64 \Rightarrow a^2b^2(1-\cos^2\theta) = 64$$

$$a^2b^2 - a^2b^2\cos^2\theta = 64$$

$$\Rightarrow \quad a^2b^2\cos^2\theta = \left(\left|\vec{a}\right|\left|\vec{b}\right|\right)^2 - 64$$

$$\Rightarrow \left(\vec{a}.\vec{b}\right)^2 = 100-64 \Rightarrow \vec{a}.\vec{b} = 6.$$

23. Taking dot product of $\vec{a}+\vec{b}+\vec{c} = 0$ with $\vec{a}, \vec{b}$ and $\vec{c}$, we get

$$\vec{a}.\vec{b}+\vec{a}.\vec{c} = -\vec{a}.\vec{a} = -\left|\vec{a}\right|^2 = -9$$

$$\vec{b}.\vec{a}+\vec{b}.\vec{c} = -\vec{b}.\vec{b} = -\left|\vec{b}\right|^2 = -25$$

and $\vec{c}.\vec{a}+\vec{c}.\vec{b} = -\vec{c}.\vec{c} = -\left|\vec{c}\right|^2 = -49$.

Solving these three equations for the three possible dot products $\vec{a}.\vec{b}, \vec{b}.\vec{c}$ and $\vec{c}.\vec{a}$ we get $\vec{a}.\vec{b} = \frac{15}{2}$.

$\therefore$ Angle between $\vec{a}$ and $\vec{b}$ is

$$\cos^{-1}\frac{\vec{a}.\vec{b}}{\left|\vec{a}\right|\left|\vec{b}\right|} = \cos^{-1}\frac{15/2}{(5)(3)} = \cos^{-1}\left(\frac{1}{2}\right) = 60°.$$

24. Let $\vec{r} = x\hat{i} + y\hat{j} + z\hat{k}$

Then $\vec{r} \times \left(\hat{i} + 2\hat{j} + \hat{k}\right) = \begin{vmatrix} \hat{i} & \hat{j} & \hat{k} \\ x & y & z \\ 1 & 2 & 1 \end{vmatrix}$

$= (y-2z)\hat{i} + (z-x)\hat{j} + (2x-y)\hat{k}.$

$\therefore\ (y-2z)\hat{i} + (z-x)\hat{j} + (2x-y)\hat{k} = \hat{i} - \hat{k}$

$\left[\because \vec{r} \times \left(\hat{i} + 2\hat{j} + \hat{k}\right) = \hat{i} - \hat{k}\right]$

$\Rightarrow y - 2z = 1, z - x = 0$ and $2x - y = -1$.

Solving these equations taking $z = t$, we get $x = t, y = 1 + 2t$ and $z = t$.

Substituting these values for $\vec{r}$ we get

$\vec{r} = t\hat{i} + (1+2t)\hat{j} + t\hat{k} = \hat{j} + t\left(\hat{i} + 2\hat{j} + \hat{k}\right).$

25. Two diagonals are given by

$\vec{AB} - \vec{BC} = 4\hat{i} - 2\hat{j} + 4\hat{k}$ and

$\vec{AB} + \vec{BC} = 2\hat{i} - 2\hat{j}$.

$\therefore\ \left|\vec{AB} - \vec{BC}\right| = 6,\ \left|\vec{AB} + \vec{BC}\right| = 2\sqrt{2}$ and

$\left(\vec{AB} - \vec{BC}\right).\left(\vec{AB} + \vec{BC}\right) = 2\hat{i} - 2\hat{j}$.

Therefore the angle between the diagonals are

$$\cos^{-1}\frac{\left(\vec{AB} - \vec{BC}\right).\left(\vec{AB} + \vec{BC}\right)}{\left|\vec{AB} - \vec{BC}\right|\left|\vec{AB} + \vec{BC}\right|}$$

$$= \cos^{-1}\frac{12}{(6)\left(2\sqrt{2}\right)} = \cos^{-1}\frac{1}{\sqrt{2}}$$

$$= \frac{\pi}{4} \text{ or } \left(\pi - \frac{\pi}{4}\right) = \frac{\pi}{4}, \frac{3\pi}{4}.$$

26. Three vectors are coplanar iff their scalar triple product i.e. the determinant formed from the components of the vectors is zero.

Therefore we must have

$$\begin{vmatrix} x & x+1 & x+2 \\ x+3 & x+4 & x+5 \\ x+6 & x+7 & x+8 \end{vmatrix} = 0$$

Performing $R_2 \to R_2 - R_1$ and $R_3 \to R_3 - R_1$, the determinant becomes

$$\begin{vmatrix} x & x+1 & x+2 \\ 3 & 3 & 3 \\ 6 & 6 & 6 \end{vmatrix}$$

Since the last two rows are proportional, their determinant is indeed zero, so the given vector are coplanar, irrespective of the values of x.

27. Three points with position vectors $\vec{r_1}, \vec{r_2}, \vec{r_3}$ are collinear iff there exists scalars x, y, z not all zero such that

$x\vec{r_1} + y\vec{r_2} + z\vec{r_3} = 0$ ...(i)

where $x + y + z = 0$ ...(ii)

Here $\vec{r_1} = l_1\vec{a} + m_1\vec{b},\ \vec{r_2} = l_2\vec{a} + m_2\vec{b}$ and

$\vec{r_3} = l_3\vec{a} + m_3\vec{b}$

$\therefore\ x\vec{r_1} + y\vec{r_2} + z\vec{r_3} = 0$

$$\Rightarrow x\left(l_1\vec{a} + m_1\vec{b}\right) + y\left(l_2\vec{a} + m_2\vec{b}\right) + z\left(l_3\vec{a} + m_3\vec{b}\right) = 0$$

$$\Rightarrow (xl_1 + yl_2 + zl_3)\vec{a} + (xm_1 + ym_2 + zm_3)\vec{b} = 0$$

But $\vec{a}$ and $\vec{b}$ are non-collinear, so their coefficient must be zero.

$\therefore\ xl_1 + yl_2 + zl_3 = 0$ ...(iii)

and $xm_1 + ym_2 + zm_3 = 0$ ...(iv)

Eliminating x, y, z between *(ii)*, *(iii)*, and *(iv)* we get

$$\begin{vmatrix} l_1 & l_2 & l_3 \\ m_1 & m_2 & ml_3 \\ 1 & 1 & 1 \end{vmatrix} = 0$$

28. Let r be the radius of the circumcircle of the polygon. Then O is the centre of this circle and for $i = 1, 2, ..., n$, $\left|\vec{OA_i}\right| = r$. The angle between adjacent radii, i.e. the angle subtended by each side of the polygon at the centre is $\frac{2\pi}{n}$. So if $\hat{n}$ is the unit vector perpendicular to the plane of the polygon, we have

$$\sum_{i=1}^{n-1} \vec{OA_i} \times \vec{OA_{i+1}}$$

$$= \sum_{i=1}^{n-1}\left(\left|\overrightarrow{OA_i}\right| \times \left|\overrightarrow{OA_{i+1}}\right| \sin\frac{\pi}{n}\right)\hat{n}$$

$$= \sum_{i=1}^{n-1}\left(r^2 \sin\frac{2\pi}{n}\right)\hat{n} = (n-1)\left(r^2 \sin\frac{2\pi}{n}\right)\hat{n}$$

$$= (n-1)\left(\overrightarrow{OA_2} \times \overrightarrow{OA_1}\right).$$

29. Let $\vec{c} = x\hat{i} + y\hat{j} + z\hat{k}$

Where $x^2 + y^2 + z^2 = 1$ ...(i)

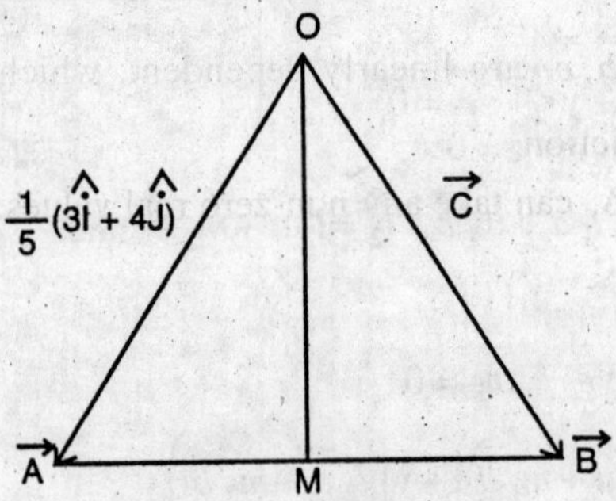

(Mid point)

Unit vector along $3\hat{i} + 4\hat{j}$ is

$$\frac{3\hat{i} + 4\hat{j}}{\sqrt{3^2 + 4^2}} = \frac{1}{5}\left(3\hat{i} + 4\hat{j}\right)$$

The bisector of these two vectors is given by

$$\vec{r} = t\left(\vec{a} + \vec{b}\right)$$

$$\Rightarrow \vec{r} = t\left\{\left(x\hat{i} + y\hat{j} + z\hat{k}\right) + \frac{1}{5}\left(3\hat{i} + 4\hat{j}\right)\right\}$$

$$= \frac{1}{5}t\left[(5x+3)\hat{i} + (5y+4)\hat{j} + 5z\hat{k}\right] \quad ...(ii)$$

But the bisector is given by

$$-\hat{i} + \hat{j} - \hat{k} = 1 \quad ...(iii)$$

Compairing *(ii)* and *(iii)*, we get

$$\frac{t}{5}(5x+3) = -1, \quad \frac{t}{5}(5y+4) = 1, \quad \frac{t}{5}.5z = -1$$

$$x = -\frac{5+3t}{5t}, \quad y = \frac{5-4t}{5t}, \quad z = -\frac{1}{t}$$

Putting in *(i)* i.e. $x^2 + y^2 + z^2 = 1$, we get

$(5 + 3t)^2 + (5 - 4t)^2 + 25 = 25t^2$

or $25t^2 - 10t + 75 = 25t^2$

or $t = \frac{15}{2}$

$$\therefore x = -\frac{55}{2}.\frac{2}{75} = -\frac{11}{25}, \quad y = \frac{10}{15}, z = -\frac{2}{15}$$

$$\therefore \vec{c} = \frac{1}{15}\left(-11\hat{i} + 10\hat{j} - 2\hat{k}\right).$$

30. $$\frac{\text{The projection of } \vec{a} \text{ on } \vec{b}}{\text{The projection of } \vec{b} \text{ on } \vec{a}} = \frac{\left(\vec{a}.\vec{b}\right)\Big/\left|\vec{b}\right|}{\left(\vec{b}.\vec{a}\right)\Big/\left|\vec{a}\right|}$$

$$= \frac{\sqrt{(2)^2 + (-3)^2 + (-6)^2}}{\sqrt{(-2)^2 + (-2)^2 + (-1)^2}}$$

$$= \frac{\sqrt{49}}{\sqrt{9}} = \frac{7}{3}.$$

31. Let the required vector ZOX plane be $\vec{c} = x\hat{i} + z\hat{k}$.

As it is a unit vector, therefore

$$\left|\vec{c}\right| = x^2 + z^2 = 1 \quad ...(i)$$

Given that $\vec{a}$ and $\vec{c}$ are inclined at an angle of 45°.

$$\therefore \cos 45° = \frac{\vec{a}.\vec{c}}{\left|\vec{a}\right|\left|\vec{c}\right|} = \frac{2x - z}{\sqrt{2^2 + 2^2 + (-1)^2}}$$

or $$\frac{1}{\sqrt{2}} = \frac{2x - z}{3}$$

or $$2x - z = \frac{3}{\sqrt{2}} \quad ...(ii)$$

Also given that $\vec{b}$ and $\vec{c}$ are inclined at an angle 60°.

$$\therefore -\frac{z}{\sqrt{2}} = \cos 60°$$

or $$-\frac{z}{\sqrt{2}} = \frac{1}{2} \text{ or } z = -\frac{1}{\sqrt{2}} \quad ...(iii)$$

From *(ii)* and *(iii)* we get $x = \frac{1}{\sqrt{2}}$

Hence the required vector is $\vec{c} = \frac{1}{\sqrt{2}}\hat{i} - \frac{1}{\sqrt{2}}\hat{k}$.

32. We have

$$\vec{r} \times \vec{b} = \vec{c} \times \vec{b}$$

$$\Rightarrow \left(\vec{r} - \vec{c}\right) \times \vec{b} = \vec{O}$$

$$\Rightarrow \vec{r} - \vec{c} = \lambda \vec{b}$$

$$\Rightarrow \vec{r} = \vec{c} + \lambda \vec{b}$$

Now $\vec{r} \cdot \vec{a} = 0$ (given)

$$\Rightarrow \left(\vec{c} + \lambda \vec{b}\right) \cdot \vec{a} = 0$$

$$\Rightarrow \lambda = -\frac{\vec{c} \cdot \vec{a}}{\vec{b} \cdot \vec{a}}$$

$$= -\frac{\left(2\hat{i} - 3\hat{j} + 4\hat{k}\right) \cdot \left(2\hat{i} + \hat{j} + \hat{k}\right)}{\left(\hat{i} + 2\hat{j} + \hat{k}\right) \cdot \left(2\hat{i} + \hat{j} + \hat{k}\right)} = -1.$$

33. We have $\vec{c} = x\vec{a} + y\vec{b} + z\left(\vec{a} \times \vec{b}\right)$

$\therefore \vec{c} \cdot \vec{a} = x$ and $\vec{c} \cdot \vec{b} = y \Rightarrow x = y = \cos\theta$.

Now $\vec{c} \cdot \vec{c} = \left|\vec{c}\right|^2$.

$$\Rightarrow \left[x\vec{a} + y\vec{b} + z\left(\vec{a} \times \vec{b}\right)\right] \cdot \left[x\vec{a} + y\vec{b} + z\left(\vec{a} \times \vec{b}\right)\right]$$

$$= \left|\vec{c}\right|^2.$$

$$\Rightarrow \quad 2x^2 + z^2 \left|\vec{a} \times \vec{b}\right|^2 = 1$$

$$\Rightarrow \quad 2x^2 + z^2 \sin^2 \frac{\pi}{2} = 1$$

$$\Rightarrow \quad 2x^2 + z^2 = 1$$

$$\Rightarrow \quad z^2 = 1 - 2\cos^2\theta \quad (\because x = \cos\theta)$$

$$\Rightarrow \quad z^2 = -\cos 2\theta.$$

34. $\begin{vmatrix} \vec{a} & \vec{b} & \vec{c} \\ \vec{a} \cdot \vec{a} & \vec{a} \cdot \vec{b} & \vec{a} \cdot \vec{c} \\ \vec{a} \cdot \vec{c} & \vec{b} \cdot \vec{c} & \vec{c} \cdot \vec{c} \end{vmatrix} = \lambda \vec{a} + \mu \vec{b} + \nu \vec{c}$

as dot product is a scalar quantity.
If $\Delta = 0$, then

$$\lambda \vec{a} + \mu \vec{b} + \nu \vec{c} = 0$$

$\Rightarrow \vec{a}, \vec{b}, \vec{c}$ are linearly dependent, which is contradiction.

Hence Δ, can take any non-zero real values.

35. Since $\left(\vec{a} - \vec{b}\right) + \left(\vec{b} - \vec{c}\right) + \left(\vec{c} - \vec{a}\right) = 0,$

therefore the vectors $\vec{a} - \vec{b}, \vec{b} - \vec{c}$ and $\vec{c} - \vec{a}$

are coplanar. Hence $\left[\vec{a} - \vec{b}, \vec{b} - \vec{c}, \vec{c} - \vec{a}\right] = 0.$

36. Given $\vec{a} \cdot \left(\vec{b} + \vec{c}\right) = 0, \quad \vec{b} \cdot \left(\vec{c} + \vec{a}\right) = 0$ and

$$\vec{c} \cdot \left(\vec{a} + \vec{b}\right) = 0$$

$$\therefore \left|\vec{a} + \vec{b} + \vec{c}\right|^2 = \left(\vec{a} + \vec{b} + \vec{c}\right)^2$$

$$= a^2 + b^2 + c^2 + 2\left(\vec{a} \cdot \vec{b} + \vec{b} \cdot \vec{c} + \vec{c} \cdot \vec{a}\right)$$

$$= a^2 + b^2 + c^2$$

$$+ \vec{a} \cdot \left(\vec{b} + \vec{c}\right) + \vec{b} \cdot \left(\vec{c} + \vec{a}\right) + \vec{c} \cdot \left(\vec{a} + \vec{b}\right)$$

($\because$ Dot product is commutative)

$= a^2 + b^2 + c^2$

$= 1^2 + 2^2 + 3^2 = 14.$

$$\therefore \left|\vec{a} + \vec{b} + \vec{b}\right| = \sqrt{14}.$$

37. Let the given vertices be A, B, C respectively and fourth vertex D with position vector $\left(x\hat{i}+y\hat{j}+z\hat{k}\right)$.

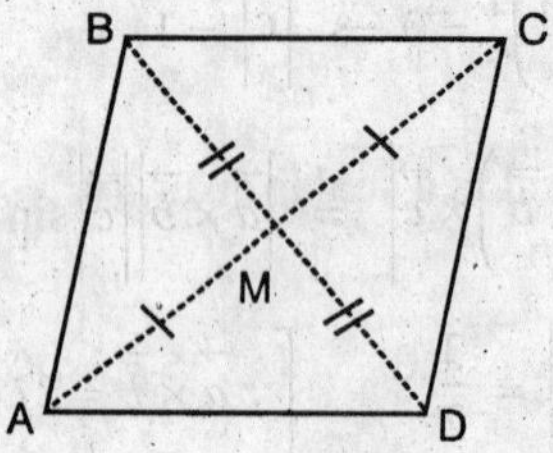

Then the position vectors of mid point of $\overrightarrow{BD}$

$$=\frac{1}{2}\left[(x+1)\hat{i}+(y+3)\hat{j}+(z+5)\hat{k}\right]$$

Position vector of mid point of $\overrightarrow{AC}$

$$=4\hat{i}+5\hat{j}+6\hat{k}.$$

$$\therefore\ \left(\frac{x+1}{2}\right)\hat{i}+\left(\frac{y+3}{2}\right)\hat{j}+\left(\frac{z+5}{2}\right)\hat{k}=4\hat{i}+5\hat{j}+6\hat{k}.$$

$$\therefore\ \frac{x+1}{2}=4,\ \frac{y+3}{2}=5 \text{ and } \frac{z+5}{2}=6.$$

$\Rightarrow x=7, y=7$ and $z=7$.

$\therefore$ Position vector of D is $7\left(\hat{i}+\hat{j}+\hat{k}\right)$.

38. We have

$$\left[\vec{a}\times\vec{b}\ \ \vec{b}\times\vec{c}\ \ \vec{c}\times\vec{a}\right]$$

$$=\left\{\left(\vec{a}\times\vec{b}\right)\times\left(\vec{b}\times\vec{c}\right)\right\}.\left(\vec{c}\times\vec{a}\right)$$

$$=\left\{\vec{d}\times\left(\vec{b}\times\vec{c}\right)\right\}.\left(\vec{c}\times\vec{a}\right), \text{ where } \vec{d}=\vec{a}\times\vec{b}.$$

$$=\left\{\left(\vec{d}.\vec{c}\right)\vec{b}-\left(\vec{d}.\vec{b}\right)\vec{c}\right\}.\left(\vec{c}\times\vec{a}\right)$$

$$=\left\{\left(\left(\vec{a}\times\vec{b}\right).\vec{c}\right)\vec{b}-\left(\left(\vec{a}\times\vec{b}\right).\vec{b}\right)\vec{c}\right\}.\left(\vec{c}\times\vec{a}\right)$$

$$=\left\{\left[\vec{a}\,\vec{b}\,\vec{c}\right]\vec{b}-\left[\vec{a}\,\vec{b}\,\vec{b}\right]\vec{c}\right\}.\left(\vec{c}\times\vec{a}\right)$$

$$=\left\{\left[\vec{a}\,\vec{b}\,\vec{c}\right]\vec{b}-(0)\,\vec{c}\right\}.\left(\vec{c}\times\vec{a}\right)$$

$$=\left[\vec{a}\,\vec{b}\,\vec{c}\right]\left(\vec{b}.\left(\vec{c}\times\vec{a}\right)\right)$$

$$=\left[\vec{a}\,\vec{b}\,\vec{c}\right]\left[\vec{a}\,\vec{b}\,\vec{c}\right]=\left[\vec{a}\,\vec{b}\,\vec{c}\right]^2.$$

39. Let $\vec{a}=\hat{i}+\hat{j}, \vec{b}=\hat{j}+\hat{k}$ and $\vec{c}=\hat{k}+\hat{i}$.

Further let $\vec{\alpha}=\dfrac{\vec{a}\times\vec{b}}{\left|\vec{a}\times\vec{b}\right|}$, $\vec{\beta}=\dfrac{\vec{b}\times\vec{c}}{\left|\vec{b}\times\vec{c}\right|}$ and $\vec{\gamma}=\dfrac{\vec{c}\times\vec{a}}{\left|\vec{c}\times\vec{a}\right|}$.

Then required volume $=\left[\vec{\alpha}\,\vec{\beta}\,\vec{\gamma}\right]$

$$=\frac{1}{\left|\vec{a}\times\vec{b}\right|\left|\vec{b}\times\vec{c}\right|\left|\vec{c}\times\vec{a}\right|}\left[\vec{a}\times\vec{b}\ \ \vec{b}\times\vec{c}\ \ \vec{c}\times\vec{a}\right]$$

$$=\frac{\left[\vec{a}\,\vec{b}\,\vec{c}\right]^2}{\left|\vec{a}\times\vec{b}\right|\left|\vec{b}\times\vec{c}\right|\left|\vec{c}\times\vec{a}\right|}$$

Now $\left[\vec{a}\,\vec{b}\,\vec{c}\right]=\begin{vmatrix}1&1&0\\0&1&1\\1&0&1\end{vmatrix}=1-1(0-1)=2$

$$\therefore\ \left[\vec{a}\,\vec{b}\,\vec{c}\right]^2=4.$$

Also $\vec{a}\times\vec{b}=\left(\hat{i}+\hat{j}\right)\times\left(\hat{j}+\hat{k}\right)=\hat{k}-\hat{j}+\hat{i}$

$\vec{b}\times\vec{c}=\left(\hat{j}+\hat{k}\right)\times\left(\hat{k}+\hat{i}\right)=\hat{i}-\hat{k}+\hat{j}$

and $\vec{c}\times\vec{a}=\left(\hat{k}+\hat{i}\right)\times\left(\hat{i}+\hat{j}\right)=\hat{j}-\hat{i}+\hat{k}$.

$$\therefore\ \left|\vec{a}\times\vec{b}\right|=\left|\vec{b}\times\vec{c}\right|=\left|\vec{c}\times\vec{a}\right|=\sqrt{3}.$$

Hence required volume $=\dfrac{2^2}{3\sqrt{3}}=\dfrac{4}{3\sqrt{3}}$.

40. We have $\vec{a}.\vec{c} = |\vec{c}|$ and $|\vec{c} - \vec{a}| = 2\sqrt{2}$

$\Rightarrow |\vec{c} - \vec{a}|^2 = 8$

$\Rightarrow |\vec{c}|^2 - 2(\vec{a}.\vec{c}) + |\vec{a}|^2 = 8$

$\Rightarrow |\vec{c}|^2 - 2|\vec{c}| + |\vec{a}|^2 = 8 \quad (\because \vec{a}.\vec{c} = |\vec{c}|)$

$\Rightarrow |\vec{c}|^2 - 2|\vec{c}| + 9 = 8 \quad (\because |\vec{a}|^2 = 9)$

$\Rightarrow (|\vec{c}| - 1)^2 = 0 \Rightarrow |\vec{c}| = 1.$

Now $|(\vec{a} \times \vec{b}) \times \vec{c}| = |\vec{a} \times \vec{b}||\vec{c}| \sin 30°$

$= \frac{1}{2}|\vec{a} \times \vec{b}| = \frac{3}{2} \quad [\because \vec{a} \times \vec{b} = 2\hat{i} - 2\hat{j} + \hat{k}].$

---

17. THREE DIMENSIONAL GEOMETRY

Rectangular Cartesian Co-ordinates : In a plane the position of a point is determined by two members x, y obtained with reference to two straight lines in the plane, generally at right angles. The position of a point in space is, however, determined by three numbers *x, y, z*.

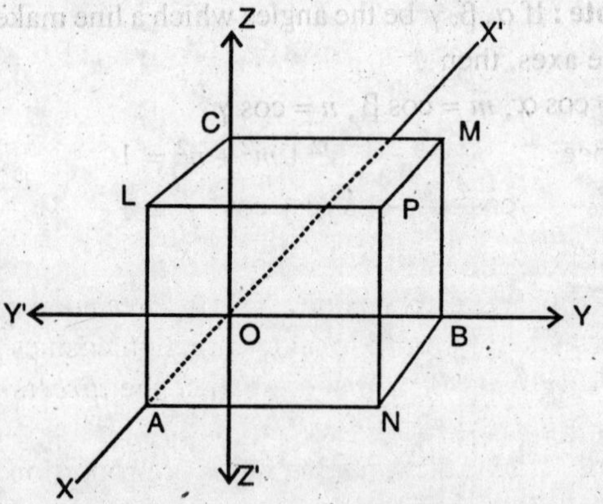

Let XOX', ZOZ' be two perpendicular straight lines. Through O, their point of intersection, called the *origin*, a line YOY' is drawn perpendicular to the plane XOZ, so that we have three mutually perpendicular straight lines XOX', YOY', ZOZ', known as rectangular co-ordinates axes. These three axes, taken in pairs, determine three planes, XOY, YOZ and ZOX mutually perpendicular to each other known as *rectangular co-ordinate planes*.

Let P be any point in space. Through P we draw planes parallel to th co-ordinates planes and let them meet the axes of co-ordinates in A, B and C. Let OA = *x*, OB = *y* and OC = *z*. The three numbers *x, y, z* taken with proper sign are called the co-ordinates of the point P. Conversely, given the co-ordinates *x, y, z* of any point with reference to a set of co-ordinates axes, then the position of the point is uniquely determined.

Distance between two points : Let the distance between two points (x_1, y_1, z_1) and (x_2, y_2, z_2) be denoted by PQ.

Then

$$PQ = \sqrt{(x_2 - x_1)^2 + (y_2 - y_1)^2 + (z_2 - z_1)^2}$$

Section Formula : Let R (*x, y, z*) divide the joint of given points P (x_1, y_1, z_1) and Q (x_2, y_2, z_2) in the ratio $m_1 : m_2$ internally.

Then $$x = \frac{m_1x_2 + m_2x_1}{m_1 + m_2}$$

$$y = \frac{m_1y_2 + m_2y_1}{m_1 + m_2}$$

$$z = \frac{m_1z_2 + m_2z_1}{m_1 + m_2}.$$

Hence the co-ordinates of the point which divides the join of (x_1, y_1, z_1) and (x_2, y_2, z_2) in the ratio $m_1 : m_2$ are

$$\left(\frac{m_1x_2 + m_2x_1}{m_1 + m_2}, \frac{m_1y_2 + m_2y_1}{m_1 + m_2}, \frac{m_1z_2 + m_2z_1}{m_1 + m_2}\right)$$

Note : 1. The co-ordinates of the mid-point of the join of (x_1, y_1, z_1), (x_2, y_2, z_2) are

$$\left(\frac{x_1 + x_2}{2}, \frac{y_1 + y_2}{2}, \frac{z_1 + z_2}{2}\right) \quad | \because m_1 = m_2$$

2. The co-ordinates of the point which divides two points (x_1, y_1, z_1), (x_2, y_2, z_2) *externally* in the ratio $m_1 : m_2$ are given by

$$x = \frac{m_1x_2 - m_2x_1}{m_1 - m_2}$$

$$y = \frac{m_1y_2 - m_2y_1}{m_1 - m_2}$$

$$z = \frac{m_1z_2 - m_2z_1}{m_1 - m_2}$$

i.e. $\left(\frac{m_1x_2 - m_2x_1}{m_1 - m_2}, \frac{m_1y_2 - m_2y_1}{m_1 - m_2}, \frac{m_1z_2 - m_2z_1}{m_1 - m_2}\right)$

Centroid of a Triangle : The co-ordinates of the centroid of the triangle whose vertices are (x_1, y_1, z_1), (x_2, y_2, z_2) and (x_3, y_3, z_3) is

$$\left(\frac{x_1 + x_2 + x_3}{3}, \frac{y_1 + y_2 + y_3}{3}, \frac{z_1 + z_2 + z_3}{3}\right)$$

Centroid of a Tetrahedron : The co-ordinates of the centroid of gravity of the tetrahedron whose vertices are (x_1, y_1, z_1), (x_2, y_2, z_2), (x_3, y_3, z_3) and (x_4, y_4, z_4) is

$$\left(\frac{x_1 + x_2 + x_3 + x_4}{4}, \frac{y_1 + y_2 + y_3 + y_4}{4}, \frac{z_1 + z_2 + z_3 + z_4}{3}\right)$$

Direction Cosines of a line : If α, β, γ be the angles that a given line makes with the positive directions of co-ordinate axes then $\cos\alpha$, $\cos\beta$, $\cos\gamma$ are called the *direction cosines* of the given line and are generally denoted by l, m, n respectively. Thus $l = \cos\alpha$, $m = \cos\beta$, $n = \cos\gamma$.

Note : 1. *Direction cosines of co-ordinates axes:* Since the line x-axis, makes with x-axis, y-axis and z-axis the angles 0°, 90° and 90° respectively, therefore its direction cosines are cos 0°, cos 90°, cos 90° i.e. 1, 0, 0.

Thus the d.c's of x-axis are 1,0, 0

Similarly d.c's of y-axis are 0,1, 0

d.c's of z-axis are 0,0, 1

2. If the direction cosines of a line PQ are l, m, n then the d.c's of QP are $-l, -m, -n$.

Relation between direction cosines

If l, m, n be the d.c's of a line OP and OP $= r$, then the co-ordinates of P are (lr, mr, nr).

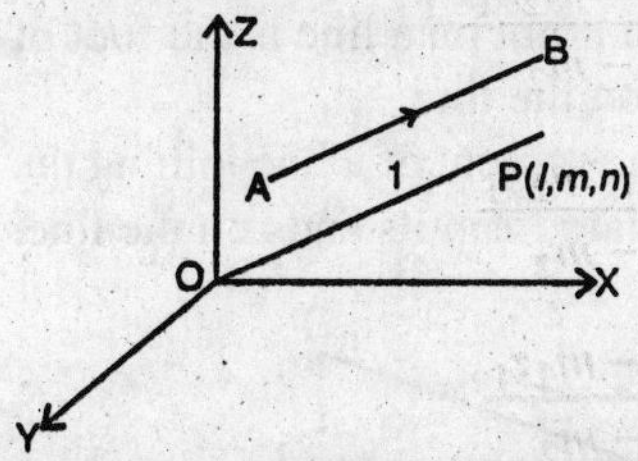

Let AB be the given line whose d.c's are l, m, n.

Through O, we draw OP parallel to AB, so that d.c's of OP are also l, m, n. Now we cut off OP = 1.

Then co-ordinates of P are (l, m, n) $[\because r = 1]$

Now by distance formula

$$\text{OP} = \sqrt{(l-0)^2 + (m-0)^2 + (n-0)^2}$$

or $\quad 1 = \sqrt{l^2 + m^2 + n^2}$

Squaring both the sides we get

$1 = l^2 + m^2 + n^2$

or $l^2 + m^2 + n^2 = 1$

i.e. the sum of the squres of the d.c's of a line is equal to one.

Note : If α, β, γ be the angles which a line makes with the axes, then

$l = \cos\alpha$, $m = \cos\beta$, $n = \cos\gamma$.

Since $\quad l^2 + m^2 + n^2 = 1$

$\therefore \quad \cos^2\alpha + \cos^2\beta + \cos^2\gamma = 1$

and thus $\sin^2\alpha + \sin^2\beta + \sin^2\gamma = 2$.

Direction ratios of a line : A set of three numbers a, b, c which are proportional to direction cosines l, m, n respectively of a line are called the *direction ratios of a line.*

Let a, b, c be the direction ratios or proportional direction cosines of a line and let l, m, n be the actual d.c's of the line.

Then $\quad \frac{l}{a} = \frac{m}{b} = \frac{n}{c} = \frac{\sqrt{(l^2 + m^2 + n^2)}}{\sqrt{(a^2 + b^2 + c^2)}}$

$$= \frac{1}{\sqrt{(a^2 + b^2 + c^2)}}$$

$[\because l^2 + m^2 + n^2 = 1]$

$\therefore \quad l = \frac{a}{\sqrt{a^2 + b^2 + c^2}}, \quad m = \frac{b}{\sqrt{a^2 + b^2 + c^2}},$

$n = \frac{c}{\sqrt{a^2 + b^2 + c^2}}.$

Note : 1. d.c's of a line are unique, but d.r's of a line are not unique.

2. If $\langle a, b, c\rangle$ are d.r's of a line, then $\langle ka, kb, kc\rangle$ are also d.r's of the same line (if $k \neq 0$).

3. If a, b, c are d.r's of a line, then $a^2 + b^2 + c^2 \neq 1$.

Direction ratios of a line joining two points : If $P(x_1, y_1, z_1)$ and $Q(x_2, y_2, z_2)$ be two given points, then the d.r's of the line are $x_2 - x_1, y_2 - y_1, z_2 - z_1$.

Angle between two lines : Let PQ, RS be the given lines and $l_1, m_1, n_1; l_2, m_2, n_2$ be their direction cosines. Let θ be the angle between them. Through O, we draw OA, OB parallel to PQ and RS respectively, then $\angle AOB = \theta$ also.

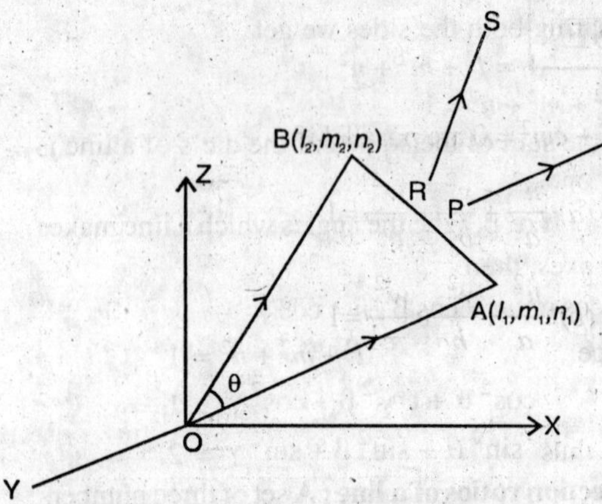

Then

$$\cos\theta = l_1l_2 + m_1m_2 + n_1n_2$$

Hence $\theta = \cos^{-1}(l_1l_2 + m_1m_2 + n_1n_2)$

Note : 1. As $\cos\theta = l_1l_2 + m_1m_2 + n_1n_2$

so $\sin\theta = \sqrt{\Sigma(l_1m_2 - m_1l_2)^2}$

and $\tan\theta = \dfrac{\sqrt{\Sigma(l_1m_2 - m_1l_2)^2}}{l_1l_2 + m_1m_2 + n_1n_2}$

2. If the lines are $\perp$, then $\theta = 90°$.

$\therefore \cos\theta = \cos 90° = 0$

or $l_1l_2 + m_1m_2 + n_1n_2 = 0$.

3. If the lines are (| |), then $\theta = 0°$ so that $\sin\theta = 0$

$\therefore \Sigma(l_1m_2 - m_1l_2)^2 = 0$

which give $\dfrac{l_1}{l_2} = \dfrac{m_1}{m_2} = \dfrac{n_1}{n_2} = \dfrac{\sqrt{(l_1^2 + m_1^2 + n_1^2)}}{\sqrt{(l_2^2 + m_2^2 + n_2^2)}}$

$= \dfrac{1}{1}$

$\therefore l_1 = l_2; m_1 = m_2; n_1 = n_2$.

Angle between two lines with respect to direction ratios : Let l_1, m_1, n_1 be the d.c's of a line whose d.r's are a_1, b_1, c_1.

$$\therefore l_1 = \frac{a_1}{\sqrt{a_1^2 + b_1^2 + c_1^2}},$$

$$m_1 = \frac{b_1}{\sqrt{a_1^2 + b_1^2 + c_1^2}},\quad n_1 = \frac{c_1}{\sqrt{a_1^2 + b_1^2 + c_1^2}}.$$

Let l_2, m_2, n_2 be the d.c's of a line whose d.r's are a_2, b_2, c_2.

$$\therefore l_2 = \frac{a_2}{\sqrt{a_2^2 + b_2^2 + c_2^2}},\quad m_2 = \frac{b_2}{\sqrt{a_2^2 + b_2^2 + c_2^2}},$$

$$n_2 = \frac{c_2}{\sqrt{a_2^2 + b_2^2 + c_2^2}}.$$

Now $\cos\theta = l_1l_2 + m_1m_2 + n_1n_2$

$$= \frac{a_1a_2 + b_1b_2 + c_1c_2}{\sqrt{a_1^2 + b_1^2 + c_1^2}\,\sqrt{a_2^2 + b_2^2 + c_2^2}}$$

Note : 1. If the lines are $\perp$, $\theta = 90°$.

$\therefore \cos 90° = 0$

or $\dfrac{a_1a_2 + b_1b_2 + c_1c_2}{\sqrt{a_1^2 + b_1^2 + c_1^2}\,\sqrt{a_2^2 + b_2^2 + c_2^2}} = 0$

or $a_1a_2 + b_1b_2 + c_1c_2 = 0$

2. If the lines are parallel then $l_1 = l_2; m_1 = m_2; n_1 = n_2$. Changing them to d.r's we get

$$\frac{a_1}{a_2} = \frac{b_1}{b_2} = \frac{c_1}{c_2}$$

3. $\sin\theta = \dfrac{\sqrt{\Sigma(a_1b_2 - b_1a_2)^2}}{\sqrt{\Sigma a_1^2}\,\sqrt{\Sigma a_2^2}}$.

4. $\tan\theta = \dfrac{\sqrt{\Sigma(a_1b_2 - b_1a_2)^2}}{\Sigma a_1a_2}$.

Projection on a line :

I. The projection of a point on a line is the foot of $\perp$ from the point on the line.

II. The projection of a segment of a line joining the feet of perpendiculars from its ends on the line.

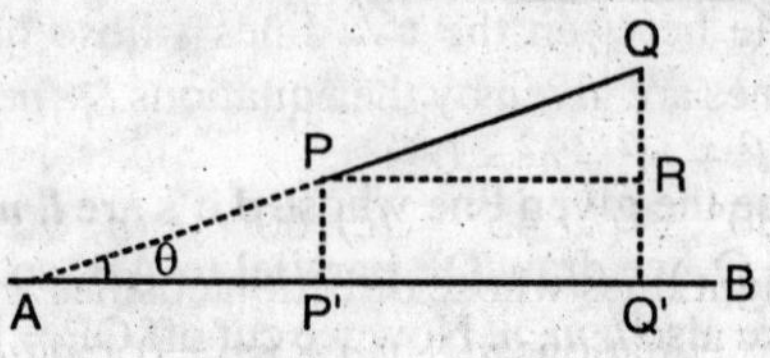

Thus P′Q′ is the projection of PQ on the line AB.

∴ Length of projection P′Q′ = PR = PQ cos θ.

where θ is the angle which the line PQ makes with PR i.e. AB.

III. The projection of the join of two points P (x_1, y_1, z_1) and Q (x_2, y_2, z_2) on a line AB whose d.c's are l, m, n is

$$P'Q' = l(x_2 - x_1) + m(y_2 - y_1) + n(z_2 - z_1).$$

EXERCISE

Mark the correct alternatives of each of the following:

1. The points (0, 7, 10), (– 1, 6, 6) and (– 4, 9, 6) form an
(a) Isosceles triangle
(b) Equilateral triangle
(c) Right angle triangle
(d) Isosceles right angle triangle

2. Given P (3, 2, –4), Q (5, 4, – 4) and R (9, 8, 10) are collinear. Then the ratio in which Q divides R is
(a) 1 : 2 (b) 2 : 1 (c) 1 : 3 (d) 3 : 1

3. The ratio in which the join of (2, 1, 5), (3, 4, 5) is divided by the plane $x + y - z = \frac{1}{2}$ is
(a) 3 : 5 (b) 5 : 3 (c) 5 : 7 (d) 7 : 5

4. Angle between the diagonals of a cube is
(a) $\theta = \cos^{-1}\left(\frac{1}{2}\right)$ (b) $\theta = \cos^{-1}\left(\frac{1}{3}\right)$
(c) $\theta = \cos^{-1}\left(\frac{1}{\sqrt{2}}\right)$ (d) $\theta = \cos^{-1}\left(\frac{1}{\sqrt{3}}\right)$

5. The edges of a rectangular parallelopiped are a, b, c. Then the angles between the four diagonals are given by
(a) $\cos^{-1} 1$
(b) $\cos^{-1} \frac{a^2 - b^2 - c^2}{a^2 + b^2 + c^2}$
(c) $\cos^{-1} \frac{a^2 \pm b^2 \pm c^2}{a^2 + b^2 + c^2}$
(d) None of these

6. Angle between the two lines whose direction cosines are given by the equations $l + m + n = 0$ and $l^2 + m^2 - n^2 = 0$ is
(a) 30° (b) 45° (c) 60° (d) 90°

7. Straight lines whose direction cosines are given by the equations $ul + vm + wn = 0$ and $al^2 + bm^2 + cm^2 = 0$ are parallel if
(a) $\frac{u^2}{a^2} + \frac{v^2}{b^2} + \frac{w^2}{c^2} = 1$
(b) $\frac{u^2}{a} + \frac{v^2}{b} + \frac{w^2}{c} = 1$
(c) $\frac{u^2}{a^2} + \frac{v^2}{b^2} + \frac{w^2}{c^2} = 0$
(d) $\frac{u^2}{a} + \frac{v^2}{b} + \frac{w^2}{c} = 0$

8. The straight lines whose direction cosines are given by the equations $al + bm + cn = 0$ and $fmn + gnl + hlm = 0$ are parallel if
(a) $\frac{f}{a} + \frac{g}{b} + \frac{h}{c} = 0$ (b) $\sqrt{af} + \sqrt{bg} + \sqrt{ch} = 0$
(c) $af + bg + ch = 0$ (d) None of these

9. The projection of a line on the co-ordinate axes are 12, 3, 4, then the length of the line is given by
(a) 17 (b) 11 (c) 13 (d) 15
[J.N.U. M.C.A.]

10. Angle between the straight line whose direction cosines are given by $l + m + n = 0$ and $2l + 2m - mn = 0$, is
(a) $\frac{\pi}{3}$ (b) $\frac{\pi}{4}$
(c) $\frac{\pi}{6}$ (d) None of these

11. The direction cosines of a line which is equally inclined to the axes are
(a) $\left(\pm\frac{1}{\sqrt{2}}, \pm\frac{1}{\sqrt{2}}, \pm\frac{1}{\sqrt{2}}\right)$
(b) (1, 1, 1)
(c) $\left(\pm\frac{1}{\sqrt{3}}, \pm\frac{1}{\sqrt{3}}, \pm\frac{1}{\sqrt{3}}\right)$

(*d*) None of these [*J.N.U. M.C.A.*]

12. If a straight line makes angles 60°, 45° and θ° respectively with the axes of co-ordinates OX, OY and OZ, then θ is equal to

(*a*) 15° (*b*) 30°
(*c*) 45° (*d*) 60°

ANSWERS

1	2	3	4	5	6	7	8	9	10
(*d*)	(*a*)	(*c*)	(*b*)	(*c*)	(*c*)	(*d*)	(*b*)	(*c*)	(*c*)
11	12								
(*c*)	(*d*)								

SOME SELECTED EXPLANATORY ANSWERS

1. Let A (0, 7, 10), B (– 1, 6, 6) and C (– 4, 9, 6) denote the given points.

Then $AB = \sqrt{(-1-0)^2+(6-7)^2+(6-10)^2}$

$= \sqrt{1+1+16} = 3\sqrt{2}$

$BC = \sqrt{(-4+1)^2+(9-6)^2+(6-6)^2}$

$= \sqrt{9+9} = 3\sqrt{2}$

$AC = \sqrt{(-4-0)^2+(9-7)^2+(6-10)^2}$

$= \sqrt{16+4+16} = 6$

Since AB = BC, the triangle ABC is isosceles.

Further $AB^2 + BC^2 = \left(3\sqrt{2}\right)^2 + \left(3\sqrt{2}\right)^2$

$= 18 + 18 = 36 = AC^2$

$\therefore \quad AB^2 + BC^2 = AC^2.$

$\therefore$ ΔABC is right angle-isosceles triangle.

2. Let Q (5, 4, – 6) divide PR in the ratio *k* : 1. Then the co-ordinates of Q are

$$\left(\frac{9k+3}{k+1}, \frac{8k+2}{k+1}, \frac{-10k-4}{k+1}\right)$$

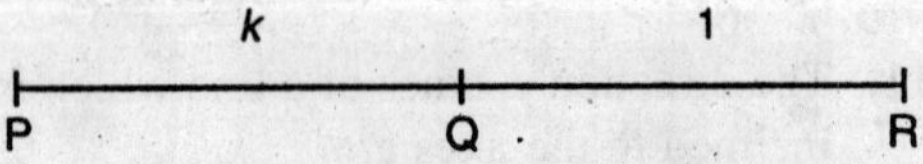

But the co-ordinates of Q are given to be (5, 4, – 6)

$\therefore$ Equating, the *x*-co-ordinates, we have

$$\frac{9k+3}{k+1} = 5 \text{ or } 9k+3 = 5k+3$$

or $4k = 2 \quad \therefore k = \frac{1}{2}.$

Hence, Q divides PR in the ratio $\frac{1}{2}:1$ or 1 : 2.

3. Let the required ratio be λ : 1. Hence the co-ordinates of the point in which the plane is cut by the join of the points (2, 1, 5), (3, 4, 3) are

$$\left(\frac{3\lambda+2}{\lambda+1}, \frac{4\lambda+1}{\lambda+1}, \frac{3\lambda+5}{\lambda+1}\right).$$

Since this point lies on the given plane, hence its co-ordinates will satisfy the equation of the plane.

$$\therefore \quad \frac{3\lambda+2}{\lambda+1} + \frac{4\lambda+1}{\lambda+1} - \frac{3\lambda+5}{\lambda+1} = \frac{1}{2}$$

or $6\lambda + 4 + 8\lambda + 2 - 6\lambda - 10 = \lambda + 1$

or $7\lambda = 5. \quad \therefore \lambda = \frac{5}{7}$

$\therefore$ The required ratio is 5 : 7.

4. Taking O, a corner of the cube as origin and OA, OB, OC the three edges through it, as axes.

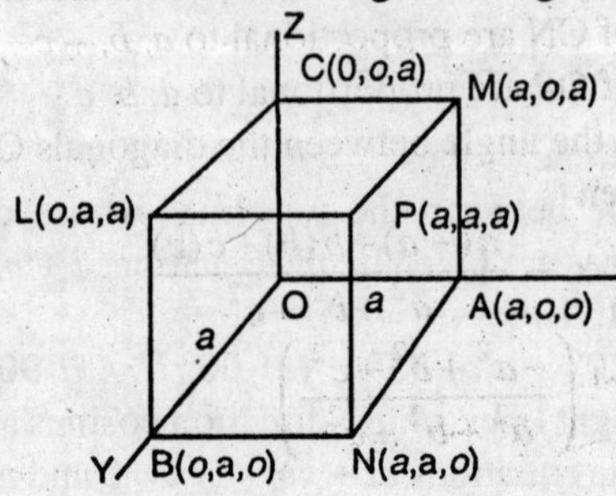

Let OA = OB = OC = a.
Then the co-ordinates of the various points are O (0, 0, 0), A (a, 0, 0), B (0, a, 0), C (0, 0, a), L (0, a, a), M (a, 0, a), N (a, a, 0), P (a, a, a).
Four diagonals are AL, BM, CN and OP.
The d.r's of the diagonal AL are $0-a, a-0, a-0$ i.e. $-a, a, a$

(using $x_2-x_1, y_2-y_1, z_2-z_1$)

or $-1, 1, 1$ (cancelling a).
Similarly d.r's of the diagonal BM are $a-0, 0-a, a-o$ i.e. $a, -a, a$ or $1, -1, 1$

(cancelling a).

If θ be the angle between the diagonals AL and BM, then

$$\cos\theta = \frac{(1)(-1)+(-1)(1)+1(1)}{\sqrt{1+1+1}\,\sqrt{1+1+1}}$$

$$\left(\because \frac{a_1a_2+b_1b_2+c_1c_2}{\sqrt{a_1^2+b_1^2+c_1^2}\,\sqrt{a_2^2+b_2^2+c_2^2}}\right)$$

$$= -\frac{1}{3}$$

$$\therefore \quad \theta = \cos^{-1}\left(-\frac{1}{3}\right) = \cos^{-1}\left(\frac{1}{3}\right).$$

Similarly the angle between other two diagonals is also the same.

5. Taking O, a corner of the rectangular parallelopiped as the origin and three edges OA, OB, OC through it as the axes. Then the co-ordinates of the various corners are
O (0, 0, 0), A (a, 0, 0), B (0, b, 0), C (0, 0, c), L (0, b, c), M (a, 0, c), N (a, b, 0), P (a, b, c).
The four diagonals are AL, BM, CN and OP.
The d.c's of AL are proportional to
$0-a, b-0, c-0$ i.e. $-a, b, c$

(using $x_2-x_1, y_2-y_1, z_2-z_1$)

Similarly d.c's of BM are proportional to $a, -b, c$
d.c's of CN are proportional to $a, b, -c$
d.c's of OP are proportional to a, b, c
If α is the angle between the diagonals OP and AL, then

$$\cos\alpha = \frac{a(-a)+b(b)+c(c)}{a^2+b^2+c^2}$$

$$\therefore \cos^{-1}\left(\frac{-a^2+b^2+c^2}{a^2+b^2+c^2}\right) \qquad ...(i)$$

Similarly angle between OP and BM

$$= \cos^{-1}\left(\frac{a^2-b^2+c^2}{a^2+b^2+c^2}\right) \qquad ...(ii)$$

Angle between OP and CN

$$= \cos^{-1}\left(\frac{a^2+b^2-c^2}{a^2+b^2+c^2}\right) \qquad ...(iii)$$

Angle between AL and BM

$$= \cos^{-1}\left(\frac{-a^2-b^2+c^2}{a^2+b^2+c^2}\right)$$

$$= \cos^{-1}\left(\frac{a^2+b^2-c^2}{a^2+b^2+c^2}\right)$$

This angle is the same as the angle between OP and CN. Similarly we can show that all other angles between other two diagonals are repeated and we get only three different angles as given by *(i)*, *(ii)* and *(iii)*. Hence angle between four diagonals are given by

$$\cos^{-1}\left(\frac{a^2\pm b^2\pm c^2}{a^2+b^2+c^2}\right).$$

6. Direction cosines of the two lines are given by

$$l+m+n=0 \qquad ...(i)$$

and $\quad l^2+m^2+n^2=0 \qquad ...(ii)$

From *(i)* we have $l=-(m+n)$
Putting this value of l in *(ii)* we get

$$(m+n)^2+m^2-n^2=0$$

or $\quad 2m^2+2mn=0$

or $\quad m(m+n)=0$

Case I

$\therefore$ when $m=0$

i.e. $\quad 0.l+m+0.n=0$

Also from *(i)* $l+m+n=0$
Soving by cross multiplication we have

$$\frac{l}{1-0}=\frac{m}{0-0}=\frac{n}{0-1}$$

or $\quad \dfrac{l}{1}=\dfrac{m}{0}=\dfrac{n}{-1}$

Case II

when $\quad m+n=0$

i.e. $\quad 0.l+m+n=0$

Also from *(i)* $l+m+n=0$

Soving by cross multiplication we have

$$\frac{l}{1-1}=\frac{m}{1-0}=\frac{n}{0-1}$$

or $\frac{l}{0}=\frac{m}{1}=\frac{n}{-1}$

Hence the d.c's of the two lines are proportional to 1, 0, – 1 and 0, 1, – 1.

If θ be the angle between the two lines, then

$$\cos\theta=\frac{1(0)+0(1)+(-1)(-1)}{\sqrt{1+0+1}\sqrt{0+1+1}}=\frac{1}{2}.$$

$\therefore \theta = 60°$.

7. The d.c's of the two lines are given by

$$ul+vm+wn=0 \qquad ...(i)$$

and $al^2+bm^2+cn^2=0$ ...(ii)

Eliminating n from *(i)* and *(ii)* and dividing throughout by m^2 we have

$$\frac{l^2}{m^2}(aw^2+cu^2)+2uvc\frac{l}{m}+(bw^2+cv^2)=0 \qquad ...(iii)$$

which is a quadratic in $\frac{l}{m}$.

If l_1, m_1, n_1 and l_2, m_2, n_2 are the d.c's of two lines, then $\frac{l_1}{m_1}, \frac{l_2}{m_2}$ are the roots of *(ii)*.

Now two lines will be parallel if

$$\frac{l_1}{l_2}=\frac{m_1}{m_2}=\frac{n_1}{n_2}$$

or if $\frac{l_1}{m_1}=\frac{l_2}{m_2}$

or if the quadratic *(iii)* has equal roots.

or if the discriminant of *(iii)* is equal to zero.

or if $4c^2u^2v^2-4(aw^2+cu^2)(bw^2+cv^2)=0$

$[\because b^2-4ac=0]$

or if $c^2u^2v^2-(abw^4+acw^2v^2+bcu^2w^2+c^2u^2v^2)=0$

or if $-w^2\left(acw^2+bcu^2+cav^2\right)=0$

if $\frac{u^2}{a}+\frac{v^2}{b}+\frac{w^2}{c}=0.$

8. The d.c's of the lines are given by

$$al+bm+cn=0 \qquad ...(i)$$

and $fmn+gnl+hlm=0$ ...(ii)

Elimination n between equation *(i)* and *(ii)* and dividing throughout by m^2 we have

$$ag\frac{l^2}{m^2}+(af+bg-ch)\frac{l}{m}+bf=0 \qquad ...(iii)$$

Then if l_1, m_1, n_1 and l_2, m_2, n_2 be the proportional d.c's of the two lines, then

$\frac{l_1}{m_1}, \frac{l_2}{m_2}$ are the root's of *(iii)*

Now, if two lines are parallel then

$$\frac{l_1}{l_2}=\frac{m_1}{m_2}=\frac{n_1}{n_2}$$

or if $\frac{l_1}{m_1}=\frac{l_2}{m_2}$

or if the roots of *(iii)* are equal

or if the discriminant of (iii) is zero.

or if $(af+bg-ch)^2-4agbf=0$

or if $af+bg-ch=\pm 2\sqrt{(agbf)}$

Taking –ive sign we get

$$af+bg-ch=-2\sqrt{agbf}$$

or $af+bg+2\sqrt{agbf}=ch$

or $\left(\sqrt{af}+\sqrt{bg}\right)^2=\left(\sqrt{ch}\right)^2$

or $\left(\sqrt{af}+\sqrt{bg}\right)=\pm\sqrt{ch}.$

Taking –ive sign we get

$$\sqrt{af}+\sqrt{bg}+\sqrt{ch}=0$$

which is the required equation.

9. Let PQ be a line of length r having d.c's $\cos\alpha$, $\cos\beta$ and $\cos\gamma$. Then projection of the line along respective co-ordinàte axes x, y, z are $r\cos\alpha$, $r\cos\beta$ and $r\cos\gamma$.

According to the problem

$$r\cos\alpha=12 \qquad ...(i)$$

$$r\cos\beta=4 \qquad ...(ii)$$

$$r\cos\gamma=3 \qquad ...(iii)$$

Squaring all the equations and adding we get

$$r^2\left(\cos^2\alpha+\cos^2\beta+\cos^2\gamma\right)=144+16+9$$

or $r^2=169$

$\left(\because \cos^2\alpha+\cos^2\beta+\cos^2\gamma=r\right)$

or $r=13.$

10. The d.c's of the two lines are given by

$$l + m + n = 0 \quad ...(i)$$

$$2l + 2m - mn = 0 \quad ...(ii)$$

From *(i)* we have $l = -(m + n)$

Putting this value of l in *(ii)*, we get

$$-2m - 2n + 2m - mn = 0$$

or $\quad -2n - mn = 0$

or $\quad -n(2 + m) = 0$

Case I

$\therefore$ when $n = 0$

we have $0.l + 0.m + 1.n = 0$

Also from *(i)* $l + m + n = 0$

Solving by cross multiplication we have

$$\frac{l}{0-1} = \frac{m}{1-0} = \frac{n}{0-0}$$

i.e. $$\frac{l}{-1} = \frac{m}{1} = \frac{n}{0}$$

Case II

when $m + 2 = 0$

i.e., $m = -2$

then *(i)* becomes $1 - 2 + n = 0$

It is satisfied by $l = 1, n = 1$ ($\because 1 - 2 + 1 = 0$)

Putting $l = 1, m = -2$ and $n = 1$ in *(ii)* we get $2 - 4 + 2 = 0$ or $0 = 0$.

$\therefore$ our choice of $l = 1, n = 1$ is correct.

Hence, direction ratios of two lines are $-1, 1, 0$ and $1, -2, 1$.

If θ is the angle between the two lines, then

$$\cos\theta = \frac{(-1)(1) + 1(-2) + 0(1)}{\sqrt{1+1+0}\sqrt{1+4+1}} = \frac{-3}{\sqrt{5}\sqrt{6}}.$$

$$\therefore \cos\theta = -\frac{\sqrt{3}}{2}$$

$$\therefore \theta = \cos^{-1}\left(\frac{\sqrt{3}}{2}\right) = \frac{\pi}{6}.$$

18. STATISTICS

Statistics : Statistics is the science which deals mainly with collection, presentation and interpretation of numerical data.

Statistical Series : An arrangemen of the data in a systematic order is called a *distribution* or a *series*. If the variable (also called *variate*) of the series is continuous, the series is called a *continuous series*. Series formed by descrete variable is called a *discrete series*. A continuous variable is one which is capable of taking all possible values between a certain limit.

Frequency : In some intervals, the number of occurence of some item is called its frequency.

Frequency Distribution : A set of numbers x_1, x_2, ..., x_n corresponding to the events E_1, E_2, ..., E_n which occur with frequencies $f_1, f_2, ..., f_n$ respecitvely, so that $f_i \geq 0$ and $x_1 < x_2 < .... < x_n$ is called the frequency distribution.

Frequency distribution are of the types :

1. Continuous Distribution : The classes of the form 1–5, 5–10, 10–15, etc. are known to be continuous distribution.

The class 0–5 means 0 or more than 0 but less than 5.

In this class lower limit = 0
upper limit = 5

Class size = upper limit – lower limit mid value of class = $\frac{1}{2}$ (upper limit + lower limit)

2. Discontinuous Distribution : The classes of the type 1–5, 6–10, 11–15, etc. are said to be discontinuous distribution. We can make them continuous by adding 0.5 to upper limit and subtracting 0.5 from the lower limit. Thus 0.5–5.5, 5.5–10.5, 10.5–15.5, etc. are in continuous form.

Measures of Central Tendency : Certain methods which reduce the given data to a single representative figure is called the measure of central tendency.

The commonly used measures of central tendency are *the mean, the median* and *the mode.*

Means :

1. *The arithmetic mean* of a set of n numbers is

$$\overline{X} = \frac{x_1 + x_2 + ... + x_n}{n} = \frac{\sum x}{n}$$

If the numbers occur f_1, f_2, ..., f_n times, respectively, then

$$\overline{X} = \frac{f_1x_1 + f_2x_2 + ... + f_nx_n}{f_1 + f_2 + ... + f_n} = \frac{\sum fx}{\sum f}$$

If the numbers are associated with a *weighting factor* $w_i \geq 0$, then

$$\overline{X} = \frac{w_1x_1 + w_2x_2 + ... + w_nx_n}{w_1 + w_2 + ... + w_n} = \frac{\sum wx}{\sum w}$$

2. *The geometric mean* of a set of *n* numbers is

$$\overline{G} = \sqrt[n]{x_1x_2....x_n}$$

If the numbers occur $f_1, f_2, ... f_n$ times, respectively then $\overline{G} = \sqrt[n]{x_1^{f_1}x_2^{f_2}....x_n^{f_n}}$

where $n = f_1 + f_2 + ... + f_n$.

3. *The harmonic mean* of a set of *n* numbers is

$$\overline{H} = \frac{1}{\left(\frac{1}{n}\right)\left(\frac{1}{x_1} + \frac{1}{x_2} + ... + \frac{1}{x_n}\right)} = \frac{n}{\sum\left(\frac{1}{x}\right)}$$

If the numbers occur f_1, f_2, ..., f_n times, respectively, then

$$\overline{H} = \frac{1}{\left(\frac{1}{n}\right)\left(\frac{f_1}{x_1} + \frac{f_2}{x_2} + ... + \frac{f_n}{x_n}\right)} = \frac{n}{\sum\left(\frac{f}{x}\right)}$$

where $n = f_1 + f_2 + ... + f_n$.

4. *The quadratic mean* of a set of n numbers is

$$\overline{Q} = \sqrt{\frac{x_1^2 + x_2^2 + ... + x_n^2}{n}} = \sqrt{\frac{\sum x^2}{n}}$$

5. *Relation*

$\overline{H} \le \overline{G} \le \overline{X}$

Median : If the data of a series are arranged in ascending or descending order of magnitude, the value of the middle term is called the *median*.

If n is the number of terms, the median is the $\left(\frac{n+1}{2}\right)$th term in case n is *odd*.

If n is even then the average of the two middle terms is given by the median.

In case case of grouped data, the median is given by the formula

$$\text{Median} = L + \frac{(U-L)}{f} \times \left(\frac{n}{2} - C\right) = L + \frac{\frac{n}{2} - C}{f} \times i$$

Where L and U are respectively the lower and upper limit of the median class.

f is the frequency of the median class.

C is cumulative frequency of the class preceding the median class.

i is the class interval and n is the total frequency.

Mode : For ungrouped data (discrete distribution)

Mode = The value of the item which occurs most frequently.

For grouped data (continuous distribution)

$$\text{Mode} = L + \frac{f_m - f_1}{(f_m - f_1) + (f_m - f_2)} \times (U - L)$$

$$= L + \frac{f_m - f_1}{2f_m - f_1 - f_2} \times h$$

Where U and L are upper and lower limit

h is width of the modal class

f is the frequency of the modal class.

f_1 is the frequency of the class preceding the modal class.

f_2 is the frequency of the class following the modal class.

Relation between Mean, Median and Mode :

$$\text{Median} = \text{Mode} + \frac{2}{3}(\text{Mean} - \text{Mode})$$

approximately.

or Mode = 3 Median – 2 Mean.

approximately.

Dispersion : The degree to which a frequency distribution of a set of numbers *tends to spread* about a point of central tendency is called the *dispersion* (Spread, variance).

Measures of Dispersion : Following are the most commonly used measures of dispersion

1. Range : It is a very crude measure of dispersion. It is the difference between the greatest and the least values of the items in a series. It is widely used for comparison of interest rates and stock prices in the market. For continuous distribution, it is the difference between the upper limit of the largest class and the lower limit of the smallest class.

2. Quartile Deviation : Quartiles are the sizes of the items which divide the series into four equal parts. The second Quartile is the *median*. The first and third quartiles also known as lower and upper Quartiles are mathematically represented by the formulas

$$Q_1 = L + \frac{\left(\frac{n}{4} - C_1\right)}{f_1} \times (U - L)$$

$$Q_3 = L + \frac{\left(\frac{3n}{4} - C_3\right)}{f_3} \times (U - L)$$

and Quartile deviation = $\frac{1}{2}(Q_3 - Q_1)$.

Where f_1 and f_3 are frequencies of first and third Quartile classes and c_1, c_3 are the cumulative frequencies of first and third classes.

Average or Mean Deviation : It is defined as the arithmetic average of the absolute values of the deviations, *i.e.*, all deviations taken positive, from the mean, mode or median.

(i) The deviation from the arithmetic mean $\overline{X}$ of each number x_j in a set of numbers $x_1, x_2, ..., x_n$ is $D_j = x_j - \overline{X}$ $j = 1, 2, ..., n$.

(ii) The mean deviation of the same set is

$$\overline{D} = \frac{|x_1 + x_2 + ... + x_n - n\overline{X}|}{n} = \frac{\sum |x_j - \overline{X}|}{n}$$

Where $|x_j - X|$ is the absolute value of D*j*.

If the numbers occur $f_1, f_2, ..., f_n$ times, then $n = f_1 + f_2 + ... + f_n$ and

$$\overline{D} = \frac{f_1|x_1 - \overline{X}| + f_2|x_2 - \overline{X}| + ... + f_n|x_n - \overline{X}|}{n}$$

$$= \frac{\sum f\,|n - \overline{X}|}{n}$$

4. Standard Deviation : The standard deviation in a set of number $x_1, x_2, ..., x_n$ is

$$\sigma = \sqrt{\frac{(x_1 - \overline{X})^2 + (x_2 - \overline{X})^2 + ... + (x_n - \overline{X})^2}{n}}$$

$$= \sqrt{\frac{\sum (x_j - \overline{X})^2}{n}}$$

If the numbers occurs $f_1, f_2, ..., f_n$ times, then $n = f_1 + f_2 + ... + f_n$ and

$$\sigma = \sqrt{\frac{f_1(x_1 - \overline{X})^2 + f_2(x_2 - \overline{X})^2 + ... + f_n(x_n - \overline{X})^2}{n}}$$

$$= \sqrt{\frac{\sum f_n(x - \overline{X})^2}{n}}$$

Variance : The square of standard deviation is called the variance (σ^2).

$$\therefore \sigma^2 = \frac{\sum (x - \overline{X})^2}{n} \text{ or } \sigma^2 = \sum f(x - \overline{X})^2$$

7. The covariance of two sets X $(x_1, x_2, ..., x_n)$, the arithmetic means of which are $\overline{X}$ and $\overline{Y}$, respectively, is

$$\sigma_{xy} = \frac{\sum (x - \overline{X})(y - \overline{Y})}{n}$$

Note : If n_i, x_i and σ_i, $i = 1, 2, ..., k$, are the sizes, means and standard deviation respectively of *k*- component series, then the standard deviation σ of the combined series of size $\sum_{i=1}^{k} n_i$ is given by

$$\sigma^2 = \frac{1}{n_1 + n_2 + ... + n_k}$$

$$\left[n_1\left(\sigma_1^2 + d_1^2\right) + n_2\left(\sigma_2^2 + d_2^2\right) + ... n_k\left(\sigma_k^2 + d_k^2\right)\right]$$

where $d_i = \overline{X}_i - \overline{X}$ and

$$\text{mean } \overline{X} = \frac{n_1\overline{X}_1 + n_2\overline{X}_2 + ... + n_k\overline{X}_k}{n_1 + n_2 + ... + n_k}$$

Coefficient of Dispersion : Different measures of dispersion discussed in the preceding section are *absolute measures* as they have been studied with references to a single series in the units of variables. But if there are more than one series of different variables, for example one of ages and the other of heights, absolute dispersion will not be helpful for their comparison. To compare them, we make use of the measures of relative dispersion. This is generally achieved by dividing the absolute measure of dispersion by the corresponding average from which it is calculated. The resulting number will be independent of the unit of measurement of the variable and is defined as the *coefficient of dispersion*.

1. For range deviation the coefficient of Range is $\frac{L - S}{L + S}$ where L and S are the largest and smallest value.

2. For quartile deviation the coefficient of dispersion is $\frac{Q_3 - Q_1}{Q_3 + Q_1}$

where Q_1 = first quartile or lower quartile.
Q_3 = thrid quartile or upper quartile.

3. Coefficient of variation = $\frac{\sigma}{\overline{X}} \times 100$

4. Coefficient of dispersion based on standard deviation is given by $\frac{\text{Standard Deviation}}{\text{Mean}} = \frac{\sigma}{\overline{X}}$.

Relation between different measure of dispersion :

1. Quartile Deviation = $\frac{2}{3}$ × Standard Deviation.

2. Mean Deviation = $\frac{4}{5}$ × Standard Deviation.

Moments : The arithmetic mean of the various powers of deviations in any distribution are called moments of the distribution. Moments are denoted by 'μ'.

1. *Moments about origin :* The rth moment of x about origin a is given by

$$\mu'_r = \frac{1}{n}\sum_i f_i (x_i - a)^r$$

where, $n = \sum_i f_i$ and r is positive integer.

$\therefore\ \mu'_0 = 1,$

$$\mu'_1 = \frac{\sum f(x-a)}{\sum f} = \frac{\sum fx}{n} - a = \overline{X} - a = d \text{ (say)}.$$

Then $\mu'_2 = \sigma^2 + d^2$.

2. *Central Moments :* The moments about arithmetic mean $\overline{X}$ of the distribution is called central moments.

The rth central moment is given by

$$\mu_r = \frac{1}{n}\sum_i f_i (X_i - \overline{X})^r$$

$$\therefore\ \mu_0 = \frac{\sum f}{\sum f} = 1$$

$$\mu_1 = \frac{\sum f(x-\overline{X})}{\sum f} = \frac{\sum fx}{n} - \overline{X} = 0$$

$$\mu_2 = \frac{1}{n}\sum_i f_i (X_i - \overline{X})^2 = \sigma^2.$$

Relation Between the Moments About the Mean and the Moments About Any Point :

I. *Moments about any point in terms of moments about the mean* $\overline{X}$.

$$\mu'_r = \mu_r + r_{c_1} d\,\mu_{r-1} + r_{c_2} d^2\,\mu_{r-2} + \dots + d^r$$

where $d = \overline{X} - a$.

Putting $r = 2, 3, 4$ etc. in above relation we get

$$\mu'_2 = \mu_2 + 2d\mu_1 + d^2 = \mu_2 + d^2 = \sigma^2 + d^2$$

$$\mu'_3 = \mu_3 + 3d\mu_2 + 3d^2\mu_1 + d^3 = \mu_3 + 3d\mu_2 + d^3$$

$$\mu'_4 = \mu_4 + 4d\mu_3 + 6d^2\mu_2 + 4d^3\mu_1 + d^4$$

$$= \mu_4 + 4d\mu_3 + 6d^2\mu_2 + d^4.$$

II. *Moments about the mean* $\overline{X}$ *in terms of moments about any point a.*

$$\mu_r = \mu'_2 - r_{c_1} d\,\mu'_{r-1} + r_{c_2} d^2\,\mu'_{r-2} - \dots + (-1)^r d^r$$

Putting $r = 2, 3, 4, \dots$ respectively we get

$$\mu_2 = \mu'_2 - 2d\mu'_1 + d^2 = \mu'_2 - d^2 = \sigma^2$$

$$\mu_3 = \mu'_3 - 3d\mu'_2 + 3d^2\mu'_1 - d^3 = \mu'_3 - 3d\mu'_2 + 2d^3$$

$$\mu_4 = \mu'_4 - 4d\mu'_3 + 6d^2\mu'_2 - 4d^3\mu'_1 + d^4$$

$$= \mu'_4 - 4d\mu'_3 + 6d^2\mu'_2 - 3d^4.$$

Skewness : Skewness is defined as lack of symmetry and is indicated in asymmetrical distribution i.e. distribution in which the values of mean, mode and median are not identical and in which quartiles are not at equal distance from the median. In such distributions the range is usually greater on one side of the mode than the other. The curve has a longer tail on one side. This behaviour of the distribution exhibits skewness.

Measures of Skewness :

1. *Absolute Skewness :*

(i) Absolute Skewness = $Q_3 + Q_2 - 2$.Median.

(ii) When Mode is not ill defined then Absolute Skewness = Mean – Mode.

(iii) When Mode is ill defined then Absolute Skewness = $3(\overline{X} - \text{Median})$.

2. *Relative Skewness :*

(i) The first coefficient of skewness due to Bowley is defined as

Coefficient of Skewness

$$= \frac{(Q_3 - \text{Median}) - (\text{Median} - Q_1)}{(Q_3 - \text{Median}) + (\text{Median} - Q_1)}$$

$$= \frac{Q_3 + Q_1 - 2\,\text{Median}}{Q_3 - Q_1}$$

(ii) The second Ceofficient of Skewness, due to Pearson, is given by

Coefficient of Skewness

$$= \frac{\text{Mean} - \text{Mode}}{\text{Standard Deviation}} = \frac{\overline{X} - \text{Mode}}{\sigma}$$

$$= \frac{3(\overline{X} - \text{Median})}{\sigma}$$

Range of this skewness is from – 1 to + 1.

For symmetrical distribution, Mean, Median and Mode are equal and so the skewness is zero.

Skewness can be positive as well as negative. If the mean is greater than *mode* or the *median*, the skewness will be positive. If it is less, skewness will be negative. In other words if the curve has longer tail on the right, then skewness is positive. The longer tail on the left indicates negative skewness.

Positively Skewd Distribution

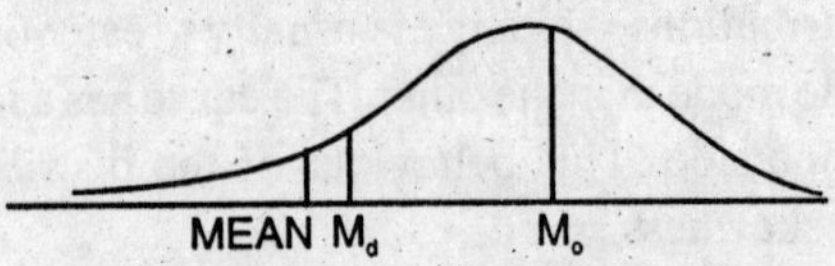

Negatively Skewed Distribution

Pearson's β and γ Coefficients : Karl Pearson defind the following four coefficients, based upon the first four moments about the mean

$$\beta \text{ coefficients} \begin{cases} \beta_1 = \dfrac{\mu_3^2}{\mu_2^3} = \dfrac{\mu_3^2}{\sigma^6} \\ \beta_2 = \dfrac{\mu_4}{\mu_2^2} = \dfrac{\mu_4}{\sigma^4} \end{cases}$$

$$\gamma \text{ coefficients} \begin{cases} \gamma_1 = \sqrt{\beta_1} = \dfrac{\mu_3}{\sigma^3} \\ \gamma_2 = \beta_2 - 3 = \dfrac{\mu_4}{\sigma_2^2} - 3 \\ \quad = \dfrac{\mu_4 - 3\sigma^4}{\mu_2^2} = \dfrac{\mu_4 - 3\sigma^4}{\sigma^4} \end{cases}$$

β_1 gives a measure of departure from symmetry and also defines a measure of skewness.

Kurtosis : The degree of flatness or peakness in a region about the mode of a frequency curve is known as kurtosis and it is denoted by β_2.

In normal distribution, $\beta_2 = 3$ or $\gamma_2 = 0$. In other words Kurtosis for the normal curves is 3 and $(\beta_2 - 3)$ defines the excess of Kurtosis.

The curve for which $\beta_2 < 3$ i.e. $\gamma_2 < 0$ are called *platykurtic* and they are flatter than the normal curve. On the other hand the curves which are more peaked than the normal curve are called *leptokurtic* and for such curves $\beta_2 > 3$ or $\gamma_2 > 0$. The normal curve is neither flat nor peaked is also called mesokurtic.

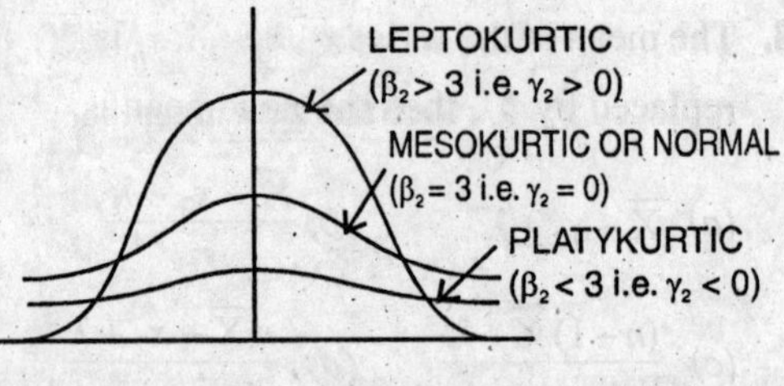

EXERCISE

Mark the correct alternative(s) of each of the following :

1. If the means of a set of observations $x_1, x_2, ..., x_n$ is $\overline{X}$, then the mean of the observations $x_i + 2i$; $i = 1, 2, 3, ..., n$ is

   (a) $\overline{X}+2$ (b) $\overline{X}+2n$

   (c) $\overline{X}+(n+1)$ (d) $\overline{X}+n$

2. The weighted AM of first n natural numbers whose weights are equal to the corresponding numbers is equal to

   (a) $2n + 1$ (b) $\frac{1}{2}(2n+1)$

   (c) $\frac{1}{3}(2n+1)$ (d) $\frac{2n+1}{6}$

3. 10 is the mean of a set of 7 observations and 5 is the mean of a set of 3 observations. The mean of the combined set is given by
(a) 15 (b) 10 (c) 8.5 (d) 7.5

4. Out of 50 students in a class, 10 were of the age of 10 years, 14 were of the age of 11 years and the remaining of 12 years. Then AM of students is
(a) 11.5 (b) 11.24
(c) 11.32 (d) None of these

5. The GM of the series 1, 2, 4, 8, 16, ..., 2^n is,
(a) $2^{\frac{n+1}{2}}$ (b) 2^{n+1}
(c) $2^{n/2}$ (d) 2^n

6. If G_1, G_2 are the geometric means of the series of observations and G is the GM of the ratios of the corresponding observations then G is equal to
(a) $\frac{G_1}{G_2}$ (b) $\log G_1 - \log G_2$
(c) $\frac{\log G_1}{\log G_2}$ (d) $\log (G_1.G_2)$

7. If a variable takes values 0, 1, 2, ..., n with frequencies 1, ${}^nC_1$, ${}^nC_2$, ..., ${}^nC_n$, then the AM is
(a) n (b) $\frac{2^n}{n}$ (c) $n+1$ (d) $\frac{n}{2}$

8. The mean of the series $x_1, x_2, ..., x_n$ is $\overline{X}$. If x_2 is replaced by λ, then the new mean is
(a) $\overline{X} - x_2 + \lambda$ (b) $\frac{\overline{X} - x_2 - \lambda}{n}$
(c) $\frac{(n-1)\overline{X} + \lambda}{n}$ (d) $\frac{n\overline{X} - x_2 + \lambda}{n}$

9. The one which is the measure of the central tendency is
(a) mode
(b) mean deviation
(c) standard deviation
(d) coefficient of correlation

10. The most stable measure of central tendency is
(a) the mean (b) the mediam
(c) the mode (d) None of these

11. A statistical measure which cannot be determined graphically is
(a) median (b) mode
(c) harmonic mean (d) mean

12. The positional average of central tendency is
(a) GM (b) HM (c) AM (d) Median

13. Which of the following is not a measure of central tendency
(a) mean (b) median
(c) mode (d) range

14. In a college of 100 teachers, the mean age is 30 years and in another college of 50 teachers, the mean age is 60. The mean age of the teachers of two colleges taken together is
(a) 40 (b) 42
(c) 45 (d) None of these
[D.U. M.C.A.]

15. In any discrete series (when all values are not same) the relationship between M.D about mean and S.D is
(a) M.D = S.D (b) M.D ≥ S.D
(c) M.D < S.D (d) M.D ≤ S.D

16. Quartile deviation of the following data 32, 45, 28, 72, 63, 59, 60 is
(a) 14.5 (b) 15 (c) 15.5 (d) 16

17. The mean deviation from the mean of the AP d, $a+d, a+2d, ..., a+2nd$ is
(a) $n(n+1)d$ (b) $\frac{n(n+1)d}{2n+1}$
(c) $\frac{n(n+1)d}{2n}$ (d) $\frac{n(n-1)}{2n+1}d$

18. The standard deviation of Q. 17 is
(a) $\frac{n(n+1)}{3}d^2$ (b) $\sqrt{\frac{n(n+1)}{3}}\,d$
(c) $\frac{n(n-1)}{3}d^2$ (d) $\sqrt{\frac{n(n-1)}{3}}\,d$

19. The standard deviation of 4, 5, 6, 7, ..., 13 is x, then the standard deviation of 14, 15, 16, ..., 23 is
(a) 2 (b) $10x$
(c) $x+10$ (d) $x+\sqrt{10}$

20. The mean of five observations is 15 and their variance is 9.2 If three observations are 16, 17 and 19, the other two are
(a) 10, 11 (b) 11, 12
(c) 12, 13 (d) None of these

21. The variance of first n natural numbers is

(a) $\frac{n^2+1}{12}$ (b) $\frac{n^2-1}{12}$

(c) $\frac{(n+1)(2n+1)}{6}$ (d) None of these

22. The variance of the following numbers 15, 25, 5, 10, 30 is

(a) 15.20 (b) 9.27
(c) 430 (d) 86

23. One series containing numbers has mean 8, variance 24 and the second series containing 5 numbers has mean 8, variance 18. Then the variance of the combined data is

(a) 20.25 (b) 26
(c) 16.5 (d) None of these

[D.U. M.C.A.]

24. The quartile deviation of 15, 60, 28, 40, 72, 30 and 50 is

(a) 16 (b) 60 (c) 28 (d) 44

25. In a distribution it is given that, mean = 20, Mode = 10, and standard deviation = 10. Then the coefficient of skewness is

(a) 0 (b) 1
(c) 10 (d) None of these

26. In a distribution, the coefficient of skewness is 0.5. If the sum of lower and upper quartiles is 120 and median in 40, then upper and lower quartiles are

(a) 50, 70 (b) 60, 60
(c) 100, 20 (d) None of these

27. The standard deviation of a distribution is 5. The value of the fourth central moment (μ_4), in order that the distribution be mesokurtic should be

(a) 3 (b) Greater than 1875
(c) 1875 (d) Less than 1875

28. The first three moments of a distribution about the value 4 are 1.5, 17 and – 30 respectively. Then the value of μ_3 equals

(a) 99.75 (b) – 99.75
(c) 109.75 (d) – 109.75

29. A data is given below :
Size of the item : 31 32 33 34 35
The value of μ_3 from the data is

(a) 0 (b) 1 (c) 2 (d) 3

30. The value of μ_2 from the data given in Q. 29 is

(a) 0 (b) 1 (c) 2 (d) 3

31. The first two moments of a distribution about the value 5 of the variable are 2 and 20 respectively. Then the variance of the distribution is

(a) 8 (b) 16 (c) 10 (d) 18

32. A data is given below
3, 6, 8, 10, 18.
Then the value of the moment μ_3 about the value 5 is

(a) 486.2 (b) 468.4
(c) 484.6 (d) 686.4

33. For a certain distribution $Q_1 = 50$, Median = 155 and $Q_9 = 260$. Then Kelly's coefficient of skewness equals to

(a) 0 (b) 1
(c) 1.5 (d) None of these

34. For a certain distribution, the arithmetic mean is 45, median is 48 and Karl Pearson's coefficient of skewness is – 0.4. Then the standard deviation of the distribution is

(a) 11.5 (b) 22.5
(c) 33.5 (d) None of these

ANSWERS

1	2	3	4	5	6	7	8	9	10
(c)	(c)	(c)	(c)	(a)	(a)	(d)	(d)	(a)	(a)
11	**12**	**13**	**14**	**15**	**16**	**17**	**18**	**19**	**20**
(c)	(d)	(d)	(a)	(d)	(c)	(b)	(b)	(a)	(b)
21	**22**	**23**	**24**	**25**	**26**	**27**	**28**	**29**	**30**
(b)	(d)	(a)	(a)	(b)	(c)	(c)	(b)	(a)	(c)
31	**32**	**33**	**34**						
(b)	(b)	(a)	(b)						

SOME SELECTED EXPLANATORY ANSWERS

1. Given $\overline{X} = \frac{x_1 + x_2 + ... + x_n}{n}$.

$\therefore \quad n\overline{X} = x_1 + x_2 + ... + x_n$.

Let $\overline{Y}$ be the mean of observations $x_i + 2i; i = 1, 2, ..., n$.

Then $\overline{Y} = \frac{(x_1 + 2.1) + (x_2 + 2.2) + (x_3 + 2.3) + ... + (x_n + 2.n)}{n}$

$= \frac{\frac{1}{n}\sum_{i=1}^{n} x_i + 2(1+2+3+....+n)}{n}$

$= \frac{1}{n}\sum_{i=1}^{n} x_i + \frac{2n(n+1)}{2n}$

$= \overline{X} + (n+1)$.

2. Required weighted mean is

$\overline{X} = \frac{1.1 + 2.2 + 3.3 + ... + n.n}{1+2+3+....+n}$

$= \frac{1^2 + 2^2 + 3^2 + ... + n^2}{1+2+3+....+n}$

$= \frac{\frac{n(n+1)(2n+1)}{6}}{\frac{n(n+1)}{2}}$

$= \frac{2n+1}{3}$.

3. Given $n_1 = 7,\ \overline{X}_1 = 10,\ n_2 = 3,\ \overline{X}_2 = 5$

$\therefore$ Combined mean $= \frac{n_1\overline{X}_1 + n_2\overline{X}_2}{n_1 + n_2}$

$= \frac{7 \times 10 + 3 \times 5}{7+3} = \frac{85}{10} = 8.5.$

4. Required AM

$= \frac{10 \times 10 + 14 \times 11 + \{50 - (10+14)\} \times 12}{10 + 14 + \{50 - (10+14)\}}$

$= \frac{10 \times 10 + 14 \times 11 + 26 \times 12}{10 + 14 + 26}$

$= \frac{566}{50} = 11.32$.

5. GM of the series $1, 2, 4, 8, ..., 2^n$

$= \{1.2.4.8....2^n\}^{1/n} = \{2^1.2^2.2^3.....2^n\}^{1/n}$

$= \left\{2^{\frac{n(n+1)}{2}}\right\}^{1/n} = 2^{\frac{n+1}{2}}$.

6. Let $x_1, x_2, ..., x_n$ and $y_1, y_2, ..., y_n$ be two series of observations with geometric means G_1 and G_2 respectively.

Then $\quad G_1 = (x_1.x_2,....x_n)^{1/n}$ and

$G_2 = (y_1 \cdot y_2,....y_n)^{1/n}$.

Since G is the geometric mean of the ratios of the corresponding observations, then

$$G = \left\{\frac{x_1}{y_1}.\frac{x_2}{y_2}.\frac{x_3}{y_3}....\frac{x_n}{y_n}\right\}^{1/n}$$

$$= \frac{(x_1.x_2.x_3....x_n)^{1/n}}{(y_1.y_2.y_3....y_n)^{1/n}} = \frac{G_1}{G_2}.$$

7. Required mean

$$\overline{X} = \frac{0.1 + 1.^nC_1 + 2.^nC_2 + 3.^nC_3 + ... + n.^nC_n}{1 + {}^nC_1 + {}^nC_2 + ... + {}^nC_n}$$

$$= \frac{\sum_{r=0}^{n} r.^nC_r}{\sum_{r=0}^{n} {}^nC_r} = \frac{\sum_{r=1}^{n} r.\frac{n}{r}.^{n-1}C_{r-1}}{\sum_{r=0}^{n} {}^nC_r}$$

$$\left[\because {}^nC_r = \frac{n}{r}.^{n-1}C_{r-1}\right]$$

$$= \frac{n\sum_{r=1}^{n} {}^{n-1}C_{r-1}}{\sum_{r=0}^{n} {}^nC_r} = \frac{n.2^{n-1}}{2^n} = \frac{n}{2}.$$

8. We have

$$\overline{X} = \frac{x_1 + x_2 + ... + x_n}{n}$$

then $\quad n\overline{X} = x_1 + x_2 + ... + x_n.$

Let $\overline{Y}$ be the new mean when x_2 is replaced by λ. Then

$$\overline{Y} = \frac{x_1 + \lambda + x_3 + ... + x_n}{n}$$

$$= \frac{(x_1 + x_2 + ... + x_n) - x_2 + \lambda}{n}$$

$$= \frac{n\overline{X} - x_2 + \lambda}{n}.$$

15. Let $\frac{x_i}{\lambda_i}$; $i = 1, 2, 3, ..., n$ be a frequency distribution.

Then $\quad S.D = \sqrt{\frac{1}{N}\sum_{i=1}^{n} f_i (x_i - \overline{X})^2}$

and $\quad M.D = \frac{1}{N}\sum_{i=1}^{n} f_i \left|x_i - \overline{X}\right|$

Let $\left|x_i - \overline{X}\right| = z;\ i = 1, 2, 3, ..., n.$

Then $(S.D)^2 - (M.D)^2 = \frac{1}{N}\sum_{i=1}^{n} f_i z_i^2 - \left(\frac{1}{N}\sum_{i=1}^{n} f_i z_i\right)^2$

$$= \sigma_z^2 \geq 0$$

$\therefore$ S.D $\geq$ M.D.

16. Arranging the values in ascending order we get 28, 32, 45, 59, 60, 63, 72.

$Q_1 = \text{Value of} \left(\frac{N+1}{4}\right)th \text{ item} = \frac{7+1}{4} = 2\text{nd item}$

i.e. 32.

$Q_2 = \text{Value of } 3\left(\frac{N+1}{4}\right)th \text{ item} = 3\left(\frac{7+1}{4}\right) = 6\text{th}$ item i.e. 63.

$$\therefore \text{ Quartile Deviation} = \frac{Q_3 - Q_1}{2} = \frac{63-32}{2}$$

$$= \frac{31}{2} = 15.5.$$

17. The mean of the series $a, a + d, a + 2d, ..., a + 2nd$ is

$$\overline{X} = \frac{1}{2n+1}[a + a + d + a + 2d + ... + a + 2nd]$$

$$= \frac{1}{2n+1}\left\{\frac{2n+1}{2}(a + a + 2nd)\right\}$$

$$= a + nd.$$

Therefore, Mean deviation from mean

$$= \frac{1}{2n+1}\sum_{r=0}^{2n}\left|(a + rd) - (a + nd)\right|$$

$$= \frac{1}{2n+1}\sum_{r=0}^{2n}\left|r - n\right| d$$

$$= \frac{1}{2n+1} : 2d\,(1 + 2 + ... + n)$$

$$= \frac{n(n+1)}{2n+1} d.$$

18. We have

$$\sigma^2 = \frac{1}{2n+1}\sum_{r=0}^{2n}\{(a + rd) - (a + nd)\}^2$$

$$= \frac{2d^2}{2n+1}(1^2 + 2^2 + ... + n^2)$$

$$= \frac{n(n+1)}{3} d^2$$

$$\therefore \ \sigma = \sqrt{\frac{n(n+1)}{3}}.d.$$

19. From the solution of Q. 18 we know that

$$\sigma = \sqrt{\frac{n\,(n+1)}{3}}\, d.$$

From the series 4, 5, 6, 7, ..., 13, we have $n = 9, d = 1$ and $\sigma = x$.

$$\therefore \quad x = \sqrt{\frac{9\,(9+1)}{3}}\,1 = \sqrt{30}$$

Also for the series 14, 15, 16, 17, ..., 23, we have $n = 9, d = 1$.

$$\therefore \quad \sigma = \sqrt{\frac{9\,(9+1)}{3}}\,1 = \sqrt{30}$$

$\therefore$ $\sigma = x$ is the required solution.

20. Mean of the observations i.e. $\frac{\sum x}{N} = 15$.

$\therefore \sum x = N \times \text{Mean} = 5 \times 15 = 75.$

Let the two missing observations be a and b

$\therefore \quad 16 + 17 + 19 + a + b = 75$

$\therefore \quad a + b = 75 - 32 = 23 \qquad ...(i)$

$$\text{Variance} = (\text{S.D})^2 = \frac{\sum d^2}{N} - \left(\frac{\sum d}{N}\right)^2$$

$$= \frac{\sum x^2}{N} - \left(\frac{\sum x}{N}\right)^2$$, taking 0 as the arbitrary origin.

i.e. $\frac{\sum x^2}{N} = \left(\frac{\sum x}{N}\right)^2 + \text{variance}$.

or $\frac{\sum x^2}{N} = (15)^2 + 9.2 = 234.2.$

$\therefore \sum x^2 = 234.2 \times 5 = 1171.$

i.e. $(16)^2 + (17)^2 + (19)^2 + a^2 + b^2 = 1171$

i.e. $256 + 284 + 361 + a^2 + b^2 = 1171$

i.e. $a^2 + b^2 = 1171 - 906$

i.e. $a^2 + b^2 = 256 \quad ...(ii)$

From (i) $a = (23 - b)$.

Substituting this value in (ii) we get

$(23 - b)^2 + b^2 = 265$

i.e. $529 - 46b + b^2 + b^2 = 265$

i.e. $2b^2 - 46b + 264 = 0$

i.e. $b^2 - 23b + 132 = 0$

i.e. $(b - 12)(b - 11) = 0$

i.e. $b = 12$ or 11

Substituting this in (i) we get $a = 11$ or 12

i.e. If $a = 11$, $b = 12$ and if $a = 12$ the $b = 11$

$\therefore$ The missing observations are 11 and 12.

21. We have

$$\sigma^2 = \frac{1}{n}\sum_{i=1}^{n} x_i^2 - \left(\frac{1}{n}\sum_{i=1}^{n} x_i\right)^2$$

$$= \frac{1}{n}(1^2 + 2^2 + 3^3 + ... + n^2) - \left\{\frac{1}{n}(1 + 2 + 3 + ... + n)\right\}^2$$

$$= \frac{1}{n}\,\frac{n(n+1)(2n+1)}{6} - \left(\frac{n+1}{2}\right)^2$$

$$= \frac{n^2 - 1}{12}.$$

22. Arranging in ascending order we get the series as 5, 10, 15, 25, 30.

Mean, $\quad \overline{X} = \frac{5 + 10 + 15 + 25 + 30}{5} = 17$

$\therefore$ Variance,

$$\sigma^2 = \frac{(5-17)^2 + (10-17)^2 + (15-17)^2 + (25-17)^2 + (30-17)^2}{5}$$

$$= \frac{430}{5} = 86.$$

23. The variance of combined data

$$\sigma^2 = \frac{1}{n_1 + n_2}\left[n_1\sigma_1^2 + n_2\sigma_2^2 + \frac{n_1 n_2}{n_1 + n_2}(\overline{X}_1 - \overline{X}_2)^2\right]$$

$$= \frac{1}{3+5}\left[(3 \times 24) + (5 \times 18) + \frac{3 \times 5}{3+5}(8-8)^2\right]$$

$$= 20.25.$$

24. Arranging the values in ascending order we get 15, 28, 30, 40, 50, 60, 72

$Q_1 = \text{Value of}\left(\frac{N+1}{4}\right) = \frac{7+1}{4} = \text{2nd item i.e. } 28.$

$Q_2 = \text{Value of } 3\left(\frac{N+1}{4}\right) = 3\left(\frac{7+1}{4}\right) = \text{6th item}$

i.e. 60.

$\therefore$ Quartile Deviation $= \frac{Q_3 - Q_1}{2}$

$$= \frac{60 - 28}{2} = \frac{32}{2} = 16.$$

25. Coefficient of Skewness

$$= \frac{\text{Mean} - \text{Mode}}{\text{Standard Deviation}}$$

$$= \frac{20 - 10}{10} = 1.$$

26. Coefficient of Skewness $= \frac{Q_3 + Q_1 - 2\,\text{Median}}{Q_3 - Q_1}$

It is given that $Q_3 + Q_1 = 120$ ...(i)
Median = 40
Coefficient of Skewness = 0.5

$$\therefore \quad 0.5 = \frac{120 - 2 \times 40}{Q_3 - Q_1}$$

or $\quad Q_3 - Q_1 = 80$ ...(ii)

Solving (i) and (ii) we get

$Q_1 = 20, Q_3 = 100.$

27. Given $\sigma = 5$

$\therefore \ \mu_2 = \sigma^2 = 25$

For mesokurtic $\beta_2 = 3$

But $\quad \beta_2 = \dfrac{\mu_4}{\mu_2^2} = 3$

or $\quad \dfrac{\mu_4}{625} = 3$

or $\quad \mu_4 = 1875.$

28. Given $\mu_1' = 1.5, \mu_2' = 17, \mu_3' = -30$

$$\text{But} \quad \mu_3 = \mu_3' - 3\mu_2'\mu_1' + 2\mu_1'^3$$
$$= -30 - 3 \times 17 \times 1.5 + 2\,(1.5)^3$$
$$= -99.75.$$

29. From the given data we get

$$\overline{X} = 33, \quad \sum (x - \bar{x}) = 0, \quad \sum (x - \bar{x})^2 = 10,$$

$$\sum (x - \bar{x})^3 = 0$$

$$\therefore \ \mu_3 = \frac{1}{n} \sum (x - \bar{x})^3 = \frac{0}{5} = 0.$$

30. From the given data we get

$$\overline{X} = 33, \quad \sum (x - \bar{x}) = 0, \quad \sum (x - \bar{x})^2 = 10,$$

$$\sum (x - \bar{x})^3 = 0$$

$$\therefore \ \mu_2 = \frac{1}{n} \sum (x - \bar{x})^2 = \frac{10}{5} = 2.$$

31. Here $a = 5$, $\mu_1' = 2, \mu_2' = 20$

But variance, $\sigma^2 = \mu_2' - (\mu_1')^2$
$= 20 - 2^2 = 16.$

32. Here $a = 5$

For computing moment μ_3 about a, we are to form table as b given below :

x	$x - a$	$(x - a)^2$	$(x - a)^3$
3	− 2	4	− 8
6	1	1	1
8	3	9	27
10	5	25	125
18	13	169	2197
Total 45	20	208	2342

$$\text{But } \mu_3 = \frac{1}{n} \sum (x - \bar{x})^3 = \frac{2342}{5} = 468.4.$$

33. Given $Q_1 = 50$; Median, $M_d = 155$; $Q_9 = 260$
Kellys Coeff. of Skewness is given by

$$S_{k_k} = \frac{Q_9 + Q_1 - 2M_d}{Q_9 - Q_1} = \frac{260 + 50 - 2 \times 155}{260 - 55} = 0.$$

34. Here $\overline{X} = 45$; $M_d = 48$ and $S_{kp} = -0.4$.

$$\text{Now } S_{kp} = \frac{3\,(\overline{X} - M_d)}{\sigma}$$

$$\therefore \ \sigma = \frac{3\,(\overline{X} - M_d)}{S_{kp}}$$

$$\text{or } \sigma = \frac{3\,(45 - 48)}{-0.4} = \frac{9}{0.4} = 22.5.$$

19. PROBABILITY

Definition : Probability is a concept which numerically measures the degree of uncertainty and therefore of certainty of the occurrence of events.

Experiment : An operation which can produce some well-defined outcomes, is an experiment.

Random Experiment : If in each trial of an experiment conducted under identical conditions, the outcome is not unique, but may be any of the possible outcomes then such an experiment is known as a random experiment.

In an random experiment

(i) all outcomes of the experiment are known in advance.

(ii) the exact outcome of any specific performance of the experiment is unpredictable i.e. not known in advance.

Sample Space : The set of all possible outcomes in a random experiment is called a sample space, provided no two or more of these outcomes can occur simultaneously and exactly one of these outcomes must occur whenever the experiment is conducted. Each element of a sample space is called a *sample point*.

Events : Any subset of a sample space is called an event. It is of two types :

(i) Simple event.

(ii) Compound event.

Simple Event : An event consisting of a single point is called an simple event.

Compound Event : It is the joint occurrence of two or more simple events.

Certain and Impossible Events : If S is a sample space, then S and null set ϕ both are events. S is called certain events and ϕ is called an impossible events.

Equally Likely Events : The given events are said to be equally likely, if none of them is expected to occur in preference to the other.

Exhaustic Events : A system of events is said to be exhaustive if on each performance of the experiment at least one of the events of the system is must to occur.

For example, on tossing a coin, the events {H} and {T} form an exhaustic system of events.

Mutually Exclusive Events : A set of events is said to be mutually exclusive if the occurrence of one of them precludes the occurrence of any of the remaining events.

In set-theoretic notation, events $A_1, A_2, ..., A_m$ are mutually exclusive if $A_i \cap A_j = \phi$ for $i \neq j$ and $1 \leq i, j \leq m$.

Algebra of Events : Let A and B be two events. Then

(i) the event "either A or B" is said to occur if at least one of A and B occurs. It *does not occur* if none of A and B occurs. We write it as 'A or B' also and represent it by $A \cup B$ or $A + B$.

(ii) the event "both A and B" is said to *occur* if both A as well as B occur simultaneously. It *does not occur* if at least one of A and B does not occur. We write it as 'A and B' also and represent it by $A \cap B$ or AB.

(iii) the event "A not" occurs if A does not occur. It *does not occur* if A occurs. We write as A'. $\overline{A}$, A^c or $S - A$ also.

(iv) the event "A but not B" is said to occur if A occurs but B does not occur. It *does not occur* if either A does not or $A \cap B$ occurs. It is represented by $A - B$.

Some Useful Results :

If $A' = S - A$, then

(i) $(A \cup B)' = A' \cap B'$

(ii) $(A \cap B)' = A' \cup B'$

(iii) $A - B = A - (A \cap B) = A \cap B'$

(iv) $A' - B = (A' \cap B') = (A \cup B)'$

(v) $A' - B' = A' \cap B = B - A$

(vi) $A \cap (B \cap C) = (A \cap B) \cup (A \cap C)$

Probability of an Event : In performance of a random experiment the occurrence of any event is always uncertain but a measure of its probable occurrence can be devised. Which then is called probability of the event. To devise this measurement following conventions are made.

(i) Probability of null event is 0.

(ii) Probability of sure event is 1.

(iii) Probability of an event which is less likely to occur is smaller than the probability of the event which is more likely to occur.

Classical Approach : In this approach the sample space is assumed to be finite, its sample points are equally likely, pair-wise mutually exclusive and taken together form an exhaustive system.

Let S denotes the sample space of a random experiment and A be an event. Then the probability of A is defined by the rational number

$$= \frac{\text{number of sample points favorable to the event A}}{\text{total number of sample points in the sample space S}} = \frac{n(A)}{n(S)}$$

Probability of A is denoted by P(A), i.e.

$P(A) = \frac{n(A)}{n(S)}$.

Some Theorem :

1. If $A \subset B$ then

 (i) $P(A) \leq P(B)$

 (ii) $P(B - A) = P(B) - P(A)$

2. $P(\phi) = 0$
3. $P(S) = 1$
4. $0 \leq P(A) \leq 1$
5. $P(A') = 1 - P(A)$
6. $P(B - A) = P[B - (\widetilde{A} \cap B)] = P(B) - P(A \cap B)$
7. $P(A \cup B) = P(A) + P(B) - P(A \cap B)$
8. $P(A \cup B) = P(A) + P(B)$ if $A \cap B = \phi$
9. $P(A \cup B \cup C) = P(A) + P(B) + P(C) - P(A \cap B) - P(B \cap C) - P(C \cap A) + P(A \cap B \cap C)$
10. $P(A) = P(A \cap B) + P(A \cap B')$
11. If $A \subset A_1 \cup A_2 \cup A_3 \cup .... \cup A_n$ and $A \cap A_1$, $A \cap A_2$, $A \cap A_3$,.... and $A \cap A_n$ are pair-wise mutually exclusive, then $P(A) = P(A \cap A_1) + P(A \cap A_2) + P(A \cap A_3) + ... + P(A \cap A_n)$.

Conditional Probability : Let S be the sample space. Let A and B be any events, $A \neq \phi$. Then probability of the event B, assuming that A is known to have occured, is called conditional probability of B restricted to the occurrence of A. It is denoted by $P\left(\frac{B}{A}\right)$

Since A is assumed to have occurred, therefore, B occur if and only if a sample point of B which is also in A results in (i.e. the event $A \cap B$ occur). Thus probability of the event B restricted to the occurrence of the event A is the same as the probability of the event $A \cap B$ while A is considered as a sample space.

$$\therefore \ P\left(\frac{B}{A}\right) = \frac{n(A \cap B)}{n(A)} = \frac{P(A \cap B)}{P(A)}.$$

Thus it follows from here that

$$P(A \cap B) = P(A).P\left(\frac{B}{A}\right).$$

If $A \neq \phi$ and $B \neq \phi$, then

$$P(A \cap B) = P(A).P\left(\frac{B}{A}\right) = P(B).P\left(\frac{A}{B}\right).$$

Independent Events : Two events are said to be *independent* if the probable occurrence or non-occurrence of any one is not effected by the occurrence or non-occurrence of the other, i.e. two events A and B are independent if $P\left(\frac{A}{B}\right) = P\left(\frac{A}{B'}\right) = P(A)$ or

$P\left(\frac{B}{A}\right) = P\left(\frac{B}{A'}\right) = P(B)$ or $P(A \cap B) = P(A).P(B)$.

Note : 1. Three events A, B and C are *independent* if $P(A \cap B \cap C) = P(A)\,P(B)\,P(C)$.

2. Three events A, B and C are called *pair-wise independent* if $P(A \cap B) = P(A)\,P(B)$.

$P(B \cap C) = P(B)\,P(C)$ and $P(C \cap A) = P(C)\,P(A)$.

3. Three independent events are always pair-wise independent, but its converse is not true.

Independent Experiments : Let there be two random experiments performed one after the other. If on repeated performances the sample space of any is not effected by the results of the other, then the two experiments are independent of each other.

i.e. *(i)* consider the tossing of a coin twice, clearly the sample space for the second toss is not effected by the results of the first toss. So the two tosses are independent random experiments.

(ii) In throwing of a die twice, the two throws are independent of each other. So the two throws are independent random experiments.

Note : In drawing of two cards, without replacement, from a well-shuffled ordinary deck of 52 playing cards, the two draws are not independent experiments.

Some Relations Between Independence and Mutually Exclusiveness of Two Events :

(i) If two events $A \neq \phi$ and $B \neq \phi$ are independent, then they are not mutually exclusive.

(ii) If two events $A \neq \phi$ and $B \neq \phi$ are mutually exclusive, then they are not independent.

(iii) If three events $A \neq \phi, B \neq \phi$ and $C \neq \phi$ are independent, then they are not mutually exclusive. Rather none of the pairs A, B; B, C and C, A is mutually exclusive.

(iv) If three events $A \neq \phi, B \neq \phi$ and $C \neq \phi$ are such that any two of these are mutually exclusive then A, B and C are not independent.

e.g. say A and B are mutually exclusive, then $P(A \cap B) = 0$ and so $P(A \cap B \cap C) \leq P(A \cap B) = 0$

i.e. $P(A \cap B \cap C) = 0$ but $P(A)\,P(B)\,P(C) \neq 0$

$\therefore$ A, B and C are not independent.

Binomial Distribution for Successive Events : Suppose p and q are the respective chances of the happening and failing of an event at a single trial. Then the chance of its happening r times (exactly) in trials is ${}^nC_r p^r q^{n-r}$ because the chance of its happening r times and failing $n - r$ times in a given order is $p^r q^{n-r}$ and there are ${}^nC_r$ such orders, which are mutually exclusive and for any such order the probability is $p^r q^{n-r}$. Therefore the required probability is

${}^nC_r\, p^r q^{n-r}$.

Baye's Theorem : Suppose $A_1, A_2, \ldots, A_n$ are mutually exclusive and exhaustive set of events. Thus they divide the sample into n parts and an events B occurs.

Then the conditional probability that A_i happen (given that B has happened) is given by

$$P\left(\frac{A_i}{B}\right) = \frac{P(A_i)\,P\left(\frac{B}{A_i}\right)}{\sum_{i=1}^{n} P(A_i).P\left(\frac{B}{A_i}\right)}$$

Note : *(i)* The events $A_1, A_2, \ldots, A_n$ are usually referred to as 'hypothesis' and the probabilities $P(A_1), P(A_2), \ldots, P(A_n)$ are known as the '*priori*' probabilities as they exist before we obtain any information from the experiment.

(ii) The probabilities $P\left(\frac{B}{A_i}\right); i = 1, 2, \ldots, n$ are called the 'likehood probabilities' as they tell us how likely the event B under consideration occur, given each and every priori probabilities.

(iii) The probabilities $P\left(\frac{A_i}{B}\right); i = 1, 2, \ldots, n$ are called the posterior probabilities as they are determined after the results of the experiment are known.

EXERCISE

Mark the correct alternative(s) of each of the following :

1. From a pack of 52 cards two are drawn at random; find the chance that one is knave and the other a queen

(a) $\frac{4}{363}$ (b) $\frac{8}{663}$ (c) $\frac{10}{663}$ (d) $\frac{4}{663}$

2. A bag contains 5 white, 7 black and 4 red balls. Then the chance that three balls drawn at random are all white is

(a) $\frac{1}{56}$ (b) $\frac{3}{56}$ (c) $\frac{1}{28}$ (d) $\frac{1}{14}$

3. In shuffling a pack of cards, four are accidently dropped. The chance that the missing cards should be one from each suit is

(a) $\frac{2017}{20825}$ (b) $\frac{2190}{20823}$

(c) $\frac{2197}{20825}$ (d) $\frac{2192}{20823}$

4. There are three works, one consisting of 3 volumes, one of 4, and the other of one volume. They are placed on a shelf at random. Then the chance that volumes of the same works are all together is

(a) $\frac{1}{140}$ (b) $\frac{1}{70}$ (c) $\frac{3}{140}$ (d) $\frac{1}{35}$

5. A and B throw with two dice; if A throw's 9, then B's chance of throwing a higher number is

(a) $\frac{1}{3}$ (b) $\frac{1}{4}$ (c) $\frac{3}{4}$ (d) $\frac{1}{6}$

6. Three cards are drawn at random from an ordinary pack. The chance that they will consist of a knave, a queen and a king is

(a) $\frac{16}{5525}$ (b) $\frac{8}{5525}$

(c) $\frac{24}{5525}$ (d) None of these

7. Three coins are tossed simultaneously the probability of getting at least one head is

(a) $\frac{3}{4}$ (b) $\frac{1}{8}$ (c) $\frac{5}{8}$ (d) $\frac{7}{8}$

8. Six boys and six girls sit in a row randomly. The probability that the boys and girls sit, alternately is

(a) $\frac{2}{231}$ (b) $\frac{5}{462}$

(c) $\frac{1}{132}$ (d) None of these

9. A bag contains 5 browns and 4 white socks. A man pulls out two socks. The probability that they are of the same colour is

(a) $\frac{1}{6}$ (b) $\frac{5}{108}$ (c) $\frac{4}{9}$ (d) $\frac{5}{18}$

10. A bag contains 17 counters marked with the numbers 1 to 17. A counter is drawn and replaced; a second drawing is then made; what is the chance that the first number is even and the second odd?

(a) $\frac{70}{289}$ (b) $\frac{72}{289}$

(c) $\frac{75}{289}$ (d) $\frac{69}{289}$

11. Four persons draw each a card from an ordinary pack. The chance that no two cards are of equal value is

(a) $\frac{2816}{4165}$ (b) $\frac{2816}{4516}$

(c) $\frac{2814}{4165}$ (d) $\frac{2814}{4516}$

12. A bag contains 5 white and 3 black balls, and 4 are successively drawn out and not replaced; what is the chance that they are alternately of different colours?

(a) $\frac{1}{7}$ (b) $\frac{1}{14}$ (c) $\frac{3}{14}$ (d) $\frac{2}{7}$

13. In three throws with a pair of dice, the chance of throwing doublets at least once is

(a) $\frac{93}{216}$ (b) $\frac{5}{12}$

(c) $\frac{91}{216}$ (d) $\frac{7}{12}$

14. M telegrams are distributed at a random over N communication channels (N>M). The probability of the event—

A = {not more than one telegram will be sent over any channel} is

(a) $\binom{N}{M}\Big/N^M$ (b) $\binom{N}{M}\Big/M^N$

(c) $\binom{N}{M}M!\Big/N^M$ (d) None of these

[J.N.U. M.C.A.]

15. If 4 whole numbers taken at random are multiplied togther, then the chance that the last digit in the product is 1, 3, 7 or 9 is

(a) $\frac{11}{625}$ (b) $\frac{13}{625}$

(c) $\frac{17}{625}$ (d) $\frac{16}{625}$

16. If two coins are tossed 5 times, what is the chance that there will be 5 heads and 5 tails?

(a) $\frac{61}{256}$ (b) $\frac{63}{256}$

(c) $\frac{65}{256}$ (d) None of these

17. A, B, C in order cut a pack of cards, replacing them after each cut, on condition that the first who cuts a spade shall win a prize. Then their respective chances are

(a) $\frac{9}{37}, \frac{12}{37}, \frac{16}{37}$ (b) $\frac{12}{37}, \frac{16}{37}, \frac{9}{37}$

(c) $\frac{16}{37}, \frac{9}{37}, \frac{12}{37}$ (d) $\frac{16}{37}, \frac{12}{37}, \frac{9}{37}$

18. In a collection of 6 mathematics books and of 4 physics books, the probability that 3 particular mathematics book will be together, is

(a) $\frac{1}{8}$ (b) $\frac{1}{10}$

(c) $\frac{1}{15}$ (d) None of these

19. Two cards are drawn from a pack of 52 cards. What is the probability that either both are red or both are kings?

(a) $\frac{55}{221}$ (b) $\frac{44}{221}$

(c) $\frac{33}{221}$ (d) $\frac{66}{221}$

20. A bag contains 10 white and 15 black balls. Two balls are drawn in succession without replacement. What is the probability that first is white and second is black?

(a) $\frac{1}{2}$ (b) $\frac{1}{4}$

(c) $\frac{3}{4}$ (d) None of these

21. A bag contains 19 tickets, numbered from 1 to 19. A ticket is drawn and then another ticket is drawn and then another ticket is drawn without replacement.

The probability that both tickets will shows even numbers is

(a) $\frac{1}{19}$ (b) $\frac{2}{19}$ (c) $\frac{3}{19}$ (d) $\frac{4}{19}$

22. The persons A and B throw a die alternately till one of them gets a 'three' and wins the game. The probability that A wins is

(a) $\frac{2}{11}$ (b) $\frac{4}{11}$

(c) $\frac{6}{11}$ (d) None of these

23. A fair coin is tossed repeatedly. If tail appears on first four tosses, then the probability of head appearing on fifth toss equals

(a) $\frac{1}{2}$ (b) $\frac{1}{32}$

(c) $\frac{31}{32}$ (d) $\frac{1}{5}$

24. There are four machines and it is known that exactly two of them are faulty. They are tested, one by one, in a random order till both the faulty machines are identified. Then the probability that only two tests are needed is

(a) $\frac{1}{3}$ (b) $\frac{1}{6}$ (c) $\frac{1}{2}$ (d) $\frac{1}{4}$

25. A coin whose faces are marked 2, 3 is thrown 5 times. What is the chance of obtaining a total of 12?

(a) $\frac{3}{16}$ (b) $\frac{5}{16}$ (c) $\frac{7}{16}$ (d) $\frac{9}{16}$

26. A coin is tossed n times, what is the chance that the head will present itself an odd number of times?

(a) $\frac{1}{2^{n-1}}$ (b) $\frac{1}{2^{n+1}}$

(c) $\frac{1}{2}$ (d) $\frac{1}{2^{n-2}}$

27. Six persons throw for a stake, which is to be won by the one who first throws head with a penny; if they throw in succession, the chance that fourth person win is

(a) $\frac{4}{15}$ (b) $\frac{4}{31}$ (c) $\frac{4}{63}$ (d) $\frac{4}{127}$

28. Counters marked 1, 2, 3 are placed in a bag and one is withdrawn and replaced. The operation being repeated three times, what is the chance of obtaining a total of 6?

(a) $\frac{5}{27}$ (b) $\frac{7}{27}$ (c) $\frac{1}{3}$ (d) $\frac{11}{27}$

29. The chance of throwing 10 exactly in one throw with 3 dice is

(a) $\frac{1}{8}$ (b) $\frac{1}{7}$

(c) $\frac{1}{14}$ (d) None of these

30. A and B throw 3 dice; if A throw 8, what is B's chance of throwing a higher number?

(a) $\frac{14}{27}$ (b) $\frac{16}{27}$ (c) $\frac{2}{3}$ (d) $\frac{20}{27}$

31. Two integers are selected at random from integers 1 to 11. If the sum is even, then the probability that both the numbers are odd is

(a) $\frac{3}{5}$ (b) $\frac{4}{5}$ (c) $\frac{1}{5}$ (d) $\frac{2}{5}$

32. A four figure number is formed of the figures 1, 2, 3, 5 with no repetitions. The probability that the number is divisible by 5 is

(a) $\frac{3}{4}$ (b) $\frac{1}{2}$ (c) $\frac{1}{4}$ (d) $\frac{1}{8}$

33. An unbiased die with faces marked 1, 2, 3, 4, 5 and 6 is rolled four times out of four face values obtained. The probability that the minimum face value is not less than 2 and the maximum face value is not greater than 5 is,

(a) $\frac{16}{81}$ (b) $\frac{1}{81}$ (c) $\frac{80}{81}$ (d) $\frac{65}{81}$

34. The numbers are chosen from 1 to 30. The probability that they are not consecutive is

(a) $\frac{144}{145}$ (b) $\frac{143}{145}$

(c) $\frac{142}{145}$ (d) None of these

35. Fifteen coupons are numbered 1, 2, 3, ..., 15. Seven coupons are selected at random one at a time with replacement. The probability that the largest number appearing on selected coupon is 9, is

(a) $\left(\frac{9}{16}\right)^6$ (b) $\left(\frac{8}{15}\right)^7$

(c) $\left(\frac{3}{5}\right)^7$ (d) None of these

36. Out of 30 consecutive integers, two are chosen at random, the probability that their sum is odd

(a) $\frac{13}{29}$ (b) $\frac{15}{29}$

(c) $\frac{17}{29}$ (d) None of these

37. If two squares are chosen at random on a chess board, the probability that they have a side in common is

(a) $\frac{1}{9}$ (b) $\frac{2}{9}$ (c) $\frac{1}{18}$ (d) $\frac{1}{6}$

38. Three squares of a chess board being chosen at random, what is the chance that two are of one colour and one of another?

(a) $\frac{4}{7}$ (b) $\frac{14}{21}$

(c) $\frac{16}{21}$ (d) $\frac{6}{7}$

39. Three letters, to each of which corresponds an envelope, are placed in the envelops at random. The probability that all the letters are not placed in the right envelops is

(a) $\frac{1}{6}$ (b) $\frac{5}{6}$ (c) $\frac{1}{3}$ (d) $\frac{2}{3}$

40. Two numbers a and b are chosen at random from the set of first 30 natural numbers. The probability that $a^2 - b^2$ is divisible by 3 is

(a) $\frac{37}{87}$ (b) $\frac{47}{87}$

(c) $\frac{57}{87}$ (d) None of these

41. If the probability that A and B will die within a year are p and q respectively, then the probability that only one of them will be alive at the end of the year is

(a) pq (b) $p(1-q)$

(c) $q(1-p)$ (d) $(p+q-2pq)$

42. A matrix is chosen at random from the set of all 2×2 matrices with element 0 and 1 only. The probability that the value of the determinant of the matrix chosen is positive, is

(a) $\frac{1}{16}$ (b) $\frac{1}{8}$ (c) $\frac{3}{16}$ (d) $\frac{1}{4}$

[D.U. M.C.A.]

43. If n integers taken at random are multipled together, then the probability that the last digit of the product is 1, 3, 7 or 9 is

(a) $\frac{2^n}{5^n}$ (b) $\frac{4^n - 2^n}{5^n}$

(c) $\frac{4^n}{5^n}$ (d) None of these

44. If 4 whole numbers taken at random are multiplied together, the probability that the last digit in the product will be 1, 3, 7 or 9 is

(a) $\frac{16}{625}$ (b) $\frac{1}{625}$

(c) $\frac{15}{625}$ (d) None of these

[D.U. M.C.A.]

45. The probability that a person tossing three fair coins will get either all heads or all tails for the second time on the 5th toss is

(a) $\frac{31}{128}$ (b) $\frac{49}{512}$

(c) $\frac{15}{64}$ (d) $\frac{27}{256}$

[J.N.U. M.C.A]

46. A fair dice is tossed repeatedly until six shows up 3 times. The probability that exactly 5 tosses are needed is

(a) $\frac{25}{1296}$ (b) $\frac{4}{432}$

(c) $\frac{125}{216}$ (d) None of these

[J.N.U. M.C.A.]

47. Two natural numbers a and b are choosen at random. The probability that $a^2 + b^2$ is divisible by 7 is

(a) $\frac{1}{7}$ (b) $\frac{1}{49}$ (c) $\frac{2}{7}$ (d) $\frac{4}{49}$

48. A box contains n enumerated articles. All the articles are taken out one by one at random. The probability that the numbers of the selected articles are in the sequence 1, 2, ..., n is

(a) $\frac{1}{n!}$ (b) $\frac{n}{n!}$

(c) $\frac{1}{n(n!)}$ (d) None of these

[J.N.U. M.C.A.]

49. A car is parked by an owner amongst 25 cars in a row, not at either end. On his return, he finds that exactly 15 places are still occupied. The probability that both the neighbouring parking places are empty is

(a) $\frac{91}{276}$ (b) $\frac{15}{164}$

(c) $\frac{15}{92}$ (d) None of these

[J.N.U. M.C.A.]

50. If four numbers are selected at random from the ten numbers 1, 2, 3, ..., 10, repetitions being allowed, then the probability that the product of the numbers is of the form $3n - 1$ or $3n + 1$, n being a non-negative integer is

(a) 0.32 *(b)* 0.24

(c) 0.192 *(d)* None of these

[J.N.U. M.C.A.]

51. The probability that a radar will detect an object is p. The probability that it will be detected in n-cycles is

(a) $1 - p^n$ *(b)* $1 - (1 - p)^n$

(c) p^n *(d)* None of these

[J.N.U. M.C.A.]

52. If p is the probability that a man aged X will die in a year, then the probability that out of n men $A_1, A_2, ..., A_n$ each aged X, A_1 will die in a year and be first to die, is

(a) $1 - (1 - p)^n$ *(b)* $(1 - p)^n$

(c) $\frac{1}{n}\left[1-(1-p)^n\right]$ *(d)* $\frac{1}{n}(1-p)^n$

53. There are four balls in a bag, but it is not known of what colours they are; one ball is drawn and found to be white; the chance that all the balls are white is

(a) $\frac{1}{10}$ *(b)* $\frac{1}{5}$ *(c)* $\frac{3}{10}$ *(d)* $\frac{2}{5}$

54. In a bag there are six balls of unknown colours; three balls are drawn and found to be black; the chance that no black ball is left in the bag is

(a) $\frac{1}{7}$ *(b)* $\frac{1}{35}$ *(c)* $\frac{2}{7}$ *(d)* $\frac{2}{35}$

55. One of a pack of 52 cards has been lost; from the remainder of the pack two cards are drawn and are found of to spades. The chance that the missing card is spade is

(a) $\frac{1}{5}$ *(b)* $\frac{11}{50}$ *(c)* $\frac{6}{25}$ *(d)* $\frac{13}{50}$

56. Chance of throwing 12 in a single throw with 3 dice is

(a) $\frac{23}{216}$ *(b)* $\frac{1}{9}$ *(c)* $\frac{25}{216}$ *(d)* $\frac{1}{8}$

57. A bag contains 7 tickets marked with the numbers 0, 1, 2, 3, ..., 6 respectively. A ticket is drawn and replaced : the chance that after 4 drawings the sum of the numbers drawn is 8 is

(a) $\frac{149}{2401}$ *(b)* $\frac{150}{2401}$

(c) $\frac{151}{2401}$ *(d)* $\frac{152}{2401}$

58. There are 10 tickets, 5 of which are blanks, and the others are marked with the numbers 1, 2, 3, 4, 5. What is the probability of drawing 10 in three trials when the tickets are replaced at every trial?

(a) $\frac{11}{1000}$ *(b)* $\frac{22}{1000}$

(c) $\frac{33}{1000}$ *(d)* None of these

59. There are 10 tickets, 5 of which are blanks, and the others are marked with the numbers 1, 2, 3, 4, 5; what is the probability of drawing 10 in three trials if the tickets are not replaced?

(a) $\frac{1}{60}$ *(b)* $\frac{1}{20}$ *(c)* $\frac{1}{12}$ *(d)* $\frac{7}{60}$

60. There are four six faced dies such that each of two dies bears the numbers 0, 1, 2, 3, 4 and 5 and the other two dies are ordinary dies bearing number 1, 2, 3, 4, 5 and 6. If all the four dies are thrown, the probability that the total of numbers coming up on all the dies is 10.

(a) $\frac{100}{1296}$ *(b)* $\frac{125}{1296}$

(c) $\frac{150}{1296}$ *(d)* $\frac{50}{1296}$

61. From a box containing 10 cards, numbered 1, 2, 3, ..., 10 four cards are drawn together. What is the probability that their sum is even?

(a) $\frac{13}{18}$ *(b)* $\frac{8}{25}$ *(c)* $\frac{7}{16}$ *(d)* $\frac{11}{21}$

[J.N.U. M.C.A.]

62. From a pack of cards two are drawn at random. What is the probability that one is a king and other is a queen?

(a) $\frac{5}{629}$ *(b)* $\frac{8}{663}$

(c) $\frac{10}{687}$ *(d)* None of these

[J.N.U. M.C.A.]

63. The probabilities that three men hit a target are respectively $\frac{1}{6}, \frac{1}{4}$ and $\frac{1}{3}$. If only one hits the target, what is the probability that it was the first man?

(a) $\frac{11}{57}$ (b) $\frac{21}{57}$ (c) $\frac{12}{67}$ (d) $\frac{13}{67}$

[J.N.U. M.C.A.]

64. On two ranches A and B each having 1000 cattle, there is an outbreak of hoof and mouth disease. The proportions of infected cattle are $\frac{1}{5}$ and $\frac{1}{4}$ respectively. One cow is chosen at random. If 70% of the infected cattle on each ranch are less than 1 year old, then the probability that the chosen cow comes from ranch B has the disease and is more than 1 year old is

(a) $\frac{1}{50}$ (b) $\frac{2}{50}$ (c) $\frac{3}{50}$ (d) $\frac{4}{50}$

[J.N.U. M.C.A.]

65. An anti aircraft gun can take a maximum of four shots at a plane moving away from it. The probability of hitting the plane at the first, second, third and fourth shot are 0.4, 0.3, 0.2 and 0.1 respectively. What is the probability that the gun hits the plane?

(a) 0.7325 (b) 0.7286
(c) 0.6976 (d) 0.6574

[J.N.U. M.C.A.]

66. Missiles are fired at a target. The probability of each missile hitting the target is p; the hits are independent of one another. Each missile which hits the target brings it down with probability r. The missiles are fired until the target is brought down or the missile reserve is exhausted. The reserve consits of n missiles ($n > 2$). Defining the event A = "at least one missile will remain in reserve", the probability P(A) is

(a) $1-(1-pr)^{n-1}$ (b) $(1-pr)^{n-1}$
(c) $(pr)^{n-1}$ (d) None of these

[J.N.U. M.C.A.]

67. Four roads lead away from a jail. A prisoner is escaping from the jail and selects a road at random. If road I is selected, the probability of escaping is $\frac{1}{8}$, for road II it is $\frac{1}{6}$. for road III it is $\frac{1}{4}$ and if road IV is selected the probability of escaping is $\frac{9}{10}$. What is the probability that the prisoner will succeed escaping?

(a) $\frac{173}{480}$ (b) $\frac{171}{408}$
(c) $\frac{171}{480}$ (d) $\frac{173}{480}$

[J.N.U. M.C.A.]

68. A problem is given to three students whose chances of solving it are $\frac{1}{2}, \frac{1}{3}$ and $\frac{1}{4}$ respectively. What is the probability that the problem will be solved?

(a) $\frac{1}{4}$ (b) $\frac{1}{2}$
(c) $\frac{3}{4}$ (d) None of these

69. If A, B and C are independent events such that P(A) = 0.2, P(B) – 0.1 and P(C) = 0.4 then $P(A \cup B \cup C)$ equals

(a) 0.9 (b) 0.008
(c) 0.560 (d) 0.568

[J.N.U. M.C.A.]

70. A and B are two independent events. The probability that both A and B occur is $\frac{1}{6}$ and the probability that neither of these is $\frac{1}{3}$. Then the probability of occurrence of A is

(a) $\frac{1}{2}$ (b) $\frac{1}{3}$ (c) $\frac{1}{5}$ (d) $\frac{1}{6}$

71. If A and B are two independent events in a given sample and the probability that both A and B occur is 0.16 while the probability that neither occurs is 0.36. The probabilities P(A) and P(B) are respectively

(a) 0.6, 0.6 (b) 0.8, 0.2
(c) 0.4, 0.4 (d) 0.9, 0.4

[J.N.U. M.C.A.]

72. In an election candidate A has 0.4 chance of winning, B has 0.3 chance, C has 0.2 chance and D has 0.1 chance. Just before the election C withdraw. The chances of other three candidates are

(a) .5, .785, 0.620 (b) .975, 0.4, 0.3
(c) 0.5, 0.375, 0.125 (d) None of these

[J.N.U. M.C.A.]

73. The probability that at least one of the events A and B occurs is 0.7 and they occur simultaneously with probability 0.2. Then $P(\overline{A})+P(\overline{B})=$

(a) 1.8 (b) 0.6
(c) 1.1 (d) 1.4

74. For any two independent events A and B, $P\{(A\cup B)\cap(\overline{A})\cap(\overline{B})\}$ is

(a) $\le\frac{1}{4}$ (b) $>\frac{1}{4}$
(c) $\frac{1}{2}$ (d) None of these

75. If $P(A\cap B)=\frac{1}{2}; P(\overline{A}\cap\overline{B})=\frac{1}{3}$, $P(A)=p, P(B)=2p$, then the value of p is given by

(a) $\frac{3}{12}$ (b) $\frac{7}{18}$
(c) $\frac{5}{12}$ (d) $\frac{7}{12}$

ANSWERS

1	2	3	4	5	6	7	8	9	10
(b)	(a)	(c)	(c)	(d)	(a)	(d)	(c)	(c)	(b)
11	12	13	14	15	16	17	18	19	20
(a)	(a)	(c)	(c)	(d)	(b)	(d)	(c)	(a)	(b)
21	22	23	24	25	26	27	28	29	30
(d)	(c)	(a)	(b)	(b)	(c)	(c)	(b)	(a)	(d)
31	32	33	34	35	36	37	38	39	40
(a)	(c)	(a)	(a)	(d)	(b)	(c)	(c)	(b)	(b)
41	42	43	44	45	46	47	48	49	50
(d)	(c)	(a)	(a)	(d)	(a)	(b)	(a)	(c)	(b)
51	52	53	54	55	56	57	58	59	60
(b)	(c)	(a)	(b)	(b)	(c)	(a)	(c)	(a)	(b)
61	62	63	64	65	66	67	68	69	70
(d)	(b)	(c)	(c)	(c)	(a)	(d)	(c)	(d)	(a)
71	72	73	74	75					
(c)	(c)	(c)	(a)	(b)					

SOME SELECTED EXPLANATORY ANSWERS

1. The total number of cases in which two cards be drawn from a pack of 52 cards are $^{52}C_2$ i.e. 1326. Also the cases favourable to the event that one is a knave and the other a queen when drawn together are $^4C_1\times{}^4C_1$ *i.e.*, 16.

Hence the required probability $=\frac{16}{1326}=\frac{8}{663}$.

2. The total number of cases in which three balls can be drawn from (5 + 7 + 4) i.e. 16 are $^{16}C_3$ or $16\times5\times7$.
The cases favourable to the event that the balls drawn are white are $^5C_3$ or 10.

Hence the required probability $=\frac{10}{16\times5\times7}=\frac{1}{56}$.

3. The possible number of cases in which any 4 cards can be dropped from a pack of cards $={}^{52}C_4$ one card from one suit can be dropped in 13 ways.
∴ One card from each suit can be dropped in 13^4 ways.

∴ Required probability $=\frac{13^4}{^{52}C_4}=\frac{2197}{20825}$.

4. In all there are (3 + 4 + 1), that is 8 volumes. The possible number of ways in which 8 volumes can be placed on shelf are 8! and favourable number of ways in which the volumes of the same works will be altogether are $3! \times 3! \times 4! \times 1!$, where the sets of the volumes can be arranged in 3! ways; and the volumes of the sets in 3!, 4! and 1! ways respectively.
Hence the required probability

$$= \frac{3! \times 3! \times 4! \times 1!}{8!} = \frac{3}{140}.$$

5. B will win if he throws any number higher than 9, that is if he throws 10, 11 or 12. The possible number of cases in which two dice can fall are 6×6 i.e. 36.
Now 10 can turn up in 3 ways i.e. when he throws any of the following combinations
6, 4; 5, 5; 4, 6
Similarly 11 can turn up as follows :
6, 5; 5, 6
And 12 can turn up only when he throws 6, 6 with each dice.
Therefore total number of favourable cases to the event are 3 + 2 + 1 i.e. 6.

$\therefore$ Required probability $= \frac{6}{36} = \frac{1}{6}$.

6. The possible number of cases in which three cards can be drawn from a pack of 52 cards are ${}^{52}C_3$.
The knave, queen and king can each be drawn in 4 ways.
Hence the favourable number of cases to the event required are $4 \times 4 \times 4$ i.e 64.
$\therefore$ The required chances

$$= \frac{64}{{}^{52}C_3} = \frac{64 \times 3!}{52 \times 51 \times 50} = \frac{16}{5525}.$$

7. Total 2^3 i.e. 8 elements are there in the sample space.

Probability of getting head is $\frac{1}{8}$.

$\therefore$ Probability of getting at least one head is

$1 - \frac{1}{8} = \frac{7}{8}$.

8. Total number of ways of sitting = 12!
If the arrangement starts with girls, the ways of sitting of girls and boys alternately are $6! \times 6!$.
Similar for the arrangement, starting with boys i.e. $6! \times 6!$.
30 total number of favourable ways $= 2 \times 6! \times 6!$

$\therefore$ Required probability $= \frac{2 \times 6! \times 6!}{12!} = \frac{1}{132}$.

9. In all there are 5 + 4 = 9 socks.
Possible number of ways of pulling two socks = ${}^9C_2 = 36$.
Same colour can be either white or brown
$\therefore$ Favourable ways $= {}^4C_2 + {}^5C_2 = 10 + 6 = 16$.

$\therefore$ Required probability $= \frac{16}{36} = \frac{4}{9}$.

10. There are 8 even and 9 odd numbers from 1 to 17.
Therefore, the chances, that the first number drawn is even is $\frac{8}{17}$ and hence the chances that the second number drawn is odd, is $\frac{9}{17}$.
Since the two events are independent, the required chances $= \frac{8}{17} \times \frac{9}{17} = \frac{72}{289}$.

11. In the first drawn, a person can draw any card of any value. When the first card has been drawn, there are 51 cards in all; the cards differing in value from the first drawn are 48.
Hence the chances that the second card is not of the same value as the first is $\frac{48}{51}$.
Again, when the first and second have been drawn there remain 50 cards; and the cards differing in value from the first and second are 44.
Therefore, the chance that the third differs from the first and second is $\frac{44}{50}$.
Similarly, the chance that the fourth differs in value from the first, second and third is $\frac{40}{49}$.
Since these events are dependent, the required chance

$$= \frac{48}{51} \times \frac{44}{50} \times \frac{40}{49} = \frac{2816}{4165}.$$

12. There are (5 + 3), that is, 8 balls, in all, in the bag. The chance that the first drawn ball is white is $\frac{5}{8}$; and the chance that the second ball is black is $\frac{3}{7}$.

After the first ball is drawn, there are 7 balls in the bag out of which 3 are black.

Similarly the chance that the third ball is white is $\frac{4}{6}$ and the chance that the fourth is black is $\frac{2}{5}$.

Since these are dependent events, the chance that they are alternately of different colours beginning with white is $\frac{5}{8}\times\frac{3}{7}\times\frac{4}{6}\times\frac{2}{5}=\frac{1}{14}$.

Similarly the chance that the balls are alternately of different colours beginning with the black is $\frac{3}{8}\times\frac{5}{7}\times\frac{2}{6}\times\frac{4}{5}=\frac{1}{14}$.

Since the two cases are mutually exclusive, the required chance $=\frac{1}{14}+\frac{1}{14}=\frac{1}{7}$.

13. There are 6 × 6 i.e. 36 possible ways of throwing two dice, out of which 6 are favourable to the event that it is a doublet.

The chance of throwing a doublet with two dice is $\frac{6}{36}=\frac{1}{6}$.

Hence the chance of failing to throw a doublet with a pair of dice is $1-\frac{1}{6}=\frac{5}{6}$. Since throwing of a doublet with two dice is independent of the number of trials and hence the chance of failing to throw a doublet three times in succession is $\left(\frac{5}{6}\right)^3$.

Hence the required chance $= 1-\left(\frac{5}{6}\right)^3=\frac{91}{216}$.

14. M telegrams can be distributed over N channels in N^M ways.

We can choose M channels out of N channels in ${}^NC_M$ ways.

Total number of ways of sending M telegram over each channel $= {}^NC_M.M!$.

$\therefore$ Required probability $=\frac{{}^NC_M.M!}{N^M}$.

15. If the last digit in the product is not 1, 3, 7 or 9, it must be 0, or 5, or even.

Therefore none of the four numbers must end in 0, 2, 4, 5, 6 or 8. Hence out of ten numbers in which any of the four numbers may end, four are favourable to the event that none of the four numbers end in 0, 2, 4, 5, 6 or 8.

Therefore the chance that each of the four numbers should not end in any of these is $\frac{4}{10}$ or $\frac{2}{5}$.

Thus the required chance $=\left(\frac{2}{5}\right)^4=\frac{16}{625}$.

16. A coin can be tossed in 2 different ways and when it is tossed 5 times, the different ways are 2^5. And similarly there are 2^5 ways for the other coin in which it can be tossed 5 times.

Since the tossing of two coins is an independent event, hence the total number of ways in which the tossing of two coins may occur is $2^5 \times 2^5$, i.e. 2^{10}.

The number of favourable ways are the same as the number of ways in which 10 things may be divided into classes containing 5 of one and 5 of another and they are $\frac{10!}{5!5!}$

$\therefore$ Required probability $=\frac{10!}{5!5!}\times\frac{1}{2^{10}}=\frac{63}{256}$.

17. There are 13 cards of spade in a complete pack of cards.

Therefore, the chance that any of them will cut a spade is $\frac{13}{52}$ i.e. $\frac{1}{4}$. The chance that it is not a spade is $1-\frac{1}{4}$ or $\frac{3}{4}$.

A will win in the following mutually exclusive ways :

(i) A wins in the first cut. So its chance is $\frac{1}{4}$.

(ii) A wins in the second cut. Then A, B, C have failed and then A cuts a spade so its chance is

$$\frac{3}{4}\times\frac{3}{4}\times\frac{3}{4}\times\frac{1}{4}=\frac{1}{4}\cdot\left(\frac{3}{4}\right)^3$$

(iii) A wins in the third cut. The A, B, C, A, B, C have failed on then A cuts a spade so its change is

$$\frac{3}{4}\times\frac{3}{4}\times\frac{3}{4}\times\frac{3}{4}\times\frac{3}{4}\times\frac{3}{4}\times\frac{1}{4}=\frac{1}{4}\cdot\left(\frac{3}{4}\right)^6$$

so on.

∴ A's respective chance of success

$$=\frac{1}{4}+\frac{1}{4}\left(\frac{3}{4}\right)^3+\frac{1}{4}\left(\frac{3}{4}\right)^6+\text{.... to infinity}$$

$$=\frac{1}{4}\cdot\frac{1}{1-\left(\frac{3}{4}\right)^3}=\frac{1}{4}\cdot\frac{1}{1-\frac{27}{64}}$$

$$=\frac{16}{37}.$$

Similarly B's respective chance of success

$$=\frac{3}{4}\times\frac{1}{4}+\left(\frac{3}{4}\right)^4\times\frac{1}{4}+\left(\frac{3}{4}\right)^7\times\frac{1}{4}+\text{.... to infinity}$$

$$=\frac{3}{16}\times\frac{1}{1-\frac{27}{64}}=\frac{12}{37}.$$

∴ Chance of C is $1-\frac{16}{37}-\frac{12}{37}=\frac{9}{37}$.

Hence there respective chances are $\frac{16}{37},\frac{12}{37},\frac{9}{37}$.

18. While solving the problem we treat those three particular mathematics book as 1. Thus total number of arrangement is 8! × 3! as they arrange among themselves also.

∴ Number of favourable ways = 8! × 3!

Total number of ways = 10!

∴ Required probability $=\frac{8!\times 3!}{10!}=\frac{1}{15}$.

19. Out of 52 cards, two cards can be drawn is $^{52}C_2$ ways.

Now there is total 26 red cards, out of which 2 red cards can be drawn in $^{26}C_2$ ways.

Since there are 4 kings, out of which 2 kings can be drawn in $^4C_2$ ways.

∴ *(i)* Probability of getting two cards which are red $=\frac{^{26}C_2}{^{52}C_2}$.

(ii) Probability of getting two kings $=\frac{^{4}C_2}{^{52}C_2}$.

(iii) There are 2 cards which are both red and kings, therefore probability of getting 2 cards which are both red and kings $=\frac{^{2}C_2}{^{52}C_2}$.

∴ Required probability = *(i)* + *(ii)* – *(iii)*

$$=\frac{^{26}C_2}{^{52}C_2}+\frac{^{4}C_2}{^{52}C_2}-\frac{^{2}C_2}{^{52}C_2}$$

$$=\frac{325}{1326}+\frac{6}{1326}-\frac{1}{1326}=\frac{55}{221}.$$

20. We can choose a white ball out of 10 white balls in $^{10}C_1$ ways.

We can choose anyone ball out of total 25 balls in $^{25}C_1$ ways.

We can choose a black ball out of 15 black balls in $^{15}C_1$ ways.

∴ Probability of getting a white ball in the first draw $=\frac{^{10}C_1}{^{25}C_1}=\frac{10}{25}=\frac{2}{5}$.

Also probability of getting a black ball in second draw when a white ball has already been drawn in first draw $=\frac{^{15}C_1}{^{24}C_1}=\frac{15}{24}=\frac{5}{8}$.

As both the events are mutually exclusive to each other, so the required probability $=\frac{2}{5}\times\frac{5}{8}=\frac{1}{4}$.

21. 19 tickets are numbered 1 to 19, in the bag.

There are all together 9 even numbered tickets viz. 2, 4, 6, 8, 10, 12, 14, 16, 18.

Therefore probability of drawing an even numbered ticket in first draw equals to $\frac{9}{19}$.

Since the ticket drawn in the first draw is not replaced, therefore second ticket drawn is from the remaining 18 tickets, out of which 8 are even numbered.

∴ Probability of drawing an even numbered ticket in the second draw is equal to $\frac{8}{18}=\frac{4}{9}$.

∴ Required probability $=\frac{9}{19}\times\frac{4}{9}=\frac{4}{19}$.

22. There are six sides of the die.

Therefore, the chance of getting 'three' is $\frac{1}{6}$.

The chance of not getting 'three' is $\frac{5}{6}$.

A will win in the following mutually exclusive ways :

(i) A wins in the firrst throw. Its chance is $\frac{1}{6}$.

(ii) A wins in the second throw. Its chance is $\frac{5}{6}\times\frac{5}{6}\times\frac{1}{6}$.

(iii) A wins in the third throw. Its chance is $\frac{5}{6}\times\frac{5}{6}\times\frac{5}{6}\times\frac{5}{6}\times\frac{1}{6}$.

So on.

∴ A's respective chance of success

$$=\frac{1}{6}+\frac{1}{6}\cdot\left(\frac{5}{6}\right)^2+\frac{1}{6}\cdot\left(\frac{5}{6}\right)^4+....$$

$$=\frac{1}{6}\cdot\frac{1}{1-\left(\frac{5}{6}\right)^2}$$

$$=\frac{1}{6}\cdot\frac{36}{11}=\frac{6}{11}.$$

23. All the trials are independent, so the probability that head appears on the fifth toss does not depend upon the previous results of the tosses.

Hence the required probability = probability of getting head $=\frac{1}{2}$.

24. Out of four machines, two machines can be chosen in ${}^4C_2 = 6$ ways.

If only two tests are required to identify faulty machines, then in first two tests faulty machines are identified.

This can be done in one way only.

So, favourable number of ways = 1

∴ Required proabability $=\frac{1}{6}$.

25. As there are 2 different ways of tossing a coin, hence the total number of different ways of tossing a coin 5 times are 2^5.

Again the number of ways of obtaining 12 with a coin whose face are marked 2 and 3 is the coefficient of x^{12} in the expansion of $\left(x^2+x^3\right)^5$.

For this coefficient arises out of the different ways in which 5 of the indices 2, 3 can be taken so as to form 12 by addition.

Now $\left(x^2+x^3\right)^5 = x^{10}(1+x)^5$

$= x^{10}(1+5x+10x^2+....)$

Hence the coefficient of x^{12} in the expansion of $\left(x^2+x^3\right)^5$ is 10.

∴ Required probability $=\frac{10}{2^5}=\frac{10}{32}=\frac{5}{16}$.

26. The chance of turning up a head $=\frac{1}{2}$ and hence the chance of not turning up head, that is of tail is $1-\frac{1}{2}=\frac{1}{2}$.

Therefore the chance of turning up head n times, $n-1$ times, $n-2$ times and so on is given by the expansion of $\left(\frac{1}{2}+\frac{1}{2}\right)^n$ and the chance of turning up head an odd number of times is given by the sum of the odd coefficients in $(1+1)^n$ divided by 2^n.

Now the sum of the odd coefficients is 2^{n-1}.

∴ Required chance $=\frac{2^{n-1}}{2^n}=\frac{1}{2}$.

27. A penny may be thrown in two different ways, out of which one is favourable to the event that it turns up head.

∴ The chance of throwing head is $1-\frac{1}{2}=\frac{1}{2}$.

Now the fourth man will win his first throw, if the first three persons fail to win.

The chance of this compound event is $\left(\frac{1}{2}\right)^3 \times \frac{1}{2}$ or $\frac{1}{2^4}$.

In his second throw his chance is $\frac{1}{2^{10}}$, because first three persons must have failed twice and fourth, fifth and sixth persons must have failed once before fourth person can have a second throw. In his third throw his chance is $\frac{1}{2^{16}}$ and so on.

Thus fourth person's chance is the sum of the infinite series $\frac{1}{2^4}+\frac{1}{2^{10}}+\frac{1}{2^{16}}+....$

$$=\frac{1}{2^4}\left(1+\frac{1}{2^6}+\frac{1}{2^{12}}+....\right)$$

$$=\frac{1}{2^4}.\left\{\frac{1}{1-\frac{1}{2^6}}\right\}$$

$$=\frac{1}{2^4}.\frac{2^6}{(2^6-1)}=\frac{4}{63}.$$

$\therefore$ Required chance $=\frac{4}{63}$.

28. As one counter may be withdrawn in 3 different ways, hence the total number of ways of withdrawing one counter are 3^3 or 27 in three operations.

Now the number of ways in which the number withdrawn will have 6 for their sum is equal to the coefficient of x^6 in the expansion of $\left(x^1+x^2+x^3\right)^3$.

For this coefficient arises out of the different ways in which 3 of the indices 1, 2, 3 can be taken so as to form 6 by addition.

$$\text{Now } \left(x+x^2+x^3\right)^3 = x^3(1+x+x^2)^3$$

$$= x^3\left(\frac{1-x^3}{1-x}\right)^3$$

We have, therefore to find the coefficient of x^3 in $\left(\frac{1-x^3}{1-x}\right)^3$ or in $\left(1-x^3\right)^3(1-x)^{-3}$ i.e. in

$(1-3x^3+6x^6-3x^9)(1+3x+6x^2+10x^3+....)$

This coefficient is equal to $(-3+10)$ or 7.

$\therefore$ Required probability $=\frac{7}{27}$.

29. There are 6 × 6 × 6, or 216 possible ways in which the three die can fall, because a single dice can fall in 6 different ways.

Now the number of ways in which the numbers thrown will have 10 for their sum is equal to the coefficient of x^{10} in the expansion of $\left(x^1+x^2+x^3+x^4+x^5+x^6\right)^3$ i.e. $x^3.\left(\frac{1-x^6}{1-x}\right)^3$.

The coefficient of x^{10} is the same as the coefficient of x^7 in $\left(\frac{1-x^6}{1-x}\right)^3$ i.e. in

$\left(1-x^6\right)^3(1-x)^{-3}$ or in $(1-3x^6+3x^{12}-x^{18})(1+3x+6x^2+10x^3+....+36x^7+....)$.

This coefficient is equal to $(-9+36)$ or 27.

$\therefore$ Required probability $=\frac{27}{216}=\frac{1}{8}$.

30. As a dice can fall in 6 different ways, hence three dice can fall in 6^3 different ways, i.e. in 216 ways.

In order to find B's chance of throwing a number higher than 8, we shall first find the chance of throwing a number less than 8.

Again the minimum sum of numbers thrown with three dice may be 3.

Hence B will lose if he throws any number from 3 to 8 inclusive. The number of ways it is possible is the sum of the coefficients of powers of x from 3 to 8 inclusive in the expansion of

$$\left(x^1+x^2+x^3+x^4+x^5+x^6\right)^3.$$

The powers of x within bracket denote the face values of the dice.

Now $\left(x+x^2+x^3+x^4+x^5+x^6\right)^3$

$= x^3\left(1+x+x^2+x^3+x^4+x^5\right)^3$

$= x^3\left(\frac{1-x^6}{1-x}\right)^3$

$= x^3\left(1-x^6\right)^3 (1-x)^{-3}$

$= x^3 (1 - 3x^6 + 3x^{12} - x^{18}) (1 + 3x + 6x^2 + 10x^3 + 15x^4 + 21x^5 + ...)$

Thus, the favourable number of ways to the event the sum of the numbers thrown is any number from 3 to 8 inclusive = 1 + 3 + 6 + 10 + 15 + 21 = 56.

$\therefore$ The probability that B losses is $\frac{56}{216}=\frac{7}{27}$.

Hence the required that B wins is $1-\frac{7}{27}=\frac{20}{27}$.

31. Out of integers from 1 to 11, there are 5 even integers and 6 odd integers.

Let A = Both the numbers choosen are odd.

B = The sum of the numbers chosen is even.

Since the sum of two integers is even if either both are even or both are odd, therefore

$P(A)=\frac{^6C_2}{^{11}C_2}; P(B)=\frac{^6C_2+{^5C_2}}{^{11}C_2}$ and

$P(A\cap B)=\frac{^6C_2}{^{11}C_2}$.

Now, required probability

$= P\left(\frac{A}{B}\right) = \frac{P(A\cap B)}{P(B)}$

$= \frac{^6C_2/^{11}C_2}{\frac{^6C_2+{^5C_2}}{^{11}C_2}} = \frac{^6C_2}{^6C_2+{^5C_2}} = \frac{15}{15+10} = \frac{3}{5}$.

32. Total number of ways in which four figure numbers can be formed is 4! = 24. A number is divisible by 5 if at units place we have 5. Therefore units place can be filled in one way and the remaining in 3! ways. Hence the total number of members divisible by 5 is 3! = 6.

So, the required probability $= \frac{6}{24}=\frac{1}{4}$.

33. If the minimum face value is not less than 2 and the minimum face value is not greater than 5, then the face value in any one throw is either 2, 3, 4 or 5.

The probability of these face values to appear in any one throw is $\frac{4}{6}=\frac{2}{3}$.

The probability that this happens in 4 throws is $\left(\frac{2}{3}\right)^4=\frac{16}{81}$.

34. Total number of ways in which 3 members can be chosen out of 30 numbers = $^{30}C_3$ = 4060.

Number of ways of choosing 3 consecutive numbers i.e. 1, 2, 3; 2, 3, 4; ...., 28, 29, 30 is 28. Therefore the number of ways in which the three numbers chosen are not consecutive is 4060 – 28 = 4032.

$\therefore$ Required probability $= \frac{4032}{4060}=\frac{144}{145}$.

35. Total number of cases of selecting seven coupons $= 15^7$, as replacement is allowed.

It is given that the largest number on the selected coupon is 9, therefore the selection is to be made from the coupons numbered 1 to 9. This can be done in 9^7 ways. Out of these 9^7 cases 8^7 cases do not contain the number 9.

Thus, favourable number of cases = $9^7 - 8^7$.

$\therefore$ Required probability $= \frac{9^7-8^7}{15^7}$.

36. The total number of ways of choosing 2 integers from 30 integers is $^{30}C_2$ = 435.

The sum of the selected numbers is odd if exactly one of them is odd and the other is even.

Therefore, favourable numberof cases = $^{15}C_1 \times {^{15}C_1}$ = 225.

Here required probability $= \frac{225}{435}=\frac{15}{29}$.

37. Total number of cases = $^{64}C_1 \times {^{63}C_1} = 64 \times 63$

For each of the four corner squares, the number of favourable cases is 2.

For each of the 24 non-corner squares on either side of chess board, the favourable number of cases is 3.

For each of the 36 remaining squares, the favourable number of cases is 4.

$\therefore$ Total number of favourable cases $= 4 \times 2 + 24 \times 3 + 36 \times 4 = 2204$.

$\therefore$ Required probability $= \dfrac{224}{64 \times 63} = \dfrac{1}{18}$.

38. There are 64 squares in a chessboard out of which 3 can be choosen in $^{64}C_3$ different ways. Again out of 64, 32 are white and 32 are black altogether.

Two of one colour and one of another may be chosen when we either choose two white and one black or two black and one white which may be choosen $^{32}C_2 \times 32$ ways.

Since these two cases are mutually exclusive,

hence the required chance $= \dfrac{2 \times {^{32}C_2} \times 32}{^{64}C_3} = \dfrac{16}{21}$.

39. Three letters can be placed in 3 envelops in 3! ways, whereas there is only one way of placing them in their right envelopes.

So, the probability that all the letters are placed in the right envelops $= \dfrac{1}{3!}$.

Hence the required probability that all letters are not placed in the right envelopes $= 1 - \dfrac{1}{3!} = \dfrac{5}{6}$.

40. We can choose any two numbers out of 1, 2, 3, ..., 30 in $^{30}C_2 = 435$ ways.

Now $a^2 - b^2$ is divisible by 3 iff either a and b both are divisible by 3 or none of a and b is divisible by 3.

Thus favourable number of cases

$= {^{10}C_2} + {^{20}C_2} = 235$.

$\therefore$ Required probability $= \dfrac{235}{435} = \dfrac{47}{87}$.

41. Here two cases arises

(i) A lives and B dies

(ii) A dies and B lives

$\therefore$ Required probability

$= p(1-q) + q(1-p) = p + q - 2pq$.

42. Each entry of the 2×2 matrix can be made with element 0, 1 in two ways. As there are in total four entry, so total number of matrix $= 2^4 = 16$. Out of all these matrices only three matrices i.e.

$\begin{bmatrix} 1 & 0 \\ 0 & 1 \end{bmatrix}, \begin{bmatrix} 1 & 0 \\ 1 & 1 \end{bmatrix}$ and $\begin{bmatrix} 1 & 1 \\ 0 & 1 \end{bmatrix}$ whose determinants are positive.

$\therefore$ Required probability $= \dfrac{3}{16}$.

43. In any number, the last digits can be any one of the numbers 0, 1, 2, 3, 4, 5, 6, 7, 8, 9. Therefore last digit of the number can be chosen in 10 ways.

$\therefore$ Total exhaustive number of ways $= 10^n$.

If the last digit be 1, 3, 7 or 9 none of the numbers can be even or end in 0 or 5.

Thus, we have a choice of 4 digits, with which each n numbers should end.

So, favourable number of ways $= 4^n$.

$\therefore$ Required probability $= \dfrac{4^n}{10^n} = \left(\dfrac{2}{5}\right)^n$.

44. If we observe very closely we will find that product of the 4 whole numbers will end with 1, 3, 7, 9 only when the last digit of each whole number is 1, 3, 7 or 9.

Thus, the probability of choosing 1, 3, 7 or 9 out of 10 digits $= \dfrac{4}{10} = \dfrac{2}{5}$.

$\therefore$ Required probability $= \dfrac{2}{5} \times \dfrac{2}{5} \times \dfrac{2}{5} \times \dfrac{2}{5} = \dfrac{16}{625}$.

45. Probability of getting all three heads $= \dfrac{1}{2} \times \dfrac{1}{2} \times \dfrac{1}{2} = \dfrac{1}{8}$.

Also probability of getting all three tails $= \dfrac{1}{8}$.

$\therefore$ Probability of getting all three heads or all the three tails in one trial $= 2 \times \dfrac{1}{8} = \dfrac{1}{4}$.

Thus, probability of not getting three heads or three tails $= 1 - \dfrac{1}{4} = \dfrac{3}{4}$.

Now in first four throws, the probability of getting all three heads or tail only once is $^4C_1 \times \left(\dfrac{3}{4}\right)^3 \times \dfrac{1}{4}$.

∴ Probability of getting all three heads or tail second times in 5th toss

$= {}^4C_1 \times \left(\frac{3}{4}\right)^3 \times \frac{1}{4} \times \frac{1}{4} = \frac{27}{256}.$

46. Probability of getting 'six' on the dice in one trial $= \frac{1}{6}$.

Probability of getting six two times out of four trial $= {}^4C_2 \times \left(\frac{5}{6}\right)^2 \times \left(\frac{1}{6}\right)^2$.

∴ Probability of getting three 'sixes' in exactly 5 tosses

$= \left[{}^4C_2 \times \left(\frac{5}{6}\right)^2 \times \left(\frac{1}{6}\right)^2\right] \times \frac{1}{6} = \frac{25}{1296}.$

47. Let $a = 7k_1 + a_1$, where $0 \le a_1 \le 6$ and $b = 7\lambda_1 + b_1$ where $0 \le b_1 \le 6$.

Then

$$a^2 + b^2 = 7\left(7k_1^2 + 7\lambda_1^2 + 2a_1k_1 + 2b_1\lambda_i\right) + a_1^2 + b_1^2$$

or $a^2 + b^2 = 7\mu + a_1^2 + b_1^2$, where $\mu \in N$.

Since each a_1 and b_1 can take values from 0 to 6. Therefore exhaustive number of cases is same as the number of ways of choosing a_1 and b_1. Thus total number of cases = 7 × 7 = 49.

Now $a^2 + b^2 = 7k + a_1^2 + b_1^2$

Thus $a^2 + b^2$ is divisible by 7 if $a_1 = b_1 = 0$

So favourable number of cases = 1.

∴ Required probability $= \frac{1}{49}$.

48. Probability of selecting article 1 out of n enumerated articles 1, 2, 3, ..., n is $\frac{1}{n}$.

Now out of remaining $(n-1)$ enumerated articles probability of selecting article 2 is $\frac{1}{n-1}$, etc.

∴ The probability that the number of selected articles taken in sequence 1, 2, 3, ..., n is

$\frac{1}{n}.\frac{1}{(n-1)}.\frac{1}{(n-2)}....\frac{1}{2}.\frac{1}{1} = \frac{1}{n!}.$

49. Empty places out of 24 places are 10, as in both the cases owner's car is ignored.

As the owner's car is not parked at either end we are to eliminate two places from both empty and non-empty place.

∴ Required probability

$= \frac{{}^{24-2}C_{10-2}}{{}^{24}C_{10}} = \frac{{}^{22}C_8}{{}^{24}C_{10}} = \frac{15}{92}.$

50. Number $3n - 1$ or $3n + 1$ means the product of the numbers are not divisible by 3 and we cannot choose those numbers which are divisible by three.

Thus eliminating 3, 6 and 9 we get total seven numbers, out of which four can be chosen in 7^4 ways where repitition is allowed. Also $3n - 1$ and $3n + 1$ where n is non-negative numbers does not include 1. So 1 cannot be product of the four numbers.

∴ Total favourable product

$= 7^4 - 1 = 2401 - 1 = 2400.$

∴ Required probability

$= \frac{2400}{10^4} = \frac{2400}{10000} = 0.24.$

51. Probability that, radar do not able to detect an object is $(1-p)$.

Also the probability that it will not be able to detect an object in n cycles $= (1-p)^n$.

∴ Required probability $= 1 - (1-p)^n$.

52. Probability that a man aged X dies in a year $= p$

∴ Probability that a man aged X, does not dies in a year $= 1 - p$

Probability that n man aged X, does not dies in a year $= (1-p)^n$

∴ Probability that at least one man dies in a year $= 1 - (1-p)^n$

Probability that out of n men, A_1 dies first $= \frac{1}{n}$.

Here the probability that A_1 dies in the year and he is first to die $= \frac{1}{n}\left[1-(1-p)^n\right]$ as both the events are independent.

53. If we consider that all numbers of white balls are in *priori* equally likely, we shall have four hypothesis :

For *(i)* all the balls in the bag may be white *(ii)* three of them may be white *(iii)* two of them may be white *(iv)* Only one of them may be white. Let the *priori* probabilities of these hypothesis be denoted by P_1, P_2, P_3, P_4 respectively. Then $P_1 = P_2 = P_3 = \frac{1}{4}$.

If all the balls in the bag are white, the chance of drawing a white ball is certain, that is 1.

If three of them are white, the chance of a white ball is $\frac{1}{2}$; if only one ball is white, the chance of drawing a white ball is $\frac{1}{4}$.

Let these probabilities be denoted by p_1, p_2, p_3, p_4 respectively.

Then $p_1 = 1,\ p_2 = \frac{3}{4}, p_3 = \frac{1}{2}, p_4 = \frac{1}{4}$.

$\therefore$ Required probability

$$= \frac{p_1P_1}{\sum_{i=1}^{4} p_iP_i} = \frac{p_1P_1}{p_1P_1 + p_2P_2 + p_3P_3 + p_4P_4}$$

$$= \frac{1.\frac{1}{4}}{1.\frac{1}{4} + \frac{3}{4}.\frac{1}{4} + \frac{1}{2}.\frac{1}{4} + \frac{1}{4}.\frac{1}{4}}$$

$$= \frac{1/4}{\frac{4}{16} + \frac{3}{16} + \frac{2}{16} + \frac{1}{16}} = \frac{4}{10} = \frac{2}{5}.$$

54. Here we may consider four hypothesis, all being equally likely. They are

(i) all the 6 balls in the bag may be black.

(ii) five of them may be black.

(iii) four of them may be black.

(iv) only three balls may be black.

Let the priori probabilities of these four hypothesis be denoted by P_1, P_2, P_3, P_4 respectively.

Then $P_1 = P_2 = P_3 = P_4 = \frac{1}{4}$.

Let p_1, p_2, p_3, p_4 denote the respective probabilities. Then the event of drawing 3 black balls are $p_1 = 1,\ p_2 = \frac{^5C_3}{^6C_3} = \frac{1}{2},\ p_3 = \frac{^4C_3}{^6C_3} = \frac{1}{5},$

$p_4 = \frac{1}{^6C_3} = \frac{1}{20}.$

$\therefore$ Required probability that no black ball is left $= \frac{p_4P_4}{\sum_{i=1}^{6} p_iP_i} = \frac{1/8}{35/80} = \frac{1}{35}$.

55. Let the probabilities of the event that the lost card is a spade or not a spade be denoted by P_1 and P_2 respectively.

Then $P_1 = \frac{1}{4}$, because there are four suits and

$P_2 = 1 - \frac{1}{4} = \frac{3}{4}$.

Let p_1 and p_2 be the probabilities of the event that two cards are spades on the supposition that the missing card is a spade or not a spade.

Then $P_1 = \frac{12}{51} \times \frac{11}{50}, P_2 = \frac{13}{51} \times \frac{12}{50}$

$\therefore$ Required probability

$$= \frac{p_1P_2}{\sum_{i=1}^{2} p_iP_i} = \frac{p_1P_2}{p_1P_1 + p_2P_2}$$

$$= \frac{\frac{12}{51} \times \frac{11}{50} \times \frac{1}{4}}{\frac{12}{51} \times \frac{11}{50} \times \frac{1}{4} + \frac{3}{4} \times \frac{13}{51} \times \frac{12}{50}} = \frac{\frac{11}{17 \times 50}}{\frac{50}{17 \times 50}}$$

$$= \frac{11}{50}.$$

56. There are 6 × 6 × 6 i.e. 216 possible ways in which three dice can fall in a single throw, because a simple die can fall in 6 ways.

Now the number of ways in which the numbers thrown will have 12 for their sum is equal to the coefficient of x^{12} in the expansion of $\left(x^1 + x^2 + x^3 + x^4 + x^5 + x^6\right)^3$; the power's of x within bracket denote the face vlaue of the die.

Now the expression

$$\left(x^1 + x^2 + x^3 + x^4 + x^5 + x^6\right)^3$$

$$= x^3\left(1 + x + x^2 + x^3 + x^4 + x^5\right)^3$$

$$= x^3\frac{\left(1 - x^6\right)^3}{(1 - x)^3}$$

$= x^3 (1-x^6)^3 (1-x)^{-3}$

The coefficient of x^{12} is the same as the coefficient of x^9 in the expansion of $(1-x^6)^3 (1-x)^{-3}$

Now coefficient of x^9 in $(1-x^6)^3 (1-x)^{-3}$

=Coefficient of x^9 in $(1-3x^6+3x^{12}-x^{18})(1+3x+6x^2+10x^3+....+55x^9+....)$

$= 55 - 30 = 25.$

$\therefore$ Required probability $= \frac{25}{216}$.

57. There are 7 possible ways of drawing a ticket. As the drawings are independent of each other, the total number of different ways are 7^4. The number of ways in which the sum of the drawing will amount to 8 is the coefficient of x^8 in the expansion of

$$(x^0+x^1+x^2+x^3+x^4+x^5+x^6)^4.$$

The powers of x within bracket denote the numbers marked on the tickets.

Now the above expression $= \left(\frac{1-x^7}{1-x}\right)^4$

$= (1-x^7)^4 (1-x)^{-4}$

$= (1-4x^7+....)(1+4x+....+165x^8+....)$

Thus coefficient of x^8 in $(1-4x^7+....)(1+4x+...., +165x^8+....) = 165-6 = 149.$

$\therefore$ Required probability $= \frac{149}{7^4} = \frac{149}{2401}$.

58. Total number of different ways of drawing three numbers on each trial is 10^3, as one number in any trial can be drawn in 10 different ways. Number of ways in which the sum of the drawings will amount to 10 is

= Coefficient of x^{10} in the expansion of

$$(x^0+x^0+x^0+x^0+x^0+x^1+x^2+x^3+x^4+x^5)^3$$

= Coefficient of x^{10} in the expansion of

$$(5+x^1+x^2+x^3+x^4+x^5)^3$$

= Coefficient of x^{10} in the expansion $(5+y)^3$ where $y = x^1+x^2+....+x^5$.

=Coefficient of x^{10} in the expansion of $5^3+3.5.y+3.5.y^2+y^3$

=Coefficient of x^{10} in the expansion of $15y^2+y^3$

($\therefore$ Coefficient of x^{10} comes from the least two terms only i.e. from $15y^2$ and y^3.)

= Coefficient of x^{10} in the expansion

$$15(x+x^2+....+x^5)^2 + (x+x^2+....+x^5)^3$$

= Coefficient of x in the expansion

$$15x^2(1-x^5)^2(1-x)^{-2} + x^3(1-x^5)^3(1-x)^{-3}$$

= Coefficient of x^{10} in expansion of $15x^2(1-2x^5+x^{10})(1+2x+3x^2+4x^3+....+9x^8+....)+x^3(1-3x^5+3x^{10}-x^{15})(1+3x+6x^2+....+36x^7+....)$

$= 15(9-8)+36-18 = 33.$

Hence required probability $= \frac{33}{1000}$.

59. As the replacement is not allowed like above problem, total number of cases are ${}^{10}C_3$; since the chances is just the same as if the three tickets were drawn simultaneously, out of which two are favourable to the event that the sum of the three drawings will amout to 10. The favourable cases consists of those in which the tickets 1, 4, 5 or the tickets 2, 3, 5 are drawn.

$\therefore$ Required probability

$$= \frac{2}{{}^{10}C_3} = \frac{2\times3\times2\times1}{10\times9\times8} = \frac{1}{60}.$$

60. Total number of cases, i.e. sample points in the sample space is $6^4 = 1296$.

Number of sample point in favour of the event

= Coefficient of x^{10} in the expansion of

$$(1+x+x^2+.....+x^5)^2.(x+x^2+.....+x^6)^2$$

= Coefficient of x^{10} in the expansion of

$$x^2(1+x+x^2+.....+x^5)^4$$

= Coefficient of x^8 in the expansion of

$$(1-x^6)^4(1-x)^{-4}$$

= Coefficient of x^8 in the expansion of $(1-4x^6+....)\left(1+4x+\frac{4\times5}{2!}x^2+\frac{4\times5\times6}{3!}x^3+....\right)$

$= {}^{11}C_8 - 4\times{}^5C_2 = 125$

$\therefore$ Required probability $= \frac{125}{1296}$.

61. Out of the total 10 cards numbered, 5 cards are numbered odd and other 5 cards numbered even. Sum of four cards can be even only when

(i) all cards are numbered odd

(ii) all cards are numbered even

(iii) out of 4 cards two are odd and two are even.

∴ Number of sample point in favour of the event $= {}^5C_4 + {}^5C_4 + {}^5C_2 \times {}^5C_2$.

∴ Required probability

$$= \frac{{}^5C_2 + {}^5C_4 + {}^5C_2 \times {}^5C_2}{{}^{10}C_4} = \frac{110}{210} = \frac{11}{21}.$$

62. Number of sample point in favour of the event $= {}^4C_1 \times {}^4C_1$

Total number of cases i.e. sample point in sample space $= {}^{52}C_2$.

63. The probabilities that each of them failed to hit the targets are $\frac{5}{6}, \frac{3}{4}, \frac{2}{3}$.

∴ Probability that the first man hit the target =

$$\frac{1}{6} + \frac{5}{6} \times \frac{3}{4} \times \frac{2}{3} \times \frac{1}{6} + \frac{5}{6} \times \frac{3}{4} \times \frac{2}{3} \times \frac{5}{6} \times \frac{3}{4} \times \frac{2}{3} \times \frac{1}{6} + \ldots$$

$$= \frac{1}{6}\left[1 + \frac{5}{72} + \left(\frac{5}{72}\right)^2 + \ldots\right]$$

$$= \frac{1}{6} \times \frac{1}{1 - \frac{5}{72}} = \frac{1}{6} \times \frac{72}{67} = \frac{12}{67}.$$

64. Ranches A, B each having 1000 cattles.

Ranches A's $\frac{1}{5}$th cattle i.e. $\frac{1}{5} \times 1000 = 200$ cattle's are infected.

∴ Ranche's A's (1000 – 200) = 800 cattle's are not infected.

Ranche's B's $\frac{1}{4}$th cattle i.e. $\frac{1}{4} \times 1000 = 250$ cattles are infected.

Now 70% of the infected cattles on each ranch are less than 1 year old.

∴ 30% of the infected cattles on each ranch are more than 1 year old.

∴ Number of cattles from ranch B which are infected and more than 1 year old is $250 \times \frac{30}{100} = 75$ Cattles.

∴ Probability that the chosen cow comes from ranch B has the disease and is more than 1 year old $= \frac{800}{1000} \times \frac{75}{1000} = \frac{3}{50}$.

65. Let P(A) = Probability that first shot hit the target.

$P(\overline{A})$ = Probablity that first shot do not hit the target.

Similarly for P(B), $P(\overline{B})$, P(C), $P(\overline{C})$, P(D) and $P(\overline{D})$

∴ Probability that it hit the target

$$= P(A) + P(\overline{A})P(B) + P(\overline{A})P(\overline{B})P(C) + P(\overline{A})P(\overline{B})P(\overline{C})P(D)$$

$$= 0.4 + (1 - 0.4) \times 0.3 + (1 - 0.4)(1 - 0.3) \times 0.2 + (1 - 0.4)(1 - 0.3)(1 - 0.2) \times 0.1$$

$$= 0.4 + 0.6 \times 0.3 + 0.6 \times 0.7 \times 0.2 + 0.6 \times 0.7 \times 0.8 \times 0.1$$

$$= 0.4 + 0.18 + 0.084 + 0.0336$$

$$= 0.6976.$$

66. The probability of hitting down the target is *pr*. At least one missile will remain in reserve means the target may be hit down in first, second, ... or $(n - 1)$th time.

∴ Required probability $= pr + (1 - pr)pr + (1 - pr)^2 pr + \ldots + (1 - pr)^{n-2} pr$

$$= pr\left[1 + (1 - pr) + (1 - pr)^2 + \ldots + (1 - pr)^{n-2}\right]$$

$$= pr.\frac{1 - (1 - pr)^{n-2}}{1 - (1 - pr)} = 1 - (1 - pr)^{n-2}.$$

67. Probability of choosing any of them at random $= \frac{1}{4}$.

∴ Probability that the prisoner will succeed escaping $= \frac{1}{4} \times \left(\frac{1}{8} + \frac{1}{6} + \frac{1}{4} + \frac{9}{10}\right) = \frac{173}{480}$.

68. Let A, B, C be the respective events of solving the problem and $\overline{A}, \overline{B}, \overline{C}$, be the respective events of not solving problems.

Now $P(A)=\frac{1}{2}$; $P(B)=\frac{1}{3}$ and $P(C)=\frac{1}{4}$.

$\therefore$ $P(\overline{A})=1-\frac{1}{2}=\frac{1}{2}$; $P(\overline{B})=1-\frac{1}{3}=\frac{2}{3}$ and

$P(\overline{C})=1-\frac{1}{4}=\frac{3}{4}$.

P [None solves the problem] = P [(not-A) and (not-B) and (not-C)]

$= P(\overline{A}\cap\overline{B}\cap\overline{C})$

$= P(\overline{A}).P(\overline{B}).P(\overline{C})$

$(\because \overline{A}, \overline{B}, \overline{C}$ are independent$)$

$= \frac{1}{2}\times\frac{2}{3}\times\frac{3}{4}=\frac{1}{4}$

Hence P [Problem will be solved] = 1 – P [None solves the problem]

$= 1-\frac{1}{4}=\frac{3}{4}$.

69. We have

$P(A\cup B\cup C) = P(A)+P(B)+P(C)-P(A\cap B)$
$-P(B\cap C)-P(C\cap A)+P(A\cap B\cap C)$
$=P(A)+P(B)+P(C)-P(A)P(B)-P(B)P(C)-$
$P(C)P(A)+P(A)P(B)P(C)$.

$(\because$ A, B, C are independent$)$

$\therefore$ Putting there respective values we get

$P(A\cup B\cup C) = 0.2+0.1+0.4-0.2\times0.1-0.1$
$\times 0.4-0.4\times0.2+0.2\times0.1\times0.4$
$=0.7-0.14+0.008=0.568$.

70. Given $P(A\cap B) = \frac{1}{6}$

and $P(\overline{A}\cap\overline{B}) = \frac{1}{3}$

Now $P(\overline{A}\cap\overline{B}) = P(\overline{A}).P(\overline{B})$
$=[1-P(A)][1-P(B)]$
$=1-P(A)-P(B)+P(A)P(B)$
$=1-P(A)-P(B)+P(A\cap B)$.

71. Proceed similar to Q. 70.

72. A's chance of winning increases and now it becomes

$0.4+\frac{0.4}{0.8}\times0.2 = 0.5$ $(\therefore .4+.3+.1=.8)$

B's chance becomes

$0.3+\frac{0.3}{0.8}\times0.2 = 0.375$.

C's chance becomes

$0.1+\frac{0.1}{0.8}\times0.2 = 0.125$.

73. Given and $P(A\cap B)=0.2$

Now $P(A\cup B) = P(A)+P(B)-(A\cap B)$

or $P(A)+P(B) = P(A\cup B)+P(A\cap B)$

or $1-P(\overline{A})+1-P(\overline{B}) = 0.7+0.2=0.9$

$\therefore$ $P(\overline{A})+P(\overline{B}) = 2-0.9=1.1$.

74. Here $P[(A\cup B)\cap(\overline{A})\cap(\overline{B})]$

$= P[(A\cup B)\cap(\overline{A}\cap\overline{B})]$

$= P[(A\cup B)\cap(\overline{A\cup B})]$

$= P(\phi)=0\le\frac{1}{4}$.

75. Given $P(\overline{A}\cap\overline{B}) = \frac{1}{3}$ or $P(\overline{A\cup B}) = \frac{1}{3}$

or $1-P(A\cup B) = \frac{1}{3}$

or $P(A\cup B) = \frac{2}{3}$

or $P(A)+P(B)P(A\cap B) = \frac{2}{3}$

or $p+2p-\frac{1}{2} = \frac{2}{3}$ or $p=\frac{7}{18}$.

or $P(A)+P(B) = 1-P(\overline{A}\cap\overline{B})+P(A\cap B)$

$= 1-\frac{1}{3}+\frac{1}{6}=\frac{5}{6}$.

or $P(A)+P(B) = \frac{5}{6}$ ...(*i*)

$\therefore$ $P(A)-P(B) = \sqrt{[P(A)+P(B)]^2-4P(A\cap B)}$

$= \sqrt{\frac{25}{36}-\frac{4}{6}}=\frac{1}{6}$

$\therefore$ or $P(A)-P(B) = \frac{1}{6}$ ...(*ii*)

Solving equation (*i*) and (*ii*) we get

$P(A)=\frac{1}{2}$ and $P(B)=\frac{1}{3}$.

20. LINEAR ALGEBRA

1. External Composition : Let U and S be two non-empty sets. A mapping $f : U \times S \to S$ is said to be an external composition of U with S. Each ordered pair (u, s) in $U \times S$ has a definite image $f(u, s)$ in S.

2. Vector Space Over a Field : A non-empty set V is said to form a vector space over a field F if

(a) there is a binary composition + on V, called addition satisfying the conditions

(i) $\alpha + \beta \in V$ for all $\alpha, \beta \in V$

(ii) $\alpha + \beta = \beta + \alpha$ for all $\alpha, \beta \in V$

(iii) $\alpha + (\beta + \gamma) = (\alpha + \beta) + \gamma$ for all $\alpha, \beta, \gamma \in V$

(iv) there exists an element θ in V such that $\alpha + \theta = \alpha$ for all α in V.

(v) for each α in V there exists an elements $-\alpha$ in V such that $\alpha + (-\alpha) = \theta$ and

(b) there is an external composition of F with V, called 'multiplication by the elements of F' satisfying the conditions

(vi) $c\alpha \in V$ for all $c \in F$, all $\alpha \in V$.

(vii) $c(d\alpha) = (cd)\alpha$ for all $c, d \in F$, all $\alpha \in V$

(viii) $c(\alpha + \beta) = c\alpha + c\beta$ for all $c \in F$, all $\alpha, \beta \in V$

(ix) $(c + d)\alpha = c\alpha + d\alpha$ for all $c, d \in F$, all $\alpha \in V$

(x) $1\alpha = \alpha$, 1 being the identity element in F.

The elements of V are called **vectors** and the elements of F are called **scalars**. The external composition of F with V is also called 'multiplication by scalars'.

Since F is a field, it has the zero element 0 and the identity element 1. Since V is a commutative group with respect to addition is the zero-element in V. This is said to be the **zero vector** or the **null vector** and is denoted by θ.

Properties : In a vector space V over a field F,

(i) $0\alpha = \theta$ for all $\alpha \in V$

(ii) $c\theta = \theta$ for all $c \in V$

(iii) $-1\alpha = -\alpha$

(iv) $c\alpha = \theta \Rightarrow c = 0$ or $\alpha = \theta$

3. Subspace : Let V be a vector space over the field F and let $W \leq V$. Then W is called a subspace of V if W itself is a vector space over F with respect to the operations of vector addition and scalar multiplication in V.

Properties

(i) A non-empty subset W of a vector space V over a field F is a subspace of V if and only if

(a) $\alpha \in W, \beta \in W \Rightarrow \alpha + \beta \in W$

(b) $\alpha \in W, c \in F \Rightarrow cd \in W$

(ii) The intersection of two subspaces of a vector space V over a field F is a subspace of V.

(iii) If U, W be two subspaces of a vector space V over a field F, then the subset $\{u + \omega | u \in u, \omega \in W\}$ forms a subspace of V.

(iv) The subspace U + W is the smallest subspace of V containing the subspace U and W.

4. Linear Combination of Vectors : Let V be a vector space over a field F. A vector β in V is said to be a linear combination of the vectors $\alpha_1, \alpha_2 \ldots\ldots \alpha_n$ in V if β can be expressed as $\beta = c_1\alpha_1 + c_2\alpha_2 + \ldots + c_n\alpha_n$ for some scalars $c_1, c_2, \ldots\ldots, c_n$ in F.

5. Linear Span : The smallest subspace containing a finite set S of vectors of a vector space V is said to be the **linear span** of S and is denoted by L(S). L(S) is said to be generated (or spanned) by the set S and S is said to be the set of **generators** of L(S).

Properties

(i) If S, T be two finite subsets of vectors of a vector space V and $S \subset T$, then $L(S) \subset L(T)$.

(ii) If S and T be two finite subsets of a vector space V over a field F and each element of T be a linear combination of the vectors of S then $L(T) \subset L(S)$.

6. Linear Dependence : A finite set of vectors $\{\alpha_1, \alpha_2, \ldots, \alpha_n\}$ of a vector space V over a field F is said to be **linearly dependent** if there exist scalars $c_1, c_2, \ldots, c_n$ not all zero, in F such that $c_1\alpha_1 + c_2\alpha_2 + \ldots + c_n\alpha_n = \theta$.

7. Linearly Independence : A finite set of vectors $\{\alpha_1, \alpha_2, \ldots, \alpha_n\}$ of a vector space V over a field F is said to be linearly independent if $c_1\alpha_1 + c_2\alpha_2 + \ldots + c_n\alpha_n = \theta$ is satisfied only if $c_1 = c_2 = \ldots = c_n = 0$.

Properties

(i) A set containing a linearly dependent set of vectors is linearly dependent.

(ii) A subset of a linearly independent set of vectors is linearly independent.

(iii) A set of vectors containing the null vector θ in a vector space V is linearly dependent.

(iv) The set consisting of a single non-zero vector α is linearly independent.

(v) If the set of vectors $\{\alpha_1, \alpha_2, \ldots, \alpha_n\}$ in a vector-space over a field F be linearly dependent, then at least one of the vectors of the set can be expressed as a linear combination of the remaining others.

(vi) If a vector-space V over a field F be spanned by a linearly dependent set $\{\alpha_1, \alpha_2, \ldots, \alpha_n\}$, then V can also be generated by a suitable proper subset of $\{\alpha_1, \alpha_2, \ldots, \alpha_n\}$. **(Deletion Theorem).**

(vii) If S be a linearly dependent finite set of generators, of a vector-space V and $S \neq \{\theta\}$, then there exists a linearly independent subset of S that generates the same space V.

(viii) If $S = \{\alpha_1, \alpha_2, \ldots, \alpha_n\}$ be a linearly independent set of generators of a vector-space V, then no proper subset S can be a spanning set of V.

8. Basis and Dimension of a Vector Space : Let V be a vector space over a field F. A set S of vectors in V is said to be a **basis** of V if and only if

(i) S is linear by independent *(ii)* S generates V. If the number of vectors in a basis of V be finite, V is said to be finite **dimensional**. The null vector-space V has no basis.

The number of vectors in a basis of a vector-space V is said to be the **dimension** or **rank** of V and is denoted by dim V. If V is the null space, it has no basis and it is said tq of dimension 0.

Properties

(i) If $\{\alpha_1, \alpha_2, \ldots, \alpha_n\}$ be a basis of a vector space V over a field F and a non-zero vector β of V is expressed as $\beta = c_1\alpha_1 + c_2\alpha_2 + \ldots + c_n\alpha_n$, $c_i \in F$, then if $c_j \neq 0$, $\{\alpha_1, \alpha_2, \ldots, \alpha_{j-1}, \beta, \alpha_{j+1}, \ldots, \alpha_n\}$ is a new basis of V.

(That is, β can be replaced α_j in the basis).

(ii) If $\{\alpha_1, \alpha_2, \ldots, \alpha_n\}$ be a basis of a finite dimensional vector space V over a field F. Then any set of linearly independent vectors of V contains at most *n* vectors.

(iii) Any two bases of a finite dimensional vector space V have the same number of vectors.

(iv) Let V be a vector space of dimension *n* over a field F. Then any linearly independent set of *n* vectors of V is a basis of V.

(v) A linearly independent set of vectors in a finite dimensional vector space V over a field F is either a basis or can be extended to a basis of V.

(vi) If $\{\alpha_1, \alpha_2, \ldots, \alpha_n\}$ be a basis of a vector space V over a field F, then every vector β in V can be expressed as a linear combination of $\alpha_1, \alpha_2, \ldots, \alpha_n$ in one and only one way.

(vii) If U be a subspace of a finite dimensional vector space V and dim V = *n* then U is finite dimensional and $\dim U \leq n$.

(viii) Let U and W be two subspaces of a finite dimensional vector space V over a field F. Then $\dim(U + W) = \dim U + \dim W - \dim(U \cap W)$.

(ix) If U and W be two subspaces of a vector space V over a field F such that $U \cap W = \{\theta\}$ and if $\{\alpha_1, \alpha_2, \ldots, \alpha_n\}$ and $\{\beta_1, \beta_2, \ldots, \beta_n\}$ be respec-

tively the bases of U and W then $\{\alpha_1, \alpha_2, \ldots, \alpha_m, \beta_1, \beta_2, \ldots, \beta_n\}$ is a basis of U + W.

(x) If V be a finite dimensional vector space and U and W are complements of each other in V, then

dim V = dim U + dim W.

9. Co-ordinatisation of Vectors : Let B = $\{\alpha_1, \alpha_2, \ldots, \alpha_n\}$ be an **ordered basis** of a vector space V over a field F. Then to each vector α in V there corresponds a well determined ordered set of n scalars $c_1, c_2, \ldots, c_n$ in F such that $\alpha = c_1\alpha_1 + c_2\alpha_2 + \ldots + c_n\alpha_n$ The ordered n-tuple $(c_1, c_2, \ldots, c_n)$ is said to be the co-ordinate vector of α relative to the **ordered basis** B and is denoted by $(\alpha)_B$.

10. Linear Mapping : Let V, W be vector spaces over a field F. A mapping $f : V \to W$ is said to be a **linear mapping** (or **linear transformation**) if it satisfies the following properties

(i) $f(\alpha + \beta) = f(\alpha) + f(\beta)$ for all $\alpha, \beta \in V$.

(ii) $f(c\alpha) = cf(\alpha)$ for all $c \in F$, all $\alpha \in V$.

In particular, if W = V, then f is said to be a **linear operator** on V.

Properties

(i) Let V, W be vector spaces over a field F and $T : V \to W$ be a linear mapping. Then

(a) $T(\theta) = \theta'$, where θ, θ' are null elements in V, W respectively

(b) $T(-\alpha) = -T(\alpha)$ for all $\alpha \in V$.

(c) $T(a_1\alpha_1 + a_2\alpha_2 + \ldots + a_n\alpha_n) = a_1 T(\alpha_1) + a_2 T(\alpha_2) + \ldots + a_n T(\alpha_n)$
Where $a_1, a_2, \ldots, a_n \in F$ and $\alpha_1, \alpha_2, \ldots, \alpha_n \in V$.

(ii) Let V, W be vector spaces over a field F and $\{\alpha_1, \alpha_2, \ldots, \alpha_n\}$ be a basis of V. If $\beta_1, \beta_2, \ldots, \beta_n$ be arbitrary vectors (not necessarily all distinct) in W, then there exists one and only one linear mapping $T : V \to W$ such that $T(\alpha_1) = \beta_1, T(\alpha_2) = \beta_2, \ldots, T(\alpha_n) = \beta_n$.

11. Kernel of a Linear Mapping : Let V, W be vector space over a field F. Let $T : V \to W$ be a linear mapping. The set of all vectors $\alpha \in V$ such that $T(\alpha) = \theta'$, θ' being the null vector in W, is said to be **Kernel** of T and is denoted by Ker (T).

Properties

(i) Ker (T) is a subspace of V.

(ii) Let $T : V \to W$ be a linear mapping. Then T is injective if and only if Ker (T) = $\{\theta\}$.

(iii) Let $T : V \to W$ be a linear mapping such that Ker (T) = $\{\theta\}$. Then the images of a linearly independent set of vectors in V are linearly independent in W.

(iv) Let $T : V \to W$ be a linear mapping. Then Im (T) is a subspace of W.

[Im (T) is the image of a linear mapping T, also called **range** of T]

(v) Let $T : V \to W$ be a linear mapping and $\{\alpha_1, \alpha_2, \ldots, \alpha_n\}$ be a basis of V. Then $\{T(\alpha_1), T(\alpha_2), \ldots, T(\alpha_n)\}$ generates Im (T).

(vi) Let V, W be vector spaces over a field F and V is finite dimensional. If $T : V \to W$ be a linear mapping then dim Ker (T) + dim Im (T) = dim V.

(vii) Let V, W be finite dimensional vector spaces over a field F. If there exists a linear mapping $T : V \to W$ which is both one-to-one and onto then dim V = dim W.

EXERCISE

Mark the correct alternative(s) of each of the following :

1. Let V be the set of all pairs (x, y) of real numbers, and let F be the field of real numbers. Addition and scalar multiplication defined as given in each part below:

$(x_1, y_1) + (x_2, y_2) = (0, y_1 + y_2)$

$k(x_1, y_1) = (kx_1, ky_1) : k \in R$.

V is not a vector space over the field of real numbers, because
(*a*) it is a abelian group
(*b*) V is not closed under the given operation
(*c*) the identity element does not exist in V
(*d*) all the above

2. Let V be the set of all pairs (x, y) of real numbers and let F be the field of real numbers. Addition and scalar multiplication defined as given in each part below
$(x_1, y_1) + (x_2, y_2) = (x_1 + x_2, y_1 + y_2)$
$k(x_1, y_1) = (k^2a, k^2b)$.
V is not a vector space over the field of real numbers, because
(*a*) V is not closed under addition
(*b*) the identity element does not exist in V
(*c*) law of scalar multiplication is not satisfied
(*d*) all the above

3. Let V be the set of all pairs (x, y) of real numbers and $F \in R$. Then which of the following is a vector space.
(*a*) $(x_1, y_1) + (x_2, y_2) = (x_1 + x_2, y_1 + y_2)$
$k(x_1, y_1) = (kx_1, y_1),\ k \in R$
(*b*) $(x_1, y_1) + (x_2, y_2) = (x_1 + x_2, y_1 + y_2)$
$k(x_1, y_1) = (|k|\, x_1, |k|\, y_1)$
(*c*) $(x_1, y_1) + (x_2, y_2) = (x_1 + y_2, y_1 + x_2)$
$k(x_1, y_1) = (kx_1, ky_1)$
(*d*) $(x_1, y_1) + (x_2, y_2) = (x_1 + x_2, y_1 + y_2)$
$k(x_1, y_1) = (kx_1, ky_1)$

4. For each of the following sets V, determine set V which is a vector space ever C with respect to co-ordinate wise addition and scalar multiplication
(*a*) $V = \{(\alpha_1, \alpha_2, \alpha_3) : \alpha_1, \alpha_2, \alpha_3$ are complex numbers and α is real$\}$
(*b*) $V = \{(\alpha_1, \alpha_2, \alpha_3) : \alpha_1, \alpha_2, \alpha_3$ are complex numbers and $\alpha_1, \alpha_2 \neq 0\}$
(*c*) $V = \{(\alpha_1, \alpha_2, \alpha_3) : \alpha_1, \alpha_2, \alpha_3$ are complex numbers and $\alpha_2 + \alpha_3 = 0\}$
(*d*) $V = \{(\alpha_1, \alpha_2, \alpha_3) : \alpha_1, \alpha_2, \alpha_3$ are complex numbers and $\alpha_2 + \alpha_3 = 1\}$

5. Which of the following sets are vector spaces over C?
(*a*) Set of all complex matrices with respect to matrix addition and multiplication of a matrix by a scalar
(*b*) The set of all 2×2 real matrices with respect to matrix-addition and multiplication of a matrix by a scalar
(*c*) The set of all 4×4 complex matrices with respect to matrix-addition and multiplication of a matrix by a scalar
(*d*) The set of all $m \times n$ complex matrices with respect to matrix-addition and multiplication of a matrix by a scalar, m and n being fixed positive integers

6. Which of the following sets of matrices is a vector space over C with respect to matrix-addition and multiplication of a matrix by scalar
(*a*) The set all matrices of the form $\begin{pmatrix} x & y \\ z & 0 \end{pmatrix}$, where $x, y, z \in C$
(*b*) The set of all matrices of the form $\begin{pmatrix} x & 0 \\ 0 & y \end{pmatrix}$, where $x, y \in C$
(*c*) The set all matrices of the form $\begin{pmatrix} x & 0 \\ 0 & 0 \end{pmatrix}$, where $x \in C$
(*d*) All the above

7. Which of the following set of vectors $\alpha = (\alpha_1, \alpha_2, \ldots, \alpha_n)$ in R^n is subspace of R^n
(*a*) all α such that $a_1 \leq 0$
(*b*) all α such that a_3 is an integer
(*c*) all α such that $a_2 + 4a_3 = 0$
(*d*) all α such that $a_1 + a_2 + \ldots + a_n = k$ (constant), $(k \neq 0)$

8. Let R be the field of real numbers. Which of the following are subspaces of V_3 (R).
(*a*) $\{(x, 2y, 3z) : x, y, z \in R\}$
(*b*) $\{(x, x, x) : x \in R\}$
(*c*) $\{(x, y, z) : x, y, z$ are rational numbers$\}$
(*d*) All the above

9. Let V be the (real) vector space of all functions f from R into R. Which of the following sets of functions is not a subspace of V?

(a) All f such that $f(x^2) = [f(x)]^2$
(b) All f such that $f(0) = f(1)$
(c) All f such that $f(-1) = 0$
(d) All f which are continuous

10. Let $V = R^3(R) = \{(x, y, z) : x, y, z \in R\}$ and W be the set of all triplets (x, y, z). Then W is a subspace of $R^3(R)$ if
(a) $x - 3y + 4z = 0$
(b) $x + y + 2z = 0$
(c) $a_1x + b_1y + c_1z = 0$
(d) All the above

11. Let V be the vector space of all functions from R to R and
$W_1 = \{f : f(4) = 3 + f(2)\}$
$W_2 = \{f : 2f(3) = f(1)\}$
$W_3 = \{f : f(5) = 0\}$. Then
(a) W_1 alone is a subspace
(b) W_2 and W_3 are subspace
(c) W_1 and W_2 are subspace
(d) W_1 and W_3 are subspace

12. If α, β, γ are linearly independent vectors in a vector space V(F). Then which of the following is linearly independent.
(a) $\alpha + \beta, \beta + \gamma, \gamma + \alpha$
(b) $\alpha + \beta, \alpha - \beta, \alpha - 2\beta + \gamma$
(c) $\alpha + \beta + \gamma, \beta + \gamma, \gamma$
(d) All the above

13. Which of the following statement is false?
(a) The set $\{1, x, x(1 - x)\}$ is a L.I set of vectors in the space of all polynomials over the real number field
(b) The vectors $2x^3 + x^2 + x + 1, x^3 + 3x^2 + x - 2, x^3 + 2x^2 - x + 3$ of $V_4(R)$ are linearly independent
(c) Set of vectors $B = \{1, 1 + x, 1 + x + x^2\}$ is a basis of P_3
(d) None of these

14. If the dimension of a vector space V(F) is n, then
(a) any $n + 1$ vectors of V are linearly dependent.
(b) any n linearly independent vectors in V form a basis of V
(c) every set of n vectors which spans V is a basis of V
(d) All the above

15. Which of the following statements are wrong. Let $V = R^2$ and let S_1, S_2, S_3 be the subspaces
$S_1 = \{a\alpha : \alpha = (1, 0)\}$
$S_2 = \{b\beta : \beta = (0, 1)\}$
$S_3 = \{c\gamma : \gamma = (1, 1)\}$
(a) V is the direct sum of S_1 and S_2
(b) V is the direct sum of S_1 and S_3
(c) V is the direct sum of S_2 and S_3
(d) V is the direct sum of S_1, S_2 and S_3

16. Which of the following statements are wrong? Let V be the set of all ordered pair $A = (a_1, a_2)$ of real numbers, with addition and scalar multiplication defined by
$(a_1, a_2) + (b_1, b_2) = (a_1 + b_1, a_2 + b_2)$
and $k(a_1, a_2) = (ka_1, 0), k \in R$
(a) The system (V, +) is an abelian group
(b) Multiplication by k is associative
i.e., $k_1(k_2A) = k_1k_2A, A \in V$
(c) Multiplication is two way distributive over addition
i.e., $k(A + B) = kA + kB$
(d) V is a real vector space.

17. Suppose U and W are subspace of the vector space $V^4(R)$, generated by the sets
$B_1 = \{(1, 1, 0, -1), (1, 2, 3, 0), (2, 3, 3, -1)\}$
$B_2 = \{(1, 2, 2, -2), (2, 3, 2, -3), (1, 3, 4, -3)\}$.
Then dim (U + W) is
(a) 2 (b) 3 (c) 4 (d) 1

18. Keeping previous question in mind, dim $(U \cap W)$ is
(a) 2 (b) 3 (c) 4 (d) 1

19. The linear mapping F, defined as
$F : R^2 \to R^2$ defined by $F(x, y) = (x + y, x + y)$.
The basis of its image U and kernel W is
(a) (1, 1) and (– 1, 1)
(b) (1, 1) and (1, – 1)
(c) (– 1, 1) and (1, 1)
(d) (1, – 1) and (– 1, 1)

20. The linear mapping F, defined as
$F : R^2 \to R^2$ defined by $F(x, y, z) = (x + y, y + z)$.
The basis of its image U and Kernel W is
(a) $\{(1, 0), (0, 1)\}$ and $\{(-1, 1, -1)\}$
(b) $\{(1, 1), (1, 1)\}$ and $\{(-1, 1, 1)\}$
(c) $\{(1, 0), (0, 1)\}$ and $\{(1, -1, 1)\}$
(d) $\{(1, 1), (0, 1)\}$ and $\{(1, -1, 1)\}$

21. In V_3 (R), where R is the field of real numbers, examine each of the following sets of vectors and find out which set of vectors is linearly independent
(a) $\{(2,1,2),(8,4,8)\}$
(b) $\{(-1,2,1),(3,0,-1),(-5,4,3)\}$
(c) $\{(2,3,5),(4,9,25)\}$
(d) $\{(1,2,-1),(3,1,5),(3,-4,7)\}$

22. The vector α in R^3 whose co-ordinate vector relative to the basis $B = \{\alpha_1 = (1,1,1), \alpha_2 = (1,1,0), \alpha_3 = (1,0,0)\}$ is (3, 2, 1) is given by
(a) $(5,6,7)$ *(b)* $(3,5,6)$
(c) $(6,5,3)$ *(d)* $(3,4,5)$

23. $U = L\{(1,2,1),(2,1,3)\}, W = \{(1,0,0),(0,1,0)\}$ and they are subspaces of R^3. Then dim $(U + W)$ and dim $(U \cap W)$ is given by
(a) 3 and 1 *(b)* 1 and 3
(c) 2 and 1 *(d)* 1 and 1

24. The linear operator T on R^3 maps the basis vectors $(1,0,0)$ $(0,1,0)$, $(0,0,1)$ to $(1,1,1)$, $(0,1,-1)$ and $(1,2,0)$ respectively. Then $T(1,1,-1)$ is
(a) $(1,0,0)$ *(b)* $(0,1,0)$
(c) $(0,0,1)$ *(d)* $(0,0,0)$

25. Let V be the vector space of all 2×2 matrices over a field F. The dimension of V(F) is
(a) 4 *(b)* 3 *(c)* 2 *(d)* 1

26. The set M of all $n \times n$ matrices over the field of real R, is a vector space over R under usual operations. The dimension of M over R is
(a) 1 *(b)* n^2 *(c)* n *(d)* $2n$

27. If $T: R^2 \to R$ is a linear map for which $T(1, 1) = 3$ and $T(0, 1) = -2$, then $T(a, b)$ is equal to
(a) $5a - 2b$ *(b)* $2a - 5b$
(c) $2a + 5b$ *(d)* $5a + 2b$

28. The rank of the linear transformation $T: R^3 \to R^3$ defined by $T(x, y, z) = (y, 0, z)$ is
(a) 3 *(b)* 2 *(c)* 1 *(d)* 0

29. If P_n (R) is the set of a polynomial of order n over R, then match List I with List II and select the correct answer using the codes given below the list.

List I *(Linear Transformation)*	*List II* *(Matrices)*
A. $T: R^3 \to R^2$ $T(x, y, z) = (x + y, y + z)$	1. $\begin{pmatrix} 1 & 0 \\ 1 & 1 \\ 0 & 1 \end{pmatrix}$
B. $T: R^3 \to P_2(R)$ $T(a, b, c) = (a + b) + (b + c)x + cx^2$	2. $\begin{pmatrix} 0 & 0 & 0 \\ 1 & 0 & 0 \\ 0 & 1 & 0 \\ 0 & 0 & 1 \end{pmatrix}$
C. $T: P_2(R) \to P_3(R)$ $T\{P(x) = xP(x)$	3. $\begin{pmatrix} 1 & 1 & 0 \\ 0 & 1 & 1 \end{pmatrix}$
D. $T: R^2 \to R^3$ $T(x, y) = (x, x + y, y)$	4. $\begin{pmatrix} 1 & 1 & 0 \\ 0 & 1 & 1 \\ 0 & 0 & 1 \end{pmatrix}$

	A	B	C	D
(a)	1	4	2	3
(b)	2	3	4	1
(c)	3	4	2	1
(d)	3	1	4	2

30. In R^3 consider the following three statements about the subject
$E = \{(1,0,0),(0,1,0),(0,0,1),(1,1,1),(1,1,0)\}$
1. E is a linearly dependent set.
2. Any three vectors of E are linearly independent
3. Any four vectors of E are linearly dependent.

Which of the above statements are correct?
(a) 1, 2, 3 *(b)* 1 and 2
(c) 1 and 3 *(d)* 2 and 3

31. If the set of all triplets (x_1, x_2, x_3) of real numbers R form a vector space V_3, then a subspace denoted by a vertical plane $y = x$ can be obtained by a linear combination of the sets
(a) (1, 1, 0) and (0, 0, 1)
(b) (1, 1, 0) and (1, 0, 0)
(c) (1, 0, 0) and (0, 1, 0)
(d) (1, 0, 1) and (0, 0, 1)

32. If $W_1 = \{0, a_2, a_3\}$ and $W_2 = \{b_1, 0, b_3\}$ are two subspaces of F^3, where F^n is a vector space of dimension *n*. Then the subspace $W_1 \cap W_2$ is isomorphic to the vector space.

(a) F^1 *(b)* F^2
(c) F^3 *(d)* $2F^4$

33. Let $F: R^3 \to R^2$ be a map given by $F(a, b, c) = (a, b)\ \forall\ a, b, c \in R^3$. The Kernel of F is

(a) $(a, 0, 0)$ *(b)* $(0, b, 0)$
(c) $(0, 0, c)$ *(d)* $(a, b, 0)$

34. If the vectors $(0, 1, a)$ $(1, a, 1)$, $(a, 1, 0)$ or linearly dependent, then the value of *a* is

(a) $0, \sqrt{2}, -\sqrt{2}$ *(b)* $0, 1, -1$
(c) $0, \sqrt{3}, -\sqrt{3}$ *(d)* $0, 2, -2$

35. Which of the following functions T from R^2 into R^2 are linear transformation

(i) $T(a, b) = (1 + a, b)$ *(ii)* $T(a, b) = (b, a)$
(iii) $T(a, b) = (a + b, a)$

(a) *(i)* and *(ii)*
(b) *(ii)* and *(iii)*
(c) *(i)* and *(iii)*
(d) None of these

36. The mapping $T: R^3 \to R^2$ is defined as $T(x, y, z) = (x + 2y + 3z, x + 3y + 2z)$ is a linear transformation from R^3 into R^2. Then its Kernel T is

(a) $L\{\alpha\}$ where $\alpha = (-1, 5, 1)$
(b) $L\{\alpha\}$ where $\alpha = (-1, 1, 5)$
(c) $L\{\alpha\}$ where $\alpha = (-5, 1, 1)$
(d) None of these

37. The mapping $T: R^3 \to R^3$ is defined as $T(x, y, z) = (y + z - x, z + x - y, x + y - z)$ is a linear transformation from R^3 into R^3. Then its range *i.e.,* Im T is

(a) $L\{(1, 0, 0), (0, 1, 0), (0, 0, 1)\}$
(b) $L\{(2, 0, 0), (0, 2, 0), (0, 0, 2)\}$
(c) $L\{(3, 0, 0), (0, 3, 0), (0, 0, 3)\}$
(d) None of these

38. With respect to standard basis vectors a linear transformation $T: R^4 \to R^3$ is given by the matrix

$$\begin{bmatrix} 3 & -1 & -1 & 1 \\ -2 & 2 & -2 & -2 \\ -1 & -1 & 3 & 1 \end{bmatrix}.$$

The dimension of Ker (T) is

(a) 1 *(b)* 2
(c) 3 *(d)* 4

[J.N.U. M.C.A.]

39. Let $B = \{\upsilon_1, \upsilon_2\}$ be an ordered basis of R^2 with $\upsilon_1 = (\cos\theta, \sin\theta)$, $\upsilon_2 = (-\sin\theta, \cos\theta)$. The co-ordinates of the point (a, b) in the ordered basis where $x, y \in R$ is

(a) $(x\cos\theta + y\sin\theta\ \ x\sin\theta + y\cos\theta)$
(b) $(-x\cos\theta + y\cos\theta, x\sin\theta - y\cos\theta)$
(c) $(x\cos\theta - y\sin\theta, x\sin\theta + y\cos\theta)$
(d) None of these

[J.N.U. M.C.A.]

40. Let $T: R^3 \to R^2$ be the linear operator defined by

$$TX = AX, \text{ where } A = \begin{bmatrix} 1 & 3 & 4 \\ 3 & 4 & 7 \\ -2 & 2 & 0 \end{bmatrix} \text{ and } X = \begin{bmatrix} x_1 \\ x_2 \\ x_3 \end{bmatrix}$$

Then the range of T and Kernel of T are given by

(a) two lines passing through the origin
(b) a plane and a line, respectively, passing through the origin
(c) two planes passing through the origin
(d) a line and a plane, respectively, passing through the origin

[J.N.U. M.C.A.]

41. Let $T: V_2(R) \to V_3(R)$ defined as $T(a, b) = (a + b, a - b, b)$ is a linear transformation from $V_2(R)$ into $V_3(R)$.

(a) zero subspace of $V_2(R)$
(b) $L\{(1, 1, 0)\}$
(c) $L\{(1, -1, 1)\}$
(d) $L\{(1, -1, 1), (1, 1, 0)\}$

ANSWERS

1	2	3	4	5	6	7	8	9	10
(d)	(c)	(d)	(c)	(c)	(d)	(c)	(d)	(a)	(c)
11	**12**	**13**	**14**	**15**	**16**	**17**	**18**	**19**	**20**
(b)	(d)	(d)	(d)	(d)	(d)	(b)	(d)	(a)	(c)
21	**22**	**23**	**24**	**25**	**26**	**27**	**28**	**29**	**30**
(c)	(c)	(a)	(d)	(c)	(c)	(a)	(b)	(c)	(c)
31	**32**	**33**	**34**	**35**	**36**	**37**	**38**	**39**	**40**
(c)	(c)	(c)	(a)	(b)	(c)	(b)	(b)	(c)	(c)
41									
(b)									

SOME SELECTED EXPLANATORY ANSWERS

7. $W=\{\alpha:\alpha\in R^n \text{ and } a_2+4a_3=0\}$

Let $\alpha=(a_1,a_2,...,a_n)$ and $\beta=(b_1,b_2,....,b_n)$ be any two members of W.

Then $a_2+4a_3=0$ and $b_2+4b_3=0$.

If $a,b\in R$, then

$a\alpha+b\beta=(aa_1+bb_1,....,aa_n+bb_n)$

We have

$(aa_2+4a_3)+b\,(b_2+4b_3)=a.0+b.0=0$

Thus

$\alpha,\beta\in W$ and $a,b\in R \Rightarrow a\alpha+b\beta\in W$.

Hence W is a subspace of R^n.

8. Let $W=\{(x,2y,3z):x,y,z\in R\}$

Let $\alpha=(x_1,2y_1,3z_1)$ and $\beta=(x_2,2y_2,3z_2)$ be any two elements of W.

Then x_1,y_1,z_1,x_2,y_2,z_2 are all real numbers.

If *a, b* are any two real numbers, then

$a\alpha+b\beta=a\,(x_1,2y_1,3z_1)+b\,(x_2,2y_2,3z_2)$

$=(ax_1+bx_2,2\,(ay_1+by_2);3\,(az_1+bz_2))\in W$

Since ax_1+bx_2, ay_1+by_2, az_1+bz_2 are real numbers, then

$a,b\in R$ and $\alpha,\beta\in W \Rightarrow a\alpha+b\beta\in W$.

$\therefore$ W is a subspace of $V_3(R)$.

Similarly we can prove for other two cases.

9. Let $W=\{f:f\in V \text{ and } f(x^2)=[f(x)]^2\}$

Let *g, h* be any two members of W.

Then $g(x^2)=[g(x)]^2$ and $h(x^2)=[h(x)]^2$.

Let $a,b\in R$.

Then $(ag+bh)\,(x^2)=(ag)\,(x^2)+(bh)\,(x^2)$

$=a[g(x)]^2+b[h(x)]^2$

Also $[(ag+bh)(x)]^2=[ag(x)+bh(x)]^2$

$=a^2[g(x)]^2+b^2[h(x)]^2+2ab\,g(x)h(x)$

Now $(ag+bh)\,(x^2)$ is not necessarily equal to $[(ag+bh)\,(x)]^2$.

Thus $ag+bh$ is not necessarily a member of W.

Hence W is not a subspace of V.

11. Let f and $g\in W_1$, so that $f(4)=3+f(2)$;

$g(4)=3+g(2)$

Now $(af+hg)\,(4)=af(4)+bg(4)$

$=[a(3+f(2))+b(3+g(2))]$

$=(af+bg)\,(2)+3\,(a+b)$

$\neq 3+(af+bg)\,(2)$ by definition.

Hence $(af+bg)\notin W_1$ $\therefore$ W_1 is not a sub-space.

$W_2=\{f:2f(3)=f(1)\}$

Here $2\,(af+bg)\,(3)=2\,(af)\,(3)+2\,(bg)\,(3)$

$=a\,(2f)\,(3)+b\,(2g)\,(3)$

$=af(1)+bg(1)$

$=(af+bg)\,(1)$

Hence by definition of W_2, $af+bg\in W_2$ which therefore is a subspace. Similarly W_3 is a subspace.

12. Let a, b, c be scalars such that

$$a(\alpha+\beta)+b(\beta+\gamma)+c(\gamma+\alpha)=\theta$$

i.e. $(a+c)\alpha+(a+b)\beta+(b+c)\gamma=\theta$ ...*(i)*

But α, β, γ are linearly independent. Therefore *(i)* gives

$$a+0.b+c=0$$
$$a+b+0.c=0$$
$$0.a+b+c=0$$

The coefficient matrix A of these equations is

$$A=\begin{bmatrix}1 & 0 & 1\\ 1 & 1 & 0\\ 0 & 1 & 1\end{bmatrix}$$

Here Rank A = 3 = the number of unknowns a, b, c.

Therefore $a=0, b=0, c=0$ is the only solution of the given equation.

Hence, $\alpha+\beta, \beta+\gamma, \gamma+\alpha$ are linearly independent.

Let a, b, c be scalars such that

$$a(\alpha+\beta)+b(\alpha-\beta)+c(\alpha-2\beta+\gamma)=\theta$$

i.e. $(a+b+c)\alpha+(a-b-2c)\beta+c\gamma=\theta$ ...*(ii)*

But α, β, γ are linearly independent. Therefore *(ii)* gives

$$a+b+c=0$$
$$a-b-2c=0$$
$$0.a+0.b+c=0$$

Only one solution of these equations is $a=0, b=0, c=0$.

Therefore the vectors $\alpha+\beta, \alpha-\beta, \alpha-2\beta+\gamma$ are linearly independent.

Similarly $\alpha+\beta+\gamma, \beta+\gamma, \gamma$ are linearly independent.

13. I. The zero vector of the vector space of all polynomials over the real number field is the zero polynomial.

Let a, b, c be scalars (i.e. real numbers) such that

$a(1)+bx+c\{x(1-x)\}=\theta$ i.e. zero polynomial

i.e. $a+(b+c)x-cx^2=\theta$ *(i)*

Now two polynomial in x are said to be equal if the coefficients of like powers of x on both sides are equal. So by the definition of the equality of two polynomial, we have from *(i)*

$$a=0, b+c=0, -c=0$$
$$\Rightarrow a=0, b=0, c=0.$$

$\therefore$ The vectors $1, x, x(1-x)$ are linearly independent over the field of real numbers.

II. The zero vector of the vector space R[x] is the zero polynomial.

Let a, b, c be scalars (i.e. real numbers) such that

$a(2x^3+x^2+x-2)+b(x^3+3x^2+x-2)+c(x^3+2x^2-x+3)=\theta$ i.e. zero polynomial.

Then $(2a+b+c)x^3+(a+3b+2c)x^2+(a+b-c)x+(a-2b+3c)=\theta$ ...*(i)*

Equating the coefficients of like powers of x on both sides of *(i)*, we get

$$2a+b+c=0$$
$$a+3b+2c=0$$
$$a+b-c=0$$
$$a-2b+3c=0 \quad ...(ii)$$

The coefficient matrix A of the system of equations *(ii)* is

$$A=\begin{bmatrix}2 & 1 & 1\\ 1 & 3 & 2\\ 1 & 1 & -1\\ 1 & -2 & 3\end{bmatrix}\sim\begin{bmatrix}1 & 3 & 2\\ 0 & 1 & 3/5\\ 0 & 0 & 1\\ 0 & 0 & 0\end{bmatrix}$$

which is in echelon form.

$\therefore$ Rank A = 3 = number of unknowns a, b, c in the system of equations *(ii)*.

Hence the system of equation (ii) has the only solution

$$a=0, b=0, c=0.$$

$\therefore$ The given set of vectors is linearly independent.

III. Let a, b, c be scalars (real numbers) such that

$$a(1)+bx+c(1+x+x^2)=0$$
$$\Rightarrow (a+c)+(b+c)x+cx^2=0$$
$$\Rightarrow a+c=0, b+c=0, c=0$$
$$\Rightarrow a=0, b=0, c=0$$

$\therefore$ The vectors $1, x, 1+x+x^2$ are linearly independent over the field of real number.

17. To determine dim (U + V), we know that

$$U+W=L(U\cup W)$$

Now $U=L(B_1), W=L(B_2)$

$$\therefore U+W=L(U\cup W)=L\{L(B_1)\cup L(B_2)\}$$

$= L\{L(B_1 \cup B_2)\} = L(B_1 \cup B_2)$.

Thus $U + W = L(B_1 \cup B_2)$

But $B_1 \cup B_2 = \{(1,1,0,-1), (1,2,3,0), (2,3,3,-1), (1,2,2,-2), (2,3,2,-3), (1,3,4,-3)\}$

For a matrix A whose rows are the generators of U + W

$$A = \begin{pmatrix} 1 & 1 & 0 & -1 \\ 1 & 2 & 3 & 0 \\ 2 & 3 & 3 & -1 \\ 1 & 2 & 2 & -2 \\ 2 & 3 & 2 & -3 \\ 1 & 3 & 4 & -3 \end{pmatrix}$$

$$\sim \begin{pmatrix} 1 & 1 & 0 & -1 \\ 0 & 1 & 3 & 1 \\ 0 & 0 & -1 & -2 \\ 0 & 0 & -1 & -2 \\ 0 & 0 & -2 & -4 \\ 0 & 0 & 0 & 0 \end{pmatrix} \quad \begin{matrix} R_2 \to R_2 - R_1 \\ R_3 \to R_3 - 2R_1 \\ R_4 \to R_4 - R_1 \\ R_5 \to R_5 - 2R_1 \\ R_6 \to R_6 - R_1 \end{matrix}$$

$$\sim \begin{pmatrix} 1 & 1 & 0 & -1 \\ 0 & 1 & 3 & 1 \\ 0 & 0 & 0 & 0 \\ 0 & 0 & -1 & -2 \\ 0 & 0 & -1 & -2 \\ 0 & 0 & -2 & -4 \end{pmatrix} \quad \begin{matrix} R_3 \to R_3 - R_2 \\ R_4 \to R_4 - R_2 \\ R_5 \to R_5 - R_2 \\ R_6 \to R_6 - 2R_2 \end{matrix}$$

$$\sim \begin{pmatrix} 1 & 1 & 0 & -1 \\ 0 & 1 & 3 & 1 \\ 0 & 0 & -1 & -2 \\ 0 & 0 & -1 & -2 \\ 0 & 0 & -2 & -4 \\ 0 & 0 & 0 & 0 \end{pmatrix}$$

$$\sim \begin{pmatrix} 1 & 1 & 0 & -1 \\ 0 & 1 & 3 & 1 \\ 0 & 0 & -1 & -2 \\ 0 & 0 & 0 & 0 \\ 0 & 0 & 0 & 0 \\ 0 & 0 & 0 & 0 \end{pmatrix} \quad \begin{matrix} R_4 \to R_4 - R_3 \\ R_5 \to R_5 - 2R_3 \end{matrix}$$

The non zero rows (1, 1, 0, – 1), (0, 1, 3, 1), (0, 0, – 1, – 2) form a basis of row space of U + W.

18. $U = L(B_1) = L\{(1, 1, 0, -1), (1, 2, 3, 0), (2, 3, 3, -1)\}$

From a matrix whose rows are the generators of U i.e.

$$\begin{pmatrix} 1 & 1 & 0 & -1 \\ 1 & 2 & 3 & 0 \\ 2 & 3 & 3 & -1 \end{pmatrix}$$

Proceed as the previous problem. Reduced echlon form is

$$\begin{pmatrix} 1 & 1 & 0 & -1 \\ 0 & 1 & 3 & 1 \\ 0 & 0 & 0 & 0 \end{pmatrix}$$

$\therefore$ {(1, 1, 0, – 1), (0, 1, 3, 1)} is a basis of U.

$\therefore$ dim U = 2. Similarly dim W = 2.

$\therefore$ dim $(U \cap W)$ = dim U + dim W – dim (U + W) = 2 + 2 – 3 = 1.

19. Let *a* map $F: R^2 \to R^2$ be defined by

$F(x, y) = (x + y, x + y)$

{(1, 0), (0, 1)} is the usual basis of R^2. The image of these vectors generate the image U.

$F(1, 0) = (1 + 0, 1 + 0) = (1, 1)$

$F(0, 1) = (1 + 0, 1 + 0) = (1, 1)$

$\therefore$ {(1, 1)} is a basis of U.

Let $F(x, y) = (x + y, x + y) = (0, 0)$

So that $x + y = 0, x + y = 0$

Take $y = 1$, then $x = -1$.

$\therefore$ {(– 1, 1)} is a basis of W.

Hence image U and kernel U are (1, 1) and (– 1, 1).

20. A map $F: R^3 \to R^2$ is given by

$$F(x, y, z) = (x + y, y + z)$$

Hence $F(1, 0, 0) = (1 + 0, 0 + 0) = (1, 0)$

$F(0, 1, 0) = (0 + 1, 1 + 0) = (1, 1)$

$F(0, 0, 1) = (0 + 0, 0 + 1) = (0, 1)$

Form of the matrix whose rows are the generators of U is

$$\begin{pmatrix} 1 & 1 \\ 1 & 1 \\ 0 & 1 \end{pmatrix} \xrightarrow{R_2 \to R_2 - R_1} \begin{pmatrix} 1 & 0 \\ 0 & 1 \\ 0 & 1 \end{pmatrix}$$

$$\xrightarrow{R_3 \to R_3 - R_2} \begin{pmatrix} 1 & 0 \\ 0 & 1 \\ 0 & 0 \end{pmatrix}$$

Thus the rows are reduced to echlon form.
$\therefore$ {(1, 0), (0, 1)} is a basis of U.
Set F (x, y, z) = (x + y, y + z) = (0, 0)
So that $x + y = 0, y + z = 0$
Upon subtraction $x - z = 0$ or $x = z = 1$ (say)
$\therefore y = -1.$
Consequently {(1, – 1, 1)} is a basis of W.

21. Let *a, b* be scalars i.e. real numbers such that
$a(2, 3, 5) + b(4, 9, 25) = (0, 0, 0)$
i.e. $(2a + 4b, 3a + 9b, 5a + 25b) = (0, 0, 0)$
$\Rightarrow 2a + 4b = 0, 3a + 9b = 0, 5a + 25b = 0$
The coefficient matrix A of these equations is

$$A = \begin{pmatrix} 2 & 4 \\ 3 & 9 \\ 5 & 25 \end{pmatrix}$$

Obviously rank A = 2 i.e. equal to the number of unknowns *a* and *b*.
Therefore these equations have the only solution $a = 0, b = 0$.
Hence the given set of vectors is linearly independent.
Others are linearly dependent vector.

22. $\alpha = 3\alpha_1 + 2\alpha_2 + \alpha_3$
$= 3(1, 1, 1) + 2(1, 1, 0) + (1, 0, 0)$
$= (6, 5, 3)$

23. Let $\alpha = (1, 2, 1)$, $\beta = (2, 1, 3)$, $\gamma = (1, 0, 0)$, $\delta = (0, 1, 0)$.
Then $\{\alpha, \beta\}$ is linearly independent.
$\therefore$ U is a subspace of R^3 of dimension 2.
$\{\gamma, \delta\}$ is linearly independent.
$\therefore$ W is a subspace of R^3 of dimension 2.
Let λ be a vector in $U \cap W$. Then $\lambda = a\alpha + b\beta$ for some real numbers *c, d*.
Also $\lambda = c\gamma + d\delta$ for some real numbers *c, d*.
$\therefore a(1, 2, 1) + b(2, 1, 3) = c(1, 0, 0) + d(0, 0, 1)$
$\Rightarrow a + 2b = c, 2a + b = 0, a + 3b = d.$

$$\therefore a = -\frac{b}{2}, c = \frac{3}{2}b, d = \frac{5}{2}b.$$

$$\therefore \lambda = \frac{3}{2}b(1,0,0) + \frac{5}{2}b(0,0,1) = b\left(\frac{3}{2}, 0, \frac{5}{2}\right)$$

$\therefore U \cap W$ is a subspace of dimension 1.
Now dim (U + W) = dim U + dim W – dim$(U \cap W)$ = 2 + 2 – 1 = 3.

24. Let $\alpha = (x_1, x_2, x_3)$ be an arbitrary element of R^2.
Then $\alpha = x_1(1, 0, 0) + x_2(0, 1, 0) + x_3(0, 0, 1)$
Now $T(\alpha) = x_1 T(1, 0, 0) + x_2 T(0, 1, 0) + x_3 T(0, 0, 1)$ since T is linear.
$= x_1(1, 1, 1) + x_2(0, 1, -1) + x_3(1, 2, 0)$
$= (x_1 + x_3, x_1 + x_2 + 2x_3, x_1 - x_2)$
$\therefore T(x_1, x_2, x_3) = (x_1 + x_3, x_1 + x_2 + 2x_3, x_1 - x_2)$
$\therefore T(1, 1, -1) = (0, 0, 0).$

25. Let $\alpha = \begin{bmatrix} 1 & 0 \\ 0 & 0 \end{bmatrix}, \beta = \begin{bmatrix} 0 & 1 \\ 0 & 0 \end{bmatrix}, \gamma = \begin{bmatrix} 0 & 0 \\ 1 & 0 \end{bmatrix},$

$\delta = \begin{bmatrix} 0 & 0 \\ 0 & 1 \end{bmatrix}$ be four elements of V.

The subset $S = \{\alpha, \beta, \gamma, \delta\}$ of V is linearly independent because
$a\alpha + b\beta + c\gamma + d\delta = 0$

$$\Rightarrow a\begin{bmatrix} 1 & 0 \\ 0 & 0 \end{bmatrix} + b\begin{bmatrix} 0 & 1 \\ 0 & 0 \end{bmatrix} + c\begin{bmatrix} 0 & 0 \\ 1 & 0 \end{bmatrix} + d\begin{bmatrix} 0 & 0 \\ 0 & 1 \end{bmatrix} = \begin{bmatrix} 0 & 0 \\ 0 & 0 \end{bmatrix}$$

$$\Rightarrow \begin{bmatrix} a & b \\ c & d \end{bmatrix} = \begin{bmatrix} 0 & 0 \\ 0 & 0 \end{bmatrix}$$

$\Rightarrow a = 0, b = 0, c = 0, d = 0.$

Also L(S) = V because if $\begin{bmatrix} a & b \\ c & d \end{bmatrix}$ is any vector in V, then we can write

$$\begin{bmatrix} a & b \\ c & d \end{bmatrix} = a\alpha + b\beta + c\gamma + d\delta$$

Therefore S is a basis of V. Since the number of elements in S is 4, therefore dim V = 4.

26. By similar process as solution of previous problem we can conclude that dimension of M over R is *n*.

27. Let $(a, b) = \lambda_1(1,1) + \lambda_2(0,1)$, where λ_1, λ_2 are arbitrary constant.
$\Rightarrow (a, b) = (\lambda_1, \lambda_1 + \lambda_2)$
$\Rightarrow \lambda_1 = a, \lambda_1 + \lambda_2 = b$
$\Rightarrow \lambda_1 = a$ and $\lambda_1 = b - a$.
Then $T(a, b) = T\{\lambda_1(1,1) + \lambda_2(0,1)\}$
$= \lambda_1 T(1,1) + \lambda_2 T(0,1)$

$= a.3 + (b - a)(-2)$
$= 3a - 2(b - a)$
$= 5a - 2b.$

28. $\{(1, 0, 0), (0, 1, 0), (0, 0, 1)\}$ is a basis of R^3.
We have $T(1, 0, 0) = (0, 0, 0)$
$T(0, 1, 0) = (1, 0, 0)$
$T(0, 0, 1) = (0, 0, 1)$
Thus the range of T is the subspace of R^3 spanned by the vectors $(1, 0, 0)$ and $(0, 0, 1)$ as $(0, 0, 0)$ is a null vector and is linearly dependent vector.
Hence rank T = dim of range of T = 2.

29. $T(x, y, z) = (x + y, y + z)$
$T(1, 0, 0) = (1, 0)$
$T(0, 1, 0) = (1, 1)$
$T(0, 0, 1) = (0, 1)$
Thus the matrix form is $\begin{pmatrix} 1 & 1 & 0 \\ 0 & 1 & 1 \end{pmatrix}$ ($\because$ rows are written along column)
$T(a, b, c) = (a + b) + (b + c)x + cx^2$
$= \{a + b, b + c, c\}$
$\therefore$ $T(1,0,0) = (1,0,0)$
$T(0,1,0) = (1,1,0)$
$T(0,0,1) = (0,1,1)$
The matrix form is
$\begin{pmatrix} 1 & 1 & 0 \\ 0 & 1 & 1 \\ 0 & 0 & 1 \end{pmatrix}$ ($\because$ rows are written along column)
$T\{P(x)\} = xP(x)$
$T\{a + bx + cx^2\} = x\{a + bx + cx^2\}$
$= \{ax + bx^2 + cx^3\}$
$\therefore$ $T(a, b, c) = (0, a, b, c)$
$T(1,0,0) = (0,1,0,0)$
$T(0,1,0) = (0,0,1,0)$
$T(0,0,1) = (0,0,0,1)$
The matrix form is $\begin{pmatrix} 0 & 0 & 0 \\ 1 & 0 & 0 \\ 0 & 1 & 0 \\ 0 & 0 & 1 \end{pmatrix}$ ($\because$ rows are written along column).

30. Consider three vectors $(0, 0, 1)$, $(1, 1, 1)$ and $(1,1, 0)$.
Relation $a_1(0,0,1) + a_2(1,1,1) + a_3(1,1,0) = \theta$
$\Rightarrow$ $a_2 + a_3 = 0$
$a_2 + a_3 = 0$
$a_1 + a_2 = 0$
Thus all of a_1, a_2 and a_3 are not equal to zero.
So any three vectors of E are not linearly independent.
Consider four vectors $(1, 0, 0)$, $(0, 1, 0)$, $(0,0,1)$ and $(1, 1, 0)$
Relation $a_1(1, 0, 0) + a_2(0, 1, 0) + a_3(0, 0, 1) + a_4(1, 1, 0) = \theta$
$\Rightarrow$ $a_1 + a_4 = 0$
$a_2 + a_4 = 0$
$a_3 = 0$
Thus all of a_1, a_2, a_3 and a_4 are not equal to zero.
So any four vectors of E are linearly dependent.

31. $y = x$ is a plane at $z = 0$.
Now let $y = x = \lambda$, where λ is any arbitrary constant.
$\therefore$ Any point on the plane is represented by the co-ordinate
$(x, y, 0) = (\lambda, \lambda, 0)$
$= \lambda(1,1,0)$
$= \lambda(1,0,0) + \lambda(0,1,0)$
Thus the subspace denoted by a vertical plane $y = x$ can be obtained by a linear combination of $(1, 0, 0)$ and $(0, 1, 0)$.

33. F is a linear tarnsformation
$\ker F = \{(a,b,c) \in R^3 : F(a,b,c) = \theta\}$
$= \{(a,b,c) \in R^3 : (a,b) = (0,0)\}$
$= \{(a,b,c) \in R^3 : a = 0, b = 0\}.$

34. Let $x, y, z \in R$. Consider the equation
$x(0, 1, a) + y(1, a, 1) + z(a, 1, 0) = \theta$
$\Rightarrow (y + az, x + ay + z, ax + y) = (0, 0, 0)$
$\Rightarrow 0.x + y + az = 0$ ...(i)
$x + ay + z = 0$ ...(ii)
$ax + y + 0.z = 0$ ...(iii)
From (i) we have $\frac{y}{a} = \frac{z}{-1} = k$ (Say)
Then $y = ak$, $z = -k$.
Putting these values in (ii) we have
$x = -a(ak) - (-k) = k(1 - a^2)$
Thus $x = k(1 - a^2), y = ak, z = -k$ ...(iv)
Substituting this in (iii) we get
$ak(1 - a^2) + ak = 0$
$\Rightarrow$ $ak(1 - a^2 + 1) = 0$
$\Rightarrow$ $ak(2 - a^2) = 0$

$\Rightarrow\ a = 0, k = 0, a^2 = 2.$

$k = 0$ is not possible.

Hence required value of a are $0, \sqrt{2}, -\sqrt{2}$.

35. I. $T(a, b) = (1 + a, b)$

Let $\alpha = (a_1, b_1),\ \beta = (a_2, b_2) \in V_2(R)$

Then $T(\alpha) = T(a_1, b_1) = (1 + a_1, b_1)$

$T(\beta) = T(a_2, b_2) = (1 + a_2, b_2)$

Also let $a, b \in R$. Then $a\alpha + b\beta \in V_2(R)$ and

$$T(a\alpha + b\beta) = T[a(a_1, b_1) + b(a_2, b_2)]$$
$$= T(aa_1 + ba_2, ab_1 + bb_2)$$
$$= (1 + aa_1 + ba_2, ab_1 + bb_2) \quad ...(i)$$

Also $aT(\alpha) + bT(\beta)$

$= aT(a_1, b_1) + bT(a_2, b_2)$

$= a(1 + a_1, b_1) + b(1 + a_2, b_2)$

$= (a + aa_1, ab_1) + (b + ba_2, bb_2)$

$= (a + b + aa_1 + ba_2, ab_1 + bb_2) \quad ...(ii)$

From *(i)* and *(ii)* we conclude that

$T(a\alpha + b\beta) \neq aT(\alpha) + bT(\beta)$

$\therefore$ T is not a linear transformation.

II. $T(a, b) = (b, a)$.

Let $\alpha = (a_1, b_1),\ \beta = (a_2, b_2) \in V_2(R)$

Then $T(\alpha) = T(a_1, b_1) = (b_1, a_1)$

$T(\beta) = T(a_2, b_2) = (b_2, a_2)$

Also let $a, b \in R$. Then $a\alpha + b\beta \in V_2(R)$ and

$$T(a\alpha + b\beta) = T[a(a_1, b_1) + b(a_2, b_2)]$$
$$= T(aa_1 + ba_2, ab_1 + bb_2)$$
$$= (ab_1 + bb_2, aa_1 + ba_2)$$
$$= a(b_1, a_1) + b(b_2, a_2)$$
$$= aT(a_1, b_1) + bT(a_2, b_2)$$

$\therefore$ T is a linear transformation.

III. $T(a, b) = (a + b, a)$

Let $\alpha = (a_1, b_1),\ \beta = (a_2, b_2) \in V_2(R)$

Then $T(\alpha) = T(a_1, b_1) = (a_1 + b_1, a_1)$

$T(\beta) = T(a_2, b_2) = (a_2 + b_2, a_2)$

Also let $a, b \in R$. Then $a\alpha + b\beta \in V_2(R)$ and

$$T(a\alpha + b\beta) = T[a(a_1, b_1) + b(a_2, b_2)]$$

$= T(aa_1 + ba_2, ab_1 + bb_2)$

$= [a(a_1 + b_1) + b(a_2 + b_2), aa_1 + ba_2]$

$= [a(a_1 + b_1), aa_1] + [b(a_2 + b_2), ba_2]$

$= a(a_1 + b_1, a_1) + b(a_2 + b_2, a_2)$

$= aT(\alpha) + bT(\beta)$

$\therefore$ T is a linear transformation.

36. Given $T(x, y, z) = (x + 2y + 3z, x + 3y + 2z)$

Let $(a, b, c) \in \ker(T)$

Then $(a + 2b + 3c, a + 3b + 2c) = (0, 0)$

$\Rightarrow\ a + 2b + 3c = 0 \quad ...(i)$

$a + 3b + 2c = 0 \quad ...(ii)$

Subtracting *(i)* from *(ii)* we get

$b - c = 0 \Rightarrow b = c = k$ (say)

Then $a = -5k$.

$\therefore (a, b, c) = (-5k, k, k) = k(-5, 1, 1) = L(\alpha)$

where $\alpha = (-5, 1, 1)$.

37. Given

$T(x, y, z) = (y + z - x, z + x - y, x + y - z)$

Now T is linear transformation from $R^3 \to R^3$.

$\{(1, 0, 0), (0, 1, 0), (0, 0, 1)\}$ is a basis for R^3.

We have $T(1, 0, 0) = (-1, 1, 1)$

$T(0, 1, 0) = (1, -1, 1)$

$T(0, 0, 1) = (1, 1, -1)$

In matrix form it is written as

$$A = \begin{pmatrix} -1 & 1 & 1 \\ 1 & -1 & 1 \\ 1 & 1 & -1 \end{pmatrix}$$

$$\sim \begin{pmatrix} 1 & 1 & -1 \\ 1 & -1 & 1 \\ -1 & 1 & 1 \end{pmatrix} \quad R_1 \to R_3$$

$$\sim \begin{pmatrix} 1 & 1 & -1 \\ 2 & 0 & 0 \\ 0 & 2 & 0 \end{pmatrix} \quad \begin{matrix} R_2 \to R_2 + R_1 \\ R_3 \to R_3 + R_1 \end{matrix}$$

$$\sim \begin{pmatrix} 0 & 0 & -1 \\ 2 & 0 & 0 \\ 0 & 2 & 0 \end{pmatrix} \quad \begin{matrix} C_1 \to C_1 + C_3 \\ C_2 \to C_2 + C_3 \end{matrix}$$

$$\sim \begin{pmatrix} 0 & 0 & 2 \\ 2 & 0 & 0 \\ 0 & 2 & 0 \end{pmatrix} \quad R_1 \to 2R_1$$

Here $\{(0,0,2), (2,0,0), (0,2,0)\} \in R^3$ and they are linearly independent. Also they span hole of its range.

38. Let

$$A = \begin{pmatrix} 3 & -1 & -1 & 1 \\ -2 & 2 & -2 & -2 \\ -1 & -1 & 3 & 1 \end{pmatrix}$$

$$\sim \begin{pmatrix} 3 & -1 & -1 & 1 \\ 4 & 0 & -4 & 0 \\ -4 & 0 & 4 & 0 \end{pmatrix} \begin{matrix} R_2 \to 2R_1 + R_2 \\ R_3 \to R_3 - R_1 \end{matrix}$$

$$\sim \begin{pmatrix} 3 & -1 & -1 & 1 \\ 4 & 0 & -4 & 0 \\ 0 & 0 & 0 & 0 \end{pmatrix} R_3 \to R_2 + R_3.$$

Now dim of range of T + dim of null space of T = dim of $R^4 = 4$.

$\Rightarrow \quad \rho(T) + \ker(T) = 4$

$\Rightarrow \quad \ker(T) = 4 - \rho(T)$

$= 4 - 2 = 2.$

39. Here $(a, b) = xv_1 + yv_2$

$= x(\cos\theta, \sin\theta) + y(-\sin\theta, \cos\theta)$

$= (x\cos\theta - y\sin\theta, x\sin\theta + y\cos\theta)$

where $x, y \in R$.

40. Given $T: IR^3 \to IR^3$ a linear operator defined by $TX = AX$.

where $A = \begin{bmatrix} 1 & 3 & 4 \\ 3 & 4 & 7 \\ -2 & 2 & 0 \end{bmatrix}$ and $X = \begin{bmatrix} x_1 \\ x_2 \\ x_3 \end{bmatrix}$

It implies mapping

$T(x_1, x_2, x_3) = (x_1 + 3x_2 + 4x_3, 3x_1 + 4x_2 + 7x_3, -2x_1 + 2x_2)$

Now $(u, v, w) \in$ null space of T

$\Rightarrow T(u, v, w) = (0, 0, 0)$

$\Rightarrow (u + 3v + 4w, 3u + 4v + 7w, -2u + 2v + 0w) = (0, 0, 0)$

$A = \begin{bmatrix} 1 & 3 & 4 \\ 3 & 4 & 7 \\ -2 & 2 & 0 \end{bmatrix}$ and $X = \begin{bmatrix} x_1 \\ x_2 \\ x_3 \end{bmatrix}$

$$\Rightarrow \begin{aligned} u + 3v + 4w &= 0 \\ 3u + 4v + 7w &= 0 \\ -2u + 2v + 0.w &= 0 \end{aligned} \qquad ...(i)$$

The null space of T is the solution space of the sytem of linear equations.

The matrix form of the equation *(i)* is given by

$$\begin{pmatrix} 1 & 3 & 4 \\ 3 & 4 & 7 \\ -2 & 2 & 0 \end{pmatrix}\begin{pmatrix} x_1 \\ x_2 \\ x_3 \end{pmatrix} = \begin{pmatrix} 0 \\ 0 \\ 0 \end{pmatrix}$$

$$\Rightarrow \begin{pmatrix} 1 & 3 & 4 \\ 0 & -5 & -5 \\ 0 & 8 & 8 \end{pmatrix}\begin{pmatrix} x_1 \\ x_2 \\ x_3 \end{pmatrix} = \begin{pmatrix} 0 \\ 0 \\ 0 \end{pmatrix}$$

$$\Rightarrow \begin{pmatrix} 1 & 3 & 4 \\ 0 & 1 & 1 \\ 0 & 1 & 1 \end{pmatrix}\begin{pmatrix} x_1 \\ x_2 \\ x_3 \end{pmatrix} = \begin{pmatrix} 0 \\ 0 \\ 0 \end{pmatrix}$$

$$\Rightarrow \begin{pmatrix} 1 & 3 & 4 \\ 0 & 1 & 1 \\ 0 & 0 & 0 \end{pmatrix}\begin{pmatrix} x_1 \\ x_2 \\ x_3 \end{pmatrix} = \begin{pmatrix} 0 \\ 0 \\ 0 \end{pmatrix}$$

$$\Rightarrow \begin{aligned} x_1 + 3x_2 + 4x_3 &= 0 \\ x_2 + x_2 &= 0 \end{aligned}$$

Above two equations represents two planes and they together represents a straight line.

Also range of T represents a plane passing through origin.

41. T is a linear transformation from $V_2(R)$ into $V_3(R)$

Now $\{(1, 0), (0, 1)\}$ is a basis of $V_2(R)$

We have $T(1, 0) = (1 + 0, 1 - 0, 0) = (1, 1, 0)$

and $T(0, 1) = (0 + 1, 0 - 1, 1) = (1 - 1, 1)$.

The vectors $T(1, 0), T(0, 1)$ span the range of T.

Thus the range of T is the subspace of $V_3(R)$ spanned by the vectors $(1, 1, 0), (1, -1, 1)$.

Now the vectors $(1, 1, 0), (1, -1, 1) \in V_3(R)$ are linearly independent because if $x, y \in R$, then

$$x(1, 1, 0) + y(1, -1, 1) = (0, 0, 0)$$

$$\Rightarrow \quad (x + y, x - y, y) = (0, 0, 0)$$

$\Rightarrow x + y = 0, x - y = 0, y = 0$

$\Rightarrow x = 0, y = 0$

$\therefore$ The vectors $(1, 1, 0), (1, -1, 1)$ form a basis for range of T.

Hence rank T = dim of range of T = 2.

Nullity of T = dim of $V_2(R)$ – rank T = 2 – 2 = 0

$\therefore$ Null space of T must be the zero subspace of $V_2(R)$.